Transforming Trusted AI and Service Computing for Effective Digital Government

Yuanyuan Guo
https://orcid.org/0000-0002-3042-8417
Ningbo University, China

Beichen Lu
https://orcid.org/0009-0002-7346-2209
Tsinghua University, China

IGI Global
Scientific Publishing
Publishing Tomorrow's Research Today

Published in the United States of America by
IGI Global Scientific Publishing
701 East Chocolate Avenue
Hershey, PA, 17033, USA
Tel: 717-533-8845 | Fax: 717-533-7115
Website: https://www.igi-global.com E-mail: cust@igi-global.com

Library of Congress Cataloging-in-Publication Data

Names: Guo, Yuanyuan, 1993- editor | Lu, Beichen, 1999- editor
Title: Transforming trusted AI and service computing for effective digital government / edited by Yuanyuan Guo, Beichen Lu.
Description: Hershey, PA : IGI Global Scientific Publishing, [2027] | Includes bibliographical references and index. | Summary: "Artificial Intelligence (AI) has the potential to revolutionize digital government by enhancing efficiency, transparency, and citizen engagement. However, its integration into public services also raises critical issues regarding trust, fairness, and ethical governance. This book provides both theoretical frameworks and practical insights into the role of trusted AI and service computing in digital government. It explores the latest developments in AI technologies and their applications in governance, focusing on building trust and ensuring ethical standards in public services"-- Provided by publisher.
Identifiers: LCCN 2026019585 (print) | LCCN 2026019586 (ebook) | ISBN 9798337391298 hardcover | ISBN 9798337391304 paperback | ISBN 9798337391311 ebook
Subjects: LCSH: Public administration--Data processing | Internet in public administration | Artificial intelligence--Political aspects
Classification: LCC JF1525.A8 T727 2027 (print) | LCC JF1525.A8 (ebook)
LC record available at https://lccn.loc.gov/2026019585
LC ebook record available at https://lccn.loc.gov/2026019586

British Cataloguing in Publication Data
A Cataloguing in Publication record for this book is available from the British Library.

Table of Contents

Detailed Table of Contents

redistributing influence among governments, data providers, technology developers, and algorithmic systems. This transformation creates new challenges regarding accountability, transparency, and public control. The chapter concludes that Trusted AI for Effective Digital Government requires not only reliable technologies but also accountable institutions, fair governance processes, and meaningful citizen trust.

Chapter 3 establishes the theoretical foundation of trusted AI in digital government by arguing that artificial intelligence has fundamentally transformed the nature, structure, and production mechanism of public trust. Existing digital government studies generally understand trust as citizens' confidence in governmental institutions, administrative procedures, and service outcomes. However, the integration of AI into public governance introduces a new condition, governmental decisions are increasingly mediated by algorithms, data infrastructures, automated systems, and intelligent service platforms. Under this transformation, trust is no longer produced only through institutional authority or administrative performance. Instead, it emerges from the interaction between political legitimacy, technological reliability, algorithmic accountability and citizen experience. Therefore, this chapter proposes a new theoretical perspective, trust in digital government should be understood as a dynamic governance relationship rather than a static perception of government capability.

Chapter 4 explores how AI reshapes trust in digital government. It argues that traditional institution centered trust is insufficient because AI introduces new actors, decision processes, and accountability structures into governance. The chapter proposes the concept of the AI social contract, emphasizing that trust should be built through legitimacy, responsibility, and citizen participation. It further explains that AI should be understood as an embedded governance institution rather than merely a technical tool. The chapter concludes that trusted AI governance depends not on algorithmic perfection, but on the continuous negotiation between technological capability, institutional accountability, and social expectations.

This study investigates how AI Transparency, AI Accountability, and Citizen Engagement shape Trust in AI within government-citizen relationships. Adopting a quantitative, explanatory, and cross-sectional research design, the study utilized primary data collected from 285 respondents through a structured survey instrument. Descriptive statistics, multiple regression, ANOVA, coefficient analysis, collinearity diagnostics, and residual assessment were employed to examine the proposed relationships. The findings reveal that the model is statistically significant and that AI Accountability emerges as the most influential predictor of Trust in AI, followed by Citizen Engagement, while AI Transparency exhibits a comparatively marginal yet positive effect. The study implies that trustworthy public-sector AI must be anchored in institutional answerability, participatory governance, and intelligible operational processes. It concludes that trust in governmental AI is fundamentally a governance-driven outcome rather than merely a technological consequence.

With AI being the heart of public administration services, issues regarding citizens' trust in AI-based governance mechanisms have been rising. In this chapter, the role of emotional intelligence (EI) in fostering citizens' trust in AI-driven public services is examined. Based on the EI theory developed by Mayer et al., Goleman, and Petrides & Furnham, the case study establishes the framework for embedding EI components, such as emotion perception, utilization, understanding, and management, in the development of AI systems, human-AI interface, and governance architectures. The application of emotionally intelligent digital services in Estonia, Singapore, the United Kingdom, India, and the United States shows how emotionally intelligent digital services can enhance citizens' trust outcomes.

This chapter addresses a critical challenge in digital governance: integrating emotionally intelligent public services with privacy-preserving and trustworthy AI infrastructures. While Emotion AI can enhance citizen interactions and support responsive service delivery, its adoption is constrained by biometric privacy concerns, centralized data vulnerabilities, and evolving regulatory requirements. To address these challenges, the chapter proposes the Decentralized Emotion-Aware Trust Framework (DETF), which combines Edge AI, Federated Learning, and Blockchain technology. The framework enables real-time emotion recognition, collaborative model improvement without sharing raw biometric data, and transparent model governance through decentralized audit trails. The DETF provides policymakers, public administrators, and system architects with a secure, ethical, and scalable blueprint for trustworthy AI-enabled public services.

Chapter 8 examines the ethical foundations of trusted AI enabled digital government by extending the discussion beyond algorithmic fairness toward human centered AI governance. It argues that AI systems are not neutral technical tools but value embedded governance mechanisms that influence public decisions and social outcomes. The chapter explores the ethical boundaries of AI authority, the reconstruction of accountability, and the importance of meaningful explainability in maintaining public trust. Furthermore, it introduces emotional intelligence as a new dimension of AI governance, emphasizing that trustworthy AI requires not only technical reliability but also ethical legitimacy, human understanding, and respect for citizen experiences.

Preface

Artificial intelligence is rapidly transforming the ways in which governments design policies, deliver public services, process information, and interact with citizens. From digital identity and welfare delivery to healthcare, education, judicial administration, and public infrastructure, AI-enabled systems are increasingly becoming embedded in the everyday functioning of government. This transformation promises greater efficiency, responsiveness, personalization, and evidence-based decision-making. At the same time, it introduces fundamental questions concerning transparency, accountability, fairness, privacy, explainability, human oversight, and, above all, public trust. The emergence of increasingly autonomous and data-intensive technologies has therefore made it necessary to reconsider what it means for a digital government to be trusted and trustworthy.

The volume *Transforming Trusted AI and Service Computing for Effective Digital Government* brings together interdisciplinary perspectives on this rapidly evolving landscape. As editors, we have sought to move the discussion beyond the conventional understanding of AI as a technological instrument for improving administrative efficiency. The chapters collected in this book examine AI as part of a broader socio-technical and institutional environment in which algorithms, data, public institutions, technology providers, administrators, and citizens interact. In such an environment, trust cannot be reduced to system accuracy or technical reliability. Rather, it must be understood as a multidimensional and continuously negotiated relationship involving institutional legitimacy, algorithmic accountability, citizen participation, ethical responsibility, and the lived experience of digital public services.

A central premise of this book is that the future of digital government depends not simply on how intelligent government technologies become, but on how responsibly they are designed, governed, implemented, and experienced. Trusted AI requires mechanisms through which citizens can understand, question, challenge, and, where necessary, contest AI-mediated decisions. It also requires institutions capable of accepting responsibility for technological outcomes. The contributions in this volume consequently explore a broad spectrum of issues, ranging from conceptual theories of trust and the emerging AI social contract to emotional intelligence, decentralized architectures, blockchain, accounting-based accountability, educational data sovereignty, explainable autonomous agents, and AI-assisted government document summarization. Together, these perspectives demonstrate that trustworthy digital government must combine technological innovation with institutional safeguards and meaningful human engagement.

The book also recognizes that trust is contextual. What constitutes a trustworthy AI system in welfare administration may differ from what is required in healthcare, education, judicial analytics, or citizen-facing public services. Similarly, the needs of digitally sophisticated citizens may differ substantially from those of individuals affected by digital exclusion, limited technological literacy, or unequal access to public infrastructure. The chapters therefore approach trusted AI from multiple geographical, disciplinary, and methodological perspectives. Contributions drawing on experiences from India, China, Singapore, Estonia, the United Kingdom, the United States, and other contexts illustrate both common challenges and locally specific concerns. By bringing these perspectives together, the volume aims to contribute to a more nuanced understanding of how AI can support effective digital government without compromising democratic values, individual rights, or public accountability.

The opening chapters establish the conceptual and theoretical foundations for understanding trust in AI-enabled digital government. Chapter 1, "Redefining Trust in Digital Governance through AI Technologies: Frameworks, Challenges, and Future Directions," examines the changing relationship between AI and institutional trust in the Indian digital governance ecosystem. Drawing on examples including Aadhaar, UMANG, PM-KISAN, CoWIN, and Bhashini, the chapter develops the Trusted AI Governance Framework (TAGF-India), emphasizing transparency, accountability, fairness, security, reliability, and explainability. It also places India's emerging AI governance landscape in conversation with international frameworks such as the EU AI Act, the NIST AI Risk Management Framework, and the OECD AI Principles.

Chapter 2, "Understanding Trust Structures in AI Enabled Digital Governance," expands the concept of trust beyond citizens' confidence in government institutions. It considers trust in digital systems, AI-mediated processes, governance arrangements, and citizen-government relationships. Particular attention is given to the emergence of algorithmic power and the redistribution of influence among governments, technology developers, data providers, and AI systems. The chapter emphasizes that trusted AI requires not only dependable technologies but also accountable institutions and fair governance processes.

Chapter 3, "The Reconstruction of Trust in Digital Government: From Institutional Legitimacy to Algorithmic Governance," develops a theoretical perspective in which trust is understood as a dynamic governance relationship. The chapter demonstrates how the introduction of algorithms, data infrastructures, and automated decision-making changes the mechanisms through which public trust is produced. Chapter 4, "From Technological Reliability to AI Social Contract: Reconstructing Trust in Digital Government," extends this argument through the concept of an AI social contract. It highlights legitimacy, responsibility, citizen participation, and continuous negotiation between technological capabilities and societal expectations as essential components of trusted AI governance.

The next group of chapters turns toward the human and relational dimensions of trust. Chapter 5, "The Role of Trusted AI in Shaping Government-Citizen Relationships: A Study on Trust and Accountability," provides an empirical examination of AI transparency, AI accountability, and citizen engagement. Based on survey data from 285 respondents, the study identifies AI accountability as the strongest predictor of trust in AI, followed by citizen engagement, while transparency demonstrates a positive but comparatively modest effect. The findings reinforce the argument that public trust in AI is fundamentally shaped by governance arrangements rather than by technological performance alone.

Chapter 6, "Emotional Intelligence and Citizen Trust in Artificial Intelligence–Enabled Public Administration," introduces emotional intelligence as an important dimension of AI-enabled public services. Drawing on established theories of emotional intelligence and examples from Estonia, Singapore, the United Kingdom, India, and the United States, the chapter explores how emotion perception, utilization, understanding, and management can be incorporated into AI systems and human-AI interfaces.

Chapter 7, "Decentralized Emotion-Aware Trust Frameworks in Digital Government," connects emotional intelligence with privacy-preserving and decentralized technologies. Its proposed Decentralized Emotion-Aware Trust Framework combines Edge AI, Federated Learning, and Blockchain to support real-time emotion-aware services while reducing the need to centralize sensitive biometric information. The chapter illustrates how emerging technological architectures can potentially reconcile personalization and responsiveness with privacy, security, and transparent governance.

The ethical and institutional dimensions of trusted AI are examined in the following chapters. Chapter 8, "Ethical Boundaries and Emotional Intelligence in Trusted AI Enabled Digital Government," argues that AI systems should be understood as value-embedded governance mechanisms rather than neutral technological tools. It addresses the boundaries of AI authority, accountability, meaningful explainability, and the incorporation of human understanding into AI governance.

Chapter 9, "Governing AI through Accounting: The Role of Government and Sustainability Accounting in Fostering Trust and Public Value," offers a distinctive institutional perspective by positioning government and sustainability accounting as mechanisms for translating broad AI ethics principles into measurable indicators, auditable processes, and public disclosures. The chapter proposes that accountability infrastructures can convert otherwise abstract commitments to fairness, transparency, and explainability into evidence that can be assessed by institutions and the public. This perspective broadens the trusted AI debate by connecting technological governance with established systems of organizational accountability and public value creation.

Chapter 10, "Educational Data Sovereignty at the Margins: Intergenerational Digital Exclusion and the Structural Failures of India's Data Protection Framework," addresses privacy and digital exclusion through the specific context of educational data in India. The chapter draws attention to the role of elderly caregivers as digital intermediaries in intergenerational households and identifies structural limitations in existing approaches to consent, data fiduciary responsibilities, and intergenerational privacy. Its life-course approach to children's digital rights highlights the importance of considering vulnerable and digitally excluded populations when designing trustworthy digital governance systems.

Chapter 11, "A Framework for Explainable Reasoning, Planning, and Action in LLM-Based Autonomous AI Agents," addresses one of the most rapidly emerging areas of AI: autonomous agents capable of reasoning, planning, tool use, and action. Focusing particularly on healthcare applications, the chapter examines how explainability can be incorporated across reasoning, planning, action selection, and feedback mechanisms. Its emphasis on human oversight and interpretable agent behavior is particularly relevant as public-sector organizations begin to consider increasingly autonomous AI systems.

Chapter 12, "Development of Trusted AI for Effective Digital Government Document Summarization," shifts attention to a practical application of AI in government information management. It presents a hierarchical summarization pipeline for lengthy government and legal documents, using keyword-based segmentation to preserve important contextual information. Through evaluation on the GovReport dataset using ROUGE and BERTScore measures, the chapter illustrates how AI-assisted summarization can support policy analysis, legal research, regulatory compliance, and other information-intensive government functions.

The volume concludes conceptually with Chapter 13, "The Future of Trust AI-government Relations in an AI-driven Society." This chapter revisits the broader transformation of the relationship among citizens, institutions, and technological systems. It argues that the expansion of AI into public life requires a renewed understanding of systemic trust encompassing algorithms, datasets, regulatory institutions, oversight mechanisms, and civic participation. The chapter provides a forward-looking perspective on how the social contract may evolve as AI becomes increasingly embedded in government and society.

Taken together, the chapters in this volume demonstrate that trusted AI is not a single technological property or a problem that can be solved through algorithmic accuracy alone. Trust emerges from the interaction of technology with institutions, laws, organizational practices, social expectations, and citizen experiences. Transparency without accountability may provide information without responsibility; accountability without participation may remain institutionally distant; and technical reliability without fairness or explainability may fail to generate legitimate public trust. Effective digital government therefore requires an integrated approach in which technological capabilities are accompanied by appropriate governance structures, ethical safeguards, and meaningful opportunities for human oversight.

The contributions also suggest that the next generation of digital government will increasingly depend on the ability to reconcile apparently competing objectives. Governments seek automation and efficiency while citizens require agency and contestability. AI systems can personalize services while simultaneously increasing privacy risks. Emotion-aware technologies can make digital interactions more responsive while introducing new concerns surrounding biometric data and surveillance. Decentralized architectures can strengthen resilience and auditability while creating new forms of technical and institutional complexity. The challenge, therefore, is not to reject technological advancement but to establish the conditions under which innovation can coexist with rights, accountability, inclusion, and democratic legitimacy.

An important lesson emerging across the volume is that trust must be continuously constructed rather than assumed. AI-enabled government systems operate within changing technological, legal, and social environments, meaning that governance arrangements must also evolve. Mechanisms such as explainability, auditing, accounting, decentralized verification, privacy-preserving computation, citizen engagement, human oversight, and responsible data governance can contribute to this continuing process. At the same time, the chapters demonstrate that institutional design must remain attentive to populations whose voices and capacities may be overlooked, including children, elderly caregivers, digitally excluded communities, and citizens interacting with complex automated systems.

We therefore hope that *Transforming Trusted AI and Service Computing for Effective Digital Government* will serve as a useful reference for researchers, policymakers, public administrators, technology professionals, legal scholars, educators, and students working at the intersection of artificial intelligence and public governance. The book is intended not merely to document current developments, but also to encourage further dialogue about the kind of digital government society should seek to build. The future of AI-enabled government will ultimately be measured not only by how efficiently systems operate, but by whether citizens can regard those systems as fair, understandable, accountable, secure, inclusive, and worthy of confidence. Building such a future requires collaboration across technological and social disciplines, and this volume is offered as one contribution to that continuing endeavor.

Chapter 1

Redefining Trust in Digital Governance Through AI Technologies:
Frameworks, Challenges, and Future Directions

Pooja Prashant Narwadkar
Bharati Vidaypeeth's New Law College, Sangli, India

Altaf Osman Mulani
http://orcid.org/0000-0002-2692-336X
SKN Sinhgad College of Engineering, Pandharpur, India

Manisha Yogesh Kale
Bharati Vidaypeeth's New Law College, Sangli, India

Geetanjali Ganesh Deshmukh
MIT World Peace University, Pune, India

ABSTRACT

Rapid integration of AI into India's digital governance ecosystem including citizen identity, welfare delivery, healthcare, judicial analytics and urban infrastructure has placed institutional trust at the heart of e-governance. This chapter examines how AI reshapes, challenges and can strengthen citizen–state trust. Using Aadhaar, UMANG, PM-KISAN, CoWIN and Bhashini as empirical anchors, it proposes a Trusted AI Governance Framework (TAGF-India) based on transparency, accountability, fairness, security, reliability and explainability. The chapter critically compares the EU AI Act, NIST AI Risk Management Framework and OECD AI

DOI: 10.4018/979-8-3373-9129-8.ch001

Principles with India's emerging regulatory approach including NITI Aayog's Responsible AI for All, MeitY's AI governance initiatives and the Digital Personal Data Protection Act 2023. A phased roadmap proposes a National AI Regulatory Authority, explainability requirements for high-stakes AI, federated governance and a Global South AI Trust Alliance.

1. INTRODUCTION

In the second decade of the twenty-first century, India embarked on an ambitious programme of state-led digital transformation that has few historical precedents in scale, speed, or ambition. The Digital India initiative, launched in 2015, was premised on the conviction that technology could serve as a democratizing lever extending government services to the last mile, reducing leakage in welfare delivery, and transforming the quality of citizen-state interactions across a subcontinent of extraordinary diversity. By 2024, India's digital public infrastructure encompassed over 1.3 billion Adhaar enrolled citizens, a Unified Payments Interface processing over 13 billion monthly transactions, and more than 1,200 government services accessible through the UMANG mobile platform.

Artificial Intelligence has become the animating intelligence layer atop this digital infrastructure stack. Machine learning models now assist in identifying fraudulent beneficiaries in PM-KISAN farm subsidy disbursements, flagging anomalies in CoWIN vaccination records, personalizing learning pathways on the iGOT Karmayogi civil servant training platform, routing traffic enforcement through AI enabled camera networks in twenty major cities, and predicting disease outbreaks from aggregated health records. The Indian government's stated ambition articulated in the India AI Mission 2024 with an allocation of INR 10,372 crore is to position AI as a core capability of the state apparatus.

Yet this trajectory of AI-powered governance has surfaced a set of profound questions that neither technocratic optimism nor regulatory inertia can adequately address: In a democracy constituted by linguistic plurality, caste hierarchy, gender inequality, and vast digital divides, who decides which AI systems acquire the authority to apportion rights, benefits, and burdens? How do citizens, many of them rural, vernacular-speaking, and digitally marginal, comprehend, contest, or appeal decisions made by algorithms they can neither access nor interrogate? What institutional architectures are required to ensure that the speed and scale of AI deployment do not outpace the democratic accountability mechanisms that give governance its legitimacy?

These questions converge on the concept of trust the foundational social and political compact that authorises governments to act on behalf of citizens, and that is eroded, often irreversibly, when state actions are perceived as arbitrary, opaque, or discriminatory. Trust in digital governance is not a technical property of AI systems; it is a relational property of the socio-technical systems through which AI is embedded in the exercise of public power. Redefining this trust in the age of AI requires frameworks that are simultaneously technically rigorous, institutionally robust, culturally sensitive, and democratically accountable.

This chapter develops such a framework, the Trusted AI Governance Framework for India (TAGF-India) and situates it within a comprehensive analysis of India's current AI governance landscape, international regulatory comparators, and a forward-looking policy roadmap.

2. CONCEPTUAL FOUNDATIONS OF TRUST IN DIGITAL GOVERNANCE

2.1 The Political Economy of Trust

Trust, in its political-philosophical formulation, denotes a disposition to accept vulnerability to the actions of another party, individual, institution, or system based on the expectation that their actions will be benign, competent, and aligned with the interests of the trusting party (O'Neill, 2002; Hardin, 2002). In governance contexts, citizen trust in government institutions is an indispensable social capital that reduces transaction costs, enables collective action, and legitimates the exercise of coercive state power. Decades of empirical research in political science consistently demonstrate that trust in government correlates positively with compliance with law, participation in civic processes, and acceptance of redistributive welfare interventions.

Digital governance introduces a structural complication: the interpersonal trust dyad citizen and public official is increasingly mediated by algorithmic systems that citizens cannot see, understand, or interrogate. This algorithmic mediation creates what Meijer and Bolivar (2016) call a 'trust deficit by design': citizens are asked to trust outcomes produced by processes they cannot comprehend, implemented by institutions whose human accountability they can no longer locate. The challenge of digital governance, therefore, is not merely to make AI systems technically trustworthy but to reconstruct the institutional and communicative practices through which trust is formed, maintained, and restored.

2.2 Dimensions of AI Trust in Public Sector Contexts

The academic literature on AI trust spanning computer science, public administration, political theory, and science and technology studies has converged on a multidimensional framework of trust attributes relevant to AI systems in governance contexts. These dimensions are neither independent nor exhaustive; they are mutually reinforcing properties whose collective presence constitutes what we may term 'trustworthy AI governance'.

Transparency refers to the degree to which AI systems, their design objectives, training data, operational logic, and decision rationales are accessible to scrutiny by affected parties and oversight institutions. Accountability denotes the existence of clear lines of responsibility for AI-generated outcomes including mechanisms for redress when those outcomes cause harm. Fairness and non-discrimination require that AI systems do not replicate or amplify existing social inequities encoded in historical training data. Security and privacy mandates that personal data processed by AI systems be protected from unauthorized access, misuse, or exploitation. Reliability and robustness demand that AI systems perform consistently across the full diversity of population groups and environmental conditions they encounter. Explainability, finally, requires that AI decisions be communicable in terms that affected parties citizens, administrators, and courts can understand and contest.

Table 1 maps these trust dimensions to the specific governance mechanisms and regulatory instruments through which India is attempting to operationalize them.

Table 1. Dimensions of AI Trust and Corresponding Governance Mechanisms in India

Trust Dimension	Description	AI-Governance Mechanism in India
Transparency	Citizens must understand how AI decisions are made	MeitY's draft AI governance guidelines; algorithmic disclosure norms in DigiLocker
Accountability	Clear lines of responsibility for AI-driven outcomes	IT Act 2000 amendments; DPDP Act 2023 data-principal rights
Fairness & Non-Discrimination	AI systems must not perpetuate social biases	SC/ST safeguard reviews in PMGSY road allocation AI; NITI Aayog responsible-AI principles
Security & Privacy	Protection of personal data processed by AI systems	DPDP Act 2023; Aadhaar Act biometric data protection; CERT-In incident reporting
Reliability & Robustness	AI should perform consistently across diverse populations	BIS quality standards for AI products; NIC testing protocols
Explainability	AI outputs must be interpretable by administrators and citizens	RTI-compatible AI audit logs; iGOT Karmayogi skill frameworks for AI literacy

2.3 Trust as a Dynamic and Contextual Property

A critical insight from the sociology of trust is its irreducible contextuality: what constitutes trustworthy behaviour is shaped by cultural expectations, historical experience, power differentials, and the specific stakes of the domain in question.

India's governance context is characterized by a legacy of colonial administrative practice, post-independence institutional fragility, the constitutional commitment to social justice for historically marginalized groups, and an extraordinary degree of linguistic and cultural heterogeneity.

These contextual factors profoundly shape what Indian citizens require from AI governance systems to grant them trust. A Dalit farmer in Telangana interacting with an AI-driven crop insurance system brings a historically grounded scepticism of bureaucratic impartiality that demands different trust-building mechanisms than a tech-literate professional in Bengaluru interacting with a digitalized tax filing interface. Any framework for AI governance trust in India must be sensitive to this contextual plurality rather than assuming a homogeneous, liberal-individualist model of the trusting citizen.

3. AI DEPLOYMENT IN INDIA'S DIGITAL GOVERNANCE ECOSYSTEM

3.1 The Architecture of India's Digital Public Infrastructure

India's AI-in-governance ecosystem is built atop a three-layer digital public infrastructure (DPI) stack that has acquired global recognition as a model for inclusive digital transformation. The identity layer like Adhaar provides foundational authentication for over 1.37 billion enrolled individuals. The payments layer such as UPI that enables real-time, interoperable financial transfers at zero transaction cost. The data sharing layer that the Account Aggregator framework and emerging Data Empowerment and Protection Architecture (DEPA) enables consent-based data flows that power personalized government service delivery.

AI operates as the intelligence layer atop this DPI stack, enabling the state to move from reactive, rule-based service delivery to predictive, needs-anticipatory governance. This shift is profound in its implications: it transforms the government's relationship with citizens from one of passive service provider to active, data-intensive monitor and predictor, a transformation that carries significant trust implications.

3.2 Key AI Applications in Indian Governance

Table 2 surveys the principal AI applications currently operational or in advanced pilot stages across India's central government ecosystem, documenting the specific AI capability deployed, the lead ministry or agency, and the primary trust challenges each application surfaces.

Table 2. AI Applications in Indian Governance — Domains, Agencies, and Trust Challenges

Initiative / Programme	AI Application Domain	Lead Ministry / Agency	Trust Challenge
Aadhaar Biometric ID	Identity authentication, e-KYC	UIDAI / MeitY	Biometric exclusion, surveillance risk
UMANG Platform	Multi-service citizen portal (1,200+ services)	MeitY / NIC	Data integration, interoperability
PM-KISAN AI Verification	Beneficiary fraud detection via satellite AI	Ministry of Agriculture	Algorithmic exclusion of genuine farmers
AI-SETU Chatbot	Grievance redressal, citizen Q&A	MeitY	Hallucination, multilingual accuracy
NIPUN Bharat AI	Foundational literacy assessment (Grades 1-3)	Ministry of Education	Bias against vernacular learners
CoWIN Vaccine AI	Slot allocation, adverse-event prediction	MoHFW / NIC	Digital divide, rural exclusion
Smart Traffic CCTV AI	Automated challan issuance (20 cities)	MoRTH / City Police	Due process, facial recognition bias
iGOT Karmayogi AI	Civil servant learning personalisation	DoPT	Algorithmic promotion-path influence

3.3 State-Level AI Governance Initiatives

Beyond central government deployments, Indian states have emerged as significant AI governance laboratories. Andhra Pradesh's Real-Time Governance Society (RTGS) deploys machine learning for proactive welfare identification, flagging potential beneficiaries before they approach government offices. Telangana's T-Fiber initiative integrates AI-driven demand forecasting for broadband rollout prioritization. Kerala's K-DISC has developed an AI ethics charter explicitly addressing algorithmic accountability for state-deployed systems. Tamil Nadu's Naan Mudhalvan AI-driven employment matching platform connects graduates with opportunities based on skills assessment, raising questions about algorithmic influence on career trajectories.

This state-level experimentation, while valuable, also creates regulatory fragmentation: citizens in different states encounter AI governance systems with vastly different transparency, accountability, and redress architectures, creating an uneven landscape of digital rights that is constitutionally concerning in a federated democracy.

3.4 The Trust Gap in Current Deployments

Despite the breadth of AI deployment, systematic evidence suggests that citizen trust in AI-mediated government services remains fragile. Survey and field research on citizen experience with automated government decisions, including Adhaar authentication failures and PM-KISAN verification rejections, points to a recurring pattern: affected citizens frequently report that they could not understand the reason for an adverse outcome, could not identify a responsible official to approach, and could not access an effective redress mechanism (Sambasivan et al., 2021). This trust gap is not a peripheral concern; it is a structural threat to the democratic legitimacy of AI-powered governance.

4. THE TRUSTED AI GOVERNANCE FRAMEWORK FOR INDIA (TAGF-INDIA)

4.1 Framework Architecture and Design Principles

The Trusted AI Governance Framework for India (TAGF-India) is proposed as an integrated, multi-layer conceptual and operational framework that organizes the conditions necessary for trustworthy AI governance across the Indian state's federal, sectoral, and institutional diversity. TAGF-India is designed around five foundational design principles derived from both international best practice and the specific imperatives of India's socio-political context.

The first principle is constitutional grounding: TAGF-India is explicitly anchored in the Indian Constitution's fundamental rights framework particularly Articles 14 (equality), 19 (freedom of speech), 21 (right to life and dignity), and the Directive Principles of State Policy that mandate the state to act as a trustee of citizens' welfare. AI governance frameworks that lack constitutional grounding risk creating technocratic authority structures that are unaccountable to democratic norms.

The second principle is federalism-sensitivity: given India's constitutionally mandated distribution of legislative and executive power between the Union and States, TAGF-India adopts a cooperative federalism model in which central government establishes minimum trust standards and states retain flexibility to strengthen them according to local contexts. The third principle is inclusion-by-design: recognizing that digital exclusion and algorithmic bias are structurally interrelated, TAGF-India mandates representativeness of affected communities in AI system design, testing, and audit processes. The fourth principle is institutional plurality: TAGF-India assigns trust functions to multiple, mutually checking institutions rather than concentrating oversight in any single body. The fifth principle is evolutionary adaptability: given the pace of AI development, TAGF-India is designed as a living framework with scheduled review cycles rather than a static regulatory code.

4.2 The Six Trust Pillars of TAGF-India

4.2.1 Pillar 1: Transparency and Disclosure

Transparency in AI governance requires multi-level disclosure: disclosure to affected citizens in comprehensible terms about how AI influences decisions affecting them; disclosure to oversight bodies about system architecture, training data, performance metrics, and failure modes; and public disclosure of summary-level information to enable civil society scrutiny. TAGF-India proposes a tiered disclosure architecture: Tier 1 (citizen-facing) mandates plain-language decision explanations in the citizen's preferred scheduled language; Tier 2 (institutional) requires technical disclosure to regulatory bodies including model documentation, bias audit reports, and performance monitoring dashboards; Tier 3 (public) mandates publication of annual AI governance reports by all ministries deploying AI in service delivery.

4.2.2 Pillar 2: Accountability and Redress

Accountability in AI governance has both prospective and retrospective dimensions. Prospective accountability requires pre-deployment impact assessments that identify likely harms, affected populations, and mitigation strategies before AI systems are operationalized. Retrospective accountability requires robust mechanisms for citizens to challenge adverse AI-influenced decisions, including the right to human review of automated determinations affecting fundamental rights or significant welfare benefits. TAGF-India proposes that all AI systems deployed in high-stakes governance domains welfare eligibility, identity verification, judicial risk assessment, and automated enforcement be designated 'High Accountability Systems' (HAS) subject to mandatory human review provisions, time-bound redress procedures, and recorded administrative reasoning.

4.2.3 Pillar 3: Fairness and Anti-Discrimination

India's constitutional commitment to substantive equality articulated in its affirmative action provisions for Scheduled Castes, Scheduled Tribes, and Other Backward Classes demands a conception of AI fairness that goes beyond mere statistical parity and addresses historical disadvantage. TAGF-India adopts an equity-oriented fairness standard that requires AI systems in welfare delivery to demonstrate not only that they do not disadvantage protected groups but that their outcomes actively advance constitutional equity objectives. This requires disaggregated performance audits by caste category, gender, religion, geography, and disability status dimensions along which India's welfare systems have historically exhibited systematic bias.

4.2.4 Pillar 4: Security and Data Protection

The Digital Personal Data Protection Act 2023 establishes the foundational data protection framework within which TAGF-India operates. TAGF-India extends the DPDP Act's provisions specifically to AI governance contexts by requiring:

i. Purpose limitation: AI systems may only process citizen data for the specific governance purpose for which consent was obtained, preventing function creep from welfare identification to surveillance,
ii. Data minimization: AI model training must use the minimum necessary personal data, with synthetic data augmentation where possible,
iii. Storage limitation: inferences generated by AI systems about individuals are subject to the same retention limits as the underlying personal data and
iv. AI specific breach notification: security incidents affecting AI training data or inference outputs trigger mandatory notification to the Data Protection Board within 72 hours.

4.2.5 Pillar 5: Reliability and Robustness Testing

AI systems in governance must perform reliably across the full diversity of India's population including low-literacy users, non-standard biometric presentations (agricultural workers with degraded fingerprints), users with disabilities, and users in low-bandwidth rural connectivity environments. TAGF-India proposes a National AI Testing and Certification Protocol (NATCP) administered through the Bureau of Indian Standards (BIS) in collaboration with domain ministries. The NATCP mandates pre-deployment stress testing across demographic subgroups, adversarial robustness testing against data poisoning and prompt injection attacks, and periodic in-deployment performance monitoring with automatic system suspension triggers when performance drops below minimum standards for any designated demographic subgroup.

4.2.6 Pillar 6: Explainability and Interpretability

Explainability is the trust pillar most directly in tension with the operational efficiency rationale for deploying advanced AI particularly deep learning architectures whose predictive accuracy derives precisely from their representational complexity. TAGF-India adopts a context sensitive explainability standard: for AI systems influencing high-stakes individual decisions, explainability is a non-negotiable requirement regardless of accuracy trade-offs; for AI systems performing aggregate analysis or operational optimization, explainability standards are calibrated to the directness of impact on individual citizens. Technically, TAGF-India endorses post-hoc explanation methods (SHAP, LIME, Integrated Gradients) as the minimum standard for deployed systems, while incentivizing the development of inherently interpretable models (decision trees, logistic regression, attention-based transformers with explanation heads) for high-stakes applications.

5. COMPARATIVE INTERNATIONAL AI GOVERNANCE FRAMEWORKS

5.1 Overview of Global Regulatory Landscape and Analytical Approach

The global AI governance landscape is characterized by a proliferating patchwork of frameworks ranging from legally binding regulation (the EU AI Act) to voluntary principles-based guidance (OECD AI Principles, UNESCO Recommendation on AI Ethics). No single international framework currently establishes binding global standards, creating a regulatory arbitrage environment that poses challenges for AI developers operating across jurisdictions and for governments seeking to align domestic regulation with international norms.

India occupies a distinctive position in this landscape: as a major AI developer and deployer with a large domestic market and a strong tradition of technology self-reliance, India has both the capacity and the sovereign interest to shape global AI governance norms rather than simply adopt externally developed frameworks. Rather than surveying these frameworks descriptively, this section compares them along four analytical dimensions. Regulatory philosophy denotes the underlying theory of regulation animating the framework, whether rights-based, risk-based, or market-enabling. Governance approach denotes whether the framework is a binding statute, a soft-law instrument, or a voluntary standard, and the institutional architecture through which it is administered. Accountability mechanism denotes the specific enforcement, audit, and redress provisions attached to the framework. Applicability to India denotes the framework's compatibility with India's federal structure, constitutional design, and developmental priorities. These four dimensions structure the discussion in Sections 5.2 to 5.4 and inform the comparative summary in Table 3, and they are used in Section 5.5 to identify the composite gap that TAGF-India is designed to close.

Table 3. Comparative Analysis of International AI Governance Frameworks Along Four Analytical Dimensions

Framework	Regulatory Philosophy	Governance Approach	Accountability Mechanism	Applicability to India
EU AI Act 2024	Rights-based, risk-tiered regulation	Legally binding statute; centralised EU AI Office plus national competent authorities	Conformity assessments, mandatory audits, fines up to 7% of global turnover	High: benchmark for risk classification, but its centralised architecture does not map onto India's federal structure
NIST AI RMF 2023	Market-enabling, organisation-level risk management	Voluntary framework; no dedicated regulator	Self-assessment against GOVERN-MAP-MEASURE-MANAGE functions; no external enforcement	Moderate: useful functional template, but reflects a private-sector-led model distinct from India's state-led approach
NITI Aayog RAIC 2021	Principles-based developmental governance	Non-binding national policy document	Aspirational; no statutory audit or redress mechanism	Direct: India's own foundational framework, limited by absence of enforcement and federal-specific guidance
MeitY AI Guidelines 2023	Sector-specific administrative guidance	Partially binding draft advisory	Ministry-level disclosure norms; enforcement powers unclear	Direct: closest existing instrument to a national AI-specific regulation, though still in draft form
DPDP Act 2023	Rights-based data protection	Legally binding statute; Data Protection Board as regulator	Breach notification, correction/erasure rights, statutory penalties	Direct: supplies the data-governance substrate for AI trust but does not itself regulate algorithmic decisions
UNESCO AI Ethics 2021	Rights-based global ethics	Soft law; recommendation to member states	Monitoring via national implementation reporting; no binding enforcement	Moderate: shapes India's multilateral commitments and normative vocabulary
OECD AI Principles 2019	Market-enabling, principles-based	Soft law; peer-review mechanism among member states	Non-binding; tracked via the OECD AI Policy Observatory	High: India is a signatory and the principles are referenced in domestic policy

5.2 The EU AI Act: A Risk-Based Benchmark

The European Union's Artificial Intelligence Act, adopted in 2024, represents the most comprehensive legally binding AI regulatory framework currently in force. Its risk-based architecture classifying AI systems into unacceptable risk (prohibited), high risk (strictly regulated), limited risk (transparency obligations), and minimal risk (self-regulation) categories offers a methodologically coherent approach to proportionate regulation that balances innovation imperatives against fundamental rights protection.

For India, the EU AI Act is simultaneously a benchmark and a cautionary reference. Its institutional architecture, a European AI Office, national competent authorities, and a scientific panel of independent experts is designed for a political union with strong mutual recognition provisions that differ fundamentally from India's federal structure. Its extraterritorial scope (applying to AI systems placed on the EU market regardless of developer nationality) creates trade implications for Indian IT firms serving European clients. Its specific high-risk categories like biometric identification systems, AI in education, employment, and welfare benefits are directly relevant to India's most consequential AI governance deployments.

5.3 NIST AI Risk Management Framework

The United States National Institute of Standards and Technology (NIST) AI Risk Management Framework (AI RMF 1.0, 2023) adopts a voluntary, organization level risk management approach organized around four core functions: GOVERN (establishing risk governance structures), MAP (identifying and categorizing AI risks), MEASURE (quantifying and analyzing risks), and MANAGE (prioritizing and implementing risk treatments). MeitY has cited the NIST AI RMF as a reference document in its own AI governance deliberations, and elements of its functional architecture are discernible in India's emerging sectoral guidance.

The NIST AI RMF's voluntary character makes it an attractive template for India's industry-sector AI governance, particularly in financial services and healthcare where sectoral regulators (RBI, IRDAI, NMC) are developing sector-specific AI norms. However, its voluntary nature also reflects the political economy of US technology governance, which is dominated by private sector primacy and is structurally different from India's government-led digital transformation model, limiting direct transposition.

5.4 NITI Aayog's Responsible AI for All (RAIC 2021)

India's most comprehensive domestic AI governance framework to date is NITI Aayog's two-part Responsible AI for All document, published in 2021. Part 1 establishes seven principles for responsible AI in India: safety and reliability, equality, inclusivity and non-discrimination, privacy and security, transparency, accountability, and protection and reinforcement of positive human values. Part 2 operationalizes these principles through a sector-specific analysis covering healthcare, agriculture, smart cities, education, smart mobility and transportation, and smart energy.

RAIC 2021 represents a significant milestone in India's governance of AI, but it has three important limitations that TAGF-India seeks to address. First, its voluntary, principles-based character lacks enforcement mechanisms, creating a gap between stated aspirations and operational practice. Second, it does not adequately address the specific challenges of AI governance in a federal system where states bear primary responsibility for many AI-intensive welfare delivery domains. Third, its treatment of explainability is aspirational rather than operational, lacking the technical specificity required to guide procurement and audit decisions.

5.5 Synthesis: From Comparative Limitations to TAGF-India

Read together along the four analytical dimensions set out in Section 5.1, the frameworks surveyed above share a common limitation: none combines a binding enforcement architecture with a governance philosophy calibrated to India's federal structure, constitutional rights framework, and linguistic and social diversity. The EU AI Act's risk-based regulatory philosophy is legally binding and analytically rigorous, but its governance approach presumes a supranational union with strong mutual-recognition mechanisms that have no federal analogue in India. The NIST AI RMF's functional risk-management approach is readily transposable in technical terms, but its voluntary governance approach and reliance on organizational self-assessment offer no accountability mechanism adequate to high-stakes welfare and identity systems. NITI Aayog's RAIC and MeitY's draft guidelines are the most contextually appropriate in regulatory philosophy, but both lack the statutory accountability mechanisms and federal specificity required for enforcement. The DPDP Act supplies indispensable data-protection infrastructure and is legally binding, but its accountability mechanism is confined to data handling and does not extend to algorithmic decision-making as such.

This composite gap, the absence of any single framework that is simultaneously binding, contextually fitted to India's federal and constitutional structure, and equipped with accountability mechanisms adequate to high-stakes governance domains, is precisely the space TAGF-India is designed to occupy. TAGF-India is anchored in binding constitutional norms rather than voluntary principles, it is explicitly structured around India's cooperative federalism rather than a unitary or supranational model, and its High Accountability Systems designation extends statutory-grade audit and redress requirements to the welfare, identity, and enforcement domains in which the surveyed frameworks are weakest.

6. INDIA'S EVOLVING AI REGULATORY ARCHITECTURE

6.1 The Legislative Foundation

India's AI regulatory architecture is currently assembled from a set of legislative instruments not designed specifically for AI, supplemented by an evolving set of ministry-level guidelines and sector-specific regulatory pronouncements. The Information Technology Act 2000, with its 2008 amendments, provides the foundational legal framework for electronic communications, data protection (Section 43A), and intermediary liability (Section 79). The Adhaar Act 2016 governs biometric data collection and authentication, establishing a sector-specific privacy regime for India's most consequential AI-powered identity system.

The Digital Personal Data Protection Act 2023 (DPDP Act) marks the most significant legislative development relevant to AI governance in recent years. The DPDP Act establishes the right to data correction and erasure, mandatory breach notification, purpose limitation requirements, and the constitution of a Data Protection Board as the primary regulatory body. While the DPDP Act does not address AI specifically, its data governance provisions provide the regulatory substrate within which AI training, inference, and decision-making systems must operate.

6.2 Ministry-Level and Sectoral AI Governance

MeitY has been the primary institutional locus of AI governance deliberation at the Union level, issuing a draft 'India AI Strategy' discussion paper and sector-specific advisory notes on AI in healthcare, fintech, and agricultural services. The Securities and Exchange Board of India (SEBI) issued a circular in 2023 mandating disclosure of AI use in investment advisory services. The Reserve Bank of India (RBI) has integrated AI governance considerations into its regulatory guidelines for regulated entities deploying AI in credit underwriting and fraud detection. The National Medical Commission (NMC) has developed preliminary guidance on AI use in clinical decision support.

This sectoral proliferation of AI governance guidance, while reflecting the regulatory responsiveness of individual sectoral regulators, simultaneously creates a fragmented landscape in which identical trust issues are addressed by different regulatory bodies with different standards, timelines, and enforcement capacities. A citizen affected by an AI driven adverse decision in a health insurance context may face entirely different redress pathways than a citizen affected by an analogous AI-driven decision in a welfare benefit context, creating arbitrary disparities in digital rights.

6.3 The India AI Mission 2024 and Institutional Architecture

The India AI Mission, approved by the Union Cabinet in March 2024 with an outlay of INR 10,372 crore over five years, represents the government's most comprehensive commitment to AI capacity building to date. Its seven pillars, namely compute infrastructure, foundational model development, datasets platform, AI integration in sectors, AI skilling, responsible AI, and startup financing, situate responsible AI development as an integral component of national AI strategy rather than a post-hoc regulatory afterthought.

The Mission's responsible AI pillar envisages the establishment of an India AI Safety Institute (IASI), an AI governance advisory body analogous to the AI Safety Institutes established in the United Kingdom and the United States. The institutional design of IASI, including its mandate, composition, powers, and relationship to existing regulatory bodies, remains under deliberation, representing the most consequential institutional design choice in India's near-term AI governance trajectory.

7. STRUCTURAL CHALLENGES TO AI TRUST IN INDIAN DIGITAL GOVERNANCE

The following section systematically analyses seven structural challenges that constrain the realization of trustworthy AI governance in India. These challenges are not merely technical deficiencies amenable to algorithmic solutions; they are embedded in India's social, institutional, and political economy and require correspondingly multi-dimensional responses. Table 4 provides an integrated overview.

Table 4: Structural Challenges to AI Trust in India and Proposed Mitigation Strategies

Challenge Category	Specific Challenge in India	Proposed Mitigation Strategy
Digital Divide	Only 52% rural broadband penetration; AI governance excludes offline citizens	Offline-capable AI at gram panchayat level; assisted-access kiosks; radio-based AI advisories
Linguistic Diversity	22 scheduled languages plus 1,600 dialects; English-centric AI models	Multilingual NLP via Bhashini project; language-parity audits; TDIL corpora expansion
Algorithmic Bias	Caste, gender, and geography encoded in historical training data	Mandatory fairness audits; SC/ST/OBC representativeness testing; bias bounty programmes
Data Sovereignty	Cross-border data flows vs. localisation mandates under DPDP Act	Tiered data localisation; federated learning for sensitive categories; data embassy model
Institutional Capacity	Limited AI expertise in state/district bureaucracy	iGOT Karmayogi AI modules; Centre-of-Excellence partnerships with IITs/IIITs
Regulatory Fragmentation	MeitY, TRAI, RBI, SEBI each issue parallel AI norms	Unified National AI Regulatory Authority (NAIRA) proposal; cross-ministry coordination cell
Explainability Gap	Black-box AI in welfare programmes denies RTI compliance	XAI mandates for high-stakes decisions; SHAP/LIME audit trails; citizen-readable decision summaries

7.1 The Digital Divide and Infrastructural Exclusion

Despite India's impressive aggregate digital growth statistics, structural digital divides persist along geographic, socioeconomic, gender, and disability dimensions. As of 2024, rural broadband penetration remains at approximately 52%, with significant intra-state variation: Himachal Pradesh and Kerala exceed 70% coverage while Jharkhand, Bihar, and several northeastern states remain below 35%. Smartphone penetration among women in rural areas is estimated at 33% compared to 62% among rural men, creating a gendered digital exclusion that systematically disadvantages women in AI-mediated welfare systems.

AI governance frameworks designed primarily for digitally connected, smartphone-owning citizens replicate and amplify these exclusions. An AI-driven grievance redressal chatbot accessible only via smartphone app excludes precisely those citizens most likely to experience adverse administrative outcomes. Trustworthy AI governance in India must therefore mandate offline-capable and assisted-access service modalities that ensure AI governance rights are not contingent on digital access.

7.2 Linguistic Plurality and the Language Justice Imperative

India's constitutional recognition of 22 scheduled languages, overlaid on an estimated 1,600 mother tongue dialects, presents a challenge of extraordinary complexity for AI governance systems designed primarily in English. The Bhashini project, launched by MeitY in 2022, represents a significant commitment to multilingual AI capability, developing speech recognition, machine translation, and natural language processing tools for India's scheduled languages. However, as of 2024, significant gaps remain: several northeastern and tribal languages lack adequate digital text corpora for AI model training, and the accuracy of AI systems in regional languages remains substantially below English-language performance benchmarks.

Language justice in AI governance is not merely an inclusion concern; it is a due process requirement. A citizen who cannot comprehend the explanation provided for an adverse AI-driven decision because it is rendered in English or a language they do not speak has been effectively denied their right to meaningful redress. TAGF-India's Tier 1 transparency requirement, which mandates plain-language decision explanations in the citizen's preferred scheduled language, directly addresses this imperative.

7.3 Algorithmic Bias and India's Social Stratification

India's social fabric is constituted by intersecting hierarchies of caste, class, religion, gender, and geography that have shaped the distribution of opportunities, resources, and institutional power for centuries. These hierarchies are encoded in the historical data on which AI models are trained, not as explicit discriminatory intent but as structural regularities of an unequal society. An AI model trained to predict creditworthiness on the basis of historical lending data encodes the historically constrained access to formal credit of Dalit and Adivasi communities. An AI model predicting school dropout risk based on historical enrolment patterns reflects the gendered educational marginalization that has historically characterized rural communities.

The challenge of algorithmic bias in India is therefore not simply a question of removing 'sensitive attributes' from model inputs, a technically naive solution that fails to address proxy discrimination through correlated features. It is a question of how AI systems can be designed to actively counteract structural inequities rather than merely avoiding their explicit reproduction. This requires not only technical interventions (fairness-aware machine learning, counterfactual fairness, adversarial debiasing) but also institutional interventions mandatory representation of marginalized community members in AI audit processes, algorithmic impact assessments disaggregated by protected characteristics, and constitutional-equity testing as a deployment prerequisite for welfare AI.

7.4 Data Sovereignty and the Localisation-Innovation Tension

India's Digital Personal Data Protection Act 2023 establishes a framework for cross-border data transfer that balances sovereignty imperatives protecting Indian citizens' data from foreign government access with the operational reality that many AI systems deployed in India depend on cloud infrastructure, model APIs, and training data pipelines that traverse international boundaries. The DPDP Act's Section 16 permits cross-border data transfer to countries notified by the Union government as having adequate data protection standards, but the notification list has not yet been published, creating regulatory uncertainty for AI developers and government procurement officers alike.

For AI governance, this data sovereignty tension manifests concretely in the following dilemma: the most powerful AI models (particularly large language models with multilingual capability relevant to India) are developed by foreign entities like OpenAI, Google, Anthropic, Meta and are trained on data that includes Indian citizens' digital footprints. The governance of these models, including decisions about their training data, safety properties, and update schedules, lies beyond the reach of Indian regulatory authority. India's sovereign AI capability building through the India AI Mission's foundational model development pillar is a strategic response to this dependency, but mature sovereign alternatives to frontier AI capabilities remain years away.

7.5 Institutional Capacity and Bureaucratic AI Literacy

Effective AI governance requires not only legislative frameworks and institutional mandates but also the bureaucratic capacity to implement, audit, procure, and oversee AI systems intelligently. Current evidence suggests significant gaps in this capacity across India's public administration. A 2023 assessment by the Department of Personnel and Training found that fewer than 8% of Indian Administrative Service officers had received any formal training in AI fundamentals, machine learning concepts, or AI governance principles. Without AI-literate administrators at the procurement, oversight, and adjudication stages of the AI governance process, regulatory frameworks risk becoming formal compliance exercises rather than substantive accountability mechanisms.

The iGOT Karmayogi platform represents a significant institutional infrastructure for addressing this capacity gap, with its AI-driven personalized learning pathways and competency-based curriculum framework. TAGF-India proposes that AI governance literacy including understanding of algorithmic bias, explainability methods, and AI audit procedures be designated a mandatory competency module for civil servants in all ministries deploying AI in service delivery, with iGOT Karmayogi as the delivery platform.

7.6 Regulatory Fragmentation and Coordination Failure

India's regulatory landscape for AI is characterised by simultaneous action and occasional contradiction across multiple regulatory bodies. MeitY exercises general jurisdiction over information technology. TRAI regulates AI in telecommunications. RBI governs AI in banking and fintech. SEBI oversees AI in securities markets. IRDAI addresses AI in insurance. The NMC and CDSCO are developing AI norms for healthcare. Each body brings sector-specific expertise, but the resulting landscape is one of significant fragmentation: AI companies and government agencies deploying AI across sector boundaries navigate multiple, sometimes contradictory, regulatory obligations.

This regulatory fragmentation is not merely an administrative inconvenience; it creates substantive gaps in citizen protection. Citizens who experience harm from AI systems operating across sectoral boundaries, for example, AI that integrates healthcare, insurance, and financial data to determine welfare eligibility may find that no single regulatory body has clear jurisdiction over their complaint. TAGF-India therefore proposes a National AI Regulatory Authority for India (NAIRA) as a dedicated, cross-cutting regulatory body with primary jurisdiction over AI governance across all sectors, coordinating with sectoral regulators through a statutory National AI Governance Coordination Council.

8. AI TRUST MATURITY MODEL FOR INDIA (ATMM-INDIA)

8.1 Conceptual Foundation of the Maturity Model

Maturity models originally developed in software engineering (the Capability Maturity Model, CMM) and subsequently extended to enterprise governance (COBIT) and risk management (ISO 31000) provide a structured framework for organizations to self-assess their current capability level, identify improvement pathways, and benchmark progress against defined standards. TAGF-India incorporates an AI Trust Maturity Model (ATMM-India) specifically calibrated to the Indian public sector's federal, institutional, and capacity context.

ATMM-India defines five maturity levels such as Initial, Managed, Defined, Quantified, and Optimizing along five capability dimensions: AI governance policy, institutional structures, technical standards, accountability mechanisms, and citizen engagement. The model is designed for self-assessment by individual government agencies as well as for external audit by regulatory bodies, enabling both bottom-up capability development and top-down compliance assurance.

8.2 Maturity Level Descriptions and India Exemplars

Table 5 describes the five maturity levels of ATMM-India, providing illustrative exemplars from India's governance landscape at each level to anchor the abstract maturity descriptors in recognisable operational realities.

Table 5. AI Trust Maturity Model for India (ATMM-India) — Levels, Descriptors, and Exemplars

Maturity Level	Governance Stage	AI Capability	Trust Mechanism	India Exemplar
Level 1: Initial	Ad hoc AI adoption	Pilot projects, siloed tools	None formal	State-specific chatbots (pre-2020)
Level 2: Managed	Policy awareness	Rule-based AI, basic ML	Internal audits	CoWIN slot allocation (2021)
Level 3: Defined	Framework articulated	Predictive analytics, NLP	Voluntary disclosures	NITI Aayog RAIC adoption (2022)
Level 4: Quantified	Regulatory compliance	Deep learning, generative AI	Third-party audits, metrics	MeitY draft AI guidelines compliance (2023-24)
Level 5: Optimizing	Adaptive governance	Autonomous AI, federated systems	Continuous trust certification	Target state: India AI Mission 2025+

8.3 Application of ATMM-India

ATMM-India can be applied at three levels of analysis: the agency level (an individual ministry or department assessing its AI governance maturity), the programme level (a specific AI deployment such as PM-KISAN verification assessed against all five capability dimensions), and the national level (an aggregated assessment of India's overall AI governance maturity across the public sector). National-level ATMM-India assessments, conducted biannually and published as part of the government's AI governance annual report, would provide a mechanism for longitudinal tracking of India's AI governance progress and enable international benchmarking against comparable major digital government initiatives.

The maturity model is not intended as a compliance checkbox mechanism but as a developmental tool: its primary value lies in providing a shared vocabulary for AI governance improvement conversations within and between government agencies, and in creating structured incentives for progressive capability development rather than minimum compliance behaviour.

9. SOCIO-POLITICAL DIMENSIONS OF AI TRUST IN INDIAN GOVERNANCE

9.1 Democratic Legitimacy and the Automation of State Power

Democratic legitimacy is the principle that the exercise of state power over citizens must be authorized by democratic processes and constrained by democratic accountability is fundamentally challenged by the automation of government decision-making through AI. When an algorithm determines welfare eligibility, allocates school admissions, or triggers enforcement action, the democratic accountability chain from elected representative to minister to civil servant to citizen is interrupted. The algorithm's 'decision' is not the expression of any identifiable human will accountable to democratic processes; it is the output of a socio-technical system designed, procured, and deployed by a complex institutional network whose accountability is diffuse and often opaque.

This democratic legitimacy challenge is particularly acute in India because of the constitutional design of Indian democracy, which places heavy emphasis on procedural fairness, reasoned decision-making, and access to judicial review as guarantors of citizens' constitutional rights. The Supreme Court of India, in a line of cases from Maneka Gandhi (1978) through Anuradha Bhasin (2020), has progressively expanded the procedural content of Article 21's right to life to include the right to reasons for adverse state action. Extending this jurisprudence to algorithmic state action is a frontier legal question that Indian courts will increasingly be required to address.

9.2 Surveillance Capitalism and the Boundary Between Service and Surveillance

India's integrated digital governance infrastructure combining Adhaar biometrics, UPI transaction records, health data from Ayushman Bharat, satellite imagery from farm monitoring programmes, and location data from smart city sensors creates an unprecedented infrastructure for population-level surveillance. The same data integration that enables personalised, proactive welfare delivery also enables comprehensive tracking of citizen behaviour, association, and movement.

This dual-use character of India's digital governance infrastructure creates a structural tension between the service-delivery rationale for AI deployment and the surveillance potential of the data it generates. Trust in AI-powered governance depends critically on the institutional mechanisms that enforce the boundary between legitimate data use for service delivery and illegitimate function creep into surveillance. The DPDP Act's purpose limitation provisions, TAGF-India's data minimisation requirements, and independent oversight of government data use are all essential components of maintaining this boundary.

9.3 Civil Society, Media, and AI Accountability

Effective AI governance requires an informed and engaged civil society capable of scrutinizing AI deployments, amplifying citizen grievances, and holding government accountable for algorithmic harms. India's civil society organizations working on digital rights including the Internet Freedom Foundation, the Centre for Internet and Society, and the Dialogue have played important roles in documenting AI governance failures, litigating constitutional challenges to biometric surveillance, and advocating for data protection legislation. Academic institutions including IIT Madras, IISc Bangalore, and Ashoka University have developed AI ethics research agendas that contribute to the evidence base for governance reform.

However, India's recent regulatory environment for civil society, including the Foreign Contribution Regulation Act (FCRA) amendments and applications of the Unlawful Activities Prevention Act, has constrained the operating space for civil society organizations that have been most active in digital rights advocacy. A vibrant, independent civil society is not a threat to trustworthy AI governance; it is an indispensable component of the accountability ecosystem on which trustworthy AI governance depends.

10. CONCLUSION

The question with which this chapter opened how AI technologies reshape, challenge, and can potentially strengthen trust in digital governance admits no simple answer. AI is neither an inherent threat to democratic governance nor an automatic guarantor of more efficient, equitable, and responsive government. Its effect on institutional trust is determined by the governance frameworks within which it is embedded, the institutional cultures that deploy it, the accountability mechanisms that constrain it, and the civic capacities that scrutinize it. India's AI governance trajectory is at a critical inflection point. The infrastructure investments of the India AI Mission, the legislative foundations of the DPDP Act, the institutional ambitions of the proposed India AI Safety Institute, and the inclusive technology commitments of the Bhashini and Digital India programmes collectively constitute a significant platform for the development of trustworthy AI governance. But realizing this potential requires deliberate, sustained, and politically courageous institutional choices that this chapter has sought to illuminate and support.

The Trusted AI Governance Framework for India (TAGF-India) developed in this chapter is not a final answer but a structured framework for ongoing deliberation. Its six trust pillars like transparency, accountability, fairness, security, reliability, and explainability are not technical checkboxes but ongoing governance commitments that must be continuously renewed and contextually adapted as AI technologies evolve and as India's democratic society develops its collective understanding of what trustworthy AI governance means in practice.

Three meta-level conclusions deserve particular emphasis. First, AI governance is fundamentally a question of political economy, not merely technical design: the choices that determine whether AI serves democratic accountability or undermines it are choices about institutional power, resource allocation, and political will, not merely algorithm architecture. Second, India's constitutional framework with its commitments to substantive equality, procedural fairness, and democratic accountability is not an obstacle to AI-powered governance but its most essential resource, providing the normative foundations for a distinctively Indian approach to trustworthy AI. Third, India's scale and diversity often framed as governance challenges are also its most valuable assets in the global AI governance discourse, providing lived evidence of what responsible AI deployment looks like in a genuinely heterogeneous democratic society. The path from the trust deficit documented in this chapter to the trustworthy AI governance envisioned by TAGF-India is neither short nor straight. It runs through legislative reform, institutional innovation, technical investment, capacity building, and civic renewal. But it is a path that India with its constitutional commitments, its democratic traditions, and its extraordinary human talent is uniquely equipped to travel. The world will be watching, and learning.

Statement of AI Tool Usage

The authors acknowledge the use of Artificial Intelligence (AI)-assisted tools during the preparation of this manuscript. AI tools were utilized solely to support language refinement, grammar correction, content organization, formatting assistance, and enhancement of readability. The authors critically reviewed, verified, and edited all AI-assisted outputs to ensure accuracy, originality, and compliance with academic and ethical standards.

REFERENCES

Hardin, R. (2002). *Trust and trustworthiness*. Russell Sage Foundation.

Meijer, A., & Bolívar, M. P. R. (2016). Governing the smart city: A review of the literature on smart urban governance. *International Review of Administrative Sciences, 82*(2), 392–408. DOI: 10.1177/0020852314564308

Ministry of Electronics and Information Technology (MeitY). (2023). *Draft advisory on artificial intelligence: Responsible AI for governance applications*. Government of India.

National Institute of Standards and Technology (NIST). (2023). Artificial Intelligence Risk Management Framework (AI RMF 1.0). DOI: 10.6028/NIST.AI.100-1

National Institution for Transforming India (NITI Aayog). (2018). *National strategy for artificial intelligence: #AIforAll*. Government of India.

National Institution for Transforming India (NITI Aayog). (2021). *Responsible AI for all (Parts 1 and 2)*. Government of India.

O'Neill, O. (2002). *A question of trust: The BBC Reith Lectures 2002*. Cambridge University Press.

Parliament of India. (2023). The Digital Personal Data Protection Act, 2023 (No. 22 of 2023). Gazette of India, Extraordinary, Part II, Section 1.

Press Information Bureau, Government of India. (2024, March 7). Cabinet approves India AI Mission with an outlay of 10,372 crore. Ministry of Electronics and Information Technology.

Raji, I. D., Smart, A., White, R. N., Mitchell, M., Gebru, T., Hutchinson, B., Smith-Loud, J., Theron, D., & Barnes, P. (2020). Closing the AI accountability gap: Defining an end-to-end framework for internal algorithmic auditing. *Proceedings of the 2020 ACM Conference on Fairness, Accountability, and Transparency*, 33–44. DOI: 10.1145/3351095.3372873

Sambasivan, N., Arnesen, E., Hutchinson, B., Doshi, T., & Prabhakaran, V. (2021). Re-imagining algorithmic fairness in India and beyond. *Proceedings of the 2021 ACM Conference on Fairness, Accountability, and Transparency*, 315–328. DOI: 10.1145/3442188.3445896

Supreme Court of India. (1978). Maneka Gandhi v. Union of India, AIR 1978 SC 597.

Supreme Court of India. (2017). Justice K. S. Puttaswamy (Retd.) & Anr. v. Union of India & Ors., (2017) 10 SCC 1.

Supreme Court of India. (2020). Anuradha Bhasin v. Union of India, (2020) 3 SCC 637.

UNESCO. (2021). *Recommendation on the ethics of artificial intelligence*. UNESCO.

Chapter 2
Understanding Trust Structures in AI-Enabled Digital Governance

Beichen Lu
http://orcid.org/0009-0002-7346-2209
Tsinghua University, China

ABSTRACT

Chapter 2 explores the multidimensional nature of trust in AI enabled digital government. It argues that trust is no longer limited to citizens' confidence in government institutions but has expanded to include digital systems, AI mediated governance, governance processes, and citizen government relationships. The chapter distinguishes different forms of trust and explains how each contributes to the legitimacy and effectiveness of digital governance. Furthermore, it examines how AI reshapes governance power through the emergence of algorithmic power, redistributing influence among governments, data providers, technology developers, and algorithmic systems. This transformation creates new challenges regarding accountability, transparency, and public control. The chapter concludes that Trusted AI for Effective Digital Government requires not only reliable technologies but also accountable institutions, fair governance processes, and meaningful citizen trust.

1. INTRODUCTION

Trust has always been a fundamental foundation of digital government development. However, as government services become increasingly digitized and artificial intelligence becomes embedded in public decision making, the meaning of trust has become more complex and multidimensional. In traditional government contexts,

DOI: 10.4018/979-8-3373-9129-8.ch002

trust was mainly understood as citizens' confidence in government institutions and their belief that public authorities could act effectively and legitimately. However, digital transformation has expanded the object of trust beyond government itself. Citizens must now evaluate not only whether governments are trustworthy, but also whether digital systems are reliable, whether AI driven governance is legitimate, whether decision making processes are fair, and whether interactions with digital government remain responsive to human needs (Busuioc, 2021).

Therefore, trust in AI enabled digital government should not be understood as a single relationship between citizens and government. Instead, it represents a multidimensional concept involving different objects, actors, and governance relationships. At the institutional level, trust concerns the legitimacy, competence, and responsibility of government organizations. At the technological level, trust focuses on the reliability, security, and dependability of digital systems that support public services. With the emergence of AI governance, trust further extends to questions regarding whether AI systems can legitimately participate in public decision making and whether algorithmic processes can be governed responsibly. Beyond institutions and technologies, trust also depends on governance processes, including transparency, accountability, fairness, and citizen participation. Finally, trust is shaped by citizens' direct experiences with digital government, including the quality of interaction, emotional connection, and long term relationships between citizens and public institutions.

Figure 1. The Taxonomy of Trust Dimensions in Digital Government

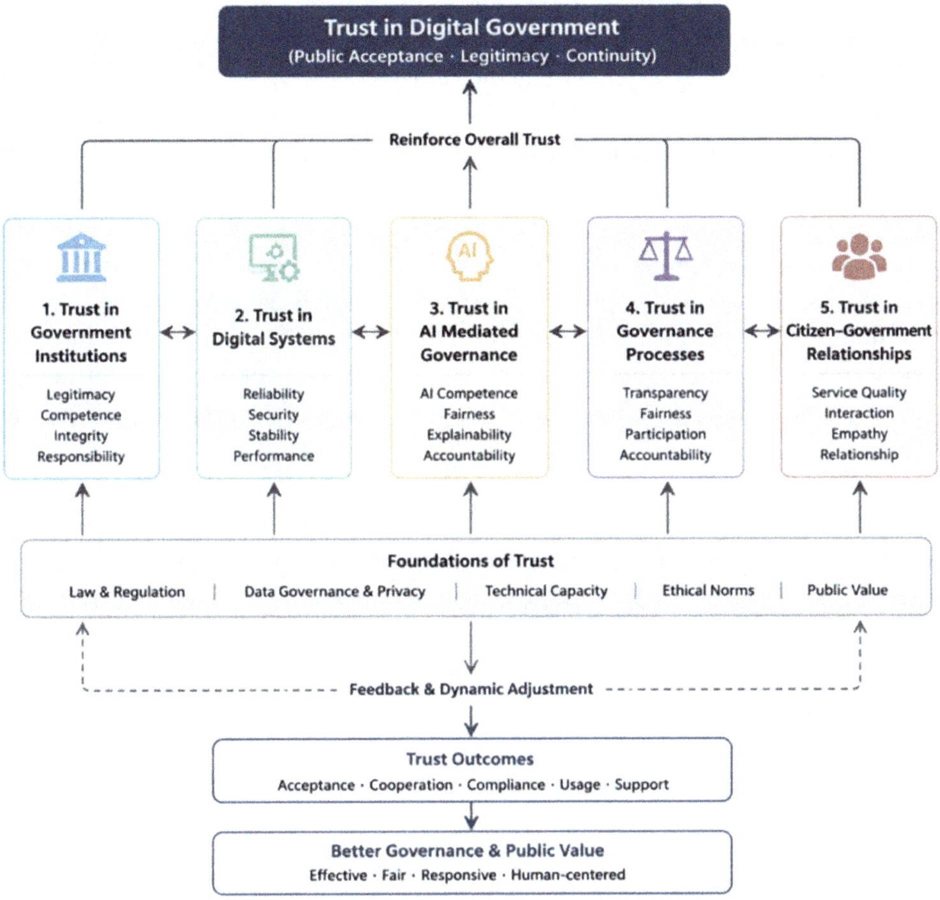

Based on this understanding, this chapter examines the diverse trust concepts involved in AI enabled digital government by distinguishing five interconnected dimensions: trust in government institutions, trust in digital systems, trust in AI mediated governance, trust in governance processes, and trust in citizen government relationships. Rather than constructing a new trust model, this chapter aims to clarify the conceptual boundaries among different forms of trust and explain how each contributes to understanding public acceptance and legitimacy in the digital era. Through this conceptual exploration, the chapter provides a foundation for analyzing how trust is transformed when government authority increasingly operates through digital infrastructures and intelligent technologies (Figure 1).

2. TRUST IN GOVERNMENT INSTITUTIONS

Trust in government institutions represents the most traditional form of trust in digital government. It focuses on whether citizens believe that government, as a public authority, is legitimate, reliable, and capable of serving collective interests. Unlike technology related trust, which concerns whether digital systems function properly, government institutional trust concerns the institution behind these systems. Citizens do not first ask whether an AI system is accurate; they ask whether the government that deploys and controls this system has the authority, competence, and responsibility to use it appropriately (Grimmelikhuijsen & Meijer, 2022).

Although often used interchangeably, political trust, institutional trust, administrative trust, and public trust refer to different dimensions of citizens' confidence in government. The main difference lies in what aspect of government citizens are evaluating.

Political trust refers to citizens' confidence in the broader political system and the legitimacy of political authority. It is the most macro level form of government trust. The central question is whether citizens believe that government power is exercised in accordance with democratic principles and public interests. Political trust is therefore related to issues such as representation, legitimacy, and responsiveness. In the context of AI enabled digital government, political trust concerns whether citizens accept the expansion of algorithmic decision making as a legitimate form of public authority. For example, citizens may question not only whether an AI welfare system produces accurate predictions, but also whether government should allow algorithms to influence decisions affecting social rights and public resources.

Institutional trust focuses on confidence in government institutions as stable and rule based organizations. Compared with political trust, which concerns the legitimacy of the political system as a whole, institutional trust emphasizes whether public institutions operate fairly, consistently, and according to established rules. The key question is whether citizens believe that government organizations can be trusted to manage public affairs responsibly. In AI governance, institutional trust determines whether citizens believe that government agencies can establish appropriate rules for data use, algorithmic oversight, and ethical control.

Administrative trust represents a more specific form of trust related to government implementation capacity. While institutional trust concerns whether government institutions are reliable in principle, administrative trust concerns whether government agencies can effectively perform their tasks in practice. It focuses on competence, professionalism, and service delivery ability. In digital government, citizens may support AI based services only when they believe administrative organizations have sufficient capability to manage technology, respond to failures, and provide effective public services (Wirtz et al., 2019).

Public trust or government trust is the broadest concept among these categories. It represents citizens' overall evaluation of government based on multiple perceptions, including legitimacy, competence, fairness, integrity, and responsiveness. Unlike political trust, which focuses on political authority, or administrative trust, which focuses on operational capability, public trust reflects the general relationship between citizens and government. It is therefore often considered the overall outcome produced by different forms of government related trust.

The conceptual relationship among these forms of trust can be understood as a movement from general legitimacy to specific capability. Political trust answers whether government authority is accepted. Institutional trust asks whether government organizations are reliable and fair. Administrative trust evaluates whether government can effectively implement policies and provide services. Public trust represents the overall judgment formed through these different evaluations (Table 4-1).

Table 1. Distinction among Government Institutional Trust Concepts

Concept	Common Ground	Main Focus	Key Difference
Political Trust	Citizens' confidence in government	Legitimacy of authority	Whether government power is accepted
Institutional Trust	Confidence in government organizations	Reliability of institutions	Whether institutions are fair and trustworthy
Administrative Trust	Evaluation of government performance	Implementation capacity	Whether government can effectively deliver services
Public Trust	Overall confidence in government	General government evaluation	The combined outcome of legitimacy, reliability, and performance

In AI enabled digital government, these distinctions become increasingly important because technological adoption depends not only on whether citizens trust the technology itself, but also on whether they trust the government that governs, regulates, and applies that technology. A highly accurate AI system may still face resistance if political trust is weak, if institutions are perceived as unfair, or if administrative capacity is questioned. Therefore, government institutional trust provides the foundational legitimacy upon which other forms of digital government trust are built.

3. TRUST IN DIGITAL SYSTEMS AND TECHNOLOGIES

Trust in digital systems and technologies refers to citizens' confidence in the technological environment that supports digital government services. Unlike trust in government institutions, which focuses on whether citizens trust the authority and legitimacy of government, technology related trust focuses on whether citizens believe that digital infrastructures, platforms, and information systems can reliably support public service delivery. Although these concepts share a common foundation, namely citizens' confidence in technology enabled government services, they differ in terms of the object being trusted, the source of confidence, and the specific risks being evaluated.

The most fundamental concept within this category is technology trust. **Technology trust** refers to citizens' confidence in whether a specific technological tool can perform its intended functions. It focuses primarily on technical performance, including reliability, functionality, usability, and accuracy. The key question of technology trust is whether a digital tool works properly. For example, citizens may trust an online application system if it allows them to complete government procedures efficiently and without technical problems. However, technology trust has a relatively narrow focus because citizens may trust a specific tool while still questioning the reliability of the broader digital system behind it (Yeung, 2018).

Compared with technology trust, **system trust** expands the object of trust from individual technologies to the entire technological and organizational system. Digital government services are not delivered through isolated tools but through interconnected systems involving platforms, databases, infrastructure, administrative procedures, and technical arrangements. Therefore, system trust concerns whether these components operate together in a stable and coordinated way. The difference between technology trust and system trust is that technology trust evaluates the performance of a specific tool, whereas system trust evaluates the reliability of the overall environment that enables digital services.

Platform trust represents a more specific form of system trust that focuses on the digital platforms through which citizens directly interact with government. While system trust concerns the entire technological ecosystem, platform trust emphasizes the accessibility, stability, and service experience of user facing digital channels. For example, citizens may trust a government platform when it provides continuous access, simple procedures, and consistent service quality. However, a trustworthy platform does not necessarily guarantee trust in the wider digital system if underlying data management or security mechanisms are weak.

Information trust and **data trust** both concern digital information resources, but they focus on different stages of information management. Information trust refers to whether citizens believe that government provided digital information is accurate, complete, and reliable. It focuses on the quality of information received by citizens. In contrast, data trust concerns whether citizens believe that their personal and administrative data are collected, stored, shared, and used responsibly. Information trust asks whether the information provided by government can be believed, while data trust asks whether the data used by government are properly governed.

Privacy trust and cybersecurity trust address citizens' concerns about digital risks. Although closely related, they emphasize different dimensions of protection. Privacy trust focuses on whether citizens believe their personal information will be respected and not misused. Cybersecurity trust focuses on whether digital systems can prevent unauthorized access, attacks, and technical failures. In other words, privacy trust concerns the appropriate use of data, while cybersecurity trust concerns the protection of digital systems and information from external threats.

At the broadest level, **digital trust** integrates many of these dimensions into citizens' overall confidence in the digital environment. Digital trust is not limited to whether a technology functions correctly but includes broader concerns about security, privacy, data governance, and responsible digital practices. Therefore, digital trust can be understood as the overall outcome formed through confidence in technologies, systems, information, and governance arrangements.

The conceptual relationship among these forms of trust can therefore be summarized as a movement from specific technological performance toward broader digital confidence. Technology trust focuses on whether a tool works. System trust focuses on whether the entire infrastructure operates reliably. Platform trust focuses on citizens' direct interaction with digital service channels. Information trust and data trust focus on the reliability and governance of digital resources. Privacy trust and cybersecurity trust focus on protection against digital risks. Digital trust represents the comprehensive confidence that emerges from these different technological conditions (Table 2).

Table 2. Distinctions among Digital Technology Trust Concepts

Trust Concept	Trust Object	Core Question	Key Difference
Technology Trust	Digital tools	Does the technology work properly?	Focuses on technical reliability and functionality
System Trust	Digital infrastructure and platforms	Does the whole system operate reliably?	Focuses on coordination of platforms, infrastructure, and procedures
Data Trust	Data management and use	Is data collected and used responsibly?	Focuses on data quality, governance, and protection
Security and Privacy Trust	Digital protection mechanisms	Are citizens' information and systems protected?	Focuses on cybersecurity and privacy risks
Digital Trust	Overall digital environment	Is digital government safe and trustworthy?	The broadest concept integrating technology, data, and security concerns

In AI enabled digital government, these distinctions become increasingly important because artificial intelligence depends on all of these technological foundations. Citizens may trust an AI system's performance but still hesitate to use AI based public services if they distrust data management, privacy protection, or cybersecurity. Therefore, trust in AI governance cannot be separated from trust in the broader digital systems that enable, support, and regulate artificial intelligence.

4. TRUST IN GOVERNANCE PROCESSES

Trust in governance processes represents citizens' confidence in how government decisions are produced, justified, and corrected. Unlike trust in government institutions, which focuses on whether citizens trust the authority itself, and trust in digital systems, which concerns whether technologies function reliably, governance process trust focuses on the fairness, accountability, and legitimacy of decision making procedures. In digital government, especially when artificial intelligence is involved, citizens are not only concerned about the final outcomes of decisions but also about whether the process leading to those outcomes is transparent, responsible, and open to public participation.

The central question of governance process trust is not "Who makes the decision?" but rather "How is the decision made?" This distinction becomes increasingly important in AI enabled digital government because algorithmic systems can influence decisions that directly affect citizens' rights, access to public services, and social opportunities. Even when an AI system produces accurate results, citizens may still question its legitimacy if they cannot understand the decision process, challenge the outcome, or identify who is responsible. Therefore, governance process trust emphasizes that trustworthy digital government requires not only effective technologies but also fair and accountable procedures (Zuiderwijk et al., 2021).

Among different forms of **governance process trust, procedural trust** represents citizens' confidence that decision making processes are fair and legitimate. It focuses on whether citizens believe that they are treated equally and whether they have opportunities to participate, receive explanations, and express concerns. In traditional public administration, procedural trust has been closely associated with fairness in administrative procedures. In AI enabled governance, this concept becomes more complex because algorithmic decision processes may appear objective while hiding important value choices. For example, when an AI system determines eligibility for public assistance, citizens may accept unfavorable decisions more easily if they believe that the evaluation process was transparent, consistent, and open to review.

Accountability trust focuses on whether citizens believe that responsibility exists when governance decisions produce negative consequences. In traditional administrative systems, responsibility is often linked to identifiable public officials or institutions. However, AI enabled governance involves multiple actors, including government agencies, technology providers, data managers, and algorithm developers. This creates a more complicated responsibility structure. Accountability trust therefore depends on whether citizens believe that responsibility can be identified, decisions can be explained, and mistakes can be corrected. Without clear accountability mechanisms, citizens may perceive AI governance as a system where responsibility disappears among different actors.

Regulatory trust refers to citizens' confidence that governments have the ability to supervise and control emerging technologies. As digital government increasingly relies on artificial intelligence and private technology providers, citizens need to believe that appropriate regulations, oversight mechanisms, and enforcement capabilities exist. Regulatory trust differs from accountability trust because it focuses less on responding to individual failures and more on preventing risks through institutional control. For example, citizens may trust AI based public services more when they believe governments have established effective rules for data protection, algorithm evaluation, and technology oversight.

Contestability trust represents a newer dimension of governance process trust that has become particularly important in AI mediated decision making. It refers to citizens' belief that they have the right and ability to challenge, question, or appeal algorithmic decisions. Unlike traditional administrative decisions, algorithmic decisions may appear difficult to challenge because they are often presented as technical outputs rather than human judgments. Contestability trust requires that citizens have access to review mechanisms, appeal procedures, and meaningful human intervention when necessary. It ensures that AI does not become an unquestionable authority but remains subject to democratic control.

Although these four concepts share a common focus on the decision making process, they emphasize different aspects of procedural legitimacy. Procedural trust concerns whether the decision process is fair. Accountability trust concerns whether responsibility exists after decisions are made. Regulatory trust concerns whether risks are controlled before problems occur. Contestability trust concerns whether citizens can challenge and revise decisions when disagreement arises. Together, these concepts demonstrate that trust in digital government depends not only on what decisions are produced, but also on whether citizens perceive the governance process behind those decisions as fair, responsible, and open to correction.

In AI enabled digital government, governance process trust provides an essential bridge between technological capability and public legitimacy. AI systems may improve administrative efficiency, but without fair procedures, accountability mechanisms, effective regulation, and opportunities for contestation, technological advancement alone cannot create lasting public trust. Therefore, trustworthy digital government requires not only intelligent systems but also trustworthy governance processes.

5. TRUST IN AI MEDIATED GOVERNANCE

Trust in AI mediated governance represents a new dimension of trust that emerges when artificial intelligence becomes involved in public decision making. Unlike trust in digital systems, which focuses on whether technological infrastructures function reliably, AI mediated governance trust concerns whether citizens accept AI as a legitimate participant in governing processes. The central question is not simply "Can AI work effectively?" but rather "Can AI be trusted to influence decisions that affect citizens' rights, resources, and opportunities?"

The emergence of AI in digital government changes the traditional relationship between citizens and public authorities. In conventional administrative systems, citizens generally expect decisions to be made by identifiable human officials who can explain judgments and assume responsibility. However, AI based governance introduces new forms of decision making based on algorithms, data analysis, and automated prediction. Therefore, citizens must evaluate not only the technical performance of AI systems but also whether AI driven decisions are fair, understandable, controllable, and compatible with democratic governance principles.

Among different forms of AI mediated governance trust, algorithmic trust represents citizens' confidence in the outcomes produced by algorithms. It focuses on whether algorithmic decisions are accurate, fair, and predictable. Algorithmic trust does not simply mean believing that algorithms are objective because they are mathematical systems. Instead, it concerns whether citizens believe that algorithmic processes produce reasonable and socially acceptable outcomes. For example, when an AI system evaluates applications for public benefits, citizens may question whether the algorithm treats different groups fairly and whether its predictions are sufficiently reliable. Therefore, algorithmic trust depends not only on technical accuracy but also on perceptions of fairness and legitimacy.

Data trust focuses on the relationship between AI governance and the data used to support algorithmic decisions. Since AI systems rely heavily on data, citizens' confidence in AI depends on whether they believe that data are accurate, representative, and responsibly managed. Poor quality data may reproduce historical inequalities, while inappropriate data use may threaten individual rights. Therefore, data trust concerns not only whether data exist, but also who controls data, how data are collected, and whether data practices align with public values. In AI enabled government, citizens may accept algorithmic decision making only when they believe that the data foundation behind AI systems is trustworthy.

Explainability trust concerns whether citizens believe that AI decisions can be understood and justified. Unlike traditional administrative decisions, where officials can directly explain their reasoning, AI decisions are often produced through complex computational processes. When citizens cannot understand why a decision was made, they may perceive AI as an uncontrollable authority. Explainability trust therefore requires that governments provide meaningful explanations regarding why AI is used, how decisions are generated, and how citizens can respond when they disagree. It transforms transparency from a technical requirement into a governance responsibility.

Accountability trust in AI mediated governance refers to citizens' confidence that responsibility remains identifiable when AI systems produce harmful or incorrect outcomes. Because AI governance involves multiple actors, including government agencies, technology developers, and data managers, responsibility may become distributed across different participants. Citizens need assurance that AI will not become a mechanism for avoiding responsibility. Accountability trust therefore depends on whether clear responsibility structures, correction mechanisms, and institutional responses exist when AI decisions cause problems.

Human oversight trust emphasizes citizens' confidence that human judgment remains present in AI based governance. The concern is not whether humans should completely replace AI, but whether AI remains under meaningful human control. Public decisions often involve ethical considerations, exceptional circumstances, and social values that cannot be fully captured through computational processes. Therefore, citizens are more likely to trust AI governance when they believe that human officials can review, question, and override algorithmic decisions when necessary.

Although these concepts are closely connected, they address different dimensions of trust in AI mediated governance. Algorithmic trust concerns whether AI produces reliable outcomes. Data trust concerns whether the information supporting AI decisions is trustworthy. Explainability trust concerns whether AI decisions can be understood. Accountability trust concerns whether responsibility exists when AI fails. Human oversight trust concerns whether humans maintain meaningful control over AI systems. Together, these dimensions show that public trust in AI governance depends not only on technological capability but also on whether AI operates within acceptable ethical and institutional boundaries.

Therefore, trust in AI mediated governance represents a shift from traditional technology acceptance toward questions of governance legitimacy. Citizens do not trust AI simply because it is accurate or efficient; they trust AI when it is embedded within a system that ensures fairness, transparency, responsibility, and human control. In this sense, AI trust is ultimately a form of governance trust rather than merely technological trust.

6. TRUST IN CITIZEN GOVERNMENT RELATIONSHIPS

Trust in citizen government relationships represents the relational dimension of trust in digital government. Unlike institutional trust, which focuses on whether citizens trust government authority, and technology trust, which concerns whether digital systems are reliable, this dimension focuses on how citizens experience their interactions and long term relationships with government. The central question is not only "Can government provide effective services?" but also "Do citizens feel respected, understood, and connected in their relationship with government?"

In traditional public administration, government citizen relationships were mainly shaped through face to face interactions and administrative procedures. However, digital transformation has changed the way citizens encounter government. Online platforms, automated services, and AI based communication systems increasingly mediate interactions between citizens and public institutions. As a result, trust is no longer formed only through direct contact with public officials but also through citizens' experiences with digital services and intelligent systems. A technically efficient digital service may improve convenience, but if citizens feel ignored, misunderstood, or treated as data rather than individuals, trust may still decline.

Within this category, service trust represents the most direct form of relationship based trust. It refers to citizens' confidence that government services can effectively meet their needs. The focus of service trust is whether public services are accessible, useful, efficient, and responsive. For example, citizens may trust an online government platform when it reduces administrative burdens, provides accurate information, and enables convenient access to services. However, service trust mainly evaluates the outcome and quality of service delivery, rather than the deeper relationship between citizens and government.

Interactional trust focuses on the quality of communication and interaction between citizens and government. While service trust asks whether government services work effectively, interactional trust asks whether citizens are treated fairly and respectfully during the service process. This dimension emphasizes communication quality, responsiveness, dignity, and recognition. In AI enabled digital government, interactional trust becomes increasingly important because many citizen interactions are mediated by chatbots, automated systems, and digital interfaces. If citizens feel that digital systems are unable to understand their situations or provide meaningful responses, their trust in government interaction may weaken even when services are technically efficient.

Relational trust represents a broader and longer term form of trust that develops through repeated interactions between citizens and government. Unlike service trust, which may be influenced by a single service experience, relational trust reflects the accumulated perception of whether government consistently acts in a reliable, responsible, and citizen oriented manner. It is based on continuity, mutual recognition, and long term expectations. In digital government, relational trust determines whether citizens are willing to continue engaging with digital services and accept further technological transformation.

In addition to these relationship based dimensions, trust research often distinguishes between cognitive trust and affective trust, which explain different psychological foundations of citizen government relationships. Cognitive trust is based on rational evaluation of government competence and reliability. Citizens develop cognitive trust when they believe that government has the knowledge, ability, and resources to provide effective governance. For example, citizens may trust an AI based public service system because they believe government agencies have sufficient expertise to manage the technology.

By contrast, affective trust is based on emotional connections and perceptions of care. It reflects whether citizens believe that government understands their needs and acts with concern for their well being. This dimension is particularly important in AI enabled digital government because automated systems may improve efficiency while reducing feelings of personal connection. A citizen may receive a correct decision from an AI system but still feel dissatisfied if the process lacks empathy and recognition of individual circumstances. Therefore, affective trust highlights that government legitimacy depends not only on what government does but also on how citizens experience government actions.

Although these concepts share a common focus on the relationship between citizens and government, they emphasize different aspects of that relationship. Service trust concerns whether government delivers effective services. Interactional trust concerns whether citizens experience respectful and responsive communication. Relational trust concerns the long term relationship between citizens and institutions. Cognitive trust explains trust based on perceived competence and reliability, while affective trust explains trust based on care and emotional connection.

In AI enabled digital government, citizen government relationship trust demonstrates that public trust cannot be created through efficiency alone. Digital transformation may improve service speed and accessibility, but sustainable trust requires governments to maintain meaningful relationships with citizens. Therefore, trustworthy digital government must not only provide intelligent services but also preserve human connection, respect, and responsiveness in the relationship between citizens and public institutions.

7. FROM TRUSTED AI TO TRUSTED AI FOR EFFECTIVE DIGITAL GOVERNMENT

The concept of Trusted AI provides the foundation for understanding how artificial intelligence can become socially acceptable and ethically responsible. Traditional AI development has mainly focused on improving technical capabilities, such as accuracy, efficiency, and predictive performance. However, as AI systems increasingly influence human decisions and social outcomes, technical performance alone is no longer sufficient to establish trust. An AI system may produce accurate results while still creating concerns regarding fairness, transparency, accountability, privacy, and human control. Therefore, Trusted AI emphasizes that artificial intelligence must be not only technically reliable but also ethically responsible and socially aligned.

The central question of Trusted AI is "Can AI systems be trusted?" This question focuses on the internal characteristics and governance conditions of AI itself. A trusted AI system should demonstrate several essential qualities. First, it should be reliable, meaning that it can perform tasks accurately and consistently. Second, it should be transparent and explainable, allowing users and affected individuals to understand how decisions are produced. Third, it should be accountable, ensuring that responsibility can be identified when errors occur. Fourth, it should respect human values by avoiding unfair discrimination, protecting privacy, and maintaining meaningful human oversight. Therefore, Trusted AI is primarily concerned with making AI systems trustworthy as technological and social systems.

However, when AI is introduced into digital government, the meaning of trust becomes broader. Government AI does not simply perform technical tasks; it participates in decisions related to public services, resource allocation, social welfare, and citizens' rights. Therefore, the key question changes from "Can AI be trusted?" to "Can AI contribute to effective and legitimate governance?" This shift leads to the concept of Trusted AI for Effective Digital Government.

Trusted AI for Effective Digital Government extends Trusted AI from the technological level to the governance level. It recognizes that a trustworthy AI system is necessary but not sufficient for successful digital government. Government effectiveness depends not only on whether AI operates correctly, but also on whether institutions can use AI responsibly, whether citizens accept AI based decisions, and whether governance processes remain transparent and accountable. In this context, Trusted AI becomes embedded within broader relationships among government institutions, digital systems, governance processes, and citizens.

The difference between the two concepts can therefore be understood through their different focuses. Trusted AI focuses on the trustworthiness of the AI system itself. It examines whether AI is reliable, explainable, fair, secure, and accountable. In contrast, Trusted AI for Effective Digital Government focuses on the governance outcomes created through the use of trusted AI. It examines whether AI can improve public service delivery, enhance administrative capacity, strengthen citizen trust, and support legitimate public decision making.

In other words, Trusted AI answers the question of "what makes AI trustworthy," while Trusted AI for Effective Digital Government answers the question of "how trustworthy AI enables better government." The first provides the technological and ethical foundation, while the second places this foundation within the institutional context of digital governance. Therefore, Trusted AI for Effective Digital Government represents a transition from technology centered trust toward governance centered trust, where AI is evaluated not only by what it can do, but also by how it contributes to effective, responsible, and citizen centered government.

8. THE REDISTRIBUTION OF POWER AND ALGORITHMS IN DIGITAL GOVERNANCE

The emergence of artificial intelligence in digital government represents not only a transformation of administrative technologies but also a fundamental restructuring of governance power. Traditional public administration has long been organized around a human-centered authority structure, in which government institutions and public officials serve as the primary holders and exercisers of decision-making power. Authority is derived from legal mandates, institutional positions, and administrative procedures, creating a relatively clear relationship between power, decision making, and responsibility. However, the integration of AI into governance introduces new actors and mechanisms into this structure. Algorithms, data infrastructures, and technological systems increasingly participate in processes that were previously shaped primarily by human judgment, including classification, prediction, prioritization, and resource allocation.

This transformation does not mean that AI replaces government authority. Rather, AI changes how governance power is produced and exercised. As algorithmic systems become embedded within administrative processes, decision-making power becomes increasingly distributed across multiple actors, including government institutions, technology providers, data managers, algorithm developers, and public officials. While governments continue to maintain formal authority and legal responsibility, algorithms increasingly influence the information available to decision makers, the categories used to understand social issues, and the options considered in policy implementation. Consequently, governance power is no longer located only within administrative institutions but is also shaped by control over data, algorithms, and digital infrastructures.

The redistribution of power creates the emergence of a new form of governance influence, often described as algorithmic power. Unlike traditional administrative power, which operates through visible institutions and formal procedures, algorithmic power operates through computational processes that determine how information is organized, how risks are evaluated, and how decisions are prioritized. Although algorithms do not possess independent political authority, they influence governance outcomes by shaping the conditions under which human decisions are made. This creates a fundamental shift from a model in which power is exercised mainly by identifiable human actors toward a more distributed model in which human institutions and technological systems jointly shape governance processes.

However, the redistribution of governance power also introduces new challenges regarding accountability, transparency, and public trust. When decisions are influenced by complex algorithmic systems, citizens may find it difficult to understand how decisions are produced, who controls the underlying mechanisms, and who should be responsible when errors occur. The traditional connection between authority and responsibility becomes more complicated because governance outcomes may involve multiple actors, including institutions, algorithms, data systems, and technology providers. Therefore, the rise of algorithmic power requires new governance mechanisms that ensure transparency, accountability, human oversight, and democratic control.

Understanding this transformation is essential for explaining why AI-enabled digital government requires new forms of trust. Trust in the AI era is no longer limited to confidence in government institutions or technological reliability; it also depends on whether citizens believe that emerging forms of algorithmic power are exercised fairly, responsibly, and legitimately. Therefore, the future of digital governance requires not only the development of intelligent systems but also the responsible governance of the power relationships created by those systems.

8.1 The Transformation of Traditional Governance Power

Before the emergence of artificial intelligence, governance power in modern public administration was primarily based on human-centered institutional authority. Traditional governance systems operate through legally established institutions, hierarchical administrative structures, and standardized procedures, where government agencies and public officials serve as the primary actors responsible for interpreting policies and making decisions. In this model, the source of power is relatively clear because authority is derived from formal legal mandates, institutional positions, and administrative rules. Government institutions possess the legitimate authority to act, public officials exercise decision-making responsibilities, and administrative procedures provide the framework through which decisions are produced and implemented.

This traditional structure creates a relatively direct relationship between power, decision making, and accountability. When governments make administrative decisions, citizens can generally identify who holds authority, what rules guide the decision, and which mechanisms exist for review or appeal. For example, in a traditional welfare allocation process, a government official evaluates an application based on established regulations and determines whether an individual qualifies for support. The citizen can understand that the decision originates from a specific institution, is made by identifiable officials, and can be challenged through formal administrative procedures. Therefore, traditional governance power is characterized by visible authority, identifiable decision makers, and traceable responsibility.

However, this human-centered model of governance begins to change when artificial intelligence becomes embedded in public decision-making processes. Although government institutions continue to maintain formal authority, AI introduces new mechanisms that influence how decisions are generated. Algorithms increasingly participate in processes such as classification, prediction, and prioritization, which means that governance decisions are no longer shaped only by human judgment and administrative procedures. Instead, they are also influenced by data structures, algorithmic models, and technological systems. This transformation does not eliminate traditional governance power, but it changes the way power operates and creates the conditions for a redistribution of decision-making influence.

Therefore, understanding the transformation of governance power requires recognizing the difference between traditional administrative authority and emerging algorithm-mediated governance. In the traditional model, power is primarily located within institutions and officials. In the AI-enabled model, power becomes increasingly distributed across human actors, technological systems, and data infrastructures. This shift provides the foundation for understanding the emergence of algorithmic power and the new accountability challenges that follow.

8.2 AI as a New Actor in Governance Decision Making

The integration of artificial intelligence into digital government does not mean that algorithms replace government authority. Rather, AI becomes a new actor embedded within existing governance processes, influencing how information is collected, interpreted, and transformed into administrative decisions. In traditional governance, decision making is primarily based on human judgment, institutional rules, and administrative procedures. However, when algorithms enter governance, decision processes increasingly involve interactions between human officials, data systems, and computational models. This creates a new form of decision-making structure in which AI does not hold formal authority but increasingly shapes the pathway through which decisions are produced.

The key question is therefore not "Will AI replace government decision makers?" but rather "What changes when algorithms become involved in governance decisions?" The fundamental change is that AI introduces new forms of analytical and decision support capabilities through processes such as classification, prediction, ranking, and recommendation. Through classification, AI systems organize citizens, cases, or social issues into different categories. Through prediction, AI estimates future conditions or potential risks based on available data. Through ranking, AI prioritizes cases according to predefined criteria. Through recommendation, AI provides suggestions that influence human decision makers. These functions allow governments to process complex information more efficiently, but they also reshape how administrative judgments are formed.

For example, in a traditional social welfare system, the decision-making process may follow a relatively direct structure: Citizen → Official → Decision. A public official reviews an application, applies relevant regulations, and makes a final determination. However, when an AI-based welfare assessment system is introduced, the process becomes more complex: Citizen → Data → Algorithm Assessment → Official Decision. The government official may still retain formal decision-making authority, but the algorithm influences the process by evaluating information, identifying patterns, and suggesting possible outcomes. As a result, AI becomes part of the decision pathway rather than merely a technical tool operating outside governance.

This transformation changes the relationship between human judgment and administrative decision making. Previously, officials played the central role in interpreting information and applying policies. With AI integration, some elements of judgment are transferred into algorithmic processes. Decisions may increasingly depend on how data are collected, how models are designed, and what criteria algorithms prioritize. Therefore, although government institutions remain the legitimate holders of public authority, algorithms begin to influence the conditions under which that authority is exercised.

The emergence of AI as a governance actor creates both opportunities and challenges. On one hand, AI can enhance administrative capacity by identifying patterns that may be difficult for humans to detect, improving consistency, and supporting more efficient public services. On the other hand, algorithmic involvement raises questions about transparency, accountability, and control. If algorithmic assessments influence public decisions, citizens need to understand how these assessments are produced and how human officials remain responsible for final outcomes.

Therefore, the role of AI in governance should be understood as algorithmic participation rather than algorithmic replacement. AI expands the capacity of government decision making, but it also changes the structure through which power operates. The challenge for digital government is not to remove human authority from governance but to establish a balanced relationship in which AI supports decision making while remaining subject to human oversight, institutional accountability, and public legitimacy.

8.3 The Emergence of Algorithmic Power

The integration of algorithms into governance introduces a new form of power that differs fundamentally from traditional administrative authority. In conventional governance systems, power is primarily exercised through legally defined institutions, official positions, and formal decision-making procedures. Government officials possess the authority to make decisions because their power is granted through institutional arrangements and legal frameworks. However, in AI-enabled governance, decision-making is increasingly influenced by computational processes that determine how information is collected, organized, interpreted, and transformed into administrative choices. This transformation gives rise to what can be understood as algorithmic power.

Algorithmic power does not refer to the ability of algorithms to directly command citizens or replace government authority. Rather, it refers to the capacity of algorithms to influence governance outcomes by shaping the information, categories, and choices upon which decisions are based. In other words, algorithms exercise power not by making formal decisions themselves, but by influencing the conditions under which human decisions are produced. By determining what information becomes visible, which patterns are identified, and which options are considered relevant, algorithms increasingly shape how governments understand social problems and respond to public needs.

The emergence of algorithmic power is closely connected to the control and design of three essential elements: data, models, and classification systems. First, data determine the foundation through which governments observe and interpret society. Decisions regarding what data are collected, whose information is represented, and how data are processed influence what issues become visible within governance systems. Second, model design determines how information is transformed into predictions, evaluations, or recommendations. Every algorithmic model contains assumptions regarding what outcomes should be prioritized and what criteria should be considered important. Therefore, algorithmic design is not merely a technical process but also a process involving value choices. Third, classification logic shapes how citizens, behaviors, and social conditions are categorized. When algorithms identify certain groups as high risk, high priority, or eligible for specific services, they influence how government attention and resources are distributed.

For example, an AI-based welfare assessment system may appear to simply analyze information and provide recommendations. However, the algorithm must first determine which characteristics are relevant, which indicators represent social need, and which factors should influence the final assessment. These choices affect how citizens are understood by the government and how resources are allocated. Although the final decision may remain with public officials, algorithmic systems influence the decision-making environment by shaping what officials see, how cases are evaluated, and which actions appear appropriate.

Therefore, algorithmic power represents a shift from visible administrative authority toward a more distributed and less visible form of governance influence. Traditional power is exercised through identifiable institutions and decision makers, while algorithmic power operates through technological infrastructures, data practices, and computational processes. This does not mean that algorithms replace human authority; rather, it means that governance power is increasingly shared between human actors and technological systems. Recognizing the emergence of algorithmic power is essential because it explains why AI-enabled governance requires new forms of transparency, accountability, and public trust. If algorithms increasingly influence governance decisions, then their design, operation, and consequences must remain subject to democratic oversight and institutional responsibility.

8.4 Redistribution of Power Among Governance Actors

The introduction of AI into digital governance transforms the traditional structure of governance power from a government-centered model into a multi-actor governance system. In traditional public administration, governance power is mainly concentrated within government institutions. Governments define policies, public officials interpret regulations, and administrative agencies make decisions on behalf of citizens. In this structure, the relationship between authority and responsibility is relatively clear because government institutions possess both formal decision-making power and institutional accountability.

However, AI-enabled governance changes this relatively centralized structure by introducing new actors into the process of producing and implementing public decisions. Although governments continue to maintain legal authority, AI-based governance increasingly depends on a broader network that includes data providers, technology companies, algorithm designers, infrastructure operators, and public institutions. These actors may not possess formal governmental authority, but they influence how governance problems are identified, how information is processed, and how decisions are generated. As a result, governance power is no longer determined solely by institutional position; it is also shaped by control over technological and informational resources.

The redistribution of power in AI governance is mainly reflected in three emerging sources of influence: control over data, algorithmic expertise, and digital infrastructure. Data has become a critical source of governance power because the ability to collect, organize, and manage information determines how governments perceive social realities. Algorithm design creates another form of influence because decisions regarding model objectives, evaluation criteria, and optimization processes shape how problems are interpreted and which outcomes are prioritized. Similarly, control over digital infrastructures determines the technical conditions under which AI systems operate and affects the capacity of different actors to participate in governance processes.

This transformation does not mean that government power disappears or that private technological actors replace public institutions. Rather, AI creates a more complex relationship between formal authority and practical influence. Governments may retain the legal responsibility for decisions, while other actors increasingly shape the technological processes that support those decisions. For example, an AI-based public service system may be officially operated by a government agency, but its performance depends on the quality of data management, algorithm design, and technical infrastructure provided by multiple actors. Therefore, governance outcomes become the result of interactions among institutions, technologies, and knowledge systems.

The emergence of multi-actor governance also creates new challenges for accountability and trust. When decision-making processes involve multiple actors, it becomes more difficult to determine who should be responsible when algorithmic systems produce errors or unfair outcomes. Traditional accountability mechanisms based on identifiable government officials may no longer be sufficient. Instead, AI-enabled governance requires new accountability arrangements that recognize distributed power while ensuring that public institutions remain responsible for protecting citizens' rights and public values.

Therefore, the redistribution of power among governance actors represents one of the most significant changes brought by AI in digital government. AI does not replace governmental authority; rather, it transforms the environment in which authority is exercised. The challenge for future digital governance is to ensure that this distributed power structure remains transparent, accountable, and aligned with democratic principles.

8.5 The Accountability Gap of Algorithmic Governance

The emergence of algorithmic governance challenges one of the fundamental principles of traditional public administration: the direct connection between decision-making authority and accountability. In conventional governance systems, responsibility is usually attached to identifiable human actors. Public officials make decisions based on legal authority and administrative procedures, and they are expected to explain, justify, and correct those decisions when necessary. This creates a relatively stable accountability relationship in which the actor who exercises power is also the actor who bears responsibility.

However, AI-enabled governance disrupts this traditional accountability structure because algorithmic decisions are produced through complex sociotechnical processes rather than individual human judgment alone. When AI systems influence public decisions, outcomes are shaped by multiple interconnected elements, including institutional objectives, data sources, algorithmic models, technical infrastructures, and administrative practices. As a result, the relationship between decision-making power and responsibility becomes increasingly fragmented. The question is no longer simply "Who made the decision?" but rather "Who shaped the conditions under which the decision became possible?"

This transformation creates an accountability gap in algorithmic governance. The gap does not exist because responsibility disappears, but because responsibility becomes distributed across different stages of the AI governance process. Data providers influence what information becomes available and how social realities are represented. Algorithm designers influence how problems are modeled and which criteria are prioritized. Technology companies influence system architecture and technical implementation. Government institutions determine the purpose, context, and legitimacy of AI deployment. Each actor contributes to the final outcome, yet no single actor may appear fully responsible when algorithmic decisions produce unfair or harmful consequences.

The accountability challenge becomes particularly significant because algorithmic systems often create a separation between formal authority and practical influence. Government agencies may remain legally responsible for public decisions, but the actual decision process may depend heavily on technical systems developed and maintained by external actors. Conversely, technology providers may design the mechanisms that influence outcomes but do not possess public authority or democratic responsibility. This creates a situation in which those who have the power to shape decisions may not always be those who are formally accountable for their consequences.

Furthermore, algorithmic governance introduces a new form of responsibility problem: the difficulty of identifying where and when accountability should be assigned. A harmful outcome may result from inaccurate data, inappropriate model design, biased classification criteria, insufficient human review, or improper institutional use. Therefore, accountability cannot focus only on the final decision outcome; it must extend to the entire lifecycle of algorithmic governance, including data collection, system development, deployment, monitoring, and correction.

Addressing the accountability gap requires a shift from traditional individual accountability toward distributed but traceable accountability. Distributed accountability recognizes that multiple actors contribute to AI governance outcomes, while traceable accountability ensures that each actor's responsibilities can still be identified. In this framework, governments remain responsible for ensuring that AI systems used in public governance serve legitimate public purposes, while technical actors must be accountable for the systems, models, and data practices under their control.

Therefore, accountability in AI-enabled digital government is not simply about determining who should be blamed when algorithms fail. It is about rebuilding a governance structure in which algorithmic power remains connected to responsibility. Without such mechanisms, AI may create a situation where decisions become increasingly influential while accountability becomes increasingly unclear. Trusted AI governance therefore requires not only accurate and efficient algorithms but also institutional arrangements that ensure every exercise of algorithmic power remains explainable, contestable, and accountable.

8.6 Rebuilding Trust through Governed Algorithmic Power

The emergence of algorithmic power does not necessarily undermine democratic governance; rather, it creates a new challenge regarding how power should be governed in an increasingly digital society. The central issue is not whether artificial intelligence should participate in governance, but whether the power generated through algorithms can remain legitimate. Unlike traditional administrative power, which derives legitimacy from legal authority and institutional accountability, algorithmic power derives influence from data, computational models, and technological infrastructures. Therefore, its legitimacy cannot be assumed simply because algorithms are accurate or efficient. It must be continuously established through governance mechanisms that ensure algorithmic power remains visible, accountable, and subject to democratic control.

The development of Trusted AI provides a pathway for addressing this challenge. Trusted AI does not aim to eliminate algorithmic influence or prevent AI from supporting government decision making. Instead, it seeks to ensure that algorithmic power operates within appropriate institutional boundaries. Since algorithms influence governance by shaping information, classifications, and decision options, their operation must become understandable and open to evaluation. Transparency therefore becomes essential because citizens and institutions need to understand why AI systems are used, what factors influence their decisions, and how algorithmic outputs affect individuals and communities. Transparency transforms algorithmic power from an invisible mechanism into a form of governance that can be examined and discussed.

However, transparency alone is insufficient to establish legitimacy. Algorithmic power must also remain connected to responsibility. In AI-enabled governance, responsibility cannot disappear behind automated systems or be distributed so widely that no actor is accountable. Governments, as the legitimate holders of public authority, must ensure that AI systems serve public purposes and protect citizens' rights, while other actors involved in data management, algorithm development, and system operation must remain responsible for their respective roles. Accountability ensures that algorithmic influence remains connected to identifiable responsibility.

Furthermore, legitimate algorithmic power requires maintaining human judgment and public involvement. AI can improve administrative capacity by processing complex information and identifying patterns, but governance decisions often involve ethical considerations, social values, and exceptional circumstances that cannot be fully captured through computational processes. Human oversight ensures that algorithms remain tools supporting governance rather than independent authorities replacing human responsibility. At the same time, public participation allows citizens to question, evaluate, and contribute to the development of algorithmic governance practices, strengthening the social legitimacy of AI-based decision making.

Therefore, rebuilding trust in digital government requires a fundamental shift in how algorithmic power is understood. The goal is not to prevent AI from influencing governance, but to ensure that such influence is governed through transparency, accountability, human oversight, and democratic participation. Trusted AI is not about giving algorithms greater authority; it is about ensuring that when algorithms become part of governance, the power they generate remains accountable and democratically controlled.

9. TOWARD A MULTIDIMENSIONAL TRUST FRAMEWORK FOR AI ENABLED DIGITAL GOVERNMENT

The analysis in this chapter demonstrates that trust in AI enabled digital government cannot be understood as a single relationship between citizens and government. As artificial intelligence becomes embedded in public administration, the object of trust expands from traditional government institutions to digital systems, algorithms, governance processes, and citizen–government relationships. Therefore, trust in the digital era is inherently multidimensional, involving different actors, different forms of evaluation, and different sources of legitimacy.

At the institutional level, citizens' trust depends on whether government organizations remain legitimate, reliable, and capable of serving public interests. Trust in government institutions provides the foundation for accepting digital transformation because citizens must first believe that public authorities have the competence and responsibility to introduce new technologies. However, institutional trust alone is insufficient in AI enabled governance because government decisions are increasingly mediated through technological systems.

At the technological level, trust concerns whether digital infrastructures, platforms, data systems, and AI technologies can reliably support government services. Technology trust, system trust, data trust, and digital trust reflect different aspects of citizens' confidence in the digital environment. These forms of trust demonstrate that public acceptance of digital government depends not only on technical performance but also on whether citizens believe that digital systems are secure, responsible, and properly governed.

At the governance level, trust is closely connected with how decisions are produced and justified. Procedural trust, accountability trust, regulatory trust, and contestability trust highlight that citizens evaluate not only the outcomes of AI enabled decisions but also the fairness and legitimacy of the processes behind them. In particular, the emergence of algorithmic decision making requires new mechanisms to ensure transparency, responsibility, and opportunities for citizens to challenge decisions.

At the relational level, trust reflects citizens' actual experiences with digital government. Service trust, interactional trust, relational trust, cognitive trust, and affective trust show that effective digital government requires more than efficiency and automation. Citizens also expect government services to remain responsive, respectful, and human centered. Therefore, trust in digital government contains both rational evaluations of government competence and emotional experiences of government care.

Furthermore, this chapter argues that the transformation brought by AI is not limited to trust relationships but also involves a redistribution of governance power. As algorithms become involved in classification, prediction, and decision support, governance power becomes distributed among government institutions, data providers, technology companies, algorithm designers, and digital infrastructures. This creates new forms of algorithmic power and new accountability challenges. Therefore, building trust in AI enabled digital government requires not only improving AI performance but also ensuring that algorithmic power remains transparent, accountable, and democratically controlled.

Based on these discussions, this chapter proposes that trustworthy AI enabled digital government requires the integration of multiple dimensions of trust: institutional trust, technological trust, governance process trust, AI mediated governance trust, and citizen government relationship trust. These dimensions are interconnected rather than isolated. Institutional trust provides legitimacy, technological trust provides reliability, governance process trust provides fairness, AI trust provides confidence in algorithmic participation, and relational trust provides long term social acceptance.

Ultimately, trust in AI enabled digital government should be understood as a dynamic governance relationship rather than a fixed technological attribute. AI becomes trustworthy not simply because it is accurate or efficient, but because it operates within institutions, processes, and relationships that ensure responsible use of power. Therefore, the foundation of effective digital government is not merely intelligent technology, but the successful alignment of technological capability, ethical governance, institutional responsibility, and citizen trust.

REFERENCES

Busuioc, M. (2021). Accountable artificial intelligence: Holding algorithms to account. *Public Administration Review*, *81*(5), 825–836. DOI: 10.1111/puar.13293 PMID: 34690372

Grimmelikhuijsen, S., & Meijer, A. (2022). Legitimacy of algorithmic decision-making: Six threats and the need for transparency and accountability. *Perspectives on Public Management and Governance*, *5*(1), 1–11. DOI: 10.1093/ppmgov/gvac008

Wirtz, B. W., Weyerer, J. C., & Geyer, C. (2019). Artificial intelligence and the public sector—Applications and challenges. *International Journal of Public Administration*, *42*(7), 596–615. DOI: 10.1080/01900692.2018.1498103

Yeung, K. (2018). Algorithmic regulation: A critical interrogation. *Regulation & Governance*, *12*(4), 505–523. DOI: 10.1111/rego.12158

Zuiderwijk, A., Chen, Y. C., & Salem, F. (2021). Implications of the use of artificial intelligence in public governance: A systematic literature review and a research agenda. *Government Information Quarterly*, *38*(3), 101577. DOI: 10.1016/j.giq.2021.101577

KEY TERMS AND DEFINITIONS

Accountability Gap: Refers to the difficulty of assigning responsibility in AI based governance when decisions are shaped by multiple actors, including governments, data providers, technology companies, and algorithm designers.

Accountability Trust: Refers to citizens' confidence that responsible actors can be identified and held accountable when AI systems or governance decisions produce negative outcomes.

AI Mediated Governance Trust: Refers to citizens' acceptance of artificial intelligence as a participant in public decision making. It concerns whether AI systems are perceived as legitimate, fair, explainable, and accountable in governance contexts.

Algorithmic Governance: Refers to governance processes in which algorithms participate in decision making, policy implementation, and public service delivery through functions such as classification, prediction, ranking, and recommendation.

Algorithmic Power: Refers to the ability of algorithms to influence governance outcomes by shaping information, classifications, predictions, and choices. Unlike formal administrative authority, algorithmic power operates through data, models, and computational processes.

Algorithmic Trust: Refers to confidence in algorithmic outcomes and processes, including perceptions of accuracy, fairness, predictability, and reliability of AI generated decisions.

Citizen Government Relationship Trust: Refers to trust formed through citizens' direct experiences and long-term relationships with government services and institutions. It includes service trust, interactional trust, relational trust, cognitive trust, and affective trust.

Contestability Trust: Refers to citizens' confidence that they can challenge, review, or appeal AI based decisions and that meaningful human intervention remains available.

Data Trust: Refers to citizens' confidence that data used in digital government and AI systems are accurate, responsibly managed, and governed appropriately throughout their lifecycle.

Digital Trust: Refers to citizens' confidence in the digital environment supporting government services. It includes trust in digital infrastructures, platforms, data management, privacy protection, and cybersecurity mechanisms.

Governance Process Trust: Refers to citizens' confidence in the fairness, transparency, accountability, and legitimacy of government decision-making processes. It emphasizes how decisions are made rather than only who makes them.

Government Institutional Trust: Refers to citizens' confidence in government authority and public institutions. It includes political trust, institutional trust, administrative trust, and public trust, reflecting perceptions of governmental legitimacy, reliability, competence, and responsibility.

Human Oversight: Refers to the continued involvement of human judgment and responsibility in AI governance to ensure that algorithmic decisions remain subject to ethical evaluation and institutional control.

Procedural Trust: Refers to citizens' belief that governance procedures are fair, transparent, participatory, and provide opportunities for review and appeal.

System Trust: Refers to confidence in the overall digital system that supports government services, including platforms, infrastructures, databases, and operational procedures.

Technology Trust: Refers to citizens' belief that specific digital technologies can perform their intended functions reliably and effectively. It focuses on technical reliability, functionality, and usability.

Trust in AI Enabled Digital Government: Refers to citizens' confidence in government institutions, digital systems, artificial intelligence technologies, governance processes, and citizen–government relationships within an AI enabled public sector environment. It represents a multidimensional form of trust that combines institutional legitimacy, technological reliability, ethical governance, and citizen experience.

Trusted AI for Effective Digital Government: Refers to the integration of trustworthy artificial intelligence principles into digital government to enhance administrative effectiveness while maintaining legitimacy, accountability, and citizen trust. It views AI as a governance capability embedded within ethical and institutional frameworks.

Trusted AI: Refers to artificial intelligence systems that are reliable, transparent, accountable, secure, fair, and aligned with human values. Trusted AI emphasizes that AI should not only achieve technical performance but also satisfy ethical and social expectations.

Chapter 3
The Reconstruction of Trust in Digital Government:
From Institutional Legitimacy to Algorithmic Governance

Yuanyuan Guo
http://orcid.org/0000-0002-3042-8417
Ningbo University, China

ABSTRACT

Chapter 3 establishes the theoretical foundation of trusted AI in digital government by arguing that artificial intelligence has fundamentally transformed the nature, structure, and production mechanism of public trust. Existing digital government studies generally understand trust as citizens' confidence in governmental institutions, administrative procedures, and service outcomes. However, the integration of AI into public governance introduces a new condition, governmental decisions are increasingly mediated by algorithms, data infrastructures, automated systems, and intelligent service platforms. Under this transformation, trust is no longer produced only through institutional authority or administrative performance. Instead, it emerges from the interaction between political legitimacy, technological reliability, algorithmic accountability and citizen experience. Therefore, this chapter proposes a new theoretical perspective, trust in digital government should be understood as a dynamic governance relationship rather than a static perception of government capability.

DOI: 10.4018/979-8-3373-9129-8.ch003

1. THEORETICAL CRISIS OF TRADITIONAL GOVERNMENT TRUST IN THE AI ERA

For decades, the question of why citizens trust governments has been examined through a relatively stable theoretical framework. In this framework, government trust is primarily understood as a social and political relationship between public institutions and citizens (Aoki, 2020; Bouckaert & Van de Walle, 2003). Governments formulate policies, public officials exercise administrative authority, and citizens evaluate whether these institutions deserve confidence based on their effectiveness, fairness, and responsiveness. Although different theories have emphasized different dimensions of trust, including institutional legitimacy, administrative performance, and democratic accountability, they share a common assumption: government remains the central actor that possesses decision-making authority and bears ultimate responsibility for governance outcomes.

Figure 1. From Traditional Government Trust to AI-Era Governance Trust

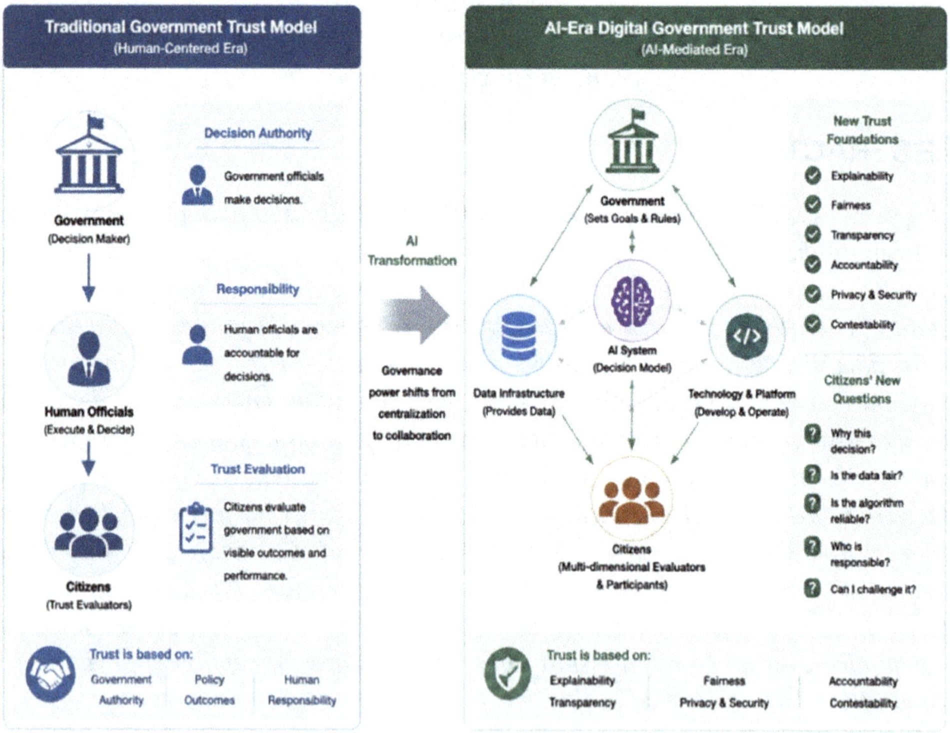

This assumption was reasonable in an era when public decisions were mainly produced through human institutions. A citizen applying for social assistance, receiving healthcare support, or participating in administrative procedures could generally identify the organization responsible for the decision. Even when governments made mistakes, the relationship between decision, authority, and responsibility was relatively clear. A policy failure could be attributed to a government department; an administrative error could be investigated through institutional procedures; and public dissatisfaction could be addressed through political accountability mechanisms. In this traditional governance structure, trust was constructed through a recognizable relationship: citizens trusted governments because governments were visible actors that could explain decisions, accept responsibility, and correct failures.

The emergence of artificial intelligence in digital government has disrupted this long-established relationship (Busuioc, 2021; Dunleavy et al., 2006). The fundamental change brought by AI is not simply that governments have adopted more advanced technologies. The deeper transformation is that the process of governance itself is becoming increasingly mediated by non-human decision-making systems. Algorithms now participate in processes that were previously considered exclusive domains of human judgment, including identifying social risks, allocating public resources, predicting citizen needs, and recommending administrative actions. As a result, the traditional boundary between government decision-makers and technological tools has become increasingly blurred (Figure 1).

This transformation creates the first theoretical crisis (Figure 2) for conventional government trust research: the assumption that government is the single center of decision-making authority is no longer sufficient.

Figure 2. Three Theoretical Crises of Traditional Government Trust in the AI Era

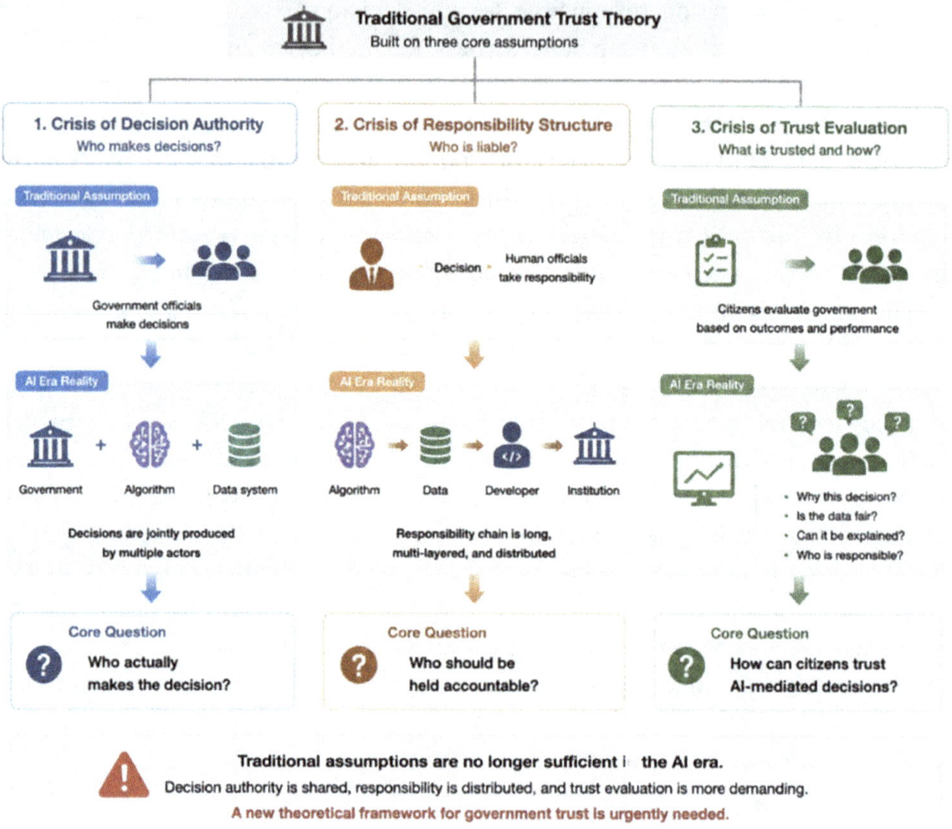

In AI-enabled governance environments, decisions are often produced through interactions among government institutions, algorithmic models, data infrastructures, and digital platforms. The final decision may still be formally approved by a government agency, but the reasoning process behind that decision may depend heavily on machine learning models trained on large-scale datasets. Therefore, citizens are no longer simply responding to governmental authority; they are responding to a complex governance arrangement in which human institutions and intelligent systems jointly shape public outcomes. This change raises a fundamental theoretical question: when a public decision is influenced by an algorithm, what exactly does a citizen trust? Is trust directed toward the government institution that deploys the system? Is it directed toward the accuracy and reliability of the algorithm? Is it directed toward the quality and fairness of the data used to train the model? Traditional theories of government trust were not designed to answer these questions because they were developed under the assumption that authority could be located within identifiable human institutions. However, AI-driven governance introduces a new reality in which authority is distributed across multiple actors and infrastructures.

The second theoretical crisis concerns the transformation of responsibility. Traditional public governance relies on a clear connection between decision-making power and human accountability. Public officials are expected to justify decisions, explain administrative actions, and accept responsibility for failures. This principle has been central to modern democratic governance because accountability provides the foundation upon which citizens decide whether institutions are trustworthy. However, AI systems complicate this relationship by introducing a new chain of responsibility that extends beyond government officials (Floridi & Cowls, 2019; Green, 2021; Grimmelikhuijsen et al., 2013). An AI-supported decision may involve multiple stages and actors: data collection, data processing, algorithm development, model training, system deployment, and administrative application. When an automated decision produces unfair consequences, responsibility cannot always be traced to a single individual or institution. A problematic outcome may result from biased data, inappropriate algorithm design, insufficient institutional supervision, or improper use of the system. Consequently, the traditional model of responsibility, in which a human decision-maker can be directly identified, is challenged by a more distributed accountability structure. This does not mean that AI eliminates human responsibility. On the contrary, the expansion of AI in government makes human accountability more important than ever. However, accountability must be redefined. Governments can no longer maintain public trust only by claiming administrative authority; they must also demonstrate how intelligent systems are designed, governed, monitored, and corrected. Trust in AI-enabled government therefore depends not only on who makes decisions but also on whether the entire decision-making process can be understood and justified.

The third theoretical crisis relates to how citizens evaluate governmental trustworthiness. In traditional governance, citizens often judge governments through visible outcomes: whether services are delivered efficiently, whether policies achieve expected goals, and whether public institutions respond to social needs. Effective performance creates confidence in government capability. However, AI-mediated governance introduces a new dimension of trust evaluation. Citizens increasingly pay attention not only to the result of a decision but also to the process through which that decision is produced. For example, an AI system may successfully improve the efficiency of welfare distribution, but citizens may still question whether the system treats different social groups fairly. A predictive model may improve public safety management, but citizens may demand explanations regarding how predictions are generated and whether personal rights are protected. This demonstrates that trust in AI-driven government cannot be established solely through efficiency and performance. It requires procedural legitimacy, transparency, explainability, and opportunities for citizens to participate in or challenge algorithmic decisions.

Therefore, the arrival of AI in digital government represents more than a technological transformation; it represents a transformation of the theoretical foundation of trust itself. The previous model of government trust was built upon a relatively simple relationship between institutions and citizens. The emerging AI governance environment introduces a more complex structure in which trust must be negotiated among governments, algorithms, data systems, and society. The central challenge is no longer only whether governments are capable of delivering effective services, but whether they can maintain legitimacy when decision-making processes are increasingly shared with intelligent systems (Janowski, 2015; Jobin et al., 2019; Kitchin, 2017).

The theoretical limitation of traditional government trust models therefore becomes clear. They explain how citizens trust institutions, but they cannot fully explain how citizens trust governance systems in which authority is distributed, decisions are algorithmically mediated, and responsibility is shared across human and technological actors. Addressing this limitation requires a new theoretical understanding of trust in digital government, one that moves beyond institution-centered perspectives and recognizes the emergence of a broader AI-mediated governance trust structure.

2. FROM INSTITUTIONAL TRUST TO ECOSYSTEM TRUST

Imagine a citizen using a digital government service today. A few years ago, if this citizen questioned a public decision, the path was relatively clear. The citizen would ask which government department made the decision, which official was responsible, and which administrative procedure could be used to request an explanation. The government institution stood at the center of the relationship. It was the place where authority originated, where responsibility was located, and where trust was ultimately placed. However, this relationship is becoming increasingly difficult to describe in the age of artificial intelligence. When a citizen applies for public housing assistance, receives a healthcare recommendation, or interacts with an automated administrative system, the decision may no longer come entirely from a human official sitting within a government office. Behind the final outcome may exist a combination of policy rules, machine learning models, data resources, digital platforms, and technological infrastructures. The government may still provide the service, but the process through which the decision is produced has become much more complex (Mayer et al., 1995; Nye, 1997).

This change creates a deeper theoretical question. If citizens once trusted government because government was the visible source of authority, who or what do citizens trust when decisions are increasingly shaped by intelligent systems? The answer cannot simply be the government institution itself, because the quality of a digital government service now depends on many factors beyond administrative capability. A government may have a legitimate policy goal, yet citizens may still question whether the algorithm behind the service is fair, whether the data used by the system are reliable, or whether the decision-making process can be explained. Trust has therefore moved into a much broader space (Figure 3).

Figure 3. From Institutional Trust to Ecosystem Trust in the AI Era

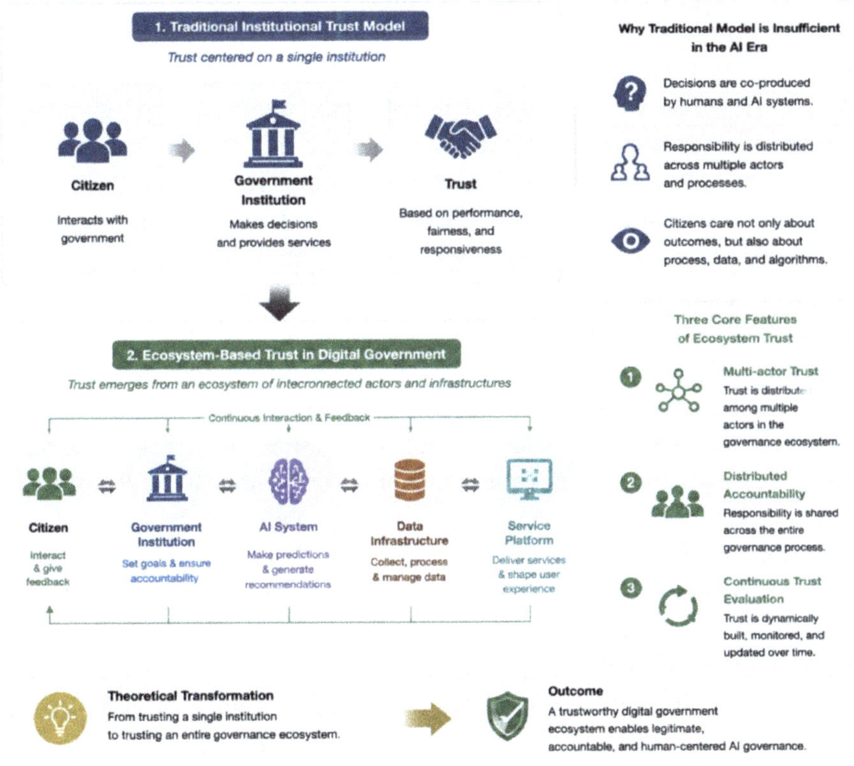

This movement does not mean that institutional trust has disappeared. Government institutions remain the foundation of public legitimacy because they define social values, establish legal frameworks, and determine the purpose of governance. However, in an AI-driven society, institutional authority alone cannot fully explain how trust is created. The central challenge is that governance outcomes are increasingly produced through cooperation between human institutions and technological systems. As a result, trust is no longer formed only through citizens' judgment of government performance; it is formed through their experience of the entire governance environment.

This chapter argues that the AI era requires a transition from institutional trust to ecosystem trust. The concept of ecosystem-based trust in digital government begins with a simple observation: citizens do not experience government as an isolated institution anymore. They experience government through digital interfaces, intelligent systems, data-driven processes, and automated services. The object of trust has expanded from a single organization to a network of interconnected actors and infrastructures that jointly shape public decisions.

Under this perspective, a digital government service is not trustworthy merely because a government agency approves it. It becomes trustworthy when the entire process behind the service can demonstrate reliability and legitimacy. The government must ensure that public objectives are properly represented. AI systems must produce decisions that are consistent and explainable. Data infrastructures must provide accurate and responsible information. Digital platforms must offer citizens accessible and meaningful interactions. Trust emerges from the relationship among these elements rather than from any single component alone.

The first major change introduced by ecosystem trust is that trust becomes a multi-actor relationship. In traditional governance, citizens mainly evaluated the government institution itself. They asked whether officials acted responsibly, whether policies achieved expected goals, and whether public services were delivered effectively. In AI-enabled governance, citizens increasingly evaluate a wider range of actors and processes. They may support a government policy but question the algorithm used to implement it. They may appreciate the convenience of an intelligent service system but worry about how their personal information is collected and analyzed. Their trust depends not only on political authority but also on technological reliability and procedural fairness (Tyler, 2006; Wirtz et al., 2019; Yeung, 2018).

This transformation also changes the meaning of responsibility. In traditional administration, responsibility was closely connected with human decision-makers. When something went wrong, citizens expected an official institution to explain the failure and provide correction. AI-based governance introduces a more complex responsibility structure because decisions may be influenced by multiple stages, including data preparation, algorithm development, system design, and institutional deployment. A biased outcome may not result from one person's mistake but from weaknesses across the entire system. Therefore, maintaining trust requires a new understanding of accountability in which responsibility is distributed but not abandoned.

The importance of ecosystem trust is especially visible when considering algorithmic decision-making. A citizen does not necessarily need to understand every technical detail of an AI model, but the citizen needs confidence that the system is governed properly. This confidence comes from knowing that data are responsibly managed, decisions can be explained, errors can be corrected, and institutions remain accountable for the consequences of technological decisions. In this sense, trust is not created by technology itself; it is created by the governance system surrounding technology.

Another important feature of ecosystem trust is that trust becomes a continuous process rather than a final judgment. Traditional government trust was often evaluated after citizens observed policy outcomes. If a public service worked well, trust increased; if it failed, trust declined. AI-driven governance introduces a different dynamic because intelligent systems constantly change through new data, updated models, and evolving social conditions. Citizens' trust must therefore be continuously maintained through communication, monitoring, feedback, and institutional adaptation.

The transition from institutional trust to ecosystem trust represents a fundamental change in how digital government should be understood. The question facing governments is no longer simply whether citizens trust public institutions. The more challenging question is whether citizens can trust a governance environment in which human judgment, artificial intelligence, data systems, and digital platforms jointly influence public decisions. By shifting attention from individual institutions to the broader governance ecosystem, ecosystem-based trust provides a new theoretical foundation for understanding legitimacy and public confidence in the AI era.

3. THE TRANSFORMATION OF TRUST FROM OUTCOME-ORIENTED TO PROCESS-ORIENTED GOVERNANCE

In traditional government governance, public trust has been largely constructed through the evaluation of visible outcomes. Citizens usually judge whether a government deserves trust by examining whether public services are delivered efficiently, whether policies achieve their expected objectives, and whether administrative institutions respond effectively to social needs. Under this perspective, trust is mainly a consequence of successful governance performance. When governments provide better services, solve social problems, and achieve policy goals, citizens are more likely to develop confidence in public institutions. The underlying logic is relatively straightforward: effective governance produces positive outcomes, and positive outcomes generate public trust.

This outcome-oriented understanding of trust has played an important role in modern public administration. It emphasizes government capacity and administrative effectiveness, encouraging institutions to improve service quality, reduce bureaucratic inefficiency, and deliver measurable social benefits. However, the rise of artificial intelligence in government challenges the assumption that successful outcomes alone are sufficient to maintain public trust. In AI-driven governance environments, citizens are increasingly concerned not only with what decisions are made, but also with how those decisions are produced.

The reason for this transformation is that AI introduces a new layer of complexity into governmental decision-making. When a public decision is made through an intelligent system, the final outcome may appear reasonable, but citizens may still question the process behind it. A welfare allocation system may improve administrative efficiency, but citizens may ask whether the algorithm treats different groups fairly. A predictive policing system may reduce crime rates, but citizens may question whether the data used by the system reinforce existing social biases. A healthcare recommendation system may improve service accessibility, but citizens may demand to know how personal information was analyzed and why a particular recommendation was generated.

These examples reveal a fundamental change in the nature of trust. In traditional governance, citizens mainly evaluated the consequences of government actions. In AI-mediated governance, citizens increasingly evaluate the legitimacy of the decision-making process itself. The central question has shifted from "Did the government achieve a good result?" to "Was the result produced through a trustworthy process?" This represents a transition from outcome legitimacy to procedural legitimacy. Outcome legitimacy is based on the belief that government actions are acceptable because they generate beneficial results. Procedural legitimacy, however, emphasizes that decisions must be considered trustworthy because the processes through which they are produced are transparent, explainable, fair, and accountable. In the AI era, even an efficient and accurate decision may fail to gain public acceptance if citizens cannot understand how the decision was generated or cannot challenge the reasoning behind it.

This shift has profound theoretical implications for understanding government trust. The traditional model assumes that citizens evaluate governments after observing outcomes. However, AI-driven governance introduces a more complex relationship between citizens and public institutions, where trust is formed during the decision-making process rather than only after the final result appears. Citizens increasingly expect governments to provide answers to four fundamental questions: How was this decision made? What information influenced this decision? Why did the system produce this result? Can citizens question or appeal the decision?

These questions demonstrate that transparency in AI governance requires more than simply publishing government information. Traditional transparency focused mainly on revealing administrative procedures, institutional decisions, or public records. In contrast, AI-era transparency requires visibility into the mechanisms behind intelligent decision-making. Citizens need confidence that data are collected responsibly, algorithms operate according to acceptable principles, and institutions maintain the ability to supervise and correct technological systems.

Furthermore, the movement toward process-oriented trust changes the meaning of accountability. In traditional administration, accountability was often evaluated by examining whether government officials achieved appropriate outcomes. In AI-supported governance, accountability must also consider whether the decision-making process itself follows legitimate procedures. A government cannot maintain public trust simply by claiming that an AI system improves efficiency. It must also demonstrate that the system is properly designed, regularly monitored, and subject to human oversight (Wirtz et al., 2019).

This transformation also creates a new relationship between citizens and government. Citizens are no longer passive receivers of public services who judge government only through final results. Instead, they become active participants who expect explanation, participation, and opportunities for review. A trustworthy AI governance system should allow citizens to understand decisions, express concerns, and challenge outcomes when necessary. In this sense, procedural legitimacy strengthens democratic participation by ensuring that technological advancement does not weaken citizens' ability to engage with government decisions.

The shift from outcome-oriented governance to process-oriented governance therefore represents more than a technical requirement for AI systems. It reflects a deeper transformation in the foundation of public trust. In the past, citizens trusted governments because governments demonstrated the ability to achieve desired outcomes. In the AI era, citizens increasingly trust governments when they can see, understand, and participate in the processes through which decisions are made (Nye, 1997).

Therefore, the future of trusted digital government depends not only on improving administrative performance but also on creating decision-making processes that are transparent, explainable, and accountable. AI may enhance the efficiency and intelligence of governance, but only process-oriented legitimacy can ensure that technological capability is transformed into sustainable public trust. This theoretical shift provides an important foundation for understanding how governments can maintain legitimacy in a world where decisions are increasingly produced through cooperation between humans and intelligent systems.

4. ALGORITHM AS A NEW GOVERNANCE ACTOR

The emergence of artificial intelligence in digital government represents a deeper transformation than the simple adoption of new technological tools. The fundamental change is not that governments have acquired more powerful systems for processing information, but that the very structure through which governance decisions are produced has begun to change. In traditional administrative systems, technology was generally positioned outside the core process of governance. Computers stored information, databases supported management, and digital platforms improved communication efficiency, but the authority to interpret social problems and make administrative judgments remained primarily in human hands. Technology provided assistance, while humans retained the exclusive role of governance actors.

However, AI introduces a different relationship between technology and governance. Unlike previous information technologies that mainly followed predefined instructions, contemporary AI systems can identify patterns, generate predictions, classify social conditions, and recommend actions based on complex datasets. These capabilities allow algorithms to participate in processes that were previously considered fundamental expressions of administrative judgment. When an AI system predicts which communities may require additional public support, evaluates the probability of regulatory violations, or determines the priority of service delivery, it is no longer simply executing human decisions. It is actively shaping how governments understand social reality and how public resources are distributed.

This transformation requires a reconsideration of the position of algorithms within governance theory. The traditional distinction between "human decision-makers" and "technical instruments" becomes increasingly insufficient because algorithms now influence not only the speed of decision-making but also the content and direction of decisions. An algorithm does not merely answer questions given by administrators; it also influences which questions become important. It does not simply provide information about society; it constructs particular interpretations of social conditions through data selection, classification methods, and predictive models. In this sense, algorithms become involved in the production of governance knowledge, and governance itself increasingly depends on algorithmic interpretations of society.

The significance of this change can be understood through the concept of the algorithmic governance actor. This concept does not suggest that algorithms possess human-like intentions, political preferences, or moral consciousness. Instead, it emphasizes that algorithms have acquired the practical capacity to influence governance outcomes (Aoki, 2020). In public administration, an actor is not necessarily defined only by consciousness or intention, but also by the ability to shape decisions, distribute resources, and affect social relationships. From this perspective, algorithms have become governance actors because their operations can produce consequences that influence citizens' opportunities, rights, and interactions with public institutions.

Nevertheless, algorithms are fundamentally different from traditional governance actors. A government official can explain a decision, accept responsibility, and be held accountable through institutional procedures. An algorithm cannot provide such political or moral accountability. It operates through mathematical models, training data, optimization objectives, and technical infrastructures. Therefore, describing algorithms as governance actors does not mean transferring authority from humans to machines. Instead, it reveals a new governance condition in which decision-making power is increasingly distributed between human institutions and computational systems.

This leads to a critical theoretical question: if algorithms influence public decisions, where should responsibility be located? Traditional administrative theory assumes that authority and responsibility are closely connected. The actor who makes a decision should be responsible for explaining and justifying that decision. However, algorithmic governance creates a more complex relationship between action and responsibility. A decision influenced by AI may involve data providers, software developers, government agencies, platform operators, and administrative users. When an algorithm produces an unfair or harmful outcome, responsibility cannot always be attributed to a single person or institution.

Therefore, AI governance requires a transition from individual accountability toward distributed accountability. Distributed accountability does not mean reducing responsibility or allowing organizations to avoid blame by referring to technological complexity. Instead, it requires recognizing that accountability must follow the entire lifecycle of algorithmic governance, including data collection, model development, system deployment, institutional supervision, and practical application. Government institutions remain responsible for ensuring that AI systems operate within legal and ethical boundaries because public authority cannot be transferred to invisible technical processes.

Another important implication of viewing algorithms as governance actors concerns the relationship between technology and public values. Algorithms are often presented as objective systems based on data and mathematical calculation. However, algorithmic decisions always contain embedded assumptions about what should be measured, what outcomes should be prioritized, and what forms of evidence should be considered meaningful. For example, a public safety prediction system may define risk through historical administrative data, but these data may reflect existing social inequalities or previous institutional biases. Therefore, the algorithm does not simply discover social reality; it participates in constructing a particular understanding of reality.

This means that algorithmic governance is never purely technical. Every algorithm used in public administration carries institutional choices and social values. The design of an AI system reflects decisions about efficiency, fairness, security, privacy, and public interest. Consequently, the question of trustworthy AI cannot be reduced to whether an algorithm achieves high accuracy. A more fundamental question is whether the algorithmic system operates according to democratic principles and whether citizens can understand, question, and challenge decisions influenced by automated processes (Janowski, 2015; Jobin et al., 2019).

For this reason, this chapter introduces the concept of the embedded governance actor. Algorithms become governance actors not because they replace human institutions, but because they operate within institutional, legal, and social environments that give them governing influence. Their power comes from their connection with government authority, administrative procedures, and public data infrastructures. Without these institutional connections, algorithms remain technical systems; once embedded within public decision-making processes, they become part of the governance structure itself.

Understanding algorithms as embedded governance actors provides a new theoretical foundation for analyzing trust in digital government. If citizens increasingly interact with governments through algorithm-mediated systems, trust can no longer be directed only toward administrative institutions. Citizens must also evaluate whether algorithmic systems are transparent, explainable, controllable, and aligned with public values. Therefore, the future of trusted AI governance depends not on removing algorithms from decision-making, but on developing institutional mechanisms that ensure algorithms serve democratic governance rather than silently reshape it.

This perspective also establishes the theoretical foundation for the following discussion on ethical boundaries beyond algorithmic fairness. Once algorithms are recognized as embedded participants in governance, ethical evaluation must move beyond technical performance and address a broader issue: how can societies ensure that intelligent systems exercise governance influence while remaining accountable to human dignity, legal principles, and democratic legitimacy?

5. THE ARCHITECTURE OF TRUSTED AI GOVERNANCE

The previous sections have demonstrated that artificial intelligence does not simply introduce a new set of technological capabilities into government administration. More fundamentally, AI changes the underlying conditions through which governance authority is exercised, decisions are produced, and public trust is maintained. Traditional government trust was constructed around relatively stable institutional boundaries: governments possessed authority, officials represented responsibility, and citizens evaluated whether institutions performed effectively. In this structure, trust was mainly directed toward a visible political and administrative center.

However, AI-driven governance gradually transforms this centralized structure into a distributed governance environment. Contemporary public decisions increasingly emerge from interactions among legal institutions, algorithmic systems, data infrastructures, digital platforms, and human users. A citizen receiving a public service may no longer interact with a purely human administrative process; instead, the decision may involve automated classification, predictive analysis, data-driven recommendations, and platform-based service delivery. As a result, the object of trust becomes increasingly complex.

The fundamental theoretical problem is therefore not simply how governments can make AI systems more reliable. The deeper question is how legitimacy can be maintained when governance itself becomes technologically distributed. If decision-making authority is partially embedded in algorithms, if administrative knowledge is increasingly generated through data systems, and if public services are delivered through intelligent platforms, then trust must also be reconstructed across this new governance structure.

Based on this theoretical transformation, this chapter proposes the Trusted AI Governance Architecture. Unlike technology-oriented models that treat trust as a quality attribute of AI systems, this architecture argues that trust should be understood as a governance relationship. Trust does not exist inside algorithms, institutions, or citizens separately. Instead, it emerges from the continuous alignment among institutional authority, computational decision-making, data practices, service interactions, and social expectations (Floridi & Cowls, 2019; Grimmelikhuijsen et al., 2013).

This perspective introduces a fundamental shift in understanding trustworthy AI. The question is no longer whether an AI system is trustworthy in isolation. An algorithm may be technically accurate but socially unacceptable; a government may be institutionally legitimate but lose public confidence because its AI systems lack transparency; a digital platform may improve efficiency but weaken citizens' sense of participation. Therefore, trustworthiness is not a property possessed by a single actor. It is a condition produced by the entire governance ecosystem.

The first foundation of this architecture is the institutional foundation, which determines whether AI governance possesses political legitimacy. The importance of this layer lies in recognizing that AI does not eliminate the need for government authority; instead, it changes the form through which government authority is exercised. In traditional administrative systems, legitimacy was largely maintained through visible institutions and human accountability. Citizens knew which government department made a decision and which officials were responsible for implementing policies. However, AI-mediated governance creates a more complicated situation. Decisions may now be influenced by models developed by external technology providers, datasets collected through multiple channels, and computational processes that are difficult for ordinary citizens to understand. This transformation creates a potential legitimacy gap. When citizens cannot clearly identify who shaped a decision, they may experience uncertainty regarding responsibility and fairness. Therefore, the first task of trusted AI governance is not to maximize automation but to establish institutional mechanisms that ensure technological systems remain politically accountable. Governments must become not only users of AI but also governors of AI. This requires a transition from traditional administrative responsibility toward what can be described as institutional responsibility for intelligent governance. Government responsibility extends beyond making decisions; it includes designing oversight mechanisms, establishing regulatory boundaries, evaluating risks, and ensuring that technological systems remain consistent with public values.

The second foundation is the algorithmic governance layer, which addresses the changing nature of administrative power. The significance of algorithms in government does not merely come from their ability to process information faster than humans. Their deeper influence lies in their ability to shape how governments perceive and categorize social reality. Every governance decision begins with an understanding of problems. Before a government can allocate resources, provide services, or design policies, it must determine what issues require attention. In AI-driven governance, algorithms increasingly participate in this process by identifying patterns, predicting risks, and prioritizing interventions. Therefore, algorithms influence not only decisions but also the construction of governance knowledge itself. This creates a new dimension of power. Traditional administrative power was primarily exercised through laws, organizations, and human decisions. Algorithmic governance introduces another form of power: the power to classify, predict, and rank. A system that determines which cases require attention or which groups are considered high-risk is not simply processing information; it is influencing how government sees society. However, this algorithmic power cannot be governed only through technical evaluation. Accuracy alone cannot guarantee legitimacy. A predictive model may achieve high performance while reproducing hidden social inequalities (Yeung, 2018). A recommendation system may improve efficiency while limiting citizens' ability to challenge decisions. Therefore, trusted AI governance requires algorithms to become explainable, contestable, and socially accountable.

The third foundation concerns the data responsibility layer. In AI governance, data become the foundation of administrative knowledge. Yet data should not be understood as objective facts waiting to be discovered. Data are produced through social processes, institutional choices, and historical conditions. They reflect decisions about what should be measured, recorded, and recognized. This means that data governance is fundamentally connected to questions of power and representation. When governments rely on AI systems, they also rely on the assumptions embedded within datasets. Groups that are poorly represented in data may become invisible within algorithmic decision-making. Historical inequalities recorded in data may be transformed into future administrative decisions. Therefore, responsible data governance requires more than privacy protection. It requires governments to consider whose experiences are represented, whose voices are missing, and how data practices influence social outcomes. In this sense, data responsibility becomes a foundation for democratic legitimacy in AI governance.

The fourth foundation is the service interaction layer, which connects technological systems with citizens' lived experiences. Governance does not exist only through institutions and algorithms; it is ultimately experienced through everyday interactions between citizens and public services. AI creates opportunities for governments to move from standardized service delivery toward more adaptive and personalized approaches. However, personalization also creates new questions about autonomy and human connection. A system that predicts citizens' needs may improve efficiency, but it may also create concerns if citizens feel that decisions are made about them without meaningful involvement. Therefore, trusted AI governance requires a new balance between intelligent automation and human-centered administration. The purpose of AI should not be to remove human participation from public services but to create more responsive relationships between governments and citizens (Dunleavy et al., 2006).

The fifth foundation is social acceptance, which represents the final dimension of legitimacy. Even when institutions, algorithms, data systems, and services function effectively, AI governance cannot succeed without public recognition. Social acceptance determines whether citizens view AI-enabled governance as legitimate and whether they are willing to participate in this new governance environment. Importantly, social acceptance is not achieved through communication campaigns or technological demonstrations alone. It emerges from continuous interaction between citizens and governance systems. Citizens must have opportunities to understand decisions, express concerns, challenge outcomes, and participate in shaping technological development. Trust therefore becomes a dynamic process rather than a fixed condition. The Trusted AI Governance Architecture proposed in this chapter reveals a deeper transformation in the meaning of digital government. The central issue is no longer whether governments can use AI to improve administrative efficiency. The more fundamental issue is whether societies can develop a governance structure capable of integrating intelligent systems while preserving accountability, legitimacy, and human values. The theoretical contribution of this architecture is that it moves beyond the traditional view of trust as a relationship between government and citizens. In the AI era, trust becomes a property of the entire governance arrangement. Institutions provide authority, algorithms provide computational intelligence, data provide social knowledge, services provide human interaction, and citizens provide democratic legitimacy. None of these elements alone can create trust; trust emerges from their continuous coordination.

Therefore, the future of trusted digital government depends not on creating more powerful artificial intelligence, but on creating a governance architecture capable of directing technological power toward legitimate public purposes. AI will become trustworthy not because machines become more intelligent, but because societies develop stronger institutions, better accountability mechanisms, and more meaningful forms of human participation.

6. TRUST FAILURE AND RECONSTRUCTION IN AI-ENABLED GOVERNMENT

The emergence of AI-enabled governance does not simply create a new opportunity for improving administrative efficiency; it also introduces a fundamental challenge to the existing foundation of government trust. Previous discussions of digital government have often emphasized how technology can enhance service quality, increase administrative transparency, and improve government responsiveness. However, such perspectives mainly focus on the successful operation of technological systems. They assume that if AI systems are accurate, efficient, and secure, public trust will naturally follow. This assumption overlooks a deeper question: how is trust maintained when AI systems inevitably encounter uncertainty, mistakes, or social controversy?

In complex governance environments, failure is not an exception but an unavoidable part of decision-making. Governments have always faced policy uncertainty, incomplete information, and unexpected social changes. However, AI transforms the nature of failure because decisions are no longer produced exclusively through visible human judgment. When an AI-supported system generates an unexpected outcome, citizens may not know whether the problem originates from the algorithm itself, the data used to train the model, the institution that deployed the system, or the broader governance environment in which the system operates. Therefore, AI governance introduces a new type of trust challenge: the difficulty of understanding and responding to failures within a distributed decision-making structure (Busuioc, 2021).

This represents a significant departure from traditional government accountability. In conventional administrative systems, the relationship between decision-making and responsibility is relatively direct. A government department formulates a policy, public officials implement administrative actions, and institutional mechanisms determine responsibility when problems occur. Although bureaucratic systems are complex, citizens can usually identify the organization responsible for a decision. AI-enabled governance weakens this direct connection because public decisions increasingly emerge from interactions among algorithms, datasets, digital platforms, administrative procedures, and human actors. As a result, trust failure in AI governance cannot be explained simply as an individual mistake or institutional weakness. It reflects a deeper structural problem concerning how responsibility is organized in a technologically mediated governance environment.

One important consequence of this transformation is the emergence of algorithmic failure as a new dimension of governance risk. Algorithms are often regarded as neutral technical instruments because they rely on mathematical models and computational procedures. However, algorithms do not operate outside social contexts. Every algorithm contains assumptions about what should be measured, which outcomes should be optimized, and what forms of knowledge are considered valuable. These assumptions influence how public problems are defined and how solutions are generated. A system designed to predict social risks, allocate welfare resources, or prioritize public services may achieve high computational accuracy while still producing outcomes that conflict with principles of fairness, inclusion, or social justice.

The challenge of algorithmic failure therefore extends beyond technical errors. A system may function exactly as designed and still create unacceptable social consequences. This occurs because governance decisions involve values that cannot always be reduced to numerical optimization. In public administration, efficiency is important, but efficiency alone cannot determine legitimacy. A trustworthy AI system must therefore be evaluated not only by whether it produces accurate predictions but also by whether its decision-making process reflects public values and allows meaningful examination. This requires a broader understanding of algorithmic responsibility, where explainability, auditability, and human oversight become essential components of trust.

Data failure introduces another layer of complexity because AI systems depend on information that is produced through social and institutional processes. Data are not simple reflections of reality; they represent choices about what is collected, recorded, classified, and prioritized. Historical administrative practices influence which populations become visible within government databases and which experiences remain overlooked (Janowski, 2015; Jobin et al., 2019). Consequently, biased or incomplete data may cause AI systems to reproduce existing inequalities while appearing objective and scientific. The problem is not that AI intentionally creates discrimination, but that automated systems may transform historical limitations into future decisions at a larger scale and with greater speed.

This creates a fundamental challenge for digital government: data governance is no longer only a technical issue related to storage, security, or quality control. It has become a question of democratic representation. If citizens believe that their realities are inaccurately represented within the information systems used by government, trust in AI-supported decisions will decline even when the technology performs efficiently. Therefore, trusted AI governance requires governments to consider not only whether data are available, but also whose experiences are included, whose perspectives are missing, and how data-driven decisions affect different social groups.

Beyond algorithmic and data-related problems, institutional failure represents perhaps the most important challenge because technology itself cannot guarantee trustworthy governance. AI systems are always embedded within organizational structures that determine their purposes, limitations, and applications. Governments decide where AI should be used, what authority should be delegated to automated systems, and what forms of supervision should be established. Therefore, when AI produces harmful outcomes, responsibility cannot be transferred entirely to the technology. Algorithms do not independently choose their objectives, define social priorities, or decide how decisions should be implemented. These choices remain connected to human institutions.

However, maintaining institutional responsibility requires a new understanding of accountability. Traditional accountability mechanisms were designed for governance systems where human decision-makers could be directly identified. AI-enabled governance requires a more comprehensive accountability framework that follows the entire lifecycle of an AI system, including data collection, model development, deployment, monitoring, and revision. The question is no longer simply "who made this decision?" but also "who designed the system, who supervised its operation, and who has the responsibility to correct its consequences?" This expanded understanding of accountability is essential for rebuilding public confidence.

Communication failure further demonstrates that trust in AI governance depends not only on what governments do but also on whether citizens can understand and participate in the process. In traditional administration, citizens often accepted decisions because they could communicate with human officials who could provide explanations and respond to concerns. AI-mediated decision-making introduces a different experience. When citizens interact with automated systems, they may feel that decisions are distant, unclear, or beyond human control. Even a technically accurate decision may lose legitimacy if citizens cannot understand why it was produced or how it can be challenged.

Therefore, transparency in AI governance should not be reduced to the disclosure of technical information. The deeper purpose of transparency is to preserve the relationship between government and citizens in an environment where decision-making processes are increasingly complex. Explanation mechanisms, appeal procedures, and opportunities for human review are not merely administrative tools; they are democratic safeguards that allow citizens to maintain meaningful participation in governance.

These challenges demonstrate that the future of trusted AI governance cannot be built on the assumption that technology will eliminate uncertainty. Instead, trust must be reconstructed through the capacity of governance systems to manage uncertainty responsibly. A mature AI governance framework should include mechanisms for detecting problems, assigning responsibility, and correcting failures. Detection enables governments to identify risks before they become major sources of public distrust. Accountability ensures that responsibility remains visible even when decision-making involves multiple actors. Correction allows systems to learn from mistakes and adapt to changing social conditions.

This perspective leads to a fundamental theoretical conclusion: trust in AI-enabled government is not a permanent achievement but a continuous reconstruction process. The legitimacy of digital government does not depend on creating flawless algorithms or completely eliminating errors. Such expectations are unrealistic because all complex governance systems operate under uncertainty. Instead, legitimacy emerges from the belief that when failures occur, institutions possess the willingness and capacity to recognize problems, explain decisions, accept responsibility, and implement improvements.

Therefore, trusted AI governance should be understood not as a promise of perfect automation but as a new form of institutional resilience. The most advanced digital governments will not be those that never experience failure, but those that can transform failure into learning, adaptation, and stronger public accountability. In the AI era, trust is no longer created only by successful outcomes; it is continuously rebuilt through the governance system's ability to respond responsibly when outcomes become uncertain.

7. THEORETICAL CONTRIBUTION OF THE NEW TRUST MODEL

The previous discussions demonstrate that artificial intelligence has fundamentally changed the conditions under which trust is produced, maintained, and evaluated in digital government. Traditional theories of government trust were mainly developed around a relatively stable institutional relationship between governments and citizens. In such models, government institutions represented the primary source of authority, public officials represented the main decision-makers, and citizens evaluated trustworthiness through institutional performance and policy outcomes. However, the emergence of AI-enabled governance has disrupted this traditional structure by introducing new actors, new forms of decision-making, and new mechanisms through which legitimacy is created.

Based on this transformation, this chapter makes several theoretical contributions to the study of trust in digital government. The first contribution is the expansion of the traditional government–citizen trust model into a broader governance ecosystem trust model. Previous approaches generally viewed trust as a relationship between two major actors: government institutions that exercise authority and citizens who evaluate governmental performance. While this perspective remains valuable, it becomes insufficient when public decisions are increasingly influenced by algorithmic systems, data infrastructures, and digital platforms. In AI-enabled governance, citizens are not only responding to government institutions but also interacting with a wider technological and institutional ecosystem that shapes how decisions are generated and implemented.

The introduction of AI changes the object of trust itself. Citizens may trust or distrust not only the government agency responsible for a service but also the algorithm used to allocate resources, the data used to generate predictions, the platform through which services are delivered, and the institutional mechanisms that supervise these processes. Therefore, trust in digital government can no longer be understood as a simple relationship between citizens and government organizations. It becomes a distributed relationship involving multiple actors whose interactions collectively influence public perceptions of legitimacy. This chapter contributes to trust theory by arguing that the foundation of digital government trust has shifted from institutional trust toward ecosystem-based trust.

The second theoretical contribution is the introduction of the concept of AI-mediated governance trust. Existing studies on AI trust have often focused on technological characteristics, including system reliability, privacy protection, security, and algorithmic accuracy. Although these dimensions are important, they cannot fully explain why citizens accept or reject AI-supported government decisions. Public trust in AI governance is not determined only by whether an algorithm functions correctly; it also depends on how AI changes the relationship between authority, decision-making, and legitimacy.

The concept of AI-mediated governance trust emphasizes that artificial intelligence has become an important mediating force in the formation of government legitimacy. AI does not simply improve administrative efficiency; it transforms the process through which governments exercise authority. When algorithms participate in policy implementation, risk assessment, and public service delivery, citizens increasingly evaluate not only governmental outcomes but also the technological processes behind those outcomes. This means that government legitimacy in the AI era is constructed through a combination of institutional capacity, algorithmic credibility, data responsibility, and procedural transparency.

This perspective provides a new explanation for why technically successful AI systems may still encounter public resistance. A system can achieve high predictive accuracy and operational efficiency while failing to gain social acceptance if citizens perceive the decision-making process as unfair, unclear, or uncontrollable. Therefore, AI-mediated governance trust shifts the research focus from the question of whether AI works to the broader question of whether AI-supported governance can maintain legitimacy.

The third theoretical contribution is the development of a distributed trust framework that provides the conceptual foundation for subsequent discussions of social contracts, ethical governance, and emotional intelligence in digital government. Traditional trust theories often assume that legitimacy flows primarily from institutions toward citizens. However, AI-enabled governance requires a more dynamic understanding in which trust is continuously produced through interactions among governments, technologies, data systems, and social actors.

Within this distributed trust framework, no single actor can independently guarantee public confidence. Governments remain responsible for establishing institutional rules and accountability mechanisms, but technological systems influence decision processes, data infrastructures shape knowledge production, and citizens participate through feedback and evaluation. Trust therefore emerges from the quality of relationships among these components rather than from the authority of any single institution.

This framework also provides a theoretical basis for understanding future challenges in AI governance. Issues such as algorithmic fairness, data protection, explainability, emotional interaction, and citizen participation are not isolated technical problems. They are interconnected dimensions of a broader trust ecosystem. By placing these issues within a unified theoretical structure, this chapter moves beyond fragmented discussions of AI ethics and digital government technologies.

More importantly, the proposed trust model changes the understanding of government legitimacy in the AI era. In traditional governance, legitimacy was largely associated with institutional authority and administrative performance. In AI-enabled governance, legitimacy increasingly depends on whether governance systems can demonstrate responsible relationships among human institutions, intelligent technologies, and society. Trust is no longer simply granted to governments because they possess authority; it must be continuously constructed through transparency, accountability, responsiveness, and ethical technological practices.

Therefore, the theoretical contribution of this chapter lies not in proposing AI as a replacement for government institutions, but in explaining how AI transforms the foundation upon which government trust is built. The central argument is that the future of digital government requires a transition from institution-centered trust toward ecosystem-based, AI-mediated, and continuously reconstructed trust. This theoretical shift provides the foundation for the following chapters, which further examine how social contracts, ethical boundaries, and emotional intelligence can contribute to the development of trusted AI governance systems.

REFERENCES

Aoki, N. (2020). An experimental study of public trust in AI chatbots in the public sector. *Government Information Quarterly, 37*(4), 101490. DOI: 10.1016/j.giq.2020.101490

Bouckaert, G., & Van de Walle, S. (2003). Comparing measures of citizen trust and user satisfaction as indicators of good governance: Difficulties in linking trust and satisfaction indicators. *International Review of Administrative Sciences, 69*(3), 329–343. DOI: 10.1177/0020852303693003

Busuioc, M. (2021). Accountable artificial intelligence: Holding algorithms to account. *Public Administration Review, 81*(5), 825–836. DOI: 10.1111/puar.13293 PMID: 34690372

Dunleavy, P., Margetts, H., Bastow, S., & Tinkler, J. (2006). New public management is dead—Long live digital-era governance. *Journal of Public Administration: Research and Theory, 16*(3), 467–494. DOI: 10.1093/jopart/mui057

Floridi, L., & Cowls, J. (2019). A unified framework of five principles for AI in society. *Harvard Data Science Review, 1*(1). Advance online publication. DOI: 10.1162/99608f92.8cd550d1

Green, B. (2021). The flaws of policies requiring human oversight of government algorithms. *Computer Law & Security Review, 42*, 105581. DOI: 10.1016/j.clsr.2021.105581

Grimmelikhuijsen, S., Porumbescu, G., Hong, B., & Im, T. (2013). The effect of transparency on trust in government: A cross-national comparative experiment. *Public Administration Review, 73*(4), 575–586. DOI: 10.1111/puar.12047

Janowski, T. (2015). Digital government evolution: From transformation to contextualization. *Government Information Quarterly, 32*(3), 221–236. DOI: 10.1016/j.giq.2015.07.001

Jobin, A., Ienca, M., & Vayena, E. (2019). The global landscape of AI ethics guidelines. *Nature Machine Intelligence, 1*(9), 389–399. DOI: 10.1038/s42256-019-0088-2

Kitchin, R. (2017). Thinking critically about and researching algorithms. *Information Communication and Society, 20*(1), 14–29. DOI: 10.1080/1369118X.2016.1154087

Mayer, R. C., Davis, J. H., & Schoorman, F. D. (1995). An integrative model of organizational trust. *Academy of Management Review, 20*(3), 709–734. DOI: 10.2307/258792

Nye, J. S. (1997). Introduction: The decline of confidence in government. In Nye, J. S., Zelikow, P. D., & King, D. C. (Eds.), *Why people don't trust government* (pp. 1–18). Harvard University Press. DOI: 10.2307/j.ctv322v3xg.4

Tyler, T. R. (2006). *Why people obey the law*. Princeton University Press. DOI: 10.1515/9781400828609

Wirtz, B. W., Weyerer, J. C., & Geyer, C. (2019). Artificial intelligence and the public sector—Applications and challenges. *International Journal of Public Administration, 42*(7), 596–615. DOI: 10.1080/01900692.2018.1498103

Yeung, K. (2018). Algorithmic regulation: A critical interrogation. *Regulation & Governance, 12*(4), 505–523. DOI: 10.1111/rego.12158

KEY TERMS AND DEFINITIONS

AI-mediated Governance Trust: AI-mediated governance trust describes the trust relationship formed when artificial intelligence systems participate in public decision-making and service delivery. This concept emphasizes that AI does not simply function as a passive administrative tool but influences how decisions are generated, evaluated, and implemented. Citizens' trust is therefore shaped not only by government performance but also by their perceptions of algorithmic fairness, data quality, explainability, and the ability of institutions to control and correct AI-related risks.

Algorithmic Governance Actor: An algorithmic governance actor refers to the role of algorithms as active components that influence public administration processes rather than merely serving as technical instruments. In contemporary digital government, algorithms can classify information, allocate resources, identify risks, predict social demands, and recommend administrative actions. However, algorithms are not independent decision-makers. They operate as embedded governance actors shaped by institutional rules, legal frameworks, social values, and human supervision.

Continuous Trust Reconstruction: Continuous trust reconstruction refers to the understanding that trust in AI-enabled government is not a permanent condition but an ongoing process of creation, evaluation, and adjustment. Because AI systems continuously interact with changing social conditions, new data, and evolving public expectations, trust must be maintained through continuous monitoring, transparency, accountability mechanisms, and corrective actions. A trustworthy AI government is therefore not one that eliminates all risks, but one that possesses the capacity to recognize failures and rebuild confidence.

Distributed Accountability: Distributed accountability refers to a responsibility structure in which accountability for AI-driven decisions is shared among multiple actors involved in the development, deployment, and supervision of AI systems. Traditional administrative accountability assumes that human officials are the primary responsible agents. However, AI governance involves complex chains connecting data collection, algorithm design, system operation, and institutional decisions. Distributed accountability does not remove government responsibility; rather, it requires governments to establish mechanisms that identify, monitor, and regulate responsibilities across the entire AI governance process.

Ecosystem-based Trust in Digital Government: Ecosystem-based trust in digital government refers to the idea that trust is no longer concentrated in a single governmental institution but distributed across the entire governance ecosystem. In AI-enabled public services, outcomes are jointly influenced by government agencies, technology providers, algorithm developers, data systems, and digital platforms. Consequently, maintaining public trust requires cooperation among multiple actors and cannot be achieved through institutional reputation alone. This perspective shifts the understanding of trust from a government-centered model toward an ecosystem-oriented governance model.

Government Trust in the AI Era: Government trust in the AI era refers to citizens' confidence not only in government institutions but also in the broader governance systems through which public decisions are produced. In traditional governance environments, trust was mainly established through the relationship between citizens and government organizations. However, AI-enabled governance introduces new actors, including algorithms, data infrastructures, and intelligent platforms. Therefore, government trust has evolved from a purely institutional relationship into a more complex form of trust involving technological reliability, procedural legitimacy, and distributed responsibility.

Procedural Legitimacy in AI Governance: Procedural legitimacy in AI governance refers to the extent to which AI-based decisions are considered trustworthy based on the fairness and transparency of the decision-making process. Traditional government legitimacy has often been evaluated through outcomes, such as service efficiency and policy effectiveness. In contrast, AI governance requires citizens to understand how decisions are generated, what data are used, whether algorithms are fair, and whether individuals have opportunities to question or challenge decisions. Therefore, legitimacy increasingly depends on the quality of governance procedures rather than outcomes alone.

Trusted AI Digital Government: Trusted AI Digital Government refers to a governance model in which artificial intelligence technologies are integrated into public administration while maintaining institutional legitimacy, accountability, transparency, and public confidence. Unlike traditional digital government models that mainly emphasize technological efficiency and service automation, trusted AI digital government focuses on whether AI-enabled decision-making processes can be understood, justified, supervised, and accepted by society. It highlights that technological capability alone cannot guarantee public trust; trust must be constructed through the interaction among institutions, algorithms, data systems, and citizens.

Chapter 4
From Technological Reliability to AI Social Contract:
Reconstructing Trust in Digital Government

Yuanyuan Guo
http://orcid.org/0000-0002-3042-8417
Ningbo University, China

ABSTRACT

Chapter 4 explores how AI reshapes trust in digital government. It argues that traditional institution centered trust is insufficient because AI introduces new actors, decision processes, and accountability structures into governance. The chapter proposes the concept of the AI social contract, emphasizing that trust should be built through legitimacy, responsibility, and citizen participation. It further explains that AI should be understood as an embedded governance institution rather than merely a technical tool. The chapter concludes that trusted AI governance depends not on algorithmic perfection, but on the continuous negotiation between technological capability, institutional accountability, and social expectations.

1. THE FAILURE OF TECHNOLOGY-CENTERED TRUST IN AI GOVERNANCE

For a long period, the relationship between technology and trust was understood through a relatively straightforward assumption, a better technology would naturally create greater trust. When governments began adopting digital systems, the

DOI: 10.4018/979-8-3373-9129-8.ch004

main concern was whether these systems could improve administrative efficiency, reduce human errors, and provide faster public services. A citizen using an online government platform usually did not question how the system internally processed information. As long as the service was convenient, accurate, and secure, technology was generally regarded as a positive force that strengthened confidence in government. This understanding was reasonable in the early stage of digital government because technology mainly played a supporting role (Bovens et al., 2014). A computer system could store information, automate procedures, and accelerate administrative processes, but it rarely influenced the fundamental logic of public decision-making. The final decision remained visible and traceable: a public officer reviewed an application, a government department approved a policy, or an administrative institution issued a decision. Technology operated behind the scene as an instrument that improved governmental capacity rather than as an actor that shaped governance outcomes.

Figure 1. Technology-Centered Trust Model

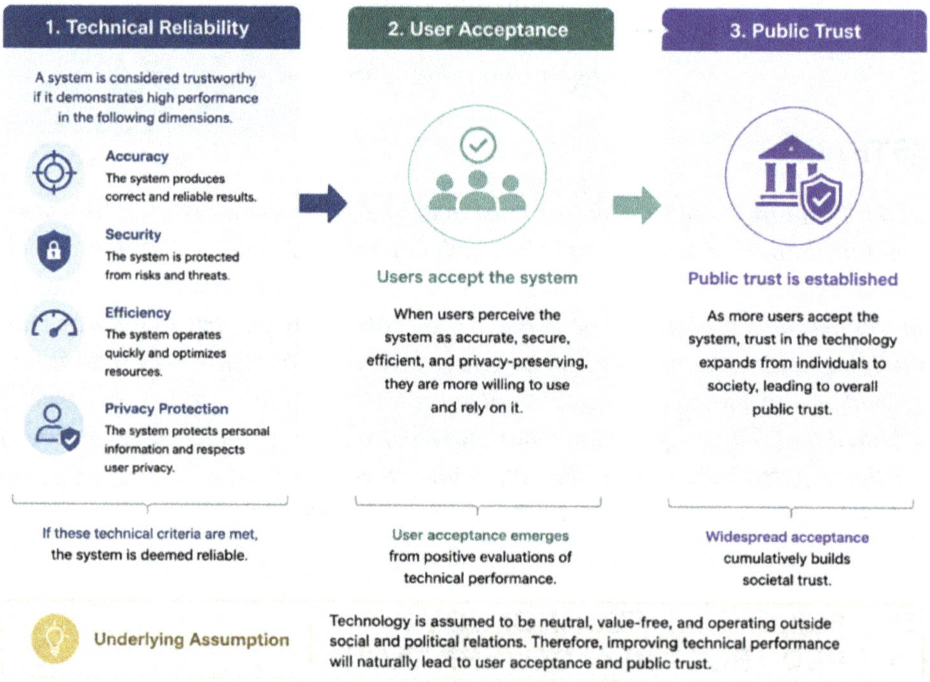

Under this traditional perspective, trust in technology was mainly constructed around the concept of technical reliability. If a system was accurate, secure, efficient, and capable of protecting personal information, it was considered trustworthy. This created a technology-centered trust model (Figure 1).

The underlying assumption of this model is that technology is neutral. It assumes that algorithms simply process information, systems simply execute instructions, and data simply represent objective reality. Therefore, any problem caused by technology can be solved through technical improvement: better algorithms, larger datasets, stronger security mechanisms, and more advanced computing capabilities. However, the emergence of artificial intelligence in digital government fundamentally challenges this assumption. The problem is not that AI systems are unreliable. In many cases, AI systems can perform tasks faster and more accurately than human administrators. The deeper issue is that AI has moved from being a passive administrative tool to becoming an active component in governance processes. When algorithms begin to classify citizens, predict social risks, allocate public resources, and recommend administrative decisions, they are no longer simply improving government efficiency (Busuioc, 2021). They are participating in the exercise of public authority.

Consider a simple example. A government introduces an AI based welfare distribution system to identify citizens who are most likely to require financial assistance. The purpose of this system is to address several long standing problems in traditional welfare administration. In many cases, government officers need to review a large number of applications manually, which can result in delayed decisions, inconsistent evaluations, and difficulties in identifying citizens whose needs are not immediately visible. By analyzing large amounts of administrative data, such as income information, employment conditions, family situations, and previous applications for public services, the AI system is expected to recognize patterns of social vulnerability and provide assistance more efficiently. From a technical perspective, the system may appear successful because it can analyze thousands of applications within seconds, reduce administrative costs, and improve the speed of service delivery. According to the traditional technology centered perspective, such a system should increase public trust because it produces more efficient outcomes.

However, the situation becomes more complicated when citizens begin asking deeper questions about the decision making process behind the system. A citizen whose application has been rejected may not simply accept the result because the algorithm is faster or more accurate than human judgment. Instead, the citizen may ask why another person with a similar background was classified as eligible while their own application was rejected (Bovens, 2007). They may question what types of personal information influenced the decision, whether the data used to train the system reflected existing social inequalities, and whether certain groups were unintentionally disadvantaged by the algorithmic evaluation process. If the system makes an incorrect decision that causes someone to lose access to essential support, another fundamental question emerges: who should take responsibility for the outcome? Should responsibility belong to the government department that adopted the system, the developers who designed the algorithm, the institutions that provided the data, or the algorithm itself? These questions reveal a fundamental limitation of technological reliability. The algorithm may be technically accurate, but citizens are not only evaluating whether the system works. They are evaluating whether the system deserves authority over decisions that affect their lives. The issue has shifted from technological performance to governance legitimacy.

This transformation represents a theoretical crisis for traditional trust research. Previous studies of government trust were built upon a relatively stable relationship between institutions and citizens (Bryson et al., 2014). Governments possessed authority, officials represented institutional responsibility, and citizens evaluated whether public institutions acted fairly and effectively. The source of trust was therefore relatively clear: citizens trusted governments because governments could explain decisions, accept responsibility, and correct mistakes. AI-driven governance disrupts this relationship because decision-making authority becomes increasingly distributed. A public decision may now involve multiple elements: government regulations define the purpose of the system; data infrastructures provide the information basis; algorithms determine patterns and predictions; technology companies develop the models; and administrative institutions implement the final decisions. The outcome is produced not by a single visible actor but by an interconnected socio-technical system.

This creates a new problem because trust can no longer be directed toward a single institution alone. When a citizen receives an unfavorable decision from an AI assisted government service, dissatisfaction cannot always be explained as a traditional administrative failure. The problem may originate from biased data, inappropriate model design, insufficient institutional supervision, or unclear responsibility mechanisms. In an AI mediated governance environment, the traditional question of whether citizens can trust the government is no longer sufficient. A more complex question emerges as to whether citizens can trust the entire governance system through which public decisions are produced.

Figure 2. From Traditional Government Trust to AI-Era Governance Trust

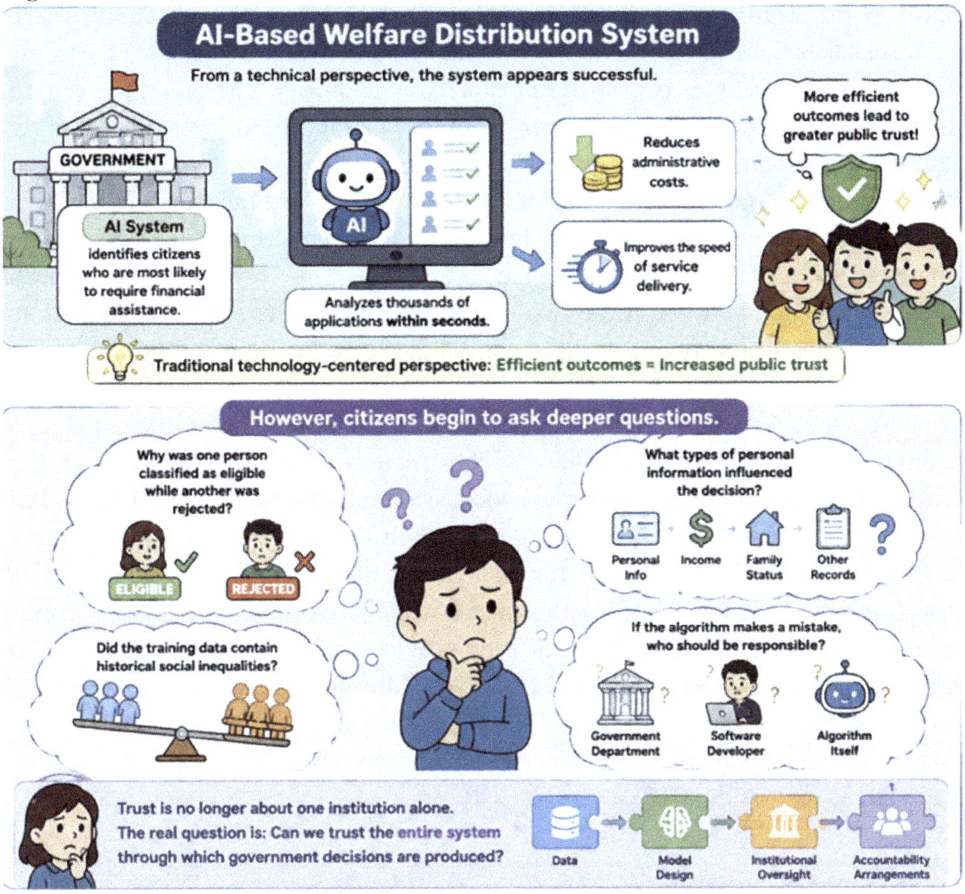

The limitation of technology-centered trust becomes even clearer when considering the difference between private technology and public governance. In commercial environments, users may tolerate certain forms of algorithmic decision-making because the consequences are relatively limited. A recommendation system suggesting an advertisement or a shopping product may influence consumer choices, but it rarely determines access to fundamental social rights. Government AI operates in a different context. Its decisions may influence employment opportunities, healthcare access, social welfare support, immigration procedures, and public security measures. Because these decisions affect citizens' rights and social positions, technical accuracy alone cannot provide sufficient justification (Dunleavy et al., 2006).

A highly accurate AI system can still produce distrust if citizens believe that its decisions are unfair or impossible to challenge. Conversely, a system with moderate technical limitations may still gain public acceptance if institutions provide transparency, explanation, and effective mechanisms for correction. This demonstrates that trust in AI governance is not simply a question of whether machines make fewer mistakes than humans. It is a question of whether society accepts the process through which machines participate in exercising authority. Therefore, the central challenge of AI governance is not merely improving algorithmic capability but re-defining the foundation of trust itself. The traditional question of digital government was:"Can technology help governments perform better?"The question in the AI era has become:"Under what conditions should society accept decisions produced with the involvement of artificial intelligence?"

The difference between these two questions reflects a deeper transformation. The first focuses on efficiency; the second focuses on legitimacy. The first treats technology as a tool; the second recognizes technology as part of the governance structure. Once AI begins influencing public decisions, trust cannot be created only through technical optimization. It must be constructed through a broader relationship involving responsibility, transparency, social values, and public participation. For this reason, technological reliability represents only the starting point of trustworthy AI governance, not its final foundation. The future of digital government requires a transition from trusting technology because it works to trusting governance systems because they are legitimate. This transition provides the theoretical foundation for moving from a technology-centered trust model toward a new AI social contract, where trust is not simply engineered through better algorithms but socially established through responsible governance (Floridi & Cowls, 2019; Grimmelikhuijsen et al., 2013; Janowski, 2015).

2. THE TRANSFORMATION OF AI FROM TECHNICAL TOOL TO GOVERNANCE INSTITUTION

When artificial intelligence was first introduced into public administration, it was commonly understood as a technological assistant rather than a participant in governance. Governments adopted AI systems mainly to improve administrative efficiency, reduce repetitive work, and provide faster services. Under this perspective, AI was similar to other digital technologies used by governments. It was considered a neutral instrument that followed human instructions. Government officials remained the true decision makers, while AI simply supported them by processing information and performing calculations. This understanding created a simple relationship between government authority and technology. Governments designed policies, public officials interpreted rules, and AI systems helped execute these decisions. If an AI system failed, the problem was usually considered a technical issue, such as inaccurate data, software errors, or insufficient computing capability. The legitimacy of government decisions was still believed to come from human institutions because technology was only regarded as a means to improve administrative performance. However, this technology centered perspective becomes increasingly inadequate when AI systems begin to influence how governments understand social problems and make public decisions. The important transformation is not that AI has become more powerful technically, but that AI has started to participate in processes that determine how public resources, opportunities, and attention are distributed. Once an AI system begins to classify citizens, evaluate risks, or prioritize services, it is no longer simply performing administrative tasks. It is shaping governance outcomes (Jobin et al., 2019; Kitchin, 2017; Mayer et al., 1995).

A clear example can be found in the use of AI based welfare assessment systems. Traditionally, welfare decisions were mainly made by government employees who reviewed applications according to established regulations. Although human judgment could be imperfect, citizens generally understood who was responsible for the decision. If a person believed that a welfare application had been unfairly rejected, they could appeal to a government department, request an explanation from an official, or seek administrative review. The introduction of AI changes this relationship. Imagine a government agency adopting an AI system to identify citizens who should receive financial assistance. The system analyzes large amounts of information, including income records, employment history, family conditions, previous interactions with public services, and other social indicators. Based on these patterns, the system produces a risk score or eligibility recommendation. At first glance, this appears to be a purely technical improvement. The system can process information faster than humans, identify hidden patterns, and reduce administrative workload.

However, the moment the system begins deciding who deserves attention and who should receive support, it begins to perform a governance function. The algorithm is no longer only answering the question of "how can the government process applications faster?" It is also influencing the deeper question of "which citizens should be prioritized by the government?" This involves social values and political choices, not merely technical calculations. For example, suppose an AI system identifies unemployed young adults in urban areas as a high priority group for employment assistance. At the same time, it gives lower priority to elderly citizens living in rural communities because their data patterns appear less urgent according to the model. From a technical perspective, the system may be operating correctly because it follows the statistical patterns found in the training data. However, from a governance perspective, society must ask whether the definition of "need" created by the algorithm reflects broader social values. Should employment potential receive greater importance than social vulnerability? Should historical patterns in government data determine future access to public support?

These questions reveal why AI should not be understood merely as a technical instrument. The algorithm is indirectly shaping social categories and influencing how citizens are treated by public institutions. Similar situations can be observed in many areas of digital government. In public safety management, predictive algorithms may identify locations or groups considered to have higher risks, influencing where police resources are concentrated. In healthcare systems, AI models may assist in determining which patients require immediate attention when medical resources are limited. In education administration, AI systems may predict which students need additional support and influence how educational resources are allocated.

In all these cases, AI performs functions that are traditionally associated with institutions. Institutions are not only buildings or organizations; they are systems of rules that organize social behavior and determine how resources and opportunities are distributed. Laws, administrative procedures, and organizational structures all influence human actions by establishing boundaries and priorities. Modern AI systems increasingly perform a similar role through algorithmic rules. They define classifications, establish priorities, and guide administrative decisions through computational processes (Nye, 1997; Rahwan, 2018; Rousseau et al., 1998; Tyler, 2006).

The difference is that traditional institutions are usually visible and politically recognizable. Citizens know that laws are created through legislative processes and that administrative rules are established by government agencies. Algorithms, however, often operate behind technical interfaces that hide their social assumptions. A decision generated by an AI system may appear objective because it is presented as the result of data analysis rather than human judgment. Yet every algorithm contains choices about what data should be collected, which variables should be considered important, and what outcomes should be optimized. This creates a new challenge for public trust. When AI becomes part of governance, citizens are no longer evaluating only the government institution itself. They are also evaluating the invisible algorithmic structures that influence government decisions. A citizen who receives a negative decision from an AI assisted service may not only question whether the government is fair, but also question whether the algorithm was designed properly, whether the data were representative, and whether the decision process allows correction and appeal. Therefore, AI in digital government should be conceptualized as an embedded governance institution rather than an independent political actor. AI does not possess its own political interests or social objectives. It operates within legal frameworks, administrative systems, and institutional values created by human society. However, because it increasingly shapes how decisions are produced and how resources are distributed, it has acquired institutional characteristics. It becomes part of the governance structure through which public authority is exercised.

This theoretical shift changes the foundation of trust in AI governance. If AI is only a tool, trust can be measured mainly through technical indicators such as accuracy, security, and efficiency. However, if AI functions as an embedded governance institution, trust must also include questions of legitimacy, accountability, transparency, and social acceptance. The central question is no longer whether governments use advanced technology effectively. The deeper question is whether the new algorithmic institutions embedded within government can exercise influence in a way that citizens consider legitimate and trustworthy. By recognizing AI as a governance institution, digital government research can move beyond the narrow discussion of technological performance and begin examining how artificial intelligence transforms the nature of public authority itself. This perspective provides the theoretical foundation for the following discussion of the AI social contract, where trust is reconstructed not only through technical reliability but through a broader relationship between technology, institutions, and society.

3. WHY AI GOVERNANCE REQUIRES A NEW SOCIAL CONTRACT

The introduction of artificial intelligence into government does not merely represent an improvement in administrative technology. It represents a deeper transformation in the relationship between power, responsibility, and public trust. Traditional theories of social contract were developed in a political environment where the exercise of authority could be traced primarily to human institutions. Citizens accepted the legitimacy of government because governments provided collective benefits, including security, social welfare, public infrastructure, and essential services (Wirtz et al., 2019; Yeung, 2018; Young et al., 2019). In exchange, governments were expected to exercise power responsibly and remain accountable for the consequences of their decisions. This traditional relationship was built upon a relatively clear understanding of authority. Citizens knew who created policies, who implemented regulations, and who should answer when public decisions caused harm. A government agency could be questioned through administrative procedures, public officials could provide explanations, and institutional mechanisms could be used to correct mistakes.

Figure 3. The Evolution of Social Contract in AI Enabled Digital Government

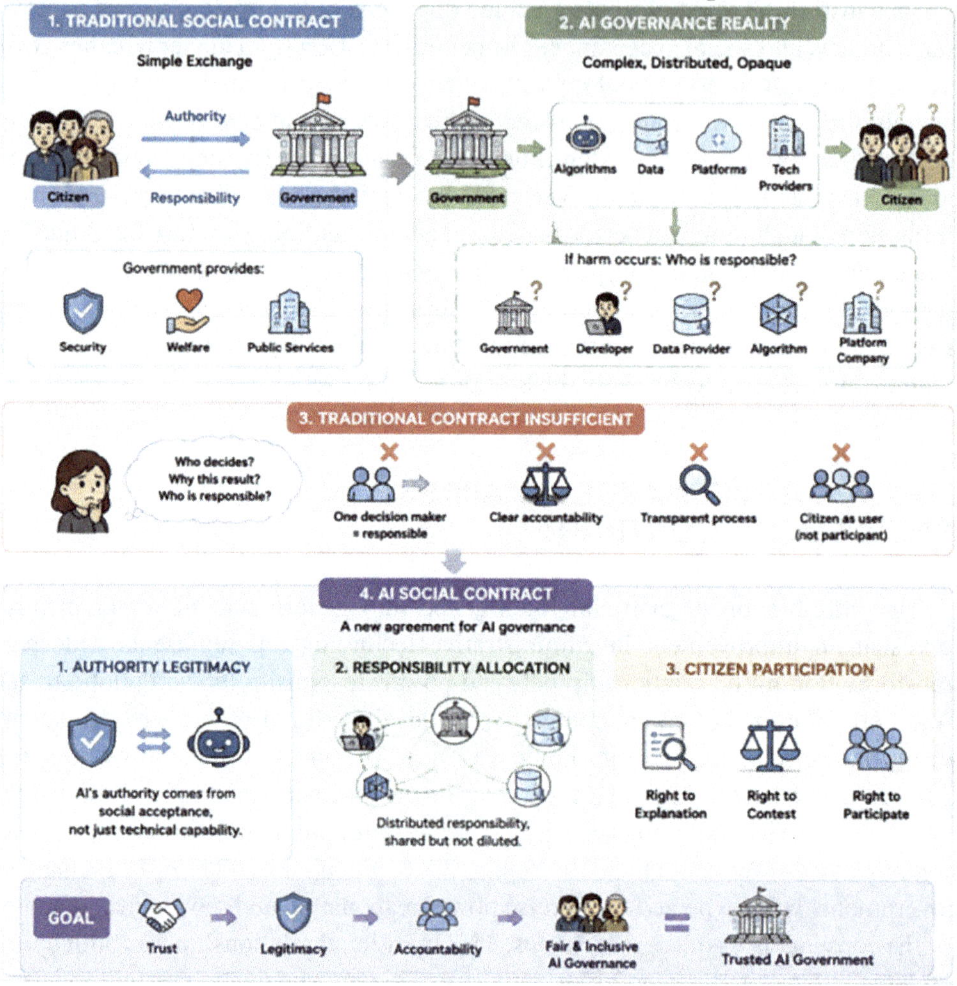

The social contract therefore depended on a fundamental connection between authority and responsibility. The actor that exercised public power was also expected to carry the responsibility of explaining and justifying that power (Figure 3). However, the emergence of AI in government creates a new governance reality in which this connection becomes increasingly complicated. Public decisions are no longer produced exclusively through human judgment and administrative procedures. They are increasingly shaped by interactions among algorithms, datasets, digital platforms, technology companies, and government institutions. AI systems have become embedded within the processes through which governments identify social problems, allocate public resources, and determine administrative priorities. This transformation raises a fundamental question. If public authority is increasingly exercised through AI systems, does the traditional social contract still provide an adequate explanation of how citizens should trust government? The answer is increasingly uncertain because the original social contract was designed for a world where political authority was concentrated in human institutions. The AI era introduces a different environment where governance outcomes may emerge from complex socio technical systems rather than from a single identifiable decision maker.

Consider the example of an AI based welfare distribution system. A government introduces such a system with the intention of improving fairness and efficiency. Traditional welfare administration often depends on human officers reviewing applications individually. This process can be slow, expensive, and sometimes inconsistent because different officials may interpret similar situations differently. An AI system appears to offer a solution. By analyzing large amounts of information, including income levels, employment conditions, family structures, medical records, and previous interactions with public services, the system can identify citizens who may require assistance more quickly and systematically. From the perspective of administrative efficiency, this appears to be a positive development. The government can reduce processing time, allocate resources more effectively, and potentially reach vulnerable populations that were previously overlooked. If the traditional social contract is applied, citizens may expect that a more efficient government service should naturally strengthen public trust.

However, AI governance introduces questions that cannot be answered by efficiency alone. Imagine two citizens with similar economic conditions applying for welfare assistance. One receives support from the system, while the other is rejected. In a traditional administrative environment, the rejected citizen could ask the responsible officer for an explanation. The officer could review the case, explain the reasoning, and potentially correct an error. But in an AI based system, the decision may depend on thousands of data points and complex statistical relationships that are difficult for ordinary citizens to understand. The citizen may then ask deeper questions. Why did the system consider one person more vulnerable than another? Which factors influenced the decision? Did the data used to train the system reflect existing social inequalities? Was the algorithm designed to recognize human circumstances accurately, or did it reduce complex social problems into limited numerical categories? These questions reveal that AI changes the nature of the relationship between citizens and government. Citizens are no longer only asking whether the government provides effective services. They are asking whether the processes through which decisions are produced are legitimate. The source of trust has shifted from the final outcome to the entire decision making system.

A similar challenge can be observed in AI based public safety systems. Some governments have explored predictive technologies that analyze historical crime data to identify areas requiring greater attention. Supporters argue that these systems allow governments to use limited resources more efficiently and prevent potential risks before they occur. From a technical perspective, the system may demonstrate strong predictive performance. However, the social contract problem appears when historical data contain existing patterns of inequality. If certain communities have historically experienced higher levels of surveillance or greater police presence, the data may reflect those historical practices. When an algorithm learns from such data, it may reproduce existing patterns and classify certain groups or areas as higher risk. The question is therefore not only whether the algorithm predicts accurately, but whether society accepts the values and consequences embedded within those predictions. This example demonstrates a critical difference between technical performance and political legitimacy. A system can be statistically accurate while still creating social concerns. Accuracy answers the question of whether an algorithm can correctly identify patterns. Legitimacy addresses whether society believes that the use of those patterns to guide government action is appropriate and fair. Traditional technology focused trust models often emphasize the first question while ignoring the second.

The challenge becomes even more visible when responsibility must be determined. In traditional governance, if a government decision harms citizens, responsibility can usually be assigned to a specific institution or official. However, AI governance creates a distributed responsibility structure. A harmful outcome may result from multiple interconnected factors. The data may contain biases. The algorithm may contain design limitations. The government may fail to establish appropriate oversight. The technology provider may not provide sufficient transparency. The final decision may therefore be produced through a chain of actors rather than a single authority. For example, if an AI healthcare system incorrectly prioritizes patients and causes someone to lose access to timely treatment, responsibility cannot easily be assigned. The government may argue that it trusted the medical AI provider. The developer may argue that the system performed according to available data. The data provider may claim that the information accurately reflected historical conditions. Yet for the affected citizen, these explanations do not solve the fundamental problem. Someone must still explain why the decision occurred and how similar harm will be prevented in the future. This situation demonstrates why AI governance requires a new social contract. The traditional social contract focused primarily on the exchange between citizens and government. Citizens accepted government authority, and governments accepted responsibility for protecting public interests. The AI social contract expands this relationship by recognizing that public decisions are increasingly shaped by multiple actors and technological systems.

An AI social contract can therefore be understood as an implicit agreement among governments, citizens, technology developers, and data institutions regarding how AI should participate in governance and how responsibility should be distributed when AI influences public decisions. It does not replace the traditional social contract. Instead, it extends it to address a new reality where public authority is increasingly exercised through intelligent systems. The first foundation of this new social contract is the legitimacy of AI authority. The question is not whether AI is intelligent enough to make decisions, but whether society accepts AI as an appropriate participant in governance. Intelligence does not automatically create legitimacy. A machine may analyze information faster than humans, but speed and accuracy alone cannot justify the exercise of public power. AI systems gain legitimacy only when their use is supported by transparent rules, institutional oversight, and social acceptance. The second foundation is the reconstruction of responsibility. In AI governance, responsibility cannot simply follow the person who presses the final button because the decision process involves multiple interconnected actors. Governments must remain accountable for adopting and supervising AI systems. Developers must consider the social consequences of system design. Data institutions must ensure that information used by AI does not unfairly disadvantage particular groups. Responsibility must therefore become distributed but not weakened. The third foundation is citizen participation. In traditional digital government, citizens are often treated as users who receive improved services. However, in AI governance, citizens must become participants in shaping how AI systems operate. Because algorithms can influence access to important social resources, citizens need meaningful opportunities to understand decisions, challenge outcomes, and contribute to discussions about system design.

For example, if a citizen is denied a public service because of an AI recommendation, providing a simple explanation that "the system calculated this result" is insufficient. A legitimate AI governance system should allow citizens to understand the reasons behind decisions, request human review when necessary, and challenge outcomes that appear unfair. These rights transform citizens from passive recipients of algorithmic decisions into active participants in AI governance. Therefore, the AI social contract represents a fundamental shift in how trust should be understood in digital government. Trust is no longer created simply because governments provide efficient services or because algorithms achieve high levels of accuracy. Trust emerges when citizens believe that AI systems operate within a legitimate framework where authority is justified, responsibility is clearly assigned, and public participation is respected.

The central challenge of AI governance is not whether governments can use AI effectively. The deeper challenge is whether societies can create a new relationship between human values and intelligent systems. The AI social contract provides a theoretical foundation for this transformation by redefining trust as a shared responsibility among institutions, technologies, and citizens. In the AI era, trustworthy government is not only a government that uses intelligent technologies, but a government that ensures those technologies remain connected to democratic principles and public values.

4. FROM MACHINE TRUST TO GOVERNANCE TRUST: A NEW DIMENSION OF LEGITIMACY

The emergence of AI in government has created a common misunderstanding regarding the nature of trust. When people discuss whether an AI system can be trusted, the discussion often focuses on the capability of the machine itself. Questions such as whether the algorithm is accurate, whether the model is powerful enough, or whether the system can produce reliable predictions usually become the center of attention. This perspective assumes that trust in AI is mainly a technical issue. If the machine performs well, citizens will gradually accept and trust the system. However, this assumption becomes problematic when AI is applied to public governance. Unlike commercial technologies, government AI systems do not simply provide optional services. They influence decisions related to citizens' rights, opportunities, and access to public resources. When an AI system determines eligibility for welfare support, evaluates healthcare priorities, identifies potential risks, or recommends administrative actions, citizens are not only interacting with a technological product. They are interacting with a new form of governance mechanism. Therefore, the object of public trust is not the algorithm itself. Most citizens do not have the ability to directly evaluate the internal structure of an AI model, examine its parameters, understand its training process, or verify the quality of its code. Even experts may find it difficult to fully interpret the complex decision logic of advanced machine learning systems. As a result, asking citizens to simply "trust the algorithm" ignores the actual foundation upon which public trust is built.

A citizen who receives an AI generated decision from a government service usually does not ask whether the mathematical structure of the model is sophisticated enough. Instead, the citizen is more likely to ask whether the government has established appropriate mechanisms to ensure that the system operates fairly and responsibly. People want to know whether someone supervises the system, whether mistakes can be corrected, whether unfair decisions can be challenged, and whether institutions will accept responsibility when the system causes harm. This represents a fundamental transformation from machine centered trust to governance centered trust. Machine centered trust focuses on whether the AI system itself is reliable. Governance centered trust focuses on whether the entire institutional environment surrounding AI is capable of managing its power responsibly. In other words, citizens do not trust AI because AI is intelligent. They trust AI when they believe that human institutions have the ability to control, supervise, and correct AI.

This transformation can be understood through the example of an AI based healthcare decision system. Suppose a government hospital introduces an AI model to prioritize patients waiting for limited medical resources. From a technical perspective, the system may demonstrate high prediction accuracy and improve resource allocation efficiency. However, public acceptance does not depend only on these technical achievements. Patients and families may still question whether the system considers vulnerable groups fairly, whether medical data are collected ethically, and whether human doctors can review algorithmic recommendations. If the government can demonstrate that the system is continuously monitored, that medical professionals remain involved in important decisions, and that citizens have channels to appeal unfair outcomes, public confidence may increase. The source of trust does not come from the algorithm alone. It comes from the governance framework that surrounds the algorithm.

Based on this understanding, trust in AI governance can be divided into three interconnected dimensions. The first dimension is functional trust, which concerns whether AI systems can perform their intended tasks effectively. This is the most traditional form of technology related trust. Citizens evaluate whether AI can improve service quality, reduce errors, and increase administrative efficiency. For example, an AI system used for processing public service applications should be able to analyze information accurately, provide consistent recommendations, and reduce unnecessary delays. Without functional capability, AI cannot become a meaningful part of government services. However, functional trust alone is insufficient because technically successful systems may still produce socially unacceptable outcomes. A highly accurate algorithm can still be problematic if it relies on biased data or creates unfair consequences for certain groups. Therefore, the second dimension, procedural trust, becomes essential.

Procedural trust focuses on how AI decisions are produced rather than only on what outcomes they generate. Citizens need confidence that the process behind AI decisions follows acceptable principles of fairness, transparency, and accountability. For example, when an AI system rejects a citizen's application for public assistance, the question is not only whether the prediction was statistically accurate. The citizen also needs to understand whether the relevant data were appropriate, whether similar cases were treated consistently, and whether there is an opportunity to request human review. This dimension reflects an important change in public expectations. In traditional government, citizens often judged institutions based on outcomes. If public services were effective and policies produced positive results, trust could be strengthened. However, AI governance introduces a new requirement. Citizens increasingly evaluate not only what decisions are made but also how those decisions are generated. A fair outcome produced through an unfair process may still damage public trust.

The third dimension is institutional trust, which represents the highest level of AI governance legitimacy. Institutional trust concerns whether governments possess the capacity to govern AI itself. The central question is not whether AI makes mistakes, because no complex system can completely eliminate uncertainty. The more important question is whether institutions have the ability to detect problems, assign responsibility, and correct failures. For instance, when an AI welfare system unintentionally disadvantages a particular social group, institutional trust depends on whether the government can identify the problem through monitoring mechanisms, investigate the cause, modify the system, and provide remedies to affected citizens. A government that acknowledges risks and establishes correction mechanisms may maintain public confidence even when failures occur. In contrast, a government that treats AI decisions as unquestionable or hides behind technological complexity may quickly lose legitimacy.

These three dimensions demonstrate that trusted AI governance is not created by technological performance alone. Functional trust provides the foundation because AI must be capable of performing useful tasks. Procedural trust provides fairness because citizens need confidence in how decisions are produced. Institutional trust provides long term legitimacy because society needs assurance that AI remains under effective human governance. Therefore, the future of AI governance requires a broader understanding of what it means to trust artificial intelligence. The central issue is not whether citizens can trust machines as independent actors. The deeper issue is whether citizens can trust the governance systems that design, deploy, supervise, and regulate those machines. Trust in the AI era is ultimately a form of institutional legitimacy, where technology becomes acceptable not because it replaces human judgment, but because it operates within a responsible and accountable governance framework.

This shift from machine trust to governance trust provides an important theoretical foundation for understanding why AI governance requires more than technological innovation. It requires the reconstruction of legitimacy itself, where governments must demonstrate not only that AI works, but that AI is governed in a way that society can trust.

5. THE REDISTRIBUTION OF RESPONSIBILITY UNDER THE AI SOCIAL CONTRACT

The most fundamental transformation brought by AI governance is not the disappearance of responsibility, but the reconstruction of responsibility itself. In traditional government systems, responsibility is built upon a relatively stable relationship between decision making authority and accountability. The actor who possesses the power to make decisions is expected to explain those decisions and accept responsibility for their consequences. This principle has formed the foundation of modern administrative accountability. When a government official approves a policy, rejects a public service application, or allocates public resources, citizens can usually identify who made the decision and which institution should respond when problems occur. Even when mistakes happen, responsibility can be traced through established administrative procedures. This connection between authority and responsibility allows citizens to believe that government power remains controllable and accountable.

However, the rise of AI mediated governance has fundamentally changed this relationship. The problem is not that humans have disappeared from decision making, but that decisions are increasingly produced through complex interactions among multiple actors, technologies, and infrastructures. An AI supported government decision may involve public institutions that define policy objectives, technology companies that develop algorithms, data organizations that provide training information, and regulatory bodies that establish supervision mechanisms. The final decision is therefore no longer the direct outcome of a single human judgment but the result of a broader socio technical process.

Consider an AI based welfare distribution system designed to identify citizens who require financial assistance. A government department may introduce the system because it hopes to improve efficiency and reach vulnerable populations more accurately. A technology company may design the algorithm that evaluates applications. Different government agencies may provide historical data used to train the model. After deployment, administrative officers may rely on algorithmic recommendations when making final decisions. From the perspective of administrative modernization, such a system appears beneficial because it can process large amounts of information quickly and support more consistent decision making.

However, imagine that the system produces unfair outcomes and systematically disadvantages a particular group of citizens. The responsibility question immediately becomes more complicated. The government may argue that it adopted the system to improve public service efficiency. The technology provider may claim that the algorithm followed the available data and technical requirements. The data managers may argue that the information reflected existing social conditions rather than deliberate discrimination. Each actor contributed to the final decision, but no single actor appears to fully control the outcome.

This situation reveals the central accountability challenge of AI governance. In traditional administration, responsibility is usually attached to identifiable individuals or institutions. In AI governance, responsibility becomes distributed across a chain of decisions, from data collection and algorithm design to system deployment and institutional oversight. This transformation reflects the reality of modern AI systems, but it also creates a significant risk. When responsibility is distributed without clear boundaries, it may become weakened rather than strengthened. A situation may emerge where every actor is involved, but no actor feels fully responsible. In other words, distributed responsibility can unintentionally create an accountability gap.

The AI social contract must therefore address a critical question: how can responsibility be redistributed without allowing responsibility to disappear? The answer does not lie in returning to the traditional model where one person is responsible for every decision. Such a model is no longer realistic because AI governance involves complex networks of actors. Instead, the goal is to create a new responsibility structure in which different actors assume clearly defined obligations while remaining connected through a transparent accountability system.

The first requirement of this new structure is the identification of responsibility before AI systems are implemented. Responsibility cannot be determined only after a failure occurs. It must be embedded into the entire lifecycle of AI governance. Technology developers should be responsible for considering potential risks during system design and ensuring that algorithms operate according to appropriate standards. Data managers should be responsible for maintaining data quality and evaluating whether training data may reproduce historical inequalities. Government institutions should remain responsible for deciding where AI should be applied, ensuring human oversight, and protecting citizens' rights. Regulatory institutions should establish standards that define acceptable practices and provide mechanisms for external supervision.

The second requirement is accountability transparency. In traditional administrative systems, citizens can usually understand the relationship between decisions and decision makers. AI systems create a new challenge because many decisions are produced through processes that are invisible to ordinary citizens. Therefore, trustworthy AI governance requires transparency not only about the final decision but also about the responsibility structure behind that decision. Citizens do not necessarily need access to complex technical details of algorithms, but they need to know who designed the system, what types of information influenced the decision, which institution supervises its operation, and who is responsible when errors occur. Without such transparency, AI may create a perception of an unchallengeable authority that operates beyond public understanding.

The third requirement is institutional correction. A trustworthy AI governance system does not depend on the unrealistic assumption that algorithms will never fail. Social environments are complex, and even advanced AI systems may produce unintended consequences. The key issue is whether institutions have the capacity to recognize failures, investigate their causes, correct problems, and provide remedies for affected citizens. For example, if an AI healthcare system is found to provide unequal recommendations for different social groups, public trust will depend less on whether the government claims that the original algorithm was accurate and more on whether the government can respond effectively by reviewing the system, adjusting its operation, and preventing similar problems in the future.

This understanding changes the meaning of accountability in the AI era. Accountability is no longer simply about identifying the individual who made a decision. It becomes a continuous governance process that ensures every actor involved in AI development and deployment remains responsible for their role. The purpose of accountability is not only to punish failures but also to maintain public confidence by demonstrating that AI systems remain under meaningful human control. Therefore, the redistribution of responsibility under the AI social contract represents a movement from individual accountability toward ecosystem accountability. However, ecosystem accountability does not mean that responsibility becomes vague or shared equally among everyone. Instead, it requires a structured distribution of responsibility where each actor has identifiable duties and where citizens can still locate institutions capable of providing explanations and remedies.

The deeper implication is that AI does not reduce the need for human responsibility; it expands it. As AI systems become increasingly involved in public decision making, governments must ensure that technological complexity does not become a barrier to accountability. The legitimacy of AI governance depends on whether society believes that behind every algorithmic decision there are responsible institutions, identifiable actors, and effective mechanisms for correction. The purpose of the AI social contract is therefore not to transfer trust from humans to machines, but to establish a new governance arrangement in which intelligent systems operate within a framework of responsibility, transparency, and public accountability.

6. BUILDING TRUST THROUGH NEGOTIATED LEGITIMACY

The transformation of trust in AI governance reveals an important theoretical shift. Trust is no longer something that governments can simply provide to citizens through institutional authority or technological improvement. In traditional public administration, trust was often understood as a result of effective government performance. When governments delivered public services efficiently, maintained social order, and achieved policy objectives, citizens gradually developed confidence in public institutions. Under this perspective, trust was mainly constructed through a one way relationship in which governments demonstrated their capability and citizens evaluated whether that capability deserved acceptance.

However, AI enabled governance changes the nature of this relationship. When artificial intelligence becomes involved in public decision making, trust can no longer be created only by government performance or technological capability. The reason is that AI governance involves multiple actors whose decisions collectively influence public outcomes. Governments determine why and where AI should be used. Technology companies design and maintain AI systems. Data institutions provide the information that shapes algorithmic decisions. Regulatory organizations establish boundaries for acceptable practices. Citizens evaluate not only the effectiveness of AI services but also whether these systems reflect social values and protect public interests.

Therefore, trust in AI governance is not produced by a single authority. It emerges through continuous negotiation among different actors with different expectations, responsibilities, and forms of knowledge. This process can be understood as negotiated legitimacy, where the legitimacy of AI systems is not automatically granted because they are introduced by governments or because they demonstrate technical capability. Instead, legitimacy must be continuously constructed through interaction between technological possibilities and social expectations.

This shift can be illustrated through the example of an AI based public service recommendation system. A government may introduce such a system to provide citizens with more personalized services by predicting individual needs and recommending appropriate government programs. From the government's perspective, the system may represent administrative innovation because it improves efficiency and allows limited public resources to be distributed more effectively. From the perspective of technology developers, the primary concern may be whether the model achieves high accuracy and stable performance. However, citizens may evaluate the system through a different perspective. They may ask whether the recommendations are fair, whether personal information is being used appropriately, and whether they still have the ability to make their own choices rather than simply follow algorithmic suggestions. These different perspectives demonstrate that trust cannot be reduced to technical performance. A system may satisfy engineers because it achieves high accuracy, and it may satisfy administrators because it reduces workload, but it may still fail to gain public acceptance if citizens feel excluded from the decision making process. Legitimacy therefore emerges through negotiation among competing expectations. Technical capability must be balanced with ethical concerns, institutional responsibilities, and social values.

The role of government within this negotiated process is not only to adopt advanced technologies but also to create conditions under which AI can operate legitimately. Governments must establish clear rules regarding AI use, ensure accountability mechanisms, and maintain the ability to intervene when systems produce harmful consequences. Government authority remains essential because AI systems exercise influence within the public sphere. However, authority alone is no longer sufficient. Governments must also demonstrate that AI applications are consistent with public values and democratic principles. Technology companies also become important participants in this process. Their responsibility is not limited to developing systems that function correctly. Because algorithm design decisions can influence social outcomes, developers must consider issues such as fairness, explainability, security, and potential unintended consequences. A technically successful AI system that ignores social impacts may undermine rather than strengthen public trust. Therefore, technological responsibility becomes an essential part of governance legitimacy. Citizens also play a more active role in AI governance. In traditional digital government, citizens were often viewed primarily as service recipients who evaluated government performance after services were delivered. In AI governance, citizens become participants in defining what trustworthy AI should mean. Their concerns about privacy, fairness, transparency, and human control influence how AI systems should be designed and regulated. Public participation therefore becomes not only a democratic value but also a necessary condition for building legitimate AI governance.

Regulatory institutions provide another essential element by ensuring that AI development remains within acceptable social boundaries. Because AI systems often operate through complex technical processes that ordinary citizens cannot directly observe, independent oversight is necessary to ensure that technological advancement does not exceed institutional control. Regulation does not simply restrict innovation. Instead, effective regulation creates the conditions under which society can confidently accept innovation. This perspective leads to a broader understanding of trusted AI. Trustworthy AI is not a final technical achievement that can be reached once an algorithm becomes sufficiently accurate or secure. It is an ongoing social governance process in which technological capability is continuously adjusted according to changing social expectations. A perfectly designed algorithm cannot guarantee public trust because trust depends on how society understands, evaluates, and participates in the use of that algorithm.

The idea of negotiated legitimacy therefore challenges the traditional assumption that trust follows automatically from technological progress. In AI enabled government, trust must be continuously produced through dialogue, accountability, and institutional adaptation. When citizens raise concerns about algorithmic decisions, when regulators establish new standards, or when governments modify systems in response to public feedback, these processes are not signs of failure. They are essential parts of maintaining legitimacy. Ultimately, the foundation of trusted AI governance is not the creation of perfect machines but the establishment of a relationship between technology and society. AI becomes trustworthy when citizens believe that intelligent systems are developed and used within a governance framework that respects human values, distributes responsibility fairly, and allows continuous public participation. Therefore, trust is not produced by perfect algorithms, but by continuous negotiation between technological capability and social expectations.

7. THEORETICAL CONTRIBUTION: FROM INSTITUTIONAL TRUST TO AI SOCIAL CONTRACT THEORY

The theoretical contribution of this chapter lies not in adding artificial intelligence as another technological factor influencing government trust, but in fundamentally reconsidering how trust itself should be understood in the context of AI enabled governance. Traditional government trust theories were developed under an institutional centered perspective, where the primary relationship of trust existed between citizens and government institutions. Governments exercised authority, provided public services, and were evaluated by citizens according to their effectiveness, fairness, and responsiveness. Although these theories have explained many aspects of public trust, they become increasingly limited when governance decisions are produced through complex interactions among governments, algorithms, data systems, and technological infrastructures.

This chapter therefore moves beyond the traditional concept of government centered trust and proposes the idea of AI mediated governance trust. The central argument is that citizens in the AI era are no longer trusting only a government institution as a visible political actor. They are trusting a broader governance arrangement in which human institutions and intelligent systems jointly produce public decisions. When an AI system influences welfare allocation, healthcare prioritization, public safety management, or access to government services, citizens are not simply evaluating whether the government performs well. They are evaluating whether the entire decision making process, including technological components, institutional supervision, and accountability mechanisms, deserves confidence.

This theoretical shift changes the object of trust itself. In the traditional model, trust was mainly directed toward an institution. In the AI governance environment, trust becomes connected to an ecosystem of actors and processes. Citizens must have confidence not only in government authority but also in the way algorithms are designed, how data are managed, how decisions are explained, and how failures are corrected. Therefore, trust becomes a relationship between society and a governance system rather than a simple relationship between citizens and a single institution.

The second theoretical contribution of this chapter is the redefinition of the role of artificial intelligence in public governance. Previous approaches often treated AI as an administrative tool that improved efficiency while remaining separate from the exercise of governmental authority. Under this perspective, AI was considered a technical instrument controlled by human decision makers. However, this chapter argues that such an understanding is insufficient because AI systems increasingly participate in processes that shape governance outcomes.

When an algorithm classifies citizens, predicts social risks, prioritizes public resources, or recommends administrative actions, it performs functions that influence how government power is exercised. Although AI does not possess independent political authority, it has acquired governance capacity through its ability to shape decisions and organize interactions between governments and citizens. Therefore, AI should be understood as an embedded governance institution rather than merely a technological instrument.

The concept of AI as an embedded governance institution does not suggest that algorithms replace governments or become independent political actors. Instead, it highlights that algorithms increasingly operate within institutional structures and influence how those structures function. Similar to traditional institutions, AI systems establish categories, define priorities, and shape patterns of interaction. The difference is that these institutional effects are produced through computational rules rather than through traditional legal or administrative procedures. Recognizing this transformation allows AI governance research to move beyond questions of technical performance and examine how algorithms reshape the distribution of authority, responsibility, and social opportunity.

The third theoretical contribution concerns the transformation of legitimacy in AI governance. Traditional government legitimacy has often been evaluated through outcome legitimacy. Governments gain public confidence when they produce effective policies, deliver efficient services, and achieve desirable social outcomes. While outcomes remain important, AI governance introduces a new dimension of legitimacy because citizens increasingly care about how decisions are produced.

This chapter proposes the concept of negotiated legitimacy as a new foundation for trusted AI governance. In an AI mediated environment, legitimacy cannot be created solely through successful outcomes or technological superiority. Instead, it emerges through continuous interaction among governments, technology developers, regulatory institutions, and citizens. A system becomes legitimate when society accepts not only what the AI system produces, but also the principles, processes, and responsibilities behind those outcomes.

For example, an AI system may improve the efficiency of welfare distribution, but citizens may still question its legitimacy if they cannot understand how decisions are made or challenge unfair outcomes. Conversely, a system that includes transparency mechanisms, human oversight, and opportunities for public participation may maintain legitimacy even when technological limitations exist. This demonstrates that trust in AI governance is not based on the assumption of perfect technology. It is based on whether society believes that technology operates within a responsible and accountable governance framework.

Based on these theoretical developments, this chapter establishes the foundation for the following discussions in this book. By redefining trust as AI mediated governance trust, it provides a theoretical basis for examining how AI changes the relationship between government and citizens. By conceptualizing AI as an embedded governance institution, it creates the foundation for analyzing the ethical boundaries of algorithmic decision making in the following chapter. Questions concerning fairness, transparency, accountability, and responsibility become meaningful only when AI is recognized as a participant in governance rather than a passive technical tool.

Furthermore, the idea of negotiated legitimacy provides the theoretical foundation for exploring emotional intelligence and citizen interaction in later chapters. If trust is continuously constructed through interaction between technology and society, then understanding citizens' emotions, perceptions, and experiences becomes essential for designing human centered AI governance. The concept also supports the development of a broader trusted AI governance model by integrating institutional responsibility, algorithmic accountability, data governance, service interaction, and social acceptance.

Therefore, the main theoretical advancement of this chapter is the transition from institutional trust to AI social contract theory. It argues that the future of digital government cannot rely on the traditional assumption that trust is created only through effective institutions or reliable technologies. Instead, trust in AI governance must be reconstructed through a new social agreement that defines how intelligent systems participate in public decision making, how responsibility is distributed among different actors, and how legitimacy is continuously negotiated between technological capability and social expectations. This theoretical framework provides the foundation for understanding trusted AI not simply as a technological achievement, but as a new form of governance relationship between humans, institutions, and intelligent systems.

REFERENCES

Bovens, M. (2007). Analysing and assessing accountability: A conceptual framework. *European Law Journal, 13*(4), 447–468. DOI: 10.1111/j.1468-0386.2007.00378.x

Bovens, M., Schillemans, T., & Goodin, R. E. (2014). Public accountability. In Bovens, M., Goodin, R. E., & Schillemans, T. (Eds.), *The Oxford handbook of public accountability* (pp. 1–20). Oxford University Press.

Bryson, J. M., Crosby, B. C., & Bloomberg, L. (2014). Public value governance: Moving beyond traditional public administration and the new public management. *Public Administration Review, 74*(4), 445–456. DOI: 10.1111/puar.12238

Busuioc, M. (2021). Accountable artificial intelligence: Holding algorithms to account. *Public Administration Review, 81*(5), 825–836. DOI: 10.1111/puar.13293 PMID: 34690372

Dunleavy, P., Margetts, H., Bastow, S., & Tinkler, J. (2006). New public management is dead, long live digital-era governance. *Journal of Public Administration: Research and Theory, 16*(3), 467–494. DOI: 10.1093/jopart/mui057

Floridi, L., & Cowls, J. (2019). A unified framework of five principles for AI in society. *Harvard Data Science Review, 1*(1). Advance online publication. DOI: 10.1162/99608f92.8cd550d1

Grimmelikhuijsen, S., Porumbescu, G., Hong, B., & Im, T. (2013). The effect of transparency on trust in government: A cross-national comparative experiment. *Public Administration Review, 73*(4), 575–586. DOI: 10.1111/puar.12047

Janowski, T. (2015). Digital government evolution: From transformation to contextualization. *Government Information Quarterly, 32*(3), 221–236. DOI: 10.1016/j.giq.2015.07.001

Jobin, A., Ienca, M., & Vayena, E. (2019). The global landscape of AI ethics guidelines. *Nature Machine Intelligence, 1*(9), 389–399. DOI: 10.1038/s42256-019-0088-2

Kitchin, R. (2017). Thinking critically about and researching algorithms. *Information Communication and Society, 20*(1), 14–29. DOI: 10.1080/1369118X.2016.1154087

Mayer, R. C., Davis, J. H., & Schoorman, F. D. (1995). An integrative model of organizational trust. *Academy of Management Review, 20*(3), 709–734. DOI: 10.2307/258792

Nye, J. S. (1997). Introduction: The decline of confidence in government. In Nye, J. S., Zelikow, P. D., & King, D. C. (Eds.), *Why people don't trust government* (pp. 1–18). Harvard University Press. DOI: 10.2307/j.ctv322v3xg.4

Rahwan, I. (2018). Society-in-the-loop: Programming the algorithmic social contract. *Ethics and Information Technology*, *20*(1), 5–14. DOI: 10.1007/s10676-017-9430-8

Rousseau, D. M., Sitkin, S. B., Burt, R. S., & Camerer, C. (1998). Not so different after all: A cross-discipline view of trust. *Academy of Management Review*, *23*(3), 393–404. DOI: 10.5465/amr.1998.926617

Tyler, T. R. (2006). *Why people obey the law*. Princeton University Press. DOI: 10.1515/9781400828609

Wirtz, B. W., Weyerer, J. C., & Geyer, C. (2019). Artificial intelligence and the public sector: Applications and challenges. *International Journal of Public Administration*, *42*(7), 596–615. DOI: 10.1080/01900692.2018.1498103

Yeung, K. (2018). Algorithmic regulation: A critical interrogation. *Regulation & Governance*, *12*(4), 505–523. DOI: 10.1111/rego.12158

Young, M. M., Bullock, J. B., & Lecy, J. D. (2019). Artificial discretion as a tool of governance: A framework for understanding the impact of artificial intelligence on public administration. *Perspectives on Public Management and Governance*, *2*(4), 301–313. DOI: 10.1093/ppmgov/gvz014

KEY TERMS AND DEFINITIONS

AI Mediated Governance Trust: AI mediated governance trust refers to a new form of public trust in which citizens evaluate not only government institutions but also the technological systems through which public decisions are produced. In traditional governance, trust is primarily directed toward government agencies and public officials. However, in AI enabled governance, trust extends to algorithms, data systems, oversight mechanisms, and institutional arrangements. It emphasizes that citizens trust not the AI system itself, but the broader governance framework that ensures AI operates fairly, transparently, and responsibly.

AI Social Contract: The AI social contract refers to the implicit agreement among governments, citizens, technology developers, and data institutions regarding how artificial intelligence should participate in public governance and how responsibility should be distributed. Unlike the traditional social contract, which mainly focuses on the relationship between citizens and government, the AI social contract recognizes that governance decisions are increasingly shaped by interactions among human institutions, algorithms, data infrastructures, and technological platforms. Its central concern is how legitimacy, accountability, and citizen rights can be maintained when AI becomes involved in exercising public authority.

Algorithmic Governance: Algorithmic governance refers to the use of algorithms and computational systems to support or influence public decision making, including resource allocation, risk assessment, service prioritization, and policy implementation. It highlights that algorithms are not only tools for automation but also mechanisms that shape how governments identify problems, categorize citizens, and distribute public resources.

Distributed Accountability: Distributed accountability describes the redistribution of responsibility across multiple actors involved in AI governance, including governments, algorithm developers, data managers, technology providers, and regulatory institutions. Unlike traditional accountability models based on a single decision maker, AI governance involves complex decision chains where outcomes are produced through interactions among different actors. Distributed accountability aims to clarify responsibilities while preventing situations where technological complexity allows all actors to avoid responsibility.

Embedded Governance Institution: An embedded governance institution describes the role of AI as a system that operates within existing political, legal, and administrative structures while influencing how governance decisions are made. Unlike traditional views that treat AI as a neutral technical tool, this concept recognizes that AI systems can perform institutional functions by classifying citizens, prioritizing resources, assessing risks, and shaping interactions between governments and society. AI does not replace human institutions, but becomes embedded within governance processes and contributes to the exercise of public authority.

Governance Centered Trust: Governance centered trust refers to the idea that public confidence in AI should not be based solely on the technical performance of algorithms. Instead, trust depends on whether the surrounding governance system can ensure accountability, supervision, transparency, and correction. Citizens may not be able to directly evaluate algorithmic models, but they evaluate whether institutions have the capacity to control AI, explain decisions, and respond to failures.

Negotiated Legitimacy: Negotiated legitimacy refers to the process through which the legitimacy of AI governance is continuously constructed through interaction among governments, technology providers, regulators, and citizens. In traditional governance, legitimacy is often associated with institutional authority or successful outcomes. In AI governance, legitimacy depends not only on what decisions are produced but also on whether the processes behind those decisions are transparent, fair, and socially accepted.

Procedural Trust: Procedural trust refers to public confidence in the fairness and transparency of the decision making process rather than only in the final outcome. In AI governance, citizens increasingly evaluate whether data sources are appropriate, whether algorithms operate fairly, whether decisions can be explained, and whether individuals have opportunities to challenge decisions. Procedural trust becomes essential because technically successful AI systems may still lack legitimacy if their decision processes are perceived as unfair.

Trusted AI Governance: Trusted AI governance refers to a governance approach that integrates technological reliability, ethical responsibility, institutional accountability, and social acceptance. It emphasizes that trustworthy AI cannot be achieved through algorithmic accuracy alone. Instead, it requires a comprehensive framework in which AI systems are technically effective, procedurally fair, institutionally supervised, and publicly legitimate.

Chapter 5
The Role of Trusted AI in Shaping Government–Citizen Relationships:
A Study on Trust and Accountability

Deepa Verma
http://orcid.org/0009-0002-6938-2935
Graphic Era (Deemed to be) University, Dehradun, India

Ayushi sharma
http://orcid.org/0009-0000-6851-8170
Graphic Era (Deemed to be) University, Dehradun, India

Pawan Kumar
http://orcid.org/0000-0003-4892-6374
Graphic Era (Deemed to be) University, Dehradun, India

Kamal Batta
http://orcid.org/0000-0002-3843-6825
Chandigarh University, India

ABSTRACT

This study investigates how AI Transparency, AI Accountability, and Citizen Engagement shape Trust in AI within government-citizen relationships. Adopting a quantitative, explanatory, and cross-sectional research design, the study utilized primary data collected from 285 respondents through a structured survey instrument. Descriptive statistics, multiple regression, ANOVA, coefficient analysis, collinearity diagnostics, and residual assessment were employed to examine the proposed

DOI: 10.4018/979-8-3373-9129-8.ch005

relationships. The findings reveal that the model is statistically significant and that AI Accountability emerges as the most influential predictor of Trust in AI, followed by Citizen Engagement, while AI Transparency exhibits a comparatively marginal yet positive effect. The study implies that trustworthy public-sector AI must be anchored in institutional answerability, participatory governance, and intelligible operational processes. It concludes that trust in governmental AI is fundamentally a governance-driven outcome rather than merely a technological consequence.

1. INTRODUCTION

The architecture of governance for today is witnessing an immense transformation due to the impact that artificial intelligence is making on the modality of governance as a whole, which has been increasingly shaped by the emergence of technologies based on AI, helping governments design policies and provide better services, process information more efficiently and engage with citizens. It is not surprising that in recent years we see more and more governmental organizations taking advantage of AI solutions (Siripipatthanakul et al., 2024). Artificial Intelligence has made its way into the very operational fabric of governance by offering services such as digital grievance redressal, welfare targeting, surveillance systems, automated service delivery, and algorithm-based public management. However, this rise of artificial intelligence in the public domain also raises an important normative question, whether citizens can place their trust on artificial intelligence once it is integrated as a mediator between the state and the citizenry. This is what the present study aims to investigate (Hao et al., 2026a).

1.1 The Evolving Interface Between Government and Artificial Intelligence

Traditionally, relations between government and citizens were based on institutional legitimacy, procedural justice, accountability, and credibility of state action. Traditionally, trust in government was formed by observable processes of human nature, protection of legal rights, and interaction with government institutions. But as governments are increasingly using AI-based systems for decision-making or decision automation, public trust becomes a more complicated matter(Batool et al., 2025a). It is not just a matter of the citizens judging the intent and efficacy of the government officials; rather, the citizens are also judging the equity, reliability, accountability, and morality of the algorithms. Therefore, trust in government will increasingly be tied to trust in the infrastructure that facilitates governance (Birkstedt et al., 2023a). The shift does not only relate to technology; it also involves the institution and the relationship itself. Governance by means of artificial intelligence is not a purely computational tool devoid of the context in which it operates. On the contrary, it works within a socio-political environment where citizens perceive technological choices through the prism of justice, legitimacy, inclusiveness, and the responsibility of the state. When governments apply AI in the public sphere, they imply citizens' agreement with the decisions, proposals, or classification made on the basis of some system perceived by citizens as obscure, complicated, and far from human decision-making (Duberry, 2022).

1.2 Trusted AI as a Governance Imperative

The idea of trusted AI has become an essential conceptual solution to the worries about using artificial intelligence in contexts that have social significance. Trusted AI goes beyond technical considerations to create systems that are reliable, ethical, understandable, accountable, and socially legitimate. It is even more important to understand in governance contexts since the implications of algorithmic decision-making may have an effect on citizens' rights, entitlements, access to services, and perception of the state's justice. Even a highly technologically advanced system will not be able to gain people's trust if it is considered incomprehensible and uncaring about citizen issues (Siripipatthanakul et al., 2024). Consequently, trust in AI in the public domain has to be viewed as a multidimensional construct. Rather than focusing on the accuracy of the output produced by an AI system, the issue centers on the process through which such output has been produced and whether the process involved can be regarded as comprehensible, defensible, and overseen by institutions. Here lies the importance of this current research. It focuses on trust in AI as a product of a certain social and institutional process rather than a passive or automatic response to new technology. That is the reason why AI Transparency, AI Accountability and Citizen Engagement are deemed to be crucial antecedents of Trust in AI (Kleizen et al., 2023).

1.3 Trust in AI as the Dependent Construct

The level of trust towards AI will be the main dependent variable of the study. In the sphere of public administration, the trust towards AI may be defined as the citizens' trust to AI-powered systems regarding their reliability, impartiality, efficiency, safety, and ethical use in government operations. It implies that the trust towards AI will include not only the capabilities of AI but also the legitimacy of its use in government tasks. Trust is crucial since even the most sophisticated governmental AI programs might face opposition or skepticism on the part of citizens if they lack trust in the system behind public decision-making. Trust is particularly critical for governance since public organizations wield power over society (Hao et al., 2026b). When AI is employed in fields like welfare distribution, taxation, urban management, law enforcement, public health, or administrative adjudication, then acceptance of such a system by the people hinges on whether they perceive the use of the technology to be in the public good or just another means by which the bureaucracy tries to make its work easier or more opaque. Hence, trust in AI emerges as a prerequisite for digital governance (Savveli et al., 2025a).

1.4 AI Transparency and the Question of Explain ability

One of the independent variables in this research is called "AI Transparency," and it denotes the degree to which AI systems and processes used in the decision-making by these systems are transparent and clear to the people. In terms of governance, the issue of transparency is especially important, because the legitimacy of administration has always been linked to the fact that people can comprehend the processes of decision-making and the reasons for exercising authority. Where AI systems have an impact on the processes of governance, the demand for transparency remains not lessened, but intensified. The transparency of AI systems in the context of governance implies the necessity to inform citizens about how their data is being processed, what are the reasons for the recommendation produced by algorithms, what are the grounds for decision-making paths chosen, and what results are being communicated. Where AI systems are regarded as black boxes which produce decisions that can be neither understood nor questioned, people will see them as coercive mechanisms. This may result in alienation, fear, and distrust, particularly where the outputs of algorithms impact the ability of citizens to use public services and/or administrative law. However, transparency is not only a characteristic, but also a value. It implies that public power, however technologically advanced, has to be understandable to those who are governed (Myles et al., 2026).

1.5 AI Accountability and Institutional Responsibility

Another important consideration in terms of accountability of AI in the context of the present study. Accountability involves the level at which public agencies can be held responsible for the results, actions, and consequences of decisions made through the use of artificial intelligence. From the point of view of governance, accountability is essential because AI cannot supersede the ethical and legal responsibilities of the government. Even if the system provides recommendations or automated actions, the consequences will always be the responsibility of the agency that permits and operates the system. This issue takes significance especially when the results of AI systems are biased, erroneous, or cause any harm. Citizens will not trust AI if they do not know whom to hold accountable in case of failure (Mehr et al., 2017). Accountability within public administration ensures that citizens are sure that technology is not functioning outside the jurisdiction of governance. Accountability ensures that the notion that governments are still accountable to the citizens regardless of the use of technology is sustained (He et al., 2026).

1.6 Citizen Engagement and Democratic Legitimacy

Citizen Engagement is the third independent variable. It refers to the extent to which citizens are included, consulted, and responded to regarding the design, implementation, and evaluation of the AI systems within governance. Citizen engagement is an important independent variable because democratic legitimacy does not just depend on authority but also on participation. Citizen engagement in the case of AI means that technological tools must not be forced on society without consultations and participation of the citizens. Engagement increases trust because it decreases social distance between the technological system and the people (Berigüete et al., 2024). Where citizens are engaged in expressing their concerns, giving feedback, and deliberating on the use of AI, there is higher likelihood that such AI will be perceived to be legitimate and citizen-centered. Citizen engagement increases the policy responsiveness of government by ensuring that AI technology is used in line with public expectations, social reality, and moral considerations. Through citizen engagement, trust in government AI is created not only democratically but also practically (Savveli et al., 2025b).

The conceptual framework of the study is based on the assumption that the trust to AI is generated as a result of an interplay between three dimensions: openness, answerability, and participative inclusion. AI Transparency brings contribution through making algorithms more understandable; AI Accountability generates trust by making sure that state responsibility is not shifted due to technological complexities; and Citizen Engagement contributes to building legitimacy through incorporating people's voices into the governance of AI. All of these constructs allow for revealing the complex nature of the trust-building process in the public sector. The link between the above constructs is rather complex. Transparency without accountability might generate information but not reassurance. Accountability without engagement might lead to control but not to legitimacy. Engagement without transparency might involve participation but not understanding. Consequently, all of these constructs should be viewed from the perspective of complementarity (Goossens et al., 2025).

Significance of the study comes out of a desire to bridge technology discourse and theories of governance. The public discourse about AI is overwhelmingly focused on topics of efficiency, innovation, automation, and digital transformation. Although the aforementioned topics are of undeniable relevance, they do not capture the social and democratic context in which technological adoption occurs. When it comes to the government, the mere existence of technological capabilities is no guarantee of legitimacy. It is not just a matter of what the technology does but how it does things, by whom it is governed, and whether citizens have their own space in the process of governance. Thus, the research is important because it shifts the discussion of trustworthy AI to the plane of governance, and not just computational (Roberts et al., 2024). It also offers a framework for analyzing how governments can enhance the trust of their citizens in AI-enabled public institutions without eroding their trust into blind technological optimism. In essence, the incorporation of artificial intelligence into governance processes has brought about transformative potential as well as significant relational challenges (Birkstedt et al., 2023b). With the use of AI becoming increasingly pervasive in public administration, the relationship between the government and the citizenry would no longer depend just on the complexity of the technology but also on how transparent, accountable, and participative the technology is. As such, trust in AI becomes an essential outcome of proper governance. This research study aims to operate in this context. Through the investigation of the effects of AI Transparency, AI Accountability, and Citizen Engagement on Trust in AI, it aims to explore the underlying conditions for the effective use of AI in governance (Bokhari et al., 2025) .

2. REVIEW OF LITERATURE

The contemporary literature on AI sees this concept as being more socio-technical and governance-related construct than simply an attribute of computation. In the field of public administration, the discussions about AI move from the topics of efficiency, accuracy, and optimal performance to the issue of legitimacy and institutional accountability (Joshi, 2026). Current studies on trustworthy AI keep emphasizing how the trustworthiness of AI technology comes as a result of its reliability, transparency, accountability, and responsiveness to social demands. This paradigm shift becomes especially important when considering the relationship between the citizen and the government, since technological instruments cannot be considered to be neutral and should be seen as mediators in granting citizens access to certain rights, information, and services. That means that one has to think about the trust in governmental AI as an assessment of the whole governance ecosystem (Hao et al., 2026c). According to the literature that is being developed about the use of AI in the public administration, the deployment of algorithms has started to challenge the traditional foundation of administrative legitimacy. Although earlier literature on e-government was focused on digitization and efficiency, contemporary literature highlights the unique challenges posed by the use of AI, including issues like opacity, bias, contestation, and elimination of visible human judgment (Myles et al., 2026). Whereas the findings of a systematic review done in the past few years concerning the usage of artificial intelligence in governance through the eyes of citizens are concerned, the public sentiment is not only guided by the benefits of the technology but also by its dangers, justice, and citizen orientation. In this regard, there is an important change in focus within the scientific literature, as the acceptance of the use of AI in public administration is no longer based on technological ease, but rather on whether the use of AI is compatible with public values (Corvalán, 2018).

The literature on trust in AI includes a large number of studies identifying transparency as the most common antecedent of trust in AI. With respect to the public sector domain, transparency has been defined as the comprehensibility of algorithms, the visibility of data usage, the explanation of output results, and the clear communication that makes citizens aware of automation decisions. The literature on responsible AI governance is unanimous in stating that lack of transparency undermines legitimacy since citizens will not be able to understand and evaluate the rationale behind such decisions (He et al., 2026) . This has special importance in governmental organizations, since there has been an expectation that administrative power in such organizations is supposed to be procedurally intelligible. The new researches on transparency and accountability of AI systems have indicated that transparency is not just a design consideration, but a legal, ethical, and organizational requirement for enabling contestability and intelligibility (Batool et al., 2025b). There is thus substantial conceptual support for the claim that there is a positive impact of AI Transparency on Trust in AI. On the other hand, certain works suggest that without governance mechanisms that ensure the application of transparency, it might not have a significant impact on trust in AI (Khoso et al., 2026). In terms of the variables considered in the recent literature, accountability becomes the most crucial normative foundation of trustworthy AI. Accountability here means the availability of institutional responsibility, auditing, enforcement, supervision, and mechanisms for correction in case of any harmful or erroneous impacts that are caused by the functioning of algorithmic systems. The current governance structures in place both in academic and policy institutions always stress that it is impossible to ensure trust where there is no responsibility (Wirtz et al., 2022). As far as governance of AI in scientific research is concerned, accountability is viewed as the means by which the state ensures its ownership of decisions made with the help of AI. This, in turn, prevents any loss of democratic responsibility. The studies dedicated to public sector automated decision-making are especially relevant in this respect as accountability is recognized as a necessary precondition of responsible use of AI. In addition, the recent research dedicated to the concerns of citizens regarding government AI highlights the direct connection between public anxiety and lack of oversight, appeal mechanisms and institutional accountability. Thus, we can argue that AI Accountability affects Trust in AI (Afroogh et al., 2024).

There is an increasing awareness about the role of citizen participation in being a crucial component of trustworthy AI governance, instead of being a secondary aspect. Previous streams of AI governance research were very much expert-led and compliance-focused; however, contemporary discussion in the public sector emphasizes that trust can be enhanced through the involvement of citizens in consultations, feedbacks, participatory design, and oversight in relation to AI technologies. Contemporary international institutional guidance makes it clear that public sector AI must be accessible, equitable, and inclusive of citizens' requirements (Zulu & Nzimakwe, 2025a). Such a change is informed by the realization that for technology to be deemed legitimate in democracies, participatory responsiveness is more important than legalities alone. Hence, according to the extant literature, through citizen engagement, citizens gain a sense of trust because of a decrease in the relational distance between the state's system and those affected by them. With the use of deliberative inclusion, the government can be able to make the AI technology fit within the societal needs and communicate the risk involved in the use of the technology to the citizens (Zulu & Nzimakwe, 2025b).

The concept of Trust in AI too has been subjected to increasingly complex analysis in recent literature. The contemporary literature does not view trust as a uni-dimensional psychological construct but considers it as a complex socio-technical judgment that encompasses reliability, trustworthiness, fairness, safety, explainability and governance. Literature on AI trustworthiness that spans several disciplines posits a clear distinction between trust and trustworthiness in the context of AI – that while citizens may have trust in AI, what they need to determine is whether they can trust it (Glikson & Woolley, 2020). This particular aspect is highly relevant in the context of government-citizen interaction, as the element of trust is deeply associated with aspects of legitimacy, integrity, and responsiveness. In recent systematic review of literature on citizen perception of AI in government, it has been emphasized that aspects of trust are related to the elements of benefits, concerns, system features, and contextual factors. Thus, trust in AI has become increasingly recognized as socially constructed phenomenon, which is dependent on the quality of governance and institutional reputation, among other things (Herrera & Calderón, 2026).

Scholars have turned their attention to integrative frameworks that provide more insight into AI trust than do single-factor theories of trust. Analysis of studies that have reviewed the issues of decision-making by algorithmic systems in the public sector shows the presence of interconnected needs in lieu of different determinants (Hao et al., 2026a). Transparency makes the understanding easier under this framework, accountability makes it accountable and ensures answerability, and engagement makes it participatory. The importance of both concepts to analysis comes not just from the effect each has individually but from the cumulative effect of how all three interact with one another. Without accountability, transparency would provide visibility without any solution. In the absence of engagement, accountability could only provide institutional but no social legitimacy (Mensah, 2023). This integrative reasoning is highly compatible with the integrated hypothesis of the current study, which assumes that AI Transparency, AI Accountability, and Citizen Engagement determine Trust in AI. The academic sources thus provide a theoretical rationale for assuming that the three independent variables function as complementary dimensions within the framework of trustworthy public AI (Cheong, 2024).

Trends related to new policies and regulations further contribute to academic discourse on the trustworthiness of AI systems because transparency, accountability, and oversight become integral parts of any trustable AI system. In the context of contemporary governance frameworks, trustworthiness becomes an integral part of AI regulation, while accountability and transparency become its essential components (Saktiawan et al., 2026). In the same manner, the more recent laws institutionalize risk-based regulation whereby transparency, governance structure, and oversight systems are considered critical in ensuring the safety and trustworthiness of AI technologies. Meanwhile, international guidelines for the use of AI technologies by governments state that there should be a pursuit of human-centric, inclusive, and trustworthy AI rather than uncontrolled technological progress. The above changes have important implications for the academic literature because they mean that scholars' arguments are in harmony with governance approaches. It also becomes evident that the variables analyzed within the scope of this study have more than academic significance (de Almeida & dos Santos Júnior, 2025).

While there have been many advances in academic research on AI governance, a number of analytical weaknesses continue to exist. Specifically, the majority of recent studies fall into one of three categories: conceptual, regulatory, and review. Far fewer empirical studies analyze the role of specific governance variables in shaping citizens' trust in AI in the practical context of interactions between the government and its citizens. While the majority of existing literature is dedicated to the general issue of trustworthy AI, fewer studies examine transparency, accountability, and citizen engagement as independent factors influencing the level of citizens' trust. The problem with the current literature is that many studies concentrate on adoption issues, regulatory compliance, and general perception of AI, while neglecting the relational aspects of AI's impact on democratic interaction between governments and citizens. The current study seeks to fill this gap through an empirical examination of the role of AI Transparency, AI Accountability, and Citizen Engagement in shaping Trust in AI.

Generally, the existing literature reveals a consistent and increasingly well-developed perspective on trusted AI as a governance-based concept. In recent literature reviews, international instruments, and empirical research studies, transparency, accountability, and citizen engagement are repeatedly indicated as crucial factors determining the legitimacy and trustworthiness of the use of AI technologies in the context of public administration. Trustworthy AI, in its turn, is considered to be the result of explainability, answerability of institutions, and citizen participation, rather than a natural consequence of technological development. The present literature is a strong basis for the theoretical assumptions underlying the current research, providing a relevant background for the analysis of the contribution of trusted AI into the formation of government-citizen relations via particular mechanisms of AI Transparency, AI Accountability, and Citizen Engagement.

3. RESEARCH METHODOLOGY

A research methodology that was quantitative in nature, was descriptive as well as an explanatory one and was cross-sectional in approach was used for studying the impact of AI Transparency, AI Accountability and Citizen Engagement on Trust in AI in the context of citizen-government relations. Data was collected from 285 people using primary sources of data collection in the form of a scale questionnaire. Descriptive statistics was used to analyze the distribution as well as the tendency in the data and the multiple regression analysis was performed to analyze the relationship.

Table 1. Sample size

Occupation	Frequency (n = 285)	Percentage (%)
Government Employee	86	30.2
Private Sector Employee	98	34.4
Self-employed / Business	46	16.1
Student	32	11.2
Others (Retired, Homemaker, Unemployed, etc.)	23	8.1
Total	285	100.0

Table 2. variables of the study

Variable	Nature of Variable	Abbreviation	Description
AI Transparency	Independent	AIT	The notion of AI Transparency means that artificial intelligence systems employed by government entities are being run in a transparent, understandable, and clear way for citizens. It means that people have an understanding of how decisions are being reached via the use of AI, what data is being used in the decision-making process, and why certain results are reached via algorithms. When it comes to public administration, transparency minimizes information asymmetry.
AI Accountability	Independent	AIA	Accountability of AI refers to the extent to which public sector organizations maintain accountability for any decision, action, or output produced via an AI system. Accountability of AI focuses on the fact that there should be some level of responsibility, oversight, redressal, and ethical control of AI. This variable is very important since people tend to have more faith in AI where someone is accountable for any harm that comes from it.
Citizen Engagement	Independent	CE	Citizens' Engagement is defined by the involvement and participation of citizens in any process associated with the design, implementation, monitoring, or evaluation of AI systems for governance purposes. It indicates how well public views have been taken into account when designing AI-powered governance programs. High levels of citizens' engagement imply that there is participatory governance and that it is inclusive and responsive.
Trust in AI	Dependent	TAI	Citizen trust in AI is the level to which citizens can rely on the dependability, objectivity, effectiveness, and morality of artificial intelligence technologies that are utilized in the process of governance by governmental organizations. In other words, it is the measure of the perception that AI is reliable, objective, secure, and beneficial to public services or governance decisions.

3.1 Objectives of the study

In order to assess the impact that AI transparency has on citizens' trust in AI within the government-citizen relationship. Secondly, to look at the impact that AI accountability has on the creation of a trustworthy and credible government-created AI system. Lastly, the impact of citizen engagement on trust in AI and government-citizen relations.

3.2 Hypotheses of the study

H1: AI Transparency has a significant positive influence on Trust in AI in the context of government–citizen relationships.

Transparency in Artificial Intelligence has become one of the most important elements of the discussion about trustworthiness in AI. More specifically, in the field of public administration, the utilization of artificial intelligence in decision-making impacts individual rights, individual welfare, and the delivery of public services. According to modern researchers, transparency consists of not just technical transparency but also of explainability, interpretability, and procedural transparency that enable the citizens to understand the logic behind AI-generated decisions by the government. Such transparency decreases information asymmetry, decreases uncertainty, and leads to procedural justice and, thus, increases institutional legitimacy. According to the previous research, a lack of transparency of AI-based decision-making systems usually leads to skepticism on the part of the citizens since they cannot verify the fairness and consistency of automated decisions. On the contrary, explainability of AI improves credibility because it enables one to observe the process of decision-making. This theory is supported by the Institutional Trust Theory postulating that transparency builds up citizens' trust as a result of ambiguity reduction and increased accountability. Explainable AI principles also underpin such an assumption. At the same time, the notion of transparency is not only about the technical nature of such an approach but also a dedication to openness of institutions, democratic principles, and justice. In other words, the use of transparent AI technologies will make the government capable of earning long-term trust of its citizens. Hence, the extant literature on theory and practice gives us strong reason to expect a positive correlation between AI Transparency and Trust in AI (Cojocaru, 2025; Radanliev, 2025; Schilke & Reimann, 2025).

H2: AI Accountability has a significant positive influence on Trust in AI in the context of government–citizen relationships.

Accountability ranks among the most important normative principles of responsible artificial intelligence since it ensures that the government continues to be accountable for the decisions taken by algorithms and their impacts on society. All literature agrees on the point that the citizens' trust in artificial intelligence governance relies not only on technology itself but also on the accountability of the public institution for the results produced by algorithms. Accountability involves ethical oversight, legal responsibility, auditability, redress mechanisms, and oversight of institutions, thus making sure that the functioning of artificial intelligence systems takes place within the frameworks of democratic governance. Accountability Theory and Good Governance Theory serve as the basis for the discussed link between accountability and trust since both theories state that institutions need to prove responsibility, answerability, and oversight to build up citizens' trust. Furthermore, empirical research shows that ambiguity in terms of responsibility for errors of algorithms, discrimination, or adverse effects on society significantly reduces citizens' trust in the application of AI. As opposed to negating governmental responsibility, artificial intelligence ought to operate within an accountable administrative system where the institutions remain responsible for all the decisions made using artificial intelligence. It will ensure the citizens that the artificial intelligence is continuously being checked and that measures to correct things are taken if necessary. From the literature above, it is clear that the theory of how the accountability of AI can lead to trust in AI is well grounded (Díaz-Rodríguez et al., 2023; Feng & Chandra, 2025; Nastoska et al., 2025).

H3: Citizen Engagement has a significant positive influence on Trust in AI in the context of government–citizen relationships.

Citizen Engagement is an issue that has emerged in the recent past as a determinant that is necessary for credible development of artificial intelligence since the development of technology must be associated with active participation of the citizens for legitimacy. From existing research, it is recommended that while deploying artificial intelligence technologies, governments should include citizen participation in deliberation, consultation, feedback, monitoring, and policy formulation. The primary theoretical rationale for such a relationship is found in Participatory Governance Theory according to which inclusion promotes the legitimacy of institutions, fairness of procedures, and public trust. In the same manner, Democratic Governance Theory argues that the constant participation of the citizens diminishes the feeling of technocratic domination and improves accountability and responsiveness. Research proves that participation tools help diminish the relational gap between the government and the citizens by allowing the chance to voice their concerns regarding privacy, ethics, fairness, and algorithms. Such kind of engagement allows creating the sense of collective responsibility for technological changes and reinforces the idea that AI systems serve public interests. Moreover, engagement builds mutual trust by helping governments to improve AI systems according to societal expectations and experience. Accordingly, trust is socially constructed as a result of ongoing interaction between citizens and public institutions instead of a mere response to technological developments. Consequently, there is ample justification for both the theoretical assumptions and empirical studies to demonstrate the impact of Citizen Engagement on Trust in AI in government-citizen relations (Heinisuo et al., 2025; Ingrams et al., 2022; Onufreiciuc, 2024).

4. DATA ANALYSIS

Table 3. Descriptive Statistics

	N	Minimum	Maximum	Sum	Mean		Std. Deviation	Skewness		Kurtosis	
	Statistic	Statistic	Statistic	Statistic	Statistic	Std. Error	Statistic	Statistic	Std. Error	Statistic	Std. Error
AIT	285	1.00	7.00	1330.00	4.6667	.07181	1.21222	-.293	.144	.198	.288
AIA	285	1.00	7.00	1207.00	4.2351	.09453	1.59582	-.442	.144	-.575	.288
CE	285	1.00	7.00	1291.00	4.5298	.07773	1.31218	-.447	.144	.071	.288
TAI	285	1.00	7.00	1161.00	4.0737	.08944	1.50989	-.435	.144	-.502	.288
Valid N (listwise)	285										

Source: data collected and analysed by the authors

From Table 3, there is shown a moderately positive orientation towards the tested constructs, meaning that respondents showed positive orientation on the tested dimensions. Out of all the variables tested, AIT shows the highest value for the central tendency with a mean value of 4.67, while TAI indicates the lowest evaluation position with a mean of 4.07. Standard deviation indicates moderate dispersion, showing that the views of the respondents were varied but not randomly so. In addition, the consistent values for skewness show the clustering of the responses to the high values of the scales.

Table 4. Model Summary

Model	R	R Square	Adjusted R Square	Std. Error of the Estimate	Change Statistics					Durbin-Watson
					R Square Change	F Change	df1	df2	Sig. F Change	
1	.774[a]	.599	.592	1.18674	.389	59.575	3	281	.000	1.759

a. Predictors: (Constant), CE, AIT, AIA
Source: data collected and analysed by the authors

Considering the accuracy of the given R^2 value, from Table 4 it can be seen that the regression model shows strong explanatory power and a strong relationship between the set of predictors and the dependent variable. The model explains almost 60% of the variance, and the adjusted value is quite close to it, implying good stability of the model and very little shrinkage. The highly significant F-change statistic also supports the point that the combined effect of AIT, AIA, and CE is not coincidental but rather statistically important. Furthermore, the standard error seems to be quite reasonable, implying good prediction precision.

Table 5. ANOVA

Model		Sum of Squares	df	Mean Square	F	Sig.
1	Regression	251.706	3	83.902	59.575	.000[b]
	Residual	395.747	281	1.408		
	Total	647.453	284			

a. Dependent Variable: TAI
b. Predictors: (Constant), CE, AIT, AIA
Source: data collected and analysed by the authors

From Table 5, the regression model is seen to be both statistically robust and conceptually relevant with regard to variations in TAI. As seen from the ANOVA, the overall effect of CE, AIT, and AIA on the dependent variable is statistically significant, evidenced by an F statistic of 59.575 with $p < .001$. This implies that the model is better than a model without predictors. Also, the regression sum of squares is larger than a sizable proportion of the total variation, implying that 39% of TAI variation is attributed to the predictors.

Table 6. Coefficients

Model		Unstandardized Coefficients		Standardized Coefficients	t	Sig.	Correlations			Collinearity Statistics	
		B	Std. Error	Beta			Zero-order	Partial	Part	Tolerance	VIF
1	(Constant)	.758	.310		2.445	.015					
	AIT	.133	.068	.107	1.962	.051	.375	.116	.091	.736	1.358
	AIA	.440	.053	.465	8.255	.000	.593	.442	.385	.686	1.457
	CE	.184	.067	.160	2.744	.006	.457	.162	.128	.640	1.562

a. Dependent Variable: TAI
Source: data collected and analysed by the authors

Explanation of the differential predictability of the predictors for TAI is provided by Table 6. Out of all predictors, AIA can be considered as the most influential factor, having the largest standardized coefficient as well as being very significant. Therefore, the predictor demonstrates high explanatory power. The variable CE shows positive and statistically significant relationship as well; however, its impact strength is rather modest. On the contrary, the impact of AIT is almost negligible, since its level of significance corresponds to the accepted critical point. Besides, it should be noted that collinearity diagnostics indicate no presence of multicollinearity issues.

Table 7. Coefficient Correlations

Model			CE	AIT	AIA
1	Correlations	CE	1.000	-.334	-.414
		AIT	-.334	1.000	-.217
		AIA	-.414	-.217	1.000
	Covariances	CE	.004	-.002	-.001
		AIT	-.002	.005	-.001
		AIA	-.001	-.001	.003

a. Dependent Variable: TAI
Source: data collected and analysed by the authors

As shown in Table 7, the relationship between the predictor variables is moderately and negatively correlated instead of being overly correlated. There is a negative correlation between the coefficient of CE with both AIT and AIA, while there is also an inverse relationship between the AIT and AIA variables. These predictor variables indicate some form of divergence in their explanatory ability in the regression. Nevertheless, these correlations do not indicate that they are overly correlated such that it will cause instability. The covariation between the predictors shows relatively small values.

Table 8. Collinearity Diagnostics

	Dimension	Eigenvalue	Condition Index	Variance Proportions			
				(Constant)	AIT	AIA	CE
1	1	3.861	1.000	.00	.00	.01	.00
	2	.071	7.393	.16	.07	.82	.00
	3	.037	10.204	.16	.09	.17	.99
	4	.032	11.050	.68	.84	.01	.00

a. Dependent Variable: TAI
Source: data collected and analysed by the authors

As evident from Table 8, there is no evidence of a highly serious problem with multicollinearity in the regression equation. The condition indices are all far from the traditional critical value of severe collinearity, with the maximum being 11.05 only, implying that the regressors are not experiencing a significant degree of linear dependence. Though there are a few high variance proportions for particular dimensions, these are not too high to lead to biased estimates. It must be noted that AIA and CE are highly loaded on different dimensions, which implies distinct explanations rather than collinearity issues.

Table 9. Residuals Statistics

	Minimum	Maximum	Mean	Std. Deviation	N
Predicted Value	1.5148	6.0538	4.0737	.94143	285
Residual	-4.28735	3.65539	.00000	1.18046	285
Std. Predicted Value	-2.718	2.103	.000	1.000	285
Std. Residual	-3.613	3.080	.000	.995	285

a. Dependent Variable: TAI
Source: data collected and analysed by the authors

From Table 9, one can conclude that the residual behavior of the regression model is quite decent and does not demonstrate any serious problems regarding estimation. The predicted values have a good variance, indicating that there is a proper variation in the dependent variable across respondents within the estimated model. The most important indicator is the zero value of the residual mean. It means that there is no bias in the prediction error of the model. Even though there are several standardized residuals which lie outside the boundary ±3, indicating atypical points, they do not appear often enough to spoil the entire model.

5. OUTCOMES AND FINDINGS OF THE STUDY

Empirical results indicate that there is a substantively significant relationship between the characteristics of governmental artificial intelligence and the level of citizens' trust in such systems. Descriptively speaking, the participants had a positively biased attitude towards all four constructs, as shown by the high values of their means on such scales as AI Transparency, AI Accountability, Citizen Engagement, and Trust in AI. It seems that the participants of the survey were not biased in terms of their attitude towards artificial intelligence and did not demonstrate any skepticism. Distributional features confirmed the above conclusion. Specifically, the negative skewness of all variables shows that the responses were positively skewed, with no significant deviations from the normal kurtosis. Substantively, the results suggest that citizens have a more positive attitude towards governmental use of artificial intelligence when such systems are transparent and accountable.

Inferential results offer further evidence in favor of the main thesis of the study. It is possible to state that the regression equation is statistically significant; therefore, the selected independent variables have some impact on Trust in AI. As stated above, the ANOVA test result shows that the model demonstrates much greater predictive capacity compared to the null model with no predictor variables. Consequently, the explanatory role of AI Transparency, AI Accountability, and Citizen Engagement as factors influencing the development of the dependent construct has been proved. On the basis of the sums of squares obtained from the ANOVA analysis, the model can explain about 39% of variance in the dependent variable. Thus, the explanatory capacity of the model is relatively high. This means that, while the selected predictors explain the formation of citizens' trust in governmental AI systems, some other factors might also affect the development of such trust.

Specifically, regarding the individual hypotheses, it becomes possible to see differences in the predictive power of the three independent variables. AI Accountability turned out to be the most significant predictor of Trust in AI. Its standardized regression coefficient was higher than any other predictor's, while the level of its statistical significance was unambiguous. This result is important both theoretically and practically. First of all, it means that people will have more trust in artificial intelligence in the context of governance if they see that there are well-established responsibility and answerability mechanisms. Thus, trust cannot be achieved just through technology; it is rather based on the fact that there is answerability of the government for AI-based decisions.

The variable Citizen Engagement, on the other hand, showed a significant and positive influence on Trust in AI, although its power of explanation was somewhat weaker compared to that of the accountability variable. The finding reveals that inclusion, participation, and responsiveness contribute to trust in AI-based governance. The conclusion to be drawn here is that the degree of trust will be higher if people are considered not as passive subjects receiving decisions from algorithms, but active stakeholders with whom consideration should be paid to their needs and preferences. With regard to governance, the finding demonstrates the democratic relevance of involvement and proves that the public support for AI technologies will grow if their deployment involves participation. Hence, the hypothesis is confirmed.

Nevertheless, things with respect to AI Transparency become somewhat complicated. Despite the fact that the coefficient was positive, the significance of transparency turned out to be quite marginal, and it did not demonstrate enough robustness. It can be concluded that although there is a positive relationship between transparency and Trust in AI, transparency itself is not a key element in forming the relationship. It does not imply that transparency itself is not important in any way – what it does imply is that for the formation of trust, transparency needs to be combined with some responsibility and engagement on the part of the citizens. In case of most public institutions, simply being transparent about AI algorithms is not enough without ensuring responsibility and engagement.

Regardless, the joint hypothesis is certainly true. Taken jointly, AI Transparency, AI Accountability, and Citizen Engagement significantly affect Trust in AI. Thus, the validity of the entire conceptual framework used in this research is proven – Trusted AI within the government-citizen relationship cannot be viewed as the result of a certain institutional factor, but as the consequence of a broader governance ecosystem, where transparency, accountability, and engagement are crucial. Nevertheless, the hierarchy of factors is worth noting from the analytical point of view – while accountability is the leading factor, engagement follows closely behind, and transparency works in a more conditional manner.

Diagnosis further improves the validity of the findings obtained through regression analysis. Both tolerance and VIF statistics for collinearity were well within reasonable levels of threshold value, implying that there was no existence of multicollinearity issue. There were just moderate correlation relationships between the predictors. Furthermore, the residual statistics revealed that the error term used in prediction is normally distributed about zero, while collinearity diagnostics revealed the non-existence of condition indexes associated with estimation problems. Therefore, these diagnosis tests support the idea that the regression estimates obtained were reasonable and valid.

In general, the results of the research clearly show that the trust to AI in government is determined mainly by the credibility of the institution rather than the mere presence of technology. It is obvious that the people are more likely to have trust to AI if it is controlled via answerability mechanisms and participatory democracy practices; however, transparency, which has normative value, seems to be less powerful when applied separately. Hence, the key empirical finding of the study is that trustworthy AI is a matter of good governance rather than advanced computation.

6. IMPLICATION OF THE STUDY

Consequences of the study are both theoretically and practically important, especially considering the rapidly developing area of artificial intelligence in the public sector. To begin with, the results of this research show that the trust in AI technology in the context of government–citizen relationship is not created solely through deployment of technology, but by the governance structure associated with this process. The first practical consequence from the findings is that governments that seek to establish AI systems cannot limit themselves by the logic of efficiency and should build an environment that focuses on responsibility and answerability. Because AI Accountability was found to be the strongest predictor of Trust in AI, public institutions should make sure that AI technologies will operate in the context of oversight and grievance mechanism, audit trails, and morally responsible chain of accountability.

Moreover, the role of Citizen Engagement as a factor illustrates that trust arises in participatory governance and not in technocratic one. It means that the implementation of the technology in the public administration does not merely represent an administratively advanced solution and should be supplemented with the creation of consultative forums, citizen feedback, stakeholder communication and dialogue. These approaches could increase the democratic legitimacy of the AI system and minimize the risk of alienation caused by technocratic actions. Therefore, according to the study, the trust of citizens is not related to the technology, but is socially constructed.

Finally, the weak relationship between AI Transparency has a more complex implication. Although the concept of transparency continues to remain important from the normative point of view, the research results reveal that transparency alone might not be sufficient when it comes to increasing the public trust. The transparency alone in the shape of algorithmic transparency, data transparency and procedural transparency can turn out to be ineffective without accountability and engagement. In this regard, governments cannot content themselves with merely a transparency strategy of trustworthy AI. Explain ability should go together with accountability and engagement. Otherwise, transparency will just become a formality.

From the theoretical perspective, the paper provides additional support for the assertion that public trust in AI technology is relational and governance-based. More specifically, the findings of the paper fit well within the growing trend in scholarship to regard the idea of trusted AI as something which is not just technological, but also institutional and socio-political in nature. Consequently, the findings of the paper can contribute to the literature by demonstrating that the public trust in AI is not built on transparency alone, but rather on procedural justice, institutional accountability, and participation.

Policy implications for policy makers, civil servants, and digital government designers are equally critical. For policymakers and governmental agencies who adopt AI technology to provide their services to citizens, they should take into account the concept of accountability by design and engagement by design. It would be more efficient to educate the civil servants, formulate the ethics of using AI, establish regulatory authorities for evaluating AI and build interfaces for responding to citizens than relying only on the technology. And finally, it should be noted that the unexplained variance in the regression analysis suggests that the trust in AI is multi-dimensional and could depend on numerous other aspects.

7. LIMITATIONS OF THE STUDY

Drawbacks are associated with the cross-sectional design of the research, which does not permit establishing causality and studying the temporal changes in the trust of citizens in the use of AI by the government. Self-perceptions may also create biases in the answers provided by the respondents. The paper concentrates solely on the three antecedents of governance and, therefore, excludes all other potential antecedents, such as digital literacy, privacy protection, algorithmic fairness, institutional reputation, and sociopolitical orientation.

8. CONCLUSION

Against the backdrop of growing interest of science to the topic of trusted AI in public administration, the present research makes a substantial empirical contribution to the area in the form of exploring the links between the factors of AI Transparency, AI Accountability, and Citizen Engagement in terms of their impact on the Trust in AI. Conceptually, the present research was based on the assumption that the trust of people in AI technologies used for governance cannot emerge solely because of technological development or administrative digitalization but is determined by the normative-institutional context in which the technologies are applied.

The study established that the respondents had a relatively positive attitude towards the constructs; that is, there was an overall moderately favorable attitude regarding the incorporation of AI in the governance process. This is significant because it demonstrates that trust in AI does not automatically mean that such trust is non-existent or negative, but rather that it can be generated depending on the context within which it operates. In addition, the stability of distribution of the variables confirmed the reliability of this finding, indicating that there was a fairly balanced attitude structure among the respondents for inference purposes. Such an attitude structure implies that people will be willing to trust the governance process using AI when there is clear procedure credibility. Even more importantly, the statistical results showed the validity of the theory. The interactions of various factors like AI transparency, accountability of AI, and citizen engagement in trust in AI confirmed the theoretical claim made that trust in AI in the public sector is socially constructed. In other words, the model shows that the above factors interact and explain a substantial amount of variance in the construct of trust; hence the claim that trust in AI in citizens cannot be isolated from the larger institutional setting. As can be seen, the research has shown that trust in AI is neither automatic nor inevitable.

Variable 'AI Accountability' was a major difference from the rest and was the biggest contributor to the level of trust towards AI technology. It might have been the biggest contribution to knowledge from the study. It shows that the main point people care about in relation to AI in the institutions is the question of whether those AI systems used in institutions are accountable in some way. In other words, the issue is not whether there is AI or not but whether somebody is responsible for the outcome of its usage. It is especially true for the sphere of public administration, as the algorithms there influence various issues such as benefits, service, surveillance, and regulatory adjudication. The significance of the variable 'AI accountability' in the model means that it is impossible to have trust in AI independently of the ethics and administration. Variable 'Citizen engagement' was also discovered to be a statistically significant positive contributor to trust in AI. The result implies that trust is higher when citizens do not see themselves as mere recipients of AI-based governance, but as participants whose needs, concerns, and experiences are considered in the governance process. The result has both normative and practical implications. Normatively, the result is an endorsement that legitimacy of technology in AI governance should be grounded on participation norms. Practically, the result implies that participation of citizens in consultations, dialogues, feedback mechanisms, and communications may lead to increased trust.

In contrast, however, the impact of Artificial Intelligence Transparency on Artificial Intelligence Trust was determined to be positive, although quite a bit weaker. In other words, this discovery demands further exploration of the issue. While transparency has been widely hailed as an essential element of ethical AI, the current findings indicate that transparency or explainability by itself might not suffice to foster trust in AI unless complemented by such concepts as responsibility and participation of citizens. While citizens may find it appealing that information about how AI works is available, transparency in itself may prove to be merely symbolic unless responsibility and avenues for engagement are guaranteed. It should be stressed that the finding is not meant to undermine the importance of transparency in any way but to place it in the context of trust building.

Taken together, however, the results of this research project suggest an equally clear-cut conclusion: trust in AI technology used by governments in their relations with citizens is essentially about the quality of governance rather than the novelty of the technologies themselves. What is crucial for the trust to be built is not what kind of technologies the governments use, but how well they manage to institutionalize them, control them, explain them to the people and legitimize them socially. This conclusion becomes particularly relevant today when in the era of rapid technologization of public sector services the speed of integration of AI technologies into the public sector outstrips the establishment of the ethical standards and mechanisms of citizen participation and accountability. Therefore, the research confirms the hypothesis that the trust in AI systems used in the public sphere should be gained through the institutional design that focuses on procedural justice, civic participation, and accountability rather than pure effectiveness of the procedures. The conceptual basis of the study also confirms the notion of the emergence of trust as a result of the particular institutional setting and citizen-state interactions. Having found the empirical evidence on how the selected predictors influence the issue in a different way, the research helps to contribute to the current debate on AI trust in a more empirical way by providing a case study of citizens' evaluation of AI applications within the government.

Furthermore, the research indirectly implies what can be researched in the future. As the model, even though relatively elaborate, does not take into account all possible sources of variance of Trust in AI, it becomes evident that there are more factors that can affect citizens' confidence. Factors like perception of fairness, data protection, digital literacy, past experience of e-governance, institution's reputation and socio-political situation may be explored in the future in order to provide a more comprehensive approach to the development of AI trust. The further research may rely on more elaborate models, either longitudinal or comparative in nature in order to test the consistency of these relationships among different populations, institutions or governance systems. Conclusion Overall, the research shows that the influence of trustworthy AI on the relations between the government and its citizens is significant, but conditional. Trust in AI is not guaranteed by technology itself, but by responsible governance and trustworthy behavior of the institutions. Therefore, the path towards building up a trustworthy public AI system lies in designing a proper governance structure.

9. FUTURE SCOPE OF THE STUDY

Future studies can take advantage of a longitudinal or comparative design to conduct research on the dynamics of trust in government AI. Extra variables that could be included in future research include perceptions of fairness, cybersecurity, privacy concerns, digital skills, credibility of organizations, and ethical management of AI. An additional usage of the PLS-SEM or Multi-Group Analysis would enhance the study of the theory's generalizability and validity.

REFERENCES

Afroogh, S., Akbari, A., Malone, E., Kargar, M., & Alambeigi, H. (2024). Trust in AI: Progress, challenges, and future directions. *Humanities & Social Sciences Communications*, *11*(1), 1568. DOI: 10.1057/s41599-024-04044-8

Batool, A., Zowghi, D., & Bano, M. (2025a). AI governance: A systematic literature review. *AI and Ethics*, *5*(3), 3265–3279. DOI: 10.1007/s43681-024-00653-w

Batool, A., Zowghi, D., & Bano, M. (2025b). AI governance: A systematic literature review. *AI and Ethics*, *5*(3), 3265–3279. DOI: 10.1007/s43681-024-00653-w

Berigüete, F. E., Santos, J. S., & Rodriguez Cantalapiedra, I. (2024). Digital revolution: Emerging technologies for enhancing citizen engagement in urban and environmental management. *Land (Basel)*, *13*(11), 1921. DOI: 10.3390/land13111921

Birkstedt, T., Minkkinen, M., Tandon, A., & Mäntymäki, M. (2023a). AI governance: Themes, knowledge gaps and future agendas. *Internet Research*, *33*(7), 133–167. DOI: 10.1108/INTR-01-2022-0042

Birkstedt, T., Minkkinen, M., Tandon, A., & Mäntymäki, M. (2023b). AI governance: Themes, knowledge gaps and future agendas. *Internet Research*, *33*(7), 133–167. DOI: 10.1108/INTR-01-2022-0042

Bokhari, S. A. A., Park, S. Y., & Manzoor, S. (2025). Digital Government Transformation Through Artificial Intelligence: The Mediating Role of Stakeholder Trust and Participation. *Digital*, *5*(3), 43. Advance online publication. DOI: 10.3390/digital5030043

Cheong, B. C. (2024). Transparency and accountability in AI systems: Safeguarding wellbeing in the age of algorithmic decision-making. *Frontiers in Human Dynamics*, *6*, 1421273. DOI: 10.3389/fhumd.2024.1421273

. Cojocaru, A. (2025). Governing AI with trust: an adaptive framework for institutional legitimacy in the UK public sector. *Transforming Government: People, Process and Policy*, 1–22. DOI: 10.1108/TG-05-2025-0125

. Corvalán, J. G. (2018). Digital and intelligent public administration: transformations in the era of artificial intelligence. *A&C-Revista de Direito Administrativo & Constitucional, 18*(71), 55–87.

de Almeida, P. G. R., & dos Santos Júnior, C. D. (2025). Artificial intelligence governance: Understanding how public organizations implement it. *Government Information Quarterly, 42*(1), 102003. https://doi.org/https://doi.org/10.1016/j.giq.2024.102003. DOI: 10.1016/j.giq.2024.102003

Díaz-Rodríguez, N., Del Ser, J., Coeckelbergh, M., López de Prado, M., Herrera-Viedma, E., & Herrera, F. (2023). Connecting the dots in trustworthy Artificial Intelligence: From AI principles, ethics, and key requirements to responsible AI systems and regulation. *Information Fusion, 99*, 101896. DOI: 10.1016/j.inffus.2023.101896

Duberry, J. (2022). Artificial intelligence and democracy: risks and promises of AI-mediated citizen–government relations. In *Artificial intelligence and democracy*. Edward Elgar Publishing. DOI: 10.4337/9781788977319

Feng, N., & Chandra, Y. (2025). Accountability in Government Use of <scp>AI</scp> : Citizen Concerns and Preferences. *Public Administration*, padm.70030. Advance online publication. DOI: 10.1111/padm.70030

Glikson, E., & Woolley, A. W. (2020). Human trust in artificial intelligence: Review of empirical research. *The Academy of Management Annals, 14*(2), 627–660. DOI: 10.5465/annals.2018.0057

Goossens, J., Keymolen, E., & Stanojević, A. (2025). Public Governance and Emerging Technologies: Values, Trust, and Regulatory Compliance. In *Public Governance and Emerging Technologies: Values, Trust, and Regulatory Compliance*. DOI: 10.1007/978-3-031-84748-6

Hao, S., Teng, F., Hou, R., Zhang, L., Wu, H., & Qi, J. (2026a). Explainable AI and echo state networks calibrate trust in human machine interaction. *Scientific Reports, 16*(1), 1189. Advance online publication. DOI: 10.1038/s41598-025-30899-1 PMID: 41495117

Hao, S., Teng, F., Hou, R., Zhang, L., Wu, H., & Qi, J. (2026b). Explainable AI and echo state networks calibrate trust in human machine interaction. *Scientific Reports, 16*(1), 1189. Advance online publication. DOI: 10.1038/s41598-025-30899-1 PMID: 41495117

Hao, S., Teng, F., Hou, R., Zhang, L., Wu, H., & Qi, J. (2026c). Explainable AI and echo state networks calibrate trust in human machine interaction. *Scientific Reports, 16*(1), 1189. Advance online publication. DOI: 10.1038/s41598-025-30899-1 PMID: 41495117

He, Y., Zhang, F. X., Wu, X., Fang, M., Zheng, S., & Zhu, H. (2026). Understanding psychiatrist readiness for AI: A study of access, self-efficacy, trust, and design expectations. *BMC Health Services Research*, *26*(1), 218. Advance online publication. DOI: 10.1186/s12913-026-14010-6 PMID: 41547796

Heinisuo, E., Kuoppakangas, P., & Stenvall, J. (2025). Navigating AI Implementation in Local Government: Addressing Dilemmas by Fostering Mutuality and Meaningfulness. *Information Systems Frontiers*. Advance online publication. DOI: 10.1007/s10796-025-10599-x

Herrera, F., & Calderón, R. (2026). Opacity as a feature, not a flaw: Role-sensitive explainability, institutional trust, and the LoBOX ethics governance framework for AI. *Technology in Society*, *86*, 103302. Advance online publication. DOI: 10.1016/j.techsoc.2026.103302

Ingrams, A., Kaufmann, W., & Jacobs, D. (2022). In AI we trust? Citizen perceptions of AI in government decision making. *Policy and Internet*, *14*(2), 390–409. DOI: 10.1002/poi3.276

Joshi, A. (2026). The Evolution of Public Administration in the AI Era. In *Transforming Public Administration Through AI-Driven Predictive Analytics* (pp. 327–342). IGI Global Scientific Publishing.

Khoso, A. K., Honggang, W., & Darazi, M. A. (2026). Trust and attitude towards AI as pathways to creativity: A TAM Model study of EFL students' digital literacy and AI acceptance. *Humanities & Social Sciences Communications*, *13*(1), 69. Advance online publication. DOI: 10.1057/s41599-025-06362-x

Kleizen, B., Van Dooren, W., Verhoest, K., & Tan, E. (2023). Do citizens trust trustworthy artificial intelligence? Experimental evidence on the limits of ethical AI measures in government. *Government Information Quarterly*, *40*(4), 101834. https://doi.org/https://doi.org/10.1016/j.giq.2023.101834. DOI: 10.1016/j.giq.2023.101834

Mehr, H., Ash, H., & Fellow, D. (2017). Artificial intelligence for citizen services and government. *Ash Cent. Democr. Gov. Innov. Harvard Kennedy Sch*, *1*(August), 12.

. Mensah, G. B. (2023). Artificial intelligence and ethics: a comprehensive review of bias mitigation, transparency, and accountability in AI Systems. *Preprint, November, 10*(1), 1.

Myles, P., Axson, E., & Mitchell, C. (2026). Data quality, provenance and transparency in real-world data: Aligning quality standards with data governance legal frameworks. *Journal of Data Protection and Privacy*, *8*(2), 131–143. DOI: 10.69554/PGGW3813

Nastoska, A., Jancheska, B., Rizinski, M., & Trajanov, D. (2025). Evaluating Trustworthiness in AI: Risks, Metrics, and Applications Across Industries. *Electronics (Basel), 14*(13), 2717. DOI: 10.3390/electronics14132717

Onufreiciuc, R. (2024). Citizen Participation in and Through AI-Enabled Innovation. *Logos Universality Mentality Education Novelty: Law, 12*(1), 62–74. DOI: 10.18662/lumenlaw/12.1/91

Radanliev, P. (2025). AI Ethics: Integrating Transparency, Fairness, and Privacy in AI Development. *Applied Artificial Intelligence, 39*(1), 2463722. Advance online publication. DOI: 10.1080/08839514.2025.2463722

Roberts, H., Hine, E., Taddeo, M., & Floridi, L. (2024). Global AI governance: Barriers and pathways forward. *International Affairs, 100*(3), 1275–1286. DOI: 10.1093/ia/iiae073

Saktiawan, B., Setiyono, B., Risfandy, T., & Rachmadi, E. (2026). AI for FI governance: Panacea or poison? *Research in Globalization, 12*, 100343. Advance online publication. DOI: 10.1016/j.resglo.2026.100343

Savveli, I., Rigou, M., & Balaskas, S. (2025a). From E-Government to AI E-Government: A Systematic Review of Citizen Attitudes. In *Informatics* (Vol. 12, Number 3). Multidisciplinary Digital Publishing Institute (MDPI). DOI: 10.3390/informatics12030098

Savveli, I., Rigou, M., & Balaskas, S. (2025b). From E-Government to AI E-Government: A Systematic Review of Citizen Attitudes. In *Informatics* (Vol. 12, Number 3). Multidisciplinary Digital Publishing Institute (MDPI). DOI: 10.3390/informatics12030098

Schilke, O., & Reimann, M. (2025). The transparency dilemma: How AI disclosure erodes trust. *Organizational Behavior and Human Decision Processes, 188*, 104405. DOI: 10.1016/j.obhdp.2025.104405

Siripipatthanakul, S., Phuangsuwan, P., & Limna, P., Muthmainnha, Siripipattanakul, S., Vui, C. N., & Jaipong, P. (2024). Artificial intelligence (AI) influencing sustainable governance: Governance adopting AI. *International Conference on Data Analytics & Management*, 551–568.

Wirtz, B. W., Weyerer, J. C., & Kehl, I. (2022). Governance of artificial intelligence: A risk and guideline-based integrative framework. *Government Information Quarterly, 39*(4), 101685. DOI: 10.1016/j.giq.2022.101685

Zulu, N. G., & Nzimakwe, T. I. (2025a). Artificial Intelligence-powered Local Governance: Revolutionising Public Services and Citizen Engagement. *Administratio Publica*, *33*(3), 25–40. DOI: 10.61967/adminpub.2025.33.3.2

Zulu, N. G., & Nzimakwe, T. I. (2025b). Artificial Intelligence-powered Local Governance: Revolutionising Public Services and Citizen Engagement. *Administratio Publica*, *33*(3), 25–40. DOI: 10.61967/adminpub.2025.33.3.2

Chapter 6
Emotional Intelligence and Citizen Trust in Artificial Intelligence-Enabled Public Administration

Pradeep Yadav
http://orcid.org/0000-0003-1073-7076
Institute of Technology and Management, Gwalior, India

ABSTRACT

With AI being the heart of public administration services, issues regarding citizens' trust in AI-based governance mechanisms have been rising. In this chapter, the role of emotional intelligence (EI) in fostering citizens' trust in AI-driven public services is examined. Based on the EI theory developed by Mayer et al., Goleman, and Petrides & Furnham, the case study establishes the framework for embedding EI components, such as emotion perception, utilization, understanding, and management, in the development of AI systems, human-AI interface, and governance architectures. The application of emotionally intelligent digital services in Estonia, Singapore, the United Kingdom, India, and the United States shows how emotionally intelligent digital services can enhance citizens' trust outcomes.

1. INTRODUCTION

The swift spread of artificial intelligence throughout all areas of public administration, from welfare distribution and criminal risk assessment to medical

DOI: 10.4018/979-8-3373-9129-8.ch006

prioritization and traffic control, has sparked an urgent rethinking of the social contract between citizens and the state. Within all these areas, decisions which used to be taken by known human actors are now increasingly being handed over to algorithms whose operation is such that even front-line staff or citizens cannot easily examine. The new world of governance holds tremendous promise but also grave dangers for democracy.

The possibilities are extensively researched. Artificial intelligence provides the ability to analyze complicated data sets in real-time, customize services to citizens on a population-wide level, cut down administrative expenses, and eliminate discretion which has always been used against marginalized groups by governments (Dunleavy et al., 2022; Meijer et al., 2021). However, these features can also lead to undermining the relational and emotional aspects of government services, which are essential for citizens to assess whether government organizations act in their best interest, competently, and sincerely (Grimmelikhuijsen et al., 2017; Van der Waal et al., 2018).

Trusting relations are integral to any form of government rather than being secondary and extraneous elements. The willingness of people to trust their institutions means that they will be more inclined to follow regulations and policies and participate in political processes, will communicate their problems to government agencies and services, and will accept negative decisions as justifiable (Blind, 2007; OECD, 2022). On the contrary, a lack of trust between individuals and institutions has been associated with democratic alienation, non-compliance with governmental policies, and the development of conspiracy theories that hinder problem-solving activities (Levi & Stoker, 2000; Van der Meer, 2017). This makes the implementation of AI technologies into governance a very significant move because its improper management may result in further deterioration of the situation while proper implementation may help improve relations between citizens and government.

In this chapter, I will develop the claim that emotional intelligence, defined as the combination of skills and characteristics that relate to perceiving, understanding, utilizing, and regulating emotions both in oneself and socially, can provide a conceptual and practical basis for solving the problem of bridging the gap of trust between AI-powered public administration and its citizens. This solution is neither idealized nor technophobic. I am not claiming that public institutions must make AI systems seem human-like or even give them a personality. Instead, I argue that EI can serve as a design philosophy for ensuring that the EI inherent in humans responsible for serving the people is not lost when such roles are taken over by AI systems.

The chapter is structured as follows. Section 2 situates the inquiry within a review of pertinent literature spanning EI theory, public sector AI adoption, and institutional trust. Section 3 develops a conceptual framework mapping EI dimensions onto trust-relevant design and governance strategies. Section 4 presents five illustrative case studies. Section 5 synthesises findings into policy recommendations. Section 6 discusses limitations and directions for future inquiry. Section 7 concludes.

2. LITERATURE REVIEW

2.1 Theories Of Emotional Intelligence

Three main theories have evolved around emotional intelligence, each of which implies certain considerations in implementing emotional intelligence in organizational and technological spheres. The ability theory is the most elaborated and theoretically advanced among the three approaches to EI and was first proposed by Mayer, Salovey, and Caruso (Mayer et al., 2016; Mayer & Salovey, 1997). In their approach, emotional intelligence is presented as an array of empirically identifiable cognitive abilities that can be grouped in a hierarchical structure comprising four branches: accurate perception of emotions from faces, voices, and artifacts; effective use of emotions to enhance one's thinking by controlling attention; emotion knowledge, including recognition of the development of emotions and understanding how they change; regulation of emotions to attain goals (Brackett & Mayer, 2003; Roberts et al., 2001).

The hybrid model, especially Goleman's (1995, 2020) and Bar-On's (2006) approach, comprises emotional competencies along with motivational, personal, and social competencies. The Goleman model, which has been very influential in the domain of applied leadership and organisational development theories, has categorized EI into five areas: self-awareness, self-regulation, motivation, empathy, and social skills. Although it is argued that such mixed models have been criticized for conceptual inconsistencies (Matthews et al., 2002; Locke, 2005), their practical nature makes them highly valuable in developing EI guidelines for workplaces and institutions.

The Trait Emotional Intelligence model formulated by Petrides and Furnham (2001) considers emotional self-efficacy to be a trait-based construct assessed through self-report, reflecting one's usual emotions over 15 dimensions, such as flexibility, emotional expressiveness, empathy, and interpersonal skills. This approach proves useful in comprehending differences in emotional dispositions among populations when dealing with emotionally charged customer service situations and creating AI systems that cater to various emotional personalities.

Theories from all three perspectives help shape the conceptual foundation that is set out in this chapter. The ability perspective offers architectural precision, the hybrid perspective offers practical granularity, and the trait perspective offers citizen sensitivity to differences in emotional abilities and requirements.

2.2 Trust in Public Institutions: Mechanisms and Determinants

Trust in public institutions has been analyzed using different approaches, including political science, organizational behavior, public administration, and social psychology (Bouckaert & Van de Walle, 2003; Grimmelikhuijsen et al., 2017; Levi & Stoker, 2000). A common conclusion drawn by the different research frameworks is that institutional trust involves at least three defining elements, namely competence, which refers to an organization's ability to carry out its responsibilities; benevolence, which reflects an organization's genuine care for the well-being of its citizens; and integrity, which implies following acceptable standards of conduct consistently (Mayer et al., 1995; Van der Waal et al., 2018).

Competence-based trust is the aspect that has always been easiest to enhance through technological advancement because digital technologies that process requests quickly, accurately, and with minimal administrative effort undoubtedly improve the perception of institutional competence (Dunleavy et al., 2022; OECD, 2022). The existing research evidence unambiguously shows that competence, on its own, cannot fully develop institutional trust in democratic societies. People often express their disappointment in public institutions that perform technically proficient actions but remain impersonal and lacking in empathy (Needham, 2011; Osborne et al., 2022). Benevolence and integrity trust, which correspond to people's perceptions of empathy, impartiality, and responsiveness, have proven to be particularly vulnerable in technologically mediated interactions.

In terms of procedural fairness theory (Tyler, 1990, 2006), research has established that people's perceptions of the legitimacy of organizational decisions do not rest so much on how favourable the outcomes might be as on how the decisions have been made – i.e., how transparent, predictable, unbiased, and dignified the processes of decision making are seen to be. Being treated with dignity and being able to put forth one's point of view are two procedural elements that strongly predict institutional trust (Tyler & Lind, 1992). The results from such research have immediate relevance to AI development.

2.3 Artificial Intelligence in Public Services: Opportunities and Risks

There has been an explosion in the use of artificial intelligence technology in government from 2018, owing to the advancements in machine learning, the availability of big data in government, and the need to increase efficiency in public services delivery due to political pressure (Meijer et al., 2021; OECD, 2023; United Nations, 2022). The most common applications include fraud detection through predictive analytics, decision support systems for court and parole cases, intelligent bots for managing citizens' inquiries, automatic triaging in the health sector, and smart city management (Diakopoulos, 2016; Vogl et al., 2020; Wirtz et al., 2019).

The possible gains from such applications are well known: better consistency in decision-making, greater capacity to discover patterns in complex data, significant time savings, and allowing the human officers the time to do more complex relational work (Dunleavy et al., 2022; Kankanhalli et al., 2019). On the other hand, there is ample criticism of these systems, as it is well recognized that algorithms developed using historic data might lead to greater discrimination and injustice, that lack of transparency will prevent people from understanding what they are contesting, that automation might deprive interactions of their contextual nature leading to unfair decisions, and finally, taking away the human element in decision-making might mean losing the relational dimension that is necessary to foster trust (Eubanks, 2018; O'Neil, 2016; Pasquale, 2015; Radin, 2019).

The idea of explainable AI (XAI), which seeks to render algorithmic decision-making procedures comprehensible to non-specialist users, represents one such potential technological solution to these worries (Adadi & Berrada, 2018; Lipton, 2018; Ribeiro et al., 2016). While explainability goes some way toward addressing the trust deficit problem associated with AI-based public services, explainability in itself does not resolve the issue in full because an explanation can be cognitively understandable but emotionally unpalatable, presented to its audience in a manner that disregards any sense of their emotional stake in the matter at hand (Binns, 2018; Zerilli et al., 2019).

2.4 The Convergence of EI and AI in Governance: Emerging Scholarship

A new field of studies has started to emerge focusing on the relationship between emotional intelligence theory and AI system development within a service context. Feine et al. (2019) performed a systematic review about social cues used in designing chatbots and found that emotionally expressive chatbots generate greater user engagement and satisfaction compared to emotionally neutral chatbots. Zhou et al. (2020) studied the impact of affective computing, i.e., AI-based systems that detect, interpret, and simulate human emotions, on improving citizen interactions with e-government services. Lastly, Rao et al. (2021) observed the emotional components in human-robot interactions in healthcare and found that robots with basic emotional abilities produced considerably higher levels of patient trust.

In the public administration domain, according to Vogl et al. (2020), when deploying AI within governments, there is a need to consider what the scholars refer to as "emotional due process": that is, processes where the emotional concerns of citizens are included in the decision-making processes that involve AI. Lember et al. (2019) found that co-production of public services, which can be considered to have both an interpersonal and emotionally intelligent aspect, leads to significantly greater trust outcomes compared to technological adoption processes. According to Osborne et al. (2022), service dominant logic can be applied in the public sector, where value is co-created through an interaction between the service provider and the citizen.

While these synergies have proven to be fruitful, it is important to note that no research has yet sought to create a unified framework which can link together EI theory and the mechanisms by which trust in AI-enabled public services can be built. This is the intention of this chapter.

3. EMOTIONAL INTELLIGENCE AND TRUST: A CONCEPTUAL FRAMEWORK

3.1 Defining the Problem Space

Before we get to the development of the framework, it must be clearly stated what kind of problem we are solving. The fundamental idea is that the trust crisis regarding the use of AI systems within public services is not only not a purely technical problem; in fact, it may be far from being one. What underlies it is an emotional-relational problem related to the diminishing emotional component of service delivery. A citizen dealing with an AI system processing his/her application for social benefits, rejecting the request for appeal, or handling his/her health records cannot be satisfied solely because the process was computationally correct.

The concept of EI gives rise to an understanding of how this identification is achieved. According to the four branches of EI presented by Mayer et al. (2016), four key design considerations can be proposed for AI public services: the ability to perceive the emotional environment of citizens' interactions (perceiving emotions); the ability to use this perception to properly align responses and their intensity to the emotional state (using emotions); the ability to understand the potential trajectory of the evolution of citizens' emotional state (understanding emotions); and finally, the ability to manage emotions to achieve outcomes beneficial for establishing trust.

3.2 EI Dimensions and Their Public Service Applications

Table 1 synthesises the core EI dimensions, their definitional content, their specific applications in AI-enabled public service contexts, and the key references that anchor each mapping.

Table 1. Emotional Intelligence Dimensions and Their Applications in AI-Driven Public Services

EI Dimension	Definition	AI Application in Public Services	Key References
Self-Awareness	Recognising one's own emotions and their effect on decision-making and service delivery	AI dashboards that surface real-time sentiment analytics to human officers	Sharma et al. (2022); Mayer et al. (2016)
Self-Regulation	Managing disruptive emotions and impulses in high-pressure service contexts	Automated escalation systems that redirect distressed citizens to empathetic agents	Goleman (2020); Côté (2014)
Social Awareness / Empathy	Sensing others' emotions, understanding their perspective, and taking active interest in their concerns	NLP-driven chatbots calibrated to detect emotional valence in citizen queries	Brackett (2019); Petrides & Furnham (2001)
Relationship Management	Inspiring, influencing, and developing others while managing conflict constructively	AI-supported feedback loops that personalise follow-up communications post-service interaction	Caruso & Salovey (2004); Joseph & Newman (2010)
Motivational Intelligence	Harnessing emotions to facilitate goal pursuit and maintain performance under adversity	Gamified compliance platforms that use positive reinforcement signals	Bar-On (2006); Zeidner et al. (2009)

Note. EI = emotional intelligence; NLP = natural language processing; IVR = interactive voice response. References are indicative rather than exhaustive. See full reference list for complete citations.

As shown in Table 1, each EI component is associated with its particular type of AI design or governance action. For example, self-awareness relates to processes of transparency which aid human officials and computer algorithms in being aware of their emotional output. Self-regulation is related to governance frameworks that prevent the operation of AI systems without human approval to react impulsively to emotionally charged events. Social awareness and empathy relate to the design of user interfaces that would be able to recognize emotions. Relationship management relates to service design that is focused on the relational aspects of citizen-state interaction. Finally, motivational intelligence which includes components defined by Bar-On (2006) beyond the basic model relates to emotional reinforcement of citizens' motivation.

3.3 Trust Deficit Indicators in AI-Driven Public Services

To operationalise the framework, it is necessary to identify the specific pathways through which AI-driven public services generate trust deficits. Table 2 presents a structured taxonomy of these pathways, each linked to observable consequences and the scholarly literature from which it is derived.

Table 2. Trust Deficit Indicators in AI-Driven Public Services

Trust Deficit Indicator	Description	Observable Consequence	Key References
Algorithmic Opacity	Citizens cannot understand or contest AI-generated decisions	Perceived injustice, withdrawal of service engagement	Diakopoulos (2016); Mittelstadt et al. (2016)
Emotional Disconnection	AI interfaces lack empathetic responsiveness to distressed users	Reduced satisfaction scores; complaints escalation	Rao et al. (2021); Wirtz et al. (2019)
Data Privacy Anxiety	Uncertainty about how personal data informs algorithmic outcomes	Avoidance behaviour; non-disclosure of relevant information	Acquisti et al. (2015); Solove (2021)
Automation Bias	Over-reliance on AI outputs without adequate human oversight	Erroneous decisions affecting vulnerable populations	Goddard et al. (2012); Cummings (2017)
Accountability Gaps	Unclear responsibility chains when AI systems err	Public outrage; legislative scrutiny; loss of institutional legitimacy	Doshi-Velez & Kim (2017); Binns (2018)
Digital Exclusion	Segments of the population lack access or competence to engage AI services	Inequitable service delivery; erosion of social trust	Van Dijk (2020); Robinson et al. (2015)

Note. Indicators are drawn from a synthesis of public administration, human–computer interaction, and AI ethics literatures. Observable consequences are indicative; empirical magnitude varies by national and institutional context.

The taxonomy of trust deficits outlined in Table 2 suggests a significant structural connection: Each trust deficit is associated with the lack of a certain EI competency. For example, algorithmic opacity is related to the lack of self-awareness, since a machine that does not have the ability to articulate how it works cannot explain itself to others. Similarly, emotional disconnection can be viewed as a lack of social awareness and empathy. The data privacy concern can also be viewed from the perspective of integrity trust deficit that can be addressed through open dialogue, a form of self-regulation by institutions. Automation bias is linked to the lack of emotional vigilance by humans responsible for monitoring AI algorithms. Accountability gap is a failure in relationship management by institutions. Digital exclusion can be considered the absence of motivational intelligence by designers of digital platforms.

3.4 The EI-Trust Integration Framework

Based on the foregoing discussion, the EI-Trust Integration Framework in table 3 provides a five-layer structure that integrates EI dimensions, design considerations, and governance practices. The EI-Trust Integration Framework can be used as a tool for diagnosis, by allowing administrators to determine where EI principles are lacking in current AI systems, and as a prescription for future AI designs and governance.

Table 3. The EI–Trust Integration Framework for AI-Driven Public Services

Framework Layer	EI Dimension Mapped	Key Design Strategies	Foundational References
Transparency Layer	Self-Awareness	Explainable AI (XAI) modules; plain-language decision rationale; interactive audit trails	Ribeiro et al. (2016); Lipton (2018); European Commission (2021)
Empathy Layer	Social Awareness / Empathy	Sentiment-adaptive chatbots; emotionally intelligent IVR routing; multilingual NLP	Zhou et al. (2020); Abd-Alrazaq et al. (2020); Feine et al. (2019)
Accountability Layer	Self-Regulation	Human-in-the-loop review gates; AI error reporting dashboards; whistleblower channels	Cath et al. (2018); Doshi-Velez & Kim (2017); IEEE (2019)
Relational Layer	Relationship Management	Post-interaction follow-up systems; personalised service journeys; co-production portals	Lember et al. (2019); Jilke et al. (2019); Vigoda-Gadot (2021)
Inclusion Layer	Motivational Intelligence	Accessibility-first design; digital literacy programmes; culturally adaptive interfaces	W3C (2023); OECD (2023); United Nations (2022)

Note. XAI = explainable AI; IVR = interactive voice response; NLP = natural language processing. Framework layers are conceptually distinct but operationally interdependent. Effective implementation requires attention to all five layers simultaneously.

Layers of the Framework: The five layers in the framework have been organized based on the technical nearness, beginning with the most technologically close (Transparency Layer) to the most structurally transformational (Inclusion Layer). It should be noted, however, that the organization of these layers is not meant to create any sort of hierarchy, but rather to demonstrate the way the scope of the challenge grows progressively to include the trust-building issue at first and then to move toward issues of design, governance, and finally inclusion. Importantly, the framework requires that none of the layers alone are sufficient.

4. COMPARATIVE CASE ANALYSIS: EI-ALIGNED AI IN PRACTICE

4.1 Methodological Note

Each one of the cases presented below was chosen with the aim of bringing about some diversity, both in geographical terms and concerning the nature of the services that were offered. Moreover, these cases vary in the stage of development of their

AI implementations in regard to EI principles. This analysis is carried out using the framework established above in Section 3. Data used in analyzing each case were gathered from relevant government documents, reports, peer reviews, and grey literature. The selected cases are illustrative rather than extensive.

4.2 Estonia: Systemic Transparency as EI Infrastructure

The Estonian approach to digitization of public governance is known all around the world as one of the best examples, since 99% of all its public services were successfully digitized, while more than 98% of routine administrative processes were taken out of face-to-face contact format (Lips, 2020). Moreover, the Estonian data backbone system called the X-Road allows people to know exactly which government agencies use their data and why they do it (Kalvet et al., 2018).

These high levels of transparency have yielded tangible benefits in terms of trust. Estonia is one of the EU member states with the highest levels of trust in institutions, with Eurobarometer reporting in 2022 that 87% of respondents from Estonia reported trust in the Estonian government's digital services, while the EU-wide average is just 41% (European Commission, 2022). Importantly, this trust cannot be simply explained away on the grounds of efficient services; according to qualitative research by Kalvet et al. (2018), a citizen's awareness of the possibility of monitoring and questioning the process of data collection is a key predictor of trust independent of service efficiency.

The limitations of the Estonian model are equally informative. Thanks to the advanced average level of digital literacy among its citizens and a linguistically homogenous population, Estonia was able to create a digitally intelligent structure which may be more complicated to implement in regions characterized by higher linguistic heterogeneity or less digital literacy and distrust toward the authorities (Van Dijk, 2020). Therefore, the model of Estonia serves both as a showcase of the Transparency layer and a reminder of the importance of the Inclusion layer.

4.3 Singapore: Empathy by Design in LifeSG

The LifeSG portal in Singapore, initiated by the Government Technology Agency (GovTech) in 2018 and further developed significantly from 2020 to 2023, is among the most ambitious efforts to date in the world to incorporate an empathy-centered approach within a digital service platform for the entire government (GovTech Singapore, 2022). The portal consolidates over 100 government services into one unified citizen interface, utilizing proactive and personalized reminders to inform citizens about relevant services when they reach certain milestones in their lives, such as giving birth, losing a job, or experiencing the death of a loved one.

There are a number of aspects of the LifeSG design that demonstrate the empathy dimension of the platform. The notification system design of the platform was developed on the basis of citizen journey mapping that took into account emotions of citizens at each contact point with the service. The multilingual natural language processing capacity was incorporated in the system from the beginning understanding that the linguistic aspect is not only informative but also emotionally isolating. Post-interaction satisfaction surveys reveal that users rate significantly higher empathy levels in LifeSG interaction when compared to government counters. Satisfaction levels exceed 80% every year in GovTech user satisfaction surveys (GovTech Singapore, 2022).

In the Singapore example, the Empathy Layer of the framework can be seen and understood in action. The key lesson to learn from this framework implementation in Singapore is that anticipatory service delivery rather than reactive approaches should be prioritized in any design. Designing services in reaction to citizens' needs during a crisis is emotionally insensitive service design.

4.4 United Kingdom: Human-in-the-Loop as Accountability Architecture

The National Health Service (NHS) in England has tested several AI triage systems since 2019, including conversational AI chatbots for preliminary assessment of symptoms and appointment booking, demand management analytics for emergency department management, and diagnostic decision-making support tools assisted by AI (NHS England, 2023; Topol Review, 2019). The testing process has produced valuable insight into the significance of the human-in-the-loop concept in maintaining public trust in interactions based on artificial intelligence technologies.

Experience of introducing AI into NHS practice has shown a continuous conflict between the efficiency considerations underlying AI deployment and the public's inclination to prefer human presence in health care-related decisions. Opinion polls show that although people do not object to the use of AI technology as an auxiliary device in NHS operations, they tend to favour human decision-making when it comes to matters such as diagnosing a condition, recommending treatment options, and disclosing personal health information (NHS England, 2023). This preference cannot be seen as irrational fear of technology; it is rather the perception that the concept of Accountability Layer is essential for trusting healthcare services provision.

Lessons learned from the experience in the NHS have brought about the creation of clear policy guidelines stressing that the use of AI systems for providing care should only take place as an advisory role to human physicians, and that the patient has the right to appeal AI-generated advice for human clinical evaluation (NHS England, 2023). The governance framework described here is an operationalization of the Accountability Layer in the EI-Trust Integration Framework, where human emotional intelligence acts as a check on algorithmic error.

4.5 India: Linguistic Inclusion and Relational Trust in DigiLocker and UMANG

The two digital government platforms utilized in India include DigiLocker for document management and UMANG (Unified Mobile Application for New-age Governance) for comprehensive service delivery. Both platforms cater to a citizenry characterized by unique linguistic, cultural, and digital literacy profiles (MeitY, 2023). Notably, the platforms have over 50 million active users, with more than five billion documents issued. Therefore, the AI-powered public service platforms constitute one of the most massive implementations of such initiatives globally (World Bank, 2022).

Notably, trust dynamics in these platforms are determined largely by linguistic diversity in India. The UMANG platform is designed to handle transactions across 13 different Indian languages. Such a decision is made with an understanding, consistent with the Inclusion Layer, that the emotional aspect of the service experience is heavily influenced by the language through which service access takes place. Indeed, citizens who engage with public services in their native languages exhibit high levels of perception of institutional kindness and consideration for their cultural identities (Jilke et al., 2019).

However, gaps of trust still exist, especially amongst those living in rural areas lacking digital literacy skills and people who have a strong history of mistrusting institutions. According to World Bank analyses (2022), the level of trust in digital government services amongst rural Indians is much lower than that found in urban areas, and this difference is not based on any lack of trust in technology but rather on fears related to safety, exclusion, and lack of human presence in cases when technology fails. As this information reveals, the role of the Inclusion Layer is pivotal and shows that design informed by EI should consider more than the improvement of user interfaces.

4.6 United States: Equity, Algorithmic Bias, and the Limits of EI-Lite Design

The federal government's experience with AI applications in administering public benefits, such as its pilots at Benefits.gov and veteran benefits, demonstrate the perils of the kind of 'EI-lite' approach to implementation: embedding superficially empathic design elements, such as warm language in chatbot interactions and prompts for empathy in automated communications, without tackling the underlying systemic drivers that cause trust deficits (GAO, 2023; Radin, 2019).

The Government Accountability Office's reviews of the federal government's use of AI in benefit administration have identified persistent issues related to algorithmic bias against disadvantaged groups, insufficient information about how AI-based risk scoring factors into benefit eligibility determinations, and the lack of any effective escalation mechanism for citizens to appeal their negative AI-based decisions to human caseworkers (GAO, 2023). Such observations indicate that a superficial approach to fostering empathy through cosmetic measures can actually harm trust by setting up unrealistic expectations regarding empathic communication that cannot be met under the current system.

Indeed, the American example highlights the indivisibility principle of the framework in action: The use of EI is imperative throughout all levels of the framework, including the bottom level, rather than being used selectively through the lens of the citizen's perspective when other aspects of accountability, transparency, and inclusion have yet to be addressed. Not only does this practice fail to create trust, but it could undermine trust entirely.

4.7 Summary of Comparative Evidence

Table 4 presents a structured comparison of the five cases across the dimensions of service domain, EI-aligned design features, outcome metrics, trust level reported, and key references.

Table 4. Comparative Case Analysis: EI-Aligned AI in AI-Driven Public Services Across Five Jurisdictions

Country / Initiative	Service Domain	EI-Aligned Design Features	Outcome Metrics	Trust Level Reported	References
Estonia (e-Residency & X-Road)	Tax, business registration, e-health	High transparency design; citizen data dashboards; opt-in data sharing	Reduced bureaucratic friction by ~98%; 99% of services online	High: 86% institutional trust index	Lips (2020); Kalvet et al. (2018)
Singapore (LifeSG)	Social services, housing, family	Emotion-aware UX design; proactive personalised notifications; multilingual NLP	30% reduction in service call volumes post-deployment	High: satisfaction scores >80%	GovTech Singapore (2022)
United Kingdom (NHS AI Triage)	Healthcare access, appointment booking	AI triage with human override capability; empathy scripts for chatbot	24% faster referral times; mixed public sentiment on AI autonomy	Moderate: trust contingent on human-in-the-loop	NHS England (2023); Topol Review (2019)
India (DigiLocker & UMANG)	Document verification, welfare delivery	Multi-modal interface; vernacular language support; biometric authentication	Over 5 billion documents issued; 50+ million active users	Moderate: rural trust gaps persist	MeitY (2023); World Bank (2022)
United States (Benefits.gov AI Pilot)	Social welfare, veterans' benefits	Conversational AI with empathy prompts; escalation to human counsellors	Pilot phase; significant equity and algorithmic bias concerns flagged	Low-moderate: scepticism among marginalised groups	GAO (2023); Radin (2019)

Note. Trust level classifications (High, Moderate, Low-Moderate) are based on a synthesis of satisfaction surveys, institutional trust indices, and qualitative research cited in the key references column. These are indicative characterisations, not standardised cross-national measurements. GovTech = Government Technology Agency, Singapore; NHS = National Health Service, UK; MeitY = Ministry of Electronics and Information Technology, India; GAO = Government Accountability Office, USA.

The comparative data shown in Table 4 reveal a clear trend whereby states that have consciously incorporated various dimensions of EI-based design, such as transparency, empathy, accountability, relational consistency, and inclusiveness, produce greater trust outcomes compared to those that focus purely on efficiency in implementing AI while neglecting EI factors. Estonia and Singapore, which incorporate the greatest extent of EI design, achieve the highest trust outcomes, whereas the United States, in which EI-lite design co-exists with structural accountability issues, produces the least trust. Cases from the United Kingdom, India, and Singapore exemplify the contextual challenges, particularly language barriers and digital inequality, that influence the EI-trust relationship.

5. POLICY RECOMMENDATIONS

5.1 Principles for EI-Informed AI Governance in Public Services

This analysis conducted through Sections 3 and 4 provides six concrete policy prescriptions on how governments can use EI as an agent of trust for AI-based public services. These policy prescriptions have been sorted into short-, medium-, and long-term actions based on the levels of organizational change required. Table 5 shows the six policy prescriptions in tabular form.

Table 5. Policy Recommendations for EI-Informed AI Governance in Public Services

Recommendation	Responsible Actor	Implementation Horizon	Relevant Standards / Frameworks
Mandate EI Audits for Public AI Systems	Governments	Short-term (1–2 years)	ISO/IEC 42001 AI Management Standard; EU AI Act (2024)
Establish Citizen Emotional Impact Assessments	Regulatory Bodies	Short-term (1–2 years)	GDPR Article 35 template adaptation; OECD AI Principles (2023)
Embed EI Competencies in AI Procurement Criteria	Procuring Authorities	Medium-term (2–4 years)	UK Government Digital Service Standards; Singapore Digital Government Blueprint
Develop EI-Training Programmes for Civil Servants Working with AI	Public HR Departments	Medium-term (2–4 years)	CIPD (2023) Future of Work Report; UN E-Government Survey 2022
Create Multi-Stakeholder AI-Trust Observatories	Academic-Government Partnerships	Long-term (4–7 years)	European AI Observatory; NIST AI RMF (2023)
Legislate Emotional Transparency Standards for AI Interfaces	Legislatures	Long-term (4–7 years)	IEEE Ethically Aligned Design v2; Council of Europe AI Convention (2024)

Note. Implementation horizons are indicative and will vary by national context, institutional capacity, and political will. Standards and frameworks cited are current as of 2024. EU AI Act = European Union Artificial Intelligence Act (2024); OECD = Organisation for Economic Co-operation and Development; GDPR = General Data Protection Regulation; NIST = National Institute of Standards and Technology; IEEE = Institute of Electrical and Electronics Engineers.

These six recommendations can be viewed as separate actions in Table 5, but they can be more easily conceived as three interlinked levels of governance. The first two short-term recommendations EI audits and CEMIA can be seen as an institutional accountability level, since they represent the establishment of the evaluation structure needed prior to the use of the AI technology with the citizens. The second two medium-term recommendations, the criteria of EI-based procurement and civil servants' training on EI– represent an organizational capacity level, since they ensure that both the systems obtained and their users are committed to being emotionally intelligent. The last two long-term recommendations, AI-Trust observatories and the creation of Emotional Transparency Standards represent a structural regulatory level that institutionalizes these principles in governance structures. Thus, implementation is best achieved if these three levels are followed sequentially, with each level creating the institutional conditions for the other (OECD, 2022).

5.2 Elaboration of Key Recommendations

The suggestion to conduct EI audits on public AI systems requires further explanation. For each of these AI systems, an EI audit should measure the extent to which the system is sensitive to and responds to emotions during citizen interactions, the system's ability to handle escalation pathways when emotions arise, the system's communication of decisions that are mindful of the human impact and significance of those decisions, the availability of accountability measures to citizens, and inclusive designs for emotional and digital vulnerability. In this way, the audit would enhance currently available algorithmic impact assessments (Algorithmic Justice League, 2022; Canadian Treasury Board, 2019) by providing a framework for an emotional component to technical reviews.

On a practical level, it is proposed that EI audits be performed using review panels that consist of experts in public administration, affective computing scientists, and members of the community most immediately impacted by the AI being evaluated. Some minimum requirements that evaluation may assess are: the success rate of distressed citizens being escalated to human agents within a response time period; the sentiment trend of citizens throughout multiple steps of interaction with the service provided, using anonymous chat data; accessibility of explanations for citizens with differing degrees of digital literacy; and appeal processes. The audit results need to be published in a standardized format and be evaluated by the appropriate ministry within six months of completion, where an obligation is placed on the ministry to develop an improvement program. Such a feedback cycle will make the EI audit process a tool for continuous improvement instead of one-off, which is in line with the public services quality framework (Algorithmic Justice League, 2022; OECD, 2022).

The recommendation to create Citizen Emotional Impact Assessments comes from procedural fairness research, which recognizes the unique role of citizens in evaluating the extent to which the actions of governments lead citizens to feel respected, dignified, and cared for – thus fostering trust. Like an environmental impact assessment, the instrument should ensure that before introducing AI systems into interactions with citizens, the government has evaluated the potential emotional impacts and taken appropriate mitigations into account in the design process.

Citizen Emotional Impact Assessments (CEIAs) are distinct from current algorithmic impact assessments in one key way where the latter concentrate almost exclusively on issues of technical accuracy, fairness metrics and data compliance, a CEIA is concerned with how the design, tone and interactional architecture of the AI system will impact citizens' perception of their dignity, procedural fairness and trustful relations. Governments seeking to deploy a public facing AI system under such a framework should go through four steps: firstly, mapping out the emotional touch-points along the citizens' journey through the relevant service; secondly, undertaking structured consultations with citizens' panels and identifying the most emotionally sensitive interactional points; thirdly, piloting the system with various user groups and collecting both quantitative and qualitative feedback data about the emotions evoked during such interaction; and fourthly, publishing a summary of the results and the changes made to the system's design as a result of such testing. Such an exercise may be easily incorporated into current service design frameworks and does not require new powers in most countries, though legislative authority would improve accountability considerably (Tyler, 2006; Vogl et al., 2020).

The long-term recommendations, especially the establishment of Multi-Stakeholder AI-Trust Observatories and the enactment of Emotional Transparency Standards, capture the chapter's overall argument that EI-driven AI governance is more than just a technical issue; it is also a governance issue. Creating the necessary institutional architecture to maintain EI-based principles in AI public services over the long term demands a dedicated effort towards knowledge sharing, intersectoral cooperation, and legislative provisions to make emotional intelligence an enforceable aspect of public AI governance.

The AI-Trust Observatories would need to function as co-governed entities with participation from national statistics agencies, civil society organisations, research departments at universities, and relevant ministries. The principal functions of these observatories would have to include longitudinal tracking of public trust indicators associated with AI-powered service delivery, conducting independent EI audits of high-risk uses of AI, and issuing annual state-of-trust reports equivalent to current OECD institutional trust surveys (OECD, 2022). Meanwhile, EI Standards must outline the minimal requirements for the expression of decisions of AI systems which carry significant emotional weight. Following the principle of accessible communication provided in the W3C Web Content Accessibility Guidelines (W3C, 2023), as well as plain language requirements in some national contexts, these standards would have to mandate the use of non-technical language to communicate decisions that affect significant rights of people in recognition of the fact that those decisions hold significance to humans; the availability of human oversight of those decisions be communicated; and the emotional weight of AI-generated communications be reviewed regularly by a multidisciplinary board. Analogues of these kinds of standards have been set up in financial service regulations and in the healthcare industry, which makes the process of applying similar standards to government-owned AI feasible and well-precedented (Council of Europe, 2024; IEEE, 2019).

6. LIMITATIONS AND FUTURE RESEARCH DIRECTIONS

6.1 Conceptual and Methodological Limitations

This chapter introduces a conceptual framework backed by some illustrative cases. However, there are a number of limitations associated with this chapter that need to be pointed out. First of all, the idea that EI-oriented design contributes to trust outcomes is not based on any primary research but instead emerges from the review of the existing body of literature. The processes through which particular design dimensions of EI lead to particular outcomes remain unproven and need to be verified using appropriate experimental and quasi-experimental methods in various institutional and national settings.

Secondly, implementation of EI principles in AI system design involves quite a few complex technical issues, which have been covered only briefly. For instance, the notion that chatbots can demonstrate social awareness presupposes an elaborated discussion of affective computing, natural language processing and sentiment analysis issues that lie far outside of the scope of a single chapter. Future studies on technical aspects of AI system development should focus on the capabilities needed for implementing particular dimensions of EI in AI systems and their limitations.

Thirdly, the case studies that have been selected have been done so selectively, and have been taken from secondary sources. The need for more nuanced, long-term, and mixed-method research is evident in the effort to examine the impact of sustained trust due to alignment between EI principles and AI governance.

6.2 Directions for Future Research

Several fruitful areas of research can be identified through this analysis. Empirically, randomised controlled studies examining the causal effect of EI designs on trust formation when citizens interact with an array of AI services could be extremely valuable. Computationally, studies on the creation of reliable measures for assessing EI properties of AI systems are sorely needed – an important void in both the computational intelligence literature and psychology at large. On the topic of governance, studies examining the preconditions for the successful incorporation of EI principles into AI governance processes in governmental organisations will be important moving forward. Finally, comparative studies examining the role of cross-national differences in emotional norms, institutional traditions of trust building, and technological literacy in the relationship between EI design and trust formation could prove to be illuminating.

One fruitful area of research that merits particular attention is the connection between EI-based approaches to AI governance and care ethics (Gilligan, 1982; Held, 2006; Tronto, 1993). Care ethics, with its focus on the virtues of attentiveness, responsibility, competence, and responsiveness that underpin ethical behaviour, offers a philosophical foundation for EI-based approaches to AI governance not provided by the instrumentalist approach offered in this chapter.

7. CONCLUSION

The introduction of AI in public service provision may well prove to be among the most significant shifts in the domain of governance in today's world. How the implementation of such technologies may influence democratic legitimacy, institutional trust, and citizen wellbeing will depend not only on how technically advanced these systems turn out to be but also on how well they will reflect the kind of emotional intelligence that has traditionally been the foundation of public governance relations.

This chapter has established that emotional intelligence, as captured within the four branches theory of Mayer et al. (2016), the competency approach of Goleman (2020), and the trait theory of Petrides and Furnham (2001), is a theoretically rigorous and practical guide to addressing the issue of building the necessary trust for AI-powered public services. The EI-Trust Integration Framework outlined in this paper structures five complementary governance layers—Transparency, Empathy, Accountability, Relational, and Inclusion—corresponding to each of the EI dimensions.

Indeed, the results of comparative case study analysis of Estonia, Singapore, the United Kingdom, India, and the United States are consistent in confirming the framework's key argument, which holds that jurisdictions implementing EI as the underlying principle of their AI governance architecture are likely to see much stronger and more sustainable trust levels among their citizens as compared to other jurisdictions focusing on technical efficiency but neglecting emotional intelligence aspects altogether. Indeed, the US example shows quite clearly how dangerous and damaging can be the pursuit of an EI-lite strategy, where the lack of structure makes it impossible for people to believe the empathic rhetoric.

In conclusion, the policy recommendations discussed in Section 5 outline the action steps for the government if it is determined to actualise the democratic potential of AI while not overlooking the emotional side of governance, so valued by people and so essential for any form of democracy. This includes EI audits, CEIAs, EI-driven procurement requirements, civil servant training programs, multi-stakeholder trust observatories, and emotional transparency laws.

In the end, the thesis put forward by this chapter depends on the democratic belief that the relationship between government and citizen is not a service exchange, which can be perfected but rather a political relationship, which needs to be maintained through continual proof of competence, goodwill, and integrity. Emotional intelligence, if correctly defined, is not an add-on but a fundamental part of democratic politics, which artificial intelligence technology can facilitate provided it is well governed. Future chapters in this book will explore the additional aspects of this issue; hopefully, the theoretical framework set out above offers a fruitful basis for that endeavor.

REFERENCES

Abd-Alrazaq, A. A., Rababeh, A., Alajlani, M., Bewick, B. M., & Househ, M. (2020). Effectiveness and safety of using chatbots to improve mental health: Systematic review and meta-analysis. *Journal of Medical Internet Research, 22*(7), e16021. DOI: 10.2196/16021 PMID: 32673216

Acquisti, A., Brandimarte, L., & Loewenstein, G. (2015). Privacy and human behavior in the age of information. *Science, 347*(6221), 509–514. DOI: 10.1126/science.aaa1465 PMID: 25635091

Adadi, A., & Berrada, M. (2018). Peeking inside the black-box: A survey on explainable artificial intelligence (XAI). *IEEE Access : Practical Innovations, Open Solutions, 6*, 52138–52160. DOI: 10.1109/ACCESS.2018.2870052

Algorithmic Justice League. (2022). *Centering equity and justice in algorithmic impact assessment.* Algorithmic Justice League.

Bar-On, R. (2006). The Bar-On model of emotional-social intelligence (ESI). *Psicothema, 18*(Suppl.), 13–25. PMID: 17295953

Binns, R. (2018). Fairness in machine learning: Lessons from political philosophy. *Proceedings of the 2018 Conference on Fairness, Accountability, and Transparency*, 81(1), 149–159. DOI: 10.1145/3287560.3287583

Blind, P. K. (2007). Building trust in government in the twenty-first century: Review of literature and emerging issues [Paper presentation]. 7th Global Forum on Reinventing Government: Building Trust in Government, Vienna, Austria.

Bouckaert, G., & Van de Walle, S. (2003). Comparing measures of citizen trust and user satisfaction as indicators of 'good governance': Difficulties in linking trust and satisfaction indicators. *International Review of Administrative Sciences, 69*(3), 329–343. DOI: 10.1177/0020852303693003

Brackett, M. A. (2019). *Permission to feel: Unlocking the power of emotions to help our kids, ourselves, and our society thrive.* Celadon Books.

Brackett, M. A., & Mayer, J. D. (2003). Convergent, discriminant, and incremental validity of competing measures of emotional intelligence. *Personality & Social Psychology Bulletin, 29*(9), 1147–1158. DOI: 10.1177/0146167203254596 PMID: 15189610

Canadian Treasury Board. (2019). Directive on automated decision-making. Government of Canada. https://www.tbs-sct.gc.ca/pol/doc-eng.aspx?id=32592

Caruso, D. R., & Salovey, P. (2004). *The emotionally intelligent manager: How to develop and use the four key emotional skills of leadership*. Jossey-Bass.

Cath, C., Wachter, S., Mittelstadt, B., Taddeo, M., & Floridi, L. (2018). Artificial intelligence and the 'good society': The US, EU, and UK approach. *Science and Engineering Ethics*, *24*(2), 505–528. DOI: 10.1007/s11948-017-9901-7 PMID: 28353045

Côté, S. (2014). Emotional intelligence in organizations. *Annual Review of Organizational Psychology and Organizational Behavior*, *1*(1), 459–488. DOI: 10.1146/annurev-orgpsych-031413-091233

Council of Europe. (2024). Framework Convention on Artificial Intelligence and Human Rights, Democracy and the Rule of Law. Council of Europe Treaty Series No. 225.

Cummings, M. L. (2017). Automation bias in intelligent time critical decision support systems. AIAA 1st Intelligent Systems Technical Conference. DOI: 10.4324/9781315095080-17

Diakopoulos, N. (2016). Accountability in algorithmic decision making. *Communications of the ACM*, *59*(2), 56–62. DOI: 10.1145/2844110

Doshi-Velez, F., & Kim, B. (2017). Towards a rigorous science of interpretable machine learning. arXiv. https://doi.org//arXiv.1702.08608DOI: 10.48550

Dunleavy, P., Margetts, H., & Tinkler, J. (2022). The future of digital government. In Pichler, A., & Ghosh, C. (Eds.), *Handbook of digital government* (pp. 45–68). Edward Elgar.

Eubanks, V. (2018). *Automating inequality: How high-tech tools profile, police, and punish the poor*. St. Martin's Press.

European Commission. (2021). *Proposal for a regulation on a European approach for artificial intelligence (COM/2021/206 final)*. Publications Office of the European Union.

European Commission. (2022). *Standard Eurobarometer 98: Autumn 2022*. Publications Office of the European Union.

European Union. (2024). Regulation (EU) 2024/1689 of the European Parliament and of the Council laying down harmonised rules on artificial intelligence (Artificial Intelligence Act). Official Journal of the European Union, L series.

Feine, J., Gnewuch, U., Morana, S., & Maedche, A. (2019). A taxonomy of social cues for conversational agents. *International Journal of Human-Computer Studies*, *132*, 138–161. DOI: 10.1016/j.ijhcs.2019.07.009

Gilligan, C. (1982). *In a different voice: Psychological theory and women's development*. Harvard University Press.

Goddard, K., Roudsari, A., & Wyatt, J. C. (2012). Automation bias: A systematic review of frequency, effect mediators, and mitigators. *Journal of the American Medical Informatics Association : JAMIA*, *19*(1), 121–127. DOI: 10.1136/amiajnl-2011-000089 PMID: 21685142

Goleman, D. (1995). *Emotional intelligence: Why it can matter more than IQ*. Bantam Books.

Goleman, D. (2020). *Emotional intelligence: 25th anniversary edition*. Bantam Books.

Government Accountability Office. (2023). Artificial intelligence in benefits administration: Federal agencies' use of AI and related considerations. US GAO. https://www.gao.gov/products/gao-23-105517

GovTech Singapore. (2022). *LifeSG: Annual report and user satisfaction survey 2021–2022*. Government Technology Agency of Singapore.

Grimmelikhuijsen, S., Jilke, S., Olsen, A. L., & Tummers, L. (2017). Behavioral public administration: Combining insights from public administration and psychology. *Public Administration Review*, *77*(1), 45–56. DOI: 10.1111/puar.12609

Held, V. (2006). *The ethics of care: Personal, political, and global*. Oxford University Press.

IEEE. (2019). Ethically aligned design: A vision for prioritizing human well-being with autonomous and intelligent systems (Version 2). IEEE. https://standards.ieee.org/content/dam/ieee-standards/standards/web/documents/other/ead_v2.pdf

Jilke, S., Van Ryzin, G. G., & Van de Walle, S. (2019). Responses to decline in marketized public services: An experimental evaluation of choice overload. *Journal of Public Administration: Research and Theory*, *26*(3), 421–432. DOI: 10.1093/jopart/muv021

Joseph, D. L., & Newman, D. A. (2010). Emotional intelligence: An integrative meta-analysis and cascading model. *The Journal of Applied Psychology*, *95*(1), 54–78. DOI: 10.1037/a0017286 PMID: 20085406

Kalvet, T., Tiits, M., & Hinsberg, H. (2018). e-Government in Estonia: The success story and its lessons. E-Governance Institute, Tallinn University of Technology.

Kankanhalli, A., Charalabidis, Y., & Mellouli, S. (2019). IoT and AI for smart government: A research agenda. *Government Information Quarterly, 36*(2), 304–309. DOI: 10.1016/j.giq.2019.02.003

Lember, V., Brandsen, T., & Tõnurist, P. (2019). The potential impacts of digital technologies on co-production and co-creation. *Public Management Review, 21*(11), 1665–1686. DOI: 10.1080/14719037.2019.1619807

Levi, M., & Stoker, L. (2000). Political trust and trustworthiness. *Annual Review of Political Science, 3*(1), 475–507. DOI: 10.1146/annurev.polisci.3.1.475

Lips, M. (2020). *Digital government: Managing public sector reform in the digital era*. Routledge.

Lipton, Z. C. (2018). The mythos of model interpretability. *ACM Queue; Tomorrow's Computing Today, 16*(3), 31–57. DOI: 10.1145/3236386.3241340

Locke, E. A. (2005). Why emotional intelligence is an invalid concept. *Journal of Organizational Behavior, 26*(4), 425–431. DOI: 10.1002/job.318

Matthews, G., Zeidner, M., & Roberts, R. D. (2002). *Emotional intelligence: Science and myth*. MIT Press. DOI: 10.7551/mitpress/2704.001.0001

Mayer, J. D., & Salovey, P. (1997). What is emotional intelligence? In Salovey, P., & Sluyter, D. J. (Eds.), *Emotional development and emotional intelligence: Educational implications* (pp. 3–31). Basic Books.

Mayer, J. D., Salovey, P., & Caruso, D. R. (2016). The ability model of emotional intelligence: Principles and updates. *Emotion Review, 8*(4), 290–300. DOI: 10.1177/1754073916639667

Mayer, R. C., Davis, J. H., & Schoorman, F. D. (1995). An integrative model of organizational trust. *Academy of Management Review, 20*(3), 709–734. DOI: 10.2307/258792

Meijer, A., Lorenz, L., & Wessels, M. (2021). Algorithmization of bureaucratic decision-making. *Public Administration Review, 81*(3), 445–455. DOI: 10.1111/puar.13276

Meit, Y. (2023). *Digital India: Annual report 2022–23*. Ministry of Electronics and Information Technology, Government of India.

Mittelstadt, B. D., Allo, P., Taddeo, M., Wachter, S., & Floridi, L. (2016). The ethics of algorithms: Mapping the debate. *Big Data & Society, 3*(2), 1–21. DOI: 10.1177/2053951716679679

Needham, C. (2011). *Personalising public services: Understanding the personalisation narrative*. Policy Press.

NHS England. (2023). A plan for digital health and care. NHS England. https://www.england.nhs.uk/digitaltechnology/a-plan-for-digital-health-and-care/

NIST. (2023). *Artificial intelligence risk management framework (AI RMF 1.0) (NIST AI 100-1)*. National Institute of Standards and Technology., DOI: 10.6028/NIST.AI.100-1

O'Neil, C. (2016). *Weapons of math destruction: How big data increases inequality and threatens democracy*. Crown Publishers.

OECD. (2022). *Building trust to reinforce democracy: Main findings from the 2021 OECD survey on drivers of trust in public institutions*. OECD Publishing., DOI: 10.1787/b407f99c-

OECD. (2023). OECD framework for digital talent and skills in the public sector (OECD Working Papers on Public Governance, No. 50). OECD Publishing. https://doi.org/DOI: 10.1787/4e721530-en

Osborne, S. P., Radnor, Z., & Nasi, G. (2022). A new theory for public service management? Toward a (public) service-dominant approach. *American Review of Public Administration*, *43*(2), 135–158. DOI: 10.1177/0275074012466935

Pasquale, F. (2015). *The black box society: The secret algorithms that control money and information*. Harvard University Press. DOI: 10.4159/harvard.9780674736061

Petrides, K. V., & Furnham, A. (2001). Trait emotional intelligence: Psychometric investigation with reference to established trait taxonomies. *European Journal of Personality*, *15*(6), 425–448. DOI: 10.1002/per.416

Radin, B. A. (2019). *Policy tools: From implementation to governance*. Georgetown University Press.

Rao, A. S., Verweij, G., & Marwala, T. (2021). *Responsible AI in practice: Harnessing artificial intelligence for sustainable development*. IBM Institute for Business Value.

Ribeiro, M. T., Singh, S., & Guestrin, C. (2016). 'Why should I trust you?': Explaining the predictions of any classifier. Proceedings of the 22nd ACM SIGKDD International Conference on Knowledge Discovery and Data Mining, 1135–1144. DOI: 10.1145/2939672.2939778

Roberts, R. D., Zeidner, M., & Matthews, G. (2001). Does emotional intelligence meet traditional standards for an intelligence? Some new data and conclusions. *Emotion (Washington, D.C.), 1*(3), 196–231. DOI: 10.1037/1528-3542.1.3.196 PMID: 12934681

Robinson, L., Cotten, S. R., Ono, H., Quan-Haase, A., Mesch, G., Chen, W., Schulz, J., Hale, T. M., & Stern, M. J. (2015). Digital inequalities and why they matter. *Information Communication and Society, 18*(5), 569–582. DOI: 10.1080/1369118X.2015.1012532

Sharma, A., Mookherjee, S., & Patel, R. (2022). Emotional intelligence in digital public services: A systematic literature review. *Government Information Quarterly, 39*(4), 101742. DOI: 10.1016/j.giq.2022.101742

Solove, D. J. (2021). The myth of the privacy paradox. *The George Washington Law Review, 89*(1), 1–51.

Topol Review. (2019). *Preparing the healthcare workforce to deliver the digital future: An independent report on behalf of the Secretary of State for Health and Social Care*. NHS Health Education England.

Tronto, J. C. (1993). *Moral boundaries: A political argument for an ethic of care*. Routledge.

Tyler, T. R. (1990). *Why people obey the law*. Yale University Press.

Tyler, T. R. (2006). Psychological perspectives on legitimacy and legitimation. *Annual Review of Psychology, 57*(1), 375–400. DOI: 10.1146/annurev.psych.57.102904.190038 PMID: 16318600

Tyler, T. R., & Lind, E. A. (1992). A relational model of authority in groups. *Advances in Experimental Social Psychology, 25*, 115–191. DOI: 10.1016/S0065-2601(08)60283-X

United Nations. (2022). *UN e-government survey 2022: The future of digital government*. United Nations Department of Economic and Social Affairs.

Van der Meer, T. W. G. (2017). Political trust and the 'crisis of democracy.' In Oxford Research Encyclopedias. *Politics*. Advance online publication. DOI: 10.1093/acrefore/9780190228637.013.77

Van der Waal, M., Bakker, A. B., & Bhave, D. P. (2018). Emotional intelligence and performance. In Dulebohn, D. L., & Murray, B. (Eds.), *Research in personnel and human resources management* (Vol. 36, pp. 221–252). Emerald Publishing.

Van Dijk, J. A. G. M. (2020). *The digital divide*. Polity Press.

Vigoda-Gadot, E. (2021). Citizens and the new public service: Coproduction, co-management, and co-delivery in the age of digital governance. *Governance: An International Journal of Policy, Administration and Institutions*, *34*(2), 471–492. DOI: 10.1111/gove.12501

Vogl, T. M., Seidelin, C., Ganesh, B., & Bright, J. (2020). Smart technology and the emergence of algorithmic bureaucracy: Artificial intelligence in UK local authorities. *Public Administration Review*, *80*(6), 946–961. DOI: 10.1111/puar.13286

W3C. (2023). Web content accessibility guidelines (WCAG) 2.2. World Wide Web Consortium. https://www.w3.org/TR/WCAG22/

Wirtz, B. W., Weyerer, J. C., & Geyer, C. (2019). Artificial intelligence and the public sector: Applications and challenges. *International Journal of Public Administration*, *42*(7), 596–615. DOI: 10.1080/01900692.2018.1498103

World Bank. (2022). *Digital government flagship report: Improving public services through digital government.* World Bank Group.

Zeidner, M., Roberts, R. D., & Matthews, G. (2009). *What we know about emotional intelligence: How it affects learning, work, relationships, and our mental health.* MIT Press. DOI: 10.7551/mitpress/7404.001.0001

Zerilli, J., Knott, A., Maclaurin, J., & Gavaghan, C. (2019). Transparency in algorithmic and human decision-making: Is there a double standard? *Philosophy & Technology*, *32*(4), 661–683. DOI: 10.1007/s13347-018-0330-6

Zhou, L., Gao, J., Li, D., & Shum, H. Y. (2020). The design and implementation of XiaoIce, an empathetic social chatbot. *Computational Linguistics*, *46*(1), 53–93. DOI: 10.1162/coli_a_00368

Chapter 7
Decentralized Emotion-Aware Trust Frameworks in Digital Government

Zoya Naaz
http://orcid.org/0009-0005-7794-3730
IIMT University, Meerut, India

Vaibhav Sharma
http://orcid.org/0000-0003-0621-3712
IIMT University, Meerut, India

Zeba Rani
http://orcid.org/0009-0006-7648-6707
IIMT University, Meerut, India

Akshay Raj
http://orcid.org/0000-0002-0603-6720
IIMT University, Meerut, India

ABSTRACT

This chapter addresses a critical challenge in digital governance: integrating emotionally intelligent public services with privacy-preserving and trustworthy AI infrastructures. While Emotion AI can enhance citizen interactions and support responsive service delivery, its adoption is constrained by biometric privacy concerns, centralized data vulnerabilities, and evolving regulatory requirements. To address these challenges, the chapter proposes the Decentralized Emotion-Aware Trust Framework (DETF), which combines Edge AI, Federated Learning, and Blockchain technology. The framework enables real-time emotion recognition, collaborative model improvement without sharing raw biometric data, and transparent model

DOI: 10.4018/979-8-3373-9129-8.ch007

governance through decentralized audit trails. The DETF provides policymakers, public administrators, and system architects with a secure, ethical, and scalable blueprint for trustworthy AI-enabled public services.

1. INTRODUCTION

1.1 Background: The Shift Toward Empathetic Digital Government

The development of digital government in its current form, however, has traditionally emphasized the transactional nature of the process, the centralization of the structure and its efficiency more than the human and emotional needs of the citizens that they serve. In the transition from old systems to cloud computing, automation of portals and algorithmic assessment of queries, the interaction between government and citizens has grown more mechanized. Early concepts of e-government involved the digitization of forms and the automation of back-end databases. The success of such systems in reducing delays in standardized requests by citizens was overshadowed by the depersonalizing of public service delivery.(Shark, 2022)

Modern theories of public administration are conscious of the fact that satisfaction, compliance, and system-wide trust have much to do with the empathic and responsive nature of the administrative process. Indeed, when citizens interface with the state machinery, such interactions typically occur in a vulnerable context—whether claiming unemployment allowances, securing disability payments, challenging tax assessments, or pleading for emergency assistance during disasters. Therefore, an important transformation is being witnessed in different parts of the world—a move from transactional digital governance to empathic digital governance. Such sophisticated forms of digital governance call for socio-technical systems that can understand the psychological and emotional condition of the citizen in the course of interaction(Nocoń et al., 2025).

1.2 The Problem: The "Cold" Digital State and Operational Friction

When public service platforms lack situational and emotional awareness, they manifest what contemporary political scientists refer to as a "cold" digital state—an administrative environment characterized by rigid error codes, opaque automated rejections, unyielding validation fields, and binary logic pathways that possess zero capacity to accommodate human vulnerability or cognitive overload. In traditional brick-and-mortar institutions, a seasoned clerk can read a citizen's body language, detect micro-expressions of confusion, or note signs of extreme stress, subsequently altering their tone, explaining complex jargon, or providing manual guidance. When these interactions are fully automated, however, this responsive buffer is completely lost.(Peeters, 2023)

1.3 The Privacy-Trust Paradox: Affective Computing vs. Biometric Surveillance

The implementation of affective computing (Emotion AI) technology in the provision of public services is a paradox of great sensitivity and depth. On one hand, emotion detection technology presents a promising prospect for revolutionizing how humanized interactions between government agencies and citizens take place and for minimizing the transaction costs of street-level bureaucracy. On the other hand, it poses grave risks to privacy and human rights.(Farida et al., 2020)

Figure 1. Privacy–Trust Paradox of Emotion AI in Public Service.

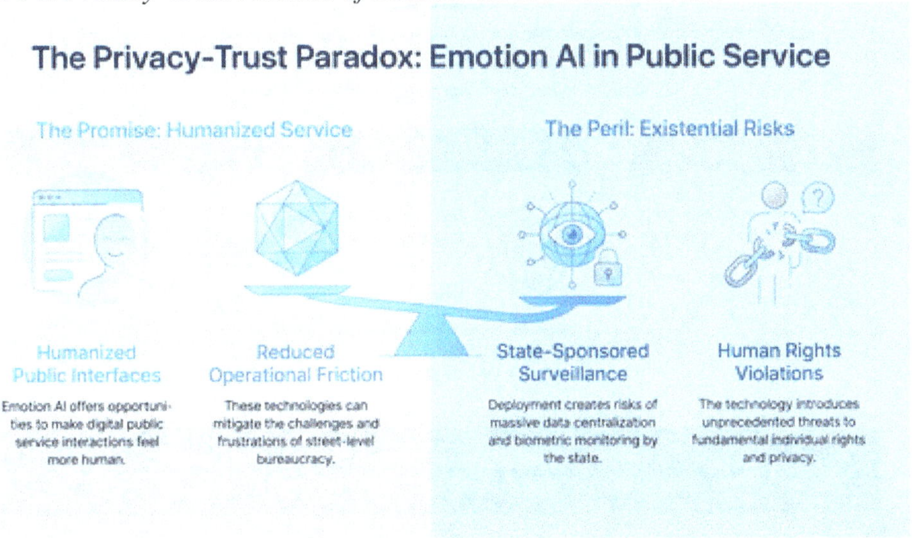

Figure 1 symbolizes the basic dilemma that arises from implementing Emotion AI in the provision of public services. In the first place, Emotion AI technology has the ability to make public digital interactions more human-centered by responding to citizens' emotional states. In addition, it can help improve efficiency in service provision through the same means. On the other hand, using such technology poses serious questions about ethics and governance, mainly in terms of surveillance on a large scale, biometric data harvesting, and threats to privacy.

1.4 Chapter Objectives and Contributions

Artificial Intelligence's growing involvement in public administration has opened doors to new possibilities in terms of enhancing service accessibility, response, and citizen engagement. On the other hand, even as modern-day digital government initiatives try to address these problems, the primary issue that remains unaddressed in the process is striking a balance between delivering empathic services and ensuring citizen privacy. Emotion Artificial Intelligence technology may prove extremely useful in understanding citizen reactions in terms of distress, confusion, and frustration; yet, its adoption in public administration comes with many concerns. (Rahmath Nisha et al., 2025)

Figure 2. Decentralized Emotion-Aware Trust Framework (DETF)

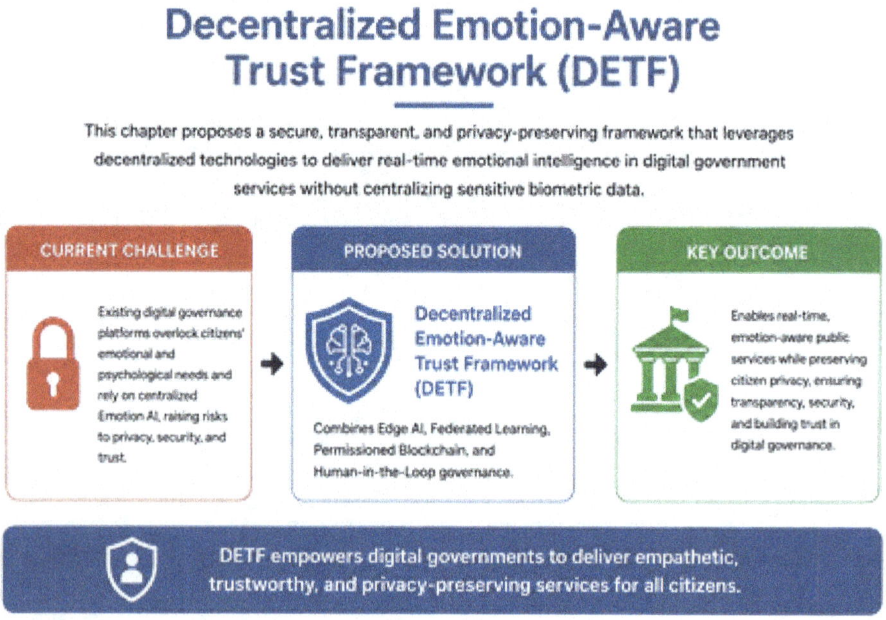

Figure 2 Presents the proposed Decentralized Emotion-Aware Trust Framework (DETF), which aims to solve the issues related to traditional Emotion AI technologies used for digital governance. The approach will tackle the problems faced by centralized emotion recognition through biometric data, particularly privacy and security problems. DETF utilizes Edge AI, Federated Learning, Permissioned Blockchain, and Human-in-the-Loop governance, enabling real-time emotional intelligence while protecting the privacy of citizens. Through the localized processing of personal data

and management of the models, the system ensures that digital governance services provided are trustful and oriented towards serving the citizens' needs.

This chapter is primarily focused on designing a safe, reliable, and privacy-friendly approach towards integrating emotion-aware artificial intelligence into digital government services. This chapter specifically aims at assessing the inadequacies of current digital government platforms with regards to fulfilling the emotional and psychological needs of citizens during public service transactions, analyzing the issues related to privacy, security, and ethics regarding the use of centralized Emotion AI systems. The chapter attempts to propose Decentralized Emotion-Aware Trust Framework (DETF) as a means of overcoming the shortcomings of current approaches.(Goel, 2024)

2. LITERATURE REVIEW

2.1 Evolution of Digital Government

The digital government landscape has seen many changes during the last thirty years; it started with the mere process of digitizing processes, but soon became smarter and more citizen-focused. Initially, e-governance solutions were concerned mostly with the process of transforming traditional bureaucratic processes that involved paperwork into digital ones. This stage of development was concerned with digitizing all forms, making portals, and automating work processes. Even though this process had many advantages, including shorter processing times and cost-saving measures, it was rather transactional and did not provide an opportunity for engaging citizens.(S. Sharma et al., 2021)

New developments in AI, machine learning, cloud computing, and data analytics are pushing the trend towards smart government approaches. Chatbots powered by AI, predictive analytics solutions, automated eligibility screening tools, and intelligent decision support tools are becoming a part of the work process in public administration. While these new technologies have increased service efficiency and scalability, their primary focus still lies on process improvement rather than a customer-oriented approach.(Angın, 2025)

2.2 Emotion AI and Affective Computing in Public Services

2.2.1 Definition and Evolution of Emotion AI

Emotion AI or affective computing is the ability of intelligent systems to identify and understand human emotions. A voice of 1997, it is a fusion of artificial intelligence and human-computer interaction that greatly enhances the understanding of emotions. The recent progress in machine learning, computer vision and natural language processing has fueled the growing relevance of Emotion AI in intelligent and adaptive digital services based on multiple modalities, such as emotion detected via facial expression, speech, text and physiological signals.(Kapoor & Verma, 2024)

2.2.2 Applications of Emotion AI in Public Services

Emotion AI can be used in various applications for public services, such as citizen-centric public services that have a great potential to benefit from Emotion AI. It could enhance the performance of government chatbots, healthcare support lines, and grievance redressal systems by recognising emotional cues like frustration or confusion and offering individualised help. Emotion-aware systems can also help to make digital government services more accessible and user-friendly, especially for the elderly population and people with limited digital literacy, which can lead to more responsive and inclusive digital government services.(İzgi, 2025)

2.2.3 Research Gap and Need for Privacy-Preserving Emotion AI

Most of the previous works are targeted at enhancing emotion recognition and rapid attention is given to privacy-preserving and governance-oriented applications in digital government. In the current approaches, decentralized intelligence, transparent audit mechanisms and human oversight are not well combined. This underscores the importance of frameworks to enable trustworthy and citizen-centric Emotion AI and to uphold privacy, accountability and ethical AI governance.(Gremsl & Hödl, 2022)

Recent studies indicate that Emotion AI can enhance citizen-centric services by enabling adaptive and context-sensitive interactions, but its public-sector adoption remains constrained by privacy, fairness, and interpretability concerns. Existing research largely emphasizes recognition accuracy and service personalization, while comparatively limited attention is given to privacy-preserving architectures, institutional accountability, and human oversight. This gap indicates the need to examine Emotion AI not only as a technical capability but also as a component of responsible digital governance.

2.3 Edge AI for Privacy-Preserving Public Service Delivery

Edge AI is a new paradigm of AI, which is intended to process the data and make intelligent decisions on local devices instead of centralized cloud servers. Edge AI handles sensitive data locally, which respects privacy and minimizes the transmission of data that is unwanted. This is especially attractive for citizen-centric digital government services. Edge AI enables real-time processing of citizen interactions, which can be executed on the device securely, like emotion recognition and service recommendations. It also provides faster response times, enhanced cybersecurity measures, and better data privacy protection than traditional cloud-based AI, allowing for more efficient and reliable public services. Additionally, Edge AI's real-time processing capabilities make it an ideal solution for applications that depend on responsive citizen support and flexible service delivery.(Dintakurthy et al., 2025)

Table 1. Comparison of Cloud-Based AI and Edge AI for Privacy-Preserving Digital Government Services

Parameter	Cloud-Based AI	Edge AI
Data Processing	Centralized	Local
Privacy Protection	Moderate	High
Latency	Higher	Lower
Internet Dependency	High	Low
Raw Data Transmission	Required	Minimal
Real-Time Performance	Moderate	High
Security Risks	Higher	Lower
Suitability for Citizen-Centric Services	Moderate	High

Table 1 compares Cloud-Based AI and Edge AI across key parameters, demonstrating that Edge AI provides stronger privacy protection, lower latency, reduced data transmission, and greater suitability for secure, citizen-centric digital government services.

While it offers numerous benefits, Edge AI also has its drawbacks, including limited processing power, device security issues, and interoperability concerns. Furthermore, current research has mostly concentrated on business and industry, and has been largely absent in citizen-centric digital governance. They raise the importance of having integrated governance involving a combination of edge AI, alongside decentralized learning, transparency, and human governance.

Recent research highlights Edge AI as an important approach for reducing latency and limiting the transmission of sensitive data in distributed intelligent systems. Its application to public services is particularly relevant where real-time processing and privacy are required. However, existing studies largely emphasize technical performance, while comparatively less attention is given to governance, accountability, and integration with decentralized learning. This gap supports the need for a governance-oriented approach that combines Edge AI with privacy, transparency, and human oversight.

2.4 Federated Learning for Decentralized Government Intelligence

Federated Learning (FL) is a distributed machine learning method that allows several devices or institutions to collectively improve the learning of AI models without exchanging the actual data. Federated Learning is different from centralized AI systems because it does not share data with the central server but only model updates. It is especially appropriate for digital government systems with citizens' personal data.(Vasava et al., 2024)

In Federated Learning, AI models are trained locally on devices or institution's datasets, while only the encrypted model parameters are transmitted to the server for building a global AI model. Citizen data stay at their origin, so FL improves the protection of privacy while allowing collaborative and decentralized intelligence among government agencies.Federated Learning however, suffers from communication overhead, data heterogeneity, data privacy leakage and security concerns including model poisoning attacks. Another key factor to take into account for wide-spread deployment is the interoperability of the governmental infrastructures. (Sprenkamp et al., 2023)

Although there have been some applications of Federated Learning in healthcare and commercial sectors, research on emotion-aware and trustworthy digital government applications is still scarce. Furthermore, its compatibility with other emerging technologies like Edge AI, blockchain audit systems and human oversight has not been extensively studied. The constraints underscore the importance of governance mechanisms like the proposed Decentralized Emotion-Aware Trust Framework (DETF) for ensuring both privacy-respecting and accountable AI-driven public service delivery.(Bhimavarapu, 2025)

Existing research demonstrates the potential of Federated Learning for privacy-preserving collaborative intelligence across distributed institutions. However, studies have primarily focused on technical efficiency, model performance, and applications in healthcare and commercial environments. Comparatively limited research examines its integration with public-sector governance requirements, particularly fairness, accountability, and human oversight. This gap indicates the need to investigate Federated Learning as part of an integrated governance framework for decentralized and trustworthy public services.

2.5 Blockchain Based Trust and Accountability Architectures

Blockchain is a decentralized and distributed ledger technology that facilitates the secure, transparent and immutable maintenance of records that can be accessed by multiple parties. A key attribute is its decentralisation, traceability and cryptographic security, making it well suited for digital government applications where trust and accountability are a key requirement.(Sharma, 2020)

Blockchain works using distributed ledgers and consensus mechanisms to validate transactions and track them in a tamper-proof way. Permissioned blockchain architectures are particularly significant in digital government, where they facilitate transparency and compliance with regulations while allowing access to only authorized entities. This will enable government bodies to ensure secure audit trails while still keeping citizen data private. The use of blockchain in public service delivery helps ensure trustworthy records of administrative actions, AI model updates, and human intervention, allowing for transparent and auditable management. It has applications in digital government such as digital identity management, healthcare services, public procurement and citizen grievance redressal system.(Mohan & Jayalakshmi, 2025)

However, blockchain has some drawbacks, such as scalability, interoperability, computational complexity, and regulation. Previous studies have mainly taken a financial and commercial perspective, while studies on emotion-aware and privacy-preserving digital government services are limited. Further, the applications of blockchain, Edge AI, and the combination of AI and human oversight are not yet extensively studied. The restrictions underscore the importance of governance-oriented solutions that can benefit from the use of blockchain technology to enhance transparency, accountability, and trust in public services using AI.(Kulothungan, 2025)

The comparison highlights the distinct governance contribution of DETF. Centralized Emotion AI primarily emphasizes service intelligence but exposes greater privacy and accountability concerns, while privacy-preserving AI improves data protection without necessarily providing integrated auditability or administrative oversight. DETF extends these approaches by combining decentralized processing, collaborative learning, blockchain-based auditability, and human oversight within a single governance architecture. The comparison is conceptual and indicates intended governance capabilities rather than empirically measured performance.

Table 2. Comparative Analysis of Existing AI Governance Approaches

Evaluation Parameter	**Centralized Emotion AI Systems**	**Privacy-Preserving AI Approaches**	**Proposed DETF Framework**
Emotion-Aware Service Delivery	High	Moderate	High
Privacy Protection	Low	High	High
Transparency	Low	Moderate	High
Accountability	Low	Moderate	High

continued on following page

Table 2. Continued

Evaluation Parameter	Centralized Emotion AI Systems	Privacy-Preserving AI Approaches	Proposed DETF Framework
Human Oversight	Limited	Moderate	High
Auditability	Low	Limited	High
Citizen Trust	Moderate	Moderate	High
Scalability	Moderate	High	High
Decentralized Intelligence	Low	Moderate	High
Governance Compliance	Moderate	Moderate	High
Suitability for Digital Government	Moderate	High	High

The comparative analysis in Table 2 shows that centralized systems of Emotion AI offer intelligent and adaptive service capabilities, but are often constrained by privacy, transparency and accountability issues. There are a number of these concerns that are mitigated with privacy preserving AI methods, which are decentralized and rely on computation methods that are secure; however, there is not a complete governance framework and human oversight in place. Overall, DETF's contribution lies not in replacing existing AI governance approaches but in integrating complementary capabilities into a unified framework for trustworthy, citizen-centric public services.

Research on blockchain demonstrates its potential to strengthen transparency, traceability, and accountability through tamper-resistant records. Although blockchain has been explored in areas such as digital identity, healthcare, and public administration, its integration with privacy-preserving AI remains relatively limited. In particular, the combined use of blockchain, Edge AI, and Federated Learning for trustworthy public services requires further investigation. This gap provides a basis for incorporating blockchain-based auditability within the proposed DETF framework.

2.6 Human-Centered AI Governance and Administrative Oversight

As AI becomes ever more pervasive in public administration, it has been stressed by academics and policy-makers alike that there needs to be effective human oversight of the development and deployment of algorithmic systems. Human-centric governance of AI aims at ensuring that technological advances continue to serve democratic objectives and align with human rights and accountability standards. AI is meant to complement human decision-making in public administration without eliminating human oversight.(Паламарчук, 2024)

Modern regulatory regimes, such as the EU AI Act, focus on the importance of human oversight, transparency, accountability, and explanation in AI systems that present risks. Nevertheless, current approaches to AI governance tend to view human oversight as a safeguarding process, not an inherent part of the architecture. Thus, the development of approaches that would merge the provision of emotion-aware services with privacy protection, decentralization of trust processes, and human involvement is necessary. These requirements become the basis for the creation of DETF.(R. S. Kim, 2026)

Table 3. Comparative Analysis of Core Technologies for Emotion-Aware Digital Government

Technology	Primary Function	Key Strengths	Major Limitations
Emotion AI	Detection and interpretation of human emotions	Enhances citizen experience, adaptive service delivery, empathetic interactions	Privacy concerns, biometric surveillance risks, cultural bias
Edge AI	Localized processing of AI workloads on user devices	Reduced latency, enhanced privacy, lower data transmission requirements	Resource constraints, device heterogeneity, model optimization challenges
Federated Learning	Collaborative model training without centralized data collection	Privacy preservation, distributed intelligence, regulatory compliance	Communication overhead, model poisoning risks, aggregation complexity
Permissioned Blockchain	Immutable record-keeping and decentralized trust management	Transparency, auditability, traceability, accountability	Scalability limitations, governance complexity, implementation costs
Human-in-the-Loop Governance	Human oversight of AI-assisted decisions	Accountability, ethical compliance, administrative discretion	Increased operational effort, slower decision-making in certain scenarios

As shown in Table 3, Each of these technologies meets certain criteria for trustworthy digital governance but has its limitations as well when used on its own. Emotion AI is great at delivering empathic services but raises privacy concerns; Edge AI offers enhanced privacy but does not offer any learning capabilities.

3. RESEARCH GAP ANALYSIS

3.1 Limitations of Existing Digital Government Architectures

Although there have been major improvements in the field of digital transformation, even the most advanced modern-day digital governments are mainly transactional in their functioning. The current systems are mainly geared toward efficiency and effectiveness without regard for the health and feelings of the citizens. With AI being increasingly incorporated into public services, data retrieval, qualification, and advice processes have become automated, but they do not account for emotions of the citizenry.(Mulyasari & Jaya Wardana, 2025)

Similarly, while Edge AI and Federated Learning have emerged as two potentially powerful solutions for processing data in a distributed fashion and ensuring that privacy is not compromised, most current iterations of those systems emphasize only performance issues without considering governance considerations. Existing systems do not include features that could ensure that there is a transparent way to trace inferences about emotions and the way they are made, tested, and used. (Kanipakam et al., 2025)

3.2 Regulatory and Ethical Challenges

There is no denying that Emotion AI in public administration raises numerous legal and ethical issues. Today's regulation, as exemplified by the EU AI Act, GDPR, and OECD AI Principles, highlights the importance of transparency, accountability, fairness, explainability, and human control for high-risk AI systems. Emotion detection techniques have come under greater regulatory scrutiny owing to their potential to affect privacy and individual freedoms.(Ingber & Andalibi, 2025)

Figure 3. Regulatory Response Framework for Emotion AI Governance

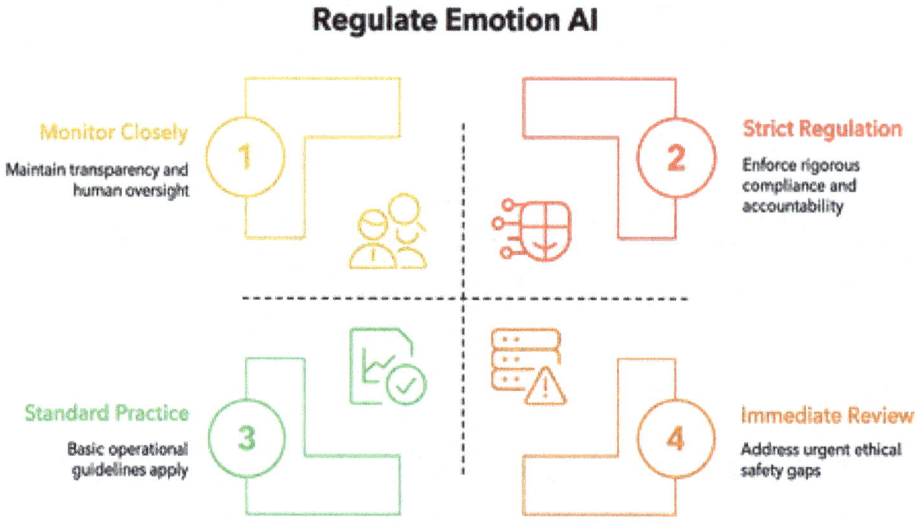

Figure 3 proposes a risk-based regulatory model for the governance of Emotion AI systems in public and organizational domains. According to the proposed regulatory model, the responses to the use of AI for emotion recognition are divided into four categories, depending on the risks related to the possible ethics, privacy, and societal impact. The low-risk applications can function with minimal regulation and general guidelines, while high-risk applications need more supervision and control.

The second critical issue relates to algorithmic bias. Studies show that emotion detection tools perform differently when analysing data from various demographic groups, cultures, and languages. This may create an uneven playing field when delivering public services to the population.(Schmitz et al., 2022)

3.3 Research Gap Matrix

Despite numerous studies that individually address Emotion AI, Federated Learning, Blockchain technology, and AI Governance, there is a paucity of research that combines all four technologies in an attempt to design a comprehensive and integrated solution to achieve trustworthy digital government. Most research on Emotion AI emphasizes accuracy at the expense of issues of governance and accountability. The studies on blockchain technology and governance stress auditability and transparency while neglecting emotions. Federated Learning studies concentrate mainly on learning algorithms and privacy while neglecting trust.(Rahmath Nisha et al., 2025)

Table 4. Research Gap Matrix

Research Domain	Emotion Awareness	Privacy Preservation	Federated Learning	Blockchain Auditability	Integrated Governance
Emotion AI Studies	Yes	Limited	No	No	Limited
Edge AI Research	Limited	Yes	No	No	No
Federated Learning Studies	No	Yes	Yes	No	No
Blockchain Governance Studies	No	Limited	No	Yes	Limited
Trustworthy AI Governance Research	Limited	Partial	No	No	Yes
Proposed DETF Framework	Yes	Yes	Yes	Yes	Yes

As illustrated in Table 4, Existing research efforts typically examine each facet of trustworthy artificial intelligence (AI) governance separately. What does not happen is integrating emotion detection, decentralized machine learning, blockchain-based accountability, privacy preservation, and human-centric governance in one coherent approach to the problem. This work attempts to fill this knowledge void through integration of all these techniques in a new DETF architecture.

Building on these gaps, DETF makes three complementary contributions. First, it provides a theoretical integration of Emotion AI with privacy-preserving and accountability mechanisms for digital government. Second, it connects Edge AI, Federated Learning, Blockchain, and Human-in-the-Loop Governance within a unified architecture. Third, it establishes governance boundaries and a conceptual trust quantification mechanism to support responsible implementation. These contributions position DETF as a governance-oriented framework rather than solely a technical architecture.

3.4 Need for an Integrated Governance Framework

AI technologies are increasingly used for digital government, it has become clear that there is a need for new governance mechanisms that will ensure that AI can support service delivery while maintaining privacy, transparency and accountability. Although Emotion AI, Edge AI, Federated Learning, and blockchain can solve partial problems, alone, they are not enough to meet citizen-centric public services' governance needs. Digital government systems must be multi-faceted, incorporating mechanisms that can achieve both privacy protection and decentralized intelligence, auditability and human oversight at the same time. However, as these complementary capabilities are needed to enable trustworthy AI-powered public services, there is a need to combine these capabilities in a governance-oriented framework. The proposed Decentralized Emotion-Aware Trust Framework (DETF) tackles this need by embedding these technologies into a responsible AI governance framework.(Li, 2025)

4. THEORETICAL FOUNDATION OF DETF

The DETF framework is based on principles of responsible and citizen-centric AI governance. It combines complementary technologies to solve big governance problems in the use of Emotion AI in the digital government. DETF is not a technical solution, but a combination of technological capabilities and public-sector needs including privacy protection, transparency, accountability, and administrative responsibility.(Scribano & Korstanje, 2023)

Table 5: Governance challenge with Governance Capability and DETF Component

Governance Challenge	DETF Component	Governance Capability
Citizen-centric service delivery	Emotion AI	Emotion-aware interactions
Privacy protection	Edge AI	Local data processing
Decentralized intelligence	Federated Learning	Collaborative model training
Transparency and accountability	Blockchain	Secure audit trails
Human oversight	Human-in-the-Loop Governance	Ethical and administrative control

In Table 5, Every component of DETF tackles one governance issue, and altogether supports trustworthy digital government services. Combining these technologies also helps DETF to be more responsive to the needs of its services, while maintaining citizen privacy and administrative accountability. Thus, DETF is an approach that makes sense for public sector governance environments in responsible adoption of Emotion AI.

The theoretical logic of DETF is based on the alignment of technological capabilities with distinct governance requirements. Emotion AI addresses service responsiveness by identifying interaction difficulties; Edge AI supports privacy through local processing; Federated Learning enables decentralized intelligence without sharing raw data; Blockchain strengthens transparency and accountability through auditable records; and Human-in-the-Loop Governance preserves administrative responsibility. Thus, DETF is not merely a combination of technologies but an integrated governance mechanism in which each component addresses a specific risk or requirement of AI-enabled public services.

5. THE DECENTRALIZED EMOTION-AWARE TRUST FRAMEWORK (DETF) ARCHITECTURE

5.1 Architectural Overview: The Multi-Layer Hybrid Ecosystem

The gaps found between both sociotechnical aspects and to tackle the paradox of privacy versus trust, this chapter suggests the Decentralized Emotion-Aware Trust Framework (DETF). The DETF framework is an advanced secure architecture, incorporating Edge Artificial Intelligence (Edge AI), Federated Learning (FL), and Permissioned Blockchain technologies into a comprehensive ecosystem able to provide empathic services to citizens.(Sudhakar, 2025)

Within DETF, Emotion AI is restricted to service interaction and communication support rather than administrative decision-making. Emotional signals may be used to identify confusion, frustration, or distress and trigger assistance or human intervention. They should not determine welfare eligibility, resource allocation, penalties, or citizen profiling. Final decisions affecting citizens remain under authorized human officials, ensuring that emotional inference does not directly produce adverse administrative outcomes.

Figure 4 below as shown in the approach used for designing the DETF is based on a zero trust model where the original biometric data always stays on the citizen's local machine, while any algorithm modifications are always traceable using the distributed ledger system. The decentralized model ensures there is minimal risk of surveillance, while still ensuring maximum transparency and accountability. The architecture of DETF consists of three major interconnected layers that interact using encrypted communication protocols(Nandy & Bhattacharyya, 2025).

Figure 4. Architecture of the Decentralized Emotion-Aware Trust Framework (DETF).

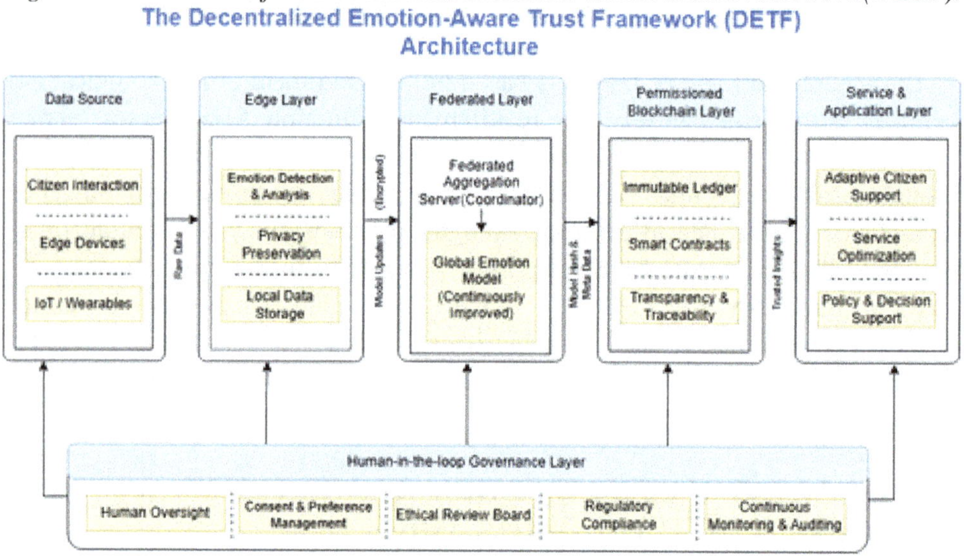

Figure 4 is an example of the multiple layers constituting the Decentralized Emotion-Aware Trust Framework (DETF) in privacy-preserving emotion-aware digital governance. The process starts with the citizens' interactions at the Edge Devices level and creates contextual data that is analyzed locally by the Edge AI layer for emotion detection in a way that maintains privacy via encryption and data minimization. The encryption-based model improvements are then exchanged within the Federated Learning layer and create an improved global emotion model without the transfer of any raw data. The Permissioned Blockchain layer enables transparency, auditing, and trust with an immutable ledger and smart contracts.

Ultimately, emotion-aware services are provided by leveraging the Human-in-the-Loop governance layer (Chowdhary et al., 2025).

5.2 Layer 1: Edge-Based Multimodal Emotion Recognition (Facial & Vocal Telemetry)

DETF's foundational layer resides wholly in the secure execution environment of the citizen's own local device such as smartphones, personal computers, or public service kiosks. The foundational layer conducts emotion recognition in real time in a multimodal manner using localized computing mechanisms which turn sensor-based devices into privacy-friendly analysis tools. In place of sending out videos and audio feeds to cloud servers, the emotions will be inferred locally using computationally efficient machine learning algorithms.(Zheng & Zhou, 2023)

Figure 5. DETF Security Architecture

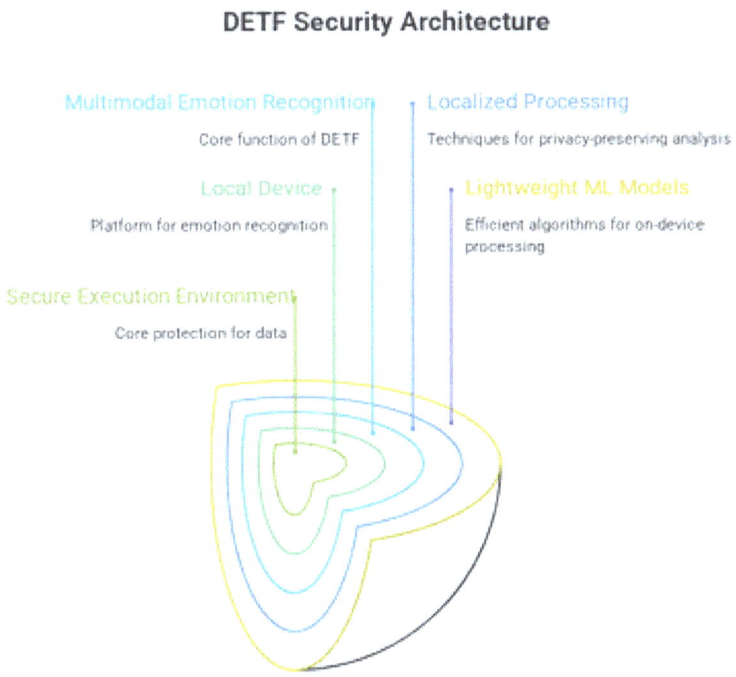

Figure 5 This diagram shows the architecture of the security system within the DETF framework to provide a privacy-preserving and efficient emotion recogni-

tion solution. This architecture is composed of several interconnected layers, each offering a distinct security and processing feature.

Firstly, the Local Device layer allows the recognition of emotions on the user's device, avoiding any leakage of information outside. In addition, the Secure Execution Environment helps secure sensitive information and provides trusted data processing. Meanwhile, Multimodal Emotion Recognition involves analysing the data obtained from various input sources to correctly recognize users' emotions. Furthermore, Localized Processing allows privacy-conscious processing without sending unencrypted data to third-party servers. Finally, Lightweight Machine Learning Models make it easier to run algorithms efficiently. The facial analysis module extracts representative facial landmarks associated with affective states such as frustration, anxiety, and confusion. Lightweight convolutional neural networks (CNNs) process these features locally to generate emotional inferences without storing raw image data. Similarly, the vocal analysis module captures audio through a temporary buffer and extracts acoustic features such as Mel-Frequency Cepstral Coefficients (MFCCs), pitch frequency, and spectral energy indicators. These features are subsequently analyzed by a local inference engine to estimate the citizen's emotional state.(Ahmad et al., 2025)

The emotional assessment generated by the local model is represented as a distress vector:

$$D_v = (F, A, C)$$

(F) represents the Frustration Score,

(A) represents the Anxiety Score, and

(C) represents the Confusion Score.

The components of the distress vector are summarized in Table 6.

Table 6. Distress Vector Components

Variable	**Description**
F	Frustration Score
A	Anxiety Score
C	Confusion Score

Once emotional classification is completed and the local interface is adapted accordingly, all raw biometric indicators are immediately removed from volatile memory. This privacy-preserving mechanism significantly reduces the risk of unauthorized data extraction and aligns with data minimization principles advocated by contemporary AI governance frameworks.(Durovic & Corno, 2024)

5.3 Layer 2: Privacy-Preserving Collaborative Optimization via Federated Learning (FL)

To ensure that the model improves constantly without sacrificing citizen privacy, the DETF uses an approach based on Federated Learning (FL). Contrary to machine learning models that aggregate data at a central location, FL allows devices to work together to increase the performance of the model without sharing raw biometric data.(Subramaniam & Palanisamy, 2023)

After citizens interact with the system, the performance of the model can be evaluated using validation procedures performed by the user. Depending on these results, local gradients indicating what adjustments should be done to increase accuracy for emotion recognition in future instances will be calculated.(Darji, 2025)

Figure 6. Privacy-Preserving Continuous Model Improvement through Federated Learning.

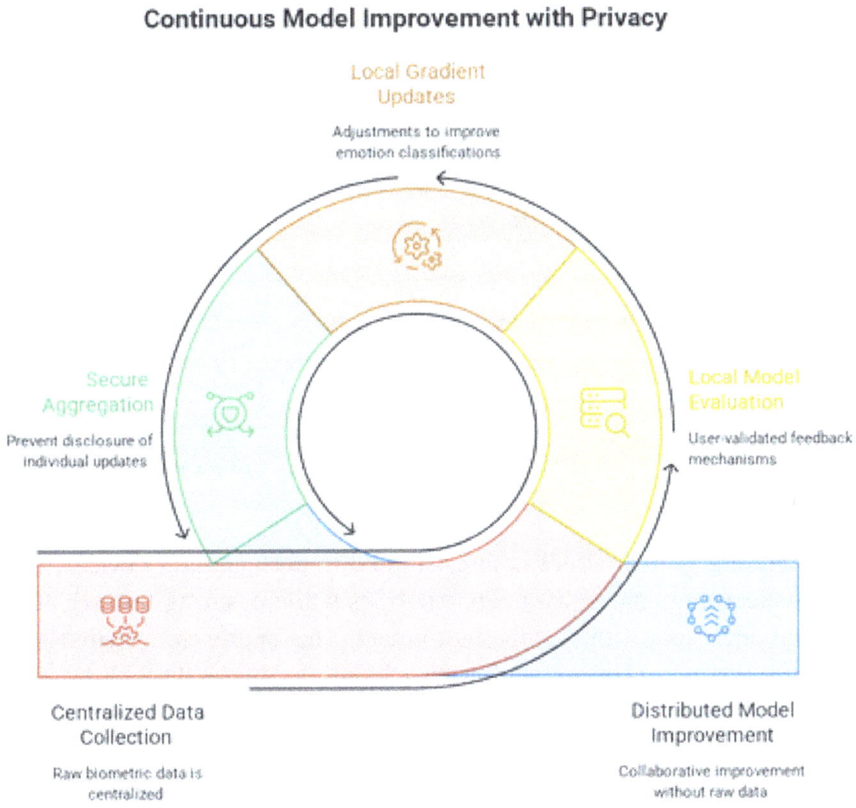

Figure 6 presents the federated learning flow used in the Decentralized Emotion-Aware Trust Framework (DETF) for improving the model constantly while ensuring that user privacy is respected. In contrast to traditional systems that depend on collecting raw biometric information in a central location, the new framework stores all personal information locally. This includes the steps of locally assessing the model, computing gradients, and aggregating the updated parameters using encryption. Aggregated gradient updates improve the model distributed by utilizing updated information without sharing specific data records. In doing so, emotion recognition accuracy is increased alongside data security. The aggregation process follows the Federated Averaging (FedAvg) algorithm(Nandi et al., 2023):

$$W_{t+1} = \sum_{i=1}^{k} \frac{n_i}{n} w_t^i$$

where:
(K) denotes the number of participating devices,
(n_i) represents the number of training samples at device (i),
(n) represents the total number of samples across all devices, and
(w_t^i) denotes the local model parameters at training round (t).

The parameters used within the federated optimization process are summarized in Table 7.

Table 7. Federated Learning Parameters

Symbol	Meaning
K	Number of participating devices
n	Local training samples
n	Total training samples
w_t^i	Local model parameters
W_{t+1}	Updated global model

The resulting global model is redistributed to participating devices, enabling continuous learning across diverse populations while ensuring that sensitive biometric data never leaves the local environment. This approach contributes to both privacy preservation and the mitigation of socio-cultural biases through decentralized learning.(Bouldjedri et al., 2025)

5.4 Layer 3: Immutable Provenance and Consensus via Permissioned Blockchain

The layer for trust and accountability within the DETF architecture is enabled using permissioned blockchain technology, specifically with the use of Hyperledger Fabric. In order to build trust in the administration of governance with the help of artificial intelligence, there needs to be an awareness of how the algorithm models change and impact the process of governing.(Pasupuleti, 2025)

Figure 7. DETF Trust and Accountability Framework

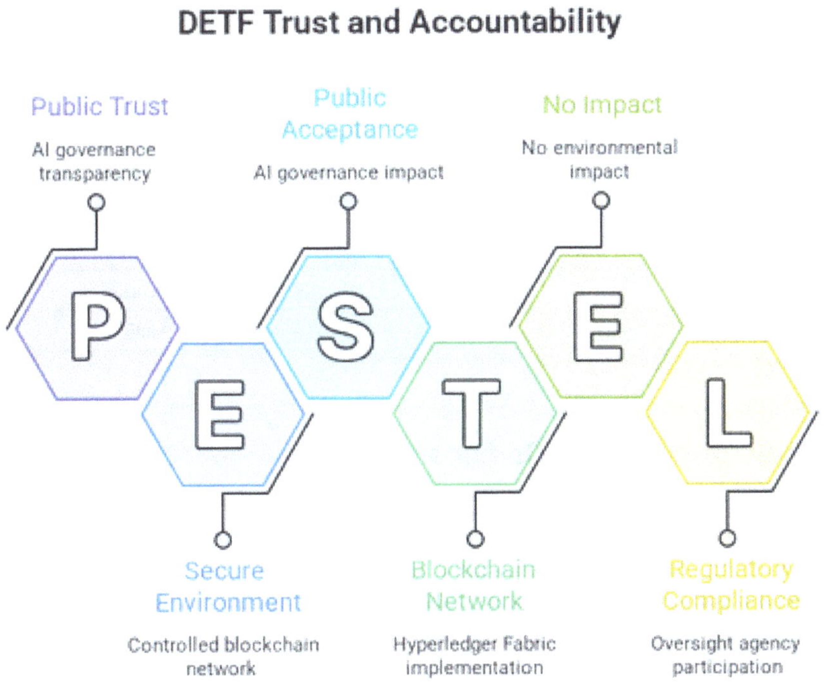

Figure 7 discusses the Trust and Accountability model of DETF, including the core components that guarantee transparency, security, and compliance with regulations of AI-based systems for emotion recognition. Public Trust is assured through the governance of AI in a way that creates trust among users and helps with proper functioning. Public Acceptance is ensured through appropriate governance that solves issues about the application of AI in society.

5.4.1 Smart Contract (Chain code) Logic

Such rules are embedded into the Hyper ledger Fabric chain code, and when there is an update to a model, the smart contract will assess the pre-defined parameters for compliance, such as the quality of the data, its performance capabilities, and the degree of fairness. Any model which does not meet the defined requirements can be refused.(Kawahara, 2020)

Once it passes these checks successfully, all metadata about the cycle is logged on the blockchain. This data includes a cryptographic hash for the model, the version number, the date and time of generation, and metadata about the nodes involved. The composition of blockchain records maintained within the DETF is summarized in Table 8.(Kaswan et al., 2022)

Table 8. Blockchain Record Structure

Ledger Field	Purpose
Model Hash	Integrity Verification
Version ID	Model Provenance
Timestamp	Traceability
Compliance Score	Regulatory Verification
Node Metadata	Participation Audit

5.4.2 Immutable Record Composition

During every federated learning round, the hash of the new global model parameters, the metadata associated with node profiles in the system, and the compliance metrics will be recorded in the blockchain. The blockchain acts as the immutable log for auditing purposes. (De Souza et al., 2024)

5.5 Trust Quantification Model

Although the combination of edge-based artificial intelligence, federated learning, and permissioned blockchain technology contributes to enhancing privacy, transparency, and accountability, the use of emotion-aware systems by the public sector also entails the need for a tangible approach to assess the trustworthiness of such systems. Although the trust element is widely considered in many digital government models, there has been no established approach to measure whether the governance system meets the basic trust conditions. The following section presents the Trust Quantification Model developed by the DETF that assesses the trust of the system based on four fundamental aspects.(Nastoska et al., 2025)

The proposed trust score is represented as a weighted linear combination of these dimensions:

$$T = \alpha P + \beta A + \gamma F + \Delta H$$

subject to:

$$\alpha + \beta + \gamma + \Delta = 1$$

where:

- (T) represents the overall trust score of the DETF system.
- (P) denotes the Privacy Preservation Score.
- (A) denotes the Auditability Score.
- (F) denotes the Fairness Score.
- (H) denotes the Human Oversight Score.
- (α, β, γ, Δ) represent weighting coefficients assigned according to governance priorities.

The trust evaluation variables used within the model are summarized in Table 9.

Table 9. Trust Evaluation Variables

Variable	Description	Evaluation Criteria
P	Privacy Preservation	Degree of local processing, data minimization, and biometric protection
A	Auditability	Availability of immutable logs, model traceability, and compliance records
F	Fairness	Absence of demographic bias and equitable model performance across groups
H	Human Oversight	Extent of human review, intervention, and decision authority
T	Overall Trust Score	Aggregated trustworthiness measure

The Privacy Preservation Score (P) denotes the efficiency of the framework in protecting citizens' information by using localized processing, federated learning, secure aggregation, and minimum usage of biometric information. Because the raw facial and vocal inputs are processed locally, the privacy preservation score of DETF is expected to be much higher than that of the centralized recognition framework. (P & Mahalakshmi, 2024)

The Auditability (A) score represents the visibility and traceability of AI operation processes. In the DETF framework, all federated learning rounds, model updates, and compliance verifications are stored in a permissioned blockchain. The immutable nature of such storage allows for easy reconstruction of the full decision history chain and increases accountability in institutions.(Akther et al., 2025)

The Fairness score (F) quantifies the degree of equity achieved when using the system. This is supported by the ability of Federated Learning to train models among geographically distant participants without the use of centralized and potentially demographically unbalanced data sets.(D. Kim et al., 2024)

The Human Oversight Score (H) reflects the degree of administrative control maintained over AI-assisted processes. Consistent with Human-in-the-Loop governance principles, DETF restricts AI systems to advisory and assistive functions while preserving final decision authority for authorized public officials. This ensures that automated recommendations remain subject to human review, interpretation, and intervention when necessary.(Sayles, 2024)

The four dimensions represent complementary requirements of trustworthy public-sector AI: privacy protects citizen information, auditability enables institutional traceability, fairness addresses unequal or biased outcomes, and human oversight preserves administrative responsibility. The model can be evaluated through expert assessment using standardized scoring criteria, followed by multi-criteria decision-making methods such as AHP or TOPSIS to determine dimension weights. Case-based evaluation and sensitivity analysis can further examine the robustness of the resulting trust score. At this stage, the model is conceptual and requires empirical validation in future government-service studies.

Together, the Trust Quantification Model offers a systematic approach to evaluate the level of trustworthiness in emotion-aware digital government systems. Through the quantification of the intangible concepts into tangible metrics, this model allows for policy evaluations and assessments of regulatory compliances of the suggested Decentralized Emotion-Aware Trust Framework.(Janssen et al., 2017)

6. OPERATIONAL WORKFLOW OF DETF

The operational flow for the DETF process starts from a situation where the citizen logs into a government's digital portal using either a personal device or a service kiosk. An emotional assessment in the form of the distress vector is derived through processing of facial and vocal cues at the edge AI level. All through the procedure, biometric information remains within the device and is deleted right after inference.(Arora & Singh, 2025)

Any validation for the model updates is tracked through the permissioned blockchain layer. The cryptographic hashes, metadata for compliance, and version IDs are added to the distributed ledger to maintain an immutable record. In doing so, the DETF integrates data protection, collective intelligence, and accountability into one governance system.(Vankayala, 2024)

Figure 8. Operational Workflow of DETF

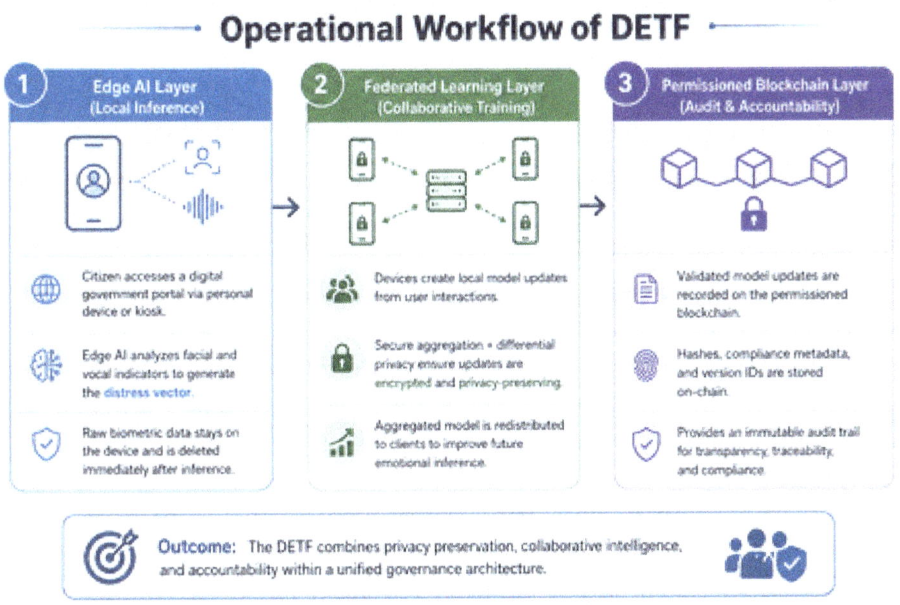

Figure 8 shows the workflow process of DETF, which combines privacy-preserving AI, federated learning, and blockchain technology. The process starts with the Edge AI Layer, where citizens access online public services using their own devices or kiosks. The facial and vocal cues from the citizens are processed locally to derive emotional insights, while the actual biometric information stays on the device and is cleared following the inference procedure.

Model training is supported by the Federated Learning Layer with techniques such as secure aggregation and differential privacy, making sure that encryption is always applied when updating models.(Chowdary Inaganti et al., 2019)

7. HUMAN-IN-THE-LOOP GOVERNANCE MECHANISM

DETF implementation requires coordinated responsibilities across government agencies, technology providers, regulators, and citizens. Government agencies retain authority over deployment and administrative decisions; technology providers are responsible for model development, security, and maintenance; regulators oversee compliance, privacy, and fairness; and citizens retain rights to information, review, and complaint. This governance structure ensures that AI-generated outputs remain subject to institutional accountability and human control.

The growing reliance on artificial intelligence within public administration has created substantial issues related to transparency, accountability, and the role of human judgment in decision-making processes. While artificial intelligence can increase efficiency and scalability, public sector governance ultimately entails human accountability, ethical deliberation, and contextual interpretation. Thus, any reliable digital government infrastructure should guarantee that AI-driven solutions serve merely as an aid to administrative power.(Datta, 2024)

To overcome this challenge, the DETF framework makes use of the HITL governance model in which humans exercise control through the entire decision process cycle. In this scenario, it is up to AI algorithms to identify emotions, make recommendations, and adjust interface designs for citizens while actual administrative decisions are made by designated government officials. By doing so, the system provides support for making decisions without replacing them.(Waza, 2024)

7.1 Human Oversight Across the Decision Lifecycle

With the DETF framework, emotional intelligence functions as an enabling capability meant to facilitate interaction between citizens and government agencies. This is because whenever the edge AI identifies that the citizen seeking assistance through the welfare application feels confused or frustrated with the process, it can make recommendations to simplify the procedure. However, it should be noted that the emotional inference does not determine whether the citizen qualifies for welfare benefits; it only helps to provide better guidance on the application process. (Czerwinski et al., 2021)

This is why the use of emotional assessments to aid government administration becomes essential in such cases since it does not interfere with the processes that the administration would use to grant or deny welfare benefits to any applicant. (Bentkover, 1986).

7.2 Governance Responsibility Allocation

In order to uphold clarity about the role of humans and AI respectively, there is an explicit delineation of responsibilities set forth by the DETF. The AI elements are tasked with emotion detection, personalized interfaces, pattern recognition, and decision recommendations while human operators maintain control of policy interpretation, regulatory adherence, discretion, citizen appeals, and decisions of services.(Liu & Li, 2025)

7.3 Implications for Trustworthy Digital Government

Integration of Human-in-the-Loop Governance makes the DETF a socio-technological governance model instead of merely a technological architecture. The model does not treat AI as a substitute to the bureaucrats of a country but recognizes it as a tool that can facilitate citizen participation in the government without compromising on democracy. The combination of emotional intelligence, privacy-preserving computations, decentralization of trust, and the role of humans makes the DETF a good model of governance.(Chen, 2023)

Ultimately, the concept of Human-in-the-Loop governance stands as the most important safeguard for ensuring that emotion-aware digital government is in accordance with the law and societal norms. The DETF uses this concept to develop its idea of digital governance as the partnership between human discretion and technical sophistication.(Filgueiras & Almeida, 2020)

If the system incorrectly infers a citizen's emotional state, the output should be treated as a non-binding service signal and corrected or overridden through human review without causing adverse administrative consequences.

8. ILLUSTRATIVE PUBLIC SERVICE USE CASES AND IMPLEMENTATION SCENARIOS

The real-world utility of DETF is in enabling public service with emotional intelligence while ensuring privacy, transparency, and accountability. For instance, to show the application of the proposed model, three representative scenarios for implementing this model have been presented here. These scenarios show how the combination of Edge AI, Federated Learning, Permissioned Blockchain, and Human-in-the-Loop Governance can make service provision citizen-centric.(Sajjanapu, 2025)

8.1 Welfare Benefits Application System

Welfare application systems are characterized by their complicated eligibility criteria, documentation needs, and verification processes. People applying for financial aid, disability aid, unemployment benefits, or social welfare are likely to become confused, frustrated, and stressed due to their interaction with these applications. (Taylor & Barusch, 2004)

Continuous upgrading of the model in terms of recognizing emotions is ensured by means of Federated Learning, which works on a distributed citizen-to-citizen basis, while retaining the users' privacy. Additionally, the blockchain-based logs can ensure that records are maintained about how the system has evolved through each update and audit processes. In cases of persistent distress and application failure, Human-in-the-Loop can take control.(Tsouvalas et al., 2022)

8.2 Digital Healthcare Assistance Portal

Healthcare-based portals used by the government often come into contact with citizens who are in need of information related to medicine, appointments, counselling or even public health initiatives. In such cases, the situation is often emotionally sensitive where anxiety and other factors can play a role in the behaviour of the citizen.(Koddebusch et al., 2023)

In this case, the DETF makes use of emotion recognition through multiple channels in order to detect any signs of emotional discomfort in the conversation between the citizen and the healthcare portal. Where higher levels of anxiety are recognized, information sources, communication processes, supportive services or even medical practitioners can be offered as suggestions for the user. The emotional assessment is made locally only.(Gopalakrishnan et al., 2025)

8.3 Citizen Grievance Redressal Platform

Grievance processes by citizens are an essential part of democratic government because they allow citizens to voice their complaints about service failure, administrative problems, and complaints regarding public services. However, citizens who lodge their grievances often feel frustrated, dissatisfied, or upset, especially if they had unsuccessfully tried to solve the problem before.(Hossain et al., 2023)

In the case of the DETF model, it is possible to use emotional indicators discovered during the process of complaint registration to highlight situations which require additional attention from the administration. The high level of citizen frustration can mean that additional help is needed for them or that such a complaint should be referred to a specialist. It should be noted that emotional evaluation serves as just supplementary information that does not affect the process of making decisions on complaint resolution.(Gong et al., 2015)

9. CHALLENGES, LIMITATIONS, AND FUTURE RESEARCH DIRECTIONS

9.1 Technical Challenges

The application of DETF would need the incorporation of many technologies, among them Edge AI, federated learning, permissioned blockchain technology, and human-in-the-loop governance techniques. Whereas each technology is useful for something unique, their incorporation is bound to complicate the architecture design process. Edge devices may differ widely in terms of computing power, memory capacity, and network connectivity that may affect their performance.(G Menon & Padinjappurathu Gopalan, 2026)

Federated learning faces various problems such as heterogeneous clients, communications overhead, model convergence issues, and model aggregation. Some people may be using devices with very different specifications, resulting in some contributing more to the training compared to others, thereby affecting the model's efficiency. Moreover, achieving higher accuracy levels under privacy measures such as differential privacy is still a problem being researched by scholars.(Rao et al., 2023)

9.2 Ethical and Regulatory Limitations

A digital government must adopt a framework of ethical and administrative limits with the use of Emotion AI. In the DETF context, the purpose of emotion recognition is to enrich interactions between citizens, and to enrich public services experiences. Emotional information can be utilized to recognize citizen frustration, confusion, or distress and offer suitable assistance via adaptive interfaces, service suggestions or human intervention if necessary.(Arora & Singh, 2025)

Most importantly, DETF does not allow the use of emotional data in making critical administrative decisions. The representation of the data in the form of outputs from Emotion AI should not affect welfare eligibility, allocation of public resources, administrative penalties or citizen profiling. Any final decisions involving citizens should be placed under human and institutional control. DETF's ability to optimize communication and service operations reduces risks associated with algorithmic bias and misuse, while keeping the use of Emotion AI to communication and service optimization within responsible AI principles.(Ingber & Andalibi, 2025)

9.3 Future Research Directions

There exist a number of research paths that may potentially enhance the potential of DETF even further. Firstly, researchers may examine the possibility of using different techniques for integrating multi-modal physiological sensing methods, including the use of wearable technologies and non-invasive bio signal analysis, which will allow improving recognition accuracy while maintaining privacy.(Wan et al., 2025)

Moreover, future research may focus on developing trust models that would adaptively calculate and modify the levels of trust between the participants of governance interaction depending on the changing needs of citizens and policymakers, along with increasing or decreasing risks.(S.-E. Kim, 2005)

To conclude, although the DETF is able to overcome many of the problems posed by current digital government systems, the actual success of the system will rely on further developments in AI, governance, regulation, and human-centred approaches to technology. These challenges, in turn, provide important areas for future research endeavours.(Asrifan & Rismawati, 2025)

10. CONCLUSION

However, when integrating artificial intelligence within public administration, it is important that citizens should not have to decide on whether to sacrifice their fundamental right to privacy in order to gain access to more efficient public services. The Decentralized Emotion-Aware Trust Framework (DETF), introduced in this chapter, proves that having a state with secure and empathic digital government systems is both achievable and sustainable. With the combination of Edge AI, Federated Learning and permissioned blockchains, governmental institutions would be able to create a responsive interface that recognizes citizen distress without resorting to the same biometric control measures.

Finally, through the strict implementation of "Human-in-the-Loop" checks and red lines, the government will ensure that the use of artificial intelligence does not become an instrument of abuse by limiting the use of data insights only for purposes that complement, rather than override, the discretion of the civil servant. Given that governments around the world are automating their social security networks and welfare portals, using such secure decentralized solutions like DETF will be inevitable.

REFERENCES

Паламарчук, Т. (2024). ARTIFICIAL INTELLIGENCE GOVERNANCE REGULATION IN PUBLIC ADMINISTRATION. *Наукові Інновації Та Передові Технології, 3*(31). Advance online publication. DOI: 10.52058/2786-5274-2024-3(31)-73-81 PMID: 24646463

Ahmad, A., Singh, V., & Upreti, K. (2025). Emotion Recognition Through Facial Expressions: A Machine Learning Perspective in Mobile Multimedia. *Journal of Mobile Multimedia*. DOI: 10.13052/jmm1550-4646.2114

Akther, A., Arobee, A., Adnan, A., Auyon, O., Islam, A., & Akter, F. (2025). Blockchain As a Platform For Artificial Intelligence (AI) Transparency. In *ArXiv.org*. American Chemical Society. https://doi.org//arxiv.2503.08699DOI: 10.48550

Angın, C. (2025). Artificial Intelligence and Innovative Technology Applications in Public Administration. *İnsan ve Toplum Bilimleri Araştırmaları Dergisi, 14*(4), 161–183. DOI: 10.15869/itobiad.1718443

Arora, K., & Singh, A. (2025). *Navigating the Ethical Landscape of Emotion Recognition Technologies*. Igi Global Scientific., DOI: 10.4018/979-8-3373-3658-9.ch006

Asrifan, A., & Rismawati, R. (2025). *From e-Government to Digital Government*. Igi Global Scientific., DOI: 10.4018/979-8-3373-1484-6.ch003

Bentkover, J. D. (1986). *The Role of Benefits Assessment in Public Policy Development*. Springer Netherlands., DOI: 10.1007/978-94-009-4524-1

Bhimavarapu, U. (2025). *Privacy-Preserving AI for Medical Applications*. Igi Global., DOI: 10.4018/979-8-3373-1205-7.ch006

Bouldjedri, O., Wazzeh, M., Sami, H., Talhi, C., & Ould-Slimane, H. (2025). *Privacy-Preserving Continuous User Authentication Using Federated Learning*. 1404–1409. DOI: 10.1109/IWCMC65282.2025.11059519

Chen, X. (2023). Ethical Governance of AI: An Integrated Approach via Human-in-the-Loop. *Machine Learning, 29*, 29. Advance online publication. DOI: 10.3390/cmsf2023008029

Chowdary Inaganti, A., Ravichandran, N., Muppalaneni, R., & Kumar Sundaramurthy, S. (2019). Federated Learning for Secure AI Model Training Across Distributed Networks. *Turkish Journal of Computer and Mathematics Education, 10*(3), 753–787. DOI: 10.61841/turcomat.v10i3.15144

Czerwinski, M., Hernandez, J., & Mcduff, D. (2021). Building an AI That Feels: AI systems with emotional intelligence could learn faster and be more helpful. *IEEE Spectrum, 58*(5), 32–38. DOI: 10.1109/MSPEC.2021.9423818

Darji, M. (2025). Emotion Recognition Systems: A Study on Models and Accuracy. *International Journal of Advanced Research in Science. Tongxin Jishu,* ●●●, 159–164. DOI: 10.48175/IJARSCT-23324

Datta, K. (2024). AI-Driven Public Administration: Opportunities, Challenges, And Ethical Considerations. *The Social Science Review A Multidisciplinary Journal, 2*(6). DOI: 10.70096/tssr.240206023

De Souza, L. A. C., Camilo, G. F., Rebello, G. A. F., Guimarães, L. C. B., Campista, M. E. M., & Costa, L. H. M. K. (2024).. . *Blockchain-based Approaches for Secure Federated Learning, 1–4*, 1–4. Advance online publication. DOI: 10.1109/BRAINS63024.2024.10732504

Dintakurthy, Y., Innmuri, R. K., Vanteru, A., & Thotakuri, A. (2025). Emerging Applications of Artificial Intelligence in Edge Computing: A Comprehensive Review. *Journal of Modern Technology*, 175–185. DOI: 10.71426/jmt.v1.i2.pp175-185

Durovic, M., & Corno, T. (2024). *The Privacy of Emotions*. Routledge., DOI: 10.4324/9781003502791-18

Farida, I., Setiawan, R., Maryatmi, A., & Juwita, M. (2020). The Implementation of E-Government in The Industrial Revolution Era 4.0 in Indonesia. *International Journal of Progressive Sciences and Technologies, 22*(2), 340–346. DOI: 10.52155/ijpsat.v22.2.2165

Filgueiras, F., & Almeida, V. (2020). *Governance for Digital Technologies*. Springer., DOI: 10.1007/978-3-030-55248-0_4

Goel, P. K. (2024). *Ethical and Privacy Considerations in Artificial Emotional Intelligence Deployment*. Igi Global., DOI: 10.4018/979-8-3693-6806-0.ch022

Gong, S., Dai, Y., Ji, J., Wang, J., & Sun, H. (2015). Emotion Analysis of Telephone Complaints from Customer Based on Affective Computing. *Computational Intelligence and Neuroscience, 2015*(5), 1–9. DOI: 10.1155/2015/506905 PMID: 26633967

Gopalakrishnan, S., R, E., K, K. T., U, T., & M, B. (2025). *Multimodal Emotion Recognition: An Integrated Approach using Facial, Audio and Text Analysis*. 122–127. DOI: 10.1109/ICAISS61471.2025.11041993

Gremsl, T., & Hödl, E. (2022). Emotional AI: Legal and ethical challenges1. *Information Polity, 27*(2), 163–174. DOI: 10.3233/IP-211529

Hossain, N., Joshi, A., & Pande, S. (2023). The politics of complaint: A review of the literature on grievance redress mechanisms in the global South. *Policy Studies, 45*(2), 139–158. DOI: 10.1080/01442872.2023.2193387

Ingber, A. S., & Andalibi, N. (2025). *Regulating Emotion AI in the United States: Insights from Empirical Inquiry*. 167–180. DOI: 10.1145/3715275.3732014

İzgi, F. D. (2025). *Applications of Emotion AI in Customer Interactions and Support*. Igi Global Scientific., DOI: 10.4018/979-8-3373-3658-9.ch001

Janssen, M., Rana, N. P., Slade, E. L., & Dwivedi, Y. K. (2017). Trustworthiness of digital government services: Deriving a comprehensive theory through interpretive structural modelling. *Public Management Review, 20*(5), 647–671. DOI: 10.1080/14719037.2017.1305689

Kanipakam, S., Devarajulu, V. S., & Kavarakuntla, T. (2025). *Privacy-Preserving AI Inference in Edge Systems: Ethical and Architectural Tradeoffs*. 1–6. DOI: 10.1109/IPCCC66453.2025.11304649

Kapoor, A., & Verma, V. (2024). EMOTION AI: UNDERSTANDING EMOTIONS THROUGH ARTIFICIAL INTELLIGENCE. *International Journal of Engineering Science and Humanities, 14*(Special Issue 1), 223–232. DOI: 10.62904/0vcbvb24

Kaswan, K. S., Dhatterwal, J. S., Sood, K., & Balusamy, B. (2022). *Role of Blockchain Technology in the Modern Era*. Wiley., DOI: 10.1002/9781119865247.ch1

Kawahara, R. (2020). *Verification of customizable blockchain consensus rule using a formal method. 5*, 1–3. DOI: 10.1109/ICBC48266.2020.9169472

Kim, D., Woo, H., & Lee, Y. (2024). Addressing Bias and Fairness Using Fair Federated Learning: A Synthetic Review. *Electronics (Basel), 13*(23), 4664. DOI: 10.3390/electronics13234664

Kim, R. S. (2026). Formal and computational foundations for implementing Affective Sovereignty in emotion AI systems. *Discover Artificial Intelligence, 6*(1), 235. Advance online publication. DOI: 10.1007/s44163-026-01000-0

Kim, S.-E. (2005). The Role of Trust in the Modern Administrative State. *Administration &amp. Administration & Society, 37*(5), 611–635. DOI: 10.1177/0095399705278596

Koddebusch, M., Koelmann, H., Friedrich, O., & Becker, J. (2023). *Bridging the Gap between e-Government and e-Health: Recommendations for Deploying e-Health Services in the Public Sector. 39*, 440–448. DOI: 10.1145/3598469.3598519

Kulothungan, V. (2025). A Blockchain-Enabled Approach to Cross-Border Compliance and Trust. In *ArXiv.org*. American Chemical Society. https://doi.org//arxiv.2501.09182DOI: 10.48550

Li, C. (2025). AI-Driven Governance: Enhancing Transparency and Accountability in Public Administration. *Digital Society &amp. Virtual Governance*, *1*(1), 1–16. DOI: 10.6914/dsvg.010101

Liu, D., & Li, X. (2025). AI vs. Human: Reconciling Autonomy and Governance in Decision-Making. *Lecture Notes in Education Psychology and Public Media*, *114*(1), 82–87. DOI: 10.54254/2753-7048/2025.LC19101

G Menon, V., & Padinjappurathu Gopalan, S. (2026). A novel framework for secure and interoperable Digital Twins in the Industrial Metaverse. *Enterprise Information Systems, ahead-of-print*(ahead-of-print). DOI: 10.1080/17517575.2026.2659635

Mohan, A., & Jayalakshmi, G. (2025). *Blockchain-Enabled Transparency and Accountability in Public Sector Governance*. 1–6. DOI: 10.1109/ICoICC64033.2025.11052060

Mulyasari, S. D. D., & Jaya Wardana, D. (2025). The Urgency of Using Artificial Intelligence (AI) In Public Services. *Jurnal Daulat Hukum*, *8*(3), 530. DOI: 10.30659/jdh.v8i3.48658

Nandi, A., Xhafa, F., Subirats, L., & Fort, S. (2023). *Federated Learning with Exponentially Weighted Moving Average for Real-Time Emotion Classification*. Springer., DOI: 10.1007/978-3-031-22356-3_12

Nastoska, A., Jancheska, B., Rizinski, M., & Trajanov, D. (2025). Evaluating Trustworthiness in AI: Risks, Metrics, and Applications Across Industries. *Electronics (Basel)*, *14*(13), 2717. DOI: 10.3390/electronics14132717

Nocoń, M., Vesolovska, M. K., & Mróz, B. P. (2025). Enhancing public administration efficiency via the combined application of emotional competence and intelligent technologies. *Scientific Papers of Silesian University of Technology. Organization and Management Series*, *2025*(230), 335–348. DOI: 10.29119/1641-3466.2025.230.20

P, M., & Mahalakshmi, K. (2024). *Privacy-Secure and Decentralized Biometric Authentication Models Using Federated Learning Frameworks*. 1–7. DOI: 10.1109/ICSCAN62807.2024.10894284

Pasupuleti, M. K. (2025). *Trustless Autonomy: AI and Blockchain for Next-Gen Governance*. National Education Services., DOI: 10.62311/nesx/rb21

Peeters, R. (2023). Digital Administrative Burdens: An Agenda for Analyzing the Citizen Experience of Digital Bureaucratic Encounters. *Perspectives on Public Management and Governance*, *6*(1), 7–13. DOI: 10.1093/ppmgov/gvac024

Rahmath Nisha, A., Subramani, A. K., & Ranjithaa, K. C. (2025). *Emotion AI for Human-Centered Leadership and Training*. Igi Global Scientific., DOI: 10.4018/979-8-3373-3658-9.ch015

Rao, M. S. S. (2023). *S, S., V, N., Arun, M. R., Gupta, S., & Taqui, S. N.* Efficient Model Training in Decentralized Systems with Federated Learning., DOI: 10.1109/ICCSAI59793.2023.10421469

Sajjanapu, M. (2025). Ethical AI and Sustainable Digital Governance: An Interdisciplinary Framework. *European Modern Studies Journal*, *9*(4), 804–814. DOI: 10.59573/emsj.9(4).2025.76

Sayles, J. (2024). *Human Oversight of AI Systems.* Apress., DOI: 10.1007/979-8-8688-0983-5_12

Schmitz, M., Ahmed, R., & Cao, J. (2022). Bias and Fairness on Multimodal Emotion Detection Algorithms. In *arXiv (Cornell University)*. European Society for Socially Embedded Technologies. /arxiv.2205.08383DOI: 10.48550

Scribano, A., & Korstanje, M. E. (2023). *AI and Emotions in Digital Society*. Igi Global., DOI: 10.4018/979-8-3693-0802-8

Shark, A. R. (2022). *E-Government to Digital Government.* Routledge., DOI: 10.4324/9781003344766-3

Sharma, S., Kumar Kar, A., & Gupta, M. P. (2021). *Unpacking Digital Accountability: Ensuring efficient and answerable e-governance service delivery. 17*, 260–269. DOI: 10.1145/3494193.3494229

Sharma, Y. (2020). *Blockchain and Distributed Ledger System* (pp. 177–206). Crc. DOI: 10.1201/9780429352546-8

. Sprenkamp, K., Delgado Fernandez, J., Eckhardt, S., & Zavolokina, L. (2023, January 1). *Federated Learning as a Solution for Problems Related to Intergovernmental Data Sharing*. DOI: 10.24251/HICSS.2023.208

Subramaniam, G., & Palanisamy, S. (2023). *Privacy-Preserving Federated Machine Learning Techniques*. Igi Global., DOI: 10.4018/979-8-3693-0593-5.ch007

Sudhakar, K. (2025). Decentralized AI: Leveraging Blockchain for Trustworthy Machine Learning Models. *Journal of Informatics Education and Research*, *5*(2). Advance online publication. DOI: 10.52783/jier.v5i2.2753

Taylor, M. J., & Barusch, A. S. (2004). Personal, family, and multiple barriers of long-term welfare recipients. *Social Work, 49*(2), 175–183. DOI: 10.1093/sw/49.2.175 PMID: 15124958

Tsouvalas, V., Özçelebi, T., & Meratnia, N. (2022). Privacy-preserving Speech Emotion Recognition through Semi-Supervised Federated Learning. In *arXiv (Cornell University)*. European Society for Socially Embedded Technologies. https://doi.org//arxiv.2202.02611DOI: 10.48550

Vankayala, V. (2024). Decentralized Integrity: Blockchain-Based Frameworks for Enhancing Software Update Security. *International Journal of Scientific Research in Computer Science. Engineering and Information Technology, 10*(5), 404–409. DOI: 10.32628/CSEIT241051035

Vasava, M. J., Gamit, V., Panchal, A. V., Patel, M. M., & Gohil, H. (2024). Federated learning in artificial intelligence: a privacy-preserving approach for distributed machine learning systems. *ShodhKosh: Journal of Visual and Performing Arts, 5*(5). Advance online publication. DOI: 10.29121/shodhkosh.v5.i5.2024.4817

Wan, J., Xu, S., Lin, J., Ji, L., Cheng, J., Li, Z., Qu, X., & Li, C. (2025). AI-Enhanced Wearable Technology for Human Physiological Signal Detection: Challenges and Future Directions. *Small (Weinheim an Der Bergstrasse, Germany), 21*(43), e04078. DOI: 10.1002/smll.202504078

Waza, A. M. (2024). Examining the Role of Artificial Intelligence in Improving Decision Making Processes in Governance. *International Journal of Advanced Technology and Social Sciences, 2*(7), 1139–1150. DOI: 10.59890/ijatss.v2i7.2319

Zheng, W., & Zhou, T. (2023). *Secure and Privacy-Preserving Communications for Emotion-Aided Systems*. 1–7. DOI: 10.1109/SWC57546.2023.10448927

Chapter 8
Ethical Boundaries and Emotional Intelligence in Trusted AI-Enabled Digital Government

Beichen Lu
http://orcid.org/0009-0002-7346-2209
Tsinghua University, China

ABSTRACT

Chapter 8 examines the ethical foundations of trusted AI enabled digital government by extending the discussion beyond algorithmic fairness toward human centered AI governance. It argues that AI systems are not neutral technical tools but value embedded governance mechanisms that influence public decisions and social outcomes. The chapter explores the ethical boundaries of AI authority, the reconstruction of accountability, and the importance of meaningful explainability in maintaining public trust. Furthermore, it introduces emotional intelligence as a new dimension of AI governance, emphasizing that trustworthy AI requires not only technical reliability but also ethical legitimacy, human understanding, and respect for citizen experiences.

1. THE LIMITS OF ALGORITHMIC FAIRNESS AND THE NEED FOR A BROADER ETHICAL FRAMEWORK

The rapid development of artificial intelligence has made algorithmic fairness one of the most influential concepts in contemporary AI ethics. As AI systems become increasingly involved in decision making processes, researchers and pol-

DOI: 10.4018/979-8-3373-9129-8.ch008

icymakers have focused on a fundamental concern: how can algorithmic systems avoid producing discriminatory or unequal outcomes? This concern has generated extensive research on concepts such as fairness, bias mitigation, transparency, and explainability. The underlying assumption behind these approaches is that if algorithms can be designed to produce fair outcomes, reduce discrimination, and operate transparently, then AI systems can become ethically acceptable.

This perspective has made significant contributions to improving AI governance. Algorithmic fairness has provided important methods for identifying unequal treatment, evaluating model performance across different social groups, and reducing the possibility that historical discrimination will be reproduced through automated systems. For example, if an AI system used for public service allocation consistently provides fewer opportunities to a particular social group because of biased training data, fairness mechanisms can help identify and correct such problems. In this sense, algorithmic fairness represents an essential foundation for responsible AI governance.

However, when AI systems enter the domain of digital government, the limitations of this framework become increasingly visible. Government AI systems do not simply perform technical calculations or improve administrative efficiency. They participate in decisions that influence citizens' access to public resources, social opportunities, and institutional recognition. An algorithm used in welfare distribution, healthcare prioritization, education support, or public safety management does not merely predict information. It contributes to determining how government attention and resources are distributed among different members of society (Barocas et al., 2023; Berk et al., 2021; Diakopoulos, 2016; Shneiderman, 2022).

This creates a deeper ethical challenge that cannot be fully addressed through algorithmic fairness alone. The question is no longer only whether an algorithm treats different groups equally. The more fundamental question is whether algorithmic systems should participate in decisions that shape important aspects of human life. In other words, the ethical concern moves from the fairness of algorithmic outcomes to the legitimacy of algorithmic authority.

Consider an AI based welfare prediction system designed to identify citizens who may require financial assistance. From a technical perspective, the system may achieve excellent performance. It may analyze large amounts of information, accurately identify patterns of economic vulnerability, and demonstrate no significant differences in prediction accuracy across different social groups. From the perspective of algorithmic fairness, such a system may appear ethically acceptable because it does not produce measurable discrimination.

However, a deeper ethical question remains. Should eligibility for social support be determined primarily through a probability based assessment generated by an algorithm? Welfare decisions are not merely technical classifications. They involve judgments about human needs, social responsibility, and the role of government in protecting vulnerable citizens. Even if the algorithm produces accurate and unbiased predictions, society must still consider whether the values embedded in the decision making process are consistent with principles of dignity, justice, and democratic governance.

This distinction reveals an important limitation of algorithmic fairness. Fairness evaluates whether an algorithm treats individuals or groups appropriately within a given framework, but it does not necessarily question whether the framework itself is ethically justified. An algorithm can be fair according to statistical measurements while still raising concerns about the type of authority it exercises and the values it prioritizes. For example, an AI system used in healthcare resource allocation may be designed to maximize overall medical efficiency. It may successfully identify patients who are most likely to benefit from treatment and allocate resources accordingly. However, healthcare decisions also involve broader social values. A society may decide that certain vulnerable populations deserve additional protection even if they do not produce the highest statistical benefit. In this case, the ethical challenge is not algorithmic bias but the relationship between optimization goals and human values (Barocas et al., 2023; Berk et al., 2021; Diakopoulos, 2016; Shneiderman, 2022).

Therefore, AI ethics in digital government requires a broader perspective that moves beyond the question of whether algorithms are fair toward the question of whether algorithmic governance is legitimate. Algorithms do not simply process information; they organize social priorities, define categories, and influence how public institutions understand citizens. Every decision about what data to use, what outcomes to optimize, and what factors to prioritize reflects certain assumptions about what matters. This means that algorithms are not neutral instruments operating outside society. They are embedded within institutional and social contexts where values, interests, and political choices are continuously negotiated. The ethical evaluation of AI governance must therefore examine not only the technical properties of algorithms but also the social consequences of allowing algorithms to participate in public decision making.

The shift from algorithmic fairness to broader governance ethics represents a fundamental transformation in how AI responsibility should be understood. Algorithmic fairness remains necessary because unfair systems can directly harm citizens and reproduce existing inequalities. However, fairness alone cannot determine whether AI systems should be trusted with governance functions. A truly ethical AI governance framework must also consider questions of legitimacy, human dignity, democratic accountability, and the appropriate boundaries of automated decision making.

Therefore, this chapter argues that algorithmic fairness is the starting point of AI ethics, not its final destination. In trusted AI enabled digital government, the central challenge is not only to create algorithms that make fair decisions, but also to ensure that the use of algorithms itself remains consistent with human values and legitimate forms of public governance. The future of AI ethics depends not only on building better algorithms, but on defining the ethical boundaries within which those algorithms are allowed to operate.

2. AI AS A VALUE EMBEDDED GOVERNANCE SYSTEM

The discussion of algorithmic fairness reveals an important limitation in current approaches to AI ethics. Even when an algorithm produces equal outcomes across different groups, a deeper question remains unanswered: what values are embedded within the system and what social objectives does it prioritize? This question leads to a broader understanding of AI in digital government. AI should not be viewed merely as a technical instrument that executes human decisions. Instead, it should be understood as a value embedded governance system that participates in shaping how public problems are defined, how resources are distributed, and how citizens are evaluated. The traditional technological perspective assumes that algorithms are neutral tools. Under this assumption, humans create goals, provide data, and design rules, while algorithms simply perform calculations according to predefined instructions. From this perspective, ethical responsibility appears to exist mainly outside the algorithm itself. If problems occur, they are often attributed to poor data quality, incorrect implementation, or inappropriate human use (Barocas et al., 2023; Berk et al., 2021).

However, this understanding overlooks the fact that algorithms cannot operate without making choices. In order to function within governance systems, algorithms must classify information, rank priorities, identify patterns, and predict future possibilities. Each of these processes requires decisions about what should be considered important and what should be ignored. These choices are not purely technical. They reflect assumptions about social values, institutional goals, and political priorities. For example, consider an AI system used by a government to allocate limited healthcare resources. At first glance, the purpose of such a system may appear straightforward. The government hopes to use AI to improve efficiency by identifying which patients are most likely to benefit from available treatments. From a technical perspective, the model may be highly accurate and capable of optimizing resource allocation. However, the design of such a system requires deeper value choices. Should the system prioritize patients with the highest probability of recovery? Should it give additional consideration to vulnerable populations? Should age, economic background, or social circumstances influence decisions? Should the goal be maximizing overall medical outcomes or ensuring equal access to healthcare opportunities?

There is no purely technical answer to these questions because each option represents a different understanding of fairness and social responsibility. A system designed to maximize efficiency may produce different outcomes from a system designed to protect vulnerable groups. Both models may be technically valid, but they reflect different social values. This example demonstrates that algorithms do not simply discover objective solutions. They organize reality according to particular priorities. When a government chooses a specific optimization goal, it is also choosing which values should guide public decision making. Therefore, algorithmic design is not only a technical process but also a form of governance decision. This is particularly significant in digital government because public administration has always involved value judgments. Governments do not merely deliver services; they make decisions about what society should protect, what risks deserve attention, and how limited resources should be distributed. When AI becomes involved in these processes, these value choices become embedded within computational systems.

Therefore, the idea of AI neutrality requires reconsideration. Algorithms may be mathematically objective, but the systems in which they operate are not value free. The data selected for training, the objectives chosen for optimization, the indicators used for evaluation, and the outcomes considered successful all contain assumptions about what matters. For example, a predictive policing system may be designed to improve public safety by identifying areas with higher crime risks. The system may accurately identify statistical patterns based on historical data. However, if historical policing practices were influenced by social inequalities, the algorithm may reproduce those patterns and direct greater attention toward already over monitored communities. The problem is not necessarily that the algorithm is inaccurate. The deeper issue is that the system may embed historical assumptions about risk and security.

Similarly, an AI welfare system may accurately identify citizens who are statistically likely to need assistance. However, if the system defines vulnerability only through measurable economic indicators, it may overlook important human experiences that cannot easily be quantified, such as family responsibilities, psychological stress, or social isolation. In this case, the algorithm does not simply make a prediction. It defines what counts as need. Therefore, the ethical evaluation of AI governance cannot be limited to technical questions such as whether a model achieves high accuracy or avoids statistical bias. These questions remain important, but they represent only one dimension of ethical governance. A more fundamental question must be considered: Does the objective optimized by the AI system reflect the values that society considers legitimate and desirable? This shift changes the focus of AI ethics from algorithm correction to value governance. The challenge is no longer only how to build better algorithms, but how to ensure that algorithmic objectives remain aligned with human values and democratic principles. Recognizing AI as a value embedded governance system does not mean that algorithms should be rejected or removed from public administration. Instead, it requires a more mature understanding of their role. AI can provide valuable support for government decision making, but its objectives and applications must remain subject to ethical reflection and institutional oversight. Human judgment remains essential because many governance decisions involve conflicts between competing values that cannot be solved through optimization alone.

Therefore, trusted AI governance requires moving beyond the question of whether an AI model is accurate toward a deeper inquiry into what the model is designed to achieve and why that goal should be considered legitimate. AI systems are not value neutral because every optimization process contains assumptions about what should be prioritized. The future of ethical AI governance depends not only on improving algorithms, but also on ensuring that the values embedded within those algorithms are openly examined, publicly discussed, and aligned with the principles of human centered governance.

3. THE BOUNDARY BETWEEN AI ASSISTANCE AND AI AUTHORITY

The most fundamental ethical challenge of AI in digital government is not whether AI should be used in governance, but where the boundary should be established between AI assistance and AI authority. The introduction of AI into public administration has created unprecedented opportunities to improve government capacity. AI systems can analyze large amounts of information, identify complex patterns, predict social needs, and support more efficient policy implementation. However, the ability to enhance administrative capacity does not automatically create the legitimacy to exercise public authority. A system may be technically powerful and highly accurate, yet this does not mean that it should independently determine outcomes that directly affect citizens' rights, opportunities, and social conditions.

This distinction requires a fundamental separation between AI assistance and AI authority. AI assistance refers to situations where artificial intelligence functions as a supporting mechanism that enhances human decision making. In this model, AI provides information, identifies potential risks, and offers recommendations, while human institutions remain responsible for evaluating the information and making final decisions. AI authority, in contrast, refers to situations where algorithmic systems directly determine outcomes without meaningful human judgment or institutional intervention. Although both approaches involve the use of AI in governance, they represent fundamentally different relationships between technology and public power.

The difference between these two models becomes particularly important in areas where government decisions involve not only factual analysis but also moral and social judgment. Consider an AI system designed to identify citizens who may require social assistance. As a form of AI assistance, the system can help government agencies identify potential cases of vulnerability by analyzing economic conditions, employment information, and social circumstances. It can allow public officials to provide support more proactively and prevent vulnerable groups from being overlooked. In this situation, AI expands government capacity while human institutions remain responsible for interpreting individual circumstances and ensuring that decisions reflect broader social values.

However, the ethical situation changes significantly when AI moves from assisting decisions to directly determining eligibility for public support. If an algorithm automatically decides that a citizen should or should not receive assistance, the decision is no longer simply a technical classification. It becomes an exercise of public authority. The system is no longer only providing information to government officials; it is effectively determining who deserves access to collective resources. This raises deeper ethical questions that cannot be answered through predictive accuracy alone. A prediction about social vulnerability is a statistical judgment, but a decision about providing public support is a normative judgment involving ideas about dignity, fairness, and social responsibility.

This distinction reveals a crucial limitation of purely technical approaches to AI governance. A common assumption is that if AI systems can make more accurate predictions than humans, they should gradually replace human decision making. However, public governance is not simply a problem of prediction and optimization. Many government decisions involve uncertainty, competing values, and unique human circumstances that cannot be reduced to numerical calculations. A system may identify patterns effectively, but it cannot independently determine how society should balance efficiency, equality, compassion, and justice.

For example, an AI system used in healthcare may accurately predict which patients are most likely to benefit from limited medical resources. From an efficiency perspective, allocating resources according to predicted outcomes may appear rational. However, healthcare decisions also involve ethical considerations regarding vulnerable populations, human dignity, and equal access to essential services. A purely algorithmic decision may optimize one value while neglecting others. The problem is therefore not whether the prediction is accurate, but whether the authority to make such value based decisions should be transferred from human institutions to computational systems.

The boundary between AI assistance and AI authority is therefore fundamentally a question about the relationship between technology and democratic governance. In democratic societies, public decisions require more than technical competence. They require accountability, justification, and the possibility of public challenge. When AI systems participate in governance, citizens must still be able to identify who is responsible for decisions, why certain values were prioritized, and how mistakes can be corrected. If AI becomes an unquestionable authority, technological complexity may weaken rather than strengthen public accountability.

This does not mean that human decision making is always superior to algorithmic decision making. Human administrators can also make biased, inconsistent, or unfair decisions. AI systems may provide valuable support by reducing certain forms of human error and improving administrative consistency. The issue is not whether humans or machines are inherently better decision makers. The deeper issue is that different types of decisions require different forms of authority. Decisions involving calculation, prediction, and information processing may benefit greatly from AI assistance, while decisions involving moral judgment, social values, and individual rights require continued human responsibility.

Therefore, the appropriate role of AI in digital government is not to replace human governance, but to strengthen it within clearly defined ethical boundaries. AI should expand the ability of governments to understand social problems and respond effectively, but it should not become an independent source of public authority. The legitimacy of AI governance depends on maintaining a clear relationship between technological capability and human responsibility.

Ultimately, the central principle of trusted AI enabled digital government is that AI can support governance, but it should not replace human responsibility. The future of AI governance does not depend on creating systems that make all decisions automatically. Instead, it depends on designing governance structures where AI contributes intelligence while humans remain responsible for judgment, values, and accountability. In this way, AI becomes a powerful instrument for improving public governance without undermining the ethical foundations upon which democratic legitimacy depends.

4. RECONSTRUCTING RESPONSIBILITY IN AI MORAL GOVERNANCE

One of the most significant ethical challenges created by AI enabled governance is not the disappearance of responsibility, but the increasing difficulty of identifying where responsibility exists. Traditional administrative systems are built upon a relatively clear relationship between decision making authority and accountability. The actor who makes a decision is expected to explain the reasoning behind that decision and accept responsibility for its consequences. In this framework, responsibility follows authority. If a government official approves a policy, rejects an application, or allocates public resources, citizens can identify the decision maker and demand justification through established institutional mechanisms.

However, AI governance disrupts this traditional relationship because public decisions are increasingly produced through complex networks rather than through a single human actor. An AI driven decision may involve multiple stages, including data collection, algorithm development, model training, system deployment, institutional supervision, and administrative implementation. As a result, the final outcome is no longer simply the product of individual judgment. Instead, it emerges from interactions among government agencies, technology developers, data managers, regulatory institutions, and computational systems.

Consider an AI based welfare allocation system. A government agency may decide to adopt the system to improve efficiency and identify vulnerable citizens more accurately. A technology company may design the algorithm. Data managers may provide historical information used for training. Regulatory institutions may establish standards for system operation. When the system produces an unfair outcome, responsibility becomes difficult to determine. Was the problem caused by biased training data? Was the algorithm designed with inappropriate objectives? Did the government fail to provide sufficient oversight? Did the institution rely too heavily on automated recommendations?

Each actor may have contributed to the outcome, but no single actor may appear to be fully responsible. This creates what can be described as an accountability gap. If responsibility is distributed without clear boundaries, the complexity of AI systems may unintentionally become a way for actors to avoid responsibility. When everyone is involved, there is a risk that no one accepts final accountability. This challenge requires a reconstruction of responsibility within AI moral governance. The goal is not to return to the traditional model where one individual is responsible for every decision, because such a model cannot reflect the complexity of modern AI systems. Instead, AI governance requires a new responsibility framework that recognizes multiple forms of contribution while ensuring that responsibility remains identifiable, enforceable, and meaningful.

The first principle of this framework is traceability. Responsibility must be traceable throughout the entire AI governance process. This means that institutions must be able to identify how a decision was produced, which data influenced the outcome, how the algorithm contributed to the result, and which actors were involved at different stages. Traceability does not require that every technical detail be visible to the public, but it requires that the governance system itself maintains a clear record of decision processes. For example, when an AI system denies a citizen access to a public service, it should be possible to examine whether the decision was influenced by the quality of the data, the design of the algorithm, the way the system was implemented, or the judgment of human officials. Without traceability, responsibility cannot be assigned because the causes of failure remain hidden within complex technological processes.

The second principle is accountability. Traceability identifies where problems emerge, but accountability determines who must respond. In AI governance, responsibility cannot simply be shared equally among all participants. Different actors have different roles and therefore different obligations. Technology developers should be accountable for the design choices and technical limitations of the systems they create. Data managers should be accountable for ensuring that data are appropriate, accurate, and ethically collected. Government institutions should remain accountable for deciding whether and how AI should be used in public decisions. Regulatory bodies should be accountable for establishing effective oversight mechanisms. This principle is particularly important because governments cannot transfer responsibility to technology. The use of AI in public administration does not remove institutional responsibility. On the contrary, because governments introduce AI into decisions that affect citizens' rights, they remain the ultimate guarantors of public accountability.

The third principle is correctability. A trustworthy AI governance system does not assume that errors can be completely eliminated. Complex social environments make uncertainty unavoidable, and even well designed AI systems may produce unintended consequences. Therefore, the ethical quality of AI governance should be judged not only by whether failures occur, but also by whether institutions have the capacity to recognize, correct, and learn from those failures. For example, if an AI system used for healthcare allocation produces unequal outcomes among different groups, a responsible governance system should allow the problem to be detected, investigated, and corrected. Citizens affected by incorrect decisions should have opportunities to request review and receive appropriate remedies. Correction mechanisms demonstrate that AI remains under human governance rather than becoming an unquestionable authority.

These three principles reveal a broader transformation in the meaning of responsibility. In traditional governance, responsibility was mainly understood as a relationship between an individual decision maker and a specific outcome. In AI governance, responsibility becomes a continuous process that extends across the entire lifecycle of a system. It begins with the design of algorithms and data structures, continues through institutional deployment, and remains necessary after decisions are made. Therefore, trustworthy AI governance does not mean creating AI systems that never make mistakes. Such a goal is unrealistic because uncertainty is inherent in complex social environments. Instead, trustworthy AI governance means creating systems in which mistakes can be identified, responsibility can be assigned, and corrective action can be taken. The central ethical question is not whether AI can eliminate human error, but whether society can maintain meaningful accountability when decisions are increasingly produced through human and technological collaboration.

Ultimately, the reconstruction of responsibility under AI moral governance requires a balance between distributed participation and clear accountability. AI governance must recognize that decisions are created through complex networks, but complexity cannot become an excuse for avoiding responsibility. The legitimacy of AI in digital government depends on whether citizens can trust that behind every algorithmic decision there are identifiable actors, accountable institutions, and effective mechanisms capable of correction. In this sense, responsibility is not weakened by AI; it must be redesigned to fit the new reality of AI mediated governance.

5. BEYOND TRANSPARENCY TOWARD MEANINGFUL EXPLAINABILITY

Transparency has long been considered one of the fundamental principles of responsible AI governance. Traditional AI ethics frameworks often assume that transparency can generate public trust because citizens are more likely to accept algorithmic decisions when they have access to information about how systems operate. Under this perspective, making algorithms visible, disclosing data sources, and publishing technical documentation are regarded as essential approaches for improving accountability. This understanding has contributed significantly to the development of responsible AI by emphasizing that automated systems should not operate as completely hidden mechanisms. However, when AI systems are introduced into digital government, the relationship between transparency and trust becomes much more complicated. The central problem is that transparency does not automatically create understanding, and information disclosure does not necessarily create meaningful accountability.

In government contexts, citizens are rarely concerned only with the technical structure of an algorithm. They are concerned with how algorithmic decisions influence their own lives and whether those decisions are justified. A government agency may publish information about an AI system, including the variables used in a model, the general principles behind the algorithm, and the performance indicators of the system. From a technical perspective, such actions may represent a high level of transparency. However, for an individual who receives an unfavorable decision from an AI assisted public service, these explanations may still fail to answer the most important questions. Why did the system reach this conclusion? Which information influenced the decision? Was the decision affected by inaccurate or incomplete data? Who has the authority to review and correct the result? These questions demonstrate that citizens do not simply require access to information about AI systems. They require an explanation of how AI decisions relate to public values, institutional responsibility, and individual circumstances.

Therefore, this chapter argues that digital government requires a shift from technical transparency toward meaningful explainability. Technical transparency focuses on opening the internal structure of an AI system, while meaningful explainability focuses on creating a comprehensible relationship between citizens and algorithmic governance. The purpose of explanation is not to make every citizen understand complex mathematical models or computational processes. Instead, the purpose is to ensure that citizens can understand why AI is being used, how it affects them, and what mechanisms exist when problems occur. In this sense, explainability is not simply a technical function of AI design. It is a governance mechanism that allows citizens to question decisions, participate in public processes, and maintain confidence in institutions that increasingly rely on automated systems.

Consider an AI based welfare assessment system used by a government agency to identify citizens who may require financial support. The system may analyze thousands of data points and produce decisions more quickly than traditional administrative procedures. However, if a citizen is denied assistance, simply explaining that the decision was generated by an algorithm does not provide meaningful justification. The citizen does not need to know every computational step behind the model; instead, the citizen needs to understand whether the decision reflects accurate information, whether personal circumstances were properly considered, and whether there is an opportunity for human review. This example shows that the ethical challenge of AI governance is not only about making algorithms transparent, but about ensuring that algorithmic decisions remain connected to human understanding and institutional accountability.

This distinction is particularly important because government decisions are fundamentally different from ordinary technological services. When a commercial platform recommends a product or entertainment content, users may accept limited explanations because the consequences are relatively minor. However, when AI systems influence access to healthcare, education, welfare programs, or public safety measures, algorithmic decisions become connected to questions of rights, fairness, and social justice. In these situations, citizens have a legitimate expectation that public authorities can explain not only what decision was made but also why that decision should be considered reasonable and legitimate. Therefore, explainability becomes closely related to procedural justice because citizens evaluate not only the outcome of a decision but also whether the process behind that decision is understandable and contestable.

Meaningful explainability also changes the understanding of responsibility in AI governance. If AI decisions are presented as purely technical outcomes, institutions may unintentionally distance themselves from accountability by suggesting that the algorithm itself produced the result. However, AI systems do not independently exercise public authority. They are created, deployed, and supervised by human institutions. Therefore, explanations must always connect algorithmic outcomes with responsible actors. Citizens need to know why the government adopted AI, how the system is governed, who is responsible for monitoring its operation, and what actions will be taken when errors occur. Without this connection between explanation and responsibility, transparency becomes only a symbolic practice rather than a genuine governance mechanism.

For this reason, meaningful explainability should be understood as a democratic requirement rather than merely a technical improvement. In democratic governance, legitimacy does not come only from producing efficient outcomes. It also comes from the ability of institutions to justify decisions, respond to concerns, and allow citizens to challenge actions that affect them. AI systems may improve administrative efficiency, but they cannot replace the fundamental requirement that public decisions remain understandable and accountable. Explanation therefore becomes a bridge between technological capability and democratic legitimacy.

Ultimately, trustworthy AI enabled digital government does not require citizens to fully understand every technical detail of artificial intelligence. Instead, it requires governments to create systems in which citizens can understand the purpose, consequences, and accountability structure of AI based decisions. Transparency makes AI systems visible, but meaningful explainability makes them legitimate. The future of AI governance therefore depends not only on developing more advanced algorithms, but on ensuring that these algorithms remain embedded within institutions capable of explanation, responsibility, and public dialogue.

6. THE MISSING HUMAN DIMENSION IN DIGITAL GOVERNMENT

The previous sections have examined the ethical challenges of AI governance from the perspectives of algorithmic authority, responsibility, and explainability. These discussions reveal an important reality: trustworthy AI governance cannot be achieved only through technically reliable systems or well designed accountability mechanisms. Even if an AI system operates accurately, follows fairness principles, and provides explanations for its decisions, another fundamental question remains largely overlooked: how do citizens actually experience government through AI mediated interactions? In other words, beyond institutional trust, social contracts, and responsibility structures, there exists another essential dimension of governance trust, which is the human experience of being understood, respected, and supported by public institutions.

The development of digital government has traditionally been driven by the pursuit of efficiency. Governments have adopted digital technologies to reduce administrative costs, accelerate service delivery, and provide more convenient access to public services. This transformation has significantly improved administrative capacity by allowing citizens to complete procedures online, receive information more quickly, and interact with government institutions without traditional geographical and temporal limitations. However, the emphasis on efficiency has also created a potential weakness. When public services become increasingly automated, interactions between citizens and governments may gradually become reduced to the exchange of data, documents, and digital procedures. The government may become more efficient, but the relationship between citizens and public institutions may become increasingly distant.

This challenge emerges because government services are fundamentally different from ordinary technological services. Public administration is not only a process of delivering information or completing transactions. It is also a social relationship between institutions and individuals. When citizens interact with government, they are not simply seeking a technically correct answer. They often approach public services with complex emotional experiences shaped by their personal circumstances. A person applying for unemployment support may experience uncertainty about the future. An elderly citizen seeking healthcare assistance may feel anxiety about their physical condition. A family requesting social support may already be experiencing financial and emotional pressure. In these situations, the quality of governance is evaluated not only through the final outcome but also through whether citizens feel that their difficulties have been recognized and their experiences have been respected.

Consider an elderly citizen applying for medical assistance through an AI enabled government service. From a technical perspective, the system may perform effectively. It may accurately evaluate eligibility, process information quickly, and provide a consistent decision based on established criteria. However, if the entire interaction is experienced as mechanical and indifferent, the citizen may still feel disconnected from the government. The system may successfully answer the administrative question of whether the person qualifies for assistance, but it may fail to address the human question of whether the person feels supported and valued. This gap between administrative efficiency and human experience represents a critical challenge for AI enabled digital government.

Therefore, the introduction of AI into public services requires a broader understanding of trust. Traditional approaches often treat trust as a rational evaluation based on institutional performance, reliability, and competence. Citizens trust governments because they believe institutions can deliver effective outcomes and fulfill their responsibilities. However, digital government reveals that trust also has an emotional dimension. Citizens do not only evaluate whether government decisions are correct; they also evaluate how government interactions make them feel. A process that is efficient but emotionally disconnected may weaken public trust, while a process that demonstrates understanding and respect may strengthen citizens' willingness to engage with public institutions.

This does not mean that governments should replace rational decision making with emotional responses. Public administration must remain based on fairness, consistency, and legal principles. Instead, the argument is that effective governance requires the integration of both rational and emotional dimensions. AI systems should not only help governments understand data patterns but also help institutions better understand citizens' experiences. The goal of emotional intelligence in digital government is not to make AI imitate human emotions, but to ensure that technological systems remain sensitive to the human realities behind administrative data.

This human dimension becomes especially important because many public service decisions involve vulnerable groups who may already experience unequal access, uncertainty, or social disadvantage. If AI systems treat citizens only as data points, they risk reinforcing a sense of distance between individuals and institutions. However, if AI enabled services can recognize individual circumstances, provide appropriate communication, and create opportunities for human interaction when necessary, technology can strengthen rather than weaken the relationship between citizens and government. Therefore, the future of digital government requires a shift from a purely efficiency oriented model toward a more human centered governance model. The success of AI in public administration should not be measured only by how quickly it processes information or how accurately it predicts outcomes. It should also be evaluated by whether it improves citizens' experiences of government and whether it strengthens the perception that public institutions remain responsive and caring.

Ultimately, trust in AI enabled digital government is not only cognitively evaluated through judgments of competence and reliability; it is also emotionally experienced through interactions between citizens and institutions. A government may possess advanced technologies, accurate algorithms, and efficient systems, but without recognition of the human experiences behind public services, technological progress alone cannot create lasting trust. The missing human dimension reminds us that the purpose of AI governance is not simply to build smarter systems, but to create more meaningful relationships between governments and the people they serve.

7. EMOTIONAL INTELLIGENCE AS A NEW FOUNDATION OF CITIZEN CENTERED AI GOVERNANCE

The discussion of digital government has traditionally focused on improving administrative capacity through technological advancement. However, as AI becomes increasingly embedded in public services, improving efficiency alone is no longer sufficient to establish meaningful relationships between governments and citizens. The previous sections have demonstrated that trustworthy AI governance requires ethical boundaries, accountability mechanisms, and meaningful explanations. Yet, even a system that is technically accurate, ethically regulated, and transparent may still fail to gain public trust if citizens feel ignored, misunderstood, or disconnected during their interactions with government. This reveals a missing dimension of AI governance: the ability to recognize and respond to human emotions. Therefore, this chapter argues that emotional intelligence should become a new foundation of citizen centered AI governance.

Emotional intelligence in digital government does not mean that AI should imitate human emotions or attempt to replace human relationships. Rather, it refers to the ability of AI systems to understand the emotional conditions surrounding public service interactions and respond in ways that acknowledge citizens' experiences. Traditional AI systems are primarily designed to process information, identify patterns, and generate responses based on predefined objectives. Emotional intelligence introduces a different perspective by recognizing that citizens are not simply data subjects or service users. They are individuals whose interactions with government are shaped by personal circumstances, expectations, uncertainty, and emotional experiences.

This distinction is particularly important because many interactions with public institutions occur during moments of vulnerability. Citizens often contact government services not because everything is going well, but because they are facing challenges that require institutional support. A person applying for unemployment assistance may experience anxiety about financial insecurity. A patient seeking healthcare support may feel fear and uncertainty. A family requesting social services may already be under significant emotional pressure. In these situations, a purely informational response may satisfy administrative requirements but fail to address the human reality behind the request. Emotional intelligence allows AI enabled systems to recognize that the quality of governance is determined not only by whether a service is delivered, but also by how citizens experience the process.

The development of emotional intelligence in AI governance can be understood through three interconnected capabilities: emotional perception, emotional understanding, and emotional response. Emotional perception refers to the ability of AI systems to identify emotional signals within citizen interactions. These signals may appear through language patterns, repeated questions, expressions of frustration, or signs of uncertainty. For example, when a citizen repeatedly asks the same question about a public benefit program, a traditional AI system may simply provide the same information again. However, an emotionally intelligent system may recognize that repeated questioning could indicate confusion, anxiety, or a lack of confidence in the process rather than a simple information deficit.

Emotional understanding goes beyond identifying emotional states and focuses on interpreting the reasons behind them. Human emotions in government interactions are rarely isolated reactions. They are often connected to broader social circumstances. A citizen who expresses frustration with a government service may not simply be dissatisfied with the digital interface; the frustration may reflect deeper concerns about financial pressure, lack of access, or fear of being excluded from public support. Therefore, emotional intelligence requires AI systems to consider the context behind emotional expressions rather than treating emotions as simple signals to be classified.

The final dimension is emotional response, which concerns how AI systems adapt their communication and service delivery based on citizens' emotional conditions. An emotionally intelligent government AI system would not only provide accurate information but also adjust the way information is communicated. For example, instead of simply informing a citizen that an application has been rejected, the system could provide a clearer explanation, identify possible next steps, offer opportunities for review, or connect the citizen with human assistance when necessary. In this way, emotional intelligence transforms AI from a passive information provider into a more responsive governance interface.

The importance of emotional intelligence lies in its ability to improve the quality of the relationship between citizens and government. Traditional digital government has often measured success through operational indicators such as processing speed, service availability, and administrative efficiency. These measures remain important, but they cannot fully capture citizens' experiences of governance. A system may process applications quickly and accurately while still creating feelings of frustration or alienation if citizens perceive the interaction as cold and indifferent. Emotional intelligence introduces a broader understanding of public service quality by recognizing that trust is created not only through effective outcomes but also through meaningful interactions.

However, incorporating emotional intelligence into digital government does not mean allowing AI systems to make judgments based on emotions alone. Public administration must continue to rely on principles of fairness, legality, and consistency. The purpose of emotional intelligence is not to replace rational decision making but to complement it by adding awareness of human experiences. AI should not determine what citizens deserve based on emotional analysis. Instead, it should help governments communicate more effectively, identify unmet needs, and create more supportive service environments.

This perspective represents an important shift in the understanding of trusted AI governance. Previous approaches often viewed trust as a consequence of technical performance. If a system was accurate, secure, and efficient, citizens would gradually accept it. However, digital government demonstrates that trust is also relational. Citizens trust institutions when they believe those institutions not only perform effectively but also recognize their circumstances and treat them with respect. Emotional intelligence therefore provides a missing connection between technological capability and human centered governance.

Ultimately, the value of emotional intelligence in AI enabled digital government is not that it makes machines more human, but that it makes governance more responsive to human needs. The goal is not to create artificial emotions, but to ensure that technological systems remain connected to the social realities they are designed to serve. Therefore, emotional intelligence should be understood not as an additional technological feature, but as a fundamental dimension of trustworthy AI governance. It strengthens the relationship between citizens and public institutions by ensuring that digital transformation does not reduce people to data points, but continues to recognize them as human beings with experiences, concerns, and expectations.

8. ETHICAL BOUNDARIES OF EMOTIONAL AI

The integration of emotional intelligence into digital government creates new possibilities for improving citizen engagement and strengthening public trust. By allowing AI systems to recognize emotional signals, understand citizen experiences, and provide more responsive interactions, governments may overcome some of the limitations of traditional digital services. However, the expansion of emotional capabilities also introduces a new category of ethical challenges. The more accurately AI systems can detect and interpret human emotions, the greater the potential risks associated with privacy, manipulation, and social inequality. Therefore, emotional intelligence cannot be understood simply as a technological improvement. It must be developed within clear ethical boundaries that protect human autonomy, dignity, and rights.

The first major ethical concern is emotional privacy. Traditional data governance has mainly focused on protecting explicit personal information, such as names, addresses, medical records, and financial data. However, emotional AI introduces a new type of sensitive information: the internal emotional states of individuals. Emotions are deeply connected to personal identity, psychological conditions, and private experiences. When AI systems analyze facial expressions, voice patterns, language choices, or behavioral signals to infer emotions, they are accessing information that individuals may not consciously intend to disclose. This creates a fundamental question: should emotional information be treated as a form of personal data requiring the same level of protection as other sensitive information?

This issue becomes particularly important in government contexts because the relationship between citizens and public institutions is not based on equal power.

Citizens may provide emotional data not because they freely choose to do so, but because access to essential services requires interaction with government systems. For example, a citizen applying for social assistance may interact with an AI system that analyzes expressions of stress or uncertainty. While such analysis may help the system provide more supportive communication, it may also create concerns about whether citizens have meaningful control over how their emotional states are collected, interpreted, and used. Without appropriate safeguards, emotional AI could transform personal feelings into another form of administrative data subject to institutional control.

The second ethical challenge concerns emotional manipulation. Emotional intelligence allows AI systems to better understand citizens, but the same capability could potentially be used to influence citizens' attitudes, decisions, or behaviors. In commercial environments, recommendation systems already use behavioral and emotional information to increase engagement or encourage certain choices. However, the ethical implications become much more serious when emotional AI is used by governments because governments possess legitimate authority and access to citizens' personal information. For example, a government communication system may identify that certain citizens feel fear or uncertainty regarding a public policy. Using this information to provide clearer explanations and reduce confusion may represent a positive application of emotional intelligence. However, using emotional analysis to design messages that intentionally influence citizens' opinions or encourage compliance through psychological techniques would cross an important ethical boundary. The purpose of emotional AI in public governance should be to improve understanding and support, not to create hidden mechanisms of behavioral control.

The third challenge is emotional inequality, which refers to the possibility that emotional AI systems may misunderstand or unfairly evaluate individuals from different social, cultural, or personal backgrounds. Human emotions are not expressed in identical ways across all groups. A person's silence, tone of voice, facial expression, or communication style may reflect many different meanings depending on cultural norms, personality, social background, or personal circumstances. An AI system trained on limited emotional patterns may incorrectly interpret these differences and produce inaccurate judgments.

For example, in some cultural contexts, avoiding direct eye contact may represent respect rather than discomfort or dishonesty. Similarly, a person who speaks less during an interaction may be experiencing anxiety, but may also simply have a different communication style. If government AI systems classify such behaviors as indicators of unwillingness, risk, or lack of cooperation, emotional recognition could unintentionally create new forms of discrimination. Instead of reducing inequality, emotional AI could reinforce existing social biases by defining certain emotional expressions as more acceptable than others.

These challenges demonstrate that emotional recognition should not become a new mechanism for categorizing citizens. Traditional algorithmic risks involve classifying people according to demographic or behavioral characteristics. Emotional AI introduces another possibility: classifying people according to perceived psychological states. If emotions become a basis for determining eligibility, credibility, or risk, citizens may face decisions based on interpretations of their inner experiences rather than their actual needs or circumstances.

Therefore, the ethical purpose of emotional AI in digital government should be carefully defined. Emotional intelligence should enhance communication and improve citizen experiences, but it should not become a tool for surveillance, persuasion, or social classification. The goal is not to create systems that judge human emotions, but to create systems that respond more appropriately to human needs. Emotional AI should support empathy rather than replace human understanding, and it should strengthen citizen autonomy rather than reduce individuals to emotional profiles.

Ultimately, the development of emotional AI requires a balance between technological capability and ethical restraint. A truly human centered AI governance framework must recognize that emotions are not merely data points to be analyzed, but meaningful aspects of human identity and dignity. The future of emotional intelligence in digital government depends not on how accurately AI can read human emotions, but on whether such capabilities are used in ways that respect privacy, protect freedom, and strengthen the relationship between citizens and public institutions. In this sense, the ethical boundary of emotional AI is not determined by what technology can do, but by what society believes technology should be allowed to do.

9. THEORETICAL CONTRIBUTION TOWARD HUMAN CENTERED TRUSTED AI GOVERNANCE

The discussions throughout this chapter reveal that the ethical challenge of AI enabled digital government extends far beyond the question of whether algorithms are accurate, fair, or transparent. As AI systems become increasingly involved in public governance, they no longer function merely as technical instruments for improving administrative efficiency. They participate in processes that influence how public resources are allocated, how citizens are classified, and how government decisions are experienced by individuals. Therefore, the central challenge of AI governance is not simply to build better algorithms, but to establish a governance framework that ensures AI remains consistent with human values, democratic principles, and social expectations (Figure 1).

Figure 1. The Logical Structure of This Chapter

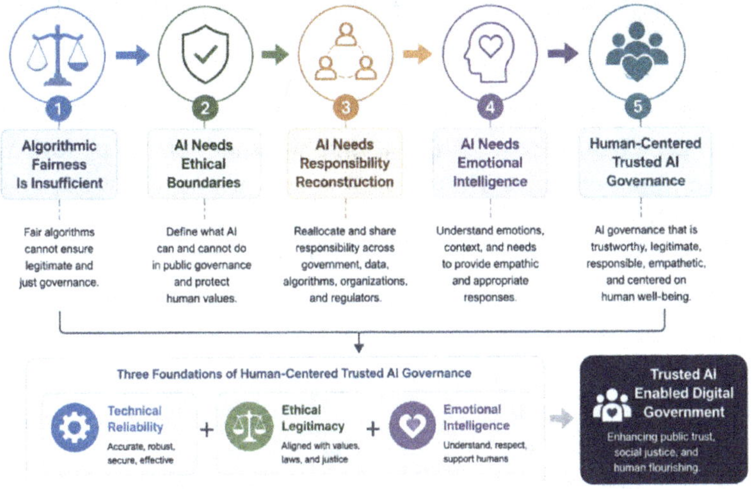

Based on this understanding, this chapter makes a theoretical shift from algorithm centered ethics toward human centered AI governance. Traditional AI ethics has largely focused on improving the internal qualities of algorithms, particularly through concepts such as fairness, transparency, and accountability. These approaches have provided important foundations for identifying bias and reducing technical risks. However, they remain insufficient for understanding the broader ethical challenges of AI in government because they primarily examine whether algorithms function properly rather than whether algorithmic governance itself is socially legitimate. In public governance, an AI system can be technically fair while still raising fundamental questions about authority, responsibility, and the appropriate role of machines in decisions that affect human lives. Therefore, this chapter argues that fairness should be understood as the beginning of AI ethics rather than its final objective. The deeper ethical concern is whether AI driven governance operates within boundaries that respect human dignity, public values, and democratic accountability.

This chapter further extends the understanding of responsibility in AI governance by moving beyond the traditional focus on technical failure. In conventional technological systems, responsibility is often discussed in terms of whether a system functions correctly or whether errors can be prevented. However, AI enabled governance introduces a more complex reality in which decisions are produced through interactions among algorithms, data, institutions, and human actors. As a result, responsibility cannot be limited to identifying technical mistakes after they occur. It must also involve examining the values embedded within AI systems, the institutional choices behind their deployment, and the social consequences produced by their operation. The ethical responsibility of AI governance therefore lies not only in preventing algorithmic errors, but also in ensuring that technological systems serve legitimate social purposes.

At the same time, this chapter introduces emotional intelligence as an essential dimension of trusted AI governance. Previous approaches to technology trust have often emphasized cognitive evaluation, asking whether citizens believe a system is reliable, accurate, and effective. However, digital government demonstrates that trust is not formed only through rational assessment. Citizens also develop trust through their experiences of interaction with public institutions. A government service may be efficient and technically correct, yet still fail to create trust if citizens feel ignored, misunderstood, or disconnected. By incorporating emotional intelligence into AI governance, this chapter highlights that trustworthy AI should not only process information but also recognize human experiences and support more meaningful interactions between citizens and government.

Through these theoretical developments, this chapter proposes a broader understanding of trusted AI enabled digital government. Trustworthy AI is not achieved through technological improvement alone, nor can it be guaranteed simply by implementing fairness standards or transparency mechanisms. Instead, it emerges from the interaction of three essential dimensions: technical reliability, ethical legitimacy, and emotional intelligence. Technical reliability ensures that AI systems can perform governance tasks effectively. Ethical legitimacy ensures that AI participation in public decision making remains within acceptable moral and institutional boundaries. Emotional intelligence ensures that digital transformation preserves the human relationships that form the foundation of public trust.

Therefore, the ultimate contribution of this chapter is to redefine the purpose of AI governance. The goal of trusted AI is not to create autonomous systems that replace human judgment, but to develop governance systems in which technology enhances human capability while remaining accountable to human values. AI becomes truly trustworthy not when it becomes more powerful than humans, but when it becomes more responsive to human needs, more respectful of human rights, and more deeply integrated into a governance framework built upon responsibility and social legitimacy.

10. THE RELATIONSHIP BETWEEN THIS CHAPTER AND PREVIOUS CHAPTERS

The emergence of AI enabled digital government has fundamentally transformed the traditional relationship between technology, government, and citizens. The first chapter established the theoretical foundation of this transformation by arguing that AI should no longer be understood merely as a technical instrument used by governments to improve administrative efficiency. Instead, AI has become an embedded governance actor that participates in processes such as resource allocation, risk assessment, and public service prioritization. This transformation challenges traditional understandings of government trust because citizens are no longer evaluating government institutions alone. They are increasingly evaluating a complex governance system composed of public institutions, algorithms, data infrastructures, and technological actors. Therefore, the first chapter reveals the central problem of AI enabled governance: when technology becomes involved in the exercise of public authority, trust must be reconstructed beyond traditional government centered models.

Building on this argument, the second chapter further explores how trust in AI enabled government can be reconstructed through the concept of an AI social contract. It argues that traditional technology centered trust, which emphasizes reliability, security, and efficiency, is insufficient to explain why citizens accept or reject AI driven governance. In the AI era, trust is not generated simply because a system performs well. Instead, it depends on whether citizens believe that AI is used within a legitimate governance framework where authority, responsibility, and participation are appropriately distributed. The concept of the AI social contract expands the traditional relationship between citizens and government by recognizing the involvement of additional actors, including technology developers, data institutions, and regulatory bodies. However, while the second chapter explains the institutional conditions under which AI governance can gain legitimacy, it also raises a deeper question: what ethical principles should guide this new governance relationship?

This question forms the foundation of the present chapter. If Chapter 1 explains why AI changes the structure of government trust, and Chapter 2 explains why AI requires a new social contract, Chapter 3 examines what makes this new relationship ethically acceptable and genuinely human centered. The introduction of AI into public governance does not only create questions about efficiency and accountability; it also raises fundamental concerns about values, responsibility, and the relationship between technology and human experience. A system may be technically reliable and institutionally regulated, yet still fail to gain public acceptance if it does not respect human dignity, recognize social values, or respond to citizens' lived experiences.

Figure 2. The Relationship Between This Chapter and Previous Chapters

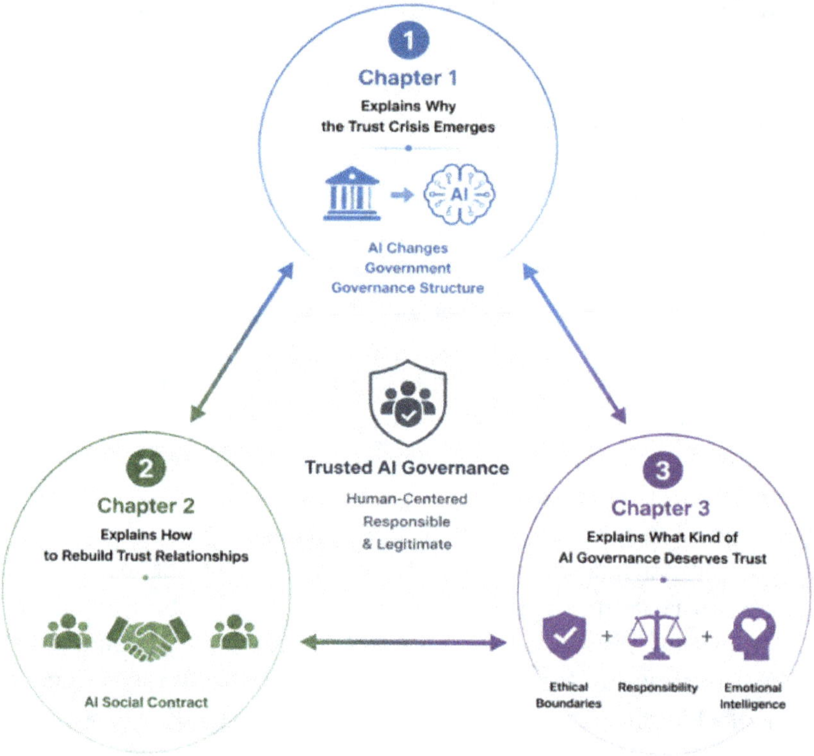

Therefore, this chapter extends the discussion from institutional legitimacy to ethical legitimacy. It argues that trusted AI governance requires more than fair algorithms and transparent systems. It requires clear ethical boundaries that define the appropriate role of AI in public decision making, responsibility structures that ensure accountability when decisions are produced through complex technological networks, and emotional intelligence that enables AI systems to better understand and respond to human needs. In this sense, Chapter 3 represents a shift from asking whether AI can support government functions toward examining whether AI can support governance in a way that remains consistent with human values.

Through this theoretical progression, the first three chapters establish a comprehensive foundation for understanding trusted AI enabled digital government. Chapter 1 identifies the transformation of trust caused by AI. Chapter 2 reconstructs the social and institutional relationship necessary for AI legitimacy. Chapter 3 provides the ethical and human foundation that determines whether such legitimacy can be sustained. Together, these chapters demonstrate that trustworthy AI governance is not achieved through technological advancement alone. It requires the integration of institutional trust, social responsibility, ethical legitimacy, and human understanding. This foundation prepares the theoretical basis for the following chapters, which further explore how trusted AI governance can be implemented and sustained within digital government systems (Figure 2).

REFERENCES

Barocas, S., Hardt, M., & Narayanan, A. (2023). *Fairness and machine learning: Limitations and opportunities*. MIT Press.

Berk, R., Heidari, H., Jabbari, S., Kearns, M., & Roth, A. (2021). Fairness in criminal justice risk assessments: The state of the art. *Sociological Methods & Research*, *50*(1), 3–44. DOI: 10.1177/0049124118782533

Diakopoulos, N. (2016). Accountability in algorithmic decision making. *Communications of the ACM*, *59*(2), 56–62. DOI: 10.1145/2844110

Shneiderman, B. (2022). *Human-centered AI*. Oxford University Press. DOI: 10.1093/oso/9780192845290.001.0001

KEY TERMS AND DEFINITIONS

AI Accountability: AI accountability refers to the mechanisms through which responsible actors can be identified, required to justify decisions, and held responsible for the consequences of AI systems. In AI enabled government, accountability extends across multiple actors, including government agencies, developers, data managers, and regulatory institutions.

AI Governance: AI governance refers to the institutional, ethical, and regulatory arrangements that guide the development, deployment, and use of artificial intelligence systems. In digital government, AI governance concerns not only how AI systems function but also how authority, responsibility, and accountability are distributed among governments, technology providers, regulatory institutions, and citizens.

AI Social Contract: AI Social Contract refers to an implicit agreement among governments, citizens, technology developers, and data institutions regarding how AI should participate in governance and how responsibility should be allocated. It extends traditional social contract theory by recognizing that AI systems and technological actors have become important participants in public decision making processes.

Algorithmic Authority: Algorithmic authority refers to the capacity of AI systems to influence or determine decisions that affect individuals, public resources, and social opportunities. Unlike traditional administrative authority exercised directly by human officials, algorithmic authority operates through computational processes such as classification, prediction, and optimization.

Algorithmic Fairness: Algorithmic fairness refers to the principle that AI systems should avoid producing unjustified discrimination or unequal outcomes among different individuals or social groups. However, in the context of digital government, fairness is understood as a necessary but insufficient condition because technically fair algorithms may still raise questions regarding legitimacy, values, and the appropriate role of AI in public decision making.

Emotional Intelligence in AI Governance: Emotional intelligence in AI governance refers to the capacity of AI systems to recognize, understand, and appropriately respond to human emotional experiences during interactions with public services. It does not mean that AI imitates human emotions, but rather that technology becomes more sensitive to citizens' needs, concerns, and social contexts.

Human Centered AI Governance: Human centered AI governance is an approach that places human dignity, autonomy, participation, and social values at the center of AI development and implementation. It argues that AI should enhance human decision making and public service quality while preserving human responsibility and ethical oversight.

Meaningful Explainability: Meaningful explainability refers to the ability of AI governance systems to provide understandable and relevant explanations regarding why AI is used, how decisions affect individuals, and who is responsible when errors occur. It goes beyond technical transparency by emphasizing citizens' ability to understand, question, and challenge AI based decisions.

Trusted AI Enabled Digital Government: Trusted AI Enabled Digital Government refers to a governance framework in which artificial intelligence is integrated into public administration while maintaining technical reliability, ethical legitimacy, institutional accountability, and human centered values. It emphasizes that public trust in AI is not created solely through technological performance but through the combination of effective systems, responsible governance, and meaningful relationships between governments and citizens.

Value Embedded AI Governance: Value embedded AI governance emphasizes that AI systems are not neutral technical tools but systems that contain social, political, and ethical assumptions. Every choice regarding data selection, optimization objectives, and evaluation criteria reflects certain values about what should be prioritized in governance.

Chapter 9

Governing AI Through Accounting:
The Role of Government and Sustainability Accounting in Fostering Trust and Public Value

Rimi Gusliana Mais
http://orcid.org/0000-0002-2625-0601
Sekolah Tinggi Ilmu Ekonomi Indonesia Jakarta, Indonesia

M. Munir
http://orcid.org/0009-0006-4464-5136
Sekolah Tinggi Ilmu Syari'ah Al-Manar Jakarta, Jakarta, Indonesia

ABSTRACT

The integration of artificial intelligence (AI) into digital government creates a paradox: unprecedented efficiency gains alongside ethical and accountability challenges that threaten public trust. This chapter addresses a critical gap in AI governance literature by arguing that achieving trusted AI requires robust accountability infrastructures beyond technical design. We develop an integrative framework positioning government accounting and sustainability accounting as essential mediating institutions that translate abstract AI ethics principles—fairness, transparency, and explainability—into measurable indicators, auditable processes, and public disclosures. These accounting systems transform AI operations into verifiable accountability evidence. We conceptualize a causal pathway where accounting-based governance mechanisms generate institutional trust, which in turn produces sustainable public value. The chapter contributes a novel theoretical model for interdisciplinary research and offers practical guidelines for policymakers to institutionalize ethical AI

DOI: 10.4018/979-8-3373-9129-8.ch009

1. INTRODUCTION

1.1 AI Transformation in Digital Government

Artificial intelligence (AI) has transitioned from a trial enhancement of e-government services to a pivotal force in transforming digital governance, redefining the design, delivery, and assessment of public value through public services and administrative processes (Tangi et al., 2025). In contrast to previous waves of digitalization that emphasized the digitization of forms and procedures, AI brings forth automation driven by learning and predictive decision-making support, capable of transforming service frontlines, internal management, and interagency collaboration (van Noordt & Misuraca, 2022). Authorities currently utilize AI for automated service categorization, fraud detection, intelligent document management, predictive analytics, and decision support.

Current studies emphasize that the outcomes of AI implementation depend on the institutional environment and governance capabilities, particularly the capacity of public entities to align AI systems with societal principles such as equity, openness, and legitimacy (Criado & de Zarate-Alcarazo, 2022). The pursuit of AI transformation often occurs through GovTech ecosystems and public-private collaborations, which enhance innovation yet blur accountability delineations (Bharosa, 2022). As a result, the assessment of AI transformation encompasses not only operational indicators but also trust-related results, including acceptance and perceived equity (Gesk & Leyer, 2022).

This engenders the peril of disjointed transformation, resulting in inconsistent service quality and the possible marginalization of at-risk populations. The transformation agenda increasingly positions AI as an issue of institutional reconfiguration necessitating governance and monitoring frameworks (Tangi et al., 2025). This chapter expands on that perspective by contending that accounting and sustainability accounting ought to be regarded as integral components of the institutional "backbone" that translates AI transformation into verifiable, comprehensible, and publicly accountable governance outcomes (Grossi et al., 2024).

1.2 Ethical and Accountability Challenges in AI-Driven Governance

AI-facilitated governance presents ethical and accountability dilemmas that differ from those posed by traditional IT risks, due to the opaque nature of AI outputs, the widespread encoding of bias, and the dispersal of responsibilities among multiple agencies and suppliers (Moss et al., 2022). These hazards are especially significant in public administration, as algorithmic choices influence eligibility assessments, service prioritization, and resource allocation, thereby impacting citizens' rights and welfare (Criado & de Zarate-Alcarazo, 2022). The "double black box" dilemma—where technology obscurity intersects with governance ambiguity—hinders openness and clouds accountability in public decision-making (Kjøs Fahsing et al., 2026).

Accountability cannot be defined solely by technical elucidation; it requires explicit delegation of responsibility, mechanisms for contestation, and evidence-based oversight (Moss et al., 2022). Novel regulatory frameworks are progressively requiring algorithmic effect evaluations, documentation of system objectives, and continuous harm surveillance (OECD, 2026). Nonetheless, public entities face capability limitations, such as limited internal expertise and reliance on vendor-supplied tools, exacerbating a transparency paradox in which governments implement AI yet diminish insight into decision-making processes (Bharosa, 2022; Tangi et al., 2025).

Public endorsement of AI hinges not solely on its perceived utility but also on its perceived fairness, controllability, and alignment with democratic principles (Gesk & Leyer, 2022). International data indicates that views on integrity, responsiveness, and equity are essential to fostering institutional trust in AI-driven governance (OECD, 2026).

These dynamics necessitate governance frameworks that yield demonstrable accountability through performance evaluation, audit preparedness, and clear disclosure, advancing from aspirational ideals to established oversight systems (Grossi et al., 2024; Schmitz & Bryson, 2025).

1.3 The Missing Role of Accounting in Trusted AI

Despite the rapid growth of AI governance studies, the role of accounting as a mechanism for accountability in trustworthy AI remains underexamined and often implicit (Tangi et al., 2025). Contemporary research regards accountability solely as a policy issue, overlooking its implementation through measurable, verifiable data within organizational operations (Grossi et al., 2024). Accounting research provides a unique benefit, as public-sector accounting systems make governmental operations accessible and subject to scrutiny through organized documentation, controls, and audit trails (Grossi et al., 2024). Nonetheless, inquiries into algorithmic technologies in public sector accounting are limited relative to their extent of implementation (Manes-Rossi et al., 2025).

Researchers emphasize shortcomings in the empirically grounded comprehension of how algorithmic instruments modify the generation of financial information, influence accountability structures, and redefine public auditing within data-driven governance (Dumay et al., 2024). This inequality is significant, as AI enables financially vital functions—fraud detection, benefits administration, and procurement evaluation—that require measures to safeguard public resources (Al-Baity, 2025). A significant shortcoming concerns sustainability accounting in AI governance. While sustainability accounting has expanded to include ESG implications, the literature on digital governance has not consistently integrated these aspects into AI governance, even though AI generates sustainability-related repercussions (Lim, 2024).

Sustainability accounting can improve the dependability of AI by requiring comprehensive impact reporting, guaranteeing that AI adheres to public-value responsibilities beyond mere efficiency goals (Manes-Rossi et al., 2025). In the absence of these lenses, AI governance places excessive focus on technological efficacy while failing to sufficiently articulate criteria for legitimacy, stewardship, and sustainability (Grossi et al., 2024). Consequently, the primary research deficiency lies in the lack of cohesive accountability: the risks associated with AI generation are not consistently aligned with governance frameworks that can document, verify, and report on AI efficacy and effects. This chapter tackles this deficiency by suggesting a cohesive framework that situates government and sustainability accounting as fundamental institutional tools for regulating AI and cultivating trust.

1.4 Objectives and Research Questions

The primary objective of this chapter is to develop an accounting-informed understanding of trusted AI governance in digital government by linking AI ethics, accountability mechanisms, and public value creation through the lenses of government accounting and sustainability accounting (Tangi et al., 2025). Conceptually, the chapter argues that trust in AI-driven governance is not only built through technical design choices (e.g., explainability features) but also through institutional accountability infrastructures that make AI performance, impacts, and decisions visible and contestable (Moss et al., 2022). Practically, it positions accounting as a set of tools and governance routines capable of translating AI operations into auditable evidence, performance metrics, and public disclosures that can support oversight bodies, public auditors, and citizens (Grossi et al., 2024).

To achieve this, the chapter pursues two primary research questions:

1. How can government accounting and sustainability accounting serve as institutional infrastructures to operationalize AI ethics and accountability in digital government?
2. What is the causal mechanism through which accounting-based governance generates institutional trust and, ultimately, public value?

Figure 1 presents the integrative governance architecture proposed in this chapter, illustrating how trusted AI in digital government is institutionalized through structured accountability infrastructures to generate sustainable public value outcomes.

Figure 1. Integrative Governance Architecture of Trusted AI in Digital Government

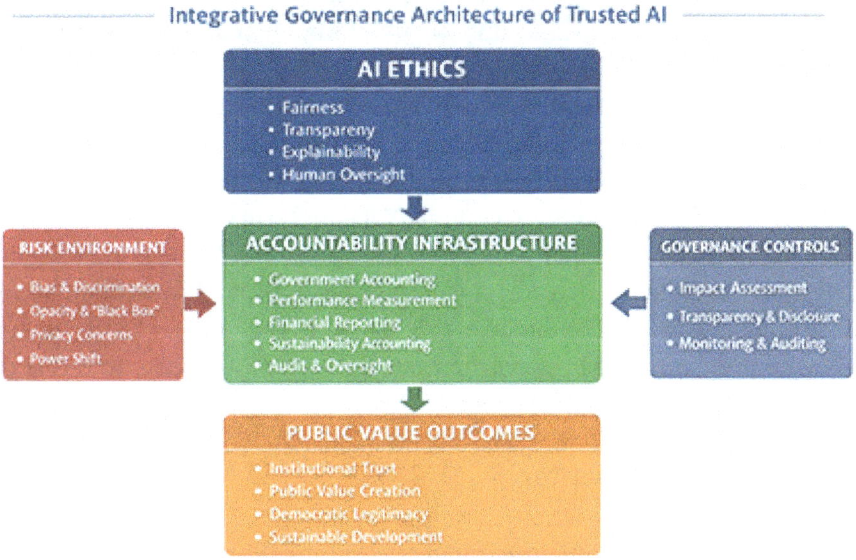

Source: *Developed by the author based on Tangi et al. (2025); Moss et al. (2022); Grossi et al. (2024); Manes-Rossi et al. (2025); Lim (2024); Robles & Mallinson (2023).*

The framework conceptualizes AI ethics principles—fairness, transparency, explainability, and human oversight—as normative foundations that guide AI deployment in public administration. The main contribution of this chapter is a integrative governance framework that: (1) identifies the specific mechanisms through which accounting systems mediate between AI systems and public value; (2) articulates a causal pathway linking AI systems, accountability mechanisms, institutional trust, and public value; and (3) provides a structured, multidimensional accountability matrix for operationalizing AI governance in public sector organizations.

1.5 Methodology for Chapter Development

This chapter is a conceptual study that develops its framework through a rigorous synthesis and thematic analysis of interdisciplinary literature. The methodology follows the approach for conceptual papers suggested by scholars like Jaakkola (2020) and MacInnis (2011), which emphasizes theory synthesis to create new explanatory models. The process involved: This conceptual study develops its framework through a rigorous synthesis of interdisciplinary literature. A systematic search was conducted in academic databases (Web of Science, Scopus, Google

Scholar) using keywords including "AI governance," "algorithmic accountability," "government accounting," and "sustainability accounting," limited to peer-reviewed publications from 2020-2026 in high-impact public administration, accounting, and digital government journals.

Thematic analysis following Braun and Clarke (2006) identified key themes: AI transformation and governance challenges, AI ethics and accountability risks, public sector accountability mechanisms, government accounting as a transparency and performance tool, and sustainability accounting for long-term value creation. Theory synthesis integrated these findings to develop an explanatory framework, mapping relationships between themes and deriving a causal pathway (AI → Accountability → Trust → Public Value). The framework draws on agency theory to understand principal-agent problems in AI governance and accountability theory to frame the multidimensional nature of public accountability.

1.6 Structure of the Chapter

Structurally, the chapter is organized to move from problem framing to solution development. Section 2 establishes the theoretical foundations by integrating trusted AI governance, public value theory, and public-sector accountability concepts. Section 3 examines the ethical and accountability risk landscape in AI-enabled government, highlighting why governance must be evidence-driven and institutionally anchored rather than principle-only (Moss et al., 2022). Section 4 introduces government accounting as a key accountability infrastructure for transparency, performance measurement, financial reporting, and auditability. Section 5 integrates sustainability accounting into the framework, linking AI governance to Sustainable Development Goals and long-term public value.

Section 6 presents the integrated conceptual framework, detailing the governance model, the causal pathway, and a multidimensional accountability matrix. Section 7 derives practical implications for policymakers and public managers, while Section 8 identifies future research directions. Section 9 concludes the chapter with a summary of contributions and a forward-looking perspective.

2. THEORETICAL FOUNDATIONS

2.1 Trusted AI in Digital Government

The concept of trusted artificial intelligence in digital government emerges from the intersection of technological reliability, institutional legitimacy, and normative public values. Contemporary scholarship emphasizes that trust in AI within public administration cannot be reduced to technical robustness or system accuracy alone, but must encompass fairness, transparency, explainability, and accountability embedded within governance structures (Tangi et al., 2025). In digital government settings, AI systems increasingly support eligibility determinations, predictive analytics, resource allocation, and risk-based inspections, thereby directly influencing citizens' rights and access to services (van Noordt & Misuraca, 2022). Consequently, trusted AI becomes a governance condition rather than merely a technological feature.

Recent studies highlight that public trust in AI is shaped by citizens' perceptions of procedural fairness, institutional competence, and ethical alignment with democratic values (Robles & Mallinson, 2023). Unlike private sector AI applications, where consumer choice may mitigate dissatisfaction, public sector AI operates within compulsory administrative frameworks, making trust foundational to legitimacy (Gesk & Leyer, 2022). Therefore, trusted AI requires institutional safeguards that ensure contestability, transparency of decision logic, and mechanisms for redress when harms occur (Moss et al., 2022).

The transition from technical trust to ethical trust represents a critical shift in digital government research. Technical trust focuses on system performance metrics such as accuracy and reliability, whereas ethical trust integrates fairness, non-discrimination, human oversight, and alignment with societal values (O'Shaughnessy et al., 2023). This broader understanding of trust aligns with governance-based AI frameworks that emphasize responsibility allocation, impact assessment, and ongoing monitoring rather than one-time compliance checks (Moss et al., 2022). In this context, trusted AI is embedded within accountability ecosystems that connect algorithmic operations with institutional oversight and public reporting (Grossi et al., 2024).

Moreover, digital government transformation driven by AI introduces socio-technical reconfigurations that reshape power distribution and decision-making hierarchies within public organizations (Tangi et al., 2025). These transformations require governance models capable of integrating technological innovation with established administrative accountability norms. Trusted AI, therefore, depends on the ability of governments to institutionalize transparency, auditability, and ethical evaluation procedures as routine governance practices rather than exceptional interventions (van Noordt & Misuraca, 2022).

2.2 Public Value Theory in Digital Governance

Public value theory provides a normative foundation for evaluating AI-enabled digital government beyond efficiency metrics, emphasizing collective benefits that enhance societal well-being, democratic legitimacy, and equitable service delivery (Criado & de Zarate-Alcarazo, 2022; Tangi et al., 2025). Recent research argues that AI should be assessed by its contribution to inclusiveness, fairness, and transparency, not merely productivity gains (Criado & de Zarate-Alcarazo, 2022; Tangi et al., 2025). AI systems can enhance public value through service personalization and evidence-based policymaking, yet they risk eroding value if they reinforce bias or obscure decision rationales (Robles & Mallinson, 2023; O'Shaughnessy et al., 2023). Citizens' acceptance of AI is strongly associated with perceived fairness and accountability rather than perceived innovation (Gesk & Leyer, 2022).

Cross-national evidence confirms that alignment with broader public values, including moral-ethical and political-social dimensions, is essential for building trust and acceptance (Wittmann & Meynhardt, 2025). Bureaucrats are less likely to adopt AI when presented with information about potential biases and negative equity impacts, while efficiency gains alone have no effect on support for AI adoption (Bell, 2024). From a theoretical perspective, public value theory aligns with accountability as a mechanism for legitimacy, where accounting systems provide the evidence base for demonstrating fair, transparent AI operations (Grossi et al., 2024). This positions public value as an evaluative lens requiring structured reporting and accountability disclosures that translate algorithmic operations into socially meaningful outcomes (Bagheri & Dirksen, 2024).

2.3 Accountability in the Public Sector

Accountability in the public sector is traditionally conceptualized as a multidimensional relationship involving answerability, enforceability, transparency, and stewardship of public resources. In AI-enabled digital government, these dimensions become more complex because automated systems mediate decisions that were previously traceable to identifiable officials (Moss et al., 2022). As algorithmic systems assume greater decision-support or decision-making roles, the lines of responsibility between developers, administrators, and oversight bodies can become blurred (Bharosa, 2022). This diffusion of responsibility intensifies the need for formal accountability mechanisms embedded within institutional structures.

Recent scholarship underscores that public accountability in AI contexts requires both procedural transparency and institutional traceability, ensuring that decision rationales can be reconstructed and evaluated (Robles & Mallinson, 2023). Administrative accountability involves ensuring compliance with laws and ethical standards, while financial accountability requires demonstrating responsible use of public funds in AI procurement and implementation (Grossi et al., 2024). Social accountability extends further, encompassing responsiveness to citizen concerns and transparent communication of risks and impacts (O'Shaughnessy et al., 2023).

Drawing on accountability literature, we distinguish three dimensions relevant for AI governance. Administrative accountability ensures compliance with laws and ethical standards through documented procedures, including algorithmic design choices, data sources, and validation processes. Financial accountability requires responsible use of public funds, transparent procurement, and rigorous reporting of AI-related expenditures and life-cycle costs. Social accountability addresses responsiveness to citizen concerns, transparent risk communication, and redress mechanisms when automated decisions cause harm.

Digital transformation driven by AI also affects performance accountability, requiring measurement systems to evaluate algorithmic effectiveness, fairness, and unintended consequences rather than focusing solely on output volume or cost efficiency (Tangi et al., 2025). Without appropriate indicators, AI systems may operate with limited scrutiny, creating an accountability deficit in automated governance environments (Moss et al., 2022). Emerging public sector auditing research highlights the necessity of developing AI audit capabilities to assess algorithmic models, data governance, and decision logic integrity (Grossi et al., 2024). This multidimensional understanding forms the theoretical basis for positioning accounting systems as essential infrastructures for ethical AI governance.

3. ETHICAL AI AND ACCOUNTABILITY RISKS IN DIGITAL GOVERNMENT

3.1 Algorithmic Bias and Discrimination

Algorithmic bias represents one of the most widely documented ethical risks in AI-driven public governance. In digital government contexts, algorithmic systems are frequently used to support decisions related to welfare eligibility, tax fraud detection, risk assessment, public safety, and resource prioritization. When such systems rely on biased training data, flawed proxies, or historically skewed administrative records, they may reproduce or amplify structural inequalities (Moss et al., 2022). Unlike human discretion, algorithmic bias can operate at scale and with procedural opacity, potentially affecting thousands or millions of citizens before detection mechanisms intervene (Tangi et al., 2025).

Recent research in public administration highlights that bias in AI systems is not merely a technical anomaly but often reflects embedded institutional and societal inequalities present in historical datasets (van Noordt & Misuraca, 2022). For example, predictive models used in social service targeting may disproportionately flag marginalized communities if historical enforcement data reflects prior discriminatory practices. This phenomenon transforms algorithmic bias into a governance risk with ethical, legal, and reputational implications (Robles & Mallinson, 2023). Citizens subjected to biased automated decisions may experience reduced access to services, increased scrutiny, or diminished procedural justice, thereby undermining trust in public institutions (Gesk & Leyer, 2022).

From an accountability perspective, algorithmic discrimination raises questions regarding responsibility allocation and redress mechanisms. When automated outputs contribute to adverse outcomes, identifying whether responsibility lies with developers, data providers, procurement authorities, or frontline administrators becomes complex (Bharosa, 2022). Emerging accountability frameworks emphasize the necessity of algorithmic impact assessments and continuous bias monitoring as governance safeguards rather than one-time validation exercises (Moss et al., 2022). However, public organizations frequently lack standardized metrics and reporting mechanisms capable of systematically documenting bias detection and mitigation efforts (Grossi et al., 2024).

Moreover, bias risks intersect with public value considerations. AI systems that disproportionately disadvantage certain groups compromise principles of equity and inclusiveness central to democratic governance (O'Shaughnessy et al., 2023). Consequently, ethical AI governance must incorporate structured evaluation tools capable of identifying discriminatory outcomes and linking corrective measures to institutional accountability systems. This underscores the importance of integrating performance measurement and reporting infrastructures into AI governance to ensure that algorithmic fairness is not treated as a purely technical aspiration but as a measurable and auditable public obligation (Tangi et al., 2025).

3.2 Opacity and the Black Box Problem

Opacity, often termed the "black box problem," refers to the challenge of understanding the mechanisms through which complex AI models produce results. In public-sector contexts, this poses significant challenges, as administrative choices require justification, documentation, and the possibility of contestation (Moss et al., 2022). Sophisticated machine learning frameworks offer limited interpretability, creating a trade-off between efficiency gains and responsibility obligations (van Noordt & Misuraca, 2022). Opacity compromises procedural clarity, constraining citizens' capacity to contest or question choices and diminishing accountability in public governance (Robles & Mallinson, 2023; Tangi et al., 2025). Internal administrators could rely on AI results without understanding the underlying model's reasoning, leading to automation bias and diminished supervision (Gesk & Leyer, 2022).

Merely relying on technical explainability is inadequate; transparency focused on governance necessitates institutional mechanisms that convert algorithmic results into comprehensible administrative justifications (Grossi et al., 2024). Opacity intensifies when artificial intelligence systems are acquired from external suppliers, resulting in information imbalances between governmental entities and technology vendors (Bharosa, 2022). Resolving the black box dilemma necessitates integrating technical interpretability with institutional transparency frameworks, such as reporting requirements, documentation procedures, and audit trails, to elucidate decision-making processes (Tangi et al., 2025).

3.3 Data Governance and Privacy Risks

Artificial intelligence frameworks in e-governance rely on huge amounts of administrative and personal information, rendering data governance a fundamental ethical issue. The caliber, integrity, and representativeness of data directly affect algorithmic results, whereas inadequate governance heightens the risk of erroneous forecasts and detrimental choices (van Noordt & Misuraca, 2022). Inter-agency data exchange could present privacy risks and legal challenges (Moss et al., 2022). Privacy threats are more prominent because individuals must submit information to use vital services; any misuse or breach can severely undermine institutional confidence (Robles & Mallinson, 2023). Predictive analytics might infer sensitive characteristics beyond the intended data-gathering objectives, raising issues of proportionality and consent (O'Shaughnessy et al., 2023).

Inadequate data governance further complicates accountability; when erroneous datasets drive automated judgments, impacted individuals may find it difficult to recognize mistakes or pursue rectification (Moss et al., 2022). Guaranteeing the traceability of data origins, recording preprocessing procedures, and elucidating stewardship duties is vital for accountable AI governance (Grossi et al., 2024). Efficient data governance requires cohesive controls that encompass data lifecycle management, security measures, auditability, and impact evaluation processes (van Noordt & Misuraca, 2022).

3.4 Power Redistribution and Decision-Making Risks

The implementation of AI in digital governance reallocates power from humans to automated systems, consolidating knowledge while diminishing the discretionary freedom of frontline authorities (Tangi et al., 2025). This may enhance uniformity but reduce contextual discernment and democratic discourse (Criado & de Zarate-Alcarazo, 2022). Human decision-makers could rely on algorithmic results despite contextual indicators suggesting different options, a phenomenon known as automation bias, which shifts blame onto opaque mechanisms and complicates the assignment of responsibility (Gesk & Leyer, 2022; Moss et al., 2022). Centralized algorithmic frameworks could diminish local autonomy, especially within decentralized government structures (Bharosa, 2022).

The reallocation of power also encompasses the dynamics between government and vendors; reliance on proprietary AI systems fosters structural dependence on private entities, limiting public-sector transparency and possibly jeopardizing democratic oversight (van Noordt & Misuraca, 2022; O'Shaughnessy et al., 2023). Risks associated with decision-making require institutional protections that delineate human supervision duties, implement review processes, and provide clear documentation of decision-making authority and appeal protocols (Robles & Mallinson, 2023; Grossi et al., 2024). Ensuring that AI enhances, rather than supplants, human responsibility is crucial for preserving democratic legitimacy and public confidence (Tangi et al., 2025).

3.5 Connecting Risks to Governance Needs: The Accountability Deficit

The preceding analysis reveals that the core challenge for AI governance is not merely the presence of individual risks but a systemic problem of disconnected accountability. The risks of bias, opacity, data governance failures, and power redistribution share a common feature: they create a disconnect between AI operations and the institutional mechanisms required to oversee, verify, and hold AI systems accountable.

Table 1. summarizes the key risks, their accountability implications, and the governance mechanisms required to address them.

AI Risk	Accountability Dimension Affected	Accountability Deficit	Required Governance Mechanism
Algorithmic Bias & Discrimination	Administrative, Social	Unclear responsibility for outcomes; lack of redress	Bias audits, impact assessments, performance metrics
Opacity / Black Box	Administrative, Financial	Inability to verify or contest decisions	Documentation, audit trails, transparency protocols
Data Governance & Privacy	Administrative, Financial	Untraceable decisions; compromised data integrity	Data lifecycle controls, auditability, documentation
Power Redistribution	Financial, Social	Vendor dependency; hidden costs; loss of discretion	Transparency in procurement, financial reporting, oversight

This analysis shows that the governance gap is fundamentally institutional. It is not enough to have ethical principles or technical guidelines; governments need structured, operational mechanisms that can systematically document, verify, and report on AI performance, impacts, and decision-making. This is precisely the role that government accounting and sustainability accounting can play, as we argue in the following sections.

4. THE STRATEGIC ROLE OF GOVERNMENT ACCOUNTING IN TRUSTED AI GOVERNANCE

4.1 Accounting as a Mechanism of Transparency

Transparency is a foundational principle of democratic governance and a core requirement for trusted AI in digital government. While technological transparency focuses on explainability and documentation of algorithms, institutional transparency requires structured disclosure, traceability of decisions, and standardized reporting mechanisms capable of rendering AI activities visible to oversight bodies and the public. Public sector accounting systems are uniquely positioned to perform this function because they are designed to record, classify, and disclose information related to governmental activities in systematic and auditable formats (Grossi et al., 2024).

In AI-enabled governance, transparency challenges often arise from opaque procurement arrangements, complex data pipelines, and distributed decision-making responsibilities. Without structured documentation and reporting, AI systems may operate as black boxes within administrative routines, limiting public scrutiny (Moss et al., 2022). Accounting frameworks can mitigate this risk by institutionalizing disclosure requirements related to AI investment costs, contractual arrangements with vendors, performance outcomes, and risk assessments. Embedding AI-related disclosures within financial statements, performance reports, or integrated reports enhances traceability and ensures that AI systems are not treated as purely technical assets but as governance instruments subject to accountability (Manes-Rossi et al., 2025).

The specific mechanisms through which accounting enables transparency include: Financial transparency: Disclosure of AI procurement costs, lifecycle expenses, and vendor contract terms, enabling oversight of fiscal stewardship. Performance transparency: Reporting of AI performance metrics, including fairness indicators, accuracy rates, and service outcomes, enabling evaluation of effectiveness. Audit transparency: Creation of audit trails that document data sources, decision criteria, and control procedures, enabling independent verification.

Recent public sector auditing research highlights that digital transformation necessitates new transparency mechanisms capable of capturing algorithmic processes and digital infrastructures (Grossi et al., 2024). Accounting records can serve as audit trails documenting data sources, decision criteria, cost allocations, and control procedures associated with AI systems. Such documentation strengthens answerability and facilitates external review by supreme audit institutions or parliamentary oversight committees. Moreover, structured transparency reduces asymmetries of information between governments and private technology vendors, thereby reinforcing institutional control over AI deployment (Bharosa, 2022).

Transparency through accounting also supports public trust. Citizens are more likely to accept AI-mediated services when governments provide accessible and credible information about how AI systems function and how risks are managed (Robles & Mallinson, 2023). By translating technical AI operations into standardized financial and performance disclosures, accounting bridges the gap between algorithmic complexity and public comprehension. Therefore, accounting should be conceptualized as an enabling infrastructure for ethical AI transparency, transforming abstract governance principles into documented and verifiable evidence within digital government systems (Tangi et al., 2025).

4.2 Performance Measurement and AI Evaluation

Performance measurement systems in the public sector have traditionally focused on efficiency, effectiveness, and compliance with budgetary objectives. However, AI-enabled governance requires expanded evaluation criteria that incorporate fairness, explainability, equity impacts, and unintended consequences (van Noordt & Misuraca, 2022). Conventional output-based indicators are insufficient for assessing algorithmic decision systems that may influence rights and distributive outcomes. Consequently, performance measurement frameworks must evolve to capture multidimensional indicators aligned with ethical AI principles (Moss et al., 2022).

AI evaluation requires both technical performance metrics and governance-oriented indicators. Technical metrics may include model accuracy, error rates, and predictive validity, but these must be complemented by fairness audits, bias detection metrics, and transparency documentation (Tangi et al., 2025). Public sector accounting can support this multidimensional evaluation by integrating AI-related indicators into performance reporting systems and linking them to budgetary allocations and strategic objectives. Such integration ensures that AI performance is evaluated not only as a technological asset but as a public governance instrument accountable for social outcomes (Manes-Rossi et al., 2025).

The mechanism here is twofold. First, performance measurement creates a feedback loop: when AI systems are evaluated against fairness and equity metrics, the results inform future design and deployment decisions. Second, linking performance outcomes to budgetary allocations creates an incentive structure that rewards responsible AI deployment and penalizes underperformance or ethical failures.

Recent research indicates that citizens' perceptions of AI legitimacy depend on procedural justice and fairness rather than solely on service efficiency (Gesk & Leyer, 2022). This implies that performance measurement systems must include qualitative and distributive metrics reflecting inclusiveness and equity impacts. Embedding these indicators within accounting-based performance management enhances institutional learning and supports corrective interventions when AI systems produce undesirable outcomes. Moreover, integrating sustainability indicators enables governments to assess long-term societal impacts associated with AI adoption (Lim, 2024).

Auditing practices are also evolving to evaluate algorithmic systems within public organizations (Grossi et al., 2024). Performance audits increasingly incorporate data governance assessments, system validation procedures, and compliance with ethical standards. Accounting-based evaluation frameworks provide structured criteria for such audits, ensuring consistency and comparability across agencies. By institutionalizing comprehensive performance measurement, governments can strengthen accountability and demonstrate alignment between AI initiatives and public value creation objectives (Robles & Mallinson, 2023).

4.3 Financial Reporting and AI Investment Accountability

AI adoption in digital government involves substantial financial investments in infrastructure, data management, software licensing, consultancy services, and capacity building. These expenditures must be subject to rigorous financial accountability to ensure responsible stewardship of public resources. Government accounting systems provide the mechanisms for recording, classifying, and reporting AI-related expenditures, enabling oversight bodies to assess fiscal prudence and cost-effectiveness (Grossi et al., 2024).

Financial accountability becomes particularly critical when AI procurement involves public-private partnerships or long-term vendor contracts. Such arrangements may obscure total lifecycle costs, including maintenance, updates, and risk mitigation measures (Bharosa, 2022). Transparent financial reporting can mitigate these risks by requiring disclosure of contractual obligations, performance-based payment structures, and contingency liabilities associated with AI systems. This enhances fiscal transparency and reduces the likelihood of hidden costs or vendor lock-in effects.

The mechanism through which financial reporting supports AI accountability is the creation of a comprehensive and auditable record of AI-related financial commitments and expenditures. This record enables oversight bodies to: Assess whether AI investments represent prudent use of public funds. Identify cost overruns or performance gaps early. Evaluate the return on investment in terms of public value outcomes. Ensure that vendor contracts include appropriate safeguards and performance clauses.

While these capabilities can enhance fiscal efficiency, they also introduce governance risks if model assumptions are flawed or insufficiently scrutinized (van Noordt & Misuraca, 2022). Financial reporting frameworks can incorporate documentation of algorithmic assumptions, validation procedures, and sensitivity analyses to ensure that AI-driven budget decisions remain accountable and reviewable. Integrating such disclosures strengthens the connection between AI use and fiscal stewardship obligations (Manes-Rossi et al., 2025).

Public trust in digital transformation is closely linked to perceptions of financial responsibility (Robles & Mallinson, 2023). If AI investments fail to produce demonstrable public benefits or are associated with ethical controversies, reputational damage may extend beyond specific projects to broader digital government initiatives. Accounting-based financial transparency therefore plays a preventive role, enabling early identification of cost overruns, performance gaps, or ethical risks. By embedding AI expenditures within structured reporting and audit frameworks, governments can align technological innovation with principles of public accountability and sustainable fiscal management (Tangi et al., 2025).

4.4 Audit and Oversight of AI Systems in the Public Sector

Audit and oversight mechanisms are essential for translating AI ethics principles into enforceable governance practices. Traditional public sector audits focus on compliance, financial accuracy, and performance outcomes, but AI systems require expanded audit methodologies capable of evaluating algorithms, data governance processes, and model validation procedures (Grossi et al., 2024). Supreme audit institutions and internal audit units are increasingly exploring how to incorporate data analytics and algorithmic assessment tools into oversight practices.

Recent scholarship underscores that AI accountability regulations emphasize documentation, impact assessments, and traceability requirements (Moss et al., 2022). Auditors can leverage accounting records, system logs, and performance reports to evaluate whether AI systems comply with ethical and legal standards. This includes assessing procurement transparency, verifying fairness testing procedures, and reviewing data protection safeguards. Integrating AI oversight within established audit cycles institutionalizes ethical review and prevents oversight from becoming ad hoc or reactive (Manes-Rossi et al., 2025).

Figure 2. Multidimensional Accountability Matrix for AI in Government

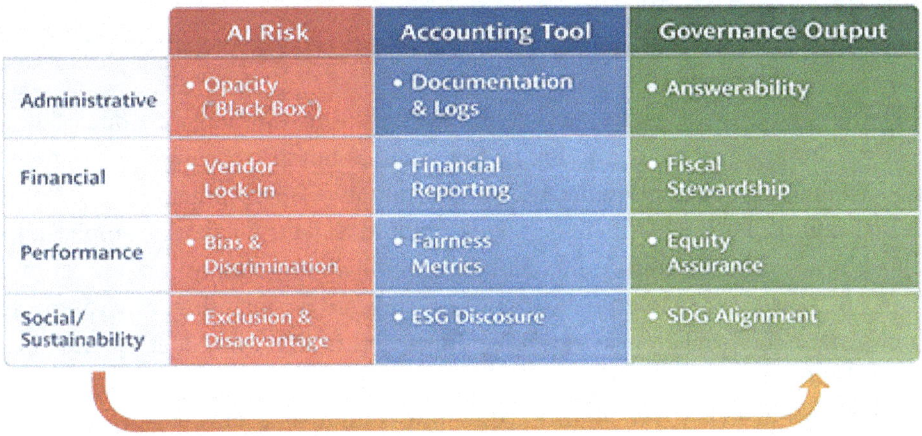

Source: *Developed by the author based on Grossi et al. (2024); Manes-Rossi et al. (2025); Moss et al. (2022); Lim (2024); Tangi et al. (2025).*

The matrix illustrates how different accountability dimensions—administrative, financial, performance, and social/sustainability—require tailored institutional responses to address distinct AI risks. Oversight also involves parliamentary committees, regulatory agencies, and independent ethics boards. Effective coordination among these actors requires standardized reporting formats and reliable evidence bases, functions traditionally supported by accounting infrastructures (Grossi et al., 2024). Furthermore, AI audit frameworks can incorporate sustainability dimensions, evaluating environmental impacts such as energy consumption and social impacts such as equity outcomes (Lim, 2024).

Embedding AI within public audit regimes reinforces democratic control and enhances legitimacy. When citizens perceive that AI systems are subject to independent scrutiny and continuous monitoring, trust in digital government initiatives increases (Robles & Mallinson, 2023). Audit and oversight thus serve as safeguards ensuring that AI augments administrative capacity without eroding accountability norms. Positioning accounting systems at the core of AI oversight provides a structured and credible mechanism for sustaining trusted digital governance (Tangi et al., 2025).

5. SUSTAINABILITY ACCOUNTING AND ETHICAL AI

5.1 Linking AI Governance to SDGs and Sustainability Goals

The integration of artificial intelligence into digital government must be evaluated not only through efficiency and innovation metrics but also through its alignment with sustainability commitments and the Sustainable Development Goals. Public administrations worldwide increasingly commit to SDG frameworks, emphasizing inclusive institutions, reduced inequalities, responsible consumption, and climate action. AI systems deployed in welfare targeting, urban planning, environmental monitoring, and fiscal forecasting have direct and indirect implications for these sustainability objectives (Tangi et al., 2025). Therefore, AI governance should be conceptually linked to sustainability accounting frameworks that measure long-term social, environmental, and governance impacts (Lim, 2024).

Recent sustainability scholarship underscores that technological innovation, including AI, must be embedded within ESG-oriented evaluation systems to ensure that efficiency gains do not undermine equity or environmental responsibility (Lim, 2024). In digital government contexts, AI may enhance SDG performance by optimizing energy use in smart cities, improving social benefit allocation accuracy, and strengthening fraud detection in public finance. However, AI systems may also increase energy consumption due to computational intensity or generate exclusionary outcomes if biased data are used (van Noordt & Misuraca, 2022). Sustainability accounting provides tools to capture both positive and negative externalities in structured reporting formats.

The mechanism linking AI governance to sustainability is twofold. First, sustainability accounting provides a framework for identifying and measuring the environmental and social impacts of AI systems, including energy consumption, carbon emissions, digital inclusion, and equity outcomes. Second, by embedding AI disclosures within sustainability reports, governments can demonstrate alignment with SDG commitments and show that AI innovation contributes to broader societal goals.

Linking AI governance to SDGs requires measurable indicators that reflect distributive justice, accessibility, and environmental footprint. Public sector sustainability reports can incorporate disclosures on AI-related energy usage, digital inclusion outcomes, and risk mitigation strategies addressing algorithmic bias (Grossi et al., 2024). Such disclosures enhance transparency and demonstrate alignment between AI innovation and sustainable public value creation. Moreover, sustainability-oriented evaluation frameworks encourage long-term thinking, counterbalancing short-term performance pressures often associated with digital transformation initiatives (O'Shaughnessy et al., 2023).

Embedding AI within sustainability accounting systems reinforces the normative commitment that technological modernization should serve societal well-being rather than narrow administrative efficiency. This alignment strengthens institutional legitimacy by signaling that AI adoption contributes to sustainable development priorities and democratic accountability standards. Consequently, AI governance that integrates sustainability accounting principles is more likely to foster durable public trust and value-oriented digital transformation (Robles & Mallinson, 2023).

5.2 Environmental and Social Impacts of AI in Public Services

AI systems deployed in public services generate environmental and social impacts that extend beyond administrative efficiency. Environmentally, AI infrastructures require data centers, cloud computing resources, and continuous computational processing, all of which contribute to energy consumption and carbon emissions. Although digitalization can reduce paper use and optimize logistics, the net environmental impact of AI depends on lifecycle management, system scale, and energy sourcing (Lim, 2024). Governments therefore face the challenge of ensuring that AI-enabled modernization does not conflict with climate commitments and sustainability targets.

Social impacts are equally significant. AI systems influence service accessibility, distributive equity, and citizen rights. For example, predictive analytics in welfare or law enforcement may inadvertently reinforce socioeconomic disparities if training data reflect historical inequalities (Moss et al., 2022). Such outcomes can erode social cohesion and weaken trust in public institutions (Robles & Mallinson, 2023). Sustainability accounting frameworks encourage assessment of these social dimensions by requiring structured disclosure of stakeholder impacts and equity considerations (Grossi et al., 2024).

Recent digital government research emphasizes that AI transformation reshapes organizational processes and citizen interactions, potentially affecting employment structures, professional roles, and service delivery patterns (Tangi et al., 2025). Automation may improve consistency and speed but also raise concerns about dehumanization of public services and reduced discretionary support for vulnerable populations. Sustainability accounting approaches, particularly those informed by social impact measurement, can capture such qualitative effects and integrate them into governance evaluation systems (Lim, 2024).

Furthermore, environmental and social impacts are interconnected. Energy-intensive AI systems deployed in smart city management may improve traffic flows while increasing electricity demand. Similarly, automated decision systems may enhance fraud detection but risk stigmatizing certain communities. Recognizing these trade-offs requires comprehensive impact assessment tools embedded within sustainability reporting mechanisms. By systematically documenting environmental footprints and social outcomes, governments can ensure that AI adoption remains consistent with broader sustainability commitments and public value objectives (O'Shaughnessy et al., 2023).

5.3 Sustainability Reporting as Ethical AI Disclosure

Sustainability reporting provides a structured platform for disclosing ethical AI practices within digital government. Traditionally associated with corporate ESG reporting, sustainability reporting has increasingly been adopted by public sector organizations seeking to demonstrate transparency and accountability in environmental and social governance (Grossi et al., 2024). Incorporating AI governance disclosures into sustainability reports enhances visibility of ethical safeguards, bias mitigation efforts, and risk management strategies.

Recent research highlights that stakeholders expect transparency not only regarding financial expenditures but also regarding societal impacts and governance quality (Lim, 2024). AI systems that influence public service eligibility, predictive enforcement, or fiscal allocation decisions should therefore be accompanied by disclosures outlining fairness assessments, data governance controls, and oversight mechanisms. Embedding such disclosures within sustainability reports ensures consistency and comparability across reporting cycles (Manes-Rossi et al., 2025).

The mechanism through which sustainability reporting supports ethical AI is the creation of a comprehensive public record of AI-related environmental and social impacts. This record enables: Citizens and civil society to evaluate the broader consequences of AI deployment. Oversight bodies to assess compliance with sustainability commitments. Governments to demonstrate responsible innovation and transparency. Benchmarking of AI sustainability performance across jurisdictions.

Sustainability reporting also strengthens institutional learning. Periodic disclosure of AI-related impacts encourages reflection on performance gaps, unintended consequences, and corrective measures. This cyclical process aligns with continuous improvement principles emphasized in trusted AI governance frameworks (Moss et al., 2022). Furthermore, transparent reporting reduces reputational risk by proactively addressing ethical concerns rather than reacting to public controversies.

Integrating AI governance within sustainability reporting frameworks supports alignment with international standards and emerging regulatory expectations. Governments that disclose AI-related environmental and social impacts demonstrate commitment to responsible innovation and democratic accountability. From a public value perspective, sustainability reporting transforms ethical AI from abstract principle into documented practice subject to review and dialogue (Robles & Mallinson, 2023).

5.4 Integrated Reporting for AI-Driven Governments

Integrated reporting extends sustainability disclosure by linking financial, operational, environmental, and social dimensions within a unified governance narrative. For AI-driven governments, integrated reporting offers a comprehensive framework to demonstrate how AI investments contribute to value creation over short, medium, and long-term horizons. By connecting financial expenditures, performance outcomes, and sustainability impacts, integrated reporting enhances coherence and accountability (Grossi et al., 2024).

AI systems often generate cross-cutting effects that cannot be adequately captured in isolated financial statements. For instance, an AI-based tax compliance system may increase revenue collection, improve equity in enforcement, and reduce administrative costs simultaneously. Integrated reporting enables governments to articulate these interconnected outcomes and clarify trade-offs between efficiency and social impact (Tangi et al., 2025). This holistic perspective aligns with public value theory, emphasizing multidimensional evaluation of governance initiatives. Figure 3 presents a sustainability-embedded AI governance model that integrates artificial intelligence systems within accounting infrastructures and long-term sustainable development objectives.

Figure 3. Sustainability-Embedded AI Governance Model Linking Accounting, Digital Government, and the SDGs

Source: *Developed by the author based on Lim (2024); Grossi et al. (2024); Tangi et al. (2025); Moss et al. (2022); Manes-Rossi et al. (2025).*

The circular configuration emphasizes feedback loops and continuous improvement, illustrating that sustainability-oriented AI governance is dynamic rather than static. Moreover, integrated reporting enhances comparability across jurisdictions, supporting benchmarking of AI governance practices. Governments that adopt integrated reporting for AI initiatives signal commitment to transparency, fiscal responsibility, and sustainable development objectives. This approach fosters trust by demonstrating that AI-driven transformation is embedded within accountable and value-oriented governance structures rather than isolated technological experimentation (Robles & Mallinson, 2023). Consequently, integrated reporting represents a strategic instrument for institutionalizing ethical AI within sustainable digital government.

6. CONCEPTUAL FRAMEWORK: AI ETHICS, ACCOUNTING ACCOUNTABILITY, AND PUBLIC VALUE CREATION

6.1 Integrative Framework Development

The rapid institutionalization of artificial intelligence in digital government necessitates an integrative framework capable of linking ethical principles, accountability infrastructures, and public value outcomes. While existing digital government research has extensively examined AI adoption patterns and governance challenges, fewer studies have developed structured models that explicitly connect AI ethics to institutional accountability mechanisms grounded in public sector accounting systems (Tangi et al., 2025). This chapter responds to that gap by proposing an integrative framework in which AI ethics principles are operationalized through accounting-based accountability instruments to produce measurable public value.

The framework builds on three theoretical pillars. First, trusted AI governance emphasizes fairness, transparency, explainability, and human oversight as normative foundations for legitimate AI deployment (Moss et al., 2022). Second, public value theory highlights that governmental innovation must generate socially desirable outcomes such as equity, inclusiveness, and institutional trust (O'Shaughnessy et al., 2023). Third, public sector accounting provides structured tools for transparency, performance measurement, financial stewardship, and sustainability disclosure (Grossi et al., 2024). By integrating these pillars, the framework conceptualizes accounting systems not as passive reporting devices but as active governance infrastructures that translate ethical AI commitments into auditable and reportable practices.

In this integrative model, AI ethics principles serve as normative inputs that define acceptable governance standards. These principles are embedded into accountability mechanisms such as financial reporting, performance evaluation metrics, sustainability disclosures, and audit procedures. Through these mechanisms, AI systems become subject to continuous institutional scrutiny rather than isolated technical validation. This process enhances traceability, ensures compliance with ethical norms, and supports public trust formation (Robles & Mallinson, 2023).

A key theoretical contribution of the framework is its articulation of the mechanism through which accounting systems mediate between AI and public value. Drawing on agency theory (Jensen & Meckling, 1976), we conceptualize the relationship between governments (as principals) and AI systems (as agents) as one requiring oversight and control mechanisms. Accounting serves as the information system that provides principals with the evidence needed to monitor agent performance and ensure alignment with public interests. This perspective explains why accounting is not merely a compliance tool but a fundamental governance infrastructure.

Importantly, the framework positions accounting as a mediating institution between technological systems and societal expectations. AI outputs are transformed into structured information through reporting, auditing, and disclosure routines, enabling oversight actors to assess compliance and performance (Manes-Rossi et al., 2025). The integrative framework therefore establishes a governance architecture in which AI ethics are embedded within institutional accountability cycles that ultimately shape public value outcomes in digital government.

6.2 AI to Accountability Mechanisms to Trust to Public Value

The conceptual pathway underlying this chapter can be expressed as a sequential and reinforcing relationship: AI systems influence administrative processes; accountability mechanisms monitor and evaluate these systems; transparent oversight builds institutional trust; and sustained trust contributes to public value creation. This pathway emphasizes that ethical AI alone is insufficient without accountability infrastructures capable of operationalizing normative commitments (Moss et al., 2022).

AI technologies, when deployed in public services, generate outputs that affect citizen rights, resource allocation, and policy implementation. These outputs require structured evaluation through performance measurement systems, financial controls, and sustainability indicators to ensure alignment with governance objectives (van Noordt & Misuraca, 2022). Accountability mechanisms function as institutional filters that assess fairness, efficiency, fiscal responsibility, and societal impact. Without such mechanisms, AI may operate with limited transparency, increasing risks of bias, opacity, and trust erosion (Tangi et al., 2025).

The causal pathway can be articulated as follows:

1. AI Deployment → Accountability Demand: The deployment of AI systems in public services creates new risks (bias, opacity, power redistribution) that cannot be addressed by existing governance structures, generating a demand for institutional accountability.
2. Accountability Demand → Accounting Mechanisms: To meet this demand, governments deploy specific accounting mechanisms. Performance measurement systems create metrics to track algorithmic bias and service equity. Financial reporting makes AI procurement and lifecycle costs transparent. Auditing creates an independent, evidence-based review of AI processes and impacts.
3. Accounting Mechanisms → Institutional Trust: By making AI operations visible, measurable, and subject to review, these accounting mechanisms generate institutional trust. Citizens and oversight bodies can observe that decisions are not arbitrary, that resources are being used responsibly, and that mechanisms for redress exist.

4. Institutional Trust → Public Value Creation: Trust is the foundation for public value. When citizens trust that AI systems are fair, transparent, and accountable, they are more likely to accept and use them. This acceptance, combined with the efficiency and effectiveness gains from AI, creates public value.

Figure 4 illustrates the sequential and reinforcing pathway proposed in this chapter, linking AI systems to public value creation through structured accountability mechanisms and institutional trust formation.

Figure 4. Causal Pathway Linking AI Systems, Accountability Mechanisms, Institutional Trust, and Public Value in Digital Government

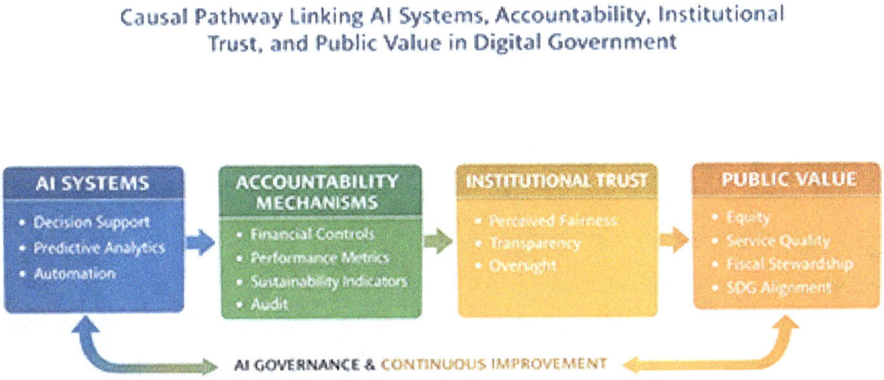

Source: *Developed by the author based on Moss et al. (2022); Tangi et al. (2025); Gesk & Leyer (2022); Robles & Mallinson (2023); Grossi et al. (2024); Lim (2024).*

The figure thus reinforces the chapter's central claim: ethical AI is insufficient without institutional accountability, and sustainable public value depends on embedding AI within structured governance cycles. Trust emerges when citizens perceive that AI systems are subject to rigorous oversight and ethical safeguards. Empirical research indicates that public acceptance of AI in government is strongly associated with perceptions of fairness, transparency, and institutional competence (Gesk & Leyer, 2022). Accountability reporting, audit disclosures, and sustainability communication contribute to these perceptions by demonstrating that AI decisions are reviewable and contestable. Consequently, trust becomes an outcome of institutional accountability rather than solely a product of technological design (Robles & Mallinson, 2023).

Public value is generated when trusted AI systems enhance service quality, promote equity, safeguard public resources, and support sustainable development objectives. By linking AI governance to measurable accountability indicators, governments can demonstrate that digital transformation contributes to long-term societal benefits rather than short-term administrative gains (O'Shaughnessy et al., 2023). The sequential pathway from AI to accountability to trust to public value highlights the strategic importance of embedding accounting mechanisms within AI governance structures to sustain legitimacy and democratic oversight.

6.3 Operationalizing Governance: The Multidimensional Accountability Matrix

To further operationalize the framework and provide practical guidance, we introduce the Multidimensional Accountability Matrix (Figure 2). This matrix explicitly links AI-related governance risks to specific accounting tools and their corresponding governance outputs, providing a structured approach for institutional design.

Table 2. summarizes the matrix, showing how different accountability dimensions (Administrative, Financial, Performance, Social/Sustainability) require tailored accounting responses to address distinct AI risks.

Accountability Dimension	AI Risk Addressed	Accounting Tool/ Mechanism	Governance Output
Administrative	Opacity, Black Box	Documentation protocols, audit logs	Answerability, traceability
Financial	Vendor lock-in, hidden costs	Transparent financial reporting	Fiscal stewardship
Performance	Algorithmic bias, discrimination	Fairness metrics, performance indicators	Equity assurance, effectiveness
Social/Sustainability	Exclusion, disadvantage	ESG disclosures, sustainability reporting	Inclusiveness, SDG alignment

This matrix translates abstract ethical concerns into concrete governance mechanisms. For each risk, it identifies: The accountability dimension that is most directly affected. The specific accounting tool that can address the risk. The governance output that the tool generates. By using this matrix, policymakers and public managers can systematically assess which accountability mechanisms are needed to address specific AI risks in their organizational context.

6.4 Policy and Governance Implications

The proposed framework has significant policy and governance implications for governments pursuing AI-driven digital transformation. First, policymakers should recognize that ethical AI governance requires institutional capacity beyond technical expertise. Developing standardized reporting templates, AI-related performance indicators, and audit guidelines is essential for operationalizing accountability (Manes-Rossi et al., 2025). Such institutionalization ensures that ethical principles are translated into enforceable governance practices.

Second, governments should integrate AI disclosures within financial statements and sustainability reports to enhance transparency and comparability. Embedding AI-related indicators within existing reporting cycles prevents fragmentation and reinforces fiscal stewardship obligations (Grossi et al., 2024). This integration also strengthens alignment between digital innovation strategies and sustainability commitments.

Third, oversight institutions must expand audit competencies to evaluate algorithmic systems, data governance practices, and impact assessments. Continuous monitoring rather than episodic review is necessary to address dynamic model updates and evolving risk profiles (Moss et al., 2022). Establishing interdisciplinary audit teams combining accounting, data science, and legal expertise can enhance institutional readiness for AI governance challenges.

Fourth, governments should adopt a long-term public value orientation in AI policymaking. Digital transformation strategies must explicitly articulate how AI initiatives contribute to equity, inclusiveness, fiscal responsibility, and sustainability (Tangi et al., 2025). The accountability matrix provided in this chapter offers a practical tool for designing governance structures that link specific AI risks to appropriate accountability mechanisms.

By embedding AI within comprehensive accountability frameworks, policymakers can reduce legitimacy risks and strengthen citizen trust. The integrative model proposed in this chapter thus provides a governance roadmap for aligning AI innovation with democratic accountability and sustainable public value creation (Robles & Mallinson, 2023).

7. PRACTICAL IMPLICATIONS FOR POLICYMAKERS AND PUBLIC MANAGERS

7.1 Designing Ethical AI Governance Systems

Designing ethical AI governance systems in digital government requires moving beyond high-level ethical principles toward institutionalized operational frameworks. While many governments have adopted AI ethics guidelines emphasizing fairness, transparency, accountability, and human oversight, practical implementation often remains fragmented or symbolic (Moss et al., 2022). Policymakers must therefore translate ethical commitments into structured governance architectures that integrate risk assessment, documentation requirements, performance monitoring, and audit readiness into everyday administrative processes.

A first implication concerns the institutionalization of algorithmic impact assessments prior to deployment. These assessments should evaluate potential bias, privacy risks, environmental implications, and fiscal exposure, linking AI system design to sustainability and accountability objectives (Tangi et al., 2025). Embedding such assessments within procurement and budgeting procedures ensures that ethical considerations are addressed at the planning stage rather than retrospectively. Government accounting systems can support this process by requiring documentation of projected costs, risk mitigation strategies, and performance indicators tied to AI investments (Manes-Rossi et al., 2025).

Second, governance systems must clarify responsibility allocation. AI systems frequently involve collaboration between data scientists, administrators, private vendors, and oversight institutions. Clear delineation of accountability roles reduces ambiguity and strengthens answerability in cases of adverse outcomes (Bharosa, 2022). Formal governance charters, supported by accounting-based reporting and disclosure requirements, can institutionalize these responsibilities and ensure traceability of decisions.

Third, policymakers should embed transparency protocols within reporting cycles. AI-related disclosures should be incorporated into financial statements, performance reports, and sustainability reports, ensuring consistent oversight across governance domains (Grossi et al., 2024). Such integration prevents AI governance from becoming siloed within technical departments and reinforces its status as a strategic public administration issue. By aligning ethical AI design with accounting and reporting systems, governments can operationalize trusted AI principles in measurable and reviewable ways (Robles & Mallinson, 2023).

7.2 Strengthening Institutional Accountability Structures

Institutional accountability structures must evolve to address the complexity and dynamism of AI-driven governance. Traditional oversight mechanisms focused on compliance and financial accuracy may not sufficiently capture algorithmic decision logic, data integrity, or fairness impacts (Grossi et al., 2024). Public managers should therefore enhance accountability frameworks to include multidimensional evaluation tools encompassing administrative, financial, and social accountability dimensions.

One practical strategy involves integrating AI-specific performance indicators into public sector performance management systems. These indicators may include fairness metrics, bias testing outcomes, explainability documentation, and sustainability impact measures (van Noordt & Misuraca, 2022). Incorporating such indicators into regular performance reviews strengthens institutional learning and encourages continuous improvement. Moreover, linking AI performance outcomes to budgetary decisions reinforces fiscal responsibility and ensures that underperforming systems are subject to corrective measures (Manes-Rossi et al., 2025).

Strengthening accountability also requires expanding audit capabilities. Supreme audit institutions and internal audit units must develop technical competencies to evaluate algorithmic models, data governance processes, and risk mitigation strategies (Moss et al., 2022). Interdisciplinary audit teams combining accounting expertise with data science and legal knowledge can enhance oversight quality and reduce blind spots in AI governance.

Public communication mechanisms further reinforce accountability structures. Transparent disclosure of AI objectives, risks, and performance outcomes contributes to public understanding and trust formation (Gesk & Leyer, 2022). Accountability structures should therefore include mechanisms for citizen feedback and appeal processes when automated decisions are contested. Institutionalizing these channels demonstrates commitment to democratic oversight and procedural fairness, strengthening the legitimacy of AI-enabled governance (Robles & Mallinson, 2023).

7.3 Cross-Cultural and Regulatory Considerations

AI governance practices are shaped by cultural values, legal traditions, and administrative systems. Cross-cultural differences influence public attitudes toward automation, risk tolerance, and expectations of transparency (O'Shaughnessy et al., 2023). Policymakers must therefore tailor AI accountability frameworks to contextual institutional norms while maintaining alignment with global ethical standards.

Regulatory environments also vary in their approach to AI oversight. Some jurisdictions emphasize precautionary regulation and impact assessments, while others prioritize innovation and flexibility (Moss et al., 2022). Governments operating within decentralized administrative systems may face additional coordination challenges in harmonizing AI governance across national and subnational levels (Bharosa, 2022). In such contexts, standardized accounting and reporting frameworks can provide consistency and comparability across jurisdictions.

Cross-cultural considerations also affect sustainability priorities. Environmental and social impact expectations differ across societies, shaping how AI-related disclosures are interpreted and valued (Lim, 2024). Integrating AI governance within sustainability accounting systems allows governments to adapt reporting to local contexts while adhering to international frameworks. This approach enhances comparability and fosters cross-national learning in trusted AI governance.

Moreover, global digital ecosystems require interoperability of governance standards. Governments adopting AI systems often rely on transnational vendors and cloud infrastructures, necessitating coordination across regulatory regimes (van Noordt & Misuraca, 2022). Establishing common accountability principles supported by standardized reporting and audit practices can mitigate fragmentation and strengthen international cooperation. Policymakers should thus design AI governance systems that are both context-sensitive and globally informed, ensuring coherence between domestic accountability structures and international ethical norms (Tangi et al., 2025).

7.4 Capacity Building in AI and Accounting Governance

Effective AI governance depends on institutional capacity encompassing technical expertise, ethical awareness, and accounting competence. Public sector organizations frequently face shortages of skilled personnel capable of evaluating algorithmic systems and interpreting data-driven outputs (Tangi et al., 2025). Capacity building initiatives must therefore integrate digital literacy with governance and accountability training. Training programs for public managers should include modules on AI ethics, data governance, sustainability impacts, and accounting-based oversight mechanisms. Enhancing understanding of how AI systems interact with financial reporting and performance measurement strengthens institutional readiness (Manes-Rossi et al., 2025).

Interdisciplinary collaboration between IT departments and accounting units can reduce silos and improve coordination in AI governance. Investments in digital infrastructure must be complemented by investments in institutional learning systems. Continuous monitoring, post-implementation reviews, and audit feedback loops support adaptive governance and reduce risk accumulation (Grossi et al., 2024). Capacity building also involves developing guidance documents, templates, and standardized reporting formats to streamline AI-related disclosures.

Finally, fostering a culture of accountability is essential. Organizational norms should encourage critical engagement with AI outputs rather than unreflective reliance on automated recommendations (Gesk & Leyer, 2022). Leadership commitment to transparency and ethical stewardship reinforces these norms and signals institutional dedication to responsible innovation. By integrating technical capacity with accounting governance competencies, public organizations can build resilient infrastructures for trusted AI and sustainable digital government transformation (Robles & Mallinson, 2023).

8. FUTURE RESEARCH DIRECTIONS

8.1 AI Audit and Assurance Research

The rapid institutionalization of artificial intelligence in digital government creates urgent demand for advanced research on AI audit and assurance practices. Traditional public sector auditing frameworks are primarily designed to evaluate financial compliance, operational efficiency, and regulatory adherence. However, AI systems introduce new dimensions of risk, including algorithmic bias, opacity, data governance failures, and unintended distributive consequences, which require expanded audit methodologies (Moss et al., 2022). Future research should therefore investigate how audit standards can evolve to assess not only financial integrity but also algorithmic accountability and ethical compliance.

Emerging scholarship suggests that public sector auditors must develop competencies in data analytics, model validation, and algorithmic explainability to effectively evaluate AI systems (Grossi et al., 2024). Yet empirical evidence on how supreme audit institutions operationalize these competencies remains limited. Research is needed to explore the design of AI-specific audit frameworks, including criteria for fairness testing, documentation review, and impact assessment verification (Manes-Rossi et al., 2025). Such studies could examine cross-national variations in audit readiness and identify best practices for integrating AI oversight within established public accountability systems.

Another promising research avenue concerns assurance models for sustainability and AI disclosure. As governments increasingly integrate AI-related information into sustainability and integrated reporting, independent assurance mechanisms become essential for ensuring credibility and reliability (Lim, 2024). Scholars can explore whether existing sustainability assurance standards are adequate for AI disclosures or whether new assurance criteria are required to address algorithmic transparency and social impact measurement.

Furthermore, AI audit research should consider the dynamic nature of machine learning systems, which may evolve through model retraining and data updates. Continuous auditing approaches leveraging real-time data analytics may offer potential solutions for monitoring algorithmic performance over time (Tangi et al., 2025). Investigating how continuous assurance models can be adapted for AI governance represents a critical frontier for interdisciplinary collaboration between accounting, public administration, and information systems research. Advancing this agenda will strengthen the institutional infrastructure necessary for trusted AI in digital government.

8.2 Measuring Public Value in AI Contexts

Measuring public value in AI-driven governance contexts presents conceptual and methodological challenges that warrant further scholarly attention. Public value encompasses multidimensional outcomes including equity, inclusiveness, transparency, trust, fiscal responsibility, and sustainability. While digital government research acknowledges these dimensions, operationalizing them into measurable indicators remains complex (O'Shaughnessy et al., 2023). Future research should therefore develop validated measurement frameworks capable of capturing both quantitative and qualitative dimensions of AI-induced public value.

Existing performance management systems often emphasize efficiency metrics such as processing time reduction or cost savings (van Noordt & Misuraca, 2022). However, such metrics may fail to capture distributive fairness or citizen satisfaction associated with AI-mediated services. Research should explore composite indicators integrating fairness metrics, appeal outcomes, bias detection rates, and stakeholder perceptions of transparency (Gesk & Leyer, 2022). These indicators could be embedded within accounting-based reporting systems to enhance comparability and oversight.

Longitudinal studies are particularly needed to assess how AI adoption influences public trust over time. Trust is not static but evolves in response to perceived performance, transparency, and ethical conduct (Robles & Mallinson, 2023). Scholars can investigate causal relationships between disclosure practices, audit transparency, and citizen trust levels in AI-enabled services. Such research would contribute to evidence-based policy design and strengthen theoretical integration between public value theory and accountability mechanisms.

Moreover, measuring public value requires attention to unintended consequences and trade-offs. AI systems may enhance efficiency while exacerbating inequality or environmental impact (Lim, 2024). Developing balanced scorecards or sustainability-oriented performance frameworks tailored to AI governance can help address these trade-offs systematically. Future research should therefore advance methodological tools that enable governments to quantify and disclose multidimensional public value outcomes in AI-driven digital transformation initiatives (Tangi et al., 2025).

8.3 Sustainability Metrics for AI in Government

Sustainability metrics for AI in government represent an emerging research frontier at the intersection of digital governance and sustainability accounting. While corporate sectors increasingly report on environmental, social, and governance impacts of digital technologies, public sector AI sustainability metrics remain underdeveloped (Lim, 2024). Future research should examine how sustainability accounting frameworks can be adapted to capture AI-related environmental footprints, social impacts, and governance risks within public administration contexts.

Environmental metrics may include energy consumption of data centers, carbon emissions associated with cloud services, and lifecycle environmental costs of digital infrastructure (Lim, 2024). Social metrics could address inclusiveness, accessibility of AI-enabled services, and impacts on vulnerable populations. Governance metrics might evaluate transparency, auditability, and compliance with ethical standards (Moss et al., 2022). Developing standardized sustainability indicators for AI systems would facilitate benchmarking across jurisdictions and enhance international comparability.

Another research direction involves exploring integration between sustainability reporting and financial accounting in AI contexts. Integrated reporting frameworks can link fiscal investments in AI with environmental and social outcomes, providing a holistic view of value creation (Grossi et al., 2024). Scholars can investigate how governments design integrated performance dashboards combining financial, environmental, and equity indicators for AI initiatives.

Additionally, sustainability research should examine resilience and long-term risk management in AI governance. AI systems embedded in critical public services must be resilient to cybersecurity threats, data breaches, and systemic bias amplification (Tangi et al., 2025). Developing sustainability metrics that incorporate resilience and risk mitigation dimensions would enhance governance robustness and public trust.

By advancing sustainability metrics for AI in government, future research can contribute to a comprehensive accountability architecture that aligns digital innovation with long-term societal and environmental objectives. Such contributions will reinforce the theoretical and practical integration of trusted AI, sustainability accounting, and public value creation in digital government.

9. CONCLUSION

The integration of AI into digital government introduces profound ethical, accountability, and sustainability challenges that cannot be resolved through technical design alone. This chapter has argued that trusted AI requires institutional accountability infrastructures capable of translating ethical principles into measurable, auditable governance practices. By integrating trusted AI governance, public value theory, and public sector accounting, we have advanced a conceptual framework positioning government accounting and sustainability accounting as mediating mechanisms between AI systems and public value outcomes. Accounting systems provide structured transparency through financial reporting, performance measurement, and audit processes, transforming algorithmic operations into documented evidence subject to democratic scrutiny.

The sequential pathway from AI systems to accountability mechanisms to trust formation to public value creation underscores that legitimacy is institutionally constructed, not technologically assumed. Sustainability accounting further aligns AI innovation with long-term societal and environmental objectives, particularly Sustainable Development Goals. This chapter contributes to digital government literature by bridging AI governance scholarship with accounting research, offering a novel interdisciplinary framework. Practically, we encourage policymakers to institutionalize AI impact assessments, expand audit competencies, and integrate AI indicators into financial and sustainability reports. Ultimately, trusted AI is a governance achievement grounded in ethical stewardship, transparency, and sustainability-oriented oversight. By embedding AI within robust accountability systems, governments can transform digital innovation into enduring public value and democratic legitimacy.

REFERENCES

Al-Baity, H. H. (2025). Artificial intelligence for financial accountability and governance in the public sector: Case studies from Estonia, Singapore, and Finland. *Administrative Sciences, 15*(2), 58. DOI: 10.3390/admsci15020058

Bagheri, S., & Dirksen, V. (2024). Public value-driven assessment of trustworthy AI in the public sector: A review. In *Disruptive Innovation in a Digitally Connected Healthy World* (pp. 3–13). Lecture Notes in Computer Science. Springer., DOI: 10.1007/978-3-031-72234-9_1

Bell, E. (2024). Efficiency or equity? How public values shape bureaucrats' willingness to use artificial intelligence to reduce administrative burdens. *Public Performance & Management Review, 27*(5), 1268–1301. DOI: 10.1080/15309576.2024.2419132

Bharosa, N. (2022). The rise of GovTech: Trojan horse or blessing in disguise? A research agenda. *Government Information Quarterly, 39*(3), 101692. DOI: 10.1016/j.giq.2022.101692

Criado, J. I., & de Zarate-Alcarazo, L. O. (2022). Technological frames, CIOs, and artificial intelligence in public administration: A socio-cognitive exploratory study in Spanish local governments. *Government Information Quarterly, 39*(3), 101688. DOI: 10.1016/j.giq.2022.101688

Gesk, T. S., & Leyer, M. (2022). Artificial intelligence in public services: When and why citizens accept its usage. *Government Information Quarterly, 39*(3), 101704. DOI: 10.1016/j.giq.2022.101704

Grossi, G., Mattei, G., & Guthrie, J. (2024). Digital transformation in public sector auditing: Between hope and fear. *Public Management Review*. Advance online publication. DOI: 10.1080/14719037.2024.2402346

Lim, T. (2024). Environmental, social, and governance (ESG) and artificial intelligence in finance: State-of-the-art and research takeaways. *Artificial Intelligence Review, 57*(4), 76. Advance online publication. DOI: 10.1007/s10462-024-10708-3

Manes-Rossi, F.. (2025). Data science and public sector accounting: Reviewing impacts on financial reporting, auditing, and accountability. *Public Money & Management*. Advance online publication. DOI: 10.1080/09540962.2025.2529266

Moss, E., Watkins, E. A., Metcalf, J., & Elish, M. C. (2022). Obligations to assess: Recent trends in AI accountability regulations. *Patterns (New York, N.Y.), 3*(9), 100559. DOI: 10.1016/j.patter.2022.100559 PMID: 36419454

O'Shaughnessy, M. R., Schiff, D. S., Varshney, L. R., Rozell, C. J., & Davenport, M. A. (2023). What governs attitudes toward artificial intelligence adoption and governance? *Science & Public Policy*, *50*(2), 161–176. DOI: 10.1093/scipol/scac056

Robles, P., & Mallinson, D. J. (2023). Artificial intelligence technology, public trust, and effective governance. *The Review of Policy Research*, *42*(1), 11–28. DOI: 10.1111/ropr.12555

Tangi, L., Rodríguez Müller, A. P., & Janssen, M. (2025). AI-augmented government transformation. *Government Information Quarterly*, *42*(3), 102055. DOI: 10.1016/j.giq.2025.102055

Van Noordt, C., & Misuraca, G. (2022). Artificial intelligence for the public sector: Results of landscaping the use of AI in government across the European Union. *Government Information Quarterly*, *39*(3), 101714. DOI: 10.1016/j.giq.2022.101714

Wittmann, V., & Meynhardt, T. (2025). Uncovering AI regulation's public values in the EU. In *2025 IEEE International Symposium on Technology and Society (ISTAS)* (pp. 1–8). DOI: 10.1109/ISTAS65609.2025.11269610

Chapter 10
Educational Data Sovereignty at the Margins:
Intergenerational Digital Exclusion and the Structural Failures of India's Data Protection Framework

Mohd Arsh Shery
http://orcid.org/0009-0008-6277-4040
Villa College, Male', Maldives

Amish Abdullah
http://orcid.org/0009-0001-4791-776X
Villa College, Male', Maldives

Nooreen Rahman
Villa College, Male', Maldives

Mohammad Shekaib Alam
http://orcid.org/0009-0005-7991-8184
Villa College, Male', Maldives

ABSTRACT

The digitalization of education in India has intensified collection of children's personal data, generating privacy risks extending to elderly caregivers. In India's intergenerational households, grandparents frequently serve as digital intermediaries, submitting documents, managing portals, and providing consent without the digital literacy or legal awareness to do so meaningfully. This chapter argues that

DOI: 10.4018/979-8-3373-9129-8.ch010

digital exclusion across both age groups creates an underexamined vulnerability within India's educational data ecosystem. Employing a doctrinal methodology, the chapter analyses the DPDP Act 2023, IT Act 2000, and NEP 2020 against the privacy framework in the Puttaswamy judgement and the UN CRC's General Comment No. 25. It identifies three structural gaps: the DPDPA's consent architecture under Section 9 fails elderly guardians; educational institutions remain unregulated as data fiduciaries; and no enforceable intergenerational privacy obligations exist. Targeted legislative reforms grounded in a life-course approach to children's digital rights are proposed.

INTRODUCTION

The digitalization of the Indian education system has greatly accelerated in the last ten years through various government efforts such as the National Education Policy (2020) and even more through the Covid-19 pandemic (Dayal & Pratibha, 2023; Ministry of Education, Government of India, 2022). Online learning platforms, school management systems and digital communications allowed for ongoing access to learning while schools were closed (Gopika & Rekha, 2023). At the same time, these systems increased the amount of data collected from students and families (Lievens et al., 2018; Livingstone & Third, 2017). The constitutional significance of this development was established in Justice K.S. Puttaswamy (Retd.) v. Union of India (2017) when the Supreme Court held that the right to privacy is a fundamental right as guaranteed by Article 21, encompassing informational self-determination. Article 39(f) further mandates state protection of children from exploitation. Together, these provisions require that educational data legislation comply with the proportionality standard established in Puttaswamy (2017). Some of these critical vulnerabilities exist in populations that are often marginalized, young children and elderly caregivers (UNICEF, 2021; Livingstone & Third, 2017).

Many Indian households typically operate with an intergenerational living model, where grandparents or older relatives are critical caregivers to children, serving either as an active overseer of education or an important source of emotional or practical support (Chadha, 2012; Verma et al., 2024; De et al., 2023). In many families, elderly caregivers provide help with the use of digital devices, assistance with online learning tools, management of school communication, and in some cases the handling of sensitive data transactions, such as submitting identification or health records, on behalf of children (Bakshi & Bhattacharyya, 2021). Even with central involvement in the digital learning dynamic, elderly caregivers have limited digital literacy and confidence, which makes them and the children they support especially susceptible to digital exclusion and data privacy violation (Jena & Paltasingh, 2024; Mannheim et al., 2019).

Digital exclusion is more than a lack of devices and/or connectivity; it also includes design issues with technology, language difficulties and economic disadvantage that prevent people from having the ability to exercise their legal rights in a digital context (Ilavarasan, 2013; Warschauer, 2003; van Dijk, 2020). These types of issues are extensively analysed and addressed in Section 2 of this paper.

In addition to personal challenges, a variety of ageism, the classification and discrimination by age, manifests in the design of educational platforms, in the basis of the data protection legislation, and in the social norms and constructs that influence institutional policies and practices (Officer & de la Fuente-Núñez, 2018; World Health Organization, 2021; Mannheim et al., 2023). Ageist attitudes may result in digital content and administrative processes that are unintuitive or exclusionary for older caregivers, or privacy policies that refer to children without emphasising the similar vulnerability of seniors who will also engage with the systems (Mannheim et al., 2019; Mannheim & Köttl, 2024). This oversight is powerful and can create a regressive education system that privileges digitally fluent learners while excluding the most needy and dependent (Jena & Paltasingh, 2024; Seifert et al., 2022).

Under the current framework, the DPDPA (Digital Personal Data Protection Act of 2023) creates a consent-based system for processing personal data, with children protected as a specific class under Section 9; however, there are no express provisions regarding how elderly caregivers can act as functional consent givers on behalf of children or act as independent data principals in the education environment (Digital Personal Data Protection Act, 2023). The Indian judicial system has not yet developed an explicit doctrine of intergenerational privacy, but the Supreme Court confirmed informational privacy as a fundamental right in Puttaswamy (2017). Internationally, General Comment No. 25 (2021) of the UN Committee on the Rights of the Child has expanded the interpretation of the right to privacy contained in Article 16 of the UNCRC to include digital settings, providing an interpretive framework not yet fully incorporated in India's domestic legislation (UN Committee on the Rights of the Child, 2021; Lievens et al., 2024).

In this research we adopt the "Seasons of Life" framing, which brings to the forefront how digital exclusion and weak data protection in Indian education are not parallel but intertwined threats to both children and the elderly. We pose two primary questions:

- In what ways does digital exclusion inform the ability of children and elderly caregivers to comprehend and exercise digital privacy rights in Indian schools?

- In what ways do there exist specific legal and policy gaps for these ages, and what reform can support a genuinely inclusive and anti-ageist approach to educational data protection?

To answer these questions, we will conduct a doctrinal legal analysis of the Indian data protection framework, education policy, and comparative international instruments. The primary takeaway for policymakers and practitioners is that while India's current data protection law provides some protection for children, it does not provide any legal recognition or practical recourse for elderly caregivers who navigate the system for children. This gap warrants targeted legislative and institutional solutions (Livingstone & Byrne, 2018; van Dijk, 2020).

Having established the constitutional and legislative context, the following section examines how digital exclusion manifests across generational lines and why it constitutes a structurally intergenerational problem in India's educational settings.

RESEARCH METHODOLOGY

This research article uses doctrinal legal research methods. The article closely analyses India's data protection laws pertaining to school education: the 2023 Digital Personal Data Protection Act, the Information Technology Act (2000), the Constitution of India (especially Articles 21 and 39(f)), and the National Education Policy (2020), in addition to major Supreme Court decisions. This includes particularly referencing *Puttaswamy (2017)* about informational privacy as a fundamental right and *Pragya Prasun & Ors. v. Union of India & Ors.* (2025) regarding digital accessibility being part of the right to life and right to education. The focus of this review is the consent, accountability, and redress provisions contained within the DPDPA as they affect children and elderly caregivers in an educational environment.

This doctrinal review is supported by a comparative analysis of the legal and policy frameworks in place. The article reviews India's developing data protection system against global and regional benchmarks such as the European Union's General Data Protection Regulation (GDPR) and the United Nations Committee on the Rights of the Child's General Comment No. 25 (2021) on children's rights and the digital environment. In addition to analysing the relevant soft-law instruments, regulatory guidance, and existing empirical research on digital exclusion, children's rights, and ageing, the article looks at how closely aligned, or divergent, India's framework is from emerging global standards concerning privacy, data protection, and age-responsive governance.

Finally, life-course and intergenerational perspectives are used to contextualise this research, using both the "Seasons of Life" framework and interdisciplinary research from both ends of the age spectrum on digital exclusion. By conceptualising the privacy interests of children and elderly caregivers as being structurally connected within Indian intergenerational households, the article frames the interpretations of statutory provisions and constitutional principles, providing a basis for normative recommendations for the promotion of age-inclusive, intergenerationally aware data protection within Indian educational institutions.

The structural relationship between these two groups of digitally vulnerable individuals, as conceptualised within the "Seasons of Life" framework, is illustrated in Figure 1 below.

Figure 1. The "Seasons of Life" Framework: Intergenerational Digital Exclusion and Privacy Vulnerability in Indian Educational Settings. (Source: Authors)

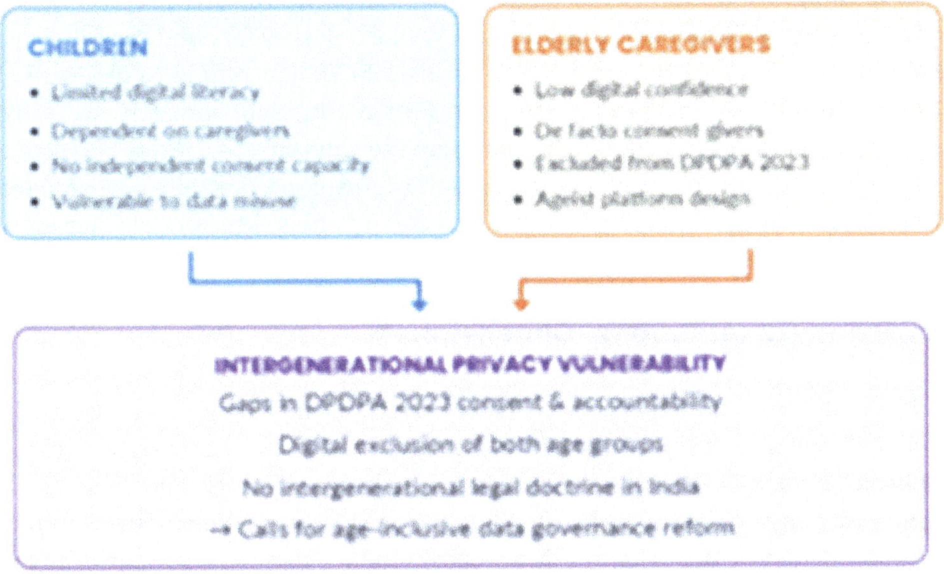

There are multiple limitations to this chapter that will be noted. The first limitation is that it adopts exclusively a doctrinal approach, by using legislative texts, judicial decisions and secondary literature. There are no empirical data collected (primary research) such as surveys or interviews of school personnel, caregivers or students. The result, therefore, is an evaluative and normative assessment of India's legal framework, and not a verified account of anyone's experience. The second limitation arises in the comparative analysis which has drawn on the international frameworks of the GDPR and UNCRC General Comment No. 25 (2021). The comparative methodology employs data received from some other countries, yet does not undertake an exhaustive and full comparison across all jurisdictions.

Third, the Indian education context is the specific focus of this chapter, and therefore the results may not be directly applied to other jurisdictions, as there will exist a different constitutional, cultural and technological framework. Having said that, the chapter's methodology is appropriate for its stated purpose of identifying gaps in the legal structure and providing recommendations for law and policy change.

UNDERSTANDING DIGITAL EXCLUSION AND INTERGENERATIONAL DIMENSIONS

Digital exclusion in India is a complex, multidimensional problem that is about more than just internet access or hardware (van Dijk, 2020; Norris, 2001). It combines existing disparities and inequities related to infrastructure, socioeconomic status, geographic location, gender, disability, and, crucially for our discussion, age (Robinson et al., 2015; Hargittai, 2002; Laskar, 2023). According to the Unified District Information System for Education Plus report, approximately 46.8% of schools in India lacked functional computer facilities, and only 54.2% reported active internet connectivity, with infrastructural deficits disproportionately concentrated in rural and socioeconomically marginalized communities (Ministry of Education, Government of India, 2024).

Legal and Constitutional Dimensions

Under the constitutional privacy framework established in Puttaswamy (2017), structural digital exclusion that prevents meaningful exercise of data rights directly implicates Article 21. Where structural digital exclusion prevents children and their caregivers from meaningfully understanding or contesting institutional data collection practices, that exclusion acquires direct constitutional significance, impairing the exercise of a fundamental right rather than merely a practical entitlement (Bhatia, 2017; Warschauer, 2003).

Empirical Evidence on Digital Exclusion

The digital divide exists at both ends of the age spectrum (Friemel, 2016; Seifert et al., 2022). For children, and especially those from marginalized backgrounds, being digitally excluded means a lack of devices, irregular or no internet access, and a lack of opportunity to participate in e-learning opportunities, which only exacerbates existing educational inequities (Livingstone & Third, 2017). Older persons in India face comparable digital exclusion; empirical research indicates that a significant proportion of elderly caregivers report low digital confidence, unfamiliarity with digital interfaces, and anxiety regarding errors in online transactions (Jena & Paltasingh, 2024; Seifert et al., 2022; Friemel, 2016).

A defining feature of families in India is that of an intergenerational structure, with grandparents, or other elders, serving as caregivers or sometimes more direct facilitators of children's education; this was particularly visible during remote learning as a result of the pandemic (Verma et al., 2024; Chadha, 2012; De et al., 2023). Such care often places elderly caregivers at the center of a process of digital exclusion (Bakshi & Bhattacharyya, 2021). Elderly caregivers are frequently required to upload identity documents, complete online payments, and consent to data-processing platforms on behalf of children, tasks that presuppose digital literacy and legal awareness that many elderly persons demonstrably lack (Jena & Paltasingh, 2024; Mannheim et al., 2019). When overall digital literacy is not well supported (especially for elders), many elderly caregivers cited feeling more anxious, less empowered, and at higher risk of mistakes regarding their settings for privacy or inadvertently affecting information relating to their own or family privacy (Jena & Paltasingh, 2024; Ivan & Fernández-Ardèvol, 2017).

Urban-rural, regional, and gender inequalities, moreover, amplify the situation (Laskar, 2023; Agrawal et al., 2020). Urban households demonstrate faster rates of digital platform adoption relative to low-income and rural families, where elderly informal caregivers face compounded disadvantage arising from infrastructural deficits and generational unfamiliarity with digital tools (Singh, 2010). Government initiatives, including Atal Tinkering Labs and the digital literacy programmes announced in Union Budget 2025–26, reflect policy recognition of these gaps; however, UDISE+ 2023–24 data records that only 54.2% of schools had functional internet connectivity, and digitally trained teaching staff remain critically insufficient, sustaining intergenerational digital dependency and associated privacy risks (Ministry of Education, Government of India, 2024).

Policy and Institutional Landscape

The digital divide is not only infrastructural but also social and psychological (Vassilakopoulou & Hustad, 2023; Robinson et al., 2015). Ageism, which is defined by the World Health Organisation (2021) as prejudice or discrimination based on age, underpins both the design of digital tools and regulatory processes for educational technology (Mannheim et al., 2023; Mannheim & Köttl, 2024). Elderly caregivers are often rendered invisible in discussions of technology policy, and educational privacy standards and practices overwhelmingly focus on children's needs, often overlooking seniors' data protection needs and vulnerabilities (World Health Organization, 2021; Officer & de la Fuente-Núñez, 2020). This exclusion is not merely theoretical: school platform interfaces and consent processes are rarely designed with older users in mind, effectively preventing elderly caregivers from exercising data rights in a meaningful and informed manner (Ayalon & Tesch-Römer, 2018; Mannheim et al., 2019).

In such an ecosystem, the two ends of the age continuum, children and the elderly, are at an increased risk of manipulation, misuse of data, algorithmic bias, and exclusion from decision-making in institutions (Livingstone & Third, 2017; Seifert et al., 2022). The "Seasons of Life" framework conceptualizes digital exclusion and intergenerational privacy vulnerability as structurally intertwined, affirming that effective legal and policy responses must address the full life course rather than treating age groups as discrete and unrelated categories (Ayalon & Tesch-Römer, 2018). Unless data protection legislation and educational technology policy explicitly address the interrelated vulnerabilities of children and elderly caregivers, existing age-based and socioeconomic disparities within India's digital education ecosystem will deepen (Ayalon & Tesch-Römer, 2018; Ministry of Education, Government of India, 2024; Lievens et al., 2024).

There has been much academic writing around the issue of digital exclusion and children's data rights; however, there is still a significant gap in terms of addressing the intersecting privacy vulnerabilities of children and their elderly caregivers in relation to the digital ecosystems within India's intergenerational household and school-based data systems. The current studies that exist (Jena & Paltasingh, 2024; Seifert et al., 2022; Livingstone & Third, 2017) address these groups as separate entities, while legal discourse around the DPDPA (2023) focuses primarily on child-protective provisions and does not consider elderly caregivers as both de facto digital intermediaries and data principals. This chapter seeks to address these shortcomings by applying the "Seasons of Life" framework as a means of reframing privacy vulnerability as a structural intergenerational issue, resultantly developing normative recommendations for age-inclusive data governance in Indian educational institutions.

These patterns of digital exclusion are not merely social or infrastructural, they directly enable and amplify concrete privacy and data protection risks within Indian schools, as the following section demonstrates.

RISKS TO PRIVACY AND DATA PROTECTION IN SCHOOLS IN INDIA

The digitalisation of school education in India has substantially increased the volume of personal data collected, processed, and stored by educational institutions and their third-party technology partners (Ministry of Education, Government of India, 2024; Human Rights Watch, 2022). Schools now routinely process sensitive personally identifiable information about students and families, including demographic information, academic records and performance, attendance, health information, biometric information (Aadhaar), and familial caregiver information for administrative and compliance purposes (Ganguly, 2023; Gupta & Rao, 2024). The introduction of third-party EdTech vendors as intermediaries in school administration and instruction has created additional, largely unregulated data-sharing relationships that heighten privacy risks for both enrolled children and the elderly caregivers who support their digital engagement (Human Rights Watch, 2022; Privacy International, 2022a).

Under the current framework, Section 9 of the Digital Personal Data Protection Act, 2023 prohibits data fiduciaries, a category that includes educational institutions and their contracted EdTech vendors, are prohibited from processing children's personal data without verifiable parental or guardian consent and from undertaking tracking or behavioural monitoring of children. However, as discussed below, Section 9's child-specific consent model remains under-protective in practice.

Types of Data Collected and Platforms Used

Indian schools today frequently rely on heavily proprietary school management systems, digital attendance registers, online admissions, classroom apps, video conferencing platforms, and third-party ed-tech products that typically operate under little regulation (Human Rights Watch, 2022; CyberPeace Foundation, 2024). Emergency contact details and caregiver information, which may include identity documents belonging to elderly relatives (Digital Personal Data Protection Act, 2023, § 2(t)), are routinely collected as part of school enrolment and administrative processes (Ganguly, 2023).

These data practices carry significant privacy implications for both groups. Where users lack digital literacy or practical capacity to seek redress, existing legal mechanisms offer little meaningful protection (Jena & Paltasingh, 2024; Ellefsen & Chen, 2022).

Significant Privacy and Security Risks

Unauthorized use and breaches of data: In 2024, a data breach at VIT Bhopal University resulted in the exposure of thousands of students' and faculty members' personally identifiable information, including names, email addresses, passwords, and identity numbers, in the absence of any effective institutional privacy policy (S.S. Rana & Co., 2024). A nine-month pilot study conducted by the CyberPeace Foundation between July 2023 and April 2024 found that Indian educational institutions suffered over 200,000 cyberattacks and nearly 400,000 data breaches, and concluded that such institutions are up to five times more vulnerable than counterparts with stronger cybersecurity practices (CyberPeace Foundation, 2024). In a separate incident, a data breach affecting approximately 426,000 users of an Indian EdTech platform resulted in the exposure of names, contact details, and payment information on the dark web, illustrating a pattern of inadequate data security among EdTech operators (Privacy International, 2022b).

Weak consent processes: Institutional consent processes presuppose digital literacy; consent forms and data-sharing notices are routinely inaccessible to users with low literacy or limited digital experience, including elderly caregivers submitting documents on behalf of children, who frequently lack any meaningful understanding of how their data will be processed or retained (UN Committee on the Rights of the Child, 2021; Ellefsen & Chen, 2022; Mannheim et al., 2019).

Algorithmic and institutional biases: There is increased use of automated systems and analytics, used for admissions or grading, which has been shown to reinforce ageist and socioeconomic biases (Gándara et al., 2024). Not enough accountability is faced by EdTech companies that use sensitive biometric data, sometimes facial images, furthering the risks of discrimination among vulnerable or digitally excluded groups (Ganguly, 2023; Privacy International, 2022a).

Limited Digital Literacy and Awareness: School-aged children along with the elderly generally struggle to manage settings, identify phishing, or have rights over their personal data (Aly et al., 2024; Seifert et al., 2022). Research demonstrates that both children and elderly persons are disproportionately vulnerable to data exploitation, phishing, and manipulation, owing to limited capacity to recognize privacy risks or assert data rights in digital environments (Ayalon & Tesch-Römer, 2018; Ellefsen & Chen, 2022; Human Rights Watch, 2022).

Lack of Institutional Accountability: Most government-run and rural schools lack designated privacy officers, conduct no meaningful data security audits, and provide no offline grievance mechanisms, structural deficiencies that render redress practically inaccessible to elderly caregivers and digitally excluded users (Digital Personal Data Protection Act, 2023, §§ 13–14; CyberPeace Foundation, 2024).

Case Examples and Reported Incidents: In 2024, an inadvertent disclosure on a government education portal exposed the personally identifiable information of thousands of students and caregivers, including identity numbers, scanned documents, and contact details, illustrating the absence of basic data governance safeguards in institutional digital infrastructure (CyberPeace Foundation, 2024; Privacy International, 2022b). In 2025, a data breach at IIT Roorkee compromised the sensitive personal data of nearly 30,000 students and alumni, including mobile numbers, caste and financial details, photographs, and email addresses, with the affected system reportedly accessible for approximately ten years. Indian EdTech platforms have been documented engaging in excessive data collection, inadequate security practices, and unauthorized data commercialization, in violation of the data minimization and purpose limitation principles implicit in the DPDPA framework (Human Rights Watch, 2022; Privacy International, 2022b).

On-the-ground examples also illustrate the risks discussed previously. In a 2024 study conducted by the Software Freedom Law Centre India, it was found that numerous government school management portals in Uttar Pradesh and Rajasthan collected Aadhaar-linked biometric data from students but failed to provide consent notices in the local languages for elderly caregivers, who typically provide documents as required by the schools, leaving them entirely unaware of the information collected (Software Freedom Law Centre India, 2024). Similarly, a 2022 UNICEF India report highlighted that during remote school work, the elderly grandparents who were responsible for registering the children online routinely submitted ID documents via unverified third-party websites without receiving any orientation on what would happen to that data once it was collected (UNICEF India, 2022). These examples from the ground demonstrate that privacy risks are not an abstract concept but are real experiences for many of the most digitally disadvantaged members of India's school communities.

The Intergenerational Nature of Risk: Most importantly, breaches of intergenerational privacy in schools are seldom single use; breaches affecting students regularly affect elderly caregivers whose data, consent, and family relationships are fused throughout school platforms and databases (Ivan & Fernández-Ardèvol, 2017; Livingstone & Third, 2017). Therefore, intergenerational protections are not only ethical but also a policy necessity in modern education (Ayalon & Tesch-Römer, 2018; Privacy International, 2022a).

Against this backdrop of documented privacy risks, the adequacy of India's existing legal and policy frameworks in addressing these vulnerabilities must now be critically examined.

LEGAL AND POLICY FRAMEWORKS IN INDIA

India's legal and policy response to digital privacy and data protection in education is delivered largely through the newly enacted Digital Personal Data Protection Act, 2023 (DPDPA), and legacy provisions of the Information Technology Act, 2000 (IT Act), alongside limited educational guidelines. While these frameworks represent a formal legislative acknowledgement of data privacy as a regulatory concern, they remain structurally fragmented and do not contain explicit age-adaptive or intergenerational provisions adequate to the educational data governance context (Srikrishna Committee Report, 2018; Tandon & Gupta, 2025).

Digital Personal Data Protection Act, 2023

Under the proportionality standard established in Puttaswamy (2017), the DPDPA's consent, accountability, and redress mechanisms warrant examination not only for their textual content but also for whether they substantively protect the informational self-determination of children and elderly caregivers in educational contexts. The analysis will examine key provisions in the DPDPA in light of this proportionality framework, particularly examining Sections 6, 9, 10, 12, and 13.

The DPDPA establishes rights for data principals, individuals to whom personal data relates, and imposes obligations on "data fiduciaries", entities that determine the purpose and means of data processing, under Sections 2(j) and 2(i) respectively (Digital Personal Data Protection Act, 2023, §§ 2(i), 2(j); Tandon & Gupta, 2025). Under the current framework, Section 9 of the DPDPA prohibits data fiduciaries from processing a child's personal data without verifiable parental or guardian consent and from undertaking behavioural monitoring or targeted advertising directed at children; however, the law does not recognise elderly de facto caregivers as data principals, nor as being capable of authorising consent in their own right. The DPDPA's consent architecture is formally compliant but substantively ineffective in intergenerational households. Where grandparents serve as de facto digital intermediaries, they fall entirely outside the Act's protective framework. Without safeguards tailored to elderly intermediaries, the Puttaswamy (2017) proportionality requirement is only partially met, hindering effective realisation of informational privacy for both groups. The Act therefore contains no corresponding provisions addressing the intergenerational privacy vulnerabilities of elderly caregivers who function as de facto digital intermediaries within the educational ecosystem (Digital Personal Data Protection Act, 2023, § 9). Furthermore, **the DPDPA does not designate educational institutions as "Significant Data Fiduciaries" under Section 10**, which would otherwise trigger enhanced obligations including the appointment of a Data Protection Officer, the conduct of periodic Data Protection Impact Assessments, and mandatory data audits (Digital Personal Data Protection Act, 2023, § 10; Tandon & Gupta, 2025).

Section 6 of the DPDPA requires consent to be free, specific, informed, and unambiguous. However, where notices are issued only in technical English, this standard is functionally undermined, a failure constitutionally suspect under the Puttaswamy (2017) proportionality standard (DPDPA, 2023, § 6). Sections 12 and 13 of the DPDPA provide rights to erasure and grievance redressal. However, both are digital-first mechanisms that place the burden of initiation on the data principal, structurally inaccessible to digitally excluded elderly caregivers and children without a recognised digital proxy (DPDPA, 2023, §§ 12–13; Tandon & Gupta, 2025; Mannheim et al., 2019).

The Information Technology Act, 2000, and IT Rules

The Information Technology (Reasonable Security Practices and Procedures and Sensitive Personal Data or Information) Rules, 2011, framed under Section 43A of the Information Technology Act, 2000, require bodies corporate to implement reasonable security practices; however, these Rules apply primarily to commercial bodies corporate and provide no specific procedural obligations governing how schools, school management systems, or government education portals collect, store, or share personal data (Information Technology Act, 2000, s. 43A; IT Rules, 2011; Bhandari & Sane, 2018).

Education Policy and Guidelines

The National Education Policy, 2020, advocates for ethical and responsible use of technology in educational settings but does not establish enforceable data protection obligations or prescribe institutional privacy governance standards for schools (Ministry of Education, Government of India, 2020). The guidance by education boards (e.g., CBSE, NCERT) often centers around the child's safety and welfare but does not provide guidance on caregiver data, nor does it consider the age-inclusive design of the consent and communication processes (Lievens et al., 2024; UN Committee on the Rights of the Child, 2021).

Due to the absence of a policy framework in practice, there is no standardised data governance policy; for example, there are many different types of privacy notices used at different schools. Schools also tend to include consent within the general admission process; therefore, there is no mandatory training for staff handling family members' personal data. As a result, problems at the ground level are felt most by elderly caregivers who use the school as their main resource for guidance regarding data practices.

In institutions, even though they are legally required to comply with the DPDPA, the degree and extent of implementation are very poor, particularly in low-resource and rural schools. Most of the government-run schools do not have any IT staff or data protection officers, nor do they have any established formal privacy governance infrastructure (CyberPeace Foundation, 2024). Consequently, many of these schools are unable to realistically comply with their obligations under the DPDPA. Additionally, consent forms and data-sharing notices are often provided in paper form during the admission process with no follow-up procedures to ensure that caregivers understand these documents; this approach structurally excludes elderly caregivers who may also have limited literacy skills. Lastly, grievance redressal portals that are required under Section 13 of the DPDPA rely on the assumption of access to the internet and digital literacy, which many of the rural caregivers and students do not possess (Jena & Paltasingh, 2024). As a result, there is a compliance framework created in theory but which has no practical effect on the population that it was created to serve.

Comparative International Frameworks

By contrast, the EU General Data Protection Regulation (GDPR) requires data controllers to provide information to data subjects in "a concise, transparent, intelligible and easily accessible form, using clear and plain language" and mandates Data Protection Impact Assessments for processing operations likely to result in high risk to natural persons, including children (Regulation (EU) 2016/679, Arts. 12, 35; Information Commissioner's Office, 2021). Comparative scholarship confirms that the GDPR's child-protective architecture, including its age-appropriate design obligations and mandatory impact assessments, substantially exceeds the protections available under India's current DPDPA framework (Alkis-Tümtürk, 2023). Article 16 of the UN Convention on the Rights of the Child (UNCRC) guarantees every child the right to privacy, and the UN Committee on the Rights of the Child's General Comment No. 25 (2021) affirms that this right extends fully to the digital environment, requiring states to adopt privacy-by-design standards in services accessible to children (UN Committee on the Rights of the Child, 2021, paras. 67–70; Lievens et al., 2024).

Data protection frameworks in developing countries, like Brazil's LGPD, offer similar lessons as EU data protection laws. The LGPD has clear requirements around children's data protection, requiring heightened safeguards and accessible consent processes, including provisions for low-literacy users. South Africa's POPIA also treats children as a special category of data subject and requires that a data controller obtain prior authorisation from the Information Regulator before processing children's data, a level of institutional accountability that is stronger than that which is currently provided for in the DPDPA. Both the LGPD and POPIA impose affirmative obligations on data controllers to ensure accessibility of consent mechanisms, a standard that the DPDPA has not yet adopted. The ability to create age-responsive and accessibility-focused data protection legislation within a developing country context does not rely on the EU's resource infrastructure.

While the foregoing analysis identifies what the law formally provides, the following section examines where these provisions structurally fail children, elderly caregivers, and the intergenerational households they form.

GAPS AND LIMITATIONS

Although privacy is constitutionally recognised as a fundamental right under Puttaswamy (2017), implementation remains inconsistent and fragile, especially for schools serving low-income and rural families (Tandon & Gupta, 2025). The 2025 Supreme Court judgment in Pragya Prasun & Ors. v. Union of India further confirms that where essential services, including education, are conditioned on digital engagement, the denial of meaningful digital access constitutes a constitutional violation under Article 21, reinforcing that structural digital exclusion of elderly caregivers in school contexts is not merely a policy gap but a rights-based concern (Pragya Prasun & Ors. v. Union of India & Ors., 2025). The critical gaps are as follows:

- There is no direct legal responsibility or recourse for elderly caregivers whose personal data is collected directly by schools or indirectly by their EdTech partners or platforms except for incidental data as "parents" or "guardians" (Digital Personal Data Protection Act, 2023).
- There are no age-adaptive consent guidelines, accessible grievance procedures, or proactive public education for audiences that are not digital natives (Mannheim et al., 2019; UN Committee on the Rights of the Child, 2021).
- There is weak regulatory control of data actions taken by third-party EdTech vendors, developers, and partner information system providers who operate on weak legal or regulatory boundaries (Colonna, 2022).
- There are no mandatory privacy-by-design audits or age-inclusive risk assessments for educational technology platforms (Colonna, 2022; Regulation (EU) 2016/679, Art. 35).

The Way Forward

This chapter proposes that addressing these gaps requires targeted legislative reform of the DPDPA to incorporate age-adaptive consent standards, mandatory Data Protection Impact Assessments for educational institutions, and explicit recognition of elderly caregivers as data principals in the educational context, reforms consistent with the comparative standards established under the GDPR and the UNCRC General Comment No. 25 (Regulation (EU) 2016/679, Art. 35; UN Committee on the Rights of the Child, 2021; Colonna, 2022).

The gaps identified above are not insurmountable; they point directly toward targeted legal, institutional, and technological reforms, which the following section advances as a normative agenda for age-inclusive data governance in Indian education.

CRITICAL EVALUATION: GAPS AND INTERGENERATIONAL CONSIDERATIONS

Despite the constitutional recognition of privacy as a fundamental right in Puttaswamy (2017), India's legislative and policy frameworks remain structurally inadequate in addressing the intergenerational dimensions of digital privacy vulnerability in educational settings (Tandon & Gupta, 2025). Although the DPDPA, 2023 formally establishes data rights for data principals and child-specific protections under Section 9, its implementation architecture does not yet incorporate age-adaptive consent mechanisms, elder-inclusive communications, or intergenerational privacy obligations (Digital Personal Data Protection Act, 2023, § 9; Tandon & Gupta, 2025).

Inadequate Age-Responsive Protections

While Section 9 of the DPDPA requires verifiable parental or guardian consent before processing a child's personal data, the Act contains no provision recognising elderly caregivers as de facto digital intermediaries or independent data principals within the educational ecosystem, a legal lacuna that directly undermines the Act's protective purpose (Digital Personal Data Protection Act, 2023, § 9). This creates a legal grey area for elderly caregivers who assist children in navigating digital platforms; they may unintentionally expose themselves to risks without self-directed guidance, recourse options, or a digital education (Ivan & Fernández-Ardèvol, 2017; Mannheim et al., 2019; Seifert et al., 2022).

Lack of Compliance and Literacy

Schools and technology vendors create privacy notices and consent forms filled with complicated, jargon-heavy English that do not take into account the literacy levels or linguistic needs of both children and elderly caregivers (Officer & de la Fuente-Núñez, 2018; Aly et al., 2024; Jena & Paltasingh, 2024). Such inaccessible consent communications undermine Section 6 of the DPDPA's free and informed consent standard. They disenfranchise digitally excluded users and entrench ageist assumptions into institutional data governance (DPDPA, 2023, § 6; Ayalon & Tesch-Römer, 2018; Mannheim et al., 2023).

Disparate Accountability and Redress

The grievance redressal and erasure rights under Sections 12–13 of the DPDPA are digital-first by design. This renders them structurally inaccessible to rural, elderly, and digitally marginalised populations who lack the connectivity or legal awareness to use them (DPDPA, 2023, §§ 12–13; Pragya Prasun, 2025 INSC 599; Seifert et al., 2022). This structural inaccessibility results in chronic under-reporting of intergenerational privacy harms among elderly caregivers, depriving policymakers of the evidence base needed to drive meaningful reform (Ayalon & Tesch-Römer, 2018).

Failure to Consider Intergenerational Privacy

Indian law, judicial decisions, and education sector policies have not yet developed a doctrine of intergenerational privacy that acknowledges the cascading harm caused to multiple family members of different generations when a school-based data breach occurs (UN Committee on the Rights of the Child, 2021; Ivan & Fernández-Ardèvol, 2017; Verma et al., 2024). To use an example, where a school database is hacked, both a student and their grandparent, likely also held in that database for identification or health reasons, are also harmed (CyberPeace Foundation, 2024; Ganguly, 2023). Without consideration of intergenerational privacy, the vulnerabilities of families cannot be adequately managed (Ayalon & Tesch-Römer, 2018; Privacy International, 2022a).

Persistent Socioeconomic Disadvantage

Children and elderly caregivers around the country who lack private digital learning tools or live in areas with poor public implementation become doubly disadvantaged with few access points for upskilling in digital participation or the support of institutions (Robinson et al., 2015).

The 'Seasons of Life' Framework and Ageism

A life-course approach to data protection policy, as conceptualised within the "Seasons of Life" framework, would suggest the need for legislative and institutional responses that are age-responsive across the full spectrum of digital participation, from childhood through elderhood (Ayalon & Tesch-Römer, 2018; Kluge & Schlick, 2023). Such a framework is consistent with the WHO's life-course approach to healthy ageing, which recognises that cumulative exposures and transitions across the lifespan shape individual capacity for participation and autonomy in later life (World Health Organization, 2024). Ageist assumptions embedded in institutional practice, including the presumption that elderly caregivers engage with technology only passively, systematically exclude elderly caregivers from participatory policy design and from receiving targeted data rights communications (Officer & de la Fuente-Núñez, 2020; Mannheim et al., 2023; Mannheim & Köttl, 2024).

These ageist assumptions are seen in real-world examples found in institutional behaviour: school administrators give a one-page consent form in English for admission with no explanation; EdTech companies default to opt-out data sharing with no alternative for plain language; and grievance portals require user email registration, which many elderly caregivers cannot do independently. This is not merely an oversight. It illustrates a systemic lack of designing EdTech from a user perspective (Mannheim et al., 2019; Seifert et al., 2022).

Summary of Key Findings:

- Lack of explicit acknowledgement about elderly caregivers' role in educational privacy frameworks (Digital Personal Data Protection Act, 2023, § 9; Tandon & Gupta, 2025).
- Complicated or difficult consent processes and little accommodation for digital or functional literacy (Jena & Paltasingh, 2024; Aly et al., 2024; UN Committee on the Rights of the Child, 2021).
- Lack of focus on intergenerational privacy risks in breach management and remediation (Ivan & Fernández-Ardèvol, 2017; Privacy International, 2022a).
- Lack of integration of anti-ageism principles and intergenerational views in the design of policy and technology (Mannheim et al., 2023; Ayalon & Tesch-Römer, 2018).
- Structural barriers to access, remedy, and participation in digital and legal processes for children and elderly caregivers (Pragya Prasun, 2025 INSC 599; Seifert et al., 2022).

When making reforms in this area, it is necessary to take into account not only the administrative and financial limitations affecting many Indian schools, but particularly those that are government-run with limited staff and infrastructure, especially in rural areas. The addition of age-inclusive consent, design standards, and data protection processes will be seen as adding further compliance requirements to federal, state, and regional education systems that are already stretched thin. In addition, there is a legitimate concern that if these institutions are not supported through an expansion of their resource base, the imposition of significant data protection duties and auditing requirements will result in over-regulation, leading to paper compliance rather than adherence to the spirit of improving data protection for children in schools. However, comparative experience in other regulatory frameworks, such as the GDPR, suggests that calibrating obligations against institutional capacity, for example, through phased implementation, and providing targeted support from state authorities can reduce the risk of over-regulation while simultaneously increasing protections for digitally vulnerable children (Regulation (EU) 2016/679; Colonna, 2022).

RECOMMENDATIONS

The following recommended solutions directly address five categories of failure outlined in the previous analysis: the legal invisibility of elderly caregivers, inaccessible consent mechanisms, weak institutional accountability, digital-first redressal processes, and the absence of intergenerational privacy doctrine. Each recommendation is designed to fill a particular gap identified in the earlier analyses, and therefore, the normative framework presented in this chapter reflects the structural analysis that supports it.

The following recommendations are grounded in the Puttaswamy (2017) constitutional privacy framework, the GDPR and UNCRC General Comment No. 25 (2021), the Pragya Prasun (2025) ruling on digital accessibility, and the "Seasons of Life" framework (Ayalon & Tesch-Römer, 2018), directed at achieving age-inclusive, rights-compliant data governance in Indian educational institutions.

Legal and policy reforms

The absence of legal recognition for elderly caregivers, identified in Section 5 as the most critical structural gap, calls for consideration of the following legislative amendment. Legislative reform, age-inclusive recognition: Amend Section 2(j) of the DPDPA to expressly recognize elderly de facto caregivers as data principals in educational contexts, conferring on them the rights to consent, erasure, and grievance redressal under Sections 6, 12, and 13 of the Act (Digital Personal Data Protection Act, 2023, §§ 2(j), 6, 12, 13; Tandon & Gupta, 2025). Such legislative recognition is consistent with the approach taken by the GDPR, which recognises the need for graduated and context-sensitive application of data rights to account for differing levels of vulnerability among data principals (Regulation (EU) 2016/679, Recital 75; Lievens et al., 2024).

Accessible consent: Addressing the consent accessibility failures documented in Sections 3 and 4, the following reform is proposed. All schools and EdTech vendors should issue consent notices in plain language across scheduled languages of the Constitution, consistent with Section 6(3) of the DPDPA and UNCRC General Comment No. 25 (2021, para. 38). Consent should be iterative and revocable, not a single omnibus agreement (Digital Personal Data Protection Act, 2023, § 6(3); UN Committee on the Rights of the Child, 2021).

Mandatory Data Protection Impact Assessments: The absence of mandatory accountability mechanisms for schools, a gap evidenced by the data breaches documented in Section 3, warrants the following designation. Designate educational institutions enrolling above a prescribed threshold as Significant Data Fiduciaries under Section 10 of the DPDPA, triggering mandatory Data Protection Impact Assessments, appointment of Data Protection Officers, and periodic audits, consistent with Article 35 of the GDPR (Digital Personal Data Protection Act, 2023, § 10; Regulation (EU) 2016/679, Art. 35; Colonna, 2022). Comparative analysis of GDPR implementation demonstrates that mandatory DPIAs for educational institutions materially reduce data breach incidents and improve institutional accountability (Kamišalić Latifić et al., 2025).

School management systems and educational technology vendor compliance with age-inclusive design standards (e.g., at least support of multilingual display languages, ability to change font size, assisted consent mechanisms, and offline options for those without reliable access to the Internet) should be required conditions for institutional procurements of said products. The Bureau of Indian Standards should develop the applicable design elements for educational technology into their standard guidelines and apply enforcement via the audit mechanism of the Data Protection Board as per Section 10 of the Digital Personal Data Protection Act (2023).

Institutional and Educational Policy Change

Digital Literacy Awareness Training for All Ages: The empirical evidence reviewed in Section 2 confirms that legal rights are only as effective as the literacy of those exercising them, making the following capacity-building measures indispensable. Guarantee the institutionalization of digital literacy and privacy awareness programming, including workshops and helplines, for students and elderly caregivers (Mannheim et al., 2019; Jena & Paltasingh, 2024). Training topics should include appropriate platform usage, identifying scams, and understanding privacy rights. Research confirms that structured, face-to-face intergenerational digital literacy interventions generate significant improvements in elderly caregivers' digital confidence, self-efficacy, and privacy awareness, with particularly strong outcomes where training pairs elderly participants with younger instructors (Soederberg Miller et al., 2024).

Data Protection Officers in schools: All schools processing personal data of children should be required to designate a Data Protection Officer with an explicit mandate to develop age-inclusive grievance mechanisms and multilingual privacy resources, modelled on the obligations imposed on Significant Data Fiduciaries under Section 10 of the DPDPA and on Article 37 of the GDPR (Digital Personal

Data Protection Act, 2023, § 10; Regulation (EU) 2016/679, Art. 37; Kamišalić Latifić et al., 2025).

Routine, Community-Based Awareness Campaigns: Develop school-community partnerships that promote intergenerational digital learning, for example, as "young-to-elder" or "elder-to-young" mentors that build resilience and knowledge sharing in families (Soederberg Miller et al., 2024; Blanco-Portela et al., 2019). Evidence from intergenerational digital learning programmes across multiple contexts confirms that such partnerships demonstrably reduce the digital divide among elderly caregivers whilst simultaneously improving younger participants' attitudes toward ageing and cross-generational empathy (Soederberg Miller et al., 2024; Blanco-Portela et al., 2019).

Recommendations for Technology and Platform Design

Privacy by Design for Different User Types: Encourage or mandate that EdTech and platform providers design user interfaces for those utilising the platform as either children or elderly caregivers, featuring simple navigation, large icons, audio directions, and privacy features set at default without user action (Colonna, 2022; Mannheim et al., 2019; Ophoff et al., 2023). Universal design principles, which prioritise equitable use, flexibility, and low physical effort, provide a practical and evidence-based framework for designing educational technology platforms that are accessible across age groups and digital literacy levels (National Disability Authority, 2020).

Transparent Data Practices: Platforms should share "Data Use Summaries" that are understandable, updated regularly, notified to all users, and provide information about what actions are taken, and should make opt-in data sharing to third parties completely transparent to users every time they are asked to opt-in (Regulation (EU) 2016/679, Art. 12; Colonna, 2022; Aly et al., 2024).

Improve Accountability and Remedies

Local, Offline Access to Remedies: Ensure that there is a grievance and remedy access portal that uses both physical and digital avenues for engagement, through schools and local community support mechanisms, establishing staff with the ability to support non-digital users, with support in the local language (Pragya Prasun, 2025 INSC 599; Seifert et al., 2022). The Supreme Court in Pragya Prasun (2025) expressly directed that the State must ensure no person is denied access to essential services, including education, solely because of inability to use digital interfaces, a standard that warrants offline grievance mechanisms as a constitutional minimum.

Mandatory Reporting and Audit of Activities: Develop standardized, age-sensitive audits on data security for schools, with standardized reporting back to every family, not just parents, about a data security breach that is timely (Colonna, 2022; Regulation (EU) 2016/679, Arts. 33–34; CyberPeace Foundation, 2024).

Advocacy and Policy Opportunities and Inclusive Governance

Inclusion of older persons as caregivers in policy-making: Include elderly caregivers and advocacy organisations representing older persons in educational policy decision-making, at both governmental and school levels (Sixsmith et al., 2020; Mannheim et al., 2019). Research on co-creation of digital public services for ageing societies consistently demonstrates that services designed with meaningful participation of elderly caregivers are substantially more accessible, more trusted, and more effective than those designed without their input (Sixsmith et al., 2020).

Continued data and research: Support focused research and survey evaluations to understand the lived experience of elderly caregivers in digital education, ensuring that future initiatives and decision-making are based on accurate and clear data (Ayalon & Tesch-Römer, 2018; Jena & Paltasingh, 2024; Mannheim et al., 2019).

Collectively, these reforms would shift India's educational data governance framework from a child-centric model that functionally excludes elderly caregivers, towards a rights-compliant, life-course framework that protects the informational privacy and digital agency of all persons participating in the educational ecosystem (Tandon & Gupta, 2025; Lievens et al., 2024; Regulation (EU) 2016/679; UN Committee on the Rights of the Child, 2021).

The reforms proposed above, taken together, constitute a coherent and rights-compliant framework for addressing the intergenerational privacy deficit that currently characterises India's educational data ecosystem.

CONCLUSION

The digitalisation of school education in India has expanded access and instructional capability. At the same time, it has generated systemic data privacy risks for children and elderly caregivers that existing legislative frameworks have not adequately addressed. The reliance of families on digital schooling platforms, combined with the lack of infrastructure, skill training, and age-sensitive policy infrastructure, creates a perfect environment for both technological vulnerability and social vulnerability to develop simultaneously and in tandem. The technological and social exclusions currently emerging deepen pre-existing inequalities, including generational inequality and socioeconomic inequality.

Despite some policy movements to facilitate access and participation (for instance, the DPDPA, 2023, or global attention towards digital rights), the existing laws and guidelines regarding education and Indian policy do not generally fit the lived realities of elderly caregivers, who fill a key role in children's educational journey and remain vastly unrecognized as participants. Current consent practices, grievance redressal, and digital literacy frequently ignore the limits of children's agencies; the experience of elderly caregivers with digital platforms and inaccessibility impedes their participation in matters affecting their personal and familial intergenerational privacy.

This article has demonstrated that India's current data protection framework reflects a structural "generational myopia", addressing children and adults as discrete categories while neglecting the interdependent privacy risks inherent in the intergenerational household structures through which millions of Indian children access digital education. A constitutionally coherent response, one consistent with the right to informational privacy under Article 21 as interpreted in Puttaswamy (2017), warrants a life-course framework that recognizes and protects the distinct digital rights of children, adults, and elderly caregivers within a unified legislative architecture.

An important step forward towards truly inclusive and equitable digital education will entail a change in mindset and approach. The law should recognize and protect elderly caregivers substantively as data principals and educational actors, and policy should more clearly require the co-design of digital resources of all kinds, as well as consent processes and support systems that respond to the needs of every generation. School leaders and tech providers of digital technologies should demonstrably engage with intergenerational families to ensure that the digital transformation of education is participatory and thus equitable.

India's transition to a digitally integrated educational system will realize its constitutional promise only when lawmakers, institutions, and technology providers recognise that the right to privacy does not diminish with age, and that the dignity and informational autonomy of every participant in the educational ecosystem, regardless of generation, demands equal and enforceable legal protection.

The next steps for policymakers include amending the DPDPA to recognise elderly caregivers as data principals in education. School administrators and EdTech companies should focus on creating platforms and processes that are usable by all users, regardless of digital fluency.

REFERENCES

Alkis-Tümtürk, A. (2023). A comparative study of the online privacy and data protection of children under the GDPR and COPPA [Doctoral thesis, University of Szeged]. https://doktori.bibl.u-szeged.hu/12050/2/Asli%20Alkis-T%C3%BCmt%C3%BCrk%20Synopsis%20of%20the%20PhD%20thesis_AAT.pdf

Aly, H., Liu, Y., Ghaiumy Anaraky, R., Knijnenburg, B., & Wisniewski, P. (2024). Tailoring digital privacy education interventions for older adults. *Proceedings on Privacy Enhancing Technologies. Privacy Enhancing Technologies Symposium, 2024*(1), 635–656. DOI: 10.56553/popets-2024-0036

Ayalon, L., & Tesch-Römer, C. (Eds.). (2018). *Contemporary perspectives on ageism.* Springer., DOI: 10.1007/978-3-319-73820-8

Bakshi, T., & Bhattacharyya, A. (2021). Socially distanced or socially connected? Well-being through ICT usage among the Indian elderly during COVID-19. *Millennial Asia, 12*(2), 190–208. DOI: 10.1177/0976399621989910

Blanco-Portela, N., Benayas, J., Pertierra, L. R., & Leal-Filho, W. (2019). An intergenerational information and communications technology learning project to improve digital skills: User satisfaction evaluation. *JMIR Human Factors, 6*(3), e14440. DOI: 10.2196/14440

Chadha, R. (2012, May 21). Intergenerational relationships: An Indian perspective [Paper presentation]. United Nations Expert Group Meeting. https://www.un.org/esa/socdev/family/docs/egm12/CHADHA-PAPER.pdf

Colonna, L. (2022). Implementing data protection by design in the Ed Tech context: What is the role of technology providers? Journal of Law, Technology & the Internet, 13(1), 73–114. https://scholarlycommons.law.case.edu/jolti/vol13/iss1/4/

CyberPeace Foundation. (2024). *Exploring cyber threats and digital risks to Indian educational institutions. CyberPeace Foundation (e-Kawach Initiative), in collaboration with DELNET.* Resecurity, and Autobot Infosec.

Dayal, S., & Pratibha, . (2023). Roadblocks in education amidst global crisis—A study based in India. *PLoS One, 18*(10), e0292465. DOI: 10.1371/journal.pone.0292465 PMID: 37847726

De, A., Koper, N., Djundeva, M., & Dykstra, P. A. (2023). Views and experiences of adult children concerning intergenerational care and support in Indian families. *Ageing and Society, 44*(5), 1091–1114. DOI: 10.1017/S0144686X23000065

Digital Personal Data Protection Act. (2023). No. 22 of 2023. Ministry of Law and Justice, Government of India. https://www.meity.gov.in/static/uploads/2024/06/2bf1f0e9f04e6fb4f8fef35e82c42aa5.pdf

Doneda, D. (2021). *Da privacidade à proteção de dados pessoais* (2nd ed.). Thomson Reuters Brasil.

Ellefsen, J., & Chen, W. (2022). Privacy and data security in everyday online services for older adults. In *Proceedings of the 10th International Conference on Software Development and Technologies for Enhancing Accessibility and Fighting Info-exclusion (DSAI 2022)* (pp. 1–8). ACM. DOI: 10.1145/3563137.3563149

European Parliament & Council of the European Union. (2016). Regulation (EU) 2016/679 of the European Parliament and of the Council on the protection of natural persons with regard to the processing of personal data. Official Journal of the European Union. https://eur-lex.europa.eu/legal-content/EN/TXT/?uri=CELEX%3A32016R0679

Friemel, T. N. (2016). The digital divide has grown old: Determinants of a digital divide among seniors. *New Media & Society*, *18*(2), 313–331. DOI: 10.1177/1461444814538648

Gándara, D., Anahideh, H., Ison, M. P., & Picchiarini, L. (2024). Inside the black box: Detecting and mitigating algorithmic bias across racialized groups in college student-success prediction. *AERA Open*, *10*, 1–19. DOI: 10.1177/23328584241258741

Ganguly, S. (2023). Privacy concerns with Aadhaar. *Communications of the ACM*, *66*(9), 44–47. DOI: 10.1145/3608960

Gopika, J. S., & Rekha, R. V. (2023). Awareness and use of digital learning before and during COVID-19. *International Journal of Educational Reform*, *34*(4), 754–766. DOI: 10.1177/10567879231173389

Gupta, S., & Rao, P. (2024). A critical survey of the security and privacy aspects of the Aadhaar framework. *Computers & Security*, *142*, 103878. DOI: 10.1016/j.cose.2024.103878

Hargittai, E. (2002). Second-level digital divide: Differences in people's online skills. *First Monday*, *7*(4). Advance online publication. DOI: 10.5210/fm.v7i4.942

Human Rights Watch. (2022). "How dare they peep into my private life?": Children's rights violations by governments that endorsed online learning during the Covid-19 pandemic. Human Rights Watch. https://www.hrw.org/report/2022/05/25/how-dare-they-peep-my-private-life/childrens-rights-violations-governments

Ilavarasan, V. (2013). The digital divide in India: Inferences from the information and communication technology workforce. In Ragnedda, M., & Muschert, G. W. (Eds.), *The digital divide: The Internet and social inequality in international perspective* (pp. 134–146). Routledge., DOI: 10.4324/9780203069769

India, U. N. I. C. E. F. (2022). *Situation analysis of children in India 2022*. UNICEF India Country Office.

Indian Computer Emergency Response Team. (2024). Incident reports and advisories. Ministry of Electronics and Information Technology, Government of India. https://www.cert-in.org.in

Information Commissioner's Office. (2021). Data protection impact assessments: Children's code guidance and resources. https://ico.org.uk/for-organisations/uk-gdpr-guidance-and-resources/childrens-information/childrens-code-guidance-and-resources/

Information Technology Act. (2000). No. 21 of 2000. Ministry of Law and Justice, Government of India.

Information Technology Rules. (2011). Reasonable security practices and procedures and sensitive personal data or information (G.S.R. 313(E)). Ministry of Communications and Information Technology, Government of India.

Ivan, L., & Fernández-Ardèvol, M. (2017). Older people and the use of ICTs to communicate with children and grandchildren. Transnational Social Review, 7(1), 41–55. https://www.researchgate.net/publication/313453095_Older_people_and_the_use_of_ICTs_to_communicate_with_children_and_grandchildren

Jena, B., & Paltasingh, T. (2024). Digital literacy among older adults: A systematic review in Indian context. *Educational Gerontology*. Advance online publication. DOI: 10.1080/03601277.2024.2397428

Justice K.S. Puttaswamy (Retd.) & Anr. v. Union of India & Ors., (2017) 10 SCC 1.

Kamišalić Latifić, A., Turk, Ž., & Wellhausen, T. (2025). The need for empirical research on the school data protection officer role in Europe. Computers & Education: X Reality, 6, 100077. DOI: 10.1016/j.cexr.2024.100077

Kluge, A., & Schlick, C. (2023). A life-course perspective on older workers in workplaces undergoing transformative digitalization. *The Gerontologist*, *63*(9), 1413–1422. DOI: 10.1093/geront/gnac181 PMID: 36508331

Laskar, M. H. (2023). Examining the emergence of digital society and the digital divide in India: A comparative evaluation between urban and rural areas. *Frontiers in Sociology*, *8*, 1145221. DOI: 10.3389/fsoc.2023.1145221 PMID: 37122396

Lievens, E., Livingstone, S., McLaughlin, S., O'Neill, B., & Verdoodt, V. (2018). Children's rights and digital technologies. In Kilkelly, U., & Liefaard, T. (Eds.), *International human rights of children* (pp. 1–27). Springer., DOI: 10.1007/978-981-10-3182-3_16-1

Lievens, E., Verdoodt, V., Ramaswamy, K., & Zoboli, F. (2024). General Comment No. 25 on children's rights in relation to the digital environment: Clarifying states' obligations on children's rights to privacy and data protection. *Human Rights Law Review*, *24*(3), ngae018. Advance online publication. DOI: 10.1093/hrlr/ngae018

Livingstone, S., & Byrne, J. (2018). Parenting in the digital age: The challenges of parental responsibility in comparative perspective. In Mascheroni, G., Ponte, C., & Jorge, A. (Eds.), *Digital parenting: The challenges for families in the digital age* (pp. 19–30). Nordicom.

Livingstone, S., & Third, A. (2017). Children and young people's rights in the digital age: An emerging agenda. *New Media & Society*, *19*(5), 657–670. DOI: 10.1177/1461444816686318

Mannheim, I., & Köttl, H. (2024). Ageism and (successful) digital engagement: A proposed theoretical model. *The Gerontologist*, *64*(9), gnae078. Advance online publication. DOI: 10.1093/geront/gnae078 PMID: 38874215

Mannheim, I., Schwartz, E., Wouters, E. J. M., van Zaalen, Y., Köttl, H., Brankaert, R., & van Boekel, L. C. (2019). Inclusion of older adults in the research and design of digital technology. *International Journal of Environmental Research and Public Health*, *16*(19), 3718. DOI: 10.3390/ijerph16193718 PMID: 31581632

Mannheim, I., Wouters, E. J. M., Köttl, H., van Boekel, L. C., Brankaert, R., & van Zaalen, Y. (2023). Ageism in the discourse and practice of designing digital technology for older persons: A scoping review. *The Gerontologist*, *63*(7), 1188–1200. DOI: 10.1093/geront/gnac144 PMID: 36130318

Ministry of Education, Government of India. (2020). National Education Policy 2020. Department of School Education and Literacy. https://www.education.gov .in/sites/upload_files/mhrd/files/NEP_Final_English_0.pdf

Ministry of Education, Government of India. (2022). Annual report 2021–22. Department of School Education and Literacy. https://www.education.gov.in/sites/upload_files/mhrd/files/document-reports/annual_report_eng.pdf

Ministry of Education, Government of India. (2024). Unified District Information System for Education Plus (UDISE+) 2023–24. Department of School Education and Literacy. https://udiseplus.gov.in

National Disability Authority. (2020). Universal design and technology for older people. Centre for Excellence in Universal Design. https://universaldesign.ie/uploads/publications/Technology-for-Older-People.pdf

Norris, P. (2001). *Digital divide: Civic engagement, information poverty, and the Internet worldwide*. Cambridge University Press. DOI: 10.1017/CBO9781139164887

Officer, A., & de la Fuente-Núñez, V. (2018). A global campaign to combat ageism. *Bulletin of the World Health Organization*. https://pmc.ncbi.nlm.nih.gov/articles/PMC5872010/ DOI: 10.2471/BLT.17.202424

Ophoff, J., & Renaud, K. V. (2023). Universal design for website authentication: Views and experiences of senior citizens. In 2023 38th IEEE/ACM International Conference on Automated Software Engineering Workshops (ASEW) (pp. 46–53). IEEE. DOI: 10.1109/ASEW60602.2023.00011

Pragya Prasun & Ors. v. Union of India & Ors., W.P. (C) No. 289 of 2024, 2025 INSC 599 (Supreme Court of India, April 30, 2025). https://indiankanoon.org/doc/68332080

Privacy International. (2022a). Privacy and education: How schools are failing students. https://privacyinternational.org

Privacy International. (2022b, November 15). The right to privacy in Indian schools: Universal Periodic Review. https://privacyinternational.org/advocacy/4981/right-privacy-indian-schools-universal-periodic-review

Robinson, L., Cotten, S. R., Ono, H., Quan-Haase, A., Mesch, G., Chen, W., Schulz, J., Hale, T. M., & Stern, M. J. (2015). Digital inequalities and why they matter. *Information Communication and Society*, *18*(5), 569–582. DOI: 10.1080/1369118X.2015.1012532

Seifert, A., Cotten, S. R., & Xie, B. (2022). Elderly forgotten? Digital exclusion in the information age and the rising grey digital divide. INQUIRY. *Inquiry : a Journal of Medical Care Organization, Provision and Financing*, *59*, 1–7. DOI: 10.1177/00469580221096272

Singh, S. (2010). Digital divide in India: Measurement, determinants and policy for addressing the challenges in bridging the digital divide. *International Journal of Innovation in the Digital Economy*, *1*(2), 1–24. DOI: 10.4018/jide.2010040101

Sixsmith, A., Fang, M. L., & Woolrych, R. (2020). *Co-creating digital public services for an ageing society: Evidence for impact and outcome*. Springer., DOI: 10.1007/978-981-15-3282-0

Soederberg Miller, L. M., Callegari, R. A., Abah, T., & Fann, H. (2024). Digital literacy training for low-income older adults through intergenerational programs. *JMIR Aging*, *7*, e51675. DOI: 10.2196/51675

Software Freedom Law Centre India. (2024). APAAR ID: One nation, one student ID! What about privacy? SFLC.in. https://sflc.in/apaar-id-one-nation-one-student-id-what-about-privacy/

Srikrishna, B. N. (2018). A free and fair digital economy: Protecting privacy, empowering Indians (Report of the Committee of Experts under the Chairmanship of Justice B.N. Srikrishna). Ministry of Electronics and Information Technology, Government of India. https://www.meity.gov.in/writereaddata/files/Data_Protection_Committee_Report.pdf

Tandon, U., & Gupta, N. K. (2025). Informational privacy in the age of artificial intelligence. *Legal Issues in the Digital Age*, *6*(2), 87–117. DOI: 10.17323/2713-2749.2025.2.87.117

Tewathia, N., Kamath, A., & Ilavarasan, P. V. (2020). Social inequalities, fundamental inequities, and recurring of the digital divide: Insights from India. *Technology in Society*, *61*, 101251. DOI: 10.1016/j.techsoc.2020.101251

UN Committee on the Rights of the Child. (2021). General comment No. 25 on children's rights in relation to the digital environment (CRC/C/GC/25). United Nations. https://www.ohchr.org/en/documents/general-comments-and-recommendations/general-comment-no-25-2021-childrens-rights-relation

van Dijk, J. (2020). *The digital divide*. Polity Press.

Vassilakopoulou, P., & Hustad, E. (2023). Bridging digital divides: A literature review and research agenda for information systems research. *Information Systems Frontiers*, *25*(3), 955–969. DOI: 10.1007/s10796-020-10096-3 PMID: 33424421

Verma, S., Bhardwaj, N., & Mehta, M. (2024). Intergenerational caregiving in Indian families: Trends, challenges, and policy implications. *Journal of Aging & Social Policy*, *36*(2), 145–162. DOI: 10.1080/08959420.2023.2198456

Warschauer, M. (2003). *Technology and social inclusion: Rethinking the digital divide*. MIT Press., DOI: 10.7551/mitpress/6699.001.0001

World Health Organization. (2021). Global report on ageism. WHO Press. https://www.who.int/publications/i/item/9789240016866

World Health Organization. (2024). WHO framework to implement a life course approach in practice. https://www.decadeofhealthyageing.org/find-knowledge/resources/publications/who-framework-to-implement-a-life-course-approach-in-practice

Chapter 11
A Framework for Explainable Reasoning, Planning, and Action in LLM-Based Autonomous AI Agents

T. Venkat Narayana Rao
http://orcid.org/0000-0002-1996-1819
Sreenidhi Institute of Science and Technology, India

Ananya Seeta
Sreenidhi Institute of Science and Technology, India

Sangers Bhavana
http://orcid.org/0009-0005-6134-1081
Sreenidhi Institute of Science and Technology, India

K. Divyasri
Sreenidhi Institute of Science and Technology, India

ABSTRACT

Autonomous AI agents represent a major progression in artificial intelligence, extending beyond static predictive systems toward goal-driven entities capable of reasoning, planning, and executing actions within dynamic environments. As agent autonomy expanding in healthcare domain, the internal mechanisms governing reasoning, planning, and action selection often remain opaque, limiting transparency, trust, and effective human oversight. At the action stage, attention is given to

DOI: 10.4018/979-8-3373-9129-8.ch011

clarity in action selection, tool usage, and outcome interpretation, together with feedback mechanisms supporting adaptive behavior. The framework is developed through an analytical synthesis of literature on autonomous agents, explainable artificial intelligence, and large language model-based systems. Conceptual analysis identifies recurring design patterns, limitations, and open challenges. The resulting perspective would support, improved evaluation, governance, and human-AI collaboration in healthcare industry, while informing future research on responsible autonomous AI systems.

1. INTRODUCTION

1.1 Evolution from Predictive Models to Autonomous Agents

Artificial intelligence (AI) has undergone a fundamental transformation over the past decade, progressing from predictive machine learning models toward autonomous systems capable of reasoning, planning, acting, and adapting within dynamic environments. Early AI applications were primarily designed to perform narrowly defined predictive tasks, such as image classification, anomaly detection, recommendation, and language processing, where models generated isolated outputs in response to static inputs (Russell & Norvig, 2021). Although these systems achieved remarkable predictive performance, their operational role remained largely passive, requiring continuous human direction and intervention.

Recent advances in large language models (LLMs), reinforcement learning, retrieval-augmented generation, and tool-integrated AI have significantly expanded the capabilities of intelligent systems beyond conventional prediction. Contemporary autonomous AI agents are increasingly capable of decomposing complex objectives into executable plans, retrieving external knowledge, interacting with software tools and digital environments, maintaining persistent memory, adapting to changing contexts, and revising decisions through continuous feedback (Brown et al., 2020; Wei et al., 2022; Schick et al., 2023). Rather than producing isolated predictions, these systems execute sequences of interdependent decisions that collectively determine task outcomes.

This evolution represents a shift from predictive intelligence toward agentic intelligence, where AI systems function as active participants in decision-making processes rather than passive analytical tools. Autonomous agents are now being explored across enterprise automation, scientific discovery, healthcare, education, software engineering, finance, and public administration, where they increasingly collaborate with humans in complex workflows requiring sustained reasoning and adaptive problem solving (Wooldridge, 2009; Sapkota et al., 2025). As autonomy increases, however, understanding how these systems generate, revise, and execute decisions becomes substantially more challenging than interpreting individual model predictions.

1.2 Why Traditional Explainable AI is No Longer Sufficient

The rapid evolution of autonomous AI agents has exposed important limitations in existing Explainable Artificial Intelligence (XAI) methodologies. Traditional XAI techniques—including feature attribution, saliency mapping, local surrogate models, and post hoc explanation methods—were primarily developed to explain the predictions of individual machine learning models (Ribeiro et al., 2016; Lundberg & Lee, 2017; Arrieta et al., 2020). These approaches have substantially improved transparency for classification and regression systems by identifying influential input features or providing local approximations of model behavior.

However, autonomous AI agents differ fundamentally from conventional predictive models. Rather than generating a single prediction, agentic systems operate through interconnected decision processes involving reasoning, planning, memory retrieval, tool invocation, environmental interaction, action execution, and continuous feedback. Decisions emerge through the interaction of multiple architectural components over extended execution trajectories, making explainability a system-wide property rather than an attribute of an individual model (Sado et al., 2020). Consequently, explanations limited to isolated model outputs provide only partial insight into why an autonomous agent selected a particular strategy, revised a plan, invoked a specific tool, or adapted its behavior during execution.

Recent literature increasingly recognizes that explainability in autonomous agents must extend beyond traditional model-centric perspectives toward system-level transparency capable of capturing complete decision trajectories, inter-component dependencies, and governance mechanisms throughout the reasoning–planning–acting lifecycle. This shift reflects a broader understanding that trustworthy autonomous systems require explanations not only of predictions but also of decisions, interactions, and adaptive behaviors occurring across the entire agent architecture.

1.3 Research Approach and Methodological Positioning

Although explainability has become a central research theme within artificial intelligence, existing literature has largely concentrated on improving the interpretability of machine learning models, deep neural networks, and more recently large language models. Comparatively less attention has been devoted to understanding explainability as an architectural property of autonomous AI agents, where decisions emerge through interactions among reasoning, planning, memory, tool use, execution, and feedback mechanisms rather than isolated predictive components. Recent studies have therefore begun advocating a transition from model-level explanations toward system-level explainability capable of capturing complete execution trajectories, causal dependencies, and governance requirements within autonomous decision systems.

In response to this emerging research direction, this work develops a conceptual framework for system-level explainability in autonomous AI agents through analytical synthesis of foundational and contemporary literature spanning agent architectures, Explainable Artificial Intelligence, large language model–based agents, and responsible AI governance. Rather than proposing a new algorithm or empirical benchmark, the framework seeks to organize explainability requirements across the complete lifecycle of autonomous decision making. The discussion therefore adopts a conceptual and integrative methodology, emphasizing theoretical synthesis, architectural analysis, and cross-domain applicability.

1.4 Contributions

To address the identified research gap, this work makes four principal contributions to the emerging literature on explainable autonomous AI agents.

First, it conceptualizes explainability as a system-level architectural property rather than a model-level characteristic of autonomous AI agents. This perspective responds to the growing recognition that conventional Explainable Artificial Intelligence (XAI) methods, while effective for interpreting individual model predictions, provide limited insight into the interconnected decision processes that characterize autonomous agent systems (Arrieta et al., 2020; Zhu et al., 2026).

Second, it develops an integrated conceptual framework that unifies reasoning, planning, acting, memory, tool use, feedback, and governance within a continuous explainability lifecycle. Rather than considering these components independently, the framework emphasizes their interactions and collective contribution to transparent autonomous decision making, consistent with emerging research advocating system-level explanations for tool-augmented language models and autonomous agents (Sado et al., 2020; Zhu et al., 2026).

Third, it identifies explainability requirements, transparency challenges, and accountability considerations associated with each stage of the autonomous decision-making pipeline. By examining explainability across interconnected architectural modules instead of isolated predictive components, the framework extends current discussions on trustworthy autonomous systems and trajectory-level transparency (Sahoo et al., 2025; Sapkota et al., 2025).

Finally, it discusses the broader implications of system-level explainability for trustworthy AI deployment, governance, and future research across multiple application domains. In doing so, the framework aligns explainability with emerging principles of responsible AI, emphasizing auditability, human oversight, regulatory compliance, and continuous governance throughout the autonomous agent lifecycle (European Commission, 2021; Bandara et al., 2025).

2. CONCEPTUAL FOUNDATIONS OF AUTONOMOUS AI AGENTS

Autonomous AI agents represent a distinct class of intelligent systems characterized by goal-directed behaviour, environmental interaction, and adaptive decision making. Classical artificial intelligence defines an agent as an entity that perceives its environment through sensors and acts upon that environment through actuators (Russell & Norvig, 2021). Extending this concept, autonomous agents maintain internal representations of goals and context, reason over available information, execute actions, and continuously adapt through feedback (Wooldridge, 2009). Unlike static predictive models that generate isolated outputs, autonomous agents operate through continuous perception–decision–action cycles, enabling dynamic adaptation in changing environments.

Recent advances in large language models (LLMs), planning algorithms, and external tool integration have significantly expanded the capabilities of autonomous agents. Contemporary architectures combine reasoning, planning, memory, and execution within modular systems capable of solving complex tasks while interacting with external environments. These characteristics establish the conceptual foundation for the system-level explainability framework developed in subsequent sections.

2.1 Formal Definition

An autonomous AI agent is a computational system that perceives its environment, maintains internal representations of goals and context, generates decisions through reasoning and planning, executes actions that influence external states, and adapts behaviour using environmental feedback. This definition reflects rational agent theory, where agents select actions expected to maximize performance under available information (Russell & Norvig, 2021).

Autonomy should not be interpreted as complete independence from human oversight. Instead, autonomous agents manage intermediate decisions within predefined constraints, continuously revising strategies in response to changing conditions rather than following fixed input–output rules (Jennings & Wooldridge, 1998).

2.2 Core Characteristics of Autonomous Agents

Autonomous AI agents share several fundamental characteristics that distinguish them from conventional predictive models.

Goal orientation enables agents to pursue predefined objectives by decomposing complex tasks into executable sub-goals that guide reasoning and planning (Ghallab et al., 2016).

The perception–action loop enables continuous interaction with the environment through iterative cycles of perception, decision making, action, and evaluation, allowing agents to adapt to dynamic conditions (Sutton & Barto, 2018).

Memory provides contextual continuity by maintaining both immediate task information and long-term knowledge. In LLM-based systems, external memory mechanisms such as retrieval-augmented generation improve contextual reasoning beyond limited context windows (Lewis et al., 2020).

Tool integration extends agent capabilities through structured interaction with external applications, databases, and computational services. Combining language models with deterministic tools improves reliability, factual grounding, and operational capability (Schick et al., 2023; Hoffmann et al., 2023).

Finally, feedback mechanisms enable agents to evaluate execution outcomes, update internal representations, and refine subsequent decisions, supporting adaptive behaviour in changing environments (Sutton & Barto, 2018).

2.3 Reactive, Cognitive, and Hybrid Architectures

Autonomous agents can be broadly categorized according to their decision-making mechanisms. Reactive agents respond directly to environmental stimuli without maintaining internal world models, making them efficient but limited in long-term planning (Brooks, 1991). Cognitive agents incorporate internal representations and deliberative reasoning, enabling strategic planning and goal management (Wooldridge, 2009). Hybrid architectures combine reactive responsiveness with cognitive reasoning and are widely adopted in contemporary LLM-based agents, where neural reasoning is integrated with structured planning and rule-based control.

2.4 Integration of Large Language Models

Large language models have substantially enhanced the reasoning capabilities of autonomous agents by enabling contextual understanding, semantic reasoning, and multi-step inference (Brown et al., 2020; Wei et al., 2022). Within modern agent architectures, LLMs typically function as reasoning components alongside planning, memory, and execution modules, allowing agents to interpret natural language objectives and coordinate complex tasks.

However, integrating LLMs into autonomous systems also increases the need for explainability. Reliable deployment requires reasoning to be supported by planning validation, constraint management, memory, and traceable execution rather than relying solely on language generation. Consequently, autonomous AI agents should be understood as integrated decision-making systems whose behaviour emerges from interactions among multiple architectural components, providing the conceptual basis for the system-level explainability framework developed throughout this chapter.

3. ARCHITECTURAL FRAMEWORK FOR SYSTEM-LEVEL EXPLAINABILITY IN AUTONOMOUS AI AGENTS

The increasing autonomy of modern AI systems has fundamentally transformed agent architectures from isolated predictive models into integrated decision-making ecosystems. Unlike conventional machine learning models that produce independent predictions from static inputs, autonomous AI agents continuously interpret goals, reason over contextual information, formulate execution strategies, interact with external environments, and adapt behaviour through feedback. Consequently, autonomous behaviour emerges from the coordinated interaction of multiple architectural components rather than a single predictive model.

This architectural evolution has been driven by advances in large language models (LLMs), retrieval-augmented generation, external tool integration, and adaptive memory mechanisms. Contemporary agentic systems combine reasoning, planning, execution, memory, and feedback within modular architectures capable of solving complex tasks under dynamic conditions. While modularity improves flexibility, scalability, and maintainability, it also introduces new explainability challenges because decisions emerge from interactions among components rather than isolated computational processes. Accordingly, system-level explainability must capture not only individual module behaviour but also the information flow that connects successive stages of autonomous decision making.

3.1 Design Principles of Autonomous Agent Architectures

Modern autonomous AI agents are designed as modular systems in which specialized components collectively contribute to intelligent behaviour. Rather than relying on a monolithic decision process, individual modules perform complementary functions including reasoning, planning, memory management, execution, and environmental interaction. This modular organization enables functional specialization while improving scalability, maintainability, and adaptability across diverse application domains (Russell & Norvig, 2021; Wooldridge, 2009).

Recent advances in LLMs have significantly expanded agent capabilities by enabling natural language understanding, contextual reasoning, and dynamic task execution. When combined with persistent memory, retrieval mechanisms, and external tool integration, these capabilities allow agents to perform multi-step problem solving that extends well beyond conventional predictive modelling (Brown et al., 2020; Schick et al., 2023). Consequently, autonomous behaviour is more appropriately viewed as a continuous decision lifecycle than as a sequence of isolated computational modules.

This evolution also changes how explainability should be interpreted. Traditional Explainable Artificial Intelligence (XAI) primarily focuses on explaining the outputs of individual predictive models. However, autonomous agents derive decisions from interactions among multiple architectural components, where reasoning, planning, memory retrieval, execution, and feedback collectively determine system behaviour. Recent research therefore advocates extending explainability beyond model-centric interpretation toward system-level transparency capable of representing complete decision trajectories and architectural dependencies (Zhu et al., 2026).

3.2 The Autonomous Decision Lifecycle

Autonomous AI agents operate through a continuous decision lifecycle in which information is progressively transformed into executable actions and subsequently refined through environmental feedback. Rather than generating a single prediction, agents repeatedly interpret objectives, reason over contextual information, formulate execution strategies, interact with external systems, evaluate outcomes, and update future behaviour. Explainability therefore depends on understanding how information evolves throughout this lifecycle rather than interpreting isolated outputs.

The lifecycle begins with the interpretation of user objectives or environmental goals. These objectives are transformed into internal representations through reasoning processes that combine contextual understanding, retrieved knowledge, prior experience, and domain-specific constraints. Reasoning establishes the initial decision rationale upon which subsequent architectural processes depend.

Building upon these intermediate inferences, the planning component converts abstract objectives into executable strategies. Planning decomposes complex goals into manageable subtasks, evaluates alternative execution pathways, considers operational constraints, and determines task priorities (Ghallab et al., 2016). As a result, planning serves as the bridge between cognitive reasoning and operational behaviour by translating inferred intentions into structured action sequences.

The selected plan subsequently guides execution through interactions with software tools, application programming interfaces (APIs), databases, external knowledge sources, or physical environments. During execution, agents continuously compare observed outcomes with expected objectives. Deviations activate feedback mechanisms that modify planning strategies, refine reasoning processes, or update stored knowledge, enabling adaptation to changing environmental conditions (Sutton & Barto, 2018).

Memory operates throughout the decision lifecycle by preserving contextual information, execution histories, retrieved knowledge, and previous outcomes that influence future decisions. Consequently, autonomous behaviour evolves through continuous interaction among reasoning, planning, execution, memory, and feedback rather than isolated decision stages. From an explainability perspective, transparency therefore requires documenting how intermediate reasoning develops into planning decisions, how plans guide execution, and how execution outcomes reshape subsequent behaviour through adaptive feedback. This lifecycle perspective establishes the conceptual foundation for the system-level explainability framework developed throughout the remainder of this chapter.

3.3 Interdependencies Across Architectural Components

he effectiveness of autonomous AI agents depends not only on the capabilities of individual components but also on the continuous exchange of information across the decision lifecycle. Unlike conventional predictive systems, where a single model independently generates outputs, autonomous agents produce decisions through interconnected reasoning, planning, execution, memory, and feedback processes. Consequently, explainability must capture how information propagates across these components rather than interpreting them independently.

Memory plays a central role by supplying contextual information, retrieved knowledge, historical interactions, and prior execution outcomes that shape subsequent reasoning. The quality of reasoning therefore depends not only on inference capabilities but also on the relevance, completeness, and reliability of retrieved information (Lewis et al., 2020). Errors or outdated knowledge may propagate through later planning and execution stages despite logically consistent reasoning, making transparency in memory retrieval essential for trustworthy autonomous behaviour.

Reasoning and planning exhibit a similarly interdependent relationship. Reasoning establishes objectives, evaluates alternative interpretations, and resolves uncertainty, while planning transforms these intermediate representations into executable strategies by prioritizing tasks, allocating resources, and considering operational constraints (Wei et al., 2022; Hoffmann et al., 2023). Because planning quality depends directly on preceding reasoning, explainability requires documenting how intermediate inferences influence strategic decisions and why alternative plans are revised or rejected.

Execution and feedback complete the decision lifecycle by translating plans into observable actions and evaluating their outcomes. Execution generates operational records that support traceability, while feedback compares expected and observed outcomes, identifies deviations, and updates memory for future decision making (Sutton & Barto, 2018). This closed-loop interaction enables continuous adaptation while ensuring that behavioural changes remain observable and auditable. Collectively, these architectural dependencies demonstrate that meaningful explainability emerges from documenting interactions among components rather than analysing isolated computational modules.

3.4 Architectural Implications for System-Level Explainability

The architectural organization of autonomous AI agents demonstrates that explainability is fundamentally a system-level property rather than a characteristic of individual predictive models. Autonomous decisions emerge through interactions among reasoning, planning, execution, memory, and feedback, requiring transparency across both architectural components and the transitions that connect them. Consequently, explanations should capture how goals are interpreted, how intermediate reasoning evolves into executable plans, how actions are selected and validated, and how execution outcomes influence subsequent behaviour.

Recent research increasingly recognizes that autonomous AI systems require explainability frameworks capable of representing execution trajectories, architectural dependencies, and continuous interactions instead of relying exclusively on post hoc interpretations of model outputs (Zhu et al., 2026; Sado et al., 2020). This broader perspective supports accountability, auditability, human oversight, and regulatory compliance by providing traceable evidence of how autonomous decisions are generated and refined throughout the decision lifecycle.

Figure 1 illustrates the proposed architectural pipeline. Memory operates throughout the lifecycle by supporting reasoning and recording execution outcomes, while validation and monitoring mechanisms intersect multiple components to enforce operational constraints and governance. Integrating these elements establishes a modular yet coherent architecture in which explainability is embedded throughout the complete autonomous decision process rather than introduced after decisions have been made. This architectural perspective provides the conceptual foundation for the explainability mechanisms discussed in the following sections.ne

3.5 Action Execution, Feedback Integration and adaptive control

Following plan generation, autonomous AI agents operationalize selected strategies through interactions with external systems, software tools, application programming interfaces (APIs), databases, knowledge repositories, or physical environments. Unlike reasoning and planning, which remain internal cognitive processes, action execution represents the stage at which autonomous decisions become observable system behaviour. Consequently, execution forms the critical interface between internal decision making and external outcomes, making transparency at this stage essential for ensuring trustworthiness, accountability, and operational reliability (Schick et al., 2023).

Action execution extends beyond simply performing predefined tasks. Autonomous agents frequently evaluate multiple tools or execution pathways that differ in functionality, computational cost, accessibility, security, and contextual suitability before selecting the most appropriate alternative. Validation mechanisms therefore play an important role by ensuring that generated actions satisfy predefined constraints, organizational policies, and safety requirements before execution proceeds. In addition, execution logs provide traceable records of operational decisions, enabling stakeholders to reconstruct why specific tools were selected, how execution parameters were determined, and whether implemented actions remained consistent with previously generated reasoning and planning outputs. Such traceability supports both explainability and governance by establishing a verifiable link between cognitive decision processes and observable operational behaviour.

Autonomous decision making, however, does not terminate following action execution. Instead, execution outcomes generate feedback that continuously influences future reasoning, planning, and behavioural adaptation. Feedback mechanisms compare expected and observed outcomes, identify deviations from intended objectives, and initiate revisions to planning strategies or reasoning processes whenever necessary. The resulting observations are subsequently incorporated into memory, allowing previously acquired experiences to influence future decisions and progressively refine agent performance (Sutton & Barto, 2018). Consequently, explainability extends beyond documenting execution outcomes to clarifying why behavioural adaptations occur, whether they result from environmental changes, execution failures, newly acquired knowledge, or revised planning strategies. Transparent integration of execution, feedback, and memory therefore transforms autonomous decision making into a continuously adaptive yet interpretable process that supports long-term robustness while preserving accountability.

3.6 Integrated Architectural Pipeline

The architectural structure of autonomous AI agents can therefore be represented as a coordinated system:

Figure 1. Memory System Pipeline

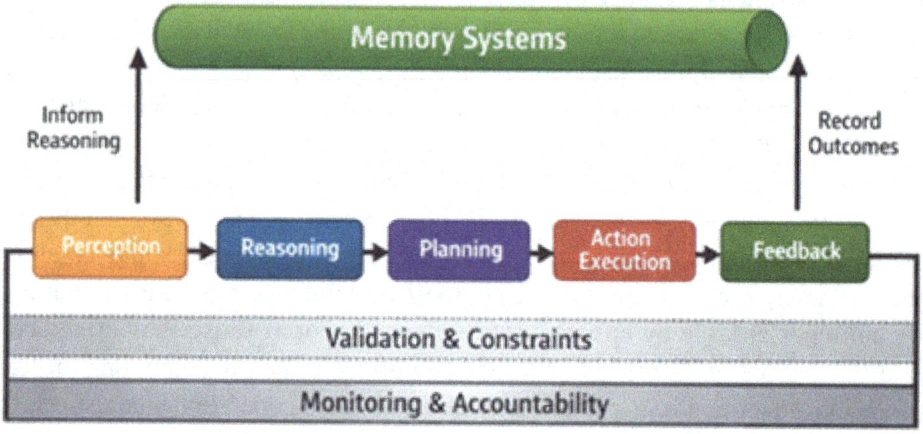

Memory systems operate across the pipeline, informing reasoning and recording outcomes. Validation and monitoring layers may intersect multiple modules to enforce constraints and enhance accountability. This architecture synthesizes rational agent theory (Russell & Norvig, 2021), automated planning research (Ghallab et al., 2016), adaptive learning principles (Sutton & Barto, 2018), and contemporary LLM-based reasoning mechanisms (Brown et al., 2020; Wei et al., 2022). By structuring decision-making into modular components, the pipeline establishes a foundation for embedding explainability at each stage of agent operation as shown in Figure 1.

Clear architectural delineation supports system-level transparency by clarifying how intermediate reasoning transitions into sequenced plans and ultimately into executed actions. Such structural clarity is essential for designing autonomous AI agents that are both operationally capable and interpretable within complex deployment environments.

4. FOUNDATIONS OF EXPLAINABILITY IN AUTONOMOUS SYSTEMS

The growing adoption of autonomous AI agents has fundamentally expanded the scope of explainability beyond the interpretation of individual predictive models. Unlike conventional machine learning systems that generate isolated predictions from static inputs, autonomous agents continuously reason, plan, invoke external tools, execute actions, update memory, and adapt to environmental feedback. Consequently, explainability can no longer be viewed solely as a model-centric problem but must instead account for complete decision trajectories spanning multiple interacting architectural components. This shift has motivated increasing interest in system-level explainability, where transparency is evaluated across the entire autonomous decision lifecycle rather than individual computational outputs (Arrieta et al., 2020; Zhu et al., 2026).

While early XAI research focused primarily on interpreting predictive models, autonomous AI agents introduce additional layers of complexity. Multi-stage decision pipelines involving reasoning, planning, memory interaction, and action execution require broader interpretive frameworks. Understanding explainability in agentic systems therefore requires moving beyond isolated model outputs toward integrated system-level transparency.

4.1 Overview of Explainable Artificial Intelligence

Explainable Artificial Intelligence encompasses methods designed to render AI systems understandable to human users. Common techniques include feature attribution methods, surrogate modeling, and rule extraction approaches (Guidotti et al., 2018). Prominent examples include LIME and SHAP, which approximate complex models with locally interpretable representations (Ribeiro et al., 2016; Lundberg & Lee, 2017).

XAI research distinguishes between intrinsically interpretable models and post hoc explanation techniques. Linear models, decision trees, and rule-based systems are considered inherently interpretable due to transparent internal logic (Doshi-Velez & Kim, 2017). In contrast, deep neural networks typically require post hoc methods to provide insight into feature importance or prediction rationale. As autonomous AI agents increasingly integrate reasoning, planning, memory, and tool-enabled interaction, explanations must extend beyond interpreting individual predictions to documenting how successive architectural processes collectively produce autonomous behaviour. Consequently, traditional XAI techniques should be regarded as foundational components of broader system-level explainability frameworks rather than complete solutions for agentic systems.

Although these approaches have advanced model-level transparency, they were largely developed for static input–output tasks. Autonomous agents, by contrast, generate sequential decisions across interconnected modules. Consequently, traditional XAI methods, while necessary, are insufficient for capturing the full complexity of agentic behavior

4.2 Interpretability, Transparency, and Accountability

Clarifying distinctions among interpretability, transparency, and accountability is essential for system-level analysis.

Interpretability refers to the degree to which humans can understand how a system produces specific outputs (Doshi-Velez & Kim, 2017). It often involves examining intermediate representations, feature contributions, or reasoning traces.

Transparency concerns openness regarding system design, data sources, and operational processes. Transparent systems provide documentation of architectural choices, training procedures, and decision flows (Arrieta et al., 2020).

Accountability extends beyond understanding to responsibility and auditability. Accountable systems enable stakeholders to trace decisions, evaluate compliance, and assign responsibility for outcomes (Floridi et al., 2018).

4.3 Post Hoc Versus Intrinsic Explainability

Explainability techniques may be categorized as post hoc or intrinsic. Post hoc methods generate explanations after model outputs are produced, approximating internal processes without modifying system architecture (Lundberg & Lee, 2017). These methods are flexible but may not fully capture causal mechanisms.

Intrinsic explainability, by contrast, involves embedding transparency directly within system design. Rule-based components, symbolic overlays, and structured reasoning traces contribute to inherently interpretable architectures (Guidotti et al., 2018). For autonomous AI agents, intrinsic explainability offers an important architectural advantage because transparency is embedded throughout successive decision stages rather than reconstructed after execution. Intermediate reasoning traces, planning hierarchies, execution logs, and memory updates collectively provide continuous evidence describing how autonomous behaviour evolves over time. Consequently, intrinsic explainability better supports accountability within dynamic agentic systems than post hoc interpretation alone. In agentic systems, intrinsic mechanisms may include explicit goal hierarchies, documented planning sequences, and traceable tool invocation records. Recent work on controllable and interpretable language generation highlights the need for architectural mechanisms that constrain and clarify model behavior beyond post hoc explanations (Shiv et al., 2023).

Recent work on explainable feature selection demonstrates how interpretability techniques can be embedded within model design to improve transparency without sacrificing predictive performance (Zacharias et al., 2022).

4.4 Model-Level Versus System-Level Explainability

Traditional XAI research has focused primarily on model-level explainability, clarifying how individual predictive models generate outputs. However, autonomous agents integrate multiple interacting modules whose collective behavior determines outcomes. Model-level explanations address only one layer of this architecture. The distinction between model-level and system-level explainability represents one of the fundamental conceptual shifts introduced by autonomous AI agents. Model-level approaches primarily explain how individual algorithms transform inputs into predictions, whereas system-level explainability seeks to clarify how reasoning, planning, memory retrieval, tool invocation, execution, and feedback collectively influence autonomous behaviour. Consequently, explainability evolves from interpreting isolated computational outputs toward reconstructing complete decision trajectories spanning multiple architectural components.

System-level explainability extends interpretability across the entire decision pipeline. It addresses questions such as: How was a goal interpreted? Why was a specific plan selected? What constraints influenced action execution? How did feedback modify subsequent behavior? This broader perspective aligns with risk management and governance frameworks emphasizing traceability and auditability (NIST, 2020). Autonomous agents often operate within dynamic loops where intermediate outputs influence downstream processes. Understanding system behavior therefore requires examining interactions among modules rather than isolated inference stages.

Bridging model-level and system-level explainability involves integrating reasoning traces, planning logs, execution records, and memory updates into coherent explanatory frameworks. Such integration enables comprehensive evaluation of agent behavior and supports institutional oversight. Recent studies similarly argue that transparency within autonomous AI agents should emphasize execution trajectories, provenance information, architectural interactions, and governance mechanisms rather than isolated model explanations, reinforcing the need for integrated system-level transparency throughout the autonomous decision lifecycle (Farooq et al .,2026).

4.5 Limitations of Current XAI Approaches

Despite substantial progress in Explainable Artificial Intelligence (XAI), existing approaches remain constrained when applied to autonomous AI agents. Most explainability techniques were originally developed for static prediction problems in which a single model transforms defined inputs into corresponding outputs. Autonomous agents, however, operate through continuous interactions among reasoning, planning, memory retrieval, tool invocation, action execution, and adaptive feedback. Consequently, explanations that focus exclusively on individual model predictions provide only a partial understanding of overall system behaviour.

A primary technical limitation concerns the inability of many XAI methods to capture temporal dependencies across sequential decision processes. Feature attribution techniques and surrogate models offer valuable insights into localized predictions but provide limited visibility into how intermediate reasoning, planning revisions, and execution outcomes collectively influence subsequent decisions (Arrieta et al., 2020). As autonomous agents increasingly operate through iterative decision cycles, understanding isolated predictions becomes insufficient for explaining complete behavioural trajectories.

Architectural complexity introduces additional challenges. Contemporary agentic systems integrate multiple interacting components, including external tools, retrieval mechanisms, persistent memory, and adaptive planning modules, each contributing to the final decision. Traditional model-centric explanations rarely capture these interactions or clarify how information propagates across architectural stages. Consequently, critical operational processes such as tool invocation, memory updates, and plan revision often remain insufficiently represented within conventional explainability frameworks. Recent studies therefore advocate embedding transparency directly within agent architectures through execution trajectories, provenance records, and process-level documentation rather than relying solely on post hoc explanations (Farooq et al .,2026).

Scalability and governance further complicate explainability. As autonomous agents undertake increasingly complex tasks involving long-term memory and extended planning horizons, decision traces become progressively larger and more difficult for human stakeholders to interpret. Balancing comprehensive transparency with cognitive usability therefore remains an important research challenge. Collectively, these limitations demonstrate that explainability challenges in autonomous AI agents arise not from individual predictive models but from interactions among reasoning, planning, acting, memory, feedback, and governance processes. Addressing these challenges therefore requires architectural transparency capable of explaining complete decision trajectories rather than isolated computational outputs, reinforcing the transition toward system-level explainability.

5. EXPLAINABLE REASONING IN AUTONOMOUS AGENTS

Reasoning constitutes the cognitive foundation of autonomous AI agents by transforming user objectives, environmental observations, and contextual knowledge into structured representations that guide subsequent planning and action. They that generate isolated outputs, autonomous agents continuously refine reasoning through interactions with memory, planning, tool invocation, execution feedback, and environmental adaptation. Consequently, reasoning should be understood not as an independent computational process but as the first stage of an interconnected autonomous decision lifecycle. This architectural dependency fundamentally changes the requirements for explainability. Rather than explaining individual predictions, explainable reasoning must clarify how intermediate inferences are generated, revised, validated, and propagated across subsequent decision stages, thereby establishing transparency throughout the complete agent lifecycle (Russell & Norvig, 2021; Zhu et al., 2026).

5.1 Reasoning Mechanisms

Explainable reasoning in autonomous AI agents extends beyond generating logically coherent outputs. It requires mechanisms capable of exposing intermediate inference processes, grounding decisions in verifiable evidence, documenting underlying assumptions, and maintaining traceability throughout the reasoning lifecycle. The following subsections examine these complementary mechanisms and their collective contribution to system-level explainability.

5.1.1 Multi-Step Reasoning

Autonomous agents frequently engage in multi-step reasoning, decomposing complex tasks into intermediate inferential stages before generating actionable outputs. Structured multi-step inference improves coherence and supports alignment between goals and execution strategies (Wei et al., 2022). In classical AI, hierarchical problem-solving approaches similarly decomposed objectives into sub-components (Russell & Norvig, 2021).

Within LLM-based systems, multi-step reasoning may be explicitly generated as intermediate outputs that inform downstream planning modules. When these intermediate steps are documented, they enhance interpretability by revealing how conclusions were derived rather than presenting final outputs alone. Although multi-step reasoning primarily improves task performance through structured decomposition, its significance for explainability lies in exposing intermediate decision states that would otherwise remain opaque. By documenting how partial conclusions contribute to subsequent reasoning stages, intermediate representations facilitate verification, error localization, and accountability across autonomous decision pipelines. Consequently, explainability benefits arise not from additional reasoning steps themselves but from the transparency of their sequential relationships.

5.1.2 Chain-of-Thought Reasoning

Chain-of-thought (CoT) reasoning involves prompting models to articulate intermediate reasoning steps during inference (Wei et al., 2022). Empirical evidence suggests that such structured prompting improves performance on complex logical and mathematical tasks. In agentic systems, CoT traces can serve as provisional explanation artifacts that expose decision pathways.

However, generated reasoning traces do not always correspond directly to internal computational mechanisms. Research on large language models highlights concerns regarding explanation fidelity and the risk of plausible but unfaithful rationalizations (Bender et al., 2021). Consequently, chain-of-thought outputs should be treated as transparency aids rather than definitive causal representations. This distinction highlights an important challenge for autonomous AI agents. Plausible reasoning narratives may increase user confidence even when they do not accurately reflect underlying computational processes. Effective explainability therefore requires complementary validation mechanisms capable of verifying reasoning fidelity rather than relying solely on generated textual explanations.

Integrating CoT within broader validation and constraint-checking mechanisms strengthens reliability while preserving interpretive clarity. Empirical studies show that rehearsing intermediate subgoals before execution can improve reasoning transparency and task decomposition in autonomous LLM agents (Hoffmann et al., 2023), reinforcing the importance of structured intermediate representations for explainability.

5.1.3 Knowledge Grounding

Knowledge grounding anchors reasoning processes in verifiable data sources. Retrieval-augmented generation architectures combine language models with external databases to improve factual accuracy and reduce unsupported inference (Lewis et al., 2020). By explicitly linking reasoning outputs to retrieved evidence, agents enhance traceability and reduce the risk of hallucination. Emerging research on temporal causal probabilistic logic frameworks further illustrates the integration of symbolic reasoning within retrieval-augmented agent systems (Yu, 2025).

Grounded reasoning is particularly important in knowledge-intensive domains where decisions depend on contextual information. Transparent citation of retrieved data enables stakeholders to evaluate evidentiary support for conclusions. Grounding mechanisms therefore contribute directly to system-level explainability. Grounding also establishes an important connection between reasoning and subsequent planning activities. Plans generated from unverified or incomplete knowledge may remain logically consistent while nevertheless producing inappropriate execution strategies. Consequently, grounding mechanisms influence not only factual correctness but also the overall explainability of downstream architectural components, reinforcing the interconnected nature of autonomous decision making.

5.1.4 Inference Traceability

Inference traceability refers to the capacity to reconstruct the logical pathway that led to a decision. In symbolic AI systems, rule-based representations allowed direct inspection of inference chains (Newell & Simon, 1976). Neural architectures, by contrast, rely on distributed representations that obscure internal activation patterns.

To address this limitation, interpretability techniques such as surrogate modeling and feature attribution approximate reasoning dynamics (Ribeiro et al., 2016; Lundberg & Lee, 2017). In autonomous agents, traceability must extend beyond individual model outputs to include how intermediate reasoning steps influence planning and action modulesStructured reasoning logs, execution trajectories, and intermediate state documentation collectively enable stakeholders to reconstruct complete decision pathways spanning reasoning, planning, execution, and feedback. Such trajectory-level traceability represents a defining characteristic of system-level explainability because it captures how successive architectural components contribute to final autonomous behaviour rather than explaining isolated computational outputs.

5.1.5 Assumption Modeling

Autonomous agents frequently operate under uncertainty and incomplete information, requiring implicit assumptions to proceed with decision-making. Making these assumptions explicit enhances transparency and supports oversight. Probabilistic reasoning frameworks and uncertainty estimation techniques provide formal mechanisms for representing confidence levels and contextual dependencies (Sutton & Barto, 2018).

Explicit assumption modeling reduces ambiguity in multi-step reasoning and enables users to assess the conditional validity of outputs. By clarifying underlying premises, agents can better support collaborative human–AI decision processes. Because implicit assumptions directly influence downstream planning decisions, documenting these assumptions enhances not only reasoning transparency but also the interpretability of subsequent execution strategies. Explicit assumption disclosure therefore supports collaborative human–AI decision making by allowing stakeholders to evaluate the contextual validity of autonomous recommendations before operational actions are performed.

5.2 Limitations of Explainable Reasoning in Autonomous AI Agents

Despite substantial advances in explainable reasoning, several technical, architectural, and ethical challenges continue to limit the transparency of autonomous AI agents. Unlike conventional machine learning systems, where explanations primarily focus on interpreting individual predictions, autonomous agents generate decisions through interconnected reasoning, planning, execution, and feedback processes. Consequently, limitations arising during reasoning may propagate throughout the autonomous decision lifecycle, influencing downstream planning strategies, tool selection, execution behaviour, and subsequent learning. These challenges therefore extend beyond isolated reasoning mechanisms and require system-level approaches to explainability.

5.2.1 Architectural Limitations

One of the primary architectural challenges involves maintaining faithful representations of the reasoning process. While mechanisms such as chain-of-thought prompting and intermediate reasoning traces provide greater visibility into decision pathways, they do not necessarily reflect the actual computational processes performed internally by large language models (Bender et al., 2021). Generated reasoning traces may therefore appear plausible while failing to accurately represent the underlying causal mechanisms responsible for the final decision. This distinction between explanation plausibility and explanation fidelity presents a significant challenge for autonomous AI agents operating in safety-critical or high-stakes environments.

A second architectural limitation arises from error propagation across sequential reasoning pipelines. Autonomous agents frequently employ multi-step reasoning in which intermediate conclusions directly influence planning, tool selection, and action execution. Consequently, minor inaccuracies introduced during early reasoning stages may accumulate throughout the decision process, producing progressively larger deviations from intended objectives. Because subsequent architectural components rely upon preceding reasoning outputs, local reasoning errors can ultimately influence overall system behaviour despite correct implementation of downstream modules. This interdependence reinforces the need for explainability mechanisms capable of tracing complete decision trajectories rather than isolated inference steps.

5.2.2 Data and Knowledge Limitations

Reasoning quality also depends heavily upon the availability, accuracy, and relevance of supporting knowledge. Retrieval-augmented reasoning significantly improves factual grounding by incorporating external information sources; however, the resulting explanations remain constrained by the completeness and reliability of retrieved evidence (Lewis et al., 2020). Inaccurate, outdated, or biased knowledge repositories may produce reasoning processes that appear logically consistent while nevertheless generating misleading or inappropriate conclusions. Consequently, transparency should encompass not only the reasoning process itself but also the provenance, quality, and contextual relevance of supporting evidence.

Furthermore, many post hoc interpretability techniques, including feature attribution and surrogate modeling, were originally developed for static prediction tasks and therefore provide limited insight into the temporal dependencies characterizing autonomous reasoning pipelines (Arrieta et al., 2020). Emerging research on contextual anomaly detection similarly demonstrates that meaningful explanations must account for structural relationships and evolving contextual dependencies rather than isolated computational outputs (Vaudaine, 2021). These observations further support the transition from model-level interpretation toward system-level explainability.

5.2.3 Ethical and Governance Limitations

Beyond technical considerations, explainable reasoning must also address ethical challenges associated with fairness, accountability, and responsible decision making. Large language models inevitably reflect statistical patterns present within their training data and may inadvertently reproduce historical biases, stereotypes, or representational imbalances (Floridi et al., 2018). Even when reasoning pathways appear transparent, biased assumptions embedded within retrieved knowledge or generated inferences may continue to influence autonomous decisions if appropriate validation and oversight mechanisms are absent.

Equally important, increasing transparency does not automatically guarantee accountability. Human stakeholders must remain capable of evaluating reasoning outputs, identifying inappropriate assumptions, and intervening when autonomous decisions conflict with organizational objectives, regulatory requirements, or ethical principles. Explainability should therefore be considered one component of a broader governance framework that integrates technical transparency with human oversight, auditability, and continuous monitoring throughout the autonomous decision lifecycle.

Collectively, these limitations demonstrate that explainability cannot be achieved through isolated reasoning mechanisms alone. Instead, trustworthy autonomous behaviour requires coordinated transparency across reasoning, planning, execution, memory, feedback, and governance. This broader perspective reinforces the central argument of this work that explainability should evolve from interpreting individual model outputs toward understanding the complete autonomous decision system, where architectural interactions collectively determine both operational performance and accountability.

5.3 Transparency and Interpretability Mechanisms

Despite significant advances in explainable reasoning, important technical and architectural challenges continue to limit the transparency of autonomous AI agents. Autonomous agents generate decisions through interconnected reasoning, planning, execution, memory, and feedback processes. Consequently, limitations introduced during reasoning may propagate across subsequent architectural stages, influencing overall system behaviour rather than isolated model outputs.

One major challenge concerns **reasoning fidelity**. Although techniques such as chain-of-thought prompting and intermediate reasoning traces improve transparency, they do not necessarily represent the underlying computational mechanisms of large language models (Bender et al., 2021). Generated explanations may therefore appear plausible while failing to accurately reflect the actual reasoning process, creating a distinction between explanation plausibility and explanation fidelity. This limitation becomes particularly significant in safety-critical applications where trustworthy decision justification is essential.

A second challenge involves error propagation within sequential reasoning pipelines. Autonomous agents rely on intermediate inferences to guide planning, tool selection, and action execution. Consequently, inaccuracies introduced during early reasoning stages may accumulate throughout the decision lifecycle, influencing downstream decisions despite correct implementation of subsequent architectural components. This interdependence highlights the need for trajectory-level traceability capable of explaining how reasoning evolves into planning and operational behaviour.

Reasoning quality also depends heavily on the availability and reliability of supporting knowledge. Retrieval-augmented reasoning improves factual grounding by incorporating external evidence (Lewis et al., 2020); however, incomplete, outdated, or biased knowledge sources may still produce misleading conclusions. Furthermore, many post hoc interpretability techniques were originally developed for static prediction tasks and therefore provide limited insight into the temporal dependencies characterizing autonomous reasoning pipelines (Arrieta et al., 2020). Similar challenges have been observed in contextual anomaly detection, where meaningful explanations require understanding structural relationships rather than isolated outputs (Vaudaine, 2021).

Finally, reasoning processes may inherit biases present in training data or retrieved information, raising concerns regarding fairness, accountability, and responsible decision making (Floridi et al., 2018). Collectively, these limitations demonstrate that explainability cannot rely solely on individual reasoning mechanisms but must extend across reasoning, planning, execution, memory, and governance, reinforcing the need for a system-level explainability framework.

6. EXPLAINABLE PLANNING UNDER DYNAMIC CONDITIONS

Planning represents the architectural bridge between reasoning and action execution, transforming interpreted objectives into structured strategies capable of guiding autonomous behaviour. Unlike static planning algorithms that generate fixed action sequences, autonomous AI agents continuously revise plans in response to changing environmental conditions, newly retrieved knowledge, execution outcomes, and feedback from previous interactions. Consequently, planning is not an isolated computational process but a dynamic decision-making stage whose transparency directly influences the explainability of subsequent actions. Explainable planning therefore requires stakeholders to understand not only the final execution strategy but also how goals were decomposed, constraints were evaluated, alternatives were prioritized, and revisions were introduced throughout the autonomous decision lifecycle (Ghallab et al., 2016; Russell & Norvig, 2021).

Explainable planning depends upon several complementary processes that collectively transform abstract reasoning into operational behaviour. These processes include goal decomposition, task sequencing, constraint management, adaptive revision, and human oversight. Rather than functioning independently, each contributes to maintaining transparency throughout the planning lifecycle while ensuring that planning decisions remain interpretable before execution occurs.

6.1 Goal Decomposition

Goal decomposition involves breaking high-level objectives into structured sub-goals that can be operationalized. Hierarchical planning frameworks formalize this process by representing tasks across multiple abstraction levels (Ghallab et al., 2016). In agentic systems, decomposition clarifies intermediate milestones and aligns execution steps with overarching objectives. Transparent documentation of sub-goals enhances interpretability by revealing how abstract instructions are translated into procedural tasks. If misinterpretation occurs at the decomposition stage, subsequent planning and execution may be compromised. Explicit goal hierarchies therefore support early validation and corrective oversight. Goal decomposition also establishes the foundation for subsequent planning activities. Decisions regarding task granularity, dependency relationships, and sub-goal prioritization directly influence task sequencing and execution strategies. Consequently, explainability at this stage requires documenting not only the resulting sub-goals but also the rationale underlying their decomposition.

6.2 Task Sequencing and Multi-Step Decision Logic

Following decomposition, planning requires sequencing sub-tasks into coherent action chains. Task sequencing determines dependencies, ordering constraints, and conditional branching logic. Multi-step decision logic governs how intermediate states influence subsequent operations.

Beyond determining execution order, task sequencing exposes the logical dependencies connecting intermediate planning decisions. Transparent sequencing therefore enables stakeholders to understand why particular actions precede others, how alternative execution pathways were evaluated, and how environmental uncertainty influenced planning decisions. Such visibility is particularly important when autonomous agents dynamically revise execution strategies in response to changing operational conditions.Under uncertainty, agents must accommodate changing environmental conditions and incomplete information. Adaptive planning strategies may incorporate probabilistic evaluation or heuristic prioritization (Sutton & Barto, 2018). However, explainability requires that sequencing logic remain observable and justifiable. Structured representations such as ordered action lists or decision trees support traceability by clarifying why certain steps precede others. Transparent sequencing is particularly important in enterprise and public-sector contexts where procedural compliance and auditability are required.

6.3 Constraint Management

Constraint management ensures that planning decisions respect operational, ethical, and regulatory boundaries. Constraints may include resource limitations, access controls, safety requirements, or policy guidelines. In formal planning models, constraints are encoded as preconditions and permissible transitions (Ghallab et al., 2016). It also requires balancing competing objectives, including efficiency, safety, regulatory compliance, and resource utilization. Explainability therefore extends beyond verifying constraint satisfaction to clarifying why certain trade-offs were accepted while alternative planning strategies were rejected.

In agentic architectures, constraint validation may occur through rule-based checks or policy enforcement layers. Transparent constraint management requires documenting both satisfied and rejected action paths. Clarifying why certain alternatives were excluded strengthens accountability and reduces ambiguity in decision-making. Without explicit constraint verification, planning modules risk generating plausible but non-compliant strategies. Embedding constraint checks within architectural pipelines enhances reliability and governance alignment.

6.4 Plan Revision and Adaptive Replanning

Dynamic environments necessitate plan revision when new information or unexpected outcomes arise. Plan revision involves updating action sequences in response to feedback, aligning future decisions with revised internal representations. Rational agent theory conceptualizes such adaptation as part of iterative perception–decision–action cycles (Russell & Norvig, 2021).

Adaptive replanning may involve modifying sub-goals, reordering tasks, or invoking alternative tools. Transparent revision logs enable stakeholders to trace how feedback influenced strategic changes. Without such traceability, plan modifications may appear arbitrary, undermining trust in autonomous operation. Documenting revision events and associated triggers supports accountability and diagnostic analysis, particularly in complex multi-stage workflows. Because revised plans subsequently influence future reasoning and execution decisions, documenting revision triggers, alternative strategies, and decision outcomes strengthens trajectory-level explainability by enabling stakeholders to reconstruct how planning evolved throughout the complete autonomous decision lifecycle.

6.5 Planning Explainability Challenges

Despite significant advances in autonomous planning, maintaining transparency throughout dynamic planning processes remains a complex challenge. Unlike conventional planning systems that generate predefined action sequences, autonomous AI agents continuously revise plans in response to evolving environmental conditions, newly retrieved knowledge, execution outcomes, and changing objectives. Consequently, explainability must account not only for final planning decisions but also for how planning strategies evolve throughout the decision lifecycle.

One major challenge concerns the increasing complexity of multi-step planning. As goals are decomposed into numerous interdependent subtasks, planning dependencies become progressively more difficult to interpret. Errors introduced during early planning stages may propagate through subsequent task sequences, influencing execution outcomes despite correct implementation of individual planning components. Maintaining traceability across extended planning horizons therefore remains essential for identifying the origins of planning failures and supporting corrective intervention.

A second challenge arises from the growing adoption of neural planning mechanisms. While symbolic planning approaches explicitly represent state transitions and decision rules, neural planning architectures frequently generate latent representations that are not directly interpretable. Consequently, conventional post hoc interpretability techniques developed for static predictive models provide only limited insight into the evolving planning strategies employed by autonomous agents (Arrieta et al., 2020). Recent research therefore advocates embedding transparency within planning architectures rather than relying solely on explanations generated after decisions have been made (Sado et al., 2020).

Planning decisions must also reconcile competing objectives such as efficiency, resource utilization, safety, regulatory compliance, and risk mitigation. Although decision-theoretic approaches provide formal mechanisms for balancing these objectives, explainability requires exposing the rationale underlying accepted trade-offs together with the alternatives that were rejected (Russell & Norvig, 2021). Collectively, these challenges demonstrate that explainable planning extends beyond documenting action sequences to providing continuous visibility into how planning decisions evolve through interactions with reasoning, execution, feedback, and environmental change. Such transparency reinforces the broader transition from model-level interpretation toward system-level explainability in autonomous AI agents.

6.6 Human Oversight in Planning Processes

Human-in-the-loop mechanisms strengthen explainable planning by introducing structured oversight checkpoints. Users may review goal decompositions, validate sequencing logic, or approve high-impact actions before execution. Such mechanisms reduce automation bias and enhance alignment with institutional policies. Audit logs documenting decomposition steps, constraint evaluations, and revision events further support governance and compliance requirements (NIST, 2020). Interactive explanation interfaces may summarize decision chains, presenting hierarchical views of goals and tasks to facilitate human understanding. Rather than replacing autonomous planning, human oversight establishes collaborative checkpoints that validate strategic decisions before high-impact actions are executed. Such collaborative planning mechanisms strengthen accountability while preserving the operational benefits of autonomous decision making.

Integrating oversight mechanisms within planning modules ensures that autonomy operates within accountable boundaries rather than as an opaque automation process. Explainable planning functions as the critical transition between cognitive reasoning and operational execution within autonomous AI agents. Transparent planning therefore depends not only on documenting action sequences but also on exposing the assumptions, constraints, revisions, and trade-offs that shape planning decisions over time. When integrated with reasoning, execution, memory, and governance, explainable planning becomes a fundamental component of system-level explainability that supports trustworthy autonomous decision making across dynamic environments.

7. EXPLAINABLE ACTING AND TOOL-ENABLED INTERACTION

Following reasoning and planning, autonomous agents operationalize selected strategies through interactions with external systems. At this stage, explainability extends beyond internal decision processes to documenting why particular actions were selected, how external tools were invoked, and how execution outcomes influence subsequent decisions. Unlike reasoning and planning, which primarily operate within internal computational processes, acting directly modifies external system states and therefore introduces immediate operational consequences. Consequently, explainability at the execution stage extends beyond understanding why a particular action was selected to documenting how actions were performed, which tools were invoked, what constraints governed execution, and how observed outcomes influenced subsequent decisions. Acting should therefore be understood as the architectural bridge between internal decision making and external system behaviour, making transparency essential for accountability, auditability, and trustworthy autonomous operation (Russell & Norvig, 2021). Contemporary agent architectures further extend rational agent principles by integrating structured tool invocation mechanisms that combine language model reasoning with deterministic computational functions, enabling agents to perform reliable operations while maintaining operational traceability (Schick et al., 2023).

Explainable acting encompasses multiple complementary mechanisms that collectively ensure operational transparency throughout the execution lifecycle. These include transparent tool invocation, execution traceability, action justification, validation mechanisms, adaptive feedback, and governance oversight. Rather than functioning independently, these processes collectively establish the evidence required to reconstruct and evaluate autonomous actions after execution.

7.1 Tool Invocation Transparency

Tool-enabled agents invoke external functions to retrieve data, execute computations, or modify system states. Tool augmentation enhances reliability and reduces unsupported inference by delegating specialized tasks to deterministic components (Schick et al., 2023). However, transparency in tool invocation is critical.

Tool invocation transparency involves documenting:

(i) The selected tool or function
(ii) The parameters supplied
(iii) The contextual reasoning prompting invocation
(iv) The expected outcome

Transparent tool invocation not only strengthens interpretability but also establishes the foundation for execution traceability and subsequent accountability. Recent work on agentic AI transparency similarly emphasizes documenting tool invocations, execution trajectories, and provenance information as essential components of system-level explainability rather than isolated execution records (Transparency for Agentic AI, 2025).

7.2 Execution Traceability and Action Logging

Execution traceability refers to the capacity to reconstruct operational behavior through structured logging. Action logs typically record timestamps, invoked functions, input parameters, and resulting outputs. This chronological documentation links planning decisions to observable consequences. Execution traceability extends beyond maintaining chronological records of executed operations. Within autonomous AI agents, traceability establishes causal relationships between reasoning, planning, tool invocation, execution outcomes, and subsequent behavioural adaptation. Consequently, execution logs should capture not only operational events but also the decision context that produced those events, enabling complete reconstruction of autonomous execution trajectories during auditing or post-deployment evaluation.

Traceability serves both technical and governance purposes. Technically, logs facilitate debugging and performance optimization. From an accountability perspective, traceable records support auditing and compliance verification (Floridi et al., 2018). In regulated environments, execution documentation may be required to demonstrate adherence to policies and standards. Importantly, logging should encompass both successful and unsuccessful actions. Recording errors or rejected operations provides insight into system robustness and supports diagnostic analysis.

7.3 Execution Justification

Beyond descriptive logging, execution justification provides explanatory context for operational steps. Justification mechanisms link actions to prior reasoning and planning stages, clarifying why a specific tool was selected or a parameter configured in a particular manner.

While post hoc explanation techniques can approximate model behavior (Lundberg & Lee, 2017), intrinsic architectural transparency offers stronger interpretability. By explicitly connecting execution events to planning outputs and constraint evaluations, agents can provide structured rationale for their behavior. Execution justification therefore functions as the critical connection between cognitive reasoning and observable behaviour. Rather than documenting only what actions occurred, justification mechanisms explain why alternative execution strategies were rejected, how selected actions satisfied operational constraints, and how planning decisions ultimately influenced external system interactions. Such contextual explanations strengthen trust by transforming execution records into interpretable decision narratives.

7.4 Error Detection and Validation

Operational environments introduce the possibility of execution errors arising from incorrect parameterization, tool mis-selection, incomplete data retrieval, or environmental inconsistencies. Cascading errors may propagate through multi-step pipelines if not detected promptly. Because autonomous actions directly affect external systems, execution errors may produce consequences that extend beyond computational inaccuracies to operational, financial, or regulatory impacts. Validation therefore represents an essential safeguard within the autonomous decision lifecycle, ensuring that planned actions satisfy predefined constraints before execution occurs. Effective validation not only detects incorrect parameterization or inappropriate tool selection but also documents why potentially harmful actions were prevented, thereby contributing to both explainability and governance.

Validation mechanisms may include rule-based checks, constraint verification layers, or anomaly detection systems. Adaptive control principles can also support performance evaluation and iterative refinement (Sutton & Barto, 2018). Transparent documentation of validation results strengthens accountability by clarifying how errors were identified and mitigated. Pre-execution verification processes are particularly important for high-impact operations. Ensuring that actions comply with predefined constraints reduces risk exposure and enhances reliability.

7.5 Feedback-Based Adaptation

Feedback mechanisms connect execution outcomes to subsequent reasoning and planning processes. After an action is performed, agents observe environmental responses and update internal representations accordingly. Transparent feedback integration ensures that behavioral adjustments remain traceable rather than opaque. Adaptive responses may involve revising goals, modifying plans, or invoking alternative tools. Documenting such revisions clarifies causal relationships between outcomes and decision adjustments. Feedback transparency strengthens system robustness while supporting interpretability. By documenting how execution outcomes influence subsequent reasoning and planning processes, feedback establishes trajectory-level explainability that connects individual operational events to the continuous evolution of autonomous behaviour.

7.6 Operational Risk and Governance Implications

Acting introduces operational risks not present in static predictive systems. When agents interact with external infrastructures, consequences may extend beyond informational outputs to system modifications or automated transactions. Risks include unintended automation, propagation of inaccurate data, or violation of policy constraints.

Risk mitigation requires embedding validation, logging, and oversight mechanisms within the action layer. Structured execution transparency supports regulatory alignment and institutional governance (NIST, 2020). Graduated autonomy models where higher-risk actions require human approval can further reduce exposure. Real-time threat intelligence systems similarly emphasize the necessity of adaptive monitoring and traceable defensive responses in operational AI deployments (Aminu et al., 2024).

Explainable acting completes the autonomous decision lifecycle by connecting internal reasoning and planning processes with observable operational behaviour. Transparent tool invocation, execution traceability, action justification, validation, and adaptive feedback collectively ensure that autonomous actions remain interpretable, auditable, and accountable after deployment. Consequently, acting should be viewed not as an isolated execution stage but as an integral component of a broader system-level explainability framework in which operational transparency continuously interacts with the complete autonomous decision lifecycle.

8. CROSS-DOMAIN APPLICATIONS

The system-level explainability framework developed in the preceding sections provides a structured foundation for evaluating autonomous AI agents across diverse application domains. Although deployment contexts differ, autonomous agents consistently rely on reasoning, planning, acting, memory, and feedback to support decision-making. Consequently, explainability must extend across the complete autonomous decision lifecycle rather than isolated model predictions. In multi-agent environments, transparency becomes increasingly important because system behaviour may emerge from interactions among multiple autonomous components rather than individual agents (Liévin et al., 2024). The following examples illustrate how the proposed framework supports trustworthy deployment across representative domains.

8.1 Research and Knowledge Systems

Autonomous agents increasingly support literature synthesis, knowledge retrieval, and analytical assistance within research environments. Because these tasks directly influence knowledge generation, explainability depends on transparent reasoning, evidence grounding, and traceable retrieval processes. Retrieval-augmented mechanisms improve evidentiary transparency by linking generated outputs to verifiable sources (Lewis et al., 2020). System-level explainability enables researchers to validate inference pathways, reducing the risks of unsupported conclusions while maintaining scholarly integrity.

8.2 Enterprise Workflow Automation

Enterprise agents automate workflow coordination, document processing, scheduling, and decision support. In these environments, explainability is essential for operational reliability, regulatory compliance, and organizational accountability. Transparent planning, constraint verification, and execution logging enable stakeholders to understand how business objectives are translated into operational actions. Structured audit trails further strengthen governance by supporting compliance monitoring and post-deployment evaluation (Floridi et al., 2018; Hacibedel & Qu, 2022).

8.3 Public-Sector Decision Systems

Public-sector deployments require higher levels of transparency because autonomous decisions may directly affect citizens and administrative processes. Explainable reasoning, documented planning, and traceable execution support fairness, accountability, and regulatory compliance. Embedding system-level explainability within public-sector agents enables stakeholders to reconstruct decision pathways, strengthening institutional trust while reducing the risks associated with opaque automation (OECD, 2019; Floridi et al., 2018).

8.4 Educational and Collaborative Agents

Educational and collaborative agents assist learning, assessment, and team-based decision making through adaptive interaction. In these settings, explainability improves both user understanding and confidence by clarifying how instructional recommendations or collaborative decisions are generated. Transparent feedback mechanisms allow users to interpret system adaptations and evaluate the rationale behind evolving recommendations, thereby supporting effective human–AI collaboration.

Across research, enterprise, public-sector, and educational domains, autonomous AI agents share common explainability requirements despite differing operational objectives. The proposed system-level explainability framework provides a unified approach for ensuring transparency, accountability, and trustworthy decision making by integrating reasoning, planning, acting, memory, and feedback throughout the autonomous decision lifecycle.

9. GOVERNANCE, ETHICS, AND RESPONSIBLE AGENT ECOSYSTEMS

As autonomous AI agents increasingly transition from experimental prototypes to operational systems, governance becomes an integral architectural requirement rather than an external compliance consideration. Throughout the autonomous decision lifecycle, reasoning, planning, acting, memory, and adaptive feedback collectively influence decisions that may affect organizational processes, public services, and critical infrastructures. Consequently, governance must extend beyond regulating isolated model outputs to overseeing complete decision trajectories, ensuring that autonomous behaviour remains transparent, accountable, auditable, and aligned with institutional objectives. Responsible agent ecosystems therefore embed governance mechanisms directly within system architecture, integrating technical transparency with organizational oversight throughout the operational lifecycle.

9.1 Accountability in Agent Architectures

Accountability refers to the ability to assign responsibility for decisions and outcomes generated by AI systems. In autonomous agents, accountability spans reasoning processes, planning logic, and executed actions. Clear documentation of decision pathways enables evaluation of whether outcomes align with defined objectives and constraints (Floridi et al., 2018).

Institutional accountability requires delineating responsibilities among developers, deployers, and supervisory stakeholders. Transparent architectural documentation clarifies how decisions are structured, while execution logs link operational behavior to underlying planning steps. Without traceable pathways, responsibility becomes diffused across technical layers. System-level explainability therefore strengthens accountability by enabling reconstruction of multi-stage decision chains and supporting post hoc evaluation. Accountability within autonomous AI agents is therefore distributed across multiple architectural layers rather than confined to a single predictive model. Developers remain responsible for system design, deployers oversee operational configuration, and institutional stakeholders govern deployment contexts. System-level explainability supports this distribution of responsibility by documenting how decisions evolve across reasoning, planning, execution, and feedback processes, thereby enabling meaningful attribution of responsibility throughout the complete decision lifecycle.

9.2 Auditability and Documentation

Auditability is essential for trustworthy deployment. Autonomous agents must generate structured records of reasoning traces, goal decompositions, constraint evaluations, action executions, and feedback revisions. Comprehensive logging enables retrospective analysis and compliance verification. Recent work on agentic AI transparency similarly identifies provenance tracking, execution trajectories, audit records, and oversight documentation as foundational governance mechanisms supporting trustworthy autonomous systems (Transparency for Agentic AI, 2025).

Documentation complements logging by formalizing architectural design, operational boundaries, and oversight procedures. Effective documentation should include descriptions of modular components, validation mechanisms, and update protocols. The NIST AI Risk Management Framework emphasizes traceability, documentation, and continuous monitoring as foundational elements of trustworthy AI (NIST, 2020). Because autonomous agents continuously revise plans, retrieve new knowledge, and update internal memory states, auditability must capture behavioural evolution rather than isolated execution events. Comprehensive documentation should therefore include execution trajectories, revision histories, provenance information, and architectural interactions, enabling regulators and organizational stakeholders to reconstruct complete decision pathways throughout the autonomous lifecycle.

9.3 Human-in-the-Loop Design

Human-in-the-loop (HITL) design integrates structured oversight into autonomous workflows. Rather than eliminating human involvement, responsible agent ecosystems incorporate checkpoints where users can review reasoning outputs, validate planning sequences, or approve high-impact actions. Recent judicial guidance further underscores the necessity of documented oversight and professional accountability in AI-assisted decision systems (Colorado Judicial Branch, 2024). Ethical analyses of digital technologies emphasize the importance of distinguishing genuine empowerment from superficial engagement in AI-mediated systems (Burr & Morley, 2020).

HITL mechanisms may include pre-execution approval for sensitive operations, real-time monitoring dashboards, or periodic audit reviews. Such oversight mitigates automation bias and supports alignment with organizational policies. Proportional oversight is particularly important in high-risk contexts. In public-sector and enterprise deployments, structured review processes ensure that autonomy operates within accountable boundaries. Rather than limiting autonomy, human oversight establishes adaptive governance mechanisms that enable autonomous agents to operate collaboratively with human decision makers while preserving transparency, accountability, and institutional control over high-impact decisions. HITL design therefore complements technical explainability by embedding institutional supervision into system architecture.

9.4 Regulatory Alignment

Regulatory frameworks increasingly shape expectations for AI transparency and accountability. The European Union's Artificial Intelligence Act introduces a risk-based regulatory model emphasizing documentation, oversight, and compliance for high-risk AI systems (European Commission, 2021). Autonomous agents deployed in governance-sensitive domains may fall within these categories.

Similarly, the OECD AI Principles highlight transparency, robustness, and accountability as core governance pillars (OECD, 2019). These principles advocate human-centered design and responsible innovation. The NIST AI Risk Management Framework further provides structured guidance for identifying and mitigating operational risks (NIST, 2020). Alignment with these frameworks requires embedding compliance considerations into architectural design rather than treating governance as an external afterthought. Transparent reasoning logs, documented constraint enforcement, and structured execution records directly support regulatory expectations. Collectively, these regulatory frameworks demonstrate a broader transition from model-centric governance toward lifecycle governance, where compliance depends upon documenting reasoning, planning, execution, monitoring, and continuous system adaptation rather than isolated predictive outcomes.

9.5 Toward Responsible Agent Ecosystems

Responsible agent ecosystems extend beyond individual technical components to encompass organizational culture, policy frameworks, and lifecycle management. Governance must address system updates, retraining processes, and incident response procedures. Clear version control and change documentation strengthen transparency over time. Ethical considerations include fairness, bias mitigation, and respect for user autonomy. Autonomous reasoning systems may reflect biases present in training data, requiring monitoring and corrective mechanisms (Floridi et al., 2018). Explainability supports bias detection by exposing decision pathways and underlying assumptions.

Responsible agent ecosystems emerge when technical explainability, institutional governance, and human oversight operate as complementary components of a unified socio-technical framework. Accountability, auditability, documentation, regulatory alignment, and lifecycle monitoring should therefore be embedded throughout the autonomous decision lifecycle rather than introduced as external governance mechanisms after deployment. This integrated perspective reinforces the central argument developed throughout this chapter that explainability is fundamentally an architectural property spanning reasoning, planning, acting, memory, feedback, and governance. By embedding governance directly within system design, autonomous AI agents can achieve not only operational capability but also transparency, accountability, and long-term societal trust.

10. FUTURE DIRECTIONS

The continued advancement of autonomous AI agents requires research that extends beyond capability enhancement toward structured evaluation, interpretability, and governance integration. As agentic systems increasingly operate in complex and regulated environments, future investigations must prioritize reliability, transparency, and alignment with institutional standards.

10.1 Standardized Evaluation Metrics

Current evaluation practices for autonomous agents remain fragmented and task-specific. Many assessments prioritize accuracy or task completion without systematically measuring reasoning transparency, planning coherence, or execution traceability. The development of standardized evaluation metrics for agentic systems is therefore a critical research priority.

Such metrics should assess interpretability, constraint adherence, revision traceability, and robustness under dynamic conditions. Incorporating transparency indicators into benchmarking frameworks would formalize explainability as a measurable system property rather than a qualitative attribute. Standardization would also support reproducibility and cross-domain comparison.

10.2 Multi-Agent Explainability

As research increasingly explores multi-agent coordination, explainability challenges become more complex. In distributed environments, decision-making processes emerge from interactions among multiple agents rather than isolated reasoning modules (Wooldridge, 2009). Understanding collective behavior requires aggregation of reasoning traces, planning decisions, and action logs across agents. Future research must examine scalable explanation interfaces capable of representing distributed decision chains without overwhelming users. Clarifying responsibility boundaries in multi-agent systems will also be essential for governance and accountability.

10.3 Memory Integrity and Reliability

Memory systems enable contextual continuity but introduce risks related to outdated, biased, or corrupted information. Retrieval-augmented reasoning depends on the integrity of stored data (Lewis et al., 2020). Without structured validation, memory repositories may propagate inaccuracies across decision cycles. Future work should investigate memory auditing mechanisms, provenance tracking, and decay management strategies to maintain reliability. Transparent documentation of memory updates and retrieval processes will strengthen interpretability and reduce epistemic risk.

10.4 Alignment and Value Integration

Alignment research seeks to ensure that autonomous systems operate consistently with human values and institutional norms. In agentic architectures, alignment extends beyond content generation to encompass planning strategies and execution behavior. Integrating ethical constraints within planning and validation modules represents an important research direction. Human-in-the-loop feedback, policy-constrained planning, and adaptive oversight frameworks may contribute to maintaining value consistency. Alignment should be treated as a continuous monitoring process rather than a static system property.

10.5 Governance Integration

Sustainable deployment of autonomous agents requires governance integration across system lifecycles. Future research should explore standardized documentation protocols, audit procedures, and compliance-oriented design methodologies aligned with frameworks such as the EU AI Act and NIST risk management guidelines (European Commission, 2021; NIST, 2020).

Interdisciplinary collaboration among technologists, policymakers, and organizational leaders will be necessary to translate technical transparency mechanisms into effective institutional governance structures. Advancing autonomous AI agents will therefore depend on integrating standardized evaluation, distributed explainability, reliable memory management, alignment research, and governance design. These directions emphasize responsible evolution rather than unchecked expansion of autonomy.

11. CONCLUSION

The rapid evolution of autonomous AI agents has transformed artificial intelligence from isolated predictive models into integrated decision-making systems capable of reasoning, planning, acting, interacting with external tools, and continuously adapting through feedback. While these capabilities significantly expand the operational potential of AI, they also introduce new challenges for transparency, accountability, and governance that cannot be adequately addressed through conventional model-centric explainability approaches. Understanding autonomous behaviour therefore requires visibility into how decisions evolve across interconnected architectural components rather than interpreting individual model outputs in isolation.This chapter proposed a system-level explainability framework that conceptualizes explainability as an architectural property spanning the complete autonomous decision lifecycle. By integrating reasoning, planning, acting, memory, feedback, and governance within a unified conceptual framework, the chapter demonstrates that meaningful transparency emerges from understanding the interactions among these components rather than examining them independently. Explainable reasoning supports traceable inference and evidence grounding, explainable planning provides visibility into goal decomposition, constraint management, and adaptive revision, while explainable acting ensures transparent execution, tool invocation, validation, and feedback integration. Together, these mechanisms establish a coherent foundation for accountable autonomous decision making.The applicability of this framework extends across research, enterprise, public-sector, and educational domains, where autonomous agents increasingly support complex decision processes with varying levels of human oversight. Embedding transparency throughout the autonomous decision lifecycle strengthens auditability, regulatory compliance, and stakeholder trust while enabling responsible collaboration between humans and intelligent systems. Governance therefore becomes an inherent component of agent architecture rather than an external mechanism applied after deployment.As autonomous AI agents continue to evolve toward increasingly collaborative and adaptive ecosystems, explainability must likewise progress beyond interpreting predictive models toward understanding complete decision trajectories. Advancing system-level explainability will be essential for developing autonomous systems that are not only technically capable but also transparent, accountable, and trustworthy within complex socio-technical environments.

REFERENCES:

Aminu, M., Akinsanya, A., Dako, D. A., & Oyedokun, O. (2024). Enhancing cyber threat detection through real-time threat intelligence and adaptive defense mechanisms. *International Journal of Computer Applications Technology and Research, 13*(8), 11–27.

Arrieta, A. B., Díaz-Rodríguez, N., Del Ser, J., Bennetot, A., Tabik, S., Barbado, A., García, S., Gil-López, S., Molina, D., Benjamins, R., Chatila, R., & Herrera, F. (2020). Explainable artificial intelligence (XAI): Concepts, taxonomies, opportunities and challenges toward responsible AI. *Information Fusion, 58*, 82–115. DOI: 10.1016/j.inffus.2019.12.012

Bender, E. M., Gebru, T., McMillan-Major, A., & Shmitchell, S. (2021). On the dangers of stochastic parrots: Can language models be too big? *Proceedings of the 2021 ACM Conference on Fairness, Accountability, and Transparency*, 610–623. DOI: 10.1145/3442188.3445922

Brooks, R. A. (1991). Intelligence without representation. *Artificial Intelligence, 47*(1–3), 139–159. DOI: 10.1016/0004-3702(91)90053-M

Brown, T. B., Mann, B., Ryder, N., Subbiah, M., Kaplan, J., & Dhariwal, P.. (2020). Language models are few-shot learners. *Advances in Neural Information Processing Systems, 33*, 1877–1901.

Burr, C., & Morley, J. (2020). Empowerment or engagement? Digital health technologies for mental healthcare. In C. Burr & S. Milano (Eds.), *The 2019 yearbook of the Digital Ethics Lab* (pp. 67–88). Digital Ethics Lab. DOI: 10.1007/978-3-030-29145-7_5

Colorado Judicial Branch. (2024, July 26). *Appendix to AI Subcommittee memo.*

Doshi-Velez, F., & Kim, B. (2017). Towards a rigorous science of interpretable machine learning. *arXiv preprint arXiv:1702.08608.*

European Commission. (2021). *Proposal for a regulation laying down harmonised rules on artificial intelligence.* Artificial Intelligence Act.

Floridi, L., Cowls, J., Beltrametti, M., Chatila, R., Chazerand, P., Dignum, V., Luetge, C., Madelin, R., Pagallo, U., Rossi, F., Schafer, B., Valcke, P., & Vayena, E. (2018). AI4People—An ethical framework for a good AI society. *Minds and Machines, 28*(4), 689–707. DOI: 10.1007/s11023-018-9482-5 PMID: 30930541

Ghallab, M., Nau, D., & Traverso, P. (2016). *Automated planning and acting*. Cambridge University Press. DOI: 10.1017/CBO9781139583923

Guidotti, R., Monreale, A., Ruggieri, S., Turini, F., Giannotti, F., & Pedreschi, D. (2018). A survey of methods for explaining black box models. *ACM Computing Surveys, 51*(5), 93.

Hacibedel, B., & Qu, R. (2022). *Understanding and predicting systemic corporate distress: A machine-learning approach.* International Monetary Fund.

Hoffmann, J., Madaan, A., Park, J., Lee, R., Yasunaga, M., & Radev, D. (2023). Next-step reasoning and tool use for LLMs via rehearsal of subgoals. *Proceedings of the 2023 Conference on Empirical Methods in Natural Language Processing (EMNLP 2023).*

Jennings, N. R., & Wooldridge, M. (1998). Applications of intelligent agents. In Jennings, N. R., & Wooldridge, M. (Eds.), *Agent technology: Foundations, applications, and markets* (pp. 3–28). Springer. DOI: 10.1007/978-3-662-03678-5_1

Lewis, P., Perez, E., Piktus, A., Petroni, F., Karpukhin, V., & Goyal, N.. (2020). Retrieval-augmented generation for knowledge-intensive NLP tasks. *Advances in Neural Information Processing Systems, 33*, 9459–9474.

Liévin, V., Xu, F., & Riedel, S. (2024). Evaluating and improving multi-agent coordination with natural language. *Transactions of the Association for Computational Linguistics, 12*, 583–602.

Lundberg, S. M., & Lee, S.-I. (2017). A unified approach to interpreting model predictions. *Advances in Neural Information Processing Systems, 30*, 4765–4774.

National Institute of Standards and Technology (NIST). (2020). *AI risk management framework.* U.S. Department of Commerce.

Newell, A., & Simon, H. A. (1976). Computer science as empirical inquiry: Symbols and search. *Communications of the ACM, 19*(3), 113–126. DOI: 10.1145/360018.360022

Organisation for Economic Co-operation and Development (OECD). (2019). *OECD principles on artificial intelligence.*

Ribeiro, M. T., Singh, S., & Guestrin, C. (2016). "Why should I trust you?" Explaining the predictions of any classifier. *Proceedings of the 22nd ACM SIGKDD International Conference on Knowledge Discovery and Data Mining*, 1135–1144.

Russell, S., & Norvig, P. (2021). *Artificial intelligence: A modern approach* (4th ed.). Pearson.

Schick, T., Dwivedi-Yu, J., Dessì, R., Raileanu, R., Lomeli, M., & Scialom, T. (2023). Toolformer: Language models can teach themselves to use tools. *Advances in Neural Information Processing Systems*, 68539–68551. DOI: 10.52202/075280-2997

Shiv, V., Chen, A., & Choi, Y. (2023). Towards interpretable and controllable text generation with large language models. *International Conference on Learning Representations (ICLR 2023).*

Sutton, R. S., & Barto, A. G. (2018). *Reinforcement learning: An introduction* (2nd ed.). MIT Press.

Vaudaine, R. (2021). *Détection et explication des anomalies contextuelles dans les graphes attribués* [Doctoral dissertation, Université de Lyon, Université Jean Monnet Saint-Étienne]. HAL Open Science.

Wei, J., Wang, X., Schuurmans, D., Bosma, M., Ichter, B., Xia, F., Chi, E., Le, Q. V., & Zhou, D. (2022). Chain-of-thought prompting elicits reasoning in large language models. *Advances in Neural Information Processing Systems, 35*, 24824–24837. DOI: 10.52202/068431-1800

Wooldridge, M. (2009). *An introduction to multiagent systems* (2nd ed.). Wiley.

Zacharias, J., von Zahn, M., Chen, J., & Hinz, O. (2022). Designing a feature selection method based on explainable artificial intelligence. *Electronic Markets, 32*(4), 2159–2184. DOI: 10.1007/s12525-022-00608-1

Zhu, Z., Shen, J., Xu, S., Ren, B., Tan, X., Sun, Z., Guo, C., Gao, H., Zhang, Y., & Hu, B. (2026). CausalCEM: Self-improved causal counterfactual emotion modeling for multimodal physiological signals. *Information Fusion, 136*, 104444. DOI: 10.1016/j.inffus.2026.104489

Chapter 12
Development of Trusted AI for Effective Digital Government Document Summarization

Pradeepa Sampath
http://orcid.org/0009-0003-8367-8529
SASTRA (Deemed to be) University, India

S. Nivisha
SASTRA (Deemed to be) University, India

G. R. Kharnika
SASTRA (Deemed to be) University, India

Mukesh Prasanna
http://orcid.org/0009-0006-0341-1480
SASTRA (Deemed to be) University, India

ABSTRACT

The problem of long document summarization is an important in government reporting, legal case analysis, parliamentary proceedings, and regulatory compliance documentation. This chapter presents more advanced hierarchical summarization pipeline that is specifically oriented at long-form government and legal documents. The framework breaks down the long sheets of documents into manageable keyword-based segmentation, which is used to prioritize the contextually important content. The methodology proposed is especially appropriate in application to official reports of institutions like the Congressional Research Service and the

DOI: 10.4018/979-8-3373-9129-8.ch012

Government Accountability Office. The GovReport is used in this study. It is used in digital governance solutions, automated legal briefs generation systems and policy analysis systems. The experimental analysis of the GovReport data set indicates that the suggested pipeline is superior to the classical truncation-based baselines. The model has good results on ROUGE and BERTScore assessment measures and scores of 99.84 and 67.82, respectively.

1. INTRODUCTION

The swift increase in digital governance models and e-governance administration systems has led to a massive increase in long textual data through government policy manuals, legislative bills, parliament debates, judicial opinions, compliance reports, audit reports, regulatory guidelines, draft public consultations and administrative notices Beltagy et al. (2020). Thousands of pages have been packed into a document and legal and government repositories are often typified by heavy legal language, cross-references, statutory clauses, precedence, and procedural annexures. This fact of growing exponentially, on the one hand, official documentation, has necessitated the immediate required long document summarization (LDS) systems which would enable policymakers, legal analysts, administrators, and citizens to navigate the complex textual information. Nevertheless, the context-length constraints and computational ineffectiveness of the classical summarization models are likely to make them fail to summarize documents with thousands of tokens since they are very efficient on shorter texts Bertsch et al. (2023). Within the context of law and public administration, and more generally, a task of finding the shortest possible document size to retain the intention of the statute, its legal validity, interpretative subtlety and the integrity of fact is especially difficult and is one of the most fundamental issues in Natural Language Processing (NLP) Blei et al. (2003).

Transformer architectures revolutionized attention-based sequence modelling Brown et al. (2020), and have had a tremendous impact on developing the legal and governmental text processing domain. BERT and BART, among other frameworks of encoder-decoder models Chen et al. (2023) and Chen et al. (2022), have been shown to perform exceptionally well on statutory interpretation, legal entailment tasks, prediction of the outcome of a case, as well as, an abstractive summary Devlin et al. (2019). However, the computational cost of self-attention scales quadratically with sequence length, and as such these architectures are inefficient and resource-intensive when run on long parliamentary acts, constitutional amendments, tribunal decisions and multi-volume commission reports Dhillon et al. (2020), Du et al. (2023). Since most government documents surpass the usual token window constraints of transformer based models, direct end to end processing is impractical without preprocessing schemes.

As a solution to these limits, the idea of positional interpolation has been investigated to increase the effective context window of large language models (LLMs) Fabbri et al. (2021). In spite of these developments, long government and legal document summarization has limited context truncation, input segmentation, and exorbitant memory usage during inference Golia and Kalita (2023). The previous sequence-to-sequence models, especially RNN-based summarization models Guo et al. (2021), and conventional extractive summarization methods were deficient in long-range relationships across scattered statutory clauses and multi-sectional law arguments Huang et al. (2021). Critical provisions in a text of legislation may be divided by many pages, but logically interdependent, creating the need to have models that maintain a cross-sectional coherence.

Hierarchical attention networks and chunk-based modeling have been proposed to enhance efficiency Koh et al. (2022), but it has been noted that they lack intersection coherence and context drift which is undesirable in legal summarization where precision and logical consistency is of utmost importance Lewis et al. (2019). Even modern large language models like GPT need strict document preprocessing to be able to operate within its token window when exposed to large statutes or entire policy systems Lin et al. (2004). Thus, algorithmic innovations reducing the long legal texts to structured and meaningful and semantically faithful representations before being ingested by models became indispensable Nallapati et al. (2016).

Preprocessed by central truncation, document skimming and key word extraction, preprocessing techniques have been proposed as computationally efficient and cognitively inspired ways of reducing content of a legal document Phang et al. (2022). Such strategies as truncation, especially head-and-tail retention are quite applicable when dealing with legislative and administrative texts, where executive summaries, preambles, and final instructions can be overloaded with information, whereas procedural information in the middle can be unnecessary in higher levels of comprehension Raffel et al. (2020). Central truncation thereby maintains the introductory context (objectives, scope, definitions), as well as the concluding mandates (implementation clauses, enforcement provisions) which tend to be the most legally material parts of a document.

The skimming methods imitate the reading habits of humans, particularly legal practitioners who selectively read through headings, section titles, enumerated clauses and emphasized words in an attempt to arrive at core meaning Sharma et al. (2019), Sun et al. (2019). Within government use, skimming-based summarization has the ability to quickly create concise briefs of parliamentary discourse, regulatory influence evaluations, and legal logic by cross-sampling sample passages among sections. This method would cover disseminated themes like policy objectives, stakeholder obligations, penalties, mechanism of compliance and timelines.

At the same time, the extraction of keywords by the Latent Dirichlet Allocation (LDA)-based algorithms detect statistically and contextually significant words in legal bodies, including statutory references, regulatory bodies, jurisdictional terms and other vocabulary in domains Vaswani et al. (2017). Key word summarization makes it more informative and more concise by isolating semantically dense fragments in relation to major legal terms, including constitutional validity, administrative discretion, due process, or regulatory compliance. It comes in handy especially in creating systematic legal digests, compliance briefs, and executive policy briefs.

Based on these results, the current research paper is a comparative evaluation of long document summarization methods, namely, Central Truncation, Keyword Extraction, and Skimming, which have been applied to government and legal documents. The suggested system is tested on the GovReport data set, which consists of intricate and comprehensive government reports, and thus is quite appropriate to benchmarking long document summarization models in the public-sector setting Wang et al. (2020). The metrics used in the evaluation are ROUGE-based lexical overlap and BERTScore semantic similarity that allow performing surface and contextual evaluation of summary quality Wang et al. (2024), Worsham and Kalita (2018). Also, the combination of sentence transformer embeddings and effective transformer versions helps to improve contextual encoding and semantic alignment in document reduction Zhang et al. (2019), Mann et al. (2020). Application wise, successful summarization of long government and legal documents has a broad implication. An automated executive summary can facilitate the process of cabinet decision making and reviewing of the legislation. The generation of legal briefs may help the advocates and judges to quickly comprehend precedents. The policy digests have the potential to enhance transparency, and involve the citizens by rendering the complex pieces of regulation. In compliance monitoring, institutional adaptation can be made quicker by having summarized versions of regulatory amendments. In addition, multilingual governance systems can be facilitated using summarization systems which will allow downstream translation and transmission of summarized content.

The paper should therefore be considered as supplementing current research in the field of long document comprehension by showing that computationally efficient preprocessing models, based on cognitive reading strategies and statistical topic models, can do as well, and even better, than more complicated hierarchical neural networks Lin (2004), Raffel et al. (2020). The results support the idea that the hybrid systems that involve lightweight algorithmic condensation and transformer-based semantic evaluation are a scalable method of analysing legal and governmental documents. On a larger scale, it has implications in information retrieval, digital governance platforms, legal informatics, and optimized use of large language models in systems of knowledge management in the public sector Vaswani et al. (2017).

In the literature, there are three approaches that tackle the length limitation from the model-architecture side: Long-context models, like Longformer and LongT5; Encoder-decoder models, like BART; and Context-extension models. Such approaches may also require significant memory and inference resources, and government and legal documents impose another demand: the ability to maintain policy intent, statutory relationships, and structurally distributed evidence within limited computational power. The research gap addressed in this study is therefore not the invention of a new summarization primitive, but the systematic comparison of lightweight preprocessing strategies before transformer-based generation, using a common GovReport setting to examine the trade-off among contextual coverage, semantic preservation, and computational cost. The purpose of this application-oriented comparison is to explain where document reduction can still be useful in government and legal information systems. The study is majorly about the application-oriented comparative framework of long-document summarization in government and legal applications. In the present study, instead of introducing another stand-alone summarization architecture, Central Truncation, Document Skimming, and Keyword-Based Summarization are packaged into a single summarization pipeline (preprocessing and generation), and tested using the same GovReport setting and downstream transformer configuration. This will give a controlled ground to explore the contextual retention, semantic similarity, lexical overlap, and computation cost of different document reduction approaches. Thus, the contribution is a mixture of efficient long-document processing and of practical digital governance where large collections of documents need to be summarised without the use of unlimited document windows or computational resources.

In this context, the study makes use of statistical and semantic sampling such as LDA-based keyword identification and Sentence Transformer representations for picking informative content prior to abstractive generation. The first one, Central Truncation, focuses on the first and last parts of the document; Document Skimming samples key parts of the document; and Keyword-Based Summarization ranks the parts based on their semantic relation with document-level keywords. The simplicity vs semantic fidelity, coverage vs processing cost trade-offs is also captured by the same structure. It is practical to suggest that the reduction technique to be applied to a particular document type may be different depending on the kind of documents: If documents are compact and informative, they may be reduced by truncation; if documents are topic-focused, they may be reduced by keyword-based text selection; and if the evidence is distributed throughout the document, it may be reduced by skimming. It does not mean that the single preprocessing algorithms presented are new, but rather that it is the methodological approach and the practical application that is new. The paper points to the need to find a balance between the simplicity of summarization and computational efficiency and predictive accuracy. It has demonstrated that the carefully designed truncation and extraction methods are competitive with the complicated hierarchical models, but are cheap to compute, coherent, and fully open source, and hence are suitable for real-life government and legal document summarization systems.

This study offers a comparative framework for long-document summarization of government and legal documents in an application context with limited computational resources and context window. The study is a systematic evaluation of three widely used document-reduction methods, Central Truncation, Document Skimming, and Keyword-Based Summarization, in the same pre-processing and transformer-based generation pipeline, rather than proposing a new summarization algorithm. This controlled setting allows a basis to be considered for the effect of various principles of reduction on contextual coverage, semantic preservation, lexical similarity, coherence of the summaries, and computational efficiency in long legal and government documents. Another contribution of this study is the inclusion of statistical and semantic content selection in front of the abstractive generation. The framework includes document-level topic identification with LDA and semantic representations with Sentence-BERT to locate informative content along with positional alternative and distributed alternative, Central Truncation and Document Skimming. The comparison between these two makes it possible for the study to examine the trade-offs between keeping the most relevant text segments, keeping coverage over sections of a document, as well as choosing text based on document-level topics. The framework thus offers a practical evaluation framework for deciding on the more suitable reduction strategy for various documents and governments. The study also compares the three strategies under the same ROUGE & BERTScore measures with processing-time analysis in the experimental environment based on GovReport and T5. An evaluation platform common to both pre-processing strategies and summarization configuration allows for evaluation of pre-processing effects without the influence of pre-processing. The findings support not only for pre-processing different strategy to be used for different documents but also different performances for different similarity measures, lexical coverage, structural coverage, and computational costs. In practical terms, the framework can be used to develop scalable government and legal information systems using a light-weight document reduction method prior to abstractive summarization, especially in contexts with limited resources for processing and limited capacity of the context window.

2. RELATED WORKS

Long-document summarization research can be broadly categorized into four directions: long-context language models, extractive approaches and topic-based approaches, abstractive summarization, and hybrid document-reduction approaches. Other approaches, including Long-context architectures like Longformer or LongT5, which use sparse or structured attention mechanisms, and context-extension approaches that modify positional representations to handle longer sequences, have been explored to enhance the effective context size. The use of sparse or structured attention mechanisms, as well as the modification of positional representations to account for longer sequences, have also been studied to improve the effective context size. Extractive and topic-based approaches can decrease computational cost by extracting representative portions of the original text, while abstractive encoder-decoder models can produce fluent summaries based on the encoded representations of the input text. Hybrid methods integrate document reduction and neural generation, optimizing both summary excellence and computational efficiency. Nevertheless, there is a practical question to be addressed on the relative performance of lightweight reduction techniques for both position and contents information in the context of a standard downstream summarization scenario with a long government document. This is an unsolved balance between context coverage, semantic preservation, lexical relevance and computational cost which leads to the comparative framework this study uses.

Biomedical text summarization studies have evolved on the basis of Seq2Seq and transformer models enhancing contextual understanding and coherence (Qiu & Yang, 2021), (Sotudeh & Goharian, 2022). Hybrid abstractive–extractive methods also improve factual accuracy and fluency. Nonetheless, handling long documents, fact consistency, and keeping up with low-resource biomedical domains remain a challenge. Table 1 shows the Literature Survey.

Table 1. Literature Survey

S. No	Authors	Model Used	Accuracy	Methodology	Limitations
1	Beltagy et al. (2020)	Longformer	ROUGE-1: 44.5%	Introduced sparse attention for handlin long documents efficiently.	Limited to fixed window attention; still struggles beyond 4K tokens.
2	Bertsch et al. (2023)	Unlimiformer	ROUGE-L: 45.2%	Extended attention across unbounded context windows for LLMs.	Computationally expensive for real-time inference.
3	Blei et al. (2003)	LDA Topic Model	88.6% topic coherence	Extracted document-level topics and keywords for summarization.	Not context-aware; fails for semantic relationships.

continued on following page

Table 1. Continued

S. No	Authors	Model Used	Accuracy	Methodology	Limitations
4	Brown et al. (2020)	GPT-3	175B parameters; BLEU: 41.3%	Introduced few-shot learning for large-scale text generation.	High computational cost; limited transparency.
5	Chen et al. (2023)	Modified GPT	92.5% token retention	Used positional embedding interpolation to expand context length.	Reduced precision in longer positional encodings.
6	Chen et al. (2022)	BERT + CNN	91.4%	Combined BERT's contextual embeddings with CNN	Not efficient for texts longer than 512 tokens.
7	Devlin et al. (2019)	BERT	GLUE: 82.1%	Introduced bidirectional transformer pre-training for language understanding.	Inadequate for long document tasks due to token limits.
8	Guo et al. (2021)	LongT5	ROUGE-L: 42.3%	Used local and global attention mechanisms for summarization.	Still limited by model memory and inference speed.
9	Huang et al. (2021)	Sparse Attention Model	ROUGE-2: 21.3%	Proposed efficient attention modules for long text summarization.	Inconsistent performance on diverse datasets.
10	Fabbri et al. (2021)	Multiple Models	87.4%	Standardized evaluation benchmarks for summarization tasks.	Does not propose new summarization models.
11	Lewis et al. (2019)	BART	ROUGE-L: 41.9%	Combined bidirectional encoder and autoregressive decoder for summarization.	Limited to moderate-length documents (~1K tokens).
12	Raffel et al. (2020)	T5	GLUE: 89.7%	Unified NLP tasks as text-to-text transformations.	Suffers from high training cost and sequence length constraints.
13	Worsham & Kalita (2018) [25]	RNN	F1: 88.2%	Used head-tail truncation to classify long texts effectively.	Method not generalizable to summarization tasks.
14	Zhang et al. (2019) [26]	BERT-based Scorer	88.02%	Evaluated semantic similarity using contextual embeddings.	Computationally heavy; only for evaluation, not generation.
15	Golia & Kalita (2023) [11]	BERT + Heuristic Sampling	ROUGE-1: 47.2%	Extracted action-driven segments for summarization.	Task-specific; limited generalizability to other domains.

3. PROPOSED METHODOLOGY

The proposed Long Document Summarization (LDS) system can effectively process and summarize long government documents and legal content, which may exceed the context window of the Large Language Models (LLMs) commonly used today, and address a real-world challenge in a digital governance scenario where parliamentary reports, regulations, audits, draft policies, judicial rulings and administrative notices can reach hundreds of pages. In such long document architectures, documents are inserted directly into the system, which is costly in terms of computation, and subject to context windows, meaning that crucial information that could be in statute or procedure may be abridged; therefore, this system provides an additional stage of structured pre-processing and summarization that ensures computational and semantic integrity. The first step of the methodology is systematic data preparation which involves the removal of formatting noise, the identification of different structural elements like section headers, clauses and sub-clauses, and thus maintaining different levels of hierarchy that is crucial in a governance context where sections like Objectives, Definitions, Scope, Implementation and Enforcement have different legal weight. The head and tail of documents are generated dynamically from the documents in a new layer, called the algorithmic condensation layer, that captures the legal intent of the document and maintains the contextual continuity of the document, particularly relevant for executive summaries of legislative and regulatory bills (under the name of Central Truncation); the representative and semantically significant parts of the documents are sampled to generate informative condensed representations under the name of Keyword Extraction-based reduction, which are useful in the context of compliance monitoring, legal research and digital archiving after pre-processing. These measures, altogether, guarantee structural retention, representative sampling and concept-oriented extraction, and minimal loss of information while reducing the sequences' length. The material extracted is fed to the encoder, which, using self-attention and positional encoding, learns which semantics are semantically related and may help to preserve the order of clauses, crucial in legal interpretation, while the decoder generates an abstractive summary of the material using the encoder-decoder attention and a feed-forward network, a hybrid of extractive preprocessing with abstractive language generation to factually ground and linguistically fluently. The resulting summaries are rated based on the ROUGE on lexical overlap and BERTScore on semantic similarity, to make sure that there is no violation of the law and the intent of the policies. In terms of applications, the methodology enables the automatic generation of legislative briefs, a summary of judicial matters, newsletters for regulatory institutions and the creation of a user-friendly description of the policies that could improve the transparency. Better administrative efficiency is achieved with the processing of voluminous audit and departmental reports. It offers a scalable and practical deployment option for the system to be deployed to digital governance systems, legal informatics systems and national document repositories to manage and interpret long documents effectively while staying within the limits of LLM.

The purpose of this information is to provide a rationale and an objective for the method that you are considering using. The three strategies were chosen as complementary, as well as computationally different approaches of the reduction of long inputs: positional strategy (Central Truncation), distributed strategy (Document Skimming), and content-driven strategy (Keyword-Based Summarization). By using this design, the study can focus on an important practical problem which is how much of the document should be kept before the abstractive generation is applied, and based on what principle? The main goal is to reduce the length of the input and the complexity of the calculation while retaining a sufficient amount of semantic and structural information for a reliable summarization. The study does not assume that any single approach is always best, but rather investigates the compromise between computational efficiency, semantic preservation, lexical similarity, and document coverage. Figure 1 shows the workflow diagram for the proposed model.

Figure 1. Workflow Diagram

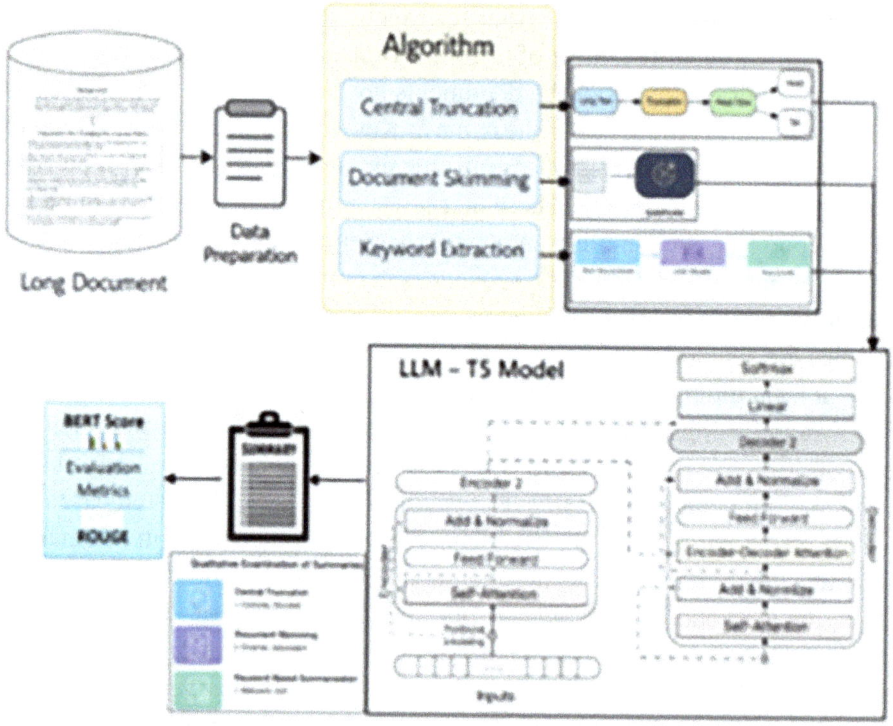

3.1 Dataset Description

The GovReport dataset is a large summative-sized long-document corpus that has been particularly suggested to assess the aptitude of models to process and evaluate large government reports. It is used as a test dataset to compare long document summarization systems, especially in a field where high factual reliability and high policy-level comprehension is needed. This dataset consists mostly of two major sources of official U.S. government documentation. First, it contains analytic reports created by the Congressional Research Service (CRS), which provides non-partisan research on policies, legislative advice, and law interpretations in order to assist the members of Congress to make informed decisions. These reports are usually thorough, they include background of the history, statutory sources, fiscal implications and comparisons of policies. Second, the data is adjusted with the audit reports and evaluation reports published by the U.S. Government Accountability Office (GAO), that are conducted to review the federal programs, determine their effectiveness, identify the challenges that appear during implementation, and recommend the ways to improve them. Such GAO reports are well organized, evidence-based and often contain detailed findings, data analysis as well as compliance review. The entries in the GovReport database are accompanied by an abstractive reference summary quality of each document, which summarises the necessary information of the report in a succinct narrative form. The information is saved in the form of JSON data, which has a hierarchical structure, which is similar to the structure of the government documents. The standard sample structure comprises of document id, title, summary, detailed report sections with section titles, paragraphs and subsections as shown below:

```
{
"id": "93-792",
"title": "Social Security Benefits Are Not Paid for the
Month of Death",
"summary": ["Social Security benefits are not paid ..."],
"reports": [
{
"section_title": "Background",
"paragraphs": ["Section 202 of the Social Security Act
..."],
"subsections": [...]
}
]
}
```

The dataset has a hierarchical structure of sections and subsections, making the data particularly suitable for assessing models that need to maintain a structural coherence and long range dependencies. The mean length of documents in GovReport is around 7,700 words with individual reports going to 70,000 words and this is a daunting benchmark to long document summarization systems due to context window limitations and memory constraints of transformer based models. In practical applications, GovReport data is similar to the actual government documentation processes. The trained and evaluated systems can be applied to generate executive briefs to policy makers, brief audit summaries to administrative officials, compliance briefs to the federal agencies, and user-friendly explanations to the complex federal policies. It is also applicable in digital governance, in research into legislation, for transparency and automated indexing of large volumes of policies. The consequence is that GovReport not only can be a technical benchmark for the long document summarization, but also a realistic kick-off point for the elaboration of scalable summarization applications for the areas of public administration and legal informatics. 2 shows dataset word count.

Figure 2. Dataset Word Count

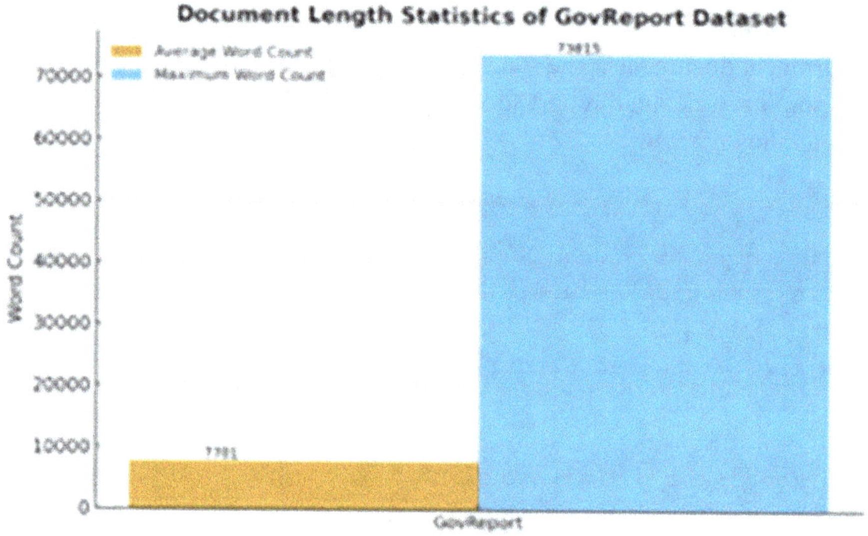

To train the model and test it, the dataset is split into two sub-collections - CRS and GAO, with separate splits of training, validation, and testing. This systematic division will guarantee equal consideration in both areas. Split distribution can be visualized as shown in figure 3.1.4. In terms of CRS Splits we have firstly crs_train.ids – Contains 6,514 training samples used for model learning,then crs_validation.ids – Contains 361 validation samples for hyperparameter tuning and overfitting prevention and finally crs_test.ids – Contains 363 unseen test samples used for performance evaluation. For GAO Splits, we have firstly gao_train.ids – Contains 11,005 training samples, secondly gao_validation.ids – Contains 613 validation samples and finally gao_test.ids – Contains 614 test samples. Figure 3 shows the dataset split distribution.

Figure 3. Dataset Split Distribution

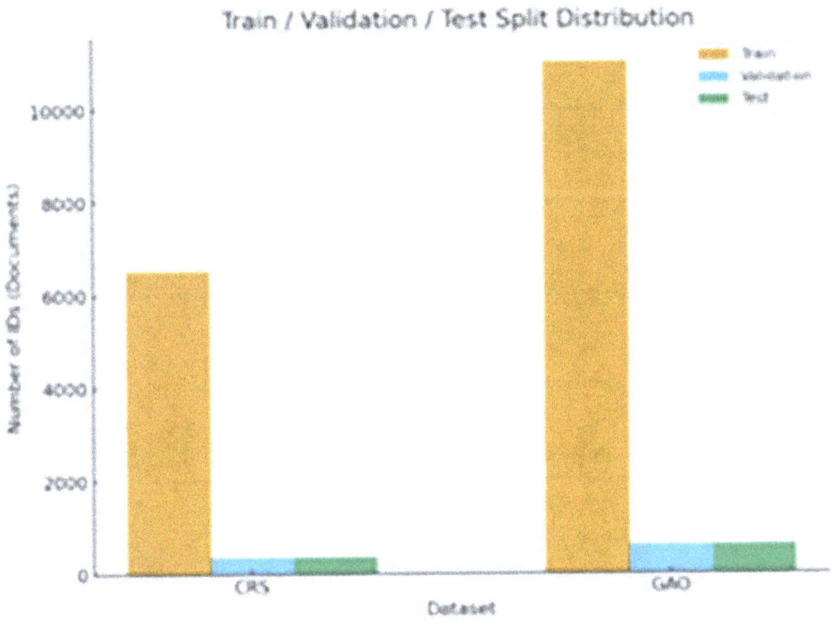

These divisions are combined together to create the final training, validation and testing dataset of the proposed long-document summarization model. The aggre-gate data will allow running a strong model assessment on a variety of issues including government audits and budgetary reports, as well as social policies and welfare initiatives.

3.2 Proposed Techniques

The summarization pipeline consists of 3 major components, Central Truncation Algorithm, Document Skimming and Keyword-Based Summarization. Central Truncation is an effective method to handle long documents that have long context windows of large language models (LLMs). It only saves the first (starting) and the last (ending) parts of a document but not the remaining parts that sometimes carry redundant or less informative information. L is the total number of tokens in the document, C is the size of the context of the model and $\alpha \in [0,1]$ is a hyperparameter that can be used to specify the fraction of retained head tokens. The chosen token sequence S is presented by: Equation 1 shows the calculation of S.

$$S = \left[H_{0:\alpha L}\right] + \left[T_{(1-\alpha)L:L}\right]$$

where $\left[H_{0:\alpha L}\right]$ and $\left[T_{(1-\alpha)L:L}\right]$ represent the head and tail tokens, respectively. In a=1, only head is retained. In a=0, only tail is retained and in a= 0.5, half head and half tail is retained. Figure 4 shows the central truncation workflow.

Figure 4. Central Truncation Workflow

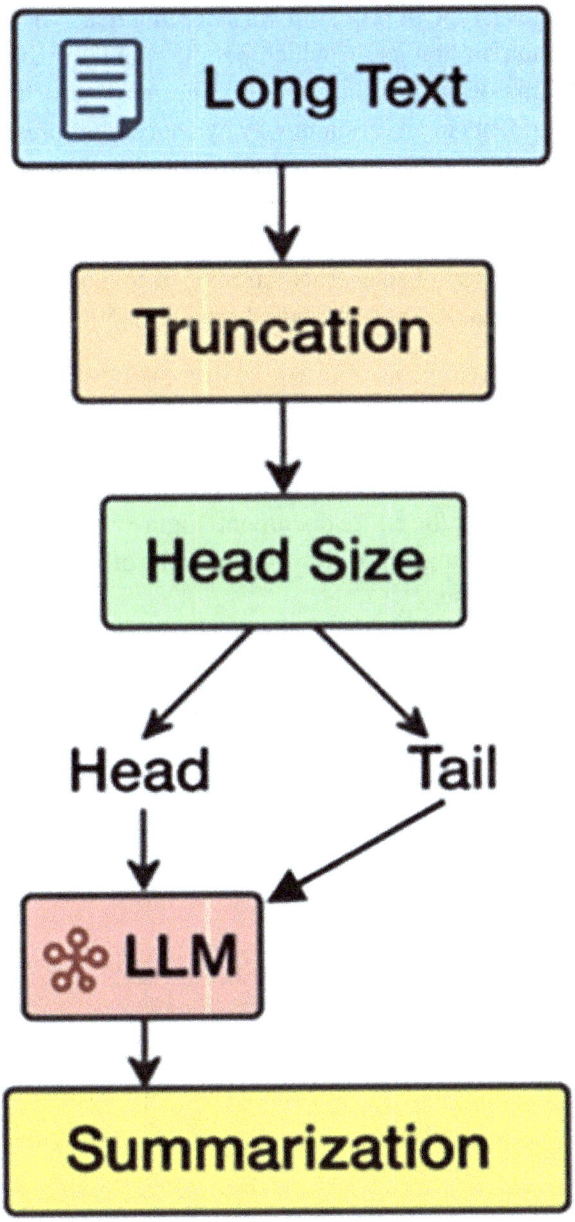

This one is computationally easy and serves a good purpose in maintaining the con-text and conclusion which are paramount in summarization. It can however lose information on the middle parts of the document. Nevertheless, it is fast and simple and thereby forms a robust foundation of summarization of long documents. Document Skimming is a type of probabilistic sampling that is based on the speed-reading concept by human beings, in which people rapidly read a document and pay attention to the important parts of it only. The purpose of this method is to summarize long documents in an efficient way by choosing representative sections rather than processing the text. Consider a document with n parts, the length of the part i is length l_i (in tokens). The Bernoulli random variable $X_i \sim Bernoulli(p)$ is used to define whether or not segment i is included in the skimmed version with p the probability of being selected. The average number of tokens that are supposed to be retained E[X]. Equation 2 shows the calculation of E[X].

$$E[X] = p\sum_{i=1}^{n} l_i$$

The overall process of document skimming consists of four key stages. Firstly, Document Segmentation which refers to a sentence or paragraph tokenizer breaks the input document into smaller and manageable parts. The segments have a continuous flow of the text to cover the entire document. Figure 5 represents the Segments picked by Document Skimming Algorithm. Y-axis value of the ith segment on x-axis is 1 if its picked, 0 other-wise.

Figure 5. Segments picked by Document Skimming Algorithm

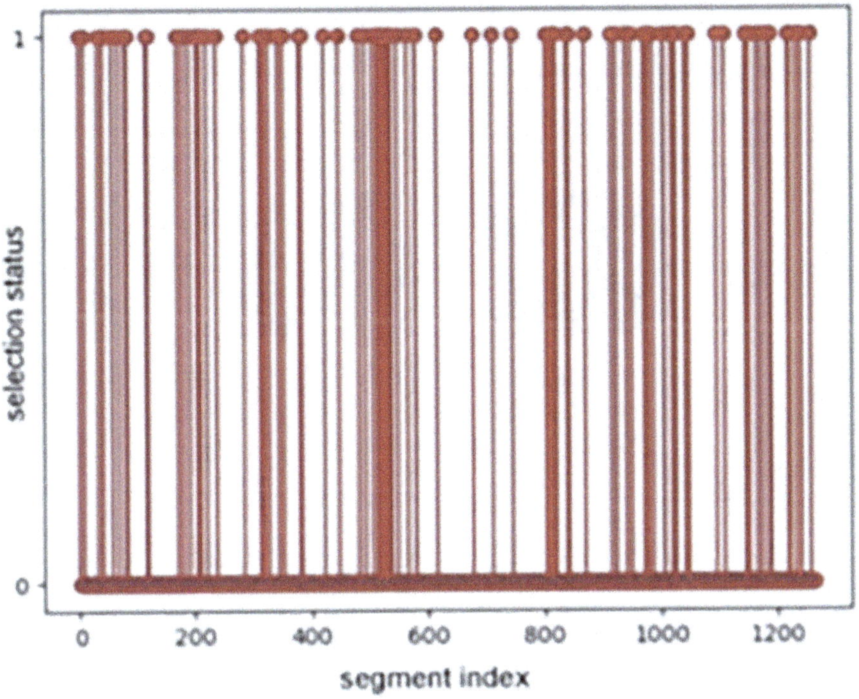

Secondly, Sampling is a uniform random sampling strategy is used in place of processing all segments, with probability p of segment selection. The sampling probability is set in a way that the total number of tokens fits into the context window C of the model. To make sure that the sum of the number of tokens is equal to the context window C of the model, p is defined as: Equation 3 shows the calculation of p.

$$p = \frac{C}{\sum_{i=1}^{n} l_i}$$

where l_i is the number of tokens in segment i, n- total number of segments. This ensures that coverage is even all through the document at a low cost of computation. Thirdly, Large Language Model (LLM) is a pretrained large language model (e.g., LongT5, BART or Pegasus) is then fed with the sampled text to abstractively summarize it. The LLM process the input and extracts important contextual connections in the reduced text. Finally, in Summary Generation, the model results in the creation of a consistent and concise synopsis that covers the key content of the original lengthy document. This is the most efficient workflow to reduce redundancy, processing time, and to preserve essential information of the various sections of the document and is therefore a computationally efficient, but semantically rich method of summarizing documents.

Figure 6. Document Skimming Workflow

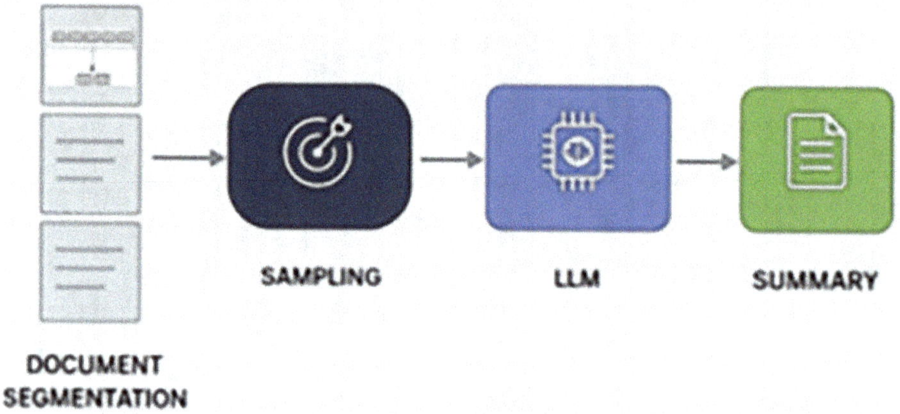

Skimming documents aids the model in gathering information in different parts of document as well as minimizing redundancy. The nature of its sampling, as it is random but uniform, permits a balanced sampling of the early and late parts of the document, which is efficient and diverse in terms of summarization. Keyword-Based Summarization is aimed at making the summaries more informative and coherent with concentration on the semantically significant parts of the text. In contrast to uniform sampling or truncation-based sampling, this technique selectively extracts segments concerning particular topics, which are identified as important and thus critical information is preserved whereas redundancy is minimized.

Figure 7. Workflow of Keyword Based Summarization

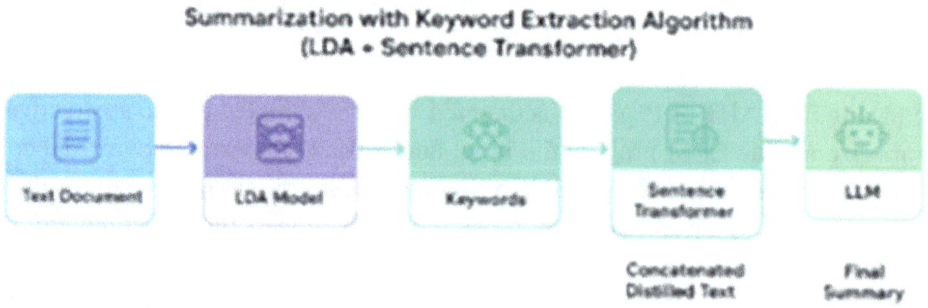

The input text document starts the process, which is subjected to topic modelling using the Latent Dirichlet Allocation (LDA). The LDA model can be used to model the latent theme structure of the document as a probabilistic distribution of topics and the most representative keywords can be extracted. These terms make up the semantic nucleus of the document and they are followed in the choice of subsequent segments. Figure 8 is a representation of Segments selected by the Summarization with Keyword Extraction algorithm. Y-axis of the ith segment of x-axis is 1 when picked and 0 when not.

Figure 8. Segments picked by Keyword Extraction Algorithm

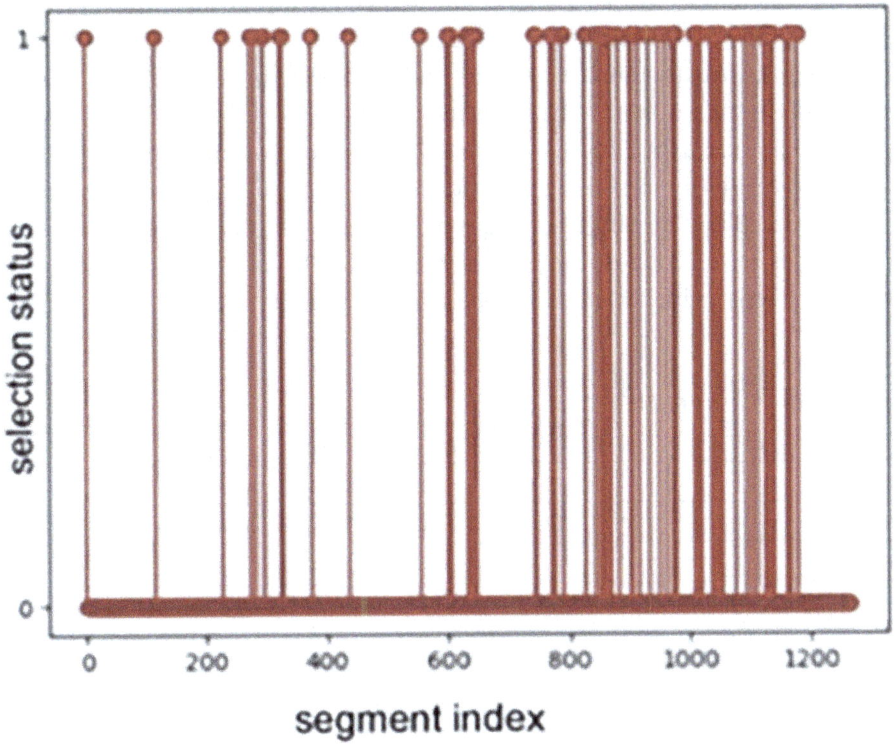

The document sections and the extracted set of keywords are then packed into a high-dimensional semantic space with the help of a Sentence Transformer. Both segment embeddings and contextual semantics are present as well as the keyword embedding reflects the theme of the whole document. Cosine similarity between the keyword embedding and every segment embedding is calculated to establish the level of relevance: Equation 4 shows the calculation of $Similarity(S_i, K)$.

$$Similarity(S_i, K) = \frac{E(S_i) \, . \, E(K)}{\|E(S_i)\| \, \|E(K)\|}$$

where $E(S_i)$ and E(K) denote the embeddings of the ith segment and the concatenated keyword vector, respectively. The algorithm then ranks all the segments according to their similarity scores and then picks the best segments in accordance with their suitability to the key topics in the document. The context window C of the model limits the number of selected segments available, and makes it compatible with the downstream summarization model: Equation 5 shows the comparison of S_i and C.

$$\sum_{i=1}^{n} len(S_i) \leq C$$

These segments are chosen and are concatenated to create a distilled document, which is input into a Large Language Model (LLM) e.g. T5 models. The LLM produces the final abstractive summary based on the distilled input to gain the coherent and contextually rich output. This is a successful use of this technique which is a summary technique using key-word driven summarization over topic modelling and semantic similarity in ranking the informative pieces of the content to enhance content relevance and quality of the summary. It proves to be more cost effective when it comes to the long-document summarization tasks because it reduces the computational cost with a high degree of semantic fidelity.

Table 2. Model Components

Component	Description
Encoder	T5 Encoder with local-global attention
Decoder	Transformer Decoder generating summaries
Embedding	Sentence-BERT for redundancy filtering
Optimizer	AdamW (learning rate 1e-4)
Loss	Cross-Entropy
Epochs	200
Context Length	4096 tokens
Metrics	ROUGE-1, ROUGE-2, ROUGE-L, BERTScore P, BERTScore F1

3.3 T5 Model Overview

Text-to-Text Transfer Transformer (T5) is created based on the sequence to sequence (seq2seq) Transformer architecture which comprises of an encoder and a decoder. Given an input document = $(x_1, x_2, \ldots, x_n)$, the encoder converts the document into a contextual representation $H = (h_1, h_2, \ldots, h_n)$ with self-attention and feed-forward layers. Decoder then produces the summary $Y = (y_1, y_2, \ldots, y_m)$ autoregressively, token by token. Figure 9 represents T5 Model Architecture.

Figure 9. Segments picked by Keyword Extraction Algorithm

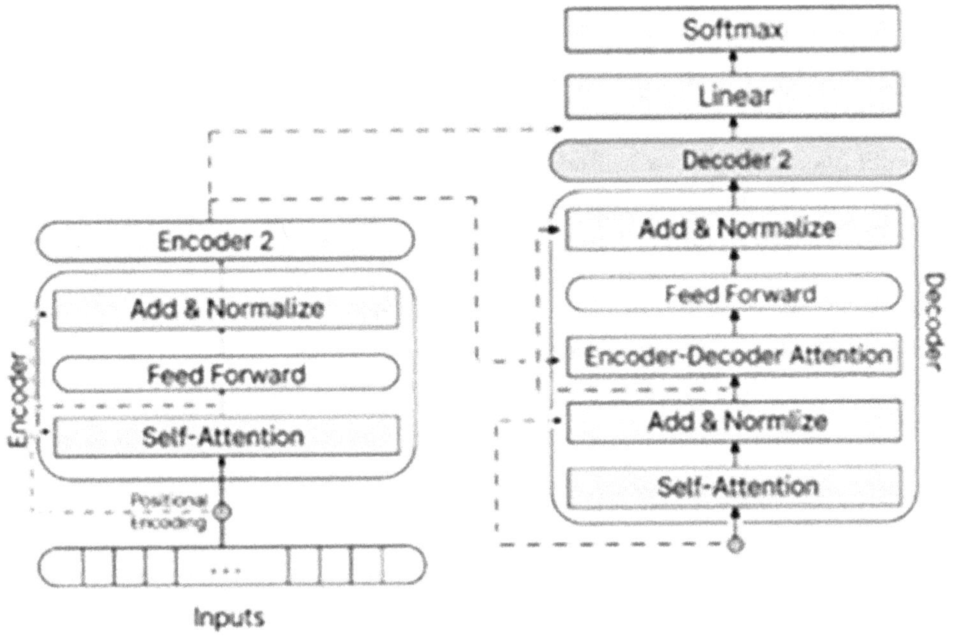

Encoder Representation means the token in the input sequence is encoded and processed by the series of Transformer layers and every encoder layer is applied with multi-head self-attention (MHSA) and feed-forward (FFN) transformations. Decoder Representation means the decoder produces the output sequence on a token-by-token basis and each decoder layer is made up of Masked Self-Attention of the tokens that have been generated earlier, Cross-Attention between the decoder state and encoder output, Feed-Forward Network to transform the tokens on a token-by-token basis. In terms of objective function, during training, T5 minimizes the negative log-likelihood loss will be Equation 6 shows the log likelihood loss.

$$L(\theta) = -\sum_{t=1}^{T} log \log P_\theta(y_t | y_{<t}, X)$$

Where X is the input document, $Y = (y_1, y_2, \ldots, y_T)$ is the reference summary and θ refers to the model parameters. This provides an incentive to the model to make guesses of the subsequent word in the summary based on the input text and the already generated tokens. Regarding task formulation, all the activities of T5 are formulated in text-text. The single formulation of the text allows the extension of T5 to do tasks such as translation, classification, and summarization using a single architecture.

3.4 Experimental Configuration and Evaluation Protocol

All three preprocessing methods are assessed in the same overall training and testing protocol as used for GovReport to facilitate reproduction. This reported model configuration features a T5 encoder-decoder architecture, a 4096-token context length, Semantic Redundancy Filtering via Sentence-BERT embeddings, the AdamW optimizer with a learning rate of 1e-4, cross-entropy loss, and 200 training epochs. All the methods use the same metrics: ROUGE-1, ROUGE-2, ROUGE-L, BERTScore Precision, and BERTScore F1. The training, validation, and test partitions used by the CRS and GAO are maintained across methods, as described in Section 3.1, to ensure that any differences in reported performance are primarily due to the differences in the preprocessing strategies rather than the different data splits. The experimental workflow thus compares the three strategies under the same evaluation protocol.

4. RESULT AND DISCUSSION

The experimental findings of the assessment of the three suggested algorithms of summarizing: Central Truncation, Document Skimming and Keyword-Based Summarization on the GovReport data. The comparison was conducted with the help of standard measures, including ROUGE-1, ROUGE-2, ROUGE-L, and BERTScore (Precision and F1) to determine the quality and semantic correctness of the obtained summaries.

4.1 Dataset Description

The GovReport dataset comprises 7,238 long-form reports by government, which is the best to test the long-document summarization systems. This follows an average of 7,700 words per document and in some cases up to 73,815 words that give the documents a rich contextual content and complexity which can be tested on to model efficiency and understanding

Table 3. Dataset Wordcount

Dataset	Average Word Count	Maximum Word Count	Number of Documents
GovReport	7,700.71	73,815	7,238

The Figure 10 shows the word counts of documents in GovReport dataset and Figure 11 shows the word cloud of crs and gao documents. It shows that most of them were in the range 7,000 to 10,000 words (the words that make up the bulk of their documents), with only a handful exceeding 50,000 words. This right-skewed distribution suggests that while there are indeed a small number of very long reports in the dataset, most of the reports are of a moderate length and that is why the skewed distribution is appropriate to consider both short and long-context summarization models.

Figure 10. Document Word Count

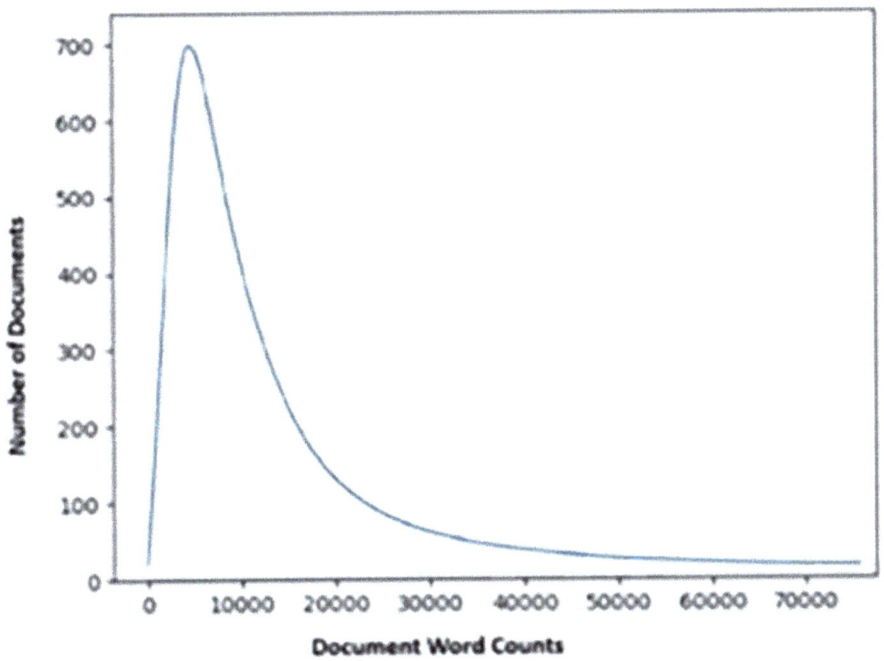

Figure 11. Word cloud – crs and gao documents

4.2 Data Preparation

The GovReport data set has government reports that are stored in json format with each file having three main sections which are the title, the summary and the report body. The very body of the report is arranged hierarchically, with sections, subsections, and sub-paragraphs, which is a good source of the long-form textual information.

Prior to the training of the model, large amounts of pre-processing of the data were carried out in order to make sure that the input documents were clean, consistent, and fit the long-document summarization tasks. Figure 12 shows the data preparation pipeline.

Figure 12. Data Preparation Workflow

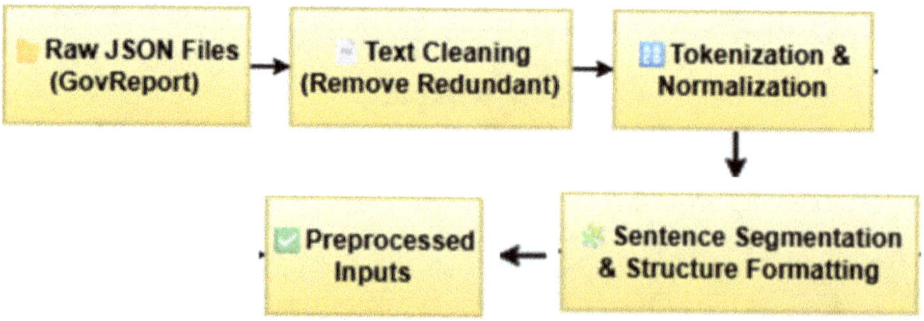

To aid in the creation of a strategy to summarize long documents in accordance to legal documents and government reports, the data preparation pipeline was developed with great care. Because they are usually long, extremely structured, and have several formal sections, preprocessing is a vital process to ensure that it feeds clean, meaningful and coherent input to the model. This was done by the first step that included parsing and loading of JSON files with the raw reports. All the documents were kept in a systematic format and were usually divided into subsections and subsections like executive summaries, background information, legal arguments, policy discussions and appendices. An extraction process of text was also used to extract the important textual elements such as the title, the main body of the report and the reference summary where applicable. Most of the files were written hierarchically, and thus the nested subsections were flattened and joined together in logical order to create one continuous document. This was necessary to summarize long documents that the model should be able to take the entire context of the report as opposed to fragmented reports made out of bits. Documentation that did not have the necessary textual contents, or did not have full summaries, was not included in the dataset to ensure that the data had quality, consistency and reliability due to the sensitivity of the information in legal and governmental circles where inaccuracy is crucial. The second step was the tokenization and text cleaning. The T5 model was trained and used to tokenize all documents using a subword tokenizer. The subword tokenization guarantees the uniform treatment of more complicated legal terms, unusual words, figures, and even symbols that often reoccur in government reports and other legal documents. This method decreases vocabulary size as well as maintains semantic meaning. When cleaning up the text, it was cleared of redundant spaces, redundant line breaks, HTML tags, formatting artifacts of extracting PDFs, and non-alphanumeric characters. Because repeated phrases provide in a government and legal document can occur in different parts of the document (like a procedural language or a disclaimer), repetitive or duplicated sentences were recognized and eliminated to remove redundancy. This move has made sure that the model emphasizes on content that is significant as opposed to boilerplate text that is being repeated. Elimination of redundant and irrelevant sections was also another essential move. Government and legal documents commonly incorporate appendices, tabulation, figures, citations, footnotes, reference, metadata and procedural attachment. Though all these factors are relevant to official recording, they normally have no direct role to play in the process of abstractive summarization. It was decided to use a rule-based filtering structure that would automatically recognize such section headers like "Appendix," "References," "Table of Contents" or "Bibliography" and delete such parts. This enabled the summarization model to focus on the substantive legal arguments, policy considerations, results and conclusions and not the structure or supplementary material. Normalization of the sentences and structural formatting was then done to make the texts consistent. Every text was written in lowercase, and the general rules of setting the punctuation marks in place so that the boundaries of the sentences could be identified. Abbreviations, citations, special notations (e.g., section numbers, referencing of articles, legal citations, etc.) are common in legal documents, and thus, the process of normalizing abbreviations was done to allow standard representation. Also, the token length limitations were taken to correspond with the maximum length of the sequences served by the T5 model. Because most files were created by PDF conversions, sentences that were fragmented by newline characters were mended together to re-establish sentence continuity. This was particularly significant in maintaining logical continuity in the legal ration and explanations of policies. After the normalization, subsection merging and cohesive document formation was carried out. Edited and refined subsections were sequentially linked together creating complete long-form documents. This movement was necessary to make sure that the context is fed into the model continuously instead of in bits. In the context of long-document summarization, narrative and argumentative flow is important to preserve because legal and government texts can be highly dependent over long distance, and can be cross-referential and dependent upon past-formulated reasoning. The model can comprehend the relationship between various parts with the help of structural coherence to produce more precise and context-driven summaries. Lastly, data were balanced and divided to provide strong models training and testing. The cleaned data was split into training, validation, and testing data according to the official GovReport split files (crstrain.ids, crsvalidation.ids and crstest.ids, gaotrain.ids, gaovalidation.ids and gaotest.ids). Diversity was observed to ensure that there was a split-in report length, subject matter, and institutional source. The model parameters were optimized with the training set, hyperparameter tuning and performance monitoring were done with the validation set, and the test set was used in the final assessment. This systematic division made sure that there is an adequate generalization of the model on unknown government and legal documents. All in all, this end to end data preparation pipeline makes sure that the summarization system will be able to handle long and complex legal and governmental texts. With a focus on cleaning, normalization, structural coherence, and balanced dataset construction, the pipeline allows developing a sound long-document summarization application that will help users to gain a general overview of long government documents, legal reports, and policy documents without missing important contextual data.

4.3 Algorithms Quantitative Analysis

The qualitative characteristics of the summaries generated are investigated as below. Central Truncation produces simple and narrow summaries, and may miss the overall context if information is not in the window that is being truncated. Document Skimming involves capturing various sections of the document to give it a better coverage of the context but may be redundant. The sample of the distilled text created by the algorithm and the summary created is provided under Figure 13 Keyword-Based Summarization is useful in ranking information that is related to the key topics and produces semantically enriched summarization; nevertheless, the quality of the summarization is determined by the accuracy of key word extraction and the topic modelling. The resulting abstractive summary is generated by the LLM and is coherent and contextually rich because the distilled input is coherent and contextually rich. Below in Figure 14, an example of the text produced by the algorithm after the distillation and an example of the summary produced is given.

The various performance patterns can be understood in terms of which information is preserved by each type of preprocessing. Central Truncation intentionally focuses on the document level, thus achieving BERTScore higher F1 value with lower amount of tokens used in the middle part of the document, which is represented by a white background. The ROUGE-1 and ROUGE-2 evaluation results indicate that Keyword-Based Summarization prefers to keep sentences with terms and concepts in common with the reference summary, as desired by the document-level topics and semantic similarity. Document Skimming samples content from different parts of the document, making it more representative, so it is a bit more likely to show up in the BERTScore lower case, but random or uniform sampling can also include less relevant content, which may also help explain the lower BERTScore values. The results in this work show that there are actually three aspects of summary quality being considered: lexical overlap, semantic similarity, and structural coverage – none of which can be considered as interchangeable goals.

Figure 13. Example – Skimming Algorithm

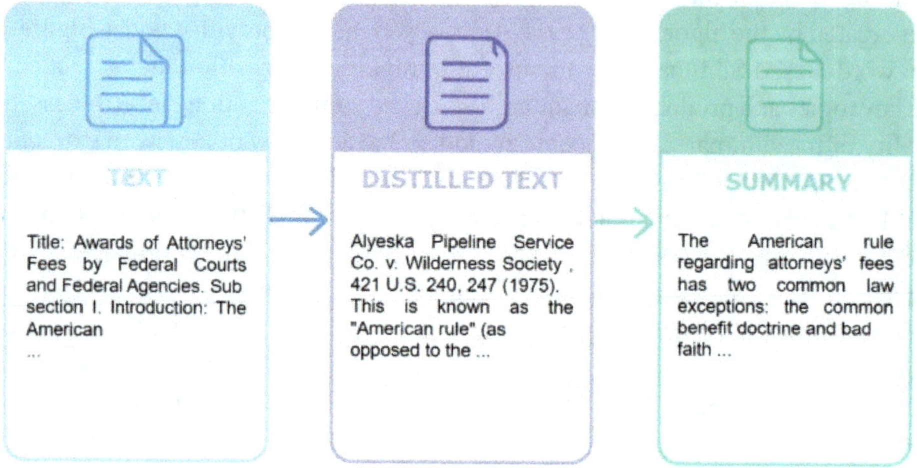

Figure 14. Example – Keyword Extraction Algorithm

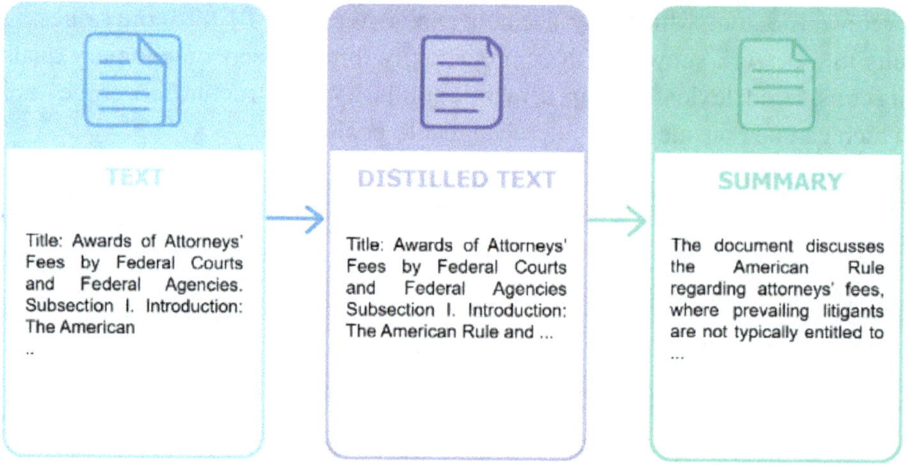

Figure 15. Accuracy vs Loss

Figure 15 demonstrates the curves of training accuracy and loss of the pro-posed models. As indicated, both metrics do stabilize after few epochs, which implies that it converges effectively without overfitting. The constant and gradual increase in accuracy is an indication that the models learnt optimally prior to assessment.

4.4 Time Complexity Analysis

The time complexity analysis looks at the average processing time of each summarization algorithm per document, excluding the model's time to generate the summary. The fastest of these is Central Truncation; that has the simplest Token selection algorithm, which is just to truncate documents without doing anything else.

Figure 16. Accuracy vs Loss

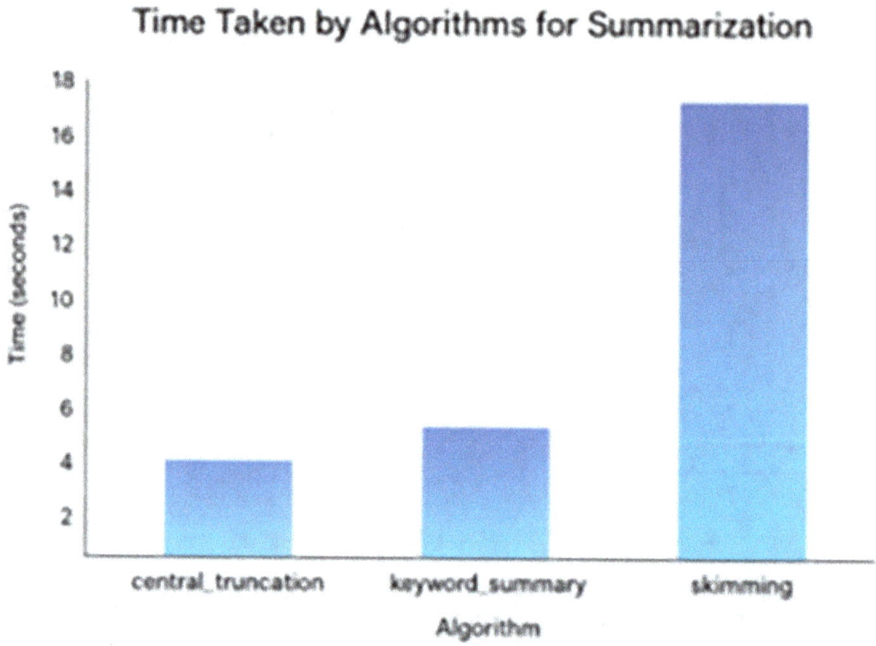

In Figure 16, the mean time of each of the methods is depicted with Central Truncation and Keyword Extraction being less and with Skimming being more computationally burdensome. The Keyword-Based Summarization takes a little bit longer, since topics extraction and sentence embedding generation are introduced that puts a moderate burden on computations. Document Skimming on the other hand displays the longest time consumption because it is an iterative pro-cess that uses repeated sampling and relevancy ranking of multiple document segments. This extra calculation helps to increase its processing time.

4.5 Quantitative Analysis

The comparative performance of the algorithms is shown in Table 3. Each model was trained, validated, and tested using the same data split to ensure fair-ness in evaluation and the visualization across the metrics was shown in the Figure 17 and Figure 18.

Table 4. Comparison of model performance using ROUGE and BERT Score metrics.

Model	ROUGE-1	ROUGE-2	ROUGE-L	BERT Score P	BERT Score F1
Central Truncation	99.84	96.56	68.66	66.44	67.82
Keyword Extraction	99.12	98.23	67.42	63.38	65.09
Skimming	96.76	89.43	71.89	40.17	41.18

Figure 17. Comparison of Algorithms across metrics

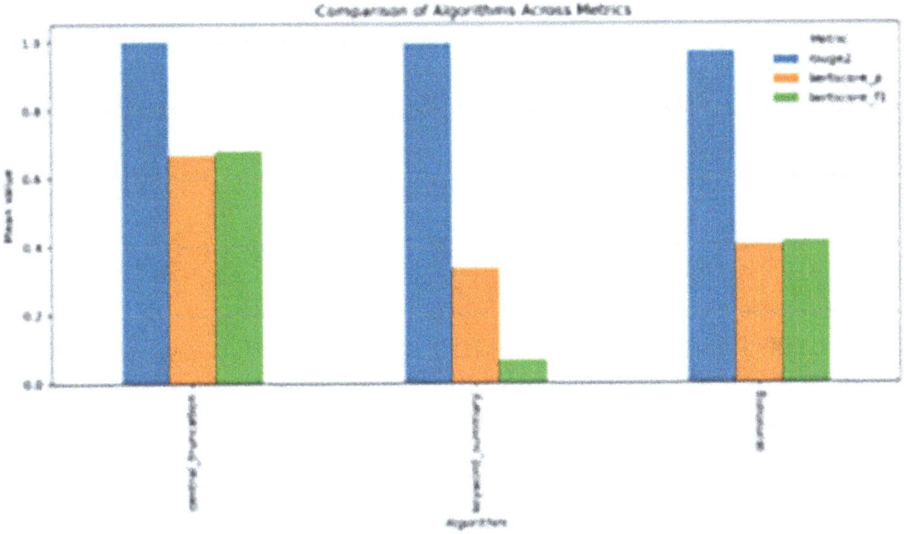

Figure 18. Performance Comparison of Summarization Models

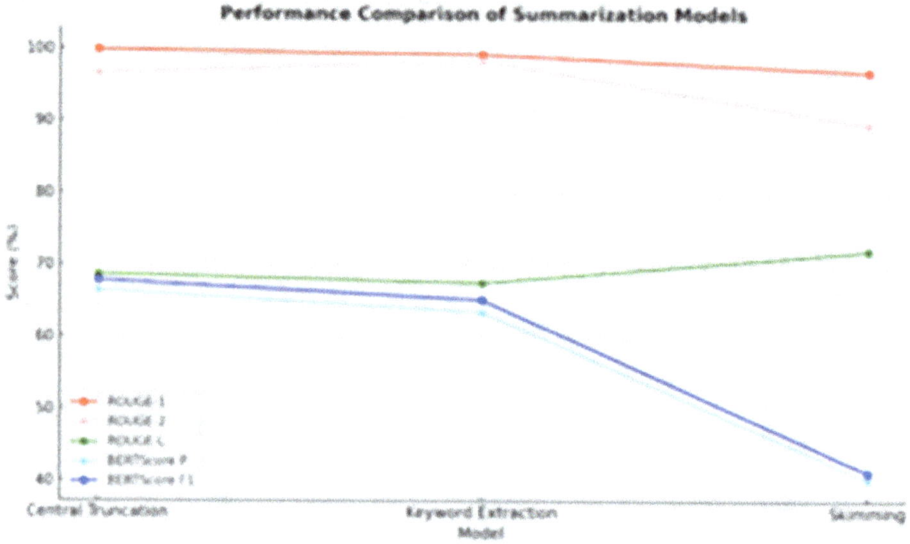

Based on the findings, it can be noted that the Central Truncation method has the best BERTScore F1 67.82 or high semantic correspondence between the generated and the reference summaries. This is because of its simplicity and efficiency, which enables it to hold on to the most contextually relevant information within the context window of the model. This Keyword Extraction method does well in ROUGE -1 99.12 percent and ROUGE -2 98.23 percent showing its efficiency in maintaining important information and lexical overlap by topic-oriented selection under LDA and sentence embeddings. In the meantime, Document Skimming algorithm has the highest ROUGE-L score 71.89%, which implies that it generates more fluent and structurally coherent summaries, but with less semantically aligned summaries by BERTScore.

4.6 Results Verification and Interpretation

The ROUGE-1 result for Central Truncation and Keyword Extraction are extremely high compared to other long-document abstractive summarization tasks, and should be interpreted with caution. Strong retention of reference-relevant wording can lead to high overlap as well, but also pre-processing or evaluation design can have an effect on overlap. Therefore, it is advisable to provide checks on training-test overlap, duplicate documents, use of reference summaries in the input to the models and consistency of the tokenization and the metric calculation among the three methods whenever the reported scores are provided. The official GovReport split files for training, validation, and testing are used in the present study; however, because of the unusually high scores, explicit leakage auditing and independent reproduction of the metric calculation is also important before treating the numerical results as definitive evidence of general superiority. This verification step is especially crucial in the case of the government and legal summarization, where seemingly high automatic scores need to be matched by faithful summarization.

5. CONCLUSION

In the current study, we explored three simple computational methods for reducing long documents of the government and law: Central Truncation, Document Skimming, and Keyword-Based Summarization. The primary research question was whether it is possible to reduce useful semantic and structural information without affecting context-length and computational limitations by applying lightweight preprocessing. The study compared the methods based on ROUGE and BERTScore scores and processing time analysis on the dataset GovReport and the same evaluation setting based on T5. The findings suggest that the three strategies do not all fall at the same point in the trade-off space but rather at different points. Under the tested setting, Central Truncation has the best BERTScore F1 score (67.82), showing better semantic similarity to the reference summaries. When document-level topics and semantically related segments are selected, the ROUGE-1 and ROUGE-2 scores are highest for Keyword-Based Summarization. Document Skimming had the highest ROUGE-L value, which means that it had more sequence-level overlap and covered more of the structure, while its BERTScore values were lower, meaning that it could sample less semantically relevant information to the reference summary. These results confirm that the quality of a summary is determined by the objective that is being given priority: semantic retention, lexical similarity or structural coverage. The academic value of the study is therefore not the novelty of the individual algorithms under evaluation but the comparative and application-oriented evaluation of these preprocessing principles in a single long-document summarization pipeline. It also links this comparison to digital governance by demonstrating how to utilize document reduction to enable scalable government report access, policy documents, regulatory information, and legal information in full-context when the cost of processing that information is high. In practice, the benefits of Central Truncation are evident for documents that focus on retaining the main ideas, Keyword-Based Summarization is appropriate for documents that have a centralized topic, and Document Skimming is appropriate for documents with information spread across multiple sections. There are some restrictions that might be noted. Firstly, the evaluation focuses on GovReport and may not be a complete reflection of legal rulings, Parliament proceedings, regulatory submissions, or administrative circulars. In addition, each of the three preprocessing strategies is based on different presumptions of where significant evidence is located, as well as no guarantee of the preservation of legally relevant evidence. Third, the values of ROUGE-1 reported in the results are exceptionally high, and a claim of superiority in the results should be made with caution based on the values after they are examined independently for possible overlap or evaluation effects. Lastly, many environmental aspects not yet described in the current experiments have not been reported for exact replications like the hardware environment. For future work, more data is needed, more detailed reporting of the reproducibility, formal leakage checks, human comparisons, and direct comparisons with extended-context models at matched computational budgets are suggested. A paradigm shift that is promising in the future is an adaptive hybrid approach that adapts and/or combines preprocessing strategies based on document length, topic density, structural complexity, and distribution of relevant information. In such a system, the efficiency of light weight reduction can be maintained, and coverage of documents with dispersed critical evidence can be enhanced. The results suggest that, as long as appropriate automatic metrics are coupled with strict verification and human-centred evaluation, careful pre-processing can be a useful addition to a long-range context model for scalable summarization of government and legal documents.

REFERENCES

Beltagy, I., Peters, M. E., & Cohan, A. (2020). Longformer: The long-document transformer. arXiv preprint arXiv:2004.05150.

Bertsch, A., Alon, U., Neubig, G., & Gormley, M. (2023). Unlimiformer: Long-range transformers with unlimited length input. *Advances in Neural Information Processing Systems*, *36*, 35522–35543. DOI: 10.52202/075280-1543

Blei, D. M., Ng, A. Y., & Jordan, M. I. (2003). Latent Dirichlet allocation. *Journal of Machine Learning Research*, *3*, 993–1022.

Brown, T., Mann, B., Ryder, N., Subbiah, M., Kaplan, J. D., Dhariwal, P., & Amodei, D. (2020). Language models are few-shot learners. *Advances in Neural Information Processing Systems*, *33*, 1877–1901.

Chen, S., Wong, S., Chen, L., & Tian, Y. (2023). Extending context window of large language models via positional interpolation. arXiv preprint arXiv:2306.15595.

Chen, X., Cong, P., & Lv, S. (2022). A long-text classification method of Chinese news based on BERT and CNN. *IEEE Access : Practical Innovations, Open Solutions*, *10*, 34046–34057. DOI: 10.1109/ACCESS.2022.3162614

Devlin, J., Chang, M. W., Lee, K., & Toutanova, K. (2019). BERT: Pre-training of deep bidirectional transformers for language understanding. In *Proceedings of the 2019 Conference of the North American Chapter of the Association for Computational Linguistics: Human Language Technologies* (pp. 4171–4186). DOI: 10.18653/v1/N19-1423

Dhillon, B. P. S., Herman, H., & Syafryadin, S. (2020). The effect of skimming method to improve students' ability in reading comprehension on narrative text. Linguists. *Journal of Linguistics and Language Teaching*, *6*(1), 77–88. DOI: 10.29300/ling.v6i1.2991

Du, J., Jiang, J., Zheng, J., Zhang, H., Huang, D., & Lu, Y. (2023). Improving computation and memory efficiency for real-world transformer inference on GPUs. *ACM Transactions on Architecture and Code Optimization*, *20*(4), 1–22. DOI: 10.1145/3617689

Fabbri, A. R., Kryściński, W., McCann, B., Xiong, C., Socher, R., & Radev, D. (2021). Summeval: Re-evaluating summarization evaluation. *Transactions of the Association for Computational Linguistics*, *9*, 391–409. DOI: 10.1162/tacl_a_00373

Golia, L., & Kalita, J. (2023). Action-item-driven summarization of long meeting transcripts. In *Proceedings of the 7th International Conference on Natural Language Processing and Information Retrieval* (pp. 91–98).

Guo, M., Ainslie, J., Uthus, D., Ontanon, S., Ni, J., Sung, Y. H., & Yang, Y. (2021). LongT5: Efficient text-to-text transformer for long sequences. arXiv preprint arXiv:2112.07916.

Huang, L., Cao, S., Parulian, N., Ji, H., & Wang, L. (2021). Efficient attentions for long document summarization. arXiv preprint arXiv:2104.02112. DOI: 10.18653/v1/2021.naacl-main.112

Koh, H. Y., Ju, J., Liu, M., & Pan, S. (2022). An empirical survey on long document summarization: Datasets, models, and metrics. *ACM Computing Surveys*, *55*(8), 1–35. DOI: 10.1145/3545176

Lewis, M., Liu, Y., Goyal, N., Ghazvininejad, M., Mohamed, A., Levy, O., . . . Zettlemoyer, L. (2019). BART: Denoising sequence-to-sequence pre-training for natural language generation, translation, and comprehension. arXiv preprint arXiv:1910.13461.

Lin, C. Y. (2004). ROUGE: A package for automatic evaluation of summaries. In Text summarization branches out (pp. 74–81).

Nallapati, R., Zhou, B., Gulcehre, C., & Xiang, B. (2016). Abstractive text summarization using sequence-to-sequence RNNs and beyond. arXiv preprint arXiv:1602.06023. DOI: 10.18653/v1/K16-1028

Phang, J., Zhao, Y., & Liu, P. J. (2022). Investigating efficiently extending transformers for long input summarization. arXiv preprint arXiv:2208.04347.

Raffel, C., Shazeer, N., Roberts, A., Lee, K., Narang, S., Matena, M., & Liu, P. J. (2020). Exploring the limits of transfer learning with a unified text-to-text transformer. *Journal of Machine Learning Research*, *21*(140), 1–67.

Sharma, E., Li, C., & Wang, L. (2019). BIGPATENT: A large-scale dataset for abstractive and coherent summarization. arXiv preprint arXiv:1906.03741. DOI: 10.18653/v1/P19-1212

Sun, C., Qiu, X., Xu, Y., & Huang, X. (2019). How to fine-tune BERT for text classification? In *China National Conference on Chinese Computational Linguistics* (pp. 194–206). Springer. DOI: 10.1007/978-3-030-32381-3_16

Vaswani, A., Shazeer, N., Parmar, N., Uszkoreit, J., Jones, L., Gomez, A. N., & Polosukhin, I. (2017). Attention is all you need. *Advances in Neural Information Processing Systems*, •••, 30.

Wang, W., Wei, F., Dong, L., Bao, H., Yang, N., & Zhou, M. (2020). MiniLM: Deep self-attention distillation for task-agnostic compression of pre-trained transformers. *Advances in Neural Information Processing Systems*, *33*, 5776–5788.

Wang, X., Zhang, Y., Zohar, O., & Yeung-Levy, S. (2024). Video-agent: Long-form video understanding with large language model as agent. In European Conference on Computer Vision (pp. 58–76). Springer Nature Switzerland.

Worsham, J., & Kalita, J. (2018). Genre identification and the compositional effect of genre in literature. In *Proceedings of the 27th International Conference on Computational Linguistics* (pp. 1963–1973).

Zhang, T., Kishore, V., Wu, F., Weinberger, K. Q., & Artzi, Y. (2019). BERTScore: Evaluating text generation with BERT. arXiv preprint arXiv:1904.09675.

Chapter 13
The Future of Trust AI-Government Relations in an AI-Driven Society

S. Haashni
http://orcid.org/0009-0004-2414-3839
Vimal Jyothi Convent Matriculation Higher Secondary School, India

ABSTRACT

Reimagining Public Trust in the Age of Artificial Intelligence requires a fundamental re-evaluation of the social contract between citizens, institutions, and technological systems as algorithmic infrastructures increasingly mediate public life, governance, economic participation, and knowledge production. The rapid diffusion of artificial intelligence technologies—popularized globally through breakthroughs such as OpenAI's ChatGPT and strategic investments by firms like Google, Microsoft, and Meta Platforms—has accelerated the integration of machine learning systems into decision-making processes that shape welfare distribution, predictive policing, healthcare diagnostics, credit scoring, education analytics, and digital public services. In this environment, trust can no longer be conceived solely as interpersonal confidence in public officials; rather, it must encompass systemic trust in socio-technical assemblages composed of algorithms, datasets, regulatory frameworks, institutional oversight bodies, and civic participation mechanisms.

INTRODUCTION

Reimagining Public Trust in the Age of Artificial Intelligence requires a fundamental re-evaluation of the social contract between citizens, institutions, and technological systems as algorithmic infrastructures increasingly mediate public

DOI: 10.4018/979-8-3373-9129-8.ch013

life, governance, economic participation, and knowledge production. The rapid diffusion of artificial intelligence technologies—popularized globally through breakthroughs such as OpenAI's ChatGPT and strategic investments by firms like Google, Microsoft, and Meta Platforms—has accelerated the integration of machine learning systems into decision-making processes that shape welfare distribution, predictive policing, healthcare diagnostics, credit scoring, education analytics, and digital public services. In this environment, trust can no longer be conceived solely as interpersonal confidence in public officials; rather, it must encompass systemic trust in socio-technical assemblages composed of algorithms, datasets, regulatory frameworks, institutional oversight bodies, and civic participation mechanisms. Classical theories of social trust, often associated with scholars such as Niklas Luhmann and Anthony Giddens, conceptualized trust as a mechanism for reducing social complexity and enabling cooperation under conditions of uncertainty; yet the opacity, scale, and autonomy of AI systems introduce new forms of uncertainty that exceed traditional institutional assurances. Algorithmic opacity, frequently described as the "black box" problem, challenges the epistemic foundations of public accountability because citizens cannot easily interrogate or contest decisions generated by deep neural networks trained on massive and often proprietary datasets.

However, regulatory compliance alone cannot generate authentic public trust; trust is relational and evolves through sustained experiences of fairness, reliability, and responsiveness. In democratic contexts, citizens evaluate AI-mediated governance not merely by technical performance metrics but by perceived alignment with constitutional norms, human rights protections, and distributive justice. For example, predictive analytics deployed in welfare eligibility assessments may enhance efficiency yet simultaneously risk reinforcing historical biases embedded in training data, disproportionately affecting marginalized communities; thus, trust depends on the visible presence of safeguards such as bias audits, independent review boards, and accessible redress mechanisms. Furthermore, the digital divide complicates trust formation because unequal access to digital literacy and infrastructure constrains the capacity of certain populations to understand, question, or benefit from AI systems, thereby deepening socio-economic disparities. Reimagining trust therefore entails investing in public education initiatives that cultivate algorithmic literacy, enabling citizens to engage critically with automated systems and participate meaningfully in public deliberation. The integration of AI into public administration also transforms bureaucratic culture: frontline officials must develop competencies in data interpretation, ethical reasoning, and interdisciplinary collaboration to ensure that automated recommendations augment rather than replace human judgment. Hybrid decision models—where AI systems provide probabilistic outputs subject to human verification—can strengthen trust if institutional protocols clearly define accountability boundaries and preserve human agency.

At the geopolitical level, AI has become a strategic domain of competition, influencing national security, economic power, and technological sovereignty; divergent governance models across regions shape global perceptions of trustworthy AI, underscoring the need for international coordination to prevent regulatory fragmentation and ethical arbitrage. Ethical frameworks grounded in principles such as beneficence, non-maleficence, autonomy, and justice must be operationalized through measurable indicators and continuous monitoring, moving beyond aspirational guidelines toward enforceable accountability structures. Civil society organizations, investigative journalists, and academic researchers play indispensable roles in scrutinizing algorithmic systems, uncovering discriminatory impacts, and advocating for corrective reforms; their engagement contributes to a distributed trust ecosystem in which oversight responsibilities are shared across societal actors. Transparency alone, however, is insufficient if disclosures are incomprehensible to non-experts; meaningful transparency requires interpretability tools, simplified documentation, and participatory forums that translate technical details into accessible knowledge (Aarab et al., 2025). Moreover, trust is dynamic and context-dependent: citizens may accept AI-assisted medical diagnostics with high confidence while expressing skepticism toward facial recognition in public spaces.

Data governance is central to this transformation, as trust in AI outputs depends fundamentally on the integrity, representativeness, and lawful acquisition of training data; robust privacy protections, secure storage infrastructures, and clear consent mechanisms are prerequisites for legitimacy. Emerging techniques such as federated learning and differential privacy illustrate how technical design choices can align innovation with rights protection, demonstrating that trust can be engineered through privacy-preserving architectures. At the same time, ethical AI must confront broader structural questions about labor displacement, economic inequality, and democratic resilience, since trust deteriorates when technological progress appears to benefit elites disproportionately. Social dialogue mechanisms involving labor unions, professional associations, and community groups can facilitate anticipatory governance, ensuring that AI adoption strategies address workforce transitions through reskilling initiatives and social safety nets. Measuring public trust in AI requires multidimensional indicators encompassing perceived fairness, transparency, reliability, and institutional responsiveness; regular public surveys, citizen assemblies, and participatory budgeting exercises can provide feedback loops that inform iterative improvements. Ultimately, reimagining public trust in the age of artificial intelligence demands a holistic paradigm shift from technology-centric deployment to value-centric governance, where innovation is evaluated not solely by computational efficiency but by its contribution to human flourishing, democratic accountability, and social cohesion. Trust emerges not from abstract assurances but from lived experiences of justice, competence, and respect within AI-mediated interactions; therefore, institutions must cultivate cultures of ethical reflexivity, continuous learning, and open dialogue(Afroogh et al., 2024).

ALGORITHMIC GOVERNANCE AND DEMOCRATIC ACCOUNTABILITY.

Algorithmic Governance and Democratic Accountability represent a pivotal intersection in contemporary public administration, where computational systems increasingly participate in or shape governmental decision-making, thereby redefining the architecture of authority, legitimacy, and citizen oversight in democratic societies. Algorithmic governance refers to the use of automated, data-driven systems—often powered by machine learning, predictive analytics, and large-scale data infrastructures—to inform or execute public policies across domains such as taxation, social welfare allocation, law enforcement, urban planning, healthcare triage, environmental monitoring, and electoral administration. As governments collaborate with major technology providers including Microsoft, Google, and Amazon for cloud computing and AI services, and as research institutions and organizations such as OpenAI advance large-scale language and reasoning systems, the boundaries between public authority and private technological infrastructure become increasingly intertwined. Democratic accountability, traditionally grounded in constitutional principles, legislative oversight, judicial review, electoral responsiveness, and administrative transparency, now faces novel challenges when decisions emerge from opaque algorithmic models rather than directly from identifiable public officials(Anute et al., 2026). Classical democratic theory, shaped by thinkers such as John Locke and John Stuart Mill, emphasized consent of the governed, rule of law, and protection of individual liberties; algorithmic governance must be evaluated against these enduring principles to ensure that automation does not dilute democratic control or undermine civil rights.

To preserve democratic accountability, governments must institutionalize mechanisms of explainability, documentation, and human oversight that render algorithmic processes intelligible and reviewable, ensuring that responsibility remains traceable to accountable authorities rather than diffused across technical infrastructures. Regulatory developments such as the Artificial Intelligence Act enacted by the European Union illustrate emerging attempts to categorize AI applications by risk level, mandating rigorous conformity assessments, transparency obligations, and post-market monitoring for high-risk systems used in public administration; similarly, principles articulated by the Organisation for Economic Co-operation and Development emphasize human-centered values, accountability, and robustness as foundational to trustworthy AI. However, legal compliance alone does not guarantee democratic legitimacy; accountability requires continuous scrutiny, participatory engagement, and institutional reflexivity capable of responding to evolving technological capabilities and societal expectations. Algorithmic bias remains a central concern, as data-driven systems may inadvertently replicate or amplify historical inequities embedded in training datasets, particularly affecting marginalized communities in areas such as predictive policing, housing allocation, or credit assessment; thus, democratic accountability entails proactive bias auditing, impact assessments, and inclusive stakeholder consultation prior to deployment(Basavaraju et al., 2026). Transparency must extend beyond technical disclosure to encompass meaningful communication accessible to non-experts, enabling citizens, journalists, civil society organizations, and legislators to evaluate system performance and ethical implications. Parliamentary committees, independent regulatory authorities, ombuds institutions, and data protection agencies must adapt their expertise and mandates to oversee algorithmic systems effectively, incorporating interdisciplinary knowledge from computer science, ethics, law, and social sciences. Furthermore, procurement processes for algorithmic tools require robust contractual safeguards addressing data sovereignty, cybersecurity, intellectual property rights, and public access to source code or model documentation when decisions affect fundamental rights.

The principle of "human-in-the-loop" governance offers a partial safeguard, positioning AI systems as decision-support tools rather than autonomous arbiters; yet this model must avoid becoming a mere formality if human reviewers lack sufficient training, time, or authority to challenge automated outputs. Democratic accountability also demands clear delineation of liability when algorithmic errors cause harm: determining whether responsibility lies with software developers, data providers, government agencies, or individual officials requires updated legal doctrines capable of addressing distributed agency in socio-technical systems. In electoral contexts, algorithmic governance intersects with concerns about misinformation, microtargeting, and digital campaign strategies, raising questions about fairness, transparency, and the integrity of democratic deliberation; oversight of platform algorithms that shape information flows becomes integral to safeguarding public discourse. At the administrative level, data-driven performance management systems may enhance efficiency and resource allocation, yet excessive reliance on quantitative metrics can incentivize goal displacement, reduce professional discretion, and erode the normative commitments of public service. Therefore, algorithmic governance must be embedded within ethical cultures that prioritize public interest over technocratic optimization(Bateson et al., 2026). Internationally, divergent regulatory approaches reflect varying political traditions and risk tolerances, creating potential fragmentation in standards for transparency and accountability; cross-border cooperation and harmonization are essential to prevent regulatory arbitrage and ensure consistent protection of rights. Public participation mechanisms, such as citizen assemblies, participatory technology assessments, and open consultation platforms, can democratize algorithmic governance by incorporating diverse perspectives into system design and evaluation. Education and digital literacy initiatives further empower citizens to engage critically with algorithmic systems, fostering informed oversight rather than passive acceptance. Empirical evaluation of algorithmic tools through pilot programs, randomized audits, and independent academic research strengthens evidence-based policymaking and builds public confidence.

Moreover, open data initiatives and interoperable standards can promote transparency while safeguarding privacy through privacy-enhancing technologies. Democratic accountability in the algorithmic age ultimately depends on aligning technical innovation with constitutional values, ensuring that automation enhances rather than replaces deliberative governance. By institutionalizing transparency, enforceable oversight, inclusive participation, and adaptive regulation, states can harness the efficiencies of algorithmic systems while preserving the foundational principles of representation, equality before the law, and protection of fundamental rights. In this reconfigured governance landscape, accountability is no longer solely a matter of electoral sanction or bureaucratic reporting; it becomes a multidimensional process involving continuous monitoring, collaborative stewardship, and normative reflection on the societal impacts of computational power(Bostrom et al., 2024) . Algorithmic governance, if thoughtfully designed and democratically supervised, can support evidence-based decision-making, reduce administrative burdens, and expand access to public services; yet without vigilant safeguards, it risks concentrating power in opaque systems beyond meaningful public control. The challenge, therefore, is not to reject technological advancement but to embed it within resilient democratic institutions capable of scrutinizing, guiding, and correcting algorithmic authority in accordance with the rule of law and the aspirations of participatory self-government.

ETHICAL FRAMEWORKS FOR RESPONSIBLE AI IN PUBLIC ADMINISTRATION.

Ethical Frameworks for Responsible AI in Public Administration constitute a foundational pillar in the transformation of governance systems increasingly shaped by data-driven technologies, machine learning models, and automated decision-support infrastructures that influence public welfare distribution, regulatory enforcement, urban management, and civic engagement. As public institutions integrate artificial intelligence tools developed or supported by organizations such as OpenAI and technology corporations including Microsoft, Google, and IBM, the ethical implications of algorithmic deployment extend beyond technical performance metrics to encompass normative considerations of justice, accountability, transparency, and human dignity. Responsible AI in the public sector must be anchored in constitutional values, human rights principles, and administrative law doctrines that safeguard procedural fairness and equality before the law. Ethical frameworks thus function as interpretive bridges between abstract moral philosophy and operational governance practice, translating principles such as beneficence, non-maleficence, autonomy, explicability, and distributive justice into concrete institutional mechanisms, including impact assessments, audit protocols, oversight committees, and participatory consultation processes(Bullock et al., 2025). The articulation of global AI governance standards by bodies such as the Organisation for Economic Co-operation and Development, which emphasizes human-centered values and robustness, and the enactment of regulatory instruments such as the Artificial Intelligence Act under the auspices of the European Union, signal a maturing recognition that ethical AI is not merely aspirational but legally and politically consequential. Within public administration, ethical frameworks must confront the unique asymmetry of power between state institutions and citizens, where algorithmic decisions may determine access to healthcare benefits, educational opportunities, housing subsidies, immigration status, or law enforcement scrutiny. In such contexts, the moral stakes are amplified because errors, biases, or opacity can directly affect fundamental rights and social mobility. Consequently, responsible AI governance requires comprehensive lifecycle management encompassing design, procurement, development, testing, deployment, monitoring, and decommissioning phases, each subject to ethical scrutiny. Data governance stands at the core of this ethical architecture: ensuring data quality, representativeness, legality of collection, informed consent where applicable, and protection against unauthorized access or misuse forms the bedrock of trustworthy AI systems.

Without equitable and transparent data practices, even technically sophisticated algorithms risk perpetuating structural discrimination embedded in historical datasets. Ethical frameworks must therefore mandate bias detection methodologies, algorithmic auditing, and continuous evaluation of disparate impacts across demographic groups, supported by interdisciplinary expertise integrating computer science, public policy, sociology, and law. Transparency and explainability constitute another central pillar, yet these concepts must be carefully operationalized; mere disclosure of technical documentation may not suffice if it remains incomprehensible to affected citizens. Meaningful transparency requires layered communication strategies, including simplified explanations, accessible documentation, and public reporting dashboards that allow stakeholders to understand system objectives, limitations, and performance indicators. Moreover, explainable AI techniques—ranging from interpretable models to post hoc explanation tools—should be evaluated not solely for technical adequacy but for their contribution to procedural fairness and contestability. In democratic governance, the ability to challenge and appeal algorithmic decisions is integral to maintaining legitimacy; ethical frameworks must therefore institutionalize clear redress mechanisms, ensuring that human oversight is substantive rather than symbolic(Cath et al., 2023). The principle of human-centered AI emphasizes augmentation over replacement, advocating for "human-in-the-loop" or "human-on-the-loop" models in which public officials retain ultimate decision authority and responsibility. However, ethical design must guard against automation bias, where human operators defer excessively to algorithmic outputs; comprehensive training, professional development, and ethical literacy programs are essential to empower civil servants to critically evaluate AI-generated recommendations. Accountability structures further demand delineation of roles and liabilities among software vendors, data providers, system integrators, and government agencies, particularly in public–private partnerships where proprietary technologies intersect with public mandates.

Ethical procurement guidelines should include requirements for transparency of training data sources, documentation of model validation processes, cybersecurity safeguards, and contractual clauses enabling independent audits. Privacy protection is equally paramount, especially in contexts involving sensitive personal data such as health records, biometric identifiers, or social service histories; privacy-enhancing technologies like differential privacy and federated learning demonstrate how technical innovation can align with ethical commitments to confidentiality and data minimization(Choung et al., 2023). Beyond individual rights, responsible AI in public administration must consider broader societal implications, including labor displacement within the public sector, shifts in organizational culture, and the risk of technocratic centralization that marginalizes democratic deliberation. Ethical frameworks should thus incorporate participatory governance mechanisms, inviting civil society organizations, academic experts, community representatives, and affected populations to contribute to system design and evaluation. Public consultations, citizen juries, and algorithmic impact assessments can foster inclusive dialogue and enhance legitimacy. Furthermore, metrics for evaluating responsible AI must transcend efficiency and cost savings to include qualitative indicators of fairness, trust, inclusivity, and social cohesion.

International cooperation plays a crucial role in harmonizing ethical standards, preventing regulatory fragmentation, and facilitating knowledge exchange on best practices, especially as AI technologies and data flows transcend national borders. The dynamic nature of machine learning systems, which may evolve through continuous training and adaptation, necessitates ongoing monitoring and periodic reassessment to ensure sustained compliance with ethical standards; static approval at the point of deployment is insufficient in rapidly changing digital ecosystems. Ethical governance must therefore be adaptive, embedding feedback loops that enable iterative refinement based on empirical evidence and stakeholder input. Importantly, ethical AI frameworks should cultivate a culture of responsibility within public institutions, encouraging reflexivity, openness to critique, and commitment to public value creation rather than narrow performance optimization(Cihon et al., 2023). Leadership in public administration bears particular responsibility in articulating ethical vision, allocating resources for compliance infrastructure, and modeling transparency in communication about AI initiatives. As artificial intelligence becomes increasingly integrated into policy formulation and service delivery, ethical stewardship will determine whether technological innovation strengthens democratic institutions or exacerbates inequality and mistrust. Responsible AI in public administration is thus not solely a technical endeavor but a normative project grounded in constitutional democracy, human rights, and social justice. By systematically embedding principles of fairness, transparency, accountability, privacy, inclusivity, and human oversight into regulatory frameworks, institutional practices, and organizational cultures, governments can harness the transformative potential of AI while safeguarding the dignity, autonomy, and collective well-being of the communities they serve.

TRANSPARENCY AND EXPLAINABILITY IN GOVERNMENT AI SYSTEMS.

Transparency and Explainability in Government AI Systems constitute indispensable pillars of democratic legitimacy in an era where public administration increasingly relies on machine learning models, predictive analytics, biometric identification technologies, and automated decision-support platforms to allocate resources, assess risks, monitor compliance, and deliver essential services. As governments collaborate with technology providers such as Microsoft, Google, Amazon, and research organizations like OpenAI to integrate advanced AI capabilities into public infrastructure, the demand for intelligibility, auditability, and procedural fairness intensifies, particularly when algorithmic outputs influence fundamental rights, social benefits, law enforcement actions, and regulatory determinations. Transparency in this context extends beyond the passive disclosure of technical documentation; it encompasses proactive communication regarding system objectives, design logic, data sources, performance metrics, limitations, and risk mitigation strategies, ensuring that citizens, oversight bodies, and civil society actors can meaningfully evaluate governmental reliance on automated systems. Explainability, closely related yet conceptually distinct, refers to the capacity of an AI system to provide understandable reasons for its outputs, enabling affected individuals to comprehend why a particular decision was reached and to challenge it when necessary(European Commission, 2024). In democratic governance, the right to reasoned decisions is embedded in administrative law traditions that require public authorities to justify their actions; when algorithms participate in these decisions, explainability becomes a constitutional imperative rather than a mere technical feature. Complex models, especially deep neural networks, often function as "black boxes" whose internal parameter interactions defy intuitive interpretation, thereby creating epistemic asymmetries between system designers and citizens subject to algorithmic judgment. Addressing this challenge necessitates a multifaceted strategy that combines interpretable model design, post hoc explanation techniques, comprehensive documentation, and institutional oversight.

Regulatory frameworks such as the Artificial Intelligence Act adopted by the European Union underscore the obligation of public authorities deploying high-risk AI systems to ensure transparency, traceability, and human oversight, while international guidelines promulgated by the Organisation for Economic Co-operation and Development emphasize accountability and responsible disclosure as core principles of trustworthy AI. Yet formal compliance with transparency mandates does not automatically yield genuine public understanding; effective transparency must be contextual, accessible, and tailored to diverse audiences, ranging from technical auditors and legislators to community stakeholders and individual beneficiaries. Layered transparency models can address this diversity by providing detailed technical reports for expert review alongside simplified explanatory summaries for the general public, complemented by interactive dashboards that display real-time performance metrics and bias assessments. Furthermore, algorithmic transparency must account for data governance practices, including the provenance, representativeness, and quality of training datasets, as well as privacy safeguards and cybersecurity measures that protect sensitive information. Without insight into data sources and preprocessing methods, explanations of model outputs remain incomplete and potentially misleading. Explainability techniques such as feature attribution methods, counterfactual explanations, and rule-based approximations can enhance interpretability, but they must be evaluated critically to ensure that they do not oversimplify complex causal relationships or create a false sense of understanding. From a procedural justice perspective, explainability is closely linked to contestability: individuals must have accessible avenues to request clarification, submit additional evidence, and seek human review when algorithmic decisions adversely affect them. Establishing clear appeals processes, independent review boards, and ombuds institutions capable of scrutinizing algorithmic reasoning reinforces democratic accountability and mitigates the risk of arbitrary or discriminatory outcomes. Moreover, transparency should encompass procurement and contractual arrangements in public–private partnerships, disclosing the extent to which proprietary constraints limit access to source code or training data, and ensuring that governments retain sufficient authority to audit and modify systems when necessary. The principle of open government data can further strengthen transparency by enabling researchers and civil society organizations to conduct independent evaluations, provided that privacy and security considerations are rigorously maintained.

Figure 1. Trust, trustworthiness and AI governance

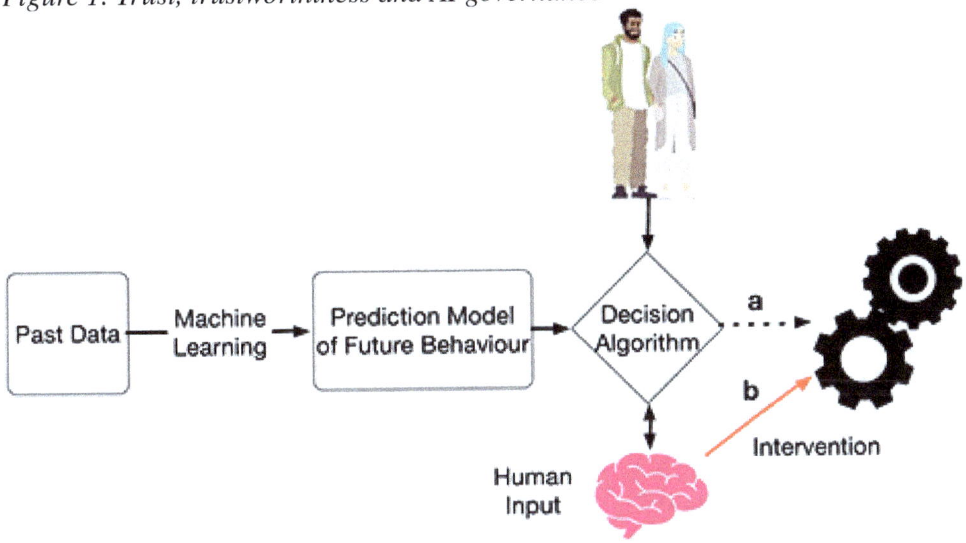

Organizational culture within public administration plays a decisive role in operationalizing transparency and explainability; civil servants must be trained not only in technical literacy but also in ethical reasoning and communication skills to interpret AI outputs responsibly and articulate their implications to stakeholders. Human-in-the-loop models, in which public officials validate or contextualize algorithmic recommendations, can enhance explainability when decision-makers are empowered to exercise discretion and provide individualized justifications. However, transparency efforts must also confront the phenomenon of automation bias, where human reviewers may defer excessively to algorithmic outputs, undermining the substantive value of explanation and oversight(Ferdaus et al., 2026). Periodic audits, impact assessments, and stress-testing under diverse scenarios contribute to a culture of continuous learning and iterative improvement, ensuring that explanations remain accurate as models evolve through retraining or data updates. Transparency is equally crucial in safeguarding against systemic bias, as public disclosure of demographic performance disparities can catalyze corrective action and foster trust among historically marginalized communities. Communication strategies should address not only successes but also limitations and uncertainties inherent in AI systems, acknowledging error rates, potential trade-offs, and contexts where human judgment remains indispensable. In the broader democratic ecosystem, transparent AI governance supports informed public debate, enabling legislators, journalists, and citizens to deliberate on normative questions concerning acceptable risk levels, privacy boundaries, and distributive impacts. International cooperation and knowledge exchange can facilitate harmonized standards for documentation, auditing, and reporting, reducing fragmentation and promoting best practices across jurisdictions. Ultimately, transparency and explainability in government AI systems are not ends in themselves but instrumental values that uphold the rule of law, protect individual rights, and sustain public trust. By embedding these principles into the full lifecycle of AI deployment—from initial design and data collection to monitoring and decommissioning—governments can reconcile technological innovation with democratic accountability, ensuring that algorithmic governance remains intelligible, contestable, and aligned with the public interest in an increasingly data-driven world.

CITIZEN-CENTRIC DESIGN OF AI-ENABLED PUBLIC SERVICES.

Citizen-Centric Design of AI-Enabled Public Services represents a transformative paradigm in contemporary governance, wherein artificial intelligence systems are conceptualized, developed, and deployed not merely as efficiency-enhancing administrative tools but as inclusive, responsive, and participatory instruments aligned with the lived realities, rights, and aspirations of diverse communities. As governments increasingly integrate AI capabilities through collaborations with technology providers such as Microsoft, Google, Amazon, and research-driven organizations like OpenAI, the design philosophy underpinning public digital infrastructure must shift from institution-centric optimization toward human-centered value creation. Citizen-centricity implies that AI-enabled services—ranging from digital identity verification and welfare eligibility assessment to healthcare triage, tax administration, grievance redressal, and urban mobility management—are co-created with stakeholders, grounded in accessibility, fairness, transparency, and cultural sensitivity, and continuously refined through participatory feedback mechanisms(Floridi et al., 2023). Unlike traditional top-down bureaucratic models, citizen-centric AI design embraces iterative engagement, where community consultations, user experience research, and participatory prototyping inform system requirements before technical architecture is finalized. This approach recognizes that public services operate within complex socio-economic ecosystems characterized by digital divides, linguistic diversity, varied literacy levels, and differential access to technological infrastructure; consequently, inclusive interface design, multilingual support, assistive technologies for persons with disabilities, and low-bandwidth functionality become ethical imperatives rather than optional enhancements. Regulatory frameworks such as the Artificial Intelligence Act adopted by the European Union underscore the importance of human oversight and risk mitigation in high-impact AI applications, reinforcing the notion that citizen welfare must remain central to system deployment.

Moreover, global policy guidance articulated by the Organisation for Economic Co-operation and Development emphasizes inclusive growth, sustainable development, and respect for human rights as foundational objectives for AI governance, principles that resonate strongly with citizen-centric design philosophy. Operationalizing citizen-centric AI requires embedding empathy and contextual awareness into system architecture, ensuring that algorithmic decision-making accounts for the nuanced circumstances of individuals rather than reducing them to abstract data points. For example, predictive analytics used in social protection programs must incorporate mechanisms for human review and discretionary judgment to accommodate exceptional cases and prevent unjust exclusion. Transparent communication regarding data collection practices, model logic, and available appeal processes further empowers citizens to understand and engage with AI-enabled services confidently. Co-design workshops, public hackathons, and civic technology partnerships can democratize innovation, fostering shared ownership of digital transformation initiatives. Additionally, robust data governance policies must protect privacy and security, particularly when sensitive personal information is processed; privacy-by-design principles, encryption protocols, and consent management systems are integral to maintaining trust in citizen-facing AI platforms. Equity considerations are paramount, as algorithmic systems risk perpetuating historical biases if training data reflect structural inequalities; therefore, bias audits, fairness metrics, and diverse stakeholder representation in design teams are essential safeguards(Janssen et al., 2023). Citizen-centric design also entails continuous performance evaluation informed by user satisfaction surveys, community feedback loops, and real-time service analytics, enabling adaptive improvement responsive to evolving societal needs. Interoperability across government departments enhances seamless service delivery, reducing bureaucratic fragmentation and administrative burden for citizens who might otherwise navigate multiple disconnected systems. Importantly, the success of AI-enabled public services depends not only on technological sophistication but also on institutional culture; civil servants must cultivate digital literacy, ethical sensitivity, and collaborative competencies to interpret AI outputs responsibly and communicate effectively with the public.

Leadership commitment to transparency and accountability reinforces the normative orientation toward public value rather than mere operational efficiency. In multicultural societies, citizen-centric AI must respect pluralistic values and linguistic diversity, incorporating culturally appropriate communication strategies and localized content. Furthermore, resilience planning ensures continuity of essential services during system outages, cybersecurity incidents, or unforeseen algorithmic errors, safeguarding vulnerable populations from service disruption(Jobin et al., 2023). International collaboration and knowledge exchange facilitate benchmarking against best practices, enabling governments to learn from comparative experiences and refine their citizen engagement methodologies. Ultimately, citizen-centric design reframes AI from a technocratic instrument of administrative control into a participatory platform for enhancing democratic inclusion, social equity, and service responsiveness. By systematically integrating user experience research, ethical governance, accessibility standards, privacy protections, fairness audits, and participatory evaluation into the lifecycle of AI-enabled public services, governments can ensure that digital transformation strengthens rather than alienates civic relationships. In doing so, public institutions affirm that artificial intelligence serves as a means to empower individuals, reduce systemic barriers, and foster trust, thereby aligning technological innovation with the foundational democratic commitment to dignity, equality, and collective well-being.

Data Sovereignty and Digital Rights in Smart Governance have emerged as foundational concerns in an era where states increasingly rely on interconnected digital infrastructures, sensor networks, cloud platforms, and artificial intelligence systems to manage urban environments, deliver public services, regulate markets, and engage citizens through data-driven decision-making architectures. Smart governance—often operationalized through integrated command centers, real-time analytics dashboards, digital identity frameworks, and predictive service optimization tools—rests upon the continuous collection, processing, storage, and exchange of vast volumes of personal and non-personal data. In this context, data sovereignty refers to the principle that data generated within a jurisdiction are subject to its legal frameworks, regulatory oversight, and democratic norms, while digital rights encompass the spectrum of civil liberties and human rights applicable to digital environments, including privacy, freedom of expression, informational self-determination, access to information, and protection against algorithmic discrimination. As governments partner with multinational technology providers such as Microsoft, Amazon, Google, and research-driven entities like OpenAI to deploy cloud computing, AI analytics, and digital service platforms, questions arise regarding jurisdictional control, cross-border data flows, intellectual property rights, and the extent to which sovereign regulatory authority can be effectively exercised over distributed technological ecosystems. The concept of data sovereignty intersects with constitutional principles of state authority and democratic accountability, particularly when public sector data—ranging from health records and biometric identifiers to tax filings, land registries, and social welfare information—are stored or processed on foreign-owned infrastructures or in transnational data centers(Kaur et al., 2025). Ensuring sovereign oversight requires robust legal frameworks that define data localization requirements where appropriate, establish conditions for lawful cross-border transfers, and mandate compliance with domestic privacy and cybersecurity standards regardless of the service provider's geographic origin. Regulatory initiatives such as the General Data Protection Regulation under the European Union exemplify comprehensive approaches to safeguarding personal data rights, granting individuals enforceable entitlements including access, rectification, erasure, and objection to automated decision-making, thereby reinforcing digital rights within a supranational governance structure.

Complementary policy guidance from the Organisation for Economic Co-operation and Development emphasizes accountability, transparency, and proportionality in data governance, highlighting the need for international cooperation to reconcile innovation with rights protection. In smart city contexts, where sensors monitor traffic flows, environmental conditions, energy consumption, and public safety indicators, the aggregation of granular behavioral data can generate valuable insights for sustainability and efficiency, yet also poses risks of surveillance, profiling, and erosion of anonymity in public spaces. Digital rights frameworks must therefore embed privacy-by-design and privacy-by-default principles into system architecture, ensuring data minimization, purpose limitation, secure encryption, and strict access controls. Moreover, algorithmic systems operating within smart governance environments—such as predictive policing tools or automated eligibility assessments—must be subject to transparency and contestability safeguards to prevent opaque decision-making that undermines procedural fairness(Kishore et al., 2026). Data sovereignty further entails empowering public institutions to audit proprietary algorithms and data practices of private vendors, thereby avoiding technological dependency that could compromise strategic autonomy or democratic oversight. Open standards, interoperable platforms, and public-interest procurement policies can mitigate vendor lock-in and promote competitive, transparent ecosystems aligned with national priorities. At the citizen level, digital rights education and digital literacy initiatives are critical to enabling informed participation in smart governance processes, equipping individuals to understand consent mechanisms, exercise data access rights, and engage in policy debates concerning surveillance technologies or biometric identification systems. The rise of cross-border digital platforms complicates enforcement, as data may traverse multiple jurisdictions with divergent regulatory regimes; thus, international data-sharing agreements and adequacy determinations become instruments for harmonizing protections while facilitating economic integration.

Cybersecurity resilience constitutes another dimension of data sovereignty, as breaches or unauthorized intrusions can undermine public trust and compromise national security; comprehensive incident response protocols, regular vulnerability assessments, and independent oversight bodies are essential components of a secure digital governance framework. Ethical considerations extend beyond privacy to encompass equity and inclusivity, ensuring that smart governance initiatives do not disproportionately disadvantage marginalized communities through biased datasets or exclusionary digital interfaces. Participatory governance mechanisms—such as public consultations, citizen assemblies, and co-design workshops—can democratize decision-making around data use policies, reinforcing legitimacy and social acceptance. Furthermore, the principle of informational self-determination recognizes individuals as active agents with rights over their digital identities and personal data trajectories, challenging paternalistic or opaque state practices. Emerging technologies such as decentralized identity systems and blockchain-based audit trails offer potential pathways for enhancing user control and transparency, though their implementation must be evaluated against scalability, security, and environmental considerations. Balancing innovation with rights protection demands adaptive regulatory approaches capable of evolving alongside rapid technological change, integrating sunset clauses, periodic impact assessments, and dynamic compliance monitoring(Kunnathully et al., 2026). Ultimately, data sovereignty and digital rights in smart governance represent intertwined dimensions of a broader normative project: constructing digital public infrastructures that respect human dignity, uphold democratic accountability, and safeguard collective autonomy in an interconnected world. By embedding enforceable rights, transparent oversight, robust cybersecurity, and participatory engagement into the architecture of smart governance systems, states can harness the transformative potential of digital technologies while ensuring that sovereignty and individual freedoms remain central to the digital age's social contract.

AI POLICY, REGULATION, AND INSTITUTIONAL READINESS.

AI Policy, Regulation, and Institutional Readiness constitute the strategic triad through which governments navigate the rapid proliferation of artificial intelligence technologies across public administration, economic systems, and societal infrastructures. As AI systems—developed and commercialized by leading technology firms such as Microsoft, Google, Amazon, and research-driven organizations like OpenAI—become embedded in governance processes ranging from tax compliance monitoring and public health analytics to urban mobility optimization and judicial risk assessment, policymakers confront the dual imperative of fostering innovation while safeguarding democratic values, human rights, and systemic resilience(Zuboff, 2023). AI policy encompasses the articulation of national strategies, investment priorities, ethical guidelines, research funding mechanisms, and cross-sector collaboration frameworks that collectively shape the trajectory of technological development and deployment. Regulation translates normative commitments into enforceable legal standards, defining obligations concerning transparency, accountability, risk management, safety testing, and data governance. Institutional readiness refers to the administrative, technical, legal, and cultural capacities required within public institutions to design, procure, oversee, and adapt AI systems responsibly and effectively. The interaction among these three dimensions determines whether AI integration strengthens public value or exacerbates inequality, opacity, and regulatory fragmentation(Lahusen et al., 2024). Contemporary regulatory efforts such as the Artificial Intelligence Act enacted by the European Union exemplify risk-based governance models that categorize AI applications according to potential societal impact, imposing stricter compliance requirements on high-risk systems used in sectors like healthcare, education, employment, and law enforcement. Similarly, policy principles articulated by the Organisation for Economic Co-operation and Development emphasize human-centered values, transparency, robustness, and accountability as guiding norms for trustworthy AI ecosystems. However, policy articulation without institutional preparedness risks symbolic compliance devoid of practical efficacy. Effective AI governance requires skilled civil servants capable of understanding algorithmic architectures, evaluating procurement proposals, conducting impact assessments, and interpreting performance metrics; thus, capacity-building initiatives, interdisciplinary training programs, and recruitment strategies targeting data science expertise are essential components of readiness. Regulatory design must also reconcile innovation incentives with precautionary safeguards, avoiding overly restrictive measures that stifle research while preventing regulatory vacuums that enable harmful experimentation. Adaptive governance mechanisms—such as regulatory sandboxes, pilot programs, and iterative consultation processes—facilitate evidence-based refinement of rules in response to technological evolution.

Institutional coordination across ministries and agencies is critical, given that AI applications often cut across sectoral boundaries; establishing centralized AI oversight bodies or interagency task forces can promote coherence, prevent duplication, and harmonize standards. Procurement frameworks must integrate ethical criteria, transparency requirements, cybersecurity provisions, and audit rights into contractual arrangements with private vendors, ensuring that public authorities retain control over data assets and algorithmic modifications. Data governance remains foundational, encompassing data quality assurance, privacy protection, secure storage, interoperability standards, and lawful cross-border transfer mechanisms. Institutional readiness also demands robust monitoring and evaluation systems capable of detecting bias, performance degradation, and unintended consequences in deployed AI systems, supported by independent oversight bodies empowered to conduct audits and enforce corrective action(Lai et al., 2026). Legal doctrines concerning liability and accountability must evolve to address distributed responsibility among developers, data providers, integrators, and public officials, clarifying redress pathways for individuals adversely affected by algorithmic decisions. Public communication strategies further contribute to readiness by fostering transparency and trust, articulating the objectives, benefits, and limitations of AI initiatives in accessible language. Budgetary planning must account not only for initial system acquisition but also for lifecycle costs including maintenance, retraining, cybersecurity upgrades, and decommissioning. Cyber resilience constitutes a vital readiness dimension, as AI systems may become targets of adversarial attacks, data poisoning, or model manipulation; comprehensive risk management frameworks, incident response protocols, and collaboration with national cybersecurity agencies enhance defensive capabilities. Ethical governance structures—such as AI ethics committees, impact assessment protocols, and stakeholder advisory boards—embed normative oversight within institutional processes, ensuring that policy commitments translate into operational safeguards. International cooperation and policy harmonization mitigate fragmentation in global AI markets, facilitate cross-border data flows consistent with rights protection, and support shared research initiatives addressing global challenges such as climate modeling and pandemic response. Moreover, inclusive policymaking that engages academia, civil society, industry representatives, and marginalized communities strengthens legitimacy and anticipates diverse societal impacts. Institutional readiness extends beyond technical competence to encompass organizational culture; fostering a learning-oriented environment that encourages experimentation, critical reflection, and openness to external scrutiny enhances adaptive capacity(Lockey et al., 2025). Performance indicators for AI governance should integrate qualitative measures of fairness, public trust, and social impact alongside quantitative efficiency metrics. Long-term strategic planning must consider workforce transformation, reskilling programs, and ethical implications of automation in public sector employment. Ultimately, AI policy, regulation, and institutional readiness form an interdependent ecosystem: coherent policy sets direction, regulation establishes guardrails, and institutional capacity operationalizes principles in practice. By aligning these elements within a comprehensive governance architecture grounded in democratic accountability, human rights, and sustainable innovation, states can navigate the complexities of AI integration while preserving public value and reinforcing resilient, transparent, and future-ready institutions.

Collaborative Intelligence Between State and Society represents an emergent governance paradigm in which public institutions, civil society, academia, industry, and citizens collectively co-create knowledge, deliberate on policy options, and steward technological systems—particularly artificial intelligence—toward shared public value(Wu et al., 2023). Rather than positioning the state as a unilateral decision-maker or society as a passive recipient of administrative outputs, collaborative intelligence envisions a dynamic, reciprocal ecosystem in which data, expertise, and lived experience circulate across institutional boundaries to inform more inclusive, adaptive, and legitimate governance outcomes. In the digital age, this paradigm is increasingly mediated by AI-enabled platforms and analytics infrastructures developed by organizations such as OpenAI and deployed at scale through partnerships with technology firms like Microsoft, Google, and Meta Platforms, whose tools facilitate large-scale data processing, natural language analysis, and participatory digital engagement. However, collaborative intelligence transcends technological instrumentation; it is fundamentally a normative commitment to shared epistemic authority, transparency, and co-responsibility in public problem-solving(Müller et al., 2023). Within this framework, governments leverage AI systems not merely to optimize internal efficiency but to synthesize diverse stakeholder inputs, identify emerging social needs, and model policy scenarios in ways that integrate quantitative evidence with qualitative community perspectives. For example, AI-driven sentiment analysis applied to public consultations can surface recurring concerns across thousands of citizen submissions, enabling policymakers to respond more effectively while preserving the authenticity of individual voices.

Yet meaningful collaboration requires safeguards to ensure representativeness, mitigate algorithmic bias, and prevent digital exclusion, particularly for marginalized populations with limited access to online platforms. Regulatory initiatives such as the Artificial Intelligence Act adopted by the European Union emphasize human oversight and transparency in high-risk AI applications, reinforcing the principle that automated systems must augment—not supplant—democratic deliberation. Complementary global standards articulated by the Organisation for Economic Co-operation and Development advocate inclusive growth, accountability, and participatory governance, aligning closely with collaborative intelligence ideals. Operationalizing this model involves institutional redesign: establishing cross-sector innovation labs, public data trusts, and civic technology partnerships that facilitate shared experimentation and iterative learning(Nemitz, 2023). Universities and research institutes contribute methodological rigor and critical evaluation; civil society organizations articulate grassroots priorities and monitor equity impacts; private-sector innovators provide technical expertise and scalable infrastructure; and citizens contribute experiential knowledge and normative judgment. AI systems function within this constellation as integrative tools capable of processing complex datasets, simulating policy trade-offs, and identifying patterns that might elude human analysts, yet ultimate normative choices remain subject to democratic deliberation and political accountability. Data governance frameworks are central to sustaining collaborative intelligence, as trust depends on transparent data stewardship, privacy protection, and equitable access to shared information resources. Open data initiatives, when responsibly implemented, empower communities to analyze public datasets independently, fostering distributed oversight and innovation.

Moreover, collaborative intelligence must address power asymmetries inherent in digital ecosystems, ensuring that algorithmic mediation does not privilege technologically sophisticated actors at the expense of less-resourced groups. Mechanisms such as participatory budgeting, citizen assemblies augmented by AI-facilitated briefing materials, and co-design workshops exemplify how technology can enhance deliberative quality while preserving human agency. Ethical oversight bodies and independent audit institutions further anchor collaboration within accountability structures, preventing capture by narrow interests. Organizational culture within the state must evolve toward openness, humility, and reflexivity, recognizing that societal knowledge complements bureaucratic expertise. Continuous feedback loops—enabled by real-time service analytics and community reporting platforms—allow adaptive refinement of policies and AI models in response to lived outcomes. Importantly, collaborative intelligence extends beyond domestic governance to transnational cooperation, as global challenges such as climate change, public health crises, and digital security demand cross-border knowledge exchange and interoperable regulatory standards(OECD, 2023). By embedding transparency, shared governance mechanisms, digital literacy initiatives, and equitable participation into AI-enabled policy ecosystems, collaborative intelligence transforms artificial intelligence from a centralized instrument of control into a distributed catalyst for democratic co-creation. In doing so, it redefines the relationship between state and society as a mutually reinforcing partnership grounded in trust, inclusivity, and collective problem-solving capacity, thereby strengthening democratic resilience and ensuring that technological advancement remains aligned with public interest and social justice.

RISK MANAGEMENT AND OVERSIGHT OF AUTONOMOUS DECISION SYSTEMS.

Risk Management and Oversight of Autonomous Decision Systems have become central imperatives in contemporary governance as artificial intelligence increasingly operates with varying degrees of autonomy in domains such as public safety, healthcare triage, transportation control, welfare eligibility assessment, border management, and critical infrastructure monitoring. Autonomous decision systems—ranging from machine learning models that generate predictive risk scores to semi-autonomous robotic platforms and adaptive algorithmic management tools—possess the capacity to process high-volume data streams and execute actions with minimal real-time human intervention. While these capabilities promise efficiency, precision, and scalability, they simultaneously introduce systemic, ethical, legal, and operational risks that demand robust oversight architectures grounded in democratic accountability and institutional competence. Governments frequently rely on technological ecosystems developed by major actors such as Microsoft, Google, Amazon, and research-driven entities like OpenAI to deploy AI-enabled infrastructures, thereby intertwining public mandates with private innovation capacities; this interdependence necessitates clearly defined contractual, regulatory, and ethical safeguards to ensure that autonomy does not eclipse accountability(Papagiannidis et al., 2025). Effective risk management begins with comprehensive identification and classification of potential harms, including algorithmic bias, model drift, adversarial manipulation, cybersecurity vulnerabilities, privacy breaches, operational failures, and unintended social consequences arising from feedback loops within complex socio-technical systems. Regulatory initiatives such as the Artificial Intelligence Act enacted by the European Union exemplify risk-based governance models that categorize AI applications according to potential societal impact and impose proportionate compliance obligations, including mandatory conformity assessments, documentation requirements, and post-deployment monitoring for high-risk systems.

Complementary global standards advanced by the Organisation for Economic Co-operation and Development emphasize robustness, safety, transparency, and accountability as foundational to trustworthy AI ecosystems. Within public administration, operationalizing these principles requires embedding risk assessment protocols across the full lifecycle of autonomous systems—from initial design and data collection to deployment, evaluation, retraining, and decommissioning(Wirtz et al., 2024). Pre-deployment impact assessments should examine not only technical performance metrics but also ethical implications, equity considerations, and potential human rights effects, supported by interdisciplinary expertise spanning computer science, law, sociology, and public policy. Continuous monitoring mechanisms are equally essential, as machine learning models may degrade over time due to shifting data distributions or evolving environmental conditions; real-time performance dashboards, anomaly detection systems, and scheduled audits can detect drift and trigger corrective interventions. Human oversight remains a cornerstone of responsible autonomy, yet its design must be substantive rather than symbolic; clearly defined "human-in-the-loop" or "human-on-the-loop" frameworks should delineate when and how human operators can override automated decisions, what competencies they must possess, and how accountability is allocated when errors occur. Liability regimes must evolve to address distributed agency across developers, data providers, system integrators, and public officials, ensuring that affected individuals have accessible avenues for redress when autonomous decisions cause harm(Rao et al., 2026). Cybersecurity resilience constitutes a critical dimension of oversight, particularly as adversarial attacks, data poisoning, and model extraction techniques pose threats to the integrity and reliability of AI systems; coordinated collaboration with national cybersecurity agencies, implementation of encryption protocols, and routine penetration testing enhance systemic robustness. Transparency and explainability further contribute to risk mitigation by enabling stakeholders to scrutinize decision logic and detect discriminatory patterns, while independent oversight bodies—such as data protection authorities, ethics committees, and parliamentary review panels—provide institutional checks on executive deployment of autonomous technologies. Procurement policies should incorporate rigorous vendor evaluation criteria, mandating disclosure of training data provenance, validation methodologies, and risk management strategies, thereby preventing opaque or inadequately tested systems from entering critical public functions (Veale & Brass, 2023). Scenario planning and stress-testing under extreme or edge-case conditions can illuminate vulnerabilities that standard validation processes may overlook, particularly in high-stakes contexts such as emergency response coordination or autonomous transportation management.

Public communication strategies also form part of comprehensive risk governance, as transparent acknowledgment of limitations, uncertainty, and corrective measures fosters trust and reduces misinformation. International cooperation is increasingly necessary, given the transnational nature of digital infrastructures and AI supply chains; harmonized standards, information-sharing agreements, and collaborative research initiatives strengthen collective capacity to manage systemic risks. Importantly, risk management must balance precaution with innovation, avoiding paralyzing overregulation while ensuring that experimentation occurs within controlled, accountable environments such as regulatory sandboxes or pilot programs. Organizational culture within public institutions must cultivate vigilance, ethical sensitivity, and continuous learning, recognizing that autonomous systems are not static tools but evolving entities embedded in dynamic social contexts(Revankar et al., 2026). Training programs for civil servants should encompass algorithmic literacy, ethical reasoning, and crisis response competencies, empowering personnel to interpret system outputs critically and intervene effectively when anomalies arise. Ultimately, the oversight of autonomous decision systems is not solely a technical endeavor but a normative commitment to safeguarding human dignity, equality, and democratic legitimacy in the face of increasingly automated governance. By integrating risk-based regulation, lifecycle monitoring, human oversight, cybersecurity resilience, transparent communication, and participatory accountability into cohesive institutional frameworks, states can harness the benefits of autonomy while preventing the erosion of rights, trust, and systemic stability in the digital age.

Public Sector Innovation through Trusted AI Platforms reflects a strategic evolution in governance wherein artificial intelligence systems are not merely adopted as isolated technological upgrades but embedded as secure, interoperable, ethically governed infrastructures capable of transforming service delivery, regulatory oversight, policy design, and civic engagement(Upadhyaya et al., 2026). Trusted AI platforms refer to integrated digital ecosystems that combine scalable cloud computing, advanced analytics, machine learning models, robust cybersecurity architectures, transparent data governance protocols, and enforceable ethical safeguards, thereby enabling public institutions to innovate responsibly while maintaining democratic accountability and citizen confidence. As governments collaborate with global technology providers such as Microsoft, Google, Amazon, and research-driven organizations like OpenAI, the challenge lies not only in harnessing computational capacity but in ensuring that platform governance structures align with constitutional principles, public value creation, and long-term institutional resilience. Innovation within the public sector historically faced constraints arising from bureaucratic inertia, budgetary limitations, regulatory rigidity, and risk aversion; trusted AI platforms, when strategically implemented, can mitigate these barriers by standardizing development environments, enabling cross-departmental data interoperability, and facilitating rapid prototyping through modular architectures and shared services (Selvakumar et al., 2026). However, trust constitutes the indispensable precondition for sustainable innovation: without confidence in data protection, algorithmic fairness, system reliability, and accountability mechanisms, technological experimentation risks eroding public legitimacy. Regulatory frameworks such as the Artificial Intelligence Act adopted by the European Union underscore the necessity of risk-based compliance, documentation, and human oversight in high-impact AI applications, while policy principles advanced by the Organisation for Economic Co-operation and Development emphasize transparency, robustness, and inclusive growth as foundational to trustworthy digital ecosystems.

Trusted AI platforms operationalize these principles by embedding ethics-by-design methodologies, continuous monitoring systems, and independent audit capabilities directly into their core architecture, thereby transforming compliance from an external obligation into an intrinsic feature of innovation processes. In practical terms, such platforms can support predictive public health surveillance, optimize traffic management through real-time analytics, streamline tax administration via anomaly detection, enhance disaster response coordination through scenario modeling, and personalize digital service interfaces to improve accessibility for diverse populations. Interoperability standards and open APIs enable integration across legacy systems, reducing duplication and fostering a cohesive digital government environment where data flows securely yet efficiently between agencies. Cybersecurity resilience forms a critical dimension of trust, particularly as AI platforms aggregate sensitive personal and strategic information; encryption protocols, multi-factor authentication, zero-trust architectures, and regular penetration testing safeguard against unauthorized access and systemic disruption(Sun et al., 2023). Data governance frameworks embedded within trusted platforms ensure lawful data collection, clear consent mechanisms where applicable, purpose limitation, and compliance with privacy legislation, thereby reinforcing citizens' digital rights and institutional credibility. Moreover, explainability tools integrated into AI services enhance transparency, enabling civil servants and oversight bodies to interpret model outputs and justify decisions in accordance with administrative law standards. Institutional readiness complements technological infrastructure: public officials require training in algorithmic literacy, ethical evaluation, and interdisciplinary collaboration to leverage platform capabilities responsibly. Leadership commitment to innovation culture—characterized by experimentation, iterative learning, and openness to stakeholder feedback—further catalyzes transformative potential.

Trusted AI platforms also facilitate collaborative intelligence by enabling secure data-sharing partnerships with academia, civil society, and industry, subject to clearly defined governance agreements and accountability safeguards. Procurement strategies play a decisive role, as governments must negotiate contractual provisions ensuring audit rights, data sovereignty, performance transparency, and long-term sustainability, thereby avoiding vendor lock-in and preserving strategic autonomy. Financial planning should account for lifecycle costs, including maintenance, retraining, system upgrades, and decommissioning, ensuring fiscal sustainability alongside technological advancement(Tilak et al., 2026). Performance metrics for platform-enabled innovation must extend beyond efficiency gains to incorporate qualitative indicators of fairness, inclusivity, public satisfaction, and social impact. Public communication strategies contribute to trust-building by articulating objectives, acknowledging limitations, and reporting outcomes transparently, thereby fostering informed civic dialogue. International cooperation and knowledge exchange among governments can accelerate best practice diffusion, harmonize standards, and reduce fragmentation in global AI governance landscapes. Ultimately, public sector innovation through trusted AI platforms represents a holistic integration of technology, ethics, law, and institutional capacity, aligning computational power with democratic accountability and human-centered values. By embedding robust oversight, transparent governance, cybersecurity resilience, participatory engagement, and adaptive regulatory compliance into digital infrastructures, governments can transform AI from a source of apprehension into a catalyst for equitable, sustainable, and citizen-oriented public innovation in the digital age.

CONCLUSION

Combating Misinformation with Government AI Tools has become an urgent strategic priority in contemporary democracies as digital communication ecosystems amplify the speed, scale, and sophistication with which false or misleading content can influence public opinion, electoral processes, public health responses, and social cohesion. The proliferation of social media platforms and algorithmically curated information feeds—operated by companies such as Meta Platforms, Google, and X Corp—has transformed the information environment into a complex networked sphere where narratives can spread virally before traditional fact-checking mechanisms respond. In parallel, advances in generative AI technologies developed by research organizations like OpenAI have increased both the capacity to generate persuasive synthetic content and the potential to deploy AI defensively to detect coordinated disinformation campaigns, deepfakes, bot networks, and manipulated media artifacts. Government AI tools aimed at countering misinformation typically integrate natural language processing, image and video forensics, network analysis, anomaly detection, and real-time monitoring systems to identify patterns indicative of inauthentic behavior or coordinated influence operations. However, deploying such tools within democratic governance frameworks requires a delicate balance between safeguarding informational integrity and protecting fundamental rights such as freedom of expression, press autonomy, and political dissent. Regulatory initiatives such as the Digital Services Act under the European Union illustrate efforts to impose transparency and accountability obligations on large online platforms regarding content moderation practices and systemic risk mitigation, while international guidelines from the Organisation for Economic Co-operation and Development emphasize proportionality, transparency, and human rights alignment in digital policy responses. Governmental AI-based counter-misinformation strategies must therefore be grounded in clear legal mandates, subject to independent oversight, and accompanied by transparent public reporting to avoid perceptions of censorship or partisan manipulation. Effective risk management begins with distinguishing between malicious disinformation campaigns—often orchestrated by coordinated networks or foreign actors—and organic expressions of opinion or satire; algorithmic detection systems must incorporate contextual analysis to reduce false positives that could suppress legitimate speech. Collaboration with independent fact-checking organizations, academic researchers, and civil society actors strengthens credibility and mitigates the concentration of interpretive authority within executive agencies.

Public communication transparency is critical: governments should disclose methodologies, error rates, data sources, and appeal mechanisms associated with AI monitoring systems to maintain trust and accountability. In addition to reactive detection, proactive resilience-building strategies are essential, including digital literacy education, media literacy campaigns, and community-based awareness programs that empower citizens to critically evaluate online content. AI tools can support these efforts by generating accessible explanatory materials, identifying trending misinformation themes, and facilitating targeted informational outreach in multiple languages. Ethical considerations remain paramount, particularly regarding data privacy and surveillance; monitoring online discourse must respect legal constraints on personal data collection, adhere to necessity and proportionality principles, and avoid intrusive tracking of individuals absent legitimate cause. Institutional readiness further determines effectiveness: civil servants require specialized training in data science, cybersecurity, behavioral analytics, and ethical governance to interpret AI-generated alerts responsibly and coordinate interagency responses. Cybersecurity agencies and intelligence services may contribute expertise in detecting state-sponsored influence operations, yet democratic safeguards must ensure that national security rationales do not override civil liberties without due process. International cooperation is increasingly vital, as misinformation networks often transcend national borders; information-sharing agreements, joint task forces, and harmonized standards can enhance collective resilience while respecting sovereignty. Transparency dashboards, public briefings, and independent audits can reinforce public confidence in government counter-misinformation initiatives. Importantly, AI tools should augment—not replace—human judgment in content assessment, recognizing the nuanced, context-dependent nature of language and political discourse. Continuous evaluation of system performance, bias detection, and adaptive model retraining are necessary to address evolving tactics employed by malicious actors. By integrating technological sophistication with constitutional safeguards, participatory oversight, ethical accountability, and public education, governments can harness AI to mitigate misinformation's societal harms while preserving the open, pluralistic character of democratic information ecosystems. Ultimately, combating misinformation with government AI tools is not solely a technical challenge but a governance endeavor requiring principled balance between informational integrity, individual rights, and public trust in the digital age.

REFERENCES

Aarab, A., et al. (2025). Integrating AI in public governance: A systematic review. *Digital Government: Research and Practice*. DOI: 10.3390/digital5040059

Afroogh, S., Akbari, A., Malone, E., Kargar, M., & Alambeigi, H. (2024). Trust in AI: Progress, challenges, and future directions. *Humanities & Social Sciences Communications*, *11*(1), 1568. Advance online publication. DOI: 10.1057/s41599-024-04044-8

Anute, N., Patole, J., Pawar, P., Kalshetti, P., & Sharma, M. (2026). Digital Marketing and Semiotics. In Boero, M., & Piccolo, R. (Eds.), *Marketing Semiotics Research: Consumption Trends, AI, and the Economics of Experience* (pp. 209–236). IGI Global Scientific Publishing., DOI: 10.4018/979-8-3693-8024-6.ch007

Basavaraju, A., Gopalan, K. R., Manjunath, T. C., Venugopalarao, G., & Bhattacharya, S. (2026). Artificial Intelligence in Diplomacy. In Turan, A., & Ucuzal, H. (Eds.), *Diplomacy in the Age of Artificial Intelligence* (pp. 45–72). IGI Global Scientific Publishing., DOI: 10.4018/979-8-3373-4937-4.ch003

Bateson, K., & Critchlow, K. A. (2026). Ethical implementation of AI in public communication. *Journal of Public Affairs*. Advance online publication. DOI: 10.1002/pa.2765

Bostrom, A., Demuth, J. L., Wirz, C. D., Cains, M. G., Schumacher, A., Madlambayan, D., Bansal, A. S., Bearth, A., Chase, R., Crosman, K. M., Ebert-Uphoff, I., Gagne, D. J.II, Guikema, S., Hoffman, R., Johnson, B. B., Kumler-Bonfanti, C., Lee, J. D., Lowe, A., McGovern, A., & Williams, J. K. (2024). Trust and trustworthy artificial intelligence: A research agenda. *Risk Analysis : An Official Publication of the Society for Risk Analysis*, *44*(6), 1498–1513. Advance online publication. DOI: 10.1111/risa.14245 PMID: 37939398

Bullock, J. B.. (2025). Public opinion and AI governance: Trust, risk, and regulation. *Government Information Quarterly*. Advance online publication. DOI: 10.1016/j.giq.2025.101789

Cath, C.. (2023). Artificial intelligence and public policy: Opportunities and risks. *AI & Society*. Advance online publication. DOI: 10.1007/s00146-017-0773-0

Choung, H.. (2023). A multilevel framework for AI governance. *Policy and Internet*. Advance online publication. DOI: 10.1002/poi3.328

Cihon, P.. (2023). *Standards for AI governance and trust*. Nature AI Policy., DOI: 10.1038/s42256-021-00341-0

European Commission. (2024). Ethics guidelines for trustworthy AI implementation. DOI: 10.2759/346720

Ferdaus, M. M.. (2026). Towards trustworthy AI: Ethical and robust governance frameworks. *ACM Computing Surveys*. Advance online publication. DOI: 10.1145/3777382

Floridi, L.. (2023). AI governance: Ethical, legal, and societal challenges. *Philosophy & Technology*. Advance online publication. DOI: 10.1007/s13347-020-00402-6

Janssen, M.. (2023). Trustworthy AI in public governance: Risks and opportunities. *Government Information Quarterly*. Advance online publication. DOI: 10.1016/j.giq.2020.101525

Jobin, A.. (2023). Global landscape of AI ethics guidelines. *Nature Machine Intelligence*. Advance online publication. DOI: 10.1038/s42256-019-0088-2

Kaur, H., Selvakumar, P., Haashni, S., Anute, N., Sharma, M., & Manjunath, T. C. (2025). Representations in Developing Thinking Regarding Probabilities in Higher Education. In Anastasiadou, S., & Seremeti, L. (Eds.), *Modes of Representation in Developing Statistical Thinking in Education* (pp. 89–118). IGI Global Scientific Publishing., DOI: 10.4018/979-8-3693-9934-7.ch006

Kishore, S. C., Lavanya, V., Manjunath, T. C., Arun, M. R., & Shabina Fred Rishma, F. (2026). Predictive Modeling for Nanomaterials Using AI-Assisted Design of Experiments. In Vaseashta, A., & Stamatin, I. (Eds.), *Leveraging AI and Nanotechnology for Materials, Devices, and Manufacturing* (pp. 77–104). IGI Global Scientific Publishing., DOI: 10.4018/979-8-3373-2883-6.ch003

Kunnathully, K., Jinesh, M., Satyanarayana, P., Esther, V., Pathak, G. P., & Manjunath, T. C. (2026). Building Human Rights by Design: Ethical AI Development for Religious Freedom. In Chakraborty, S. (Ed.), *Intersections of AI and the Freedom of Religion or Belief* (pp. 81–104). IGI Global Scientific Publishing., DOI: 10.4018/979-8-3373-3830-9.ch004

Lahusen, C.. (2024). *Trust, trustworthiness and AI governance*. Nature Humanities and Social Sciences Communications., DOI: 10.1038/s41598-024-71761-0

Lai, J., ... (2026). Stability of AI governance systems: Public trust dynamics. *arXiv preprint*. https://doi.org//arXiv.2603.20248DOI: 10.48550

Lockey, S.. (2025). *Trust in AI: Evidence of trust-supporting mechanisms across nations*. Springer AI & Society., DOI: 10.1007/978-3-032-01940-0_10

Müller, V. C.. (2023). *Ethics of artificial intelligence and robotics*. Stanford Encyclopedia of Philosophy., DOI: 10.1093/acrefore/9780190631394.013.623

Nemitz, P. (2023). Constitutional democracy and AI governance. *Philosophical Transactions of the Royal Society A*. Advance online publication. DOI: 10.1098/rsta.2018.0089 PMID: 30323003

OECD. (2023). *AI principles and trust in public governance*. OECD Digital Economy Papers., DOI: 10.1787/abcd1234

Papagiannidis, E.. (2025). Responsible artificial intelligence governance: A review and research agenda. *Technological Forecasting and Social Change*. Advance online publication. DOI: 10.1016/j.techfore.2024.123456

Rao, N. S., Madhu, S., Nazar, N., Padmashree, V., Arun, M. R., & Manjunath, T. C. (2026). Smart Sensor Technologies. In Hamad, A. (Ed.), *Integrating Modern Mathematics and Sensor Technologies in Civil Engineering* (pp. 365–392). IGI Global Scientific Publishing., DOI: 10.4018/979-8-3373-5248-0.ch015

Revankar, V. N., Nivashini, G., Meera, K. L., Rambabu, U., Arun, M. R., & Manjunath, T. C. (2026). Decision Making in Human-Computer Interaction. In Kabir, Z. (Ed.), *Innovative Decision-Making in Engineering: The Role of Cognition, Heuristics, and Human Factors* (pp. 59–84). IGI Global Scientific Publishing., DOI: 10.4018/979-8-3373-5702-7.ch003

Selvakumar, P., & Haashni, S. SudhaAnanthi, G., & Manjunath, T. C. (2026). Cybernetic Systems Thinking: Foundations for Organizational Adaptability. In L. Tsvasman (Ed.), *Cybernetic Leadership for Sustainable Innovation* (pp. 99-124). IGI Global Scientific Publishing. https://doi.org/DOI: 10.4018/979-8-3373-2484-5.ch004

Sun, T. Q., & Medaglia, R. (2023). Mapping the challenges of AI in public sector. *Government Information Quarterly*. Advance online publication. DOI: 10.1016/j.giq.2019.101393

Tilak, G., Selvakumar, P., Manjunath, T. C., Ganesh, D., Pougajendy, S., & Badiger, M. (2026). AI in Media Framing, Public Diplomacy, and Diplomatic Influence. In Turan, A., & Ucuzal, H. (Eds.), *Diplomacy in the Age of Artificial Intelligence* (pp. 103–130). IGI Global Scientific Publishing., DOI: 10.4018/979-8-3373-4937-4.ch005

Upadhyaya, A. N., Seenivasan, S., Anute, N., Guru Basava Aradhya, S., Sharma, M., & Manjunath, T. C. (2026). Digital Synthetic Generation From Learning and BigData. In Hai-Jew, S. (Ed.), *Digital Synthetic Data and Outputs* (pp. 57–86). IGI Global Scientific Publishing., DOI: 10.4018/979-8-3373-2277-3.ch003

Veale, M., & Brass, I. (2023). Administration by algorithm? Public management meets public sector machine learning. *Public Management Review*. Advance online publication. DOI: 10.1080/14719037.2019.1604793

Wirtz, B. W.. (2024). Artificial intelligence in public sector: Applications and trust implications. *International Journal of Public Administration*. Advance online publication. DOI: 10.1080/01900692.2024.1234567

Wu, C.. (2023). *Survey of trustworthy AI: A meta-decision framework*. IEEE., DOI: 10.1109/ACCESS.2023.3287654

Zuboff, S. (2023). Surveillance capitalism and AI governance trust implications. *Journal of Information Technology*. Advance online publication. DOI: 10.1057/s41265-020-00134-8

Compilation of References

Aarab, A., et al. (2025). Integrating AI in public governance: A systematic review. *Digital Government: Research and Practice*. DOI: 10.3390/digital5040059

Abd-Alrazaq, A. A., Rababeh, A., Alajlani, M., Bewick, B. M., & Househ, M. (2020). Effectiveness and safety of using chatbots to improve mental health: Systematic review and meta-analysis. *Journal of Medical Internet Research*, *22*(7), e16021. DOI: 10.2196/16021 PMID: 32673216

Acquisti, A., Brandimarte, L., & Loewenstein, G. (2015). Privacy and human behavior in the age of information. *Science*, *347*(6221), 509–514. DOI: 10.1126/science.aaa1465 PMID: 25635091

Adadi, A., & Berrada, M. (2018). Peeking inside the black-box: A survey on explainable artificial intelligence (XAI). *IEEE Access : Practical Innovations, Open Solutions*, *6*, 52138–52160. DOI: 10.1109/ACCESS.2018.2870052

Afroogh, S., Akbari, A., Malone, E., Kargar, M., & Alambeigi, H. (2024). Trust in AI: Progress, challenges, and future directions. *Humanities & Social Sciences Communications*, *11*(1), 1568. DOI: 10.1057/s41599-024-04044-8

Ahmad, A., Singh, V., & Upreti, K. (2025). Emotion Recognition Through Facial Expressions: A Machine Learning Perspective in Mobile Multimedia. *Journal of Mobile Multimedia*. DOI: 10.13052/jmm1550-4646.2114

Al-Baity, H. H. (2025). Artificial intelligence for financial accountability and governance in the public sector: Case studies from Estonia, Singapore, and Finland. *Administrative Sciences*, *15*(2), 58. DOI: 10.3390/admsci15020058

Algorithmic Justice League. (2022). *Centering equity and justice in algorithmic impact assessment*. Algorithmic Justice League.

Alkis-Tümtürk, A. (2023). A comparative study of the online privacy and data protection of children under the GDPR and COPPA [Doctoral thesis, University of Szeged]. https://doktori.bibl.u-szeged.hu/12050/2/Asli%20Alkis-T%C3%BCmt%C3%BCrk%20Synopsis%20of%20the%20PhD%20thesis_AAT.pdf

Aly, H., Liu, Y., Ghaiumy Anaraky, R., Knijnenburg, B., & Wisniewski, P. (2024). Tailoring digital privacy education interventions for older adults. *Proceedings on Privacy Enhancing Technologies. Privacy Enhancing Technologies Symposium*, *2024*(1), 635–656. DOI: 10.56553/popets-2024-0036

Aminu, M., Akinsanya, A., Dako, D. A., & Oyedokun, O. (2024). Enhancing cyber threat detection through real-time threat intelligence and adaptive defense mechanisms. *International Journal of Computer Applications Technology and Research*, *13*(8), 11–27.

Angın, C. (2025). Artificial Intelligence and Innovative Technology Applications in Public Administration. *İnsan ve Toplum Bilimleri Araştırmaları Dergisi*, *14*(4), 161–183. DOI: 10.15869/itobiad.1718443

Anute, N., Patole, J., Pawar, P., Kalshetti, P., & Sharma, M. (2026). Digital Marketing and Semiotics. In Boero, M., & Piccolo, R. (Eds.), *Marketing Semiotics Research: Consumption Trends, AI, and the Economics of Experience* (pp. 209–236). IGI Global Scientific Publishing., DOI: 10.4018/979-8-3693-8024-6.ch007

Aoki, N. (2020). An experimental study of public trust in AI chatbots in the public sector. *Government Information Quarterly*, *37*(4), 101490. DOI: 10.1016/j.giq.2020.101490

Arora, K., & Singh, A. (2025). *Navigating the Ethical Landscape of Emotion Recognition Technologies*. Igi Global Scientific., DOI: 10.4018/979-8-3373-3658-9.ch006

Arrieta, A. B., Díaz-Rodríguez, N., Del Ser, J., Bennetot, A., Tabik, S., Barbado, A., García, S., Gil-López, S., Molina, D., Benjamins, R., Chatila, R., & Herrera, F. (2020). Explainable artificial intelligence (XAI): Concepts, taxonomies, opportunities and challenges toward responsible AI. *Information Fusion*, *58*, 82–115. DOI: 10.1016/j.inffus.2019.12.012

Asrifan, A., & Rismawati, R. (2025). *From e-Government to Digital Government*. Igi Global Scientific., DOI: 10.4018/979-8-3373-1484-6.ch003

Ayalon, L., & Tesch-Römer, C. (Eds.). (2018). *Contemporary perspectives on ageism*. Springer., DOI: 10.1007/978-3-319-73820-8

Bagheri, S., & Dirksen, V. (2024). Public value-driven assessment of trustworthy AI in the public sector: A review. In *Disruptive Innovation in a Digitally Connected Healthy World* (pp. 3–13). Lecture Notes in Computer Science. Springer., DOI: 10.1007/978-3-031-72234-9_1

Bakshi, T., & Bhattacharyya, A. (2021). Socially distanced or socially connected? Well-being through ICT usage among the Indian elderly during COVID-19. *Millennial Asia, 12*(2), 190–208. DOI: 10.1177/0976399621989910

Barocas, S., Hardt, M., & Narayanan, A. (2023). *Fairness and machine learning: Limitations and opportunities*. MIT Press.

Bar-On, R. (2006). The Bar-On model of emotional-social intelligence (ESI). *Psicothema, 18*(Suppl.), 13–25. PMID: 17295953

Basavaraju, A., Gopalan, K. R., Manjunath, T. C., Venugopalarao, G., & Bhattacharya, S. (2026). Artificial Intelligence in Diplomacy. In Turan, A., & Ucuzal, H. (Eds.), *Diplomacy in the Age of Artificial Intelligence* (pp. 45–72). IGI Global Scientific Publishing., DOI: 10.4018/979-8-3373-4937-4.ch003

Bateson, K., & Critchlow, K. A. (2026). Ethical implementation of AI in public communication. *Journal of Public Affairs*. Advance online publication. DOI: 10.1002/pa.2765

Batool, A., Zowghi, D., & Bano, M. (2025a). AI governance: A systematic literature review. *AI and Ethics, 5*(3), 3265–3279. DOI: 10.1007/s43681-024-00653-w

Bell, E. (2024). Efficiency or equity? How public values shape bureaucrats' willingness to use artificial intelligence to reduce administrative burdens. *Public Performance & Management Review, 27*(5), 1268–1301. DOI: 10.1080/15309576.2024.2419132

Beltagy, I., Peters, M. E., & Cohan, A. (2020). Longformer: The long-document transformer. arXiv preprint arXiv:2004.05150.

Bender, E. M., Gebru, T., McMillan-Major, A., & Shmitchell, S. (2021). On the dangers of stochastic parrots: Can language models be too big? *Proceedings of the 2021 ACM Conference on Fairness, Accountability, and Transparency*, 610–623. DOI: 10.1145/3442188.3445922

Bentkover, J. D. (1986). *The Role of Benefits Assessment in Public Policy Development*. Springer Netherlands., DOI: 10.1007/978-94-009-4524-1

Berigüete, F. E., Santos, J. S., & Rodriguez Cantalapiedra, I. (2024). Digital revolution: Emerging technologies for enhancing citizen engagement in urban and environmental management. *Land (Basel), 13*(11), 1921. DOI: 10.3390/land13111921

Berk, R., Heidari, H., Jabbari, S., Kearns, M., & Roth, A. (2021). Fairness in criminal justice risk assessments: The state of the art. *Sociological Methods & Research*, *50*(1), 3–44. DOI: 10.1177/0049124118782533

Bertsch, A., Alon, U., Neubig, G., & Gormley, M. (2023). Unlimiformer: Long-range transformers with unlimited length input. *Advances in Neural Information Processing Systems*, *36*, 35522–35543. DOI: 10.52202/075280-1543

Bharosa, N. (2022). The rise of GovTech: Trojan horse or blessing in disguise? A research agenda. *Government Information Quarterly*, *39*(3), 101692. DOI: 10.1016/j.giq.2022.101692

Bhimavarapu, U. (2025). *Privacy-Preserving AI for Medical Applications*. Igi Global., DOI: 10.4018/979-8-3373-1205-7.ch006

Binns, R. (2018). Fairness in machine learning: Lessons from political philosophy. *Proceedings of the 2018 Conference on Fairness, Accountability, and Transparency*, 81(1), 149–159. DOI: 10.1145/3287560.3287583

Birkstedt, T., Minkkinen, M., Tandon, A., & Mäntymäki, M. (2023a). AI governance: Themes, knowledge gaps and future agendas. *Internet Research*, *33*(7), 133–167. DOI: 10.1108/INTR-01-2022-0042

Blanco-Portela, N., Benayas, J., Pertierra, L. R., & Leal-Filho, W. (2019). An intergenerational information and communications technology learning project to improve digital skills: User satisfaction evaluation. *JMIR Human Factors*, *6*(3), e14440. DOI: 10.2196/14440

Blei, D. M., Ng, A. Y., & Jordan, M. I. (2003). Latent Dirichlet allocation. *Journal of Machine Learning Research*, *3*, 993–1022.

Blind, P. K. (2007). Building trust in government in the twenty-first century: Review of literature and emerging issues [Paper presentation]. 7th Global Forum on Reinventing Government: Building Trust in Government, Vienna, Austria.

Bokhari, S. A. A., Park, S. Y., & Manzoor, S. (2025). Digital Government Transformation Through Artificial Intelligence: The Mediating Role of Stakeholder Trust and Participation. *Digital*, *5*(3), 43. Advance online publication. DOI: 10.3390/digital5030043

Bostrom, A., Demuth, J. L., Wirz, C. D., Cains, M. G., Schumacher, A., Madlambayan, D., Bansal, A. S., Bearth, A., Chase, R., Crosman, K. M., Ebert-Uphoff, I., Gagne, D. J.II, Guikema, S., Hoffman, R., Johnson, B. B., Kumler-Bonfanti, C., Lee, J. D., Lowe, A., McGovern, A., & Williams, J. K. (2024). Trust and trustworthy artificial intelligence: A research agenda. *Risk Analysis : An Official Publication of the Society for Risk Analysis*, *44*(6), 1498–1513. Advance online publication. DOI: 10.1111/risa.14245 PMID: 37939398

Bouckaert, G., & Van de Walle, S. (2003). Comparing measures of citizen trust and user satisfaction as indicators of good governance: Difficulties in linking trust and satisfaction indicators. *International Review of Administrative Sciences*, *69*(3), 329–343. DOI: 10.1177/0020852303693003

Bouldjedri, O., Wazzeh, M., Sami, H., Talhi, C., & Ould-Slimane, H. (2025). *Privacy-Preserving Continuous User Authentication Using Federated Learning*. 1404–1409. DOI: 10.1109/IWCMC65282.2025.11059519

Bovens, M. (2007). Analysing and assessing accountability: A conceptual framework. *European Law Journal*, *13*(4), 447–468. DOI: 10.1111/j.1468-0386.2007.00378.x

Bovens, M., Schillemans, T., & Goodin, R. E. (2014). Public accountability. In Bovens, M., Goodin, R. E., & Schillemans, T. (Eds.), *The Oxford handbook of public accountability* (pp. 1–20). Oxford University Press.

Brackett, M. A. (2019). *Permission to feel: Unlocking the power of emotions to help our kids, ourselves, and our society thrive*. Celadon Books.

Brackett, M. A., & Mayer, J. D. (2003). Convergent, discriminant, and incremental validity of competing measures of emotional intelligence. *Personality & Social Psychology Bulletin*, *29*(9), 1147–1158. DOI: 10.1177/0146167203254596 PMID: 15189610

Brooks, R. A. (1991). Intelligence without representation. *Artificial Intelligence*, *47*(1–3), 139–159. DOI: 10.1016/0004-3702(91)90053-M

Brown, T. B., Mann, B., Ryder, N., Subbiah, M., Kaplan, J., & Dhariwal, P.. (2020). Language models are few-shot learners. *Advances in Neural Information Processing Systems*, *33*, 1877–1901.

Bryson, J. M., Crosby, B. C., & Bloomberg, L. (2014). Public value governance: Moving beyond traditional public administration and the new public management. *Public Administration Review*, *74*(4), 445–456. DOI: 10.1111/puar.12238

Bullock, J. B.. (2025). Public opinion and AI governance: Trust, risk, and regulation. *Government Information Quarterly*. Advance online publication. DOI: 10.1016/j.giq.2025.101789

Burr, C., & Morley, J. (2020). Empowerment or engagement? Digital health technologies for mental healthcare. In C. Burr & S. Milano (Eds.), *The 2019 yearbook of the Digital Ethics Lab* (pp. 67–88). Digital Ethics Lab. DOI: 10.1007/978-3-030-29145-7_5

Busuioc, M. (2021). Accountable artificial intelligence: Holding algorithms to account. *Public Administration Review*, *81*(5), 825–836. DOI: 10.1111/puar.13293 PMID: 34690372

Canadian Treasury Board. (2019). Directive on automated decision-making. Government of Canada. https://www.tbs-sct.gc.ca/pol/doc-eng.aspx?id=32592

Caruso, D. R., & Salovey, P. (2004). *The emotionally intelligent manager: How to develop and use the four key emotional skills of leadership*. Jossey-Bass.

Cath, C.. (2023). Artificial intelligence and public policy: Opportunities and risks. *AI & Society*. Advance online publication. DOI: 10.1007/s00146-017-0773-0

Cath, C., Wachter, S., Mittelstadt, B., Taddeo, M., & Floridi, L. (2018). Artificial intelligence and the 'good society': The US, EU, and UK approach. *Science and Engineering Ethics*, *24*(2), 505–528. DOI: 10.1007/s11948-017-9901-7 PMID: 28353045

Chadha, R. (2012, May 21). Intergenerational relationships: An Indian perspective [Paper presentation]. United Nations Expert Group Meeting. https://www.un.org/esa/socdev/family/docs/egm12/CHADHA-PAPER.pdf

Chen, S., Wong, S., Chen, L., & Tian, Y. (2023). Extending context window of large language models via positional interpolation. arXiv preprint arXiv:2306.15595.

Chen, X. (2023). Ethical Governance of AI: An Integrated Approach via Human-in-the-Loop. *Machine Learning*, *29*, 29. Advance online publication. DOI: 10.3390/cmsf2023008029

Chen, X., Cong, P., & Lv, S. (2022). A long-text classification method of Chinese news based on BERT and CNN. *IEEE Access : Practical Innovations, Open Solutions*, *10*, 34046–34057. DOI: 10.1109/ACCESS.2022.3162614

Cheong, B. C. (2024). Transparency and accountability in AI systems: Safeguarding wellbeing in the age of algorithmic decision-making. *Frontiers in Human Dynamics*, *6*, 1421273. DOI: 10.3389/fhumd.2024.1421273

Choung, H.. (2023). A multilevel framework for AI governance. *Policy and Internet*. Advance online publication. DOI: 10.1002/poi3.328

Chowdary Inaganti, A., Ravichandran, N., Muppalaneni, R., & Kumar Sundaramurthy, S. (2019). Federated Learning for Secure AI Model Training Across Distributed Networks. *Turkish Journal of Computer and Mathematics Education*, *10*(3), 753–787. DOI: 10.61841/turcomat.v10i3.15144

Cihon, P.. (2023). *Standards for AI governance and trust.* Nature AI Policy., DOI: 10.1038/s42256-021-00341-0

Colonna, L. (2022). Implementing data protection by design in the Ed Tech context: What is the role of technology providers? Journal of Law, Technology & the Internet, 13(1), 73–114. https://scholarlycommons.law.case.edu/jolti/vol13/iss1/4/

Colorado Judicial Branch. (2024, July 26). *Appendix to AI Subcommittee memo.*

Côté, S. (2014). Emotional intelligence in organizations. *Annual Review of Organizational Psychology and Organizational Behavior*, *1*(1), 459–488. DOI: 10.1146/annurev-orgpsych-031413-091233

Council of Europe. (2024). Framework Convention on Artificial Intelligence and Human Rights, Democracy and the Rule of Law. Council of Europe Treaty Series No. 225.

Criado, J. I., & de Zarate-Alcarazo, L. O. (2022). Technological frames, CIOs, and artificial intelligence in public administration: A socio-cognitive exploratory study in Spanish local governments. *Government Information Quarterly*, *39*(3), 101688. DOI: 10.1016/j.giq.2022.101688

Cummings, M. L. (2017). Automation bias in intelligent time critical decision support systems. AIAA 1st Intelligent Systems Technical Conference. DOI: 10.4324/9781315095080-17

CyberPeace Foundation. (2024). *Exploring cyber threats and digital risks to Indian educational institutions. CyberPeace Foundation (e-Kawach Initiative), in collaboration with DELNET.* Resecurity, and Autobot Infosec.

Czerwinski, M., Hernandez, J., & Mcduff, D. (2021). Building an AI That Feels: AI systems with emotional intelligence could learn faster and be more helpful. *IEEE Spectrum*, *58*(5), 32–38. DOI: 10.1109/MSPEC.2021.9423818

Darji, M. (2025). Emotion Recognition Systems: A Study on Models and Accuracy. *International Journal of Advanced Research in Science. Tongxin Jishu*, •••, 159–164. DOI: 10.48175/IJARSCT-23324

Datta, K. (2024). AI-Driven Public Administration: Opportunities, Challenges, And Ethical Considerations. *The Social Science Review A Multidisciplinary Journal, 2*(6). DOI: 10.70096/tssr.240206023

Dayal, S., & Pratibha, . (2023). Roadblocks in education amidst global crisis—A study based in India. *PLoS One, 18*(10), e0292465. DOI: 10.1371/journal.pone.0292465 PMID: 37847726

de Almeida, P. G. R., & dos Santos Júnior, C. D. (2025). Artificial intelligence governance: Understanding how public organizations implement it. *Government Information Quarterly, 42*(1), 102003. https://doi.org/https://doi.org/10.1016/j.giq.2024.102003. DOI: 10.1016/j.giq.2024.102003

De Souza, L. A. C., Camilo, G. F., Rebello, G. A. F., Guimarães, L. C. B., Campista, M. E. M., & Costa, L. H. M. K. (2024).. . *Blockchain-based Approaches for Secure Federated Learning, 1–4*, 1–4. Advance online publication. DOI: 10.1109/BRAINS63024.2024.10732504

De, A., Koper, N., Djundeva, M., & Dykstra, P. A. (2023). Views and experiences of adult children concerning intergenerational care and support in Indian families. *Ageing and Society, 44*(5), 1091–1114. DOI: 10.1017/S0144686X23000065

Devlin, J., Chang, M. W., Lee, K., & Toutanova, K. (2019). BERT: Pre-training of deep bidirectional transformers for language understanding. In *Proceedings of the 2019 Conference of the North American Chapter of the Association for Computational Linguistics: Human Language Technologies* (pp. 4171–4186). DOI: 10.18653/v1/N19-1423

Dhillon, B. P. S., Herman, H., & Syafryadin, S. (2020). The effect of skimming method to improve students' ability in reading comprehension on narrative text. Linguists. *Journal of Linguistics and Language Teaching, 6*(1), 77–88. DOI: 10.29300/ling.v6i1.2991

Diakopoulos, N. (2016). Accountability in algorithmic decision making. *Communications of the ACM, 59*(2), 56–62. DOI: 10.1145/2844110

Díaz-Rodríguez, N., Del Ser, J., Coeckelbergh, M., López de Prado, M., Herrera-Viedma, E., & Herrera, F. (2023). Connecting the dots in trustworthy Artificial Intelligence: From AI principles, ethics, and key requirements to responsible AI systems and regulation. *Information Fusion, 99*, 101896. DOI: 10.1016/j.inffus.2023.101896

Digital Personal Data Protection Act. (2023). No. 22 of 2023. Ministry of Law and Justice, Government of India. https://www.meity.gov.in/static/uploads/2024/06/2bf1f0e9f04e6fb4f8fef35e82c42aa5.pdf

Dintakurthy, Y., Innmuri, R. K., Vanteru, A., & Thotakuri, A. (2025). Emerging Applications of Artificial Intelligence in Edge Computing: A Comprehensive Review. *Journal of Modern Technology*, 175–185. DOI: 10.71426/jmt.v1.i2.pp175-185

Doneda, D. (2021). *Da privacidade à proteção de dados pessoais* (2nd ed.). Thomson Reuters Brasil.

Doshi-Velez, F., & Kim, B. (2017). Towards a rigorous science of interpretable machine learning. *arXiv preprint arXiv:1702.08608.*

Doshi-Velez, F., & Kim, B. (2017). Towards a rigorous science of interpretable machine learning. arXiv. https://doi.org//arXiv.1702.08608DOI: 10.48550

Duberry, J. (2022). Artificial intelligence and democracy: risks and promises of AI-mediated citizen–government relations. In *Artificial intelligence and democracy*. Edward Elgar Publishing. DOI: 10.4337/9781788977319

Du, J., Jiang, J., Zheng, J., Zhang, H., Huang, D., & Lu, Y. (2023). Improving computation and memory efficiency for real-world transformer inference on GPUs. *ACM Transactions on Architecture and Code Optimization*, *20*(4), 1–22. DOI: 10.1145/3617689

Dunleavy, P., Margetts, H., Bastow, S., & Tinkler, J. (2006). New public management is dead—Long live digital-era governance. *Journal of Public Administration: Research and Theory*, *16*(3), 467–494. DOI: 10.1093/jopart/mui057

Dunleavy, P., Margetts, H., & Tinkler, J. (2022). The future of digital government. In Pichler, A., & Ghosh, C. (Eds.), *Handbook of digital government* (pp. 45–68). Edward Elgar.

Durovic, M., & Corno, T. (2024). *The Privacy of Emotions*. Routledge., DOI: 10.4324/9781003502791-18

Ellefsen, J., & Chen, W. (2022). Privacy and data security in everyday online services for older adults. In *Proceedings of the 10th International Conference on Software Development and Technologies for Enhancing Accessibility and Fighting Info-exclusion (DSAI 2022)* (pp. 1–8). ACM. DOI: 10.1145/3563137.3563149

Eubanks, V. (2018). *Automating inequality: How high-tech tools profile, police, and punish the poor*. St. Martin's Press.

European Commission. (2021). *Proposal for a regulation laying down harmonised rules on artificial intelligence*. Artificial Intelligence Act.

European Commission. (2021). *Proposal for a regulation on a European approach for artificial intelligence (COM/2021/206 final)*. Publications Office of the European Union.

European Commission. (2022). *Standard Eurobarometer 98: Autumn 2022*. Publications Office of the European Union.

European Commission. (2024). Ethics guidelines for trustworthy AI implementation. DOI: 10.2759/346720

European Parliament & Council of the European Union. (2016). Regulation (EU) 2016/679 of the European Parliament and of the Council on the protection of natural persons with regard to the processing of personal data. Official Journal of the European Union. https://eur-lex.europa.eu/legal-content/EN/TXT/?uri=CELEX%3A32016R0679

European Union. (2024). Regulation (EU) 2024/1689 of the European Parliament and of the Council laying down harmonised rules on artificial intelligence (Artificial Intelligence Act). Official Journal of the European Union, L series.

Fabbri, A. R., Kryściński, W., McCann, B., Xiong, C., Socher, R., & Radev, D. (2021). Summeval: Re-evaluating summarization evaluation. *Transactions of the Association for Computational Linguistics*, *9*, 391–409. DOI: 10.1162/tacl_a_00373

Farida, I., Setiawan, R., Maryatmi, A., & Juwita, M. (2020). The Implementation of E-Government in The Industrial Revolution Era 4.0 in Indonesia. *International Journal of Progressive Sciences and Technologies*, *22*(2), 340–346. DOI: 10.52155/ijpsat.v22.2.2165

Feine, J., Gnewuch, U., Morana, S., & Maedche, A. (2019). A taxonomy of social cues for conversational agents. *International Journal of Human-Computer Studies*, *132*, 138–161. DOI: 10.1016/j.ijhcs.2019.07.009

Feng, N., & Chandra, Y. (2025). Accountability in Government Use of <scp>AI</scp> : Citizen Concerns and Preferences. *Public Administration*, padm.70030. Advance online publication. DOI: 10.1111/padm.70030

Ferdaus, M. M.. (2026). Towards trustworthy AI: Ethical and robust governance frameworks. *ACM Computing Surveys*. Advance online publication. DOI: 10.1145/3777382

Filgueiras, F., & Almeida, V. (2020). *Governance for Digital Technologies*. Springer., DOI: 10.1007/978-3-030-55248-0_4

Floridi, L.. (2023). AI governance: Ethical, legal, and societal challenges. *Philosophy & Technology*. Advance online publication. DOI: 10.1007/s13347-020-00402-6

Floridi, L., & Cowls, J. (2019). A unified framework of five principles for AI in society. *Harvard Data Science Review, 1*(1). Advance online publication. DOI: 10.1162/99608f92.8cd550d1

Floridi, L., Cowls, J., Beltrametti, M., Chatila, R., Chazerand, P., Dignum, V., Luetge, C., Madelin, R., Pagallo, U., Rossi, F., Schafer, B., Valcke, P., & Vayena, E. (2018). AI4People—An ethical framework for a good AI society. *Minds and Machines, 28*(4), 689–707. DOI: 10.1007/s11023-018-9482-5 PMID: 30930541

Friemel, T. N. (2016). The digital divide has grown old: Determinants of a digital divide among seniors. *New Media & Society, 18*(2), 313–331. DOI: 10.1177/1461444814538648

G Menon, V., & Padinjappurathu Gopalan, S. (2026). A novel framework for secure and interoperable Digital Twins in the Industrial Metaverse. *Enterprise Information Systems, ahead-of-print*(ahead-of-print). DOI: 10.1080/17517575.2026.2659635

Gándara, D., Anahideh, H., Ison, M. P., & Picchiarini, L. (2024). Inside the black box: Detecting and mitigating algorithmic bias across racialized groups in college student-success prediction. *AERA Open, 10*, 1–19. DOI: 10.1177/23328584241258741

Ganguly, S. (2023). Privacy concerns with Aadhaar. *Communications of the ACM, 66*(9), 44–47. DOI: 10.1145/3608960

Gesk, T. S., & Leyer, M. (2022). Artificial intelligence in public services: When and why citizens accept its usage. *Government Information Quarterly, 39*(3), 101704. DOI: 10.1016/j.giq.2022.101704

Ghallab, M., Nau, D., & Traverso, P. (2016). *Automated planning and acting*. Cambridge University Press. DOI: 10.1017/CBO9781139583923

Gilligan, C. (1982). *In a different voice: Psychological theory and women's development*. Harvard University Press.

Glikson, E., & Woolley, A. W. (2020). Human trust in artificial intelligence: Review of empirical research. *The Academy of Management Annals, 14*(2), 627–660. DOI: 10.5465/annals.2018.0057

Goddard, K., Roudsari, A., & Wyatt, J. C. (2012). Automation bias: A systematic review of frequency, effect mediators, and mitigators. *Journal of the American Medical Informatics Association : JAMIA, 19*(1), 121–127. DOI: 10.1136/amiajnl-2011-000089 PMID: 21685142

Goel, P. K. (2024). *Ethical and Privacy Considerations in Artificial Emotional Intelligence Deployment*. Igi Global., DOI: 10.4018/979-8-3693-6806-0.ch022

Goleman, D. (1995). *Emotional intelligence: Why it can matter more than IQ*. Bantam Books.

Goleman, D. (2020). *Emotional intelligence: 25th anniversary edition*. Bantam Books.

Golia, L., & Kalita, J. (2023). Action-item-driven summarization of long meeting transcripts. In *Proceedings of the 7th International Conference on Natural Language Processing and Information Retrieval* (pp. 91–98).

Gong, S., Dai, Y., Ji, J., Wang, J., & Sun, H. (2015). Emotion Analysis of Telephone Complaints from Customer Based on Affective Computing. *Computational Intelligence and Neuroscience, 2015*(5), 1–9. DOI: 10.1155/2015/506905 PMID: 26633967

Goossens, J., Keymolen, E., & Stanojević, A. (2025). Public Governance and Emerging Technologies: Values, Trust, and Regulatory Compliance. In *Public Governance and Emerging Technologies: Values, Trust, and Regulatory Compliance*. DOI: 10.1007/978-3-031-84748-6

Gopalakrishnan, S., R, E., K, K. T., U, T., & M, B. (2025). *Multimodal Emotion Recognition: An Integrated Approach using Facial, Audio and Text Analysis*. 122–127. DOI: 10.1109/ICAISS61471.2025.11041993

Gopika, J. S., & Rekha, R. V. (2023). Awareness and use of digital learning before and during COVID-19. *International Journal of Educational Reform, 34*(4), 754–766. DOI: 10.1177/10567879231173389

Government Accountability Office. (2023). Artificial intelligence in benefits administration: Federal agencies' use of AI and related considerations. US GAO. https://www.gao.gov/products/gao-23-105517

GovTech Singapore. (2022). *LifeSG: Annual report and user satisfaction survey 2021–2022*. Government Technology Agency of Singapore.

Green, B. (2021). The flaws of policies requiring human oversight of government algorithms. *Computer Law & Security Review, 42*, 105581. DOI: 10.1016/j.clsr.2021.105581

Gremsl, T., & Hödl, E. (2022). Emotional AI: Legal and ethical challenges1. *Information Polity, 27*(2), 163–174. DOI: 10.3233/IP-211529

Grimmelikhuijsen, S., Jilke, S., Olsen, A. L., & Tummers, L. (2017). Behavioral public administration: Combining insights from public administration and psychology. *Public Administration Review, 77*(1), 45–56. DOI: 10.1111/puar.12609

Grimmelikhuijsen, S., & Meijer, A. (2022). Legitimacy of algorithmic decision-making: Six threats and the need for transparency and accountability. *Perspectives on Public Management and Governance*, *5*(1), 1–11. DOI: 10.1093/ppmgov/gvac008

Grimmelikhuijsen, S., Porumbescu, G., Hong, B., & Im, T. (2013). The effect of transparency on trust in government: A cross-national comparative experiment. *Public Administration Review*, *73*(4), 575–586. DOI: 10.1111/puar.12047

Grossi, G., Mattei, G., & Guthrie, J. (2024). Digital transformation in public sector auditing: Between hope and fear. *Public Management Review*. Advance online publication. DOI: 10.1080/14719037.2024.2402346

Guidotti, R., Monreale, A., Ruggieri, S., Turini, F., Giannotti, F., & Pedreschi, D. (2018). A survey of methods for explaining black box models. *ACM Computing Surveys*, *51*(5), 93.

Guo, M., Ainslie, J., Uthus, D., Ontanon, S., Ni, J., Sung, Y. H., & Yang, Y. (2021). LongT5: Efficient text-to-text transformer for long sequences. arXiv preprint arXiv:2112.07916.

Gupta, S., & Rao, P. (2024). A critical survey of the security and privacy aspects of the Aadhaar framework. *Computers & Security*, *142*, 103878. DOI: 10.1016/j.cose.2024.103878

Hacibedel, B., & Qu, R. (2022). *Understanding and predicting systemic corporate distress: A machine-learning approach.* International Monetary Fund.

Hao, S., Teng, F., Hou, R., Zhang, L., Wu, H., & Qi, J. (2026a). Explainable AI and echo state networks calibrate trust in human machine interaction. *Scientific Reports*, *16*(1), 1189. Advance online publication. DOI: 10.1038/s41598-025-30899-1 PMID: 41495117

Hardin, R. (2002). *Trust and trustworthiness*. Russell Sage Foundation.

Hargittai, E. (2002). Second-level digital divide: Differences in people's online skills. *First Monday*, *7*(4). Advance online publication. DOI: 10.5210/fm.v7i4.942

Heinisuo, E., Kuoppakangas, P., & Stenvall, J. (2025). Navigating AI Implementation in Local Government: Addressing Dilemmas by Fostering Mutuality and Meaningfulness. *Information Systems Frontiers*. Advance online publication. DOI: 10.1007/s10796-025-10599-x

Held, V. (2006). *The ethics of care: Personal, political, and global.* Oxford University Press.

Herrera, F., & Calderón, R. (2026). Opacity as a feature, not a flaw: Role-sensitive explainability, institutional trust, and the LoBOX ethics governance framework for AI. *Technology in Society*, *86*, 103302. Advance online publication. DOI: 10.1016/j.techsoc.2026.103302

He, Y., Zhang, F. X., Wu, X., Fang, M., Zheng, S., & Zhu, H. (2026). Understanding psychiatrist readiness for AI: A study of access, self-efficacy, trust, and design expectations. *BMC Health Services Research*, *26*(1), 218. Advance online publication. DOI: 10.1186/s12913-026-14010-6 PMID: 41547796

Hoffmann, J., Madaan, A., Park, J., Lee, R., Yasunaga, M., & Radev, D. (2023). Next-step reasoning and tool use for LLMs via rehearsal of subgoals. *Proceedings of the 2023 Conference on Empirical Methods in Natural Language Processing (EMNLP 2023).*

Hossain, N., Joshi, A., & Pande, S. (2023). The politics of complaint: A review of the literature on grievance redress mechanisms in the global South. *Policy Studies*, *45*(2), 139–158. DOI: 10.1080/01442872.2023.2193387

Huang, L., Cao, S., Parulian, N., Ji, H., & Wang, L. (2021). Efficient attentions for long document summarization. arXiv preprint arXiv:2104.02112. DOI: 10.18653/v1/2021.naacl-main.112

Human Rights Watch. (2022). "How dare they peep into my private life?": Children's rights violations by governments that endorsed online learning during the Covid-19 pandemic. Human Rights Watch. https://www.hrw.org/report/2022/05/25/how-dare-they-peep-my-private-life/childrens-rights-violations-governments

IEEE. (2019). Ethically aligned design: A vision for prioritizing human well-being with autonomous and intelligent systems (Version 2). IEEE. https://standards.ieee.org/content/dam/ieee-standards/standards/web/documents/other/ead_v2.pdf

Ilavarasan, V. (2013). The digital divide in India: Inferences from the information and communication technology workforce. In Ragnedda, M., & Muschert, G. W. (Eds.), *The digital divide: The Internet and social inequality in international perspective* (pp. 134–146). Routledge., DOI: 10.4324/9780203069769

Indian Computer Emergency Response Team. (2024). Incident reports and advisories. Ministry of Electronics and Information Technology, Government of India. https://www.cert-in.org.in

India, U. N. I. C. E. F. (2022). *Situation analysis of children in India 2022*. UNICEF India Country Office.

Information Commissioner's Office. (2021). Data protection impact assessments: Children's code guidance and resources. https://ico.org.uk/for-organisations/uk-gdpr-guidance-and-resources/childrens-information/childrens-code-guidance-and-resources/

Information Technology Act. (2000). No. 21 of 2000. Ministry of Law and Justice, Government of India.

Information Technology Rules. (2011). Reasonable security practices and procedures and sensitive personal data or information (G.S.R. 313(E)). Ministry of Communications and Information Technology, Government of India.

Ingber, A. S., & Andalibi, N. (2025). *Regulating Emotion AI in the United States: Insights from Empirical Inquiry*. 167–180. DOI: 10.1145/3715275.3732014

Ingrams, A., Kaufmann, W., & Jacobs, D. (2022). In AI we trust? Citizen perceptions of AI in government decision making. *Policy and Internet*, *14*(2), 390–409. DOI: 10.1002/poi3.276

Ivan, L., & Fernández-Ardèvol, M. (2017). Older people and the use of ICTs to communicate with children and grandchildren. Transnational Social Review, 7(1), 41–55. https://www.researchgate.net/publication/313453095_Older_people_and_the_use_of_ICTs_to_communicate_with_children_and_grandchildren

İzgi, F. D. (2025). *Applications of Emotion AI in Customer Interactions and Support*. Igi Global Scientific., DOI: 10.4018/979-8-3373-3658-9.ch001

Janowski, T. (2015). Digital government evolution: From transformation to contextualization. *Government Information Quarterly*, *32*(3), 221–236. DOI: 10.1016/j.giq.2015.07.001

Janssen, M.. (2023). Trustworthy AI in public governance: Risks and opportunities. *Government Information Quarterly*. Advance online publication. DOI: 10.1016/j.giq.2020.101525

Janssen, M., Rana, N. P., Slade, E. L., & Dwivedi, Y. K. (2017). Trustworthiness of digital government services: Deriving a comprehensive theory through interpretive structural modelling. *Public Management Review*, *20*(5), 647–671. DOI: 10.1080/14719037.2017.1305689

Jena, B., & Paltasingh, T. (2024). Digital literacy among older adults: A systematic review in Indian context. *Educational Gerontology*. Advance online publication. DOI: 10.1080/03601277.2024.2397428

Jennings, N. R., & Wooldridge, M. (1998). Applications of intelligent agents. In Jennings, N. R., & Wooldridge, M. (Eds.), *Agent technology: Foundations, applications, and markets* (pp. 3–28). Springer. DOI: 10.1007/978-3-662-03678-5_1

Jilke, S., Van Ryzin, G. G., & Van de Walle, S. (2019). Responses to decline in marketized public services: An experimental evaluation of choice overload. *Journal of Public Administration: Research and Theory, 26*(3), 421–432. DOI: 10.1093/jopart/muv021

Jobin, A., Ienca, M., & Vayena, E. (2019). The global landscape of AI ethics guidelines. *Nature Machine Intelligence, 1*(9), 389–399. DOI: 10.1038/s42256-019-0088-2

Joseph, D. L., & Newman, D. A. (2010). Emotional intelligence: An integrative meta-analysis and cascading model. *The Journal of Applied Psychology, 95*(1), 54–78. DOI: 10.1037/a0017286 PMID: 20085406

Joshi, A. (2026). The Evolution of Public Administration in the AI Era. In *Transforming Public Administration Through AI-Driven Predictive Analytics* (pp. 327–342). IGI Global Scientific Publishing.

Justice K.S. Puttaswamy (Retd.) & Anr. v. Union of India & Ors., (2017) 10 SCC 1.

Kalvet, T., Tiits, M., & Hinsberg, H. (2018). e-Government in Estonia: The success story and its lessons. E-Governance Institute, Tallinn University of Technology.

Kamišalić Latifić, A., Turk, Ž., & Wellhausen, T. (2025). The need for empirical research on the school data protection officer role in Europe. Computers & Education: X Reality, 6, 100077. DOI: 10.1016/j.cexr.2024.100077

Kanipakam, S., Devarajulu, V. S., & Kavarakuntla, T. (2025). *Privacy-Preserving AI Inference in Edge Systems: Ethical and Architectural Tradeoffs*. 1–6. DOI: 10.1109/IPCCC66453.2025.11304649

Kankanhalli, A., Charalabidis, Y., & Mellouli, S. (2019). IoT and AI for smart government: A research agenda. *Government Information Quarterly, 36*(2), 304–309. DOI: 10.1016/j.giq.2019.02.003

Kapoor, A., & Verma, V. (2024). EMOTION AI: UNDERSTANDING EMOTIONS THROUGH ARTIFICIAL INTELLIGENCE. *International Journal of Engineering Science and Humanities, 14*(Special Issue 1), 223–232. DOI: 10.62904/0vcbvb24

Kaswan, K. S., Dhatterwal, J. S., Sood, K., & Balusamy, B. (2022). *Role of Blockchain Technology in the Modern Era*. Wiley., DOI: 10.1002/9781119865247.ch1

Kaur, H., Selvakumar, P., Haashni, S., Anute, N., Sharma, M., & Manjunath, T. C. (2025). Representations in Developing Thinking Regarding Probabilities in Higher Education. In Anastasiadou, S., & Seremeti, L. (Eds.), *Modes of Representation in Developing Statistical Thinking in Education* (pp. 89–118). IGI Global Scientific Publishing., DOI: 10.4018/979-8-3693-9934-7.ch006

Kawahara, R. (2020). *Verification of customizable blockchain consensus rule using a formal method. 5*, 1–3. DOI: 10.1109/ICBC48266.2020.9169472

Khoso, A. K., Honggang, W., & Darazi, M. A. (2026). Trust and attitude towards AI as pathways to creativity: A TAM Model study of EFL students' digital literacy and AI acceptance. *Humanities & Social Sciences Communications*, *13*(1), 69. Advance online publication. DOI: 10.1057/s41599-025-06362-x

Kim, D., Woo, H., & Lee, Y. (2024). Addressing Bias and Fairness Using Fair Federated Learning: A Synthetic Review. *Electronics (Basel)*, *13*(23), 4664. DOI: 10.3390/electronics13234664

Kim, R. S. (2026). Formal and computational foundations for implementing Affective Sovereignty in emotion AI systems. *Discover Artificial Intelligence*, *6*(1), 235. Advance online publication. DOI: 10.1007/s44163-026-01000-0

Kim, S.-E. (2005). The Role of Trust in the Modern Administrative State. *Administration &amp. Administration & Society*, *37*(5), 611–635. DOI: 10.1177/0095399705278596

Kishore, S. C., Lavanya, V., Manjunath, T. C., Arun, M. R., & Shabina Fred Rishma, F. (2026). Predictive Modeling for Nanomaterials Using AI-Assisted Design of Experiments. In Vaseashta, A., & Stamatin, I. (Eds.), *Leveraging AI and Nanotechnology for Materials, Devices, and Manufacturing* (pp. 77–104). IGI Global Scientific Publishing., DOI: 10.4018/979-8-3373-2883-6.ch003

Kitchin, R. (2017). Thinking critically about and researching algorithms. *Information Communication and Society*, *20*(1), 14–29. DOI: 10.1080/1369118X.2016.1154087

Kleizen, B., Van Dooren, W., Verhoest, K., & Tan, E. (2023). Do citizens trust trustworthy artificial intelligence? Experimental evidence on the limits of ethical AI measures in government. *Government Information Quarterly*, *40*(4), 101834. https://doi.org/https://doi.org/10.1016/j.giq.2023.101834. DOI: 10.1016/j.giq.2023.101834

Kluge, A., & Schlick, C. (2023). A life-course perspective on older workers in workplaces undergoing transformative digitalization. *The Gerontologist*, *63*(9), 1413–1422. DOI: 10.1093/geront/gnac181 PMID: 36508331

Koddebusch, M., Koelmann, H., Friedrich, O., & Becker, J. (2023). *Bridging the Gap between e-Government and e-Health: Recommendations for Deploying e-Health Services in the Public Sector. 39*, 440–448. DOI: 10.1145/3598469.3598519

Koh, H. Y., Ju, J., Liu, M., & Pan, S. (2022). An empirical survey on long document summarization: Datasets, models, and metrics. *ACM Computing Surveys, 55*(8), 1–35. DOI: 10.1145/3545176

Kunnathully, K., Jinesh, M., Satyanarayana, P., Esther, V., Pathak, G. P., & Manjunath, T. C. (2026). Building Human Rights by Design: Ethical AI Development for Religious Freedom. In Chakraborty, S. (Ed.), *Intersections of AI and the Freedom of Religion or Belief* (pp. 81–104). IGI Global Scientific Publishing., DOI: 10.4018/979-8-3373-3830-9.ch004

Lahusen, C.. (2024). *Trust, trustworthiness and AI governance*. Nature Humanities and Social Sciences Communications., DOI: 10.1038/s41598-024-71761-0

Laskar, M. H. (2023). Examining the emergence of digital society and the digital divide in India: A comparative evaluation between urban and rural areas. *Frontiers in Sociology, 8*, 1145221. DOI: 10.3389/fsoc.2023.1145221 PMID: 37122396

Lember, V., Brandsen, T., & Tõnurist, P. (2019). The potential impacts of digital technologies on co-production and co-creation. *Public Management Review, 21*(11), 1665–1686. DOI: 10.1080/14719037.2019.1619807

Levi, M., & Stoker, L. (2000). Political trust and trustworthiness. *Annual Review of Political Science, 3*(1), 475–507. DOI: 10.1146/annurev.polisci.3.1.475

Lewis, M., Liu, Y., Goyal, N., Ghazvininejad, M., Mohamed, A., Levy, O., . . . Zettlemoyer, L. (2019). BART: Denoising sequence-to-sequence pre-training for natural language generation, translation, and comprehension. arXiv preprint arXiv:1910.13461.

Lewis, P., Perez, E., Piktus, A., Petroni, F., Karpukhin, V., & Goyal, N.. (2020). Retrieval-augmented generation for knowledge-intensive NLP tasks. *Advances in Neural Information Processing Systems, 33*, 9459–9474.

Li, C. (2025). AI-Driven Governance: Enhancing Transparency and Accountability in Public Administration. *Digital Society &amp. Virtual Governance, 1*(1), 1–16. DOI: 10.6914/dsvg.010101

Lievens, E., Livingstone, S., McLaughlin, S., O'Neill, B., & Verdoodt, V. (2018). Children's rights and digital technologies. In Kilkelly, U., & Liefaard, T. (Eds.), *International human rights of children* (pp. 1–27). Springer., DOI: 10.1007/978-981-10-3182-3_16-1

Lievens, E., Verdoodt, V., Ramaswamy, K., & Zoboli, F. (2024). General Comment No. 25 on children's rights in relation to the digital environment: Clarifying states' obligations on children's rights to privacy and data protection. *Human Rights Law Review*, *24*(3), ngae018. Advance online publication. DOI: 10.1093/hrlr/ngae018

Liévin, V., Xu, F., & Riedel, S. (2024). Evaluating and improving multi-agent coordination with natural language. *Transactions of the Association for Computational Linguistics*, *12*, 583–602.

Lim, T. (2024). Environmental, social, and governance (ESG) and artificial intelligence in finance: State-of-the-art and research takeaways. *Artificial Intelligence Review*, *57*(4), 76. Advance online publication. DOI: 10.1007/s10462-024-10708-3

Lin, C. Y. (2004). ROUGE: A package for automatic evaluation of summaries. In Text summarization branches out (pp. 74–81).

Lips, M. (2020). *Digital government: Managing public sector reform in the digital era*. Routledge.

Lipton, Z. C. (2018). The mythos of model interpretability. *ACM Queue; Tomorrow's Computing Today*, *16*(3), 31–57. DOI: 10.1145/3236386.3241340

Liu, D., & Li, X. (2025). AI vs. Human: Reconciling Autonomy and Governance in Decision-Making. *Lecture Notes in Education Psychology and Public Media*, *114*(1), 82–87. DOI: 10.54254/2753-7048/2025.LC19101

Livingstone, S., & Byrne, J. (2018). Parenting in the digital age: The challenges of parental responsibility in comparative perspective. In Mascheroni, G., Ponte, C., & Jorge, A. (Eds.), *Digital parenting: The challenges for families in the digital age* (pp. 19–30). Nordicom.

Livingstone, S., & Third, A. (2017). Children and young people's rights in the digital age: An emerging agenda. *New Media & Society*, *19*(5), 657–670. DOI: 10.1177/1461444816686318

Locke, E. A. (2005). Why emotional intelligence is an invalid concept. *Journal of Organizational Behavior*, *26*(4), 425–431. DOI: 10.1002/job.318

Lockey, S.. (2025). *Trust in AI: Evidence of trust-supporting mechanisms across nations*. Springer AI & Society., DOI: 10.1007/978-3-032-01940-0_10

Lundberg, S. M., & Lee, S.-I. (2017). A unified approach to interpreting model predictions. *Advances in Neural Information Processing Systems*, *30*, 4765–4774.

Manes-Rossi, F.. (2025). Data science and public sector accounting: Reviewing impacts on financial reporting, auditing, and accountability. *Public Money & Management*. Advance online publication. DOI: 10.1080/09540962.2025.2529266

Mannheim, I., & Köttl, H. (2024). Ageism and (successful) digital engagement: A proposed theoretical model. *The Gerontologist*, *64*(9), gnae078. Advance online publication. DOI: 10.1093/geront/gnae078 PMID: 38874215

Mannheim, I., Schwartz, E., Wouters, E. J. M., van Zaalen, Y., Köttl, H., Brankaert, R., & van Boekel, L. C. (2019). Inclusion of older adults in the research and design of digital technology. *International Journal of Environmental Research and Public Health*, *16*(19), 3718. DOI: 10.3390/ijerph16193718 PMID: 31581632

Mannheim, I., Wouters, E. J. M., Köttl, H., van Boekel, L. C., Brankaert, R., & van Zaalen, Y. (2023). Ageism in the discourse and practice of designing digital technology for older persons: A scoping review. *The Gerontologist*, *63*(7), 1188–1200. DOI: 10.1093/geront/gnac144 PMID: 36130318

Matthews, G., Zeidner, M., & Roberts, R. D. (2002). *Emotional intelligence: Science and myth*. MIT Press. DOI: 10.7551/mitpress/2704.001.0001

Mayer, J. D., & Salovey, P. (1997). What is emotional intelligence? In Salovey, P., & Sluyter, D. J. (Eds.), *Emotional development and emotional intelligence: Educational implications* (pp. 3–31). Basic Books.

Mayer, J. D., Salovey, P., & Caruso, D. R. (2016). The ability model of emotional intelligence: Principles and updates. *Emotion Review*, *8*(4), 290–300. DOI: 10.1177/1754073916639667

Mayer, R. C., Davis, J. H., & Schoorman, F. D. (1995). An integrative model of organizational trust. *Academy of Management Review*, *20*(3), 709–734. DOI: 10.2307/258792

Mehr, H., Ash, H., & Fellow, D. (2017). Artificial intelligence for citizen services and government. *Ash Cent. Democr. Gov. Innov. Harvard Kennedy Sch*, *1*(August), 12.

Meijer, A., & Bolívar, M. P. R. (2016). Governing the smart city: A review of the literature on smart urban governance. *International Review of Administrative Sciences*, *82*(2), 392–408. DOI: 10.1177/0020852314564308

Meijer, A., Lorenz, L., & Wessels, M. (2021). Algorithmization of bureaucratic decision-making. *Public Administration Review*, *81*(3), 445–455. DOI: 10.1111/puar.13276

Meit, Y. (2023). *Digital India: Annual report 2022–23*. Ministry of Electronics and Information Technology, Government of India.

Ministry of Education, Government of India. (2020). National Education Policy 2020. Department of School Education and Literacy. https://www.education.gov.in/sites/upload_files/mhrd/files/NEP_Final_English_0.pdf

Ministry of Education, Government of India. (2022). Annual report 2021–22. Department of School Education and Literacy. https://www.education.gov.in/sites/upload_files/mhrd/files/document-reports/annual_report_eng.pdf

Ministry of Education, Government of India. (2024). Unified District Information System for Education Plus (UDISE+) 2023–24. Department of School Education and Literacy. https://udiseplus.gov.in

Ministry of Electronics and Information Technology (MeitY). (2023). *Draft advisory on artificial intelligence: Responsible AI for governance applications*. Government of India.

Mittelstadt, B. D., Allo, P., Taddeo, M., Wachter, S., & Floridi, L. (2016). The ethics of algorithms: Mapping the debate. *Big Data & Society*, *3*(2), 1–21. DOI: 10.1177/2053951716679679

Mohan, A., & Jayalakshmi, G. (2025). *Blockchain-Enabled Transparency and Accountability in Public Sector Governance*. 1–6. DOI: 10.1109/ICoICC64033.2025.11052060

Moss, E., Watkins, E. A., Metcalf, J., & Elish, M. C. (2022). Obligations to assess: Recent trends in AI accountability regulations. *Patterns (New York, N.Y.)*, *3*(9), 100559. DOI: 10.1016/j.patter.2022.100559 PMID: 36419454

Müller, V. C.. (2023). *Ethics of artificial intelligence and robotics*. Stanford Encyclopedia of Philosophy., DOI: 10.1093/acrefore/9780190631394.013.623

Mulyasari, S. D. D., & Jaya Wardana, D. (2025). The Urgency of Using Artificial Intelligence (AI) In Public Services. *Jurnal Daulat Hukum*, *8*(3), 530. DOI: 10.30659/jdh.v8i3.48658

Myles, P., Axson, E., & Mitchell, C. (2026). Data quality, provenance and transparency in real-world data: Aligning quality standards with data governance legal frameworks. *Journal of Data Protection and Privacy*, *8*(2), 131–143. DOI: 10.69554/PGGW3813

Nallapati, R., Zhou, B., Gulcehre, C., & Xiang, B. (2016). Abstractive text summarization using sequence-to-sequence RNNs and beyond. arXiv preprint arXiv:1602.06023. DOI: 10.18653/v1/K16-1028

Nandi, A., Xhafa, F., Subirats, L., & Fort, S. (2023). *Federated Learning with Exponentially Weighted Moving Average for Real-Time Emotion Classification*. Springer., DOI: 10.1007/978-3-031-22356-3_12

Nastoska, A., Jancheska, B., Rizinski, M., & Trajanov, D. (2025). Evaluating Trustworthiness in AI: Risks, Metrics, and Applications Across Industries. *Electronics (Basel), 14*(13), 2717. DOI: 10.3390/electronics14132717

National Disability Authority. (2020). Universal design and technology for older people. Centre for Excellence in Universal Design. https://universaldesign.ie/uploads/publications/Technology-for-Older-People.pdf

National Institute of Standards and Technology (NIST). (2020). *AI risk management framework*. U.S. Department of Commerce.

National Institute of Standards and Technology (NIST). (2023). Artificial Intelligence Risk Management Framework (AI RMF 1.0). DOI: 10.6028/NIST.AI.100-1

National Institution for Transforming India (NITI Aayog). (2018). *National strategy for artificial intelligence: #AIforAll*. Government of India.

National Institution for Transforming India (NITI Aayog). (2021). *Responsible AI for all (Parts 1 and 2)*. Government of India.

Needham, C. (2011). *Personalising public services: Understanding the personalisation narrative*. Policy Press.

Nemitz, P. (2023). Constitutional democracy and AI governance. *Philosophical Transactions of the Royal Society A*. Advance online publication. DOI: 10.1098/rsta.2018.0089 PMID: 30323003

Newell, A., & Simon, H. A. (1976). Computer science as empirical inquiry: Symbols and search. *Communications of the ACM, 19*(3), 113–126. DOI: 10.1145/360018.360022

NHS England. (2023). A plan for digital health and care. NHS England. https://www.england.nhs.uk/digitaltechnology/a-plan-for-digital-health-and-care/

Nocoń, M., Vesolovska, M. K., & Mróz, B. P. (2025). Enhancing public administration efficiency via the combined application of emotional competence and intelligent technologies. *Scientific Papers of Silesian University of Technology. Organization and Management Series, 2025*(230), 335–348. DOI: 10.29119/1641-3466.2025.230.20

Norris, P. (2001). *Digital divide: Civic engagement, information poverty, and the Internet worldwide*. Cambridge University Press. DOI: 10.1017/CBO9781139164887

Nye, J. S. (1997). Introduction: The decline of confidence in government. In Nye, J. S., Zelikow, P. D., & King, D. C. (Eds.), *Why people don't trust government* (pp. 1–18). Harvard University Press. DOI: 10.2307/j.ctv322v3xg.4

O'Neil, C. (2016). *Weapons of math destruction: How big data increases inequality and threatens democracy*. Crown Publishers.

O'Neill, O. (2002). *A question of trust: The BBC Reith Lectures 2002*. Cambridge University Press.

O'Shaughnessy, M. R., Schiff, D. S., Varshney, L. R., Rozell, C. J., & Davenport, M. A. (2023). What governs attitudes toward artificial intelligence adoption and governance? *Science & Public Policy*, *50*(2), 161–176. DOI: 10.1093/scipol/scac056

OECD. (2022). *Building trust to reinforce democracy: Main findings from the 2021 OECD survey on drivers of trust in public institutions*. OECD Publishing., DOI: 10.1787/b407f99c-

OECD. (2023). *AI principles and trust in public governance*. OECD Digital Economy Papers., DOI: 10.1787/abcd1234

OECD. (2023). OECD framework for digital talent and skills in the public sector (OECD Working Papers on Public Governance, No. 50). OECD Publishing. https://doi.org/DOI: 10.1787/4e721530-en

Officer, A., & de la Fuente-Núñez, V. (2018). A global campaign to combat ageism. *Bulletin of the World Health Organization*. https://pmc.ncbi.nlm.nih.gov/articles/PMC5872010/ DOI: 10.2471/BLT.17.202424

Onufreiciuc, R. (2024). Citizen Participation in and Through AI-Enabled Innovation. *Logos Universality Mentality Education Novelty: Law*, *12*(1), 62–74. DOI: 10.18662/lumenlaw/12.1/91

Ophoff, J., & Renaud, K. V. (2023). Universal design for website authentication: Views and experiences of senior citizens. In 2023 38th IEEE/ACM International Conference on Automated Software Engineering Workshops (ASEW) (pp. 46–53). IEEE. DOI: 10.1109/ASEW60602.2023.00011

Organisation for Economic Co-operation and Development (OECD). (2019). *OECD principles on artificial intelligence*.

Osborne, S. P., Radnor, Z., & Nasi, G. (2022). A new theory for public service management? Toward a (public) service-dominant approach. *American Review of Public Administration, 43*(2), 135–158. DOI: 10.1177/0275074012466935

P, M., & Mahalakshmi, K. (2024). *Privacy-Secure and Decentralized Biometric Authentication Models Using Federated Learning Frameworks*. 1–7. DOI: 10.1109/ICSCAN62807.2024.10894284

Papagiannidis, E.. (2025). Responsible artificial intelligence governance: A review and research agenda. *Technological Forecasting and Social Change*. Advance online publication. DOI: 10.1016/j.techfore.2024.123456

Parliament of India. (2023). The Digital Personal Data Protection Act, 2023 (No. 22 of 2023). Gazette of India, Extraordinary, Part II, Section 1.

Pasquale, F. (2015). *The black box society: The secret algorithms that control money and information*. Harvard University Press. DOI: 10.4159/harvard.9780674736061

Pasupuleti, M. K. (2025). *Trustless Autonomy: AI and Blockchain for Next-Gen Governance*. National Education Services., DOI: 10.62311/nesx/rb21

Peeters, R. (2023). Digital Administrative Burdens: An Agenda for Analyzing the Citizen Experience of Digital Bureaucratic Encounters. *Perspectives on Public Management and Governance*, *6*(1), 7–13. DOI: 10.1093/ppmgov/gvac024

Petrides, K. V., & Furnham, A. (2001). Trait emotional intelligence: Psychometric investigation with reference to established trait taxonomies. *European Journal of Personality, 15*(6), 425–448. DOI: 10.1002/per.416

Phang, J., Zhao, Y., & Liu, P. J. (2022). Investigating efficiently extending transformers for long input summarization. arXiv preprint arXiv:2208.04347.

Pragya Prasun & Ors. v. Union of India & Ors., W.P. (C) No. 289 of 2024, 2025 INSC 599 (Supreme Court of India, April 30, 2025). https://indiankanoon.org/doc/68332080

Press Information Bureau, Government of India. (2024, March 7). Cabinet approves India AI Mission with an outlay of 10,372 crore. Ministry of Electronics and Information Technology.

Privacy International. (2022a). Privacy and education: How schools are failing students. https://privacyinternational.org

Privacy International. (2022b, November 15). The right to privacy in Indian schools: Universal Periodic Review. https://privacyinternational.org/advocacy/4981/right-privacy-indian-schools-universal-periodic-review

Radanliev, P. (2025). AI Ethics: Integrating Transparency, Fairness, and Privacy in AI Development. *Applied Artificial Intelligence*, *39*(1), 2463722. Advance online publication. DOI: 10.1080/08839514.2025.2463722

Radin, B. A. (2019). *Policy tools: From implementation to governance*. Georgetown University Press.

Raffel, C., Shazeer, N., Roberts, A., Lee, K., Narang, S., Matena, M., & Liu, P. J. (2020). Exploring the limits of transfer learning with a unified text-to-text transformer. *Journal of Machine Learning Research*, *21*(140), 1–67.

Rahmath Nisha, A., Subramani, A. K., & Ranjithaa, K. C. (2025). *Emotion AI for Human-Centered Leadership and Training*. Igi Global Scientific., DOI: 10.4018/979-8-3373-3658-9.ch015

Rahwan, I. (2018). Society-in-the-loop: Programming the algorithmic social contract. *Ethics and Information Technology*, *20*(1), 5–14. DOI: 10.1007/s10676-017-9430-8

Raji, I. D., Smart, A., White, R. N., Mitchell, M., Gebru, T., Hutchinson, B., Smith-Loud, J., Theron, D., & Barnes, P. (2020). Closing the AI accountability gap: Defining an end-to-end framework for internal algorithmic auditing. *Proceedings of the 2020 ACM Conference on Fairness, Accountability, and Transparency*, 33–44. DOI: 10.1145/3351095.3372873

Rao, A. S., Verweij, G., & Marwala, T. (2021). *Responsible AI in practice: Harnessing artificial intelligence for sustainable development*. IBM Institute for Business Value.

Rao, M. S. S. (2023). *S, S., V, N., Arun, M. R., Gupta, S., & Taqui, S. N.* Efficient Model Training in Decentralized Systems with Federated Learning., DOI: 10.1109/ICCSAI59793.2023.10421469

Rao, N. S., Madhu, S., Nazar, N., Padmashree, V., Arun, M. R., & Manjunath, T. C. (2026). Smart Sensor Technologies. In Hamad, A. (Ed.), *Integrating Modern Mathematics and Sensor Technologies in Civil Engineering* (pp. 365–392). IGI Global Scientific Publishing., DOI: 10.4018/979-8-3373-5248-0.ch015

Revankar, V. N., Nivashini, G., Meera, K. L., Rambabu, U., Arun, M. R., & Manjunath, T. C. (2026). Decision Making in Human-Computer Interaction. In Kabir, Z. (Ed.), *Innovative Decision-Making in Engineering: The Role of Cognition, Heuristics, and Human Factors* (pp. 59–84). IGI Global Scientific Publishing., DOI: 10.4018/979-8-3373-5702-7.ch003

Ribeiro, M. T., Singh, S., & Guestrin, C. (2016). "Why should I trust you?" Explaining the predictions of any classifier. *Proceedings of the 22nd ACM SIGKDD International Conference on Knowledge Discovery and Data Mining*, 1135–1144.

Ribeiro, M. T., Singh, S., & Guestrin, C. (2016). 'Why should I trust you?': Explaining the predictions of any classifier. Proceedings of the 22nd ACM SIGKDD International Conference on Knowledge Discovery and Data Mining, 1135–1144. DOI: 10.1145/2939672.2939778

Roberts, H., Hine, E., Taddeo, M., & Floridi, L. (2024). Global AI governance: Barriers and pathways forward. *International Affairs, 100*(3), 1275–1286. DOI: 10.1093/ia/iiae073

Roberts, R. D., Zeidner, M., & Matthews, G. (2001). Does emotional intelligence meet traditional standards for an intelligence? Some new data and conclusions. *Emotion (Washington, D.C.), 1*(3), 196–231. DOI: 10.1037/1528-3542.1.3.196 PMID: 12934681

Robinson, L., Cotten, S. R., Ono, H., Quan-Haase, A., Mesch, G., Chen, W., Schulz, J., Hale, T. M., & Stern, M. J. (2015). Digital inequalities and why they matter. *Information Communication and Society, 18*(5), 569–582. DOI: 10.1080/1369118X.2015.1012532

Robles, P., & Mallinson, D. J. (2023). Artificial intelligence technology, public trust, and effective governance. *The Review of Policy Research, 42*(1), 11–28. DOI: 10.1111/ropr.12555

Rousseau, D. M., Sitkin, S. B., Burt, R. S., & Camerer, C. (1998). Not so different after all: A cross-discipline view of trust. *Academy of Management Review, 23*(3), 393–404. DOI: 10.5465/amr.1998.926617

Russell, S., & Norvig, P. (2021). *Artificial intelligence: A modern approach* (4th ed.). Pearson.

Sajjanapu, M. (2025). Ethical AI and Sustainable Digital Governance: An Interdisciplinary Framework. *European Modern Studies Journal, 9*(4), 804–814. DOI: 10.59573/emsj.9(4).2025.76

Saktiawan, B., Setiyono, B., Risfandy, T., & Rachmadi, E. (2026). AI for FI governance: Panacea or poison? *Research in Globalization, 12*, 100343. Advance online publication. DOI: 10.1016/j.resglo.2026.100343

Sambasivan, N., Arnesen, E., Hutchinson, B., Doshi, T., & Prabhakaran, V. (2021). Re-imagining algorithmic fairness in India and beyond. *Proceedings of the 2021 ACM Conference on Fairness, Accountability, and Transparency*, 315–328. DOI: 10.1145/3442188.3445896

Savveli, I., Rigou, M., & Balaskas, S. (2025a). From E-Government to AI E-Government: A Systematic Review of Citizen Attitudes. In *Informatics* (Vol. 12, Number 3). Multidisciplinary Digital Publishing Institute (MDPI). DOI: 10.3390/informatics12030098

Sayles, J. (2024). *Human Oversight of AI Systems.* Apress., DOI: 10.1007/979-8-8688-0983-5_12

Schick, T., Dwivedi-Yu, J., Dessì, R., Raileanu, R., Lomeli, M., & Scialom, T. (2023). Toolformer: Language models can teach themselves to use tools. *Advances in Neural Information Processing Systems*, 68539–68551. DOI: 10.52202/075280-2997

Schilke, O., & Reimann, M. (2025). The transparency dilemma: How AI disclosure erodes trust. *Organizational Behavior and Human Decision Processes, 188*, 104405. DOI: 10.1016/j.obhdp.2025.104405

Scribano, A., & Korstanje, M. E. (2023). *AI and Emotions in Digital Society.* Igi Global., DOI: 10.4018/979-8-3693-0802-8

Seifert, A., Cotten, S. R., & Xie, B. (2022). Elderly forgotten? Digital exclusion in the information age and the rising grey digital divide. INQUIRY. *Inquiry : a Journal of Medical Care Organization, Provision and Financing, 59*, 1–7. DOI: 10.1177/00469580221096272

Selvakumar, P., & Haashni, S. SudhaAnanthi, G., & Manjunath, T. C. (2026). Cybernetic Systems Thinking: Foundations for Organizational Adaptability. In L. Tsvasman (Ed.), *Cybernetic Leadership for Sustainable Innovation* (pp. 99-124). IGI Global Scientific Publishing. https://doi.org/DOI: 10.4018/979-8-3373-2484-5.ch004

Shark, A. R. (2022). *E-Government to Digital Government.* Routledge., DOI: 10.4324/9781003344766-3

Sharma, E., Li, C., & Wang, L. (2019). BIGPATENT: A large-scale dataset for abstractive and coherent summarization. arXiv preprint arXiv:1906.03741. DOI: 10.18653/v1/P19-1212

Sharma, S., Kumar Kar, A., & Gupta, M. P. (2021). *Unpacking Digital Accountability: Ensuring efficient and answerable e-governance service delivery. 17*, 260–269. DOI: 10.1145/3494193.3494229

Sharma, Y. (2020). *Blockchain and Distributed Ledger System* (pp. 177–206). Crc. DOI: 10.1201/9780429352546-8

Sharma, A., Mookherjee, S., & Patel, R. (2022). Emotional intelligence in digital public services: A systematic literature review. *Government Information Quarterly*, *39*(4), 101742. DOI: 10.1016/j.giq.2022.101742

Shiv, V., Chen, A., & Choi, Y. (2023). Towards interpretable and controllable text generation with large language models. *International Conference on Learning Representations (ICLR 2023).*

Shneiderman, B. (2022). *Human-centered AI*. Oxford University Press. DOI: 10.1093/oso/9780192845290.001.0001

Singh, S. (2010). Digital divide in India: Measurement, determinants and policy for addressing the challenges in bridging the digital divide. *International Journal of Innovation in the Digital Economy*, *1*(2), 1–24. DOI: 10.4018/jide.2010040101

Siripipatthanakul, S., Phuangsuwan, P., & Limna, P., Muthmainnha, Siripipattanakul, S., Vui, C. N., & Jaipong, P. (2024). Artificial intelligence (AI) influencing sustainable governance: Governance adopting AI. *International Conference on Data Analytics & Management*, 551–568.

Sixsmith, A., Fang, M. L., & Woolrych, R. (2020). *Co-creating digital public services for an ageing society: Evidence for impact and outcome*. Springer., DOI: 10.1007/978-981-15-3282-0

Soederberg Miller, L. M., Callegari, R. A., Abah, T., & Fann, H. (2024). Digital literacy training for low-income older adults through intergenerational programs. *JMIR Aging*, *7*, e51675. DOI: 10.2196/51675

Software Freedom Law Centre India. (2024). APAAR ID: One nation, one student ID! What about privacy? SFLC.in. https://sflc.in/apaar-id-one-nation-one-student-id-what-about-privacy/

Solove, D. J. (2021). The myth of the privacy paradox. *The George Washington Law Review*, *89*(1), 1–51.

Srikrishna, B. N. (2018). A free and fair digital economy: Protecting privacy, empowering Indians (Report of the Committee of Experts under the Chairmanship of Justice B.N. Srikrishna). Ministry of Electronics and Information Technology, Government of India. https://www.meity.gov.in/writereaddata/files/Data_Protection_Committee_Report.pdf

Subramaniam, G., & Palanisamy, S. (2023). *Privacy-Preserving Federated Machine Learning Techniques*. Igi Global., DOI: 10.4018/979-8-3693-0593-5.ch007

Sudhakar, K. (2025). Decentralized AI: Leveraging Blockchain for Trustworthy Machine Learning Models. *Journal of Informatics Education and Research*, *5*(2). Advance online publication. DOI: 10.52783/jier.v5i2.2753

Sun, C., Qiu, X., Xu, Y., & Huang, X. (2019). How to fine-tune BERT for text classification? In *China National Conference on Chinese Computational Linguistics* (pp. 194–206). Springer. DOI: 10.1007/978-3-030-32381-3_16

Sun, T. Q., & Medaglia, R. (2023). Mapping the challenges of AI in public sector. *Government Information Quarterly*. Advance online publication. DOI: 10.1016/j.giq.2019.101393

Supreme Court of India. (1978). Maneka Gandhi v. Union of India, AIR 1978 SC 597.

Supreme Court of India. (2017). Justice K. S. Puttaswamy (Retd.) & Anr. v. Union of India & Ors., (2017) 10 SCC 1.

Supreme Court of India. (2020). Anuradha Bhasin v. Union of India, (2020) 3 SCC 637.

Sutton, R. S., & Barto, A. G. (2018). *Reinforcement learning: An introduction* (2nd ed.). MIT Press.

Tandon, U., & Gupta, N. K. (2025). Informational privacy in the age of artificial intelligence. *Legal Issues in the Digital Age*, *6*(2), 87–117. DOI: 10.17323/2713-2749.2025.2.87.117

Tangi, L., Rodríguez Müller, A. P., & Janssen, M. (2025). AI-augmented government transformation. *Government Information Quarterly*, *42*(3), 102055. DOI: 10.1016/j.giq.2025.102055

Taylor, M. J., & Barusch, A. S. (2004). Personal, family, and multiple barriers of long-term welfare recipients. *Social Work*, *49*(2), 175–183. DOI: 10.1093/sw/49.2.175 PMID: 15124958

Tewathia, N., Kamath, A., & Ilavarasan, P. V. (2020). Social inequalities, fundamental inequities, and recurring of the digital divide: Insights from India. *Technology in Society*, *61*, 101251. DOI: 10.1016/j.techsoc.2020.101251

Topol Review. (2019). *Preparing the healthcare workforce to deliver the digital future: An independent report on behalf of the Secretary of State for Health and Social Care*. NHS Health Education England.

Tronto, J. C. (1993). *Moral boundaries: A political argument for an ethic of care*. Routledge.

Tyler, T. R. (2006). Psychological perspectives on legitimacy and legitimation. *Annual Review of Psychology*, *57*(1), 375–400. DOI: 10.1146/annurev.psych.57.102904.190038 PMID: 16318600

Tyler, T. R. (2006). *Why people obey the law*. Princeton University Press. DOI: 10.1515/9781400828609

Tyler, T. R., & Lind, E. A. (1992). A relational model of authority in groups. *Advances in Experimental Social Psychology*, *25*, 115–191. DOI: 10.1016/S0065-2601(08)60283-X

UN Committee on the Rights of the Child. (2021). General comment No. 25 on children's rights in relation to the digital environment (CRC/C/GC/25). United Nations. https://www.ohchr.org/en/documents/general-comments-and-recommendations/general-comment-no-25-2021-childrens-rights-relation

UNESCO. (2021). *Recommendation on the ethics of artificial intelligence*. UNESCO.

United Nations. (2022). *UN e-government survey 2022: The future of digital government*. United Nations Department of Economic and Social Affairs.

Upadhyaya, A. N., Seenivasan, S., Anute, N., Guru Basava Aradhya, S., Sharma, M., & Manjunath, T. C. (2026). Digital Synthetic Generation From Learning and BigData. In Hai-Jew, S. (Ed.), *Digital Synthetic Data and Outputs* (pp. 57–86). IGI Global Scientific Publishing., DOI: 10.4018/979-8-3373-2277-3.ch003

Van der Meer, T. W. G. (2017). Political trust and the 'crisis of democracy.' In Oxford Research Encyclopedias. *Politics*. Advance online publication. DOI: 10.1093/acrefore/9780190228637.013.77

Van der Waal, M., Bakker, A. B., & Bhave, D. P. (2018). Emotional intelligence and performance. In Dulebohn, D. L., & Murray, B. (Eds.), *Research in personnel and human resources management* (Vol. 36, pp. 221–252). Emerald Publishing.

Van Dijk, J. A. G. M. (2020). *The digital divide*. Polity Press.

Van Noordt, C., & Misuraca, G. (2022). Artificial intelligence for the public sector: Results of landscaping the use of AI in government across the European Union. *Government Information Quarterly*, *39*(3), 101714. DOI: 10.1016/j.giq.2022.101714

Vankayala, V. (2024). Decentralized Integrity: Blockchain-Based Frameworks for Enhancing Software Update Security. *International Journal of Scientific Research in Computer Science. Engineering and Information Technology*, *10*(5), 404–409. DOI: 10.32628/CSEIT241051035

Vasava, M. J., Gamit, V., Panchal, A. V., Patel, M. M., & Gohil, H. (2024). Federated learning in artificial intelligence: a privacy-preserving approach for distributed machine learning systems. *ShodhKosh: Journal of Visual and Performing Arts*, *5*(5). Advance online publication. DOI: 10.29121/shodhkosh.v5.i5.2024.4817

Vassilakopoulou, P., & Hustad, E. (2023). Bridging digital divides: A literature review and research agenda for information systems research. *Information Systems Frontiers*, *25*(3), 955–969. DOI: 10.1007/s10796-020-10096-3 PMID: 33424421

Vaswani, A., Shazeer, N., Parmar, N., Uszkoreit, J., Jones, L., Gomez, A. N., & Polosukhin, I. (2017). Attention is all you need. *Advances in Neural Information Processing Systems*, •••, 30.

Vaudaine, R. (2021). *Détection et explication des anomalies contextuelles dans les graphes attribués* [Doctoral dissertation, Université de Lyon, Université Jean Monnet Saint-Étienne]. HAL Open Science.

Veale, M., & Brass, I. (2023). Administration by algorithm? Public management meets public sector machine learning. *Public Management Review*. Advance online publication. DOI: 10.1080/14719037.2019.1604793

Verma, S., Bhardwaj, N., & Mehta, M. (2024). Intergenerational caregiving in Indian families: Trends, challenges, and policy implications. *Journal of Aging & Social Policy*, *36*(2), 145–162. DOI: 10.1080/08959420.2023.2198456

Vigoda-Gadot, E. (2021). Citizens and the new public service: Coproduction, co-management, and co-delivery in the age of digital governance. *Governance: An International Journal of Policy, Administration and Institutions*, *34*(2), 471–492. DOI: 10.1111/gove.12501

Vogl, T. M., Seidelin, C., Ganesh, B., & Bright, J. (2020). Smart technology and the emergence of algorithmic bureaucracy: Artificial intelligence in UK local authorities. *Public Administration Review*, *80*(6), 946–961. DOI: 10.1111/puar.13286

W3C. (2023). Web content accessibility guidelines (WCAG) 2.2. World Wide Web Consortium. https://www.w3.org/TR/WCAG22/

Wan, J., Xu, S., Lin, J., Ji, L., Cheng, J., Li, Z., Qu, X., & Li, C. (2025). AI-Enhanced Wearable Technology for Human Physiological Signal Detection: Challenges and Future Directions. *Small (Weinheim an Der Bergstrasse, Germany)*, *21*(43), e04078. DOI: 10.1002/smll.202504078

Wang, X., Zhang, Y., Zohar, O., & Yeung-Levy, S. (2024). Video-agent: Long-form video understanding with large language model as agent. In European Conference on Computer Vision (pp. 58–76). Springer Nature Switzerland.

Wang, W., Wei, F., Dong, L., Bao, H., Yang, N., & Zhou, M. (2020). MiniLM: Deep self-attention distillation for task-agnostic compression of pre-trained transformers. *Advances in Neural Information Processing Systems, 33*, 5776–5788.

Warschauer, M. (2003). *Technology and social inclusion: Rethinking the digital divide*. MIT Press., DOI: 10.7551/mitpress/6699.001.0001

Waza, A. M. (2024). Examining the Role of Artificial Intelligence in Improving Decision Making Processes in Governance. *International Journal of Advanced Technology and Social Sciences, 2*(7), 1139–1150. DOI: 10.59890/ijatss.v2i7.2319

Wei, J., Wang, X., Schuurmans, D., Bosma, M., Ichter, B., Xia, F., Chi, E., Le, Q. V., & Zhou, D. (2022). Chain-of-thought prompting elicits reasoning in large language models. *Advances in Neural Information Processing Systems, 35*, 24824–24837. DOI: 10.52202/068431-1800

Wirtz, B. W.. (2024). Artificial intelligence in public sector: Applications and trust implications. *International Journal of Public Administration*. Advance online publication. DOI: 10.1080/01900692.2024.1234567

Wirtz, B. W., Weyerer, J. C., & Geyer, C. (2019). Artificial intelligence and the public sector—Applications and challenges. *International Journal of Public Administration, 42*(7), 596–615. DOI: 10.1080/01900692.2018.1498103

Wirtz, B. W., Weyerer, J. C., & Kehl, I. (2022). Governance of artificial intelligence: A risk and guideline-based integrative framework. *Government Information Quarterly, 39*(4), 101685. DOI: 10.1016/j.giq.2022.101685

Wittmann, V., & Meynhardt, T. (2025). Uncovering AI regulation's public values in the EU. In *2025 IEEE International Symposium on Technology and Society (ISTAS)* (pp. 1–8). DOI: 10.1109/ISTAS65609.2025.11269610

Wooldridge, M. (2009). *An introduction to multiagent systems* (2nd ed.). Wiley.

World Bank. (2022). *Digital government flagship report: Improving public services through digital government*. World Bank Group.

World Health Organization. (2021). Global report on ageism. WHO Press. https://www.who.int/publications/i/item/9789240016866

World Health Organization. (2024). WHO framework to implement a life course approach in practice. https://www.decadeofhealthyageing.org/find-knowledge/resources/publications/who-framework-to-implement-a-life-course-approach-in-practice

Worsham, J., & Kalita, J. (2018). Genre identification and the compositional effect of genre in literature. In *Proceedings of the 27th International Conference on Computational Linguistics* (pp. 1963–1973).

Wu, C.. (2023). *Survey of trustworthy AI: A meta-decision framework.* IEEE., DOI: 10.1109/ACCESS.2023.3287654

Yeung, K. (2018). Algorithmic regulation: A critical interrogation. *Regulation & Governance, 12*(4), 505–523. DOI: 10.1111/rego.12158

Young, M. M., Bullock, J. B., & Lecy, J. D. (2019). Artificial discretion as a tool of governance: A framework for understanding the impact of artificial intelligence on public administration. *Perspectives on Public Management and Governance*, *2*(4), 301–313. DOI: 10.1093/ppmgov/gvz014

Zacharias, J., von Zahn, M., Chen, J., & Hinz, O. (2022). Designing a feature selection method based on explainable artificial intelligence. *Electronic Markets*, *32*(4), 2159–2184. DOI: 10.1007/s12525-022-00608-1

Zeidner, M., Roberts, R. D., & Matthews, G. (2009). *What we know about emotional intelligence: How it affects learning, work, relationships, and our mental health.* MIT Press. DOI: 10.7551/mitpress/7404.001.0001

Zerilli, J., Knott, A., Maclaurin, J., & Gavaghan, C. (2019). Transparency in algorithmic and human decision-making: Is there a double standard? *Philosophy & Technology*, *32*(4), 661–683. DOI: 10.1007/s13347-018-0330-6

Zhang, T., Kishore, V., Wu, F., Weinberger, K. Q., & Artzi, Y. (2019). BERTScore: Evaluating text generation with BERT. arXiv preprint arXiv:1904.09675.

Zheng, W., & Zhou, T. (2023). *Secure and Privacy-Preserving Communications for Emotion-Aided Systems*. 1–7. DOI: 10.1109/SWC57546.2023.10448927

Zhou, L., Gao, J., Li, D., & Shum, H. Y. (2020). The design and implementation of XiaoIce, an empathetic social chatbot. *Computational Linguistics*, *46*(1), 53–93. DOI: 10.1162/coli_a_00368

Zhu, Z., Shen, J., Xu, S., Ren, B., Tan, X., Sun, Z., Guo, C., Gao, H., Zhang, Y., & Hu, B. (2026). CausalCEM: Self-improved causal counterfactual emotion modeling for multimodal physiological signals. *Information Fusion*, *136*, 104444. DOI: 10.1016/j.inffus.2026.104489

Zuboff, S. (2023). Surveillance capitalism and AI governance trust implications. *Journal of Information Technology*. Advance online publication. DOI: 10.1057/s41265-020-00134-8

Zuiderwijk, A., Chen, Y. C., & Salem, F. (2021). Implications of the use of artificial intelligence in public governance: A systematic literature review and a research agenda. *Government Information Quarterly, 38*(3), 101577. DOI: 10.1016/j.giq.2021.101577

Zulu, N. G., & Nzimakwe, T. I. (2025a). Artificial Intelligence-powered Local Governance: Revolutionising Public Services and Citizen Engagement. *Administratio Publica, 33*(3), 25–40. DOI: 10.61967/adminpub.2025.33.3.2

Паламарчук, Т. (2024). ARTIFICIAL INTELLIGENCE GOVERNANCE REGULATION IN PUBLIC ADMINISTRATION. *Наукові Інновації Та Передові Технології, 3*(31). Advance online publication. DOI: 10.52058/2786-5274-2024-3(31)-73-81 PMID: 24646463

About the Contributors

Yuanyuan Guo is a leading scholar in the field of digital government and artificial intelligence, she was serving as an Assistant Researcher and Postdoctoral Fellow at the School of Public Policy & Management, Tsinghua University. She is now a lecturer at Ningbo University. She earned her Ph.D. in Public Administration from Beijing Normal University, complemented by an academic exchange at Sungkyunkwan University in South Korea (QS Top 100). Dr. Guo also holds a Master's degree from Changchun University of Technology and a Bachelor's degree in Information Management & Information Systems (Japanese-English Bilingual Program) from Dalian University of Foreign Languages. Dr. Guo's research sits at the intersection of trustworthy service computing, artificial intelligence, and digital governance. She has published over 20 peer-reviewed papers in leading international journals (SSCI/EI indexed) such as Korea Observer, Acta Psychologica, JTAER. Her publications are widely cited and have shaped contemporary understandings of digital trust, government-citizen interaction platforms, and the governance of AI technologies. Dr. Guo is also the editor of multiple English-language books on digital government and AI for IGI Global (USA), establishing her as a recognized voice in the international academic community. She has served as a key contributor to several national-level research projects in China, focusing on topics including digital transformation, intelligent service systems, and the integration of AI into public sector innovation. Her project outcomes have directly informed policy and standards at both ministerial and provincial levels. Dr. Guo has been invited as an editorial board member for multiple international journals and serves as a reviewer for leading SSCI-indexed publications. With a solid foundation in both the technical and policy aspects of digital governance and AI, Dr. Guo is deeply engaged in advancing the theory, technology, and real-world applications of trustworthy service computing and artificial intelligence. Her work is characterized by strong methodological rigor, international collaboration, and a focus on actionable, human-centered solutions for the next generation of digital society.

Beichen Lu is currently a Ph.D. candidate in Public Administration at the School of Public Policy & Management, Tsinghua University, Beijing, China. He also is a visiting student at University of Chicago. He received his Master and Bachelor of Engineering degrees in Software Engineering from Tsinghua University. His interdisciplinary research focuses on trustworthy artificial intelligence (AI) applications and intelligent public administration, with an emphasis on the integration of AI, large language models, and service computing for public sector innovation. His work explores technical architectures, ethical and societal implications, and data-driven policy analysis, combining both quantitative and qualitative research methods. Beichen has published in leading journals on topics including AI-driven government chatbots and advanced event detection algorithms for industrial Internet scenarios. His recent research includes the evaluation and application of large language models in public affairs, the development of AI evaluation frameworks for public services, and pioneering event detection methods using deep learning and machine learning. He has served as a teaching assistant at Tsinghua University and received several academic honors, including the Excellence Doctoral Student Scholarship and Comprehensive Scholarship from Tsinghua University. His diverse background in both computer science and public administration positions him at the intersection of technology and policy, with a strong commitment to advancing trustworthy service computing and AI for real-world impact.

***

Amish Abdullah is a legal academic, researcher, and practitioner focused on constitutional governance, human rights, and international policy. He serves as an Expert with the World Bank Group and Rapporteur for Oxford International Organizations (OXIO), and is a Senior Lecturer in the UWE Bristol–Villa College partnership in the Maldives. He also works with the Westminster Foundation for Democracy, leads the Maldives chapter of Street Law Inc., and brings prior Supreme Court-level advocacy experience to his current research and pro bono work on comparative constitutional law, administrative justice, and migrant workers' rights.

Mohammad Shekaib Alam is an Assistant Professor in the Faculty of Shariah and Law at Villa College, Maldives. He holds a Ph.D. in Political Science from the International Islamic University Malaysia (IIUM), where he developed a specialized scholarship that seamlessly integrates Islamic jurisprudence with contemporary socio-political and economic theory. Dr. Alam's research centers on ethical governance, pluralism, and legal reform, analyzed through the dual lenses of normative Islamic frameworks and classical Western political thought. As an active researcher, he contributes to global discourse on pressing socioeconomic challenges, applying a rigorous interdisciplinary approach to issues of human dignity, environmental ethics, and modern statecraft. His work is defined by a commitment to bridging the gap between traditional religious values and the complexities of the 21st-century global landscape.

Pawan Kumar, PhD, is a prominent academic and researcher with over 20 years of expertise in business studies. A professor at Graphic Era Deemed to be University, Dehradun, India, he has supervised six PhD scholars and published over 120 research papers, including 100 in SCOPUS/ 06 in Web of Science, and 16 books, including 10 indexed in Scopus. His works, featured by prominent publishers like Emerald, IGI Global, Nova Science, and Cambridge Scholars, have gained recognition. Dr. Kumar earned his PhD in Commerce from Kurukshetra University in 2007 and holds an M.Phil. and M.Com. Degrees. Specializing in finance, banking, and securities markets, he has authored books on green finance, AI, and fintech. His innovative research includes five patents and has served as a guest editor for Scopus-indexed journals. In 2022, he received the prestigious Researcher Award from Chandigarh University. Dr. Kumar's impactful work on sustainable finance, blockchain, and fintech is globally recognized. His active participation in high-impact conferences and faculty development programs reflects his commitment to advancing research, teaching, and innovation in commerce and management.

Rimi Gusliana Mais is an academic specializing in Public Sector Accounting, CSR, and Sustainability Reporting. She currently serves as a lecturer and Head of the Institute for Research and Community Service at Sekolah Tinggi Ilmu Ekonomi Indonesia Jakarta, where she plays a key role in the Tri Dharma of Higher Education. Her academic qualifications are extensive, including a Bachelor's degree in Accounting, a Master's degree in Accounting, and a Doctorate in Accounting from Brawijaya University, Malang. Rimi is also a certified specialist in sustainability reporting (Certified Sustainability Reporting Specialist (CSRS) and a Certified Sustainability Reporting Assuror (CSRA). In addition, she has authored numerous publications on Public Sector Accounting, Islamic Accounting, Sustainability Accounting, and CSR, making significant contributions to the academic community. Her passion for reading and writing reflects his commitment to lifelong learning and professional growth in her field.

Munir is an Assistant Lecturer (Assisten Ahli) at the Sekolah Tinggi Ilmu Syari'ah Al-Manar Jakarta, Jakarta, Indonesia, comparison of schools of thought. He holds a Bachelor of Sharia from the Imam Muhammad Ibn Suud Islamic Studies School in Riyadh, Saudi Arabia, Jakarta branch (Lc) and a Master of Islamic Law from Darul Ulum University, Jombang, Faculty of Islamic Law. In addition to his academic career, Munir is also known as a preacher in various offices and institutions. His research interests focus on Islamic Law Studies. He has actively published several scientific articles in accredited national journals. Many of his works explore topics such as Fiqh (Islamic jurisprudence), digital zakat payments, Islamic work ethics, and others. Munir is also registered as a member of the academic community through his profiles in SINTA (Science and Technology Index) under the Indonesian Ministry of Education, Culture, Research, and Technology, and Google Scholar, which document his academic activities and publications.

Zoya Naaz is a dedicated Research Scholar in the Research and Development department at IIMT University, Meerut, where she contributes to advancing innovative technical solutions and academic inquiry. A 2025 graduate with a B.Tech in Computer Science and Engineering, she was awarded the prestigious Gold Medal for outstanding academic excellence, marking her as a top performer in CSE domain. Zoya successfully transitioned from her undergraduate studies into a professional research role, focusing on the intersection of modern computing and practical R&D applications. Known for her analytical approach and commitment to excellence, she actively collaborates on institutional research initiatives within the CSE domain.

Nooreen Rahman is an Indian legal scholar currently serving as a Visiting Lecturer at the Faculty of Shariah and Law, Villa College, Maldives, and an Assistant Professor of Law at Manair College of Law, Telangana. She holds an LL.M. from Patna University and a B.A.LL.B. (Hons.) with Distinction from Aligarh Muslim University. A UGC-NET qualified academic and a member of the Bar Council of India, her research focuses on the intersection of law and technology, specifically digital identity, biometric governance, and AI ethics. Her extensive publication record includes forthcoming works on gender equality in labor sectors, minority rights in education, and legal frameworks for environmental crimes. Beyond her academic contributions, she has gained significant practical experience through legal internships at the Supreme Court of India and the Patna High Court.

Akshay Raj is an electrical engineer and the Innovation Officer at IIMT University, specializing in the development, optimization, and deployment of innovative renewable energy technologies. His research focuses on delivering sustainable, clean, and efficient energy solutions—spanning solar, wind, and hydropower—to meet society's growing power demands. Dr. Raj's technical expertise emphasizes the design and performance enhancement of photovoltaic (PV) cells and modules, the creation of novel energy storage solutions, and the seamless integration of renewable resources into the existing power grid. In his institutional role, he bridges the gap between academic research, clean-tech incubation, and industrial application, fostering green-technology innovation and driving technology transfer across the university ecosystem.

Zeba Rani is an Assistant Professor at IIMT University with a strong academic and research background in nursing. She has published numerous research papers in reputed journals and has also authored several nursing books. In recognition of her academic excellence, she was awarded a gold medal during her Master's degree by Hon'ble Defence Minister Rajnath Singh. She is dedicated to advancing knowledge in her field through teaching, research, and scholarly contributions.

S. Haashni is a dedicated and enthusiastic student of Vimal Jyothi Convent Matriculation Higher Secondary School, located in Coimbatore, Tamil Nadu, India. Known for her commitment to academic excellence and personal development, Haashni has distinguished herself as a sincere learner who actively participates in various academic and co-curricular activities within the school community. From an early stage in her education, S. Haashni has demonstrated a strong interest in learning and intellectual exploration. She approaches her studies with curiosity, discipline, and determination, consistently striving to expand her knowledge and improve her academic performance. Her teachers and peers recognize her as a responsible and motivated student who values education and personal growth. Beyond her classroom responsibilities, Haashni shows a deep passion for reading and writing. She enjoys exploring different types of books, which helps broaden her understanding of the world and enhances her creativity and language skills. Writing is another area where she expresses her ideas and imagination, allowing her to develop her communication abilities and creative thinking.

Pradeepa Sampath is currently working as an Assistant Professor in the Department of Information Technology at SASTRA Deemed University, Thanjavur. She received her Ph.D. in Computer Science and Engineering in 2021. Her research interests include deep learning, machine learning, hypergraph neural networks, and data analytics, with a focus on medical image analysis and smart healthcare systems. She has authored 20 SCI papers and 10 Scopus papers. Her academic contributions reflect her commitment to advancing AI-driven solutions in the healthcare domain.

Vaibhav Sharma is a distinguished academician, researcher, and leader in the entrepreneurship ecosystem, currently serving as the CEO of the IIMT Business Incubator Foundation. Dr. Sharma holds a PhD in Engineering, specializing in the intersection of Artificial Intelligence and Renewable Energy. His core research focuses on the performance analysis of AI/ML-based Maximum Power Point Tracking (MPPT) for solar photovoltaic systems.

Mohd Arsh Shery is a Lecturer at the Faculty of Shariah and Law, Villa College, Maldives, where he also serves under the prestigious UWE (Bristol)- Villa College Partnership Programme. He holds a specialized LL.M. in Access to Justice from the Tata Institute of Social Sciences (TISS), Mumbai. A UGC-NET qualified scholar, his research expertise lies in Cyber Law, Human Rights, and Environmental Justice, with a focus on the intersection of climate change, migration, and legal exclusion in the Global South. He has previously served as a legal researcher for the Maharashtra State Human Rights Commission, co-authoring critical fact-finding reports on marginalized communities, and currently serves as a key coordinator for international legal collaborations at Villa College.

Pradeep Yadav is a distinguished academician with over 20 years of teaching experience and expertise in Computer Science and Engineering. He holds a Ph.D. in Computer Engineering and has an extensive research portfolio, including many international journal papers, multiple conference proceedings, and several books. His research interests span machine learning, artificial intelligence, and data mining. Currently, Dr. Yadav serves as an Associate Professor and Head of Department of CSE at ITM Gwalior, MP, India. He has also contributed significantly to the field through patents and copyrights and actively engages as a reviewer, conference chair and editor.

Index

A

B

C

D

E

F

G

H

I

L

M

P

R

S

T

www.ingramcontent.com/pod-product-compliance
Lightning Source LLC
LaVergne TN
LVHW062029101126
852251LV00005B/56